A PLATO READER

RIVERSIDE EDITIONS

RIVERSIDE EDITIONS

UNDER THE GENERAL EDITORSHIP OF

Gordon N. Ray

A PLATO READER

EDITED BY

RONALD B. LEVINSON

University of Maine

HOUGHTON MIFFLIN COMPANY · BOSTON

NEW YORK · ATLANTA · GENEVA, ILL. · DALLAS · PALO ALTO

FOREWORD

THIS BOOK is addressed not to specialists in Greek philosophy, but to diligent lay readers who wish to become better acquainted with the Platonic Dialogues. It is particularly addressed to those whose encounter with Plato has for the most part been indirect, e.g., through the study of history and government, or through the literature of the Platonic tradition.

In any case, the intended reader will bring with him his own more or less sharply focused image of Plato, perhaps as the marble index of Hellenic profundity and charm, perhaps as the philosophical Father of Dictatorship. We shall try to show whence these images derive and how to sharpen the contours and adjust the proportions of the images by submitting them to a direct exposure to their ultimate source, the Platonic writings.

Meanwhile we must not overlook the plain fact of experience that those who for the first time are approaching the task of "decoding" a major thinker of the ancient world will need some initial aid. Such aid is peculiarly needed here by all who are not content with mere impressionism, since Plato is one of that small number of philosophers whose rich surface color and dramatic form are apt to conceal from the uninitiated the structure of nicely articulated meanings that lie beneath.

Accordingly, I have sought through several devices to bring this elusive Greek as near as can be to our modern reach. The opening section of my Introduction is biographical, and offers acquaintance with Plato, man and thinker, in the context of his time. There will be found the minimum of historical and biographical data without which our picture of Plato would be as flat as a shadow on a cavern wall.

Following the biographical sketch is a presentation of Plato's thought in terms of eight major topics or themes. I have sought to justify my choice of themes by appeal to the high court of history. Here will be glimpsed the vast pageant of philosophers, theologians, social reformers, lyric poets, and many others, enlisted — each, of course, with his own interpretations and reservations — under the banner of Plato. There follows a sequence of sections dealing successively with each of the eight chosen themes. Then, in close illustrative coordination with these eight themes, the dialogues are presented. These include the "Socratic" dialogue *Euthyphro* and the trilogy *Apology, Crito,* and *Phaedo,* in their entirety; the *Symposium* virtually complete; and that half of the *Phaedrus* which is of the greater literary importance. The major part of the *Republic* is included, though for the sake of brevity the first two books have been replaced by brief summaries, and some

v

passages in later books have been similarly dealt with. As compensation for these omissions, the volume includes parts of six later dialogues not often represented in books of selections from Plato: the *Cratylus, Parmenides, Theaetetus, Sophist, Timaeus,* and *Laws.* These dialogues, or the selections presented, deal with topics of great contemporary interest, such as the nature of language, the validity of knowledge, the logic of negation and contradiction, and the philosophy of religion.

The more advanced reader needs no manual of instruction; he may do as he pleases; but I would advise the beginner not to venture immediately into the strange world of the dialogues. Let him at most shuttle back and forth between the eight themes and the thirteen dialogues, thus forming and, in the light of a second reading, correcting and re-forming his conception of Plato's thought.

It would be pleasant if I could assure the reader that all the interpretations of Plato which I shall offer for his instruction are universally accepted by Platonic scholars. But here, as in all fields of scholarship, there are divergent views on a number of points and broad differences in general standpoint between interpreters. My own standpoint tends to be that of an appreciator of Plato who prefers to hail his excellences rather than to condemn his blindnesses and faults, and who sees many of his imperfections as conditioned by his place and time; and I ascribe to Plato a more unified and consistent philosophy than do some other commentators. Lack of space and the technical nature of many of the issues have led to an apparent dogmatism of statement for which I beg indulgence in advance. Fuller discussion of most of the topics covered in this volume will be found in my book *In Defense of Plato* (1953), and the reader will also find there references to scholars who hold other views.

Finally, I would express my hope that the ancient thoughts and ideals of the dialogues may show themselves vigorously alive by their power to kindle in a modern reader an Eros of inquiry into the many transcultural philosophical questions upon which Time is not empowered to pronounce.

Acknowledgments

The preparation of this volume has been greatly aided by Mr. Lee Morton, my one-time student and later friend, who gave thoughtful secretarial aid, and by my wife, who amidst the rush of full-time professional activity has still found time to help greatly with problems of both form and matter.

R. B. L.

Contents

INTRODUCTION

READINGS FROM THE DIALOGUES

INTRODUCTION

By Ronald B. Levinson

I

Plato, a Biographical Sketch

The materials from which to construct a sober and substantial "Life of Plato" have not survived the centuries. In consequence, a biographer must make the maximum use of what is at his disposal, fragmentary and conjectural though it often is.

There are even legends of Plato, as there are legends of the saints. For example, we are told that he was born on Apollo's birthday, May 21 on our calendar, and was, in fact, a son of Apollo.[1] Again, it is reported that the infant Plato, lying asleep on a bed of myrtle, was visited by a swarm of bees, who deposited upon his lips the choice honey of Mount Hymettus, humming gently the while, by way of foretelling the eloquence destined to be his. Such tales, worthless as fact, are not without value as the symbolic image of the self that Plato was somehow able to project.

Similarly, the thrifty biographer must turn to account even so palpable a piece of mythology as the traditional claim that Plato was descended, on the side of his father Ariston, from the early Athenian king, Codrus, and through him, from the god Poseidon. Such ancestral distinction, fictional but socially real, was reinforced by his mother's no less honorific genealogy, which counted the great lawgiver and poet Solon as a lineal forebear. All this is part of our evidence that the young Plato was free to move in the politest circles of Athenian aristocracy. His stepfather's reported friendship with the great democrat, Pericles, attests also that he had some basis for understanding the merits of the democratic standpoint.

Born in 428/27 B.C., he received the name Aristocles; the name Plato is really a nickname from the Greek word, πλατύς (platys),[2] meaning broad, but whether in reference to his shoulders or his brow, no one can say. He grew up in the shadow of the Peloponnesian war, that fateful conflict between Sparta and Athens which had begun

---

[1] The late F. J. E. Woodbridge has turned the Platonic legend to good account in the charming first chapter of his book, *The Son of Apollo* (Boston: Houghton Mifflin, 1929).

[2] See Appendix on transliteration.

in 431 B.C. and ended only in 404 with the decisive defeat of Athens. Though explicit records fail us, there is good reason to believe that the young Plato took his share in the fighting. Aside from this, it can be inferred from his dialogues that his youth was a period of what we would call humanistic studies. There is a tradition that he wrote poetry, but after meeting Socrates cried out, "Hither, Hephaestus [the god of fire], Plato hath need of thee!" and burned his manuscripts.

One may surmise that the discussion of political issues — who should rule and how — formed the enveloping atmosphere in Plato's family household. Such a guess is confirmed on the evidence of an open letter, seventh in a collection of thirteen letters long regarded as spurious. Some among them, however, are now almost universally believed to be from Plato's own hand, and in one of these, the *Seventh Letter*, the aging Plato is heard expounding the history of his relation to Sicilian politics. He is moved to trace his relation to political affairs back to the circumstances of his early youth, both in its outer course and in its inner motivation. What is most important from our point of view may be excerpted as follows:

My experience as a young man was that of many others. I supposed that as soon as I came of age I would at once enter public life.

But, I found, the political fortunes of our city were changing in the following way. The existing government [Athenian democracy] was denounced from many quarters and there was a revolution. . . . Thirty men were established as rulers of all, vested with absolute power. Now among them, it happened, were family connections and acquaintances of mine and, what is more, they at once invited me to join them in what they thought I would find suitable activities. Considering my youth my reaction to all this was not surprising. For I fancied that they would govern the city by bringing it out of its unjust way of life into a just way.

Accordingly, I kept my eyes fixed upon them to see what they would do. And I saw those men in a short while making the previous regime look like the Golden Age. Outstanding among their misdeeds was their treatment of a man of high age who was very dear to me, Socrates, whom I would scarcely hesitate to call the justest man of his time. They directed Socrates, along with some others, to arrest a certain citizen and forcibly conduct him to his execution. Their object was to make Socrates, whether he wished it or not, a participant in their political crimes. But he did not obey, choosing to run the gravest risks rather than be a partner in their unholy deeds. In view of these acts and others of the same kind and of no less significance, I was revolted and turned my back upon the evils of the day.

But in a short while the Thirty were overthrown and along with them the whole of the existing government. Then once more but less urgently the passion for public service exerted its pull upon me. In those troubled times, many atrocities were indeed still committed but it is no wonder that amidst revolutions men should sometimes take excessive vengeance upon their enemies. Nevertheless, the restored democrats displayed great moderation. By some evil chance, however, certain men of influence haled our comrade Socrates into court on a most unholy charge, of which Socrates would be the last man in the world to be guilty. For it was on a charge of impiety that one group brought him to court and the others voted against and executed him, him the man who, at the time when they [the democrats] were suffering in exile, refused to have any part in the unholy arrest of one of the friends of the exiled democrats.

Noting these actions and the sort of man who held political office, noting too their laws and customs, the more I considered them and the older I grew, the more difficult appeared to me the task of rightly governing a state. For without friends and trustworthy associates it is impossible to accomplish anything; it was no easy matter to find friends ready to hand, since our city [Athens] was no longer run in accordance with the character and customs of our fathers; and to acquire new friends with any ease was impossible. The laws, too, both written and customary, were being increasingly corrupted with amazing speed.

Consequently I, who originally had been full of zeal to enter public life, after having looked into these matters and seen the whirligig of political ups and downs, at last grew dizzy. I continued to consider how improvements might one day be made in these matters, particularly in the basic principles of the state, but as to action I constantly awaited the favorable moment, until at last I reached the conclusion that all existing states are ill-governed, for their laws are almost incurably bad; to cure them it would take a combination of radical revision and luck. I was then forced to say in praise of the true philosophy, that through it we are enabled to discern the nature of justice, for the state and for the individual alike. It follows that there will be no cessation of evils for the human race until the class of those who have philosophized rightly and truly comes into political power, or until those who are now wielding power in the state by some divine dispensation become true philosophers.

These were my convictions when I visited Italy and Sicily for the first time. [Translation mine]

In this excerpt there are several points of outstanding interest to the biographer. Such, for example, is the hint, as I think we may call it, that Plato did for a short while hold some political office while the Thirty were in power.[3] More interesting still are the references to Socrates as Plato's friend and companion, along with the high tribute paid to him for his moral courage and integrity.

[3] An open question briefly discussed by L. A. Post, *Thirteen Epistles of Plato* (Oxford: Clarendon Press, 1925).

The modern reader may be puzzled by the letter's failure to mention Socrates as having brought philosophy to bear upon the mind of the young Plato. But we are to remember that for Plato, early and late, politics, in its broad and noble sense, was grounded on ethics. And it seems a fair inference from the letter that this ethical component came to Plato by way of his "comrade" Socrates, the master moralist. Traditionally, Plato's first teacher in philosophy was one Cratylus, whose name is affixed to a dialogue with which we are to become acquainted in this volume. Little is known of this thinker except that he upheld an extreme version of the Heraclitean doctrine of the Universal Flux, believing that nothing had sufficient fixity to be the object of knowledge. Recent opinion would turn Cratylus, however, into a fellow pupil of Plato's, thus making Socrates in every sense Plato's first philosophical inspirer.

Perhaps, too, though documents fail us, the young Plato was present at some of those intellectual bouts between Socrates and the "sophists," as they were called, which so often are depicted in the Platonic dialogues. The sophists, whose title means simply "men who know," were professional teachers of public speaking, estate management, and other skills and subjects likely to be useful to well-to-do Athenians expecting to enter public life. Some modern scholars have hailed them as great liberal thinkers, intellectually sophisticated and morally advanced, and Plato too at times credits some of them, notably Protogoras and Gorgias, with respectable intellectual status and moral uprightness. In general, however, they appear in the dialogues as foils of Socrates, far less skilled than he in argument, and as advocates either of amoral views or of uncriticized and therefore insecure customary morality.

As the *Seventh Letter* makes clear, the execution of Socrates marked a critical point in Plato's life. Turning aside from the path of politics, he spent some twelve years in foreign travel, like Odysseus seeing many cities and learning the minds of many men. Among these were, in southern Italy, the mathematician-philosopher Archytas; and in Syracuse, the tyrant or absolute monarch Dionysius I; the latter's son Dionysius, the spoilt heir apparent; and Dion, brother-in-law to the tyrant, whom Plato would seem to have inspired at this time with a passion for philosophy.

During this period also, it is commonly held, Plato composed his so-called "Socratic dialogues." Among these were such memorable works as the *Apology*, the *Crito*, and the *Phaedo*, which tell the tale of the trial, imprisonment, and death of Socrates, and a number in which Socrates is represented crossing swords with individual sophists and other claimants to knowledge such as the soothsayer Euthyphro, with resulting discomfiture of his opponent in the discussion but without the establishment of any solution to the question discussed.

Returning to Athens in 387 B.C., Plato, now in the high noon of his powers, founded his famous forerunner of the modern university and professional graduate school, the Academy. His Socratic dialogues had made him widely known throughout the Hellenic world, and his masterwork, the *Republic*, was presumably published at about this time. Students of ability, some of genius, e.g., Aristotle and the astronomer-mathematician Eudoxus, joined his staff.

This happy and fruitful way of life was interrupted by the voice of conscience, which obliged him, at the urgence of his admired friend Dion, to revisit Syracuse and undertake the education of the new ruler, Dionysius II. The *Seventh Letter* records the misgivings with which he set out on this unpromising mission, which entailed the all but impossible task of establishing in the face of hedonist living and autocratic government the rule of law and philosophic temperance. The story of this ill-starred adventure — Plato's second and third journeys to Syracuse — is not without its thrills, and may be read in the collection of his letters, supplemented by Plutarch's very readable *Life of Dion*.

The remainder of Plato's quiet life, devoted to teaching and writing, has little biographical interest. Cicero's statement about him, "Scribens mortuus est," i.e., "He died while writing," means only that Plato continued to write to the end of his days. One could wish to interpret literally and translate, "Death found him pen in hand."

We are told that Plato's fellow-Athenians gave him a splendid burial in or near the Academy and inscribed upon his tomb a number of praiseful elegiac couplets, among them one proclaiming that Apollo had produced two sons, Asclepius for the healing of bodies and Plato for the healing of souls. One other couplet merits citation. It runs in Shelley's version thus:

> Eagle! Why soarest thou above that tomb?
> To what sublime and star-y-paven home
> Floatest thou?
> I am the image of swift Plato's spirit,
> Ascending heaven — Athens does inherit
> His corpse below.

II

Eight Major Themes in Plato's Thought

If Plato's biographer complains of the paucity of available material, the anatomist of Plato's mind and thought is tempted to make the contrary complaint. He finds himself confronting a vast and various expanse, unified, indeed, but unified, one might say, multitudinously. It would be manifest folly for us to attempt to treat each unit in this tremendous whole. On the other hand, arbitrary omissions would lead to a distorted view. At this point we must introduce, as our *deus ex machina*, the theory and practice of a thematic scheme, as preliminary to the reading of the dialogues themselves.

The term "theme" is used here in no strange or metaphysic sense. Indeed, the term "idea" might almost have been used instead, but, as we shall see, "idea" is used in Plato's philosophy in a definitely technical sense. Furthermore, "theme" has certain positive advantages. It conveys, swiftly and unequivocally, two implications that are much needed here. "Theme" imputes importance and strongly suggests that this importance is reinforced by means of recurrence. A "theme" is what a thinker broaches, develops, returns to, and elaborates. It is notoriously so employed in musical composition; the parallel with the structure of a Platonic dialogue, in which a theme is stated, developed, perhaps dropped and re-introduced, is more than a surface analogy, and the same pattern may be discerned in the dialogues considered as a whole.

THE CHOICE OF THEMES

We have, I trust, identified and justified our basic term. But we may reasonably be asked, in view of the vast plurality of themes involved in Plato's writings, by what warrant or by what objective criterion we have ventured to choose as we did.

Aside from the Socratic theme, the centrality of which can hardly be questioned, the criterion shall be an appeal to history, more particularly to the history of ideas, with emphasis on those "seminal" ideas whose "adventures" — to employ the vivid language of the philosopher Alfred North Whitehead — have been most eventful in the intellectual, aesthetic, and spiritual development of the Western world.

In this appeal we can make no claim to scientific precision; tradition and the agreement of accredited scholars must be our guide. Our hope is to gain confirmation for our "major themes" by showing their affinity with those of the many contributors to our culture who have acknowledged allegiance to or have otherwise been significantly stirred by Plato's thought. Space forbids the presentation of anything like an all-inclusive list, requiring us to be content with a small number of representative men.

To whom, specifically, can we appeal? Philosophers and theologians come first to mind: Aristotle, Plato's "star pupil," who, in spite of some important divergences and many exaggerated disagreements on points of detail, has been happily styled a "Platonist in spite of himself." His theory of "Eternal Forms," a variation on the Platonic Theory of Ideas, is unintelligible without Plato in the background. We are speaking here of our Theme 2, "The Eternal Ideas," but what we have said is valid for most of the other themes, if allowance is made for the inevitable difference of emphasis between the two minds. Aristotle certainly was deeply influenced by Plato's thought on the nature of the soul, on the ideal form of the state, on education, on the structure of the universe, and on some of the topics we have grouped under the title "Knowing, Naming, and Non-Being," particularly the theory of knowledge and logic.

We turn to Plotinus, Plato's devout disciple of the third century A.D., founder of Neo-Platonism. One might define him as a "Plato entranced." Much of Plato, the social and political philosophy, he quietly ignored, but in his subtly argued and deeply felt mystical elaboration of Platonic themes, in his *Enneads,* he may be said to have done two things. First, he produced the greatest monument of theoretic mysticism in the Western world. And second, as a corollary, since his whole work professes to be an unfolding of the deeper meaning of Plato's thought, he brought forth a book destined to dominate the interpretation of Plato and Platonism, for good *and* for evil, until the arrival of critical Platonic scholarship in the nineteenth century. Plotinus' influence was exerted through the Latin version of the *Enneads* made by the famous Florentine Platonist, Marsilio Ficino (*circa* 1482 A.D.). Ficino also translated the dialogues of Plato, and by his interpretive commentaries reinforced the Plotinian conception of Plato's meaning. It was from Ficino that many "Greekless" readers, e.g., Rousseau, derived their knowledge of Plato.

By his insistent accent upon the mystical, symbolistic, and generally other-wordly elements in Plato, Plotinus disturbed the balance between "finite" and "infinite," "Europe" and "Asia," which Emerson found so admirable in the quality of Plato's mind. In compensation, however, by surrounding the name of Plato with alluringly poetic and mystic fire, Plotinus became the godfather, so to say, of the whole brood of high-flying Platonizers, in prose and verse, conspicuous on the skyline of the sixteenth and seventeenth centuries. Our theme of "Love and Beauty" and, in close association therewith, the themes of "The Psyche," "The Eternal Ideas," and "The Cosmic Frame" become here headings under which a vast literature could appropriately be entered. Among the high-flying Platonizers we may list as outstanding Giordano Bruno, Du Bellay, Edmund Spenser, and John Donne. These men did not merely assent to Plato's soaring flights. With him, they flew to the heights of philosophic love, in his *Symposium* and *Phaedrus,* and hymned the mathematical sublimities of the Creation, in his *Timaeus.*

The late sixteenth century saw the publication in France of a vastly influential book intimately related to our theme of "The Psyche," Montaigne's *Essays,* thickly studded with citations from Plato. Significant here is not the systematic development of Plato's thought, for Montaigne is notoriously desultory and whimsical. What is important is rather the mere fact that Montaigne spread on the record for his countless readers to observe, and to turn to their own use, much of Plato's deepest and most engaging wisdom. We may note in passing that Florio's English version of Montaigne is one of the most substantial sources of Shakespeare's mediated contact with Plato's mind.

But England was not dependent for Platonism upon importations from France. In 1515 there appeared in the Latin tongue a now classical descendant of Plato's "Re-formed State." This was Sir Thomas More's "Utopia," itself predestined to become the ancestor of a long line of similar socio-political reformers' dreams.

Yet another Platonic theme is prominent in Elizabethan England, that of "Education." We have almost all heard of Lady Jane Grey, whom Roger Ascham, erstwhile tutor to Queen Elizabeth, found reading Plato's dialogue on the soul (*Phaedo*) while everyone else had gone hunting. Ascham in his *Scolemaster* (published after his death in 1568), with his frequent citations from Plato, may be taken, along with his far greater Italian predecessor, Castiglione (*The Courtier,* 1528), as an impressive example of the men who have been helped by Plato toward a humane and enlightened view of the learning process and the conditions of its effectiveness. And in Castiglione's *Courtier* there is something more: a morally and aesthetically impressive portrait of the type of human excellence at which a genuine aristocracy, under the most favorable conditions, is pledged to aim. Readers of the *Republic* and the *Symposium* of Plato will have a not ill-founded feeling that they have heard something of the same sort before.

In our selective ramble we may walk silently by the eighteenth century, for in the thin cold air of its Rationalism the Platonic plant sends forth but few of its sublimer shoots. At the turn of the century, however, concomitantly with the Romantic movement of which it became a proper part, Platonism revived. Restricting attention to the English scene, we encounter the interesting fact that, barring Keats, the leading poets of the early nineteenth century were all, if not officially Platonists, at least important contributors to the Platonic revival, which stressed again the themes of "The Psyche" and "Love and Beauty." Think of Wordsworth, whose famous "immortality ode," in spite of its un-Platonic glorification of the child, is built upon an essentially Platonic base. Shelley's Platonism may sometimes, as in the *Epipsychidion*, be mingled with that glistening sensuality which Irving Babbitt deplored under the name of "Sentimental Platonism." Nevertheless, as a volume of some 500 pages has documented,[4] Shelley was profoundly absorbed in Plato from his student days onward. His translations of the *Symposium* and the *Ion* (an imaginary conversation between Socrates and a professional public reciter of Homer, notable for its theory of poetic inspiration), and the imagery and feeling-tone of such poems as *Adonais*, reveal the impact of Plato on a mind that, as Notopoulos' book makes clear, was in some important aspects akin to Plato's own.

The poets with whom we have just been consorting spoke often of such high entities as the Soul and God. But as the century advanced, the challenge of social and political problems brought a change of focus. Plato now became of interest primarily because of his drastic criticisms of a sick or unjust society. Accordingly, we find John Ruskin crusading in Plato's name against the uglinesses and iniquities occasioned by the Industrial Revolution and "justified" by an outmoded economic theory of *laissez faire*. Others, like Matthew Arnold, protested against current social "anarchy" and "barbarism," with standards and shibboleths borrowed from or inspired by Plato's polemical writings. Meanwhile, aloof in serene contemplative Oxford, Walter Pater was writing in intricately melodic prose his overly aesthetic *Plato and Platonism*, in which Plato's "City Beautiful" is hymned for its quiet beauty, its Doric charm.

We approach the end of our rather various roll call and are fortunate to find in almost our own day a thinker who rivals Aristotle in the range of interests which he shares with Plato and in his indebtedness to Plato, and who has generously acknowledged his debt. He is a "man of span," the late much loved and admired mathematician, logician, metaphysician, and ethical thinker, Alfred North Whitehead. The words in which he has just now been described, strange as it may seem, are all precisely applicable to Plato. We have already spoken of Plato the metaphysician, though not under that name, for his

4 James A. Notopoulos, *The Platonism of Shelley* (Durham, N.C.: Duke University Press, 1949).

Theory of Ideas is nothing if not metaphysics; and we have spoken of Plato as ethicist, for his ethical ideals appear in his re-formed state and educational prescriptions. His tremendous contributions to logic and his concern with mathematics will be unfolded below.

In one of Whitehead's books there is a much quoted passage to which our use of themes can appeal for precedent. "Centuries ago," he tells us in prophetic tones, "Plato divined the seven main factors interwoven in fact."[5] Of the seven, three are identical with corresponding topics on our list: "The Ideas," "The Psyche," and "The Eros" (Love). The remaining four — "The Physical Elements," "The Harmony," "The Mathematical Relations," and "The Receptacle" — are not immediately recognizable in terms that we have used. In point of fact, however, they have been accorded place as constituents of our final theme, "The Cosmic Frame."

With the discovery of this last and most substantial confirmation, we may proceed with a firmer tread to the task of setting the philosophy of Plato within the framework of our eight themes.

THEME 1: ST. SOCRATES

Some explanation should be offered for our strange procedure of converting Socrates the historical man, son of a stone-cutter and a midwife, into something so ethereal as a theme. But the anomaly is only word-deep. Are we not in the habit of doing the same thing whenever we speak of "a Milton" or "a Cromwell," thus bestowing upon the man a typicality which can be treated as a theme? Plato in his portrayal of Socrates did just that. He found a man in whom he saw embodied those qualities of character which were for Plato proper and central to the nature of man. And by his profoundly skillful literary and dramatic art he has so intertwined Socrates the man with Socrates the ideal of human excellence that the two are all but one. Who was Plato's Socrates? The man in quest of the knowledge that (so he had said) is virtue. And how are that knowledge and that virtue to be attained? Plato's implied answer is like that of a Christian who, when asked a similar question, might answer in the words of Thomas à Kempis, "Through the imitation of Christ." Plato tells us, "Through the imitation of Socrates."

Let us pursue this theme a little further. It was Erasmus who, in contemplation of the courage and humility with which the pagan Socrates met his fate, was moved to confess the impulse to exclaim, *"O, Sancte Socrates, ora pro nobis."* And the world has, on the whole,

5 Alfred North Whitehead, *Adventures of Ideas* (New York: Macmillan, 1933), p. 203.

agreed that there is a curious and impressive "somewhat" about this man, as Plato has depicted him, that in its own terms challenges comparison with sainthood whether of East or West. Shelley, it will be recalled, went still further, and with the expectable extravagance of a lyric poet called Socrates "the Jesus Christ of Greece."

This saint-like aspect of Socrates (and it is important to remember that, for all its impressiveness, it is an aspect and not the whole man) is amply represented in our readings from the dialogues. The three related works, *Apology, Crito,* and *Phaedo,* comprise a unified and moving drama, comparable, in a broad sense, to the trilogy Aeschylus composed on the theme of Prometheus. Socrates, like Prometheus, is the bringer of light or fire, and the *Apology* re-enacts the "crime" of offering men a new and unauthorized source of light. In the *Crito* we have a parallel to Aeschylus' *Prometheus Bound:* Socrates in prison chains, urged by a friend and visitor to forget his ideals as the price of getting free. And to crown the trilogy, the *Phaedo* is, in a manner, a "Socrates Unbound": here on his last day, in the company of his intimate friends and followers, Socrates finds in philosophic argument and symbolic myth the final freedom, escape from the bondage of the bodily world of sense into the realm of the spirit.

Sainthood has sometimes another element which at least appeared to be present in Socrates: a special channel of communication with the divine. Socrates is represented by Plato in the *Apology* (Stephanus page 31b-c)[b] as speaking of a divine sign which he sometimes experienced. This was the "daimonion" or "daemon-like thing" (a "daemon" in Plato's usage is a divine being lesser than a god). This sign, Socrates says, sometimes forbids him to carry out a specific act, but never bids him do one. In my own view this sign was to Socrates, as Plato conceived him, more akin to conscience than to revelation. Nevertheless it was not a reasoned conviction derived explicitly from moral principles, and it was open to interpretation by his contemporaries as a claim to special suprahuman status. We ourselves may see in it special dedication to the ideal.

But in recognizing the element of sainthood in Socrates we must be careful, for as Plato has painted him he has other traits as well,

6 Just as editions of the Bible are standardized for purposes of reference, all scholarly editions of Plato, regardless of the number of pages that they may contain, are made uniform by displaying in their margins the page numbers of the famous Stephanus edition of the sixteenth century. For greater precision, each original page in such editions is divided into five parts indicated by a,b,c,d, and e. In this book the references to the Stephanus pages will usually be given simply as, for example, "*Apology* 31b," and by looking at the numbers in the margins of the dialogue cited, the proper passages can be quickly found. It should be noted that in this book the Stephanus page divisions could not always be made to correspond exactly with those in the Jowett edition, but are not misplaced by more than a line of type.

which, though he employed them as the tools of his saintly trade, are not, one might say, part of the standard equipment of a saint. These other traits are not indeed missing from the Socrates of the trilogy, but there they are somewhat overshadowed by the interest of the drama. Just here it should be particularly helpful to turn to the short but substantial *Euthyphro*, a dialogue that brings into the sharpest focus the traits of which we are in search. Let the thoughtful reader compile his own list and compare it with the following tabulation:

In the *Euthyphro* Socrates displays a certain paradoxical duality of mind; if he is "X," then also, in some degree, he is "non-X" or even "anti-X." He is deeply earnest in his attempt to uncover the meaning of the term "piety" or "holiness," yet his earnestness is tempered by a subtle playful irony. He is skeptical and he is devout, ignorant yet obviously knowing, and so it goes. At the end of the discussion there is no conclusion, only the clearing of the field through the refutation of false assumptions and the promise of a renewed beginning. But at a deeper level much more has been accomplished. We have been shown a powerful mind at work, following a clear and logically exacting method, in pursuit of a sovereignly important goal, i.e., the finding of the point of attachment between the life of man and the nature of the divine.

Socrates, it must be remembered, had declared paradoxically both that "virtue is knowledge" and that his own wisdom consisted in his knowledge that he was ignorant. Yet he asserted without hesitation, as we shall see, that care for the soul is the highest good for man, and he held beliefs about right and wrong on the basis of which he lived and for which he was prepared to die. The knowledge which he chiefly sought to clarify and test in argument, and which in deed he asserted he possessed, was that of values.

It was, doubtless, this spectacle of mind in quest of value that kindled in the young Plato the fire of philosophy and set him to work upon what may be called his lifelong task: completing the unfinished labors of Socrates by constructing a schedule of values whose practical application to the life of man would displace current confusions and perversions. In short, the Socratic theme was the ground of Plato's thought, and his goal the acquisition of the knowledge that is virtue.

THEME 2: THE ETERNAL IDEAS

The so-called "Theory of Ideas" has always been regarded as the most central and distinctive of Plato's philosophical doctrines. As to its precise meaning, however, and the consistency with which it is maintained throughout the long reaches of the dialogues, controversy has often raged. And on the issue of its truth-value, opinion has been sharply divided between the "tender-minded" idealists, to whom it is welcome as pointing the way to a realm of supernal reality, and the "tough-minded" empiricists, to whom it appears, in Carlyle's phrase, as "transcendental moonshine." We are not called upon to settle this age-long debate; our task is to define and clarify with a minimum of technicality the Theory of Ideas to the end of uncovering the important role it plays in Plato's thought.

It needs first to be said, and said again, that "Idea" in Greek, and as used in the phrase "Theory of Ideas," has in itself nothing in common with the modern subjective use, nor does it require a mind as its inseparable locus and habitat. Plato's Ideas are, it is true, considered by him to be involved in all feats of reasoning and contemplation. Nevertheless they remain, for Plato, as we shall see below, forever Olympianly aloof in their timeless, spaceless place. Their cosmic claims will enter our discussion of Themes 7 and 8, in "Knowing, Naming, and Non-Being" and "The Cosmic Frame."

To describe the Theory of Ideas, we must begin as usual with Socrates and his attempt to define the virtue of Piety or Holiness, according to Plato's no doubt idealized report. In his conversation with Euthyphro, Socrates was in pursuit of a definitive statement which is not only true of the virtue in question but true exclusively of it. He is after the essence of Piety, stripped of all accidental accretions, and in stating his demand he employs the terminology which Plato will be seen employing to expound his Theory of Ideas. Thus Socrates speaks of "that self-same form by reason of which all holy things are holy," and of "that one Idea by reason of which both unholy and holy things are what they are, respectively." Immediately thereafter Socrates says, "Acquaint me then with that Idea, whatever it is, that I may have a model or paradigm at which to look . . ." (6d e).

It is to be observed that in this early dialogue, when he demands to be told the "Idea" of holiness, Socrates is talking logic, not metaphysics. He is not assuming a separate, self-existing entity, radiating splendor from another world in which it eternally abides. "Holiness itself," as he here employs the phrase, is not something over and above the acts and intentions which are "holy." He is seeking only the statement of a set of related concepts which will permit us to discriminate the notion of "holiness" from all other notions, and to do so in such universal terms that we can say, "If x then y" and also "If y then x."

We see thus why the man Socrates is not regarded as the only begetter of the Ideal theory. What Socrates can be shown to have done was a paving of the way along which Plato proceeded further. According to our best evidence, Socrates abstained from speculative flights into metaphysical space such as Plato was to make. To have stressed the importance of universal definition was a very present help, indeed a necessary condition of Plato's theory, and we are warranted in calling the theory an outstanding example of Plato's elaboration of his Socratic heritage.

As a preliminary tool of understanding, as a first approximation, let us identify the Theory of Ideas, as follows: The theory asserts that our sense perceptions and our concepts elaborated from them are not the true source of genuine knowledge, i.e., do not directly "mesh" with Reality. The material things of our experience are themselves not wholly and abundantly real. They are only more or less imperfect, confused, and continually changing copies (imitations) of the "Idea" (type) to which they belong. In other words, the very inadequacy of the copies testifies to the full reality of their source and fount. And that wellspring of eternal perfection, those prototypes, patterns, paradigms, and goals of aspiration are what Plato means by his word "Idea."

Assuming, then, that the basic meaning of Plato's Theory of Ideas is in the reader's mind, we must ask whether its significance is equally apparent. Plainly Plato was staking almost his all as a philosopher upon this doctrine, to which he returns ever and again.

Plato's reputed teacher Cratylus, a devotee of the famous pre-Socratic philosopher Heraclitus, had preached the doctrine of universal change or flux; in Heraclitus' own picturesque language, "All things flow," and "You cannot step twice into the same stream." To Plato's mind this philosophy of flux was neither a wholly acceptable account of the order of nature, nor yet a mistaken view awaiting refutation. Plato saw and accepted the changefulness of the world of sense but postulated, behind it and above it, a stability, a fixity, to be discovered by persistent search. Such fixity had been asserted by other earlier thinkers, notably by Parmenides, of whom we will later speak. But Parmenides had carried his principle of the Changeless One further than Plato thought fit to go, so far in fact that he denied the reality of all change, and thus of the whole world of sense.

At this point a principle such as that of the Ideas became, on Plato's view, indispensable. To revert to the metaphor of the river: the Ideas function as river banks and bridges which prevent the flux from carrying all before it. Thus the world has structure. Again, without the Ideas there would be no objective measuring rod of good and evil; each city and each citizen would claim unchallenged the right to measure value. The reign of moral relativity would be upon us; Whirl would again be king.

Returning now to our point of departure, we must express regret that Plato has not left us any full-length account of the simpler form of his theory, though, as we shall presently see, he has discussed in detail the meaning and application of its more mature and abstruse form. The outline just offered is based largely on the one dialogue that comes nearest to supplying this lack, the *Phaedo*. But before going further in our exposition it will be expedient to invite the reader to acquaint himself with the substance of that dialogue, giving special heed to Stephanus pages 72e–77, and 97b–101b.

Assuming, now, that my readers have made direct acquaintance with the *Phaedo*, I shall administer an informal and self-scored examination, distributed into three questions, the importance of which should become more apparent as we move forward to the discussion of related themes.

1. How close a relation exists between the Theory of Ideas and the belief in the pre-existence of the soul and in the soul's recollection of the Ideas as seen before birth?

2. Are there held to be Ideas of all classes of things, good, bad, and indifferent, or only of such as possess dignity or other recognized value?

3. Has Plato, either by direct statement or by implication, committed himself to the view that the Ideas are self-reflexive, i.e., that the Idea of Holiness is holy, the Ideas of Courage and of Heat respectively brave and hot?

In concluding this little study of Plato's Theory of Ideas, let me comment briefly on the three questions asked, indicating where one would look for further light on these dark matters.

Comment One: In terms of the argument in the *Phaedo*, a very close relationship exists between the Ideas and the pre-existence of the soul; they are said to stand or fall together. But with the aid of a fresh definition of "Soul" as "that which has the power of self-movement," a definition first appearing in the *Phaedrus*, a later dialogue, Plato was able to extend the function of Soul beyond the human and into the cosmic sphere, and thus to free his theory of the soul's immortality from dependence upon the ante-natal experience of the human individual.

Comment Two: That in his earlier dialogues, including the *Phaedo*, Plato tends to restrict the realm of the Ideas to entities of high dignity and value is commonly recognized. The Idea of Beauty is celebrated in more than one dialogue, and the Idea of the Good reigns over his *Republic*, a dialogue of his mature period. Yet that Plato was aware, at least in his later period, of a certain inconsistency in this matter can be seen by reading a few pages (126a–135d) from that riddling dialogue named after the great champion of Changeless Being, Parmenides. Here Parmenides, on the threshold of old age, is heard answering a challenge thrown out by Socrates, who is represented as being still in his early manhood. The argument relates to the Theory of Ideas, defended by Socrates and vigorously attacked by the older philosopher. Among the issues raised is that which we mentioned:

Are there Ideas of all things indiscriminately, of mud and blood with as good a right to existence as the rest? The discussion is vigorous and the spectacle of Plato attacking Plato is arresting. The conclusion is that such repugnant Ideas will be granted equal status by a logically mature mind.

Comment Three: The question is difficult and turns on a number of logical subtleties. We can do no more than start a discussion of the points at issue. It is past doubt that Plato often speaks the language of "self-reflection," e.g., in the *Phaedo* (100b ff.), the *Symposium* (210c f.), and above all, the *Republic* (518c, 532c). Are these passages intended to be taken at face value, or is Plato allowing himself aesthetic license when, for example, he speaks of the piercing beauty of the Idea of Beauty? Sometimes this seems to be the case, but it is possible that Plato did not till relatively late observe the problem.

Granted this flaw in Plato's gem, we need not magnify its importance; we have seen how Plato allowed his character Parmenides to uncover several flaws in his "Idealogy." We are left with the thought that Plato was realist enough to confess a fault in his own theory but idealist enough to retain faith in the essential truth of a doctrine which seemed to him the only available means of preserving cherished values from being swept into the abyss of non-being, while he still sought ways to make it logically more sound.

THEME 3: THE PSYCHE

To follow Plato through the height and depth of his speculations upon the nature of that metaphorically winged creature Psyche (the Soul) would require the agility of Shakespeare's Puck and would inevitably heap theme upon theme in dire confusion. The students at Plato's Academy were taught a method of logical subdivision, by which a large class of items was divided into its successively smaller subclasses, and we may employ a version of this method by first breaking down the concept of "Soul" into its several major constituents and then presenting a simple functional account of each, leaving to ensuing sections the task of showing the meaning of "Psyche" from their particular point of view. Our point of departure will be, as was Plato's, Socrates.

1. The Socratic "Soul"

It is at his own risk that one draws a firm dividing line between the beliefs of Socrates and those of his admiring reporter. But when, at the end of the *Apology* (40c ff.), Plato gives us a Socrates who goes no further than to present immortality as an open possibility to which a perpetual dreamless sleep is the equally probable alternative, there are good reasons for thinking that here at least Plato has stepped aside and allowed Socrates to express a view which Plato, at the date of writing, probably did not share.

That Plato did not always reserve judgment about immortality is a conclusion which forces itself upon the reader of the *Phaedo*. There Socrates retains his basic character as man and thinker, but his view of the Soul as inherently immortal and the elaborate arguments with which he defends it can hardly be explained otherwise than in the light of Plato's frequent practice of presenting as the thought of Socrates ideas which he had elaborated out of originally Socratic material. Appealing, then, to the evidence of the *Apology*, we make bold to say that Socrates, unlike his more speculative disciple, had no theory concerning the origin, nature, and destiny of the human soul.

This last statement runs a risk of being sadly misunderstood. Socrates, though reluctant to leave the marketplace of everyday observable experience, was, in practice, basically engaged in the scrutiny and "saving" of human souls, an enterprise which it was the sovereign aim of Plato to carry on. In the interest of clarity we must ask precisely what Socrates had in view in his use of this word "psyche" (Soul).

The first, best, and, for our purposes, sufficient answer is given us by some words of Socrates in the *Apology*, together with the comments of two scholars. In language that to some degree anticipates the words of Jesus: "What shall it profit a man if he gain the whole world and lose his soul?" Socrates in all earnest now, and with high moral eloquence, avers:

> Men of Athens, I honor and love you; but I shall obey God rather than you, and while I have life and strength I shall never cease from the practice and teaching of philosophy. . . . I believe that no greater good has ever happened in the State than my service to the God. For I do nothing but go about persuading you all, old and young alike, not to take thought for your persons or your properties, but first and chiefly to care about the greatest improvement of the soul. [*Apology* 29d–30b; Jowett's translation.]

Commenting on these words in his edition of the dialogue, John Burnet declares, "The call is repeated with solemn emphasis. We are to understand that this is the central thing in the teaching of Socrates."[7] In an instructive essay this same scholar traces the steps in the semantics of "psyche," starting from the "phantom souls of the Homeric poems," and concludes that none of them "can explain the new meaning given to the word by Socrates."

[7] John Burnet, *Plato's* Euthyphro, Apology of Socrates, *and* Crito (Oxford: Clarendon Press, 1924).

Werner Jaeger in his discussion of "Socrates the Teacher"[8] is in hearty accord with Burnet. On his view, Socrates inaugurated an epoch within which we still live. He had discovered the inner life and conceived the "soul" as the organizing principle that directs human existence — and elevates it — by its ability to construct a hierarchy in which spiritual goods occupy the summit. Plato shared this vision and this faith. But he philosophized beyond it in what he took to be the same direction.

2. Soul as Self-Subsistent

Here we need only to make explicit the earlier suggested contrast between the concept of "Soul" in the *Apology* and that in the *Phaedo*. One might attempt an experiment in subtraction and say: The *Phaedo* minus the *Apology* equals that of which we are in search. This operation is not so difficult as it may sound; the reader is urged to try for himself.

It would be bad pedagogy to intervene at this moment, with the "right answer." But a few suggestions may be in order. The basic difference, it seems fair to say, is that embodied in our caption, conveyed in the word "subsistent." That which subsists enjoys many immunities; it is in its essence immortal. So in the *Phaedo* the soul, once granted the status of enduring entity, is greatly extended in dignity and power. It can veritably "look before and after," recollecting its ante-natal vision of the Ideas and claiming with them a high kinship of resemblance. All this and more is what Plato sought in the *Phaedo* to have added unto the stature of the Soul.

3. The Tripartite Soul

In partial contradiction with what seems the simple, uncompounded unity of the Soul as presented in the *Phaedo* is the insistently pluralistic account in the *Republic*, which recognizes in the soul three parts, faculties, or powers: Reason, "Spirit" or emotion, and Appetite, each with its separate function, their separateness underscored by the frequent mutual conflict into which they fall.

It would be rash, however, to assert that Plato in the *Republic* has fully committed himself to the existence of three parts in the Soul. It is true that in a later dialogue, the *Timaeus* (69d, 89e), he affirms this as probable and represents only man's Reason, not the whole soul, as divine. But that he could conceive a soul which was uncompounded but yet was at variance with itself is already suggested in the *Phaedo*

---

[8] In the second volume of his monumental *Paideia*, English translation (New York: Oxford University Press, 1943), p. 38 ff.

(p. 82b ff.), where the degradation of the Soul, bewitched and polluted by evil association with the body, is contrasted with the Soul in her pristine purity. And at *Republic* 611d, the contrast between the unconflicted purity native to the Soul and the obscurement and multiple disfiguration of the Soul by communion with the body, is conveyed by the striking image of the sea-god Glaucus, whose native shape can no longer be discerned beneath the encrustation of shells and weeds and rock.

The tripartite Soul in the *Republic* is not yet a distinct conception of the Soul in addition to other concepts. It is rather Plato's device for spreading on the record in vivid fashion his insights into the actual behavior of men and the norms which he stoutly believed should govern them. Much of what has most deeply entered the lay gospels of the Western world takes its departure from the normative psychology and ethics which Plato has propounded here. This broad theme deserves a full discussion and we will return to it in our discussion of "The Re-formed State." In the section on "Knowing, Naming, and Non-Being," we shall have something to say of another neglected aspect of the Soul as Plato conceived it, the Soul as knower, a chapter in the history of epistemology, or the theory of knowledge.

4. The Soul as Self-Mover

In concluding this inventory of conceptions of the Soul we must mention one which we meet for the first time in the *Phaedrus* (245c–246a), a dialogue commonly taken as later than the *Republic*. This is the identification of Soul as the self-moving principle of movement for all bodies. The *Phaedrus* passage is included in this volume, and it is suggested that the reader begin his acquaintance with it now and return to it again when, in discussing Theme 8, "The Cosmic Frame," we shall be concerned with its bearing on Plato's view of the universe at large.

THEME 4: LOVE AND BEAUTY

Among the dialogues there are two, the *Symposium* and the *Phaedrus* (part I), in which Plato has most particularly addressed himself to the dual theme of Love and Beauty. Their philosophical depth, reinforced by the alluring style and timeless relevance of their contents, has given them a secure place among the classics of the Western world. And yet there has been no lack of critics ancient and modern to question the high and spiritual significance that the friends of Plato have discovered in them. Some of these critics have gone so far as to find in them indications that their author was a repressed neurotic whose sensual fantasies are here inadvertently exposed to view. With this possibility in mind, let us take a close look at the evidence, considering first the *Symposium,* commonly regarded as antedating the *Phaedrus.*

The *Symposium*

This dialogue reports the banquet given by the poet Agathon to celebrate the victory of his tragedy in the annual dramatic competition. Host and guests agree that there is to be no "compulsory" drinking, in view of the ravages of the night before. There is to be no "floor show"; the flute-girl is to be dismissed and the company left to their own devices. Following the suggestion of young Phaedrus — the same whom we are to meet in the dialogue that bears his name — there will be a common theme; each man will take his turn and speak in praise of Love (*Eros*), "an ancient and mighty God" but one who, Phaedrus complains, has been strangely neglected by encomiasts until now.

The six speeches that follow — seven if we include the altogether unexpected "Praise of Socrates" uttered by the wine-staggered late-comer Alcibiades — are to be read entire if their value is not to be seriously diminished. Here I propose only to formulate a few central questions, the answers to which should throw some light on Plato's philosophical and aesthetic intentions in this dialogue.

Question I: Is there any significance in the order and relative importance of the speeches?

Answer I: Indeed, yes. The distinguished Platonic scholar Paul Shorey has spoken of "the succession of speeches skillfully arranged to exhaust many aspects of the topic, to secure variety and relief, and to lead up, in the Platonic manner, to the rhetorical climax of Agathon's speech, which turns out to be not the climax after all, because a greater height of idealistic eloquence reveals itself behind in the speech of Socrates."[9]

An outstanding example of variety and relief is the speech put into the mouth of the great comic dramatist, Aristophanes — a speech which, it is commonly believed, Plato tailored nicely to Aristophanes' measure. In it the dramatist tells a truly Aristophanic myth in which the members of the first human race are said to have been spherical and to have been halved by the gods, so that each became two of our present human kind. This myth, with its broad humor tempered by pathos — the obscure longing of each severed creature for his or her long-lost other half — anticipates and paves the way for what we

[9] Paul Shorey, *What Plato Said* (Chicago: University of Chicago Press, 1933).

are to hear from Socrates concerning the high mysteries of love, taught to him, so he declares, by the priestess Diotima of Mantinea.

Question II: Did Socrates truly learn the nature of Love from Diotima?

Answer II: Probably not. The lady is a fiction designed to serve a double purpose. She lends an air of religious solemnity to the discussion and makes it possible for Socrates to correct Agathon his host without offense, by confessing that he himself was laboring under the same misconceptions as Agathon until the wise woman of Mantinea set him right.

Question III: "Diotima" makes a distinction between the lesser and the greater mysteries of Love. Explain.

Answer III: "Diotima" is using the language of the Greek mystery religions, into which the neophyte was initiated by stages. Socrates, she is represented as saying, has completed the first stage, whose password is "Creation in Beauty." Can he, she asks, complete the second and final initiation, and from the love of one beautiful body rise to love of all beautiful bodies, souls, thoughts, laws, and institutions, and finally mount to a vision of the great Sea of Beauty absolute?

Question IV: Why did Plato allow his otherwise orderly and coherent dialogue to be disrupted by the disorderly invasion of the drunken Alcibiades?

Answer IV: A fallacious question. The unity of the *Symposium* was not shattered but reinforced by the "invasion." We are here offered a little play within a play, in which the higher, purer form of Love, transcending the sensuous, finds its embodiment in Socrates.

The *Phaedrus*

> The vision of the seer who saw the Spirit of Man.
> A chariot he beheld, speeding twixt earth and heaven
> drawn by wing'd horses, and the charioteer . . .
>   Thus Plato recordeth — how Socrates told it
> to Phaedrus on a summer morning, as they sat
> beneath a lofty plane-tree by the grassy banks
> of the Ilissus, talking of the passions of men.[10]

In these lines Robert Bridges has evoked the *personae* and the *milieu* of Plato's *Phaedrus*. Moreover he has brought us within sight, so to speak, of the myth of the charioteer which, second only to the creation myth in the *Timaeus,* is the longest, most inclusive, and — as many readers would say — the masterpiece of Plato's mythopoeic imagination.

[10] Robert Bridges, *The Testament of Beauty* (New York: Oxford University Press, 1930).

It would, however, be less than honest to pass over in silence certain objections raised against Plato's myth, some on aesthetic, some on moral grounds. We may consider an example of each type, beginning with the aesthetic.

The contemporary school of the New Critics have defined and deplored, under the name of "Platonic Poetry," the pretty-pretty, exclusively poetical sort of poetry which lacks the tension that contrast, paradox, and irony provide. One of the New Critics, himself a poet, the late Wallace Stevens, has stigmatized Plato's myth in just this way. The chariot riding in the sky, the driver and the winged horses, all this he concedes is imagery arousing immediate conviction and delight. But, he is forced to say, its nobility is too noble and the vision soon fades for want of common day. The issue Stevens has raised deserves fuller discussion than is here possible.[11] But a cogent answer to the charge is available to anyone who will go further in Plato's book. There he will find the needed prose elements — blood, sweat, even the pains of teething.

The moral objections to the *Phaedrus* center on the role of homosexuality in the Platonic myth, and are equally applicable to the *Symposium*.[12] There is no question that the two dialogues explicitly accept, to the degree of celebration, a Socratic or Platonic type of male homosexual love, or (to employ the native Greek name for such love) of "paiderastia." They candidly recognize and propose improvements upon an existing practice in the Athens of Plato's day.

To evaluate Plato's handling of the theme, however, two precautions are necessary. One is to note that homosexual attachments, some merely sensual, some closer to friendly comradeship, were so prominent in Plato's world that even to conceive a society in which they were absent was difficult; Plato himself, however, almost achieved this conception in the *Laws* (837–840), where he expresses the wish that overtly sexual relations between males could become by universal custom as unthinkable as between close family members.

The other precaution is to bear in mind that *paiderastia*, as the Greeks knew it, was not one but many. There was indeed a profligate form, which was more open and more prevalent than such a practice could be in present-day society, and which was justly viewed with grave disapproval by the fathers of young sons and by upright citizens generally. However, cultural studies have shown that a form of affectionate and sensual relationship between an older and a younger man had developed in early times among the warrior class of the

[11] See my paper on the aesthetic affinities of the *Phaedrus:* "Plato's *Phaedrus* and the New Criticism," *Archiv für Geschichte der Philosophie*, 46 (1964), 293–309.

[12] This question is dealt with at some length in my book, *In Defense of Plato* (Cambridge, Mass.: Harvard University Press, 1953).

Dorian Greeks and had achieved social recognition and even honor. Again, in fifth-century Athens, among the more privileged classes, similar relations were recognized, subject to no stigma, provided the relationship was entered upon in full recognition of the duty of the older partner to promote the growth in "virtue," i.e., human excellence, as the Greeks conceived it, of the junior associate, and provided also that the association contemplated long-term stability. This is very close to the form of *paiderastia* reflected by the non-Platonic speakers in the dialogues, and similar in many ways to the form celebrated and affirmed by Plato himself through the mouth of Socrates.

And yet there is a little difference which, one may fairly say, makes all the difference. Plato does not approve overt homosexuality. It is the difference in ultimate aim between the man who, having reached a position in the world quite satisfactory by ordinary standards, comes to rest, and the man who, remembering, as Plato suggests, the vision he once enjoyed of the Eternal Forms, "strains upward like a bird." Both dialogues stress this Faustian discontent and both treat the sensual component of Love not as something to live for but rather as something to live beyond.

In another dialogue, the *Republic*, included in this volume, Plato again makes plain the firm restrictions he would impose on bodily expression of love between males (403b). And in the *Laws* (837–839) he affirms the same ideal.

What awakens Eros (Love) in the human soul, what part does Beauty play, and how can the whole course of experience be directed toward the highest ends through a progressively enlarging vision of Beauty absolute? These are the questions to which the *Symposium* and the *Phaedrus* offer thoughtful and fruitful, if not to us wholly acceptable answers. I am acquainted with no finer and deeper confirmation of what has just been said than the following words of William Hocking:

> ". . . a Greek thinker had seen that all impulses are forms of one, . . . that man is not satisfied with living; he asks the further question, Life *for what?* Plato's answer is, for creating or reproducing what we love. All desires, he teaches in the most profound psychological analysis of ancient times, . . . are forms of love; and all love is an impulse to create, stirred by a vision of beauty, whether of persons or ideas. There is something ineffably humble about love, for it confesses poverty, a want of something; . . . something ineffably proud about it, for it feels in itself the . . . capacity . . . of the artist to give durable form to his vision or that of the legislator to coin into law his idea of a better social order. Plato's belief was that this kind of creation is what all desire really wants."[13]

[13] W. E. Hocking, *Preface to Philosophy* (New York: Macmillan, 1946), pp. 13–14.

THEME 5: THE RE-FORMED STATE

It will be recalled from the biographical sketch how eagerly the youthful Plato looked forward to the day when he would actively participate in the public life of his native Athens, and how reluctantly he set aside that hope until a better time that never came. It requires no great flight of the psychological imagination to suggest some relation between the failure of his political hopes and the glowing depiction of a model Greek city-state, re-formed to Plato's measure and known as the *Republic*.

This is an amazing book, rich in content, polished in form, masterly in construction, working into an organic whole a great variety of themes: a book that Ivor Richards declares to have had more influence on the culture of the West than any other save the Bible. Whether it should be regarded as primarily political or primarily ethical (or educational, as we shall see below) it is futile to inquire, since there is no reason for thinking that Plato intended such distinctions and since in any case he has so interwoven politics, ethics, education, and even metaphysics as to make it virtually impossible to find their points of juncture.

Were we able for a moment to step into Platonopolis, we would see a city of only a few thousand citizens, its temples, shops, gymnasia, and other buildings notable for their aesthetic simplicity and charm. Who governs this city-state? A small number of men and (less often) women, singled out from among the class of citizens called "guardians," all of them bred or chosen in childhood for their superior ability, and elaborately trained. The few who are the rulers have received further and more arduous training, culminating in the vision of the Idea of the Good, of which we shall speak later. They are the Guardians *par excellence* of the city and its laws. They will determine policy within the framework of a constitution such as the *Republic* has outlined. Thus law and the rule of law enjoy an honored place in Plato's state, and this fact is not in the least contradicted by the passage (425c–427a) deploring not the sovereignty of law but the excesses of minute legislation which generate a litigious temperament in the inhabitants of less ideal cities.

There are three classes in this city, classes but not castes, since membership is determined by fitness, not by birth. The Guardians are at the summit; they are supported by a greater number of junior guardians, "auxiliaries," who constitute a military class from whose ranks the senior guardians will be recruited, according to need. Together these two classes man the government. The third class, which includes the remainder of the citizen body — the doctors, teachers, and merchants, together with the "butchers and bakers" — has no voice in the running of the state. Each one among them nevertheless has his own function which he exclusively pursues. The intended result is Justice, the health and harmony of each and all. Plato also considers that as the Guardians represent Reason, the auxiliaries Spirit or Emotion, and the remainder Desire or Appetite, their mutual relations in the ideal state correspond to Justice in the individual soul, the condition in which reason, supported by the emotions, rules over the desires.

Beyond this bare outline of Plato's ideal state, mention at least should be made of Plato's most striking departures from the Hellenic norm, such as the education of women, the state-arranged "sacred marriages" by which the best of the human stock is to be perpetuated, and the austere "communism" of the two higher classes, who will live in perpetual barracks and call nothing their individual own. Here, too, we find the most famous of Platonic doctrines, that of the philosopher-kings: "There will be no respite from evil in your cities, until either kings become philosophers or philosophers become kings." (*Republic*, 473c-d, 499b; quoted by himself from himself, as we saw, in the *Seventh Letter*.)

Such then is the city of Plato's masterwork, but the *Republic* is not the only city to have been shaped by Plato's hand. There is also the city of the *Laws*, a work which contains within its hundreds of Stephanus pages directions for founding a city in Crete with 5040 adult male citizens, in the full sense of the word "citizen." Its constitution is outlined in the dialogue by an aged "Athenian Stranger" (to all seeming, Plato himself), at the request of the Cretan Cleinias and the Spartan Megillus, as the three old men slowly pursue their way on a long summer's day from Cnossos to the cave and sanctuary of Zeus.

Something of the stiffness and plodding character of the three old men has found its way into Plato's report, partly, no doubt, involuntarily, in consequence of Plato's age — he was working on it still up to the time of his death — but also, perhaps, as his last deliberate expression of dramatic mimesis. There are also passages of solemn beauty, of moral elequence and of imagery which serve as oases for the reader in the long and sometimes arid march. As Bury has suggested, it is surely in every way an old man's book: its merits and its defects are those of age. We shall return to the *Laws* in treating Theme 8, but a few words are here in order on the relation to each other of Plato's two cities.

The two cities differ systematically. In the *Republic* the first question is ever, "Is this the best conceivable proposal?" The *Laws* asks, "Is this the best practicable proposal; will it work?" The *Laws* is

always nearer the ground; the *Republic* soars. In the Cretan city there
will be no community of property, no collective marriages. A detailed
study of the *Laws*, such as Morrow's masterly book,[14] will show the
extent to which Plato adapted his personal preferences to meet the
needs of a society consisting, as he put it, "not of gods but of men."

We have spoken of Plato's commitment to the rule of law even in
his *Republic*, where ideal rulers might be considered to obviate the
need of it. Even they, however, will be subject to the constitution
as outlined by Plato (*Republic* 458c), which he presents as itself
grounded in the moral law. In the *Laws* and the *Politicus* (a dialogue
treating of the ideal statesman), and in his recommendations for the
Syracusan state, Plato stresses his belief that, in the absence of ideal
rulers, adherence to law is best. In the *Laws* he describes a constitution embodying the principle of checks and balances seen in the
American Constitution, expressed in regulations giving every citizen
inalienable rights and subjecting every official to scrutiny of his official acts by some other organ of the state. So pervasive and recurrent
is Plato's concern with law that "Obedience to Law" might almost have
been identified as a ninth major theme.

Theme 6:   Education

One famous reader of the *Republic*, Jean Jacques Rousseau, in his
own pedagogical romance, *Émile*, was moved to proclaim the paradox
that Plato's book "is not a treatise on politics, as those who judge a
book by title only imagine. It is the best treatise on education ever
written." This often quoted dictum may need dilution, particularly in
the extent of its denial, but even so it conveys some truth in both of its
emphatic parts.

It will be remembered from the biographical sketch that Plato's
credentials as an educator were beyond question. His first awakening
to the life of the mind was in response to the stimulus of one whose
name traditionally heads the list of great teachers in the ancient world.
And we have seen that this influence was deep and lasting, as witness
the Socratic method of the analysis of concepts such as justice, which is
pursued, with variations, throughout the dialogues, and even, as the
scanty evidence at our disposal suggests, employed as the basic pedagogical instrument in Plato's own school, the Academy. Education,
it seems, was for him no tangential interest but a matter of deep
concern.

The *Republic* is indeed, as Rousseau said, an educational treatise,

[14] Glenn R. Morrow, *Plato's Cretan City* (Princeton: Princeton University
Press, 1960).

but it is also a political one, because Plato believed that the only humanly acceptable political system rests upon a base of morality, which in turn requires for its establishment a properly conducted educational system. And, as even a first reading of the *Republic* will make evident, among the duties and concerns of the Guardians of such a state, none is considered more important than the effective continuance of its educational program. In the *Laws* Plato goes even a step further and decrees that the elective office of "Superintendent of Schools" shall be regarded as the most important in the entire state.

What, then, are Plato's educational prescriptions and where in his writings are they chiefly to be found? The relevant passages in Plato's writings, both those included in the present volume and those omitted, are as follows. (1) In the *Republic:* education for all the guardians, 376c–412b, 451e–457b; advanced education for the rulers only, 498b-c, 502d–540c. (2) In the *Laws:* education for all the citizens, 788a–822c; advanced education for the members of the Night Council, 817e–818a, 951d–952b, 961d 968c.

What Plato's educational prescriptions are in detail will be left for discovery by the reader himself, but initial guidance may be supplied by the following tabulation, based on the *Republic* correlated with the *Laws*.

Plato's Major Educational Ideals

1. Education is of the whole man (or woman), body and soul.

2. Its two basic components are "gymnastic" for the body and "music" (in the broad sense, including literature) for the soul.

3. The entire process is "for the sake of the soul," though it serves the interests and satisfies all prerequisites for a well-conditioned body. In a comely sentence Plato affirms: "He who has most fitly mingled gymnastic and music and has most moderately applied them to the soul, him may we pronounce to be the most fully musical and happy man." What is here contemplated is not a mere aggregate of information or set of techniques. It is at bottom what I shall call character formation. Let the reader consider whether Plato's definition of aims is as outmoded as the old-fashioned name I have applied to it, or whether, in view of its psychological insights and concern with the forming of personality, it has rather a twentieth-century ring.

4. The educational process must be spontaneous and never forced (*Republic* 536e). In the *Laws* (819a) Plato proposes "kindergarten" methods of learning arithmetic, such as the "number-games" by which, he tells us, the Egyptian children learned it in his day.

5. The physical and cultural environment plays an important role. Its molding influence is expressed in the demand (*Republic* 401c-d)

that the young shall be surrounded by sights and sounds that transmit their grace and rhythm to the soul, "so that dwelling, so to say, in a healthful land they may receive benefit from all things about them, from whatever is conveyed to eye or ear, emanating from fair works, and coming like a health-bringing breeze from regions of wholesomeness, so that without their knowing it, from their earliest years, they are brought into friendship and concord with the beauty of reason."

6. The higher education which Plato prescribes for the chosen few both in the *Republic* and (with a difference of emphasis) in the *Laws*, is treated not as an intellectual luxury, but, in all earnest, as the basis of political order and stability.

It was Plato's most valued ideal — the cynic would say his supreme illusion — that at the summit of reality, so real as to be beyond the limited existence (or specific nature) attributable to all else, there is an Idea or Form of the Good, and that this form is accessible to a trained and gifted mind, manifesting itself suddenly but after a long preparation, "like a fire . . ." (Plato's *Seventh Letter*, 341c-d). This image of a fire is a variation on the most famous of Plato's images, the parable of the cave (*Republic* 514 ff.) in which the life of man in general is likened to a dark cave, lighted only by a little fire, in contrast to the life of the true philosopher, who has access to the cosmic fire, source of light, life, and our knowledge thereof.

The bearing of all this upon Plato's educational scheme can scarcely have been missed by a reader of the *Republic* (412a, 484, 497c-d); it is reinforced in more than one passage in the *Laws* (e.g., 962b). Somewhere in any properly ordered state there must be one or more persons — Guardians in the *Republic*, members of the Night Council in the *Laws* — who have received a higher education such as to enable their natively perceptive minds to grasp and to apply to the community the eternal principles derived from the vision of the Good.

In a more comprehensive survey, account would be taken of several other dialogues, beyond those printed in our readings. Among these are the several pages of the *Protagoras* (325c–326e), in which the famous public teacher or sophist who bore that name is shown as offering in language seemingly Plato's own a vivid account of a typical upper-class Athenian boy in the process of receiving the elementary education expected of the future Athenian citizen. It is this which Plato has altered and adapted for his guardians in the *Republic*. Some account should be taken, too, of the *Euthydemus*. Here, in broad caricature, Plato paid his ironical respects to a degraded form of pseudological training, itself a caricature of the method of Socrates, viz., the art of eristic (*eris* means "strife" or "contention") by means of which one can prove or disprove anything true or false, right or wrong. We shall have something pertinent to say of this "art" in the section on

"Knowing, Naming, and Non-Being." Finally, we should not fail to note some of Plato's later writings which are dominated by logical or methodological interests, e.g., the *Sophist* and the *Politicus* or *Statesman*, but in which in certain passages we have the luck to find the door of the Academy left deliberately ajar. From the way the young respondents in these dialogues are treated we may infer, with some security, how Plato was educating their living prototypes, the younger students at the Academy.

THEME 7: KNOWING, NAMING, AND NON-BEING

Among the showpieces in the Platonic gallery stands the famous Parable of the Cave, with which the seventh book of the *Republic* begins. We are shown the sad plight of the inmates of a cavern who must spend their entire lives in semi-darkness, chained to their seats. They are unable to turn their heads away from the inner wall of the cavern upon which, as on a motion picture screen, are projected — *how* they do not know — the flat shadow images of men and things. These images comprise the sum total of their acquaintance with reality, unless by some happy chance one of their number, freed from his chains, climbs the rugged slope and, slowly adjusting his eyes to the painful novelty of light, discovers the three-dimensional realities of the sunlit world and at last views the sun himself, "guardian of all that is in the visible world, and in a certain way the cause of all things which he [the former cave-inmate] and his fellows have been accustomed to behold."

What Plato has given us in this parable — generously adding a key to its allegory — is a magnificent pictorial exposition of the several levels or stages of "knowing" as he conceives it, together with their correlative stages of being, or, as we are more accustomed to say, of reality. Plato has here conveyed to us in concrete and dramatic form what he had earlier presented diagramatically in the famous "divided line" (*Republic* 509 ff.).

To be especially noted throughout is Plato's conviction that every level of knowing confronts a corresponding level of being. For example, to perceive a shadow requires no exercise of high intelligence and, accordingly, reveals a very minimum of reality; to envision an Eternal Form (a Platonic Idea) requires the operation of pure reason and gives us a view of a lofty peak of being.

My intention in this section is to introduce three dialogues, representative of Plato's later period, which taken together display Plato grappling with a group of logical and epistemological problems ancestrally akin to those with which philosophers of our time have been much concerned. The dialogues are the *Cratylus*, the *Theaetetus*, and the *Sophist;* the reader is advised to read the parts of them which are included in this volume (the greater portion of the *Cratylus* and of the *Theaetetus*, and the most relevant pages of the *Sophist*) in that order. In that order, too, I will introduce them here for a brief preliminary identification.

The *Cratylus*

Whoever is interested in semantics and philosophical linguistics, in the relation between thoughts and things, symbol and referent, might well make room on his book shelf for the *Cratylus*, in which are to be seen the brave beginnings of all these interests.

The major theme of the dialogue is the question — frequently debated by sophists and philosophers before and after Plato's day — "Is there a natural rightness discoverable in the names of things, or is language wholly a tissue of symbols whose meaning is determined purely by convention?"

It must be noted that there is no sympathetic magic here, no suggestion that a "name" is properly a part of the thing named. At most there is a certain naiveté in the declaration by the Socrates of the dialogue that he believes the names of things were given them by early name-givers who sought to express in them, though generally without success, the true natures of the things in question.

A further word of warning: In this dialogue, as in many others, Plato has mingled the serious with the sportive, to produce the compound known as "satire." He permits his Socrates to toss etymologies about with a fine abandon and to make the ludicrous statement that this fireworks inspiration was "rubbed off" from the soothsayer Euthyphro (probably the same rather silly person whom we meet in the short dialogue that bears his name), with whom Socrates says he has spent the morning.

How, then, are we to draw the line between Plato's philosophy and Plato's fun? There is no formula for guaranteed success. One must rely upon an "educated intuition" reinforced by wide and repeated reading and comparison of the dialogues. But two conclusions are past all reasonable doubt: in the *Cratylus* Plato has satirized the methods and results reached by those who rely on the supposed truth-values inherent in human speech, and he has eminently *not* satirized his conviction that the Eternal Ideas are prior to language, since without them nothing would exist long enough to be known. He affirms that only through our recognition of the Ideas as reflected in actuality can we know actuality or tell truth about it.

The *Theaetetus*

The priority of the Ideas gives us an easy introduction to the *Theaetetus,* a work that must be reckoned among the major displays of Plato's technical competence and originality in that branch of philosophy between logic and metaphysics which the Greeks left unnamed but which in modern parlance is called "theory of knowledge" or "epistemology," and which may be defined as a critical, analytical inquiry into the nature of knowledge, its origin, validity, and extent. This definition may serve likewise as a thumbnail answer to the question of what the *Thaetetus* is all about.

It may seem strange that in this dialogue Plato has made so little use of what bulked so large in the *Cratylus,* namely, the Theory of Ideas. But on second thought we can see good tactical reasons for his doing what he did. With the *Cratylus* presumably behind him and the "Idea-laden" *Sophist* yet to come, he chose in the *Theaetetus* a path of indirection, seeking to confirm his own positive position by sapping the foundations of rival views, as in the long and subtle dissection of Protagoras' celebrated doctrine that "man is the measure of all things"; that is, as Plato interprets it, the doctrine that whatever any man thinks or perceives is true for him, and the same for any social group. The Eternal Ideas are not directly brought into play, but a close reading of the dialogue will detect the shadow of their presence. As Cornford has shown,[15] the Ideas appear, disguised under different words, in the passage at 184a-186c where Socrates insists that there are common terms or names, such as "like" and "unlike," the meanings of which are apprehended not by the senses but only by thought. This reference serves to remind us of the heavier guns being held in reserve for use in other dialogues, notably the *Sophist,* to which we now turn.

The *Sophist*

In the *Sophist* we are offered Plato's attempt to administer the *coup de grace* to certain logical fallacies trading on the ambiguities of negative statements and, particularly, on the confusion arising from the Greek expression "non-being" or "what is not" or "nothing" (τὸ μὴ ὄν, *to mē on*).

A backward glance at the *Theaetetus* and the *Cratylus* will identify the fallacies in question. At *Theaetetus* 167a the argument of Protagoras is reinforced by an appeal to the fallacious axiom that "no

---

15 F. M. Cornford, *Plato's Theory of Knowledge* (New York: Humanities Press, 1951), p. 105.

one can think what is not" (or, as the phrase can also be understood, "what he does not think"). In a later passage of the *Theaetetus,* omitted from this volume, there is also a long but inconclusive discussion of similar fallacious arguments supporting the assertion that false opinions cannot exist. Again at *Cratylus* 429d we meet with the contention that no falsehood is possible, "for how could anyone who says what he says, yet say nothing?" Examples of this sort of verbal reasoning, reflecting the Greek delight in mental agility and acrobatics, are dramatically employed in many of the dialogues, but nowhere in such tumbling abundance as in the *Euthydemus,* commonly considered an early dialogue. Since on every page of the *Euthydemus* we find evidence of its author's understanding of the fallacies involved, we cannot take the later *Sophist* to be Plato's report of a recent discovery in the logic of language. We are, however, warranted in seeing the *Sophist* as containing Plato's first extended analysis of the relationship between thinking and linguistic expression, and in view of the recurrence of the topics involved, in seeing non-being also as a major element in Plato's thought. The Theory of the Ideas, reserved from introduction in the *Theaetetus,* here provides Plato's solution to the riddle.

THEME 8: THE COSMIC FRAME

"I had rather believe all the fables in the Legend and the Talmud, and the Alcoran, than that this universal frame is without a Mind." To this confession of faith, with which Francis Bacon begins his essay "Of Atheism," the author of the *Timaeus* and the *Laws* would have (nay, has) given his cordial assent. Evidence of Plato's concern with this theme is scattered up and down the Platonic writings, but not until rather late in his day did he set himself the task of constructing, in the *Timaeus,* a detailed symbolical-conceptual model of the World-All or Cosmos, including the animate order culminating in man,[16] and writing in the *Laws,* Book X, an essay in natural theology proving the existence of the gods, their moral excellence, and their providential care for man.

Our proper business in this concluding section is with these two "theo-cosmological" dialogues, as one might be tempted to call them. It will, however, promote understanding of them and provide a good

16 But it should be noted that the *Timaeus* was intended to form part of a trilogy to which cosmology would serve as a preface; which is to say that Plato was still a moral and political philosopher. See F. M. Cornford, *Plato's Cosmology* (New York: Harcourt, Brace, 1937), p. 20.

example of the unity of Plato's thought to consider briefly some antici-
pations of them in Plato's earlier thinking.

One outstanding example is found at *Phaedo* 97b, where the highly
Platonic Socrates recalls his passionate excitement when, as a baffled
young enquirer into the physics and chemistry of nature, he one day
chanced to hear someone reading from a book by the philosopher
Anaxagoras expounding his doctrine that Mind (*Nous*) is the source
of order and the cause of all things. How great were his expectations
of finding here a method of solving problems of every kind! For Mind
could be trusted to have arranged that each thing should be where and
and as it is best for it to be; find that "best" for any given state of
affairs and you have found the answer. But, alas, how his high hopes
tumbled after reading further in the book and finding how little use
Anaxagoras had made of his arresting insight, subordinating Mind
and treating as the true causes of things, "air, ether, water, and [he
ironically adds] many such like absurdities."

This dissatisfaction with a materialistic theory of the Cosmos, this
longing for a world view in which Mind, purpose, and value play the
leading role, set the terms and pointed to the goal that Plato made
his own in the *Timaeus* and in the *Laws*, as well as in other dialogues,
including the *Republic*.

One other instance of Plato forecasting Plato, relevant to the
Timaeus but even more so to the *Laws*, occurs in the last six Stephanus
pages of the second book of the *Republic*, where "Socrates" (i.e.,
Plato) raises and answers, to his own and Adeimantus' satisfaction, the
problem of where to draw the line between harmless and harmful
literature for consumption by the young. Socrates deplores the effect
on the plastic mind of a Grecian child of the tales commonly told him
from Homer and Hesiod, relating the misconduct not of mortal men
alone, but of heroes and even gods in the highest ranks, including Zeus
himself. To represent gods as sending upon mortals evils undeserved,
misleading them with lying dreams, encouraging violations of an oath,
bickering and even warring with one another — such depictions will
not be sanctioned in the perfected city. That all may know the legiti-
mate limits within which they must move, two canons or criteria (*ty-
poi*, says the Greek) are formulated and accepted as basic law. Freely
stated they run as follows: (1) God is good and the author of good
only; (2) God is changeless, a lover of truth, and no sender of lying
dreams.

Let us remember these canons in our reading of *Laws* X, for they
are an important part of what has been called Plato's natural theology.
Written for the *Republic*, they are yet fully suitable for the *Laws*. In
fact, they could properly, without changing a single word, be inscribed

on a tablet and set up to public view in the marketplace of either of Plato's re-formed cities.

We are now prepared to comment briefly on Plato's theo-cosmology as reflected in our two dialogues. Subordinating chronology to climactic interest, we shall consider first the *Laws* and then bring our whole discussion to an end by answering some questions crucial to an understanding of the *Timaeus*.

What, then, does *Laws* X tell us of the Universe as conceived by Plato? It will be helpful to break this enormous question into a sequence of more manageable questions, as follows:

Question I: Does this book tell us anything about the relative importance of mind (or soul) and body (matter) in the composition of the universe?

Answer I: Indeed, yes. Plato has here made his last and supreme effort to demonstrate the cosmic priority and superiority of mind to lifeless matter. To him this issue was paramount. He saw materialism as sapping the foundations of religion and morals, reducing them to the level of mere convention, products of human art, or, as we might put it, socially convenient fictions.

On an earlier page, in the discussion of the Soul, or Psyche, we touched lightly upon the concept, first formulated in the *Phaedrus,* of the soul as possessing the power of initiating motion by moving itself and thus imparting motion to the rest of the universe. A scrutiny of the argument in the *Laws* against the outright atheists (the heart of it is at 890d–896a) will show the centrality that this imputed attribute of soul has achieved in Plato's metaphysics: he now sees Soul, the self-mover, as the oldest of all things and the directing and ordering power in the Universe.

Question II: Does the book tell of any canons of theology over and above those inherited from the *Republic?*

Answer II: Yes, the two canons of the *Republic* have been added to and amplified. We are now told not merely that the gods are good but that they are "superlatively good," equipped with every good quality of mind and heart. They see all that men do, and hear all, and possess the power "to do anything that mortals and immortals have power to do," as Plato rather strangely states. The conclusion from the foregoing premises is momentous: the Divine Goodness feels a concern for the best interests of every part of the Universe, great or small; divine power assures us that this noble program is not an empty "ought."

We must, however, be careful not to read into the Platonic theology the doctrine so familiar to us of God's infinite power. At *Laws* 906a we hear of a great warfare, apparently continuous and without an ending, in which the gods and daemons are our allies. ("Daemons," in Plato's sense, are roughly like Christian angels, immortal, and intermediate between gods and men; *Symposium* 202d–e defines their functions.) This warfare is a species of Zoroastrian conflict between the good and the more numerous forces of evil. Granting that Plato is "mythologizing" here, we must remind ourselves that the myths of Plato ordinarily convey a meaning, of which the narration is only the shining vehicle. Implicit in this myth of unending conflict is the conviction that the divine power is limited and, as the *Timaeus* makes explicit, encounters a certain inexpugnable resistance to the full realization of its benevolent intent.

Question IV: Does Book X offer any account of man's place in the scheme of things?

Answer IV: There is no formal discussion here of man's place in the cosmic scheme. Nevertheless there are thrown out a sufficient number of relevant utterances to supply the material for a thumbnail "Essay on Man," as follows:

Man, the most religious of animals, is akin to the gods, whose property he is. His most arduous and noblest task is that of aiding the divine powers in the struggle against the forces of evil (906a). Justice and the other virtues reside in the gods and daemons, but a small measure of them may be clearly seen even here dwelling within us. The World-All has been providentially planned, so far as possible, with a view to the preservation and excellence of the whole, not of the parts. This ordering, however, does not forget the interest of the parts, of which man is one. Let every man know that what is best for the whole is in the end the best also for him, the part. Man is left free, since it is for him to determine by his virtuous or vicious actions whether he will rise to heavenly heights or be borne downwards to the depths (904e).

It is interesting to observe how much Stoicism owes to this Platonic "anthropology," as readers of Marcus Aurelius can hardly fail to note.

We turn now, in conclusion, to the *Timaeus*, a complex, inspiring, and historically influential work, which many readers have found the most interesting of the Platonic dialogues. Again, let the exposition take the form of question and answer, first to remove some possible stumbling blocks from the beginner's path, and finally to present Plato's central message in this work, as seen by a modern thinker.

Question I: Is Plato a monotheist? He sounds like one at *Timaeus* 27c when he speaks of calling upon God, but in the next breath he speaks of invoking the aid of gods and goddesses. And the same thing happens repeatedly. "He was good," we are told of the Divine Craftsman (the Demiurge) at *Timaeus* 29e, but later on (e.g., 41a) we hear of numerous lesser gods.

Answer I: Here we must distinguish between two levels of deity. On the one level stand the traditional Hellenic gods, Zeus, Apollo, and even Dionysus, whose symbolic worship, within the limits set by his "canons of theology," Plato would encourage in his re-formed State, but whose literal existence he would as thinker deny. We have then a polytheism of cult for the ordinary citizen. May we say that we have a monotheism of idea for the use of philosophers only? We may, with proviso. Plato's monotheism must not be mistaken for the belief in the existence of one supreme personality, comparable to the God of the Judaeo-Christian tradition; and like the Judaeo-Christian tradition he recognized an opposing principle resistant to good. Plato's ultimate god was the World Soul, with its vision of the Eternal Forms, the ruler in accord with Reason of the World-All, holy, just, and wise. And true religion was the soul's aspiration of becoming like, so far as possible, to the moral and aesthetic harmony thus achieved.

Question II: Why does Plato in the *Timaeus*, in Emerson's phrase, throw so much "mathematical dust in his reader's eyes" with all his talk of continued geometrical proportions (31b–32c), harmonic intervals (e.g. 35b–36b), and geometrical figures, e.g., the circle of the Same and of the Other (36b-c), and why does he in a later section (53c ff.) introduce triangles and, as the shapes of the ultimate particles of the elements, those regular solids — pyramids, cubes, and the rest — which to this day bear Plato's name?

Answer II: In one word the answer is "Pythagoras." If the reader will turn back to the biographical sketch he will come upon a reference to Plato's acquaintance with the mathematical philosopher Archytas, of Tarentum. This gifted man was the leading Pythagorean of his time and is reliably credited with many mathematical discoveries. There were other Pythagoreans in the Greek world of Plato's day, and the sect — for they were of the nature of a religious order — had done much to develop the science of astronomy. Plato had learned from them and had become enamored of mathematics. He loved it for its own sake, because of the beauty of its form, and valued it as the best gymnastic for the mind; he conceived the mathematical relations expressed in the motions of the heavenly bodies as evidences of the operation of Mind or Reason in the Universe, and their recognition as the proper instrument for helping the race of man to learn the lesson of order and harmony.

Question III: Scholars have held that Plato, like his pupil Aristotle, believed the Universe to be eternal — it has always existed. Why, then, does the *Timaeus* depict its construction by that Divine Artisan, the Demiurge?

Answer III: We must first of all remember that the *Timaeus* is in great part a myth. Or, we may perhaps better say, it is a mythical way of telling such truth as was available about the structure and function of the World-All. Now a "mythical way" is always a narrative way, in which are reported in their temporal relations a sequence of events. Hence a Universe mythically expounded must unavoidably have a beginning, must have come to be. It follows that there is no real inconsistency at this point between Plato's cosmology and Plato's myth. There exists a simple "transformation formula" for converting one into the other: what the mythological order reports as first in the order of time, the cosmological order reports as first in the order of Being, i.e., causally and ontologically first. In the *Timaeus* Plato has chosen to translate being into time, as at once a more intelligible and infinitely more dramatic device. His Universe, like Aristotle's, is, was, and will ever be eternal, but Plato reserves the right of mythological depiction.

Question IV: "The creation of the world — that is to say, the world of civilized order — is the victory of persuasion over force."[17] This sentence, a free translation of *Timaeus* 47e–48a, states the central thesis of Whitehead's *Adventures of Ideas*, admittedly one of the most Platonic books of our time.[17] How could creation be so achieved, and what is the opposing force of which Whitehead speaks?

Answer IV: Plato in his *Timaeus* envisages creation as the act of the Divine Craftsman in bringing harmonious order into the original chaos of unformed elements which Plato calls the "Receptacle." This chaos is conceived as filled with senseless motions or forces collectively called ἀνάγκη (*anankē*), "compulsion" or "necessity." Plato's Demiurge, in taking over chaos, has contrived to turn to account its potential resources. Looking to the Eternal Ideas as models, he has infused the formless, ever-shifting void with their patterns, not by counter-force but by persuasion. Plato's conviction that "the divine element in the world is to be conceived as a persuasive and not a coercive influence," Whitehead declares, "should be looked upon as one of the greatest intellectual discoveries in the history of religion." For it is the principle "by reason of which ideals are effective in the world, and forms of order evolve."[18] Thus we have before us a supreme example of Plato's creativity in the realm of values.

[17] Whitehead, *Adventures of Ideas*, p. 31.
[18] *Ibid.*, pp. 213–14.

Plato speaks in many voices ...

READINGS FROM THE

DIALOGUES

THE intention here is to bring Plato into closer view b
such of his dialogues (or carefully selected portions ther
adequately embody the eight themes identified and disc
Introduction.

Although the editor would have preferred to let the
without further prompting from him, there remain un
many important aspects of the themes in relation to th
dialogues that forewords often are required. Other comme
editor includes summaries of omitted parts of dialogues
are needed for continuity.

The dialogues are presented here in the most recen
the Jowett translation (*The Dialogues of Plato*, Fou
1953), by permission of the Clarendon Press and the Jowe
Trustees. Short quotations from the Jowett translation wi
torial commentary are identified by the raised letter "J."

The numbers in the margins of the Platonic text a
numbers of the Stephanus edition (see page xixn.) by wh
in the dialogues are customarily identified in citations
rupted text, the Stephanus page number is placed opposi
ning of each Stephanus page or within one line of the be
when the text is resumed after an omission or inter
Stephanus page number does not necessarily indicate th
of the Stephanus page.

Footnotes to the text that have been supplied by the p
are labeled "(L)"; all others are Jowett's or (in square bra
of the editors of the Fourth Edition.

Euthyphro

Persons of the Dialogue

SOCRATES   EUTHYPHRO

Scene: A portico before the King Archon's office

◄§ The *Euthyphro*, next to the shortest of the genuine Platonic dialogues, shows us Socrates at work as the imperturbable inquirer, "the gad-fly of Athens," stabbing the noble but sluggish steed awake. It is held to be one of that group of Plato's earlier writings called the "Socratic dialogues," in which Plato has given us the most reliable of his many portraits of his admired and beloved master. Despite its hummingbird proportions it is fully comparable, in form and content, to dialogues such as the *Lysis*, on friendship; the *Charmides*, on temperance; and, with reservations, to the search for justice as pursued in the first book of the *Republic*.

This little "scroll" is full of philosophical suggestions, most of which Plato has elaborated elsewhere. But nowhere among the dialogues do we find Plato returning to the teasing but by no means trivial problem broached by Socrates (10a) and destined to be discussed by theologians throughout the Christian centuries. The problem concerns the relation between piety and divine approval. Socrates states the issue with masterly compression: ". . . whether the pious (or holy) is beloved by the gods because it is holy, or holy because it is beloved of the gods?"

In more modern terms, the question is whether an act of piety is *per se* an act which both gods and men are morally obliged to love and admire because of the quality of its own nature. This is the first alternative. Let us examine the second. On this view the essential nature of piety is ignored and the bare fact of being approved by God fills its room. Suppose now it is asked, "Is murder wrong?" The answer of one who holds the second view could only be, "Yes, murder is a great impiety, but only because God, who could have willed otherwise, set his canon against it."

The other participant in the dialogue, Euthyphro, is represented by Plato as a pompous and self-righteous pietist, dull and incapable of logical thought. It is possible that he is the same Euthyphro mentioned in the *Cratylus* as the inspirer of Socrates' ability to suggest far-fetched etymologies of names for the gods and Homeric personages. Especially to be noted, as Jowett points out, is Euthyphro's appeal to the traditional tales of dissension among the gods and the relation of this appeal to the condemnation of Socrates, who rejected

3

the tales. Relevant also is Plato's prohibition of such tales in his ideal city of the *Republic*.

The King Archon, before whose office the scene is laid, was an Athenian state official who, though titled "King," possessed no power save in matters of religious concern, such as murder and impiety. It was before him that Socrates had been summoned, as the first pages of the dialogue inform us, to answer to the charge of impiety which led eventually to his trial and death.

2   *Euthyphro.* What can have happened, Socrates, to bring you away from the Lyceum? and what are you doing in the Porch of the King Archon? Surely you cannot be concerned in a suit before the King, like myself?

Socrates. Not in a suit, Euthyphro; prosecution is the word which the Athenians use.

Euth. What! I suppose that someone has been prosecuting you, for I cannot believe that you are the prosecutor of another.

Soc. Certainly not.

Euth. Then someone else has been prosecuting you?

Soc. Yes.

Euth. And who is he?

Soc. A young man who is little known, Euthyphro; and I hardly know him: his name is Meletus, and he is of the deme of Pitthis. Perhaps you may remember his appearance; he has a beak, and straight hair, and a beard which is ill grown.

Euth. No, I do not remember him, Socrates. But what is the charge which he brings against you?

Soc. What is the charge? Well, rather a grand one, which implies a degree of discernment far from contemptible in a young man. He says he knows how the youth are corrupted and who are their corruptors. I fancy that he must be a wise man, and seeing that I am the reverse of a wise man, he has found me out, and is going to accuse me of corrupting his generation. And of this our mother the state is to be the judge. Of all our political men he is the only one who seems to me to begin in the right way, with the cultivation of virtue in youth; like a

3   good husbandman, he makes the young shoots his first care, and clears away us whom he accuses of destroying them. This is only the first step; afterwards he will assuredly attend to the elder branches; and if he goes on as he has begun, he will be a very great public benefactor.

Euth. I hope that he may; but I rather fear, Socrates, that the opposite will turn out to be the truth. My opinion is that in attacking you he is simply aiming a blow at the heart of the state. But in what way does he say that you corrupt the young?

Soc. In a curious way, which at first hearing excites surprise: he says that I am a maker of gods, and that I invent new gods and deny the existence of the old ones; this is the ground of his indictment.

Euth. I understand, Socrates; he means to attack you about the familiar sign which occasionally, as you say, comes to you. He thinks that you are a neologian, and he is going to have you up before the court for this. He knows that such a charge is readily received by the world, as I myself know too well; for when I speak in the assembly about divine things, and foretell the future to them, they laugh at me and think me a madman. Yet every word that I say is true. But they are jealous of us all; and we must be brave and go at them.

Soc. Their laughter, friend Euthyphro, is not a matter of much consequence. For a man may be thought clever; but the Athenians, I suspect, do not much trouble themselves about him until he begins to impart his wisdom to others; and then for some reason or other, perhaps, as you say, from jealousy, they are angry.

Euth. I have no great wish to try their temper towards me in this way.

Soc. No doubt they think you are reserved in your behaviour, and unwilling to impart your wisdom. But I have a benevolent habit of pouring out myself to everybody, and would even pay for a listener, and I am afraid that the Athenians may think me too talkative. Now if, as I was saying, they would only laugh at me, as you say that they laugh at you, the time might pass gaily enough with jokes and merriment in the court; but perhaps they may be in earnest, and then what the end will be you soothsayers only can predict.

Euth. I dare say that the affair will end in nothing, Socrates, and that you will win your cause; and I think that I shall win my own.

Soc. And what is your suit, Euthyphro? are you the pursuer or the defendant?

Euth. I am the pursuer.

Soc. Of whom?

Euth. When I tell you, you will perceive another reason why **4** I am thought mad.

Soc. Why, has the fugitive wings?

Euth. Nay, he is not very volatile at his time of life.

Soc. Who is he?

Euth. My father.

Soc. My dear Sir! Your own father?

Euth. Yes.

Soc. And of what is he accused?

Euth. Of murder, Socrates.

Soc. Good heavens! How little, Euthyphro, does the common herd know of the nature of right and truth! A man must be an extraordinary man, and have made great strides in wisdom, before he could have seen his way to bring such an action.

Euth. Indeed, Socrates, he must.

Soc. I suppose that the man whom your father murdered was one of your family — clearly he was; for if he had been a stranger you would never have thought of prosecuting him.

Euth. I am amused, Socrates, at your making a distinction between one who is a member of the family and one who is not; for surely the pollution is the same in either case, if you knowingly associate with the murderer when you ought to clear yourself and him by proceeding against him. The real question is whether the murdered man has been justly slain. If justly, then your duty is to let the matter alone; but if unjustly, then proceed against the murderer, if, that is to say, he lives under the same roof with you and eats at the same table. In fact, the man who is dead was a poor dependant of mine who worked for us as a field labourer on our farm in Naxos, and one day in a fit of drunken passion he got into a quarrel with one of our domestic servants and slew him. My father bound him hand and foot and threw him into a ditch, and then sent to Athens to ask an expositor of religious law what he should do with him. Meanwhile he never attended to him and took no care about him, for he regarded him as a murderer; and thought that no great harm would be done even if he did die. Now this was just what happened. For such was the effect of cold and hunger and chains upon him, that before the messenger returned from the expositor, he was dead. And my father and family are angry with me for taking the part of the murderer and prosecuting my father. They say that he did not kill him, and that if he did, the dead man was but a murderer, and I ought not to take any notice, for that a son is impious who prosecutes a father for murder. Which shows, Socrates, how little they know what the gods think about piety and impiety.

Soc. Good heavens, Euthyphro! and is your knowledge of religion and of things pious and impious so very exact, that, supposing the circumstances to be as you state them, you are not afraid lest you too may be doing an impious thing in bringing an action against your father?

Euth. The best of Euthyphro, that which distinguishes him, 5 Socrates, from the common herd, is his exact knowledge of all such matters. What should I be good for without it?

Soc. Rare friend! I think that I cannot do better than be your disciple. Then before the trial with Meletus comes on I shall challenge him, and say that I have always had a great interest in religious questions, and now, as he charges me with rash imaginations and innovations in religion, I have become your disciple. You, Meletus, as I shall say to him, acknowledge Euthyphro to be a great theologian, and so you ought to approve of me, and not have me into court; otherwise you should begin by indicting him who is my teacher, and who will be the ruin, not of the young, but of the old; that is to say, of myself whom he instructs, and of his old father whom he admonishes and chastises. And if Meletus refuses to listen to me, but will go on, and will not shift the indictment from me to you, I cannot do better than repeat this challenge in the court.

Euth. Yes, indeed, Socrates; and if he attempts to indict me I am mistaken if I do not find a flaw in him; the court will be occupied with him long before it comes to me.

Soc. And I, my dear friend, knowing this, am desirous of becoming your disciple. For I observe that no one appears to notice you — not even this Meletus; but his sharp eyes have found me out at once, and he has indicted me for impiety. And therefore, I adjure you to tell me the nature of piety and impiety, which you said that you knew so well, in their bearing on murder and generally on offences against the gods. Is not piety in every action always the same? and impiety, again — is it not always the opposite of piety, and also the same with itself, having, as impiety, one notion or form which includes whatever is impious?

Euth. To be sure, Socrates.

Soc. And what is piety, and what is impiety?

Euth. Piety is doing as I am doing; that is to say, prosecuting anyone who is guilty of murder, sacrilege, or of any similar crime — whether he be your father or mother, or whoever he may be — that makes no difference; and not to prosecute them is impiety. And please to consider, Socrates, what a notable proof I will give you that this is the law, a proof which I have already given to others: — of the principle, I mean, that the impious, whoever he may be, ought not to go unpunished. For do not men acknowledge Zeus as the best and most righteous of the gods? — and yet they admit that he bound his 6 father (Cronos) because he wickedly devoured his sons, and that he too had punished his own father (Uranus) for a similar reason, in a nameless manner. And yet when I proceed against my father, they are angry with me. So inconsistent are they in their way of talking when the gods are concerned, and when I am concerned.

Soc. May not this be the reason, Euthyphro, why I am charged with impiety — that I cannot away with these stories about the gods? that, I suppose is where people think I go wrong. But as you who are well informed about them approve of them, I cannot do better than assent to your superior wisdom. What else can I say, confessing as I do, that I know nothing about them? Tell me, for the love of Zeus, whether you really believe that they are true.

Euth. Yes, Socrates; and things more wonderful still, of which the world is in ignorance.

Soc. And do you really believe that the gods fought with one another, and had dire quarrels, battles, and the like, as the poets say, and as you see represented in the works of great artists? The temples are full of them; and notably the robe of Athene, which is carried up to the Acropolis at the great Panathenaea, is embroidered with them throughout. Are all these tales of the gods true, Euthyphro?

Euth. Yes, Socrates; and, and as I was saying, I can tell you, if you would like to hear them, many other things about the gods which would quite amaze you.

Soc. I dare say; and you shall tell me them at some other time when I have leisure. But just at present I would rather hear from you a more precise answer, which you have not as yet given, my friend, to the question, 'What is "piety"?' When asked, you only replied, 'Doing as you do, charging your father with murder'.

Euth. And what I said was true, Socrates.

Soc. No doubt, Euthyphro; but you would admit that there are many other pious acts?

Euth. There are.

Soc. Remember that I did not ask you to give me two or three examples of piety, but to explain the general form which makes all pious things to be pious. Do you not recollect saying that one and the same form made the impious impious, the pious pious?

Euth. I remember.

Soc. Tell me what is the nature of this form, and then I shall have a standard to which I may look, and by which I may measure actions, whether yours or those of anyone else, and then I shall be able to say that such and such an action is pious, such another impious.

Euth. I will tell you, if you like.

Soc. I should very much like.

7   *Euth.* Piety, then, is that which is dear to the gods, and impiety is that which is not dear to them.

Soc. Very good, Euthyphro; you have now given me the sort of answer which I wanted. But whether what you say is true or not I cannot as yet tell, although I make no doubt that you will go on to prove the truth of your words.

Euth. Of course.

Soc. Come, then, and let us examine what we are saying. That thing or person which is dear to the gods is pious, and that thing or person which is hateful to the gods is impious, these two being the extreme opposites of one another. Was not that said?

Euth. It was.

Soc. And well said?

Euth. Yes, Socrates, I think so.

Soc. And further, Euthyphro, the gods were admitted to have enmities and hatreds and differences?

Euth. Yes, that was also said.

Soc. And what sort of difference creates enmity and anger? Suppose for example that you and I, my good friend, differ on the question which of two groups of things is more numerous; do differences of this sort make us enemies and set us at variance with one another? Do we not proceed at once to counting, and put an end to them?

Euth. True.

Soc. Or suppose that we differ about magnitudes, do we not quickly end the difference by measuring?

Euth. Very true.

Soc. And we end a controversy about heavy and light by resorting to a weighing machine?

Euth. To be sure.

Soc. But what are the matters about which differences arise that cannot be thus decided, and therefore make us angry and set us at enmity with one another? I dare say the answer does not occur to you at the moment, and therefore I will suggest that these enmities arise when the matters of difference are the just and unjust, good and evil, honourable and dishonourable. Are not these the subjects about which men differ, and about which when we are unable satisfactorily to decide our differences, you and I and all of us quarrel, when we do quarrel?

Euth. Yes, Socrates, the nature of the differences about which we quarrel is such as you describe.

Soc. And the quarrels of the gods, noble Euthyphro, when they occur, are of a like nature?

Euth. Certainly they are.

Soc. They have differences of opinion, as you say, about good and evil, just and unjust, honourable and dishonourable: there would be no quarrels among them, if there were no such differences — would there now?

Euth. You are quite right.

Soc. Does not each party of them love that which they deem noble and just and good, and hate the opposite?

Euth. Very true.

Soc. But, as you say, one party regards as just the same things as the other thinks unjust, — about these they dispute, and so there arise wars and fightings among them.

Euth. Very true.

Soc. Then the same things are hated by the gods and loved by the gods, and are both hateful and dear to them?

Euth. It appears so.

Soc. And upon this view the same things, Euthyphro, will be pious and also impious?

Euth. So I should suppose.

Soc. Then, my friend, I remark with surprise that you have not answered the question which I asked. For I certainly did not ask you to tell me what action is both pious and impious; but now it would seem that what is loved by the gods is also hated by them. And therefore, Euthyphro, in thus chastising your father you may very likely be doing what is agreeable to Zeus but disagreeable to Cronos or Uranus, and what is acceptable to Hephaestus but unacceptable to Hera, and there may be other gods who have similar differences of opinion.

Euth. But I believe, Socrates, that all the gods would be agreed as to the propriety of punishing a murderer: there would be no difference of opinion about that.

Soc. Well, but speaking of men, Euthyphro, did you ever hear anyone arguing that a murderer or any sort of evil-doer ought to be let off?

Euth. I should rather say that these are the questions which they are always arguing, especially in courts of law: they commit all sorts of crimes, and there is nothing which they will not do or say in their own defence.

Soc. But do they admit their guilt, Euthyphro, and yet say that they ought not to be punished?

Euth. No; they do not.

Soc. Then there are some things which they do not venture to say and do: for they do not venture to argue that if guilty they are to go unpunished, but they deny their guilt, do they not?

Euth. Yes.

Soc. Then they do not argue that the evil-doer should not be punished, but they argue about the fact of who the evil-doer is, and what he did and when?

Euth. True.

Soc. And the gods are in the same case, if as you assert they quarrel about just and unjust, and some of them say while others deny that injustice is done among them. For surely neither god nor man will ever venture to say that the doer of injustice is not to be punished?

Euth. That is true, Socrates, in the main.

Soc. But they join issue about the particulars — gods and men alike, if indeed the gods dispute at all; they differ about some act which is called in question, and which by some is affirmed to be just, by others to be unjust. Is not that true?

Euth. Quite true.

9 *Soc.* Well then, my dear friend Euthyphro, do tell me, for my better instruction and information, what proof have you that in the opinion of all the gods a servant who is guilty of murder, and is put

in chains by the master of the dead man, and dies because he is put in chains before he who bound him can learn from the expositors of religious law what he ought to do with him, is killed unjustly; and that on behalf of such an one a son ought to proceed against his father and accuse him of murder. How would you show that all the gods absolutely agree in approving of his act? Prove to me that they do, and I will applaud your wisdom as long as I live.

Euth. No doubt it will be a difficult task; though I could make the matter very clear indeed to you.

Soc. I understand; you mean to say that I am not so quick of apprehension as the judges: for to them you will be sure to prove that the act is unjust, and hateful to all the gods.

Euth. Yes indeed, Socrates; at least if they will listen to me.

Soc. But they will be sure to listen if they find that you are a good speaker. There was a notion that came into my mind while you were speaking; I said to myself: 'Well, and what if Euthyphro does prove to me that all the gods regarded the death of the serf as unjust, how do I know anything more of the nature of piety and impiety? for granting that this action may be hateful to the gods, still piety and impiety are not adequately defined by these distinctions, for that which is hateful to the gods has been shown to be also dear to them.' And therefore, Euthyphro, I do not ask you to prove this; I will suppose, if you like, that all the gods condemn and abominate such an action. But I will amend the definition so far as to say that what all the gods hate is impious, and what they love pious or holy; and what some of them love and others hate is both or neither. Shall this be our definition of piety and impiety?

Euth. Why not, Socrates?

Soc. Why not! certainly, as far as I am concerned, Euthyphro, there is no reason why not. But whether this premiss will greatly assist you in the task of instructing me as you promised, is a matter for you to consider.

Euth. Yes, I should say that what all the gods love is pious and holy, and the opposite which they all hate, impious.

Soc. Ought we to inquire into the truth of this, Euthyphro, or simply to accept it on our own authority and that of others — echoing mere assertions? What do you say?

Euth. We should inquire; and I believe that the statement will stand the test of inquiry.

Soc. We shall soon be better able to say, my good friend. The point which I should first wish to understand is whether the pious or holy is beloved by the gods because it is holy, or holy because it is beloved of the gods.

Euth. I do not understand your meaning, Socrates.

Soc. I will endeavour to explain: we speak of carrying and we speak of being carried, of leading and being led, seeing and being seen. You know that in all such cases there is a difference, and you know also in what the difference lies?

Euth. I think that I understand.

Soc. And is not that which is beloved distinct from that which loves?

Euth. Certainly.

Soc. Well; and now tell me, is that which is carried in this state of carrying because it is carried, or for some other reason?

Euth. No; that is the reason.

Soc. And the same is true of what is led and of what is seen?

Euth. True.

Soc. And a thing is not seen because it is visible, but conversely, visible because it is seen; nor is a thing led because it is in the state of being led, or carried because it is in the state of being carried, but the converse of this. And now I think, Euthyphro, that my meaning will be intelligible; and my meaning is, that any state of action or passion implies previous action or passion. It does not become because it is becoming, but it is in a state of becoming because it becomes; neither does it suffer because it is in a state of suffering, but it is in a state of suffering because it suffers. Do you not agree?

Euth. Yes.

Soc. Is not that which is loved in some state either of becoming or suffering?

Euth. Yes.

Soc. And the same holds as in the previous instances; the state of being loved follows the act of being loved, and not the act the state.

Euth. Certainly.

Soc. And what do you say of piety, Euthyphro: is not piety, according to your definition, loved by all the gods?

Euth. Yes.

Soc. Because it is pious or holy, or for some other reason?

Euth. No, that is the reason.

Soc. It is loved because it is holy, not holy because it is loved?

Euth. Apparently.

Soc. And it is the object of the gods' love, and is dear to them, because it is loved of them?

Euth. Certainly.

Soc. Then that which is dear to the gods, Euthyphro, is not holy, nor is that which is holy dear to the gods, as you affirm; but they are two different things.

Euth. How do you mean, Socrates?

Soc. I mean to say that the holy has been acknowledged by us to be loved because it is holy, not to be holy because it is loved.

Euth. Yes.

Soc. But that which is dear to the gods is dear to them because it is loved by them, not loved by them because it is dear to them.

Euth. True.

Soc. But, friend Euthyphro, if that which is holy were the same with that which is dear to the gods, and were loved because it is holy, then that which is dear to the gods would be loved as being dear to them; but if that which is dear to them were dear to them because loved by them, then that which is holy would be holy because loved by them. But now you see that the reverse is the case, and that the two things are quite different from one another. For one (θεοφιλές) [*theophiles*] is of a kind to be loved because it is loved, and the other (ὅσιον) [*hosion*] is loved because it is of a kind to be loved. Thus you appear to me, Euthyphro, when I ask you what is the nature of holiness, to offer an attribute only, and not the essence — the attribute of being loved by all the gods. But you still do not explain to me the nature of holiness. And therefore, if you please, I will ask you not to hide your treasure, but to start again, and tell me frankly what holiness or piety really is, whether dear to the gods or not (for that is a matter about which we will not quarrel); and what is impiety?

Euth. I really do not know, Socrates, how to express what I mean. For somehow or other the definitions we propound, on whatever bases we rest them, seem always to turn round and walk away from us.

Soc. Your words, Euthyphro, are like the handiwork of my ancestor Daedalus; and if I were the sayer or propounder of them, you might scoffingly reply that the products of my reasoning walk away and will not remain fixed where they are placed because I am a descendant of his. But now, since these propositions are your own, you must find some other gibe, for they certainly, as you yourself allow, show an inclination to be on the move.

Euth. Nay, Socrates, I think the gibe is much to the point, for you are the Daedalus who sets arguments in motion; not I, certainly, but you make them move or go round, for they would never have stirred, as far as I am concerned.

Soc. Then I must be a greater than Daedalus: for whereas he only made his own inventions to move, I move those of other people as well. And the beauty of it is, that I would rather not: for I would give the wisdom of Daedalus, and the wealth of Tantalus, to be able to detain them and keep them fixed. But enough of this. As I perceive that you are spoilt, I will myself endeavour to show you how you might instruct me in the nature of piety; and I hope that you will not grudge your labour. Tell me, then, — Is not all that is pious necessarily just?

Euth. Yes.

Soc. And is, then, all which is just pious? or, is that which is pious all just, but that which is just is only in part, and not all, pious?

Euth. I do not understand you, Socrates.

Soc. And yet I know that you are as much wiser than I am, as you are younger. But, as I was saying, revered friend, you are spoilt owing to the abundance of your wisdom. Please to exert yourself, for there is no real difficulty in understanding me. What I mean I may explain by an illustration of what I do not mean. The poet (Stasinus) sings —

> 'Of Zeus, the author and creator of all these things,
> He will not speak reproach: for where there is fear there is also reverence.'

Now I disagree with this poet. Shall I tell you in what respect?

Euth. By all means.

Soc. I should not say that where there is fear there is also reverence; for I am sure that many persons fear poverty and disease, and the like evils, but I do not perceive that they reverence the objects of their fear.

Euth. Very true.

Soc. But where reverence is, there is fear; for he who has a feeling of reverence and shame about the commission of any action, fears and is afraid of an ill reputation.

Euth. No doubt.

Soc. Then we are wrong in saying that where there is fear there is also reverence; and we should say, where there is reverence there is also fear. But there is not always reverence where there is fear; for fear is a more extended notion, and reverence is a part of fear, just as the odd is a part of number, and number is a more extended notion than the odd. I suppose that you follow me now?

Euth. Quite well.

Soc. That was the sort of question which I meant to raise when I asked whether the just is always the pious, or whether it is not the case that where there is piety there is always justice, but there may be justice where there is not piety; for justice is the more extended notion of which piety is only a part. Do you dissent?

Euth. No, I think that you are quite right.

Soc. Then, if piety is a part of justice, I suppose that we should inquire what part? If you had pursued the inquiry in the previous cases; for instance, if you had asked me what is an even number, and what part of number the even is, I should have had no difficulty in replying, a number which is not lopsided, so to speak, but represents a figure having two equal sides. Do you not agree?

Euth. Yes, I quite agree.

Soc. In like manner, I want you to tell me what part of justice is piety or holiness, that I may be able to tell Meletus not to do me injustice, or indict me for impiety, as I am now adequately instructed by you in the nature of piety or holiness, and their opposites.

Euth. Piety or holiness, Socrates, appears to me to be that part of justice which attends to the gods, as there is the other part of justice which attends to men.

Soc. That is good, Euthyphro; yet still there is a little point about 13 which I should like to have further information, What is the meaning of 'attention'? For attention can hardly be used in the same sense when applied to the gods as when applied to other things. We do so apply it, do we not? for instance, horses are said to require attention, and not every person is able to attend to them, but only a person skilled in horsemanship. Is it not so?

Euth. Certainly.

Soc. I should suppose that the art of horsemanship is the art of attending to horses?

Euth. Yes.

Soc. Nor is everyone qualified to attend to dogs, but only the huntsman?

Euth. True.

Soc. And I should also conceive that the art of the huntsman is the art of attending to dogs?

Euth. Yes.

Soc. As the art of the oxherd is the art of attending to oxen?

Euth. Very true.

Soc. In like manner holiness or piety is the art of attending to the gods? — that would be your meaning, Euthyphro?

Euth. Yes.

Soc. And is not attention always designed for the good or benefit of that to which the attention is given? As in the case of horses, you may observe that when attended to by the horseman's art they are benefited and improved, are they not?

Euth. True.

Soc. As the dogs are benefited by the huntsman's art, and the oxen by the art of the oxherd, and all other things are tended or attended for their good and not for their hurt?

Euth. Certainly, not for their hurt.

Soc. But for their good?

Euth. Of course.

Soc. And does piety or holiness, which has been defined to be the art of attending to the gods, benefit or improve them? Would you say that when you do a holy act you make any of the gods better?

Euth. No, no; that was certainly not what I meant.

Soc. And I, Euthyphro, never supposed that you did. I asked you the question about the nature of the attention, because I thought that you did not.

Euth. You do me justice, Socrates; that is not the sort of attention which I mean.

Soc. Good: but I must still ask what is this attention to the gods which is called piety?

Euth. It is such, Socrates, as servants show to their masters.

Soc. I understand — a sort of ministration to the gods.

Euth. Exactly.

Soc. Medicine is also a sort of ministration or service, having in view the attainment of some object — would you not say of health?

Euth. I should.

Soc. Again, there is the art which ministers to the ship-builder with a view to the attainment of some result?

Euth. Yes, Socrates, with a view to the building of a ship.

Soc. As there is an art which ministers to the house-builder with a view to the building of a house?

Euth. Yes.

Soc. And now tell me, my good friend, about the art which ministers to the gods: what work does that help to accomplish? For you must surely know if, as you say, you are of all men living the one who is best instructed in religion.

Euth. And I speak the truth, Socrates.

Soc. Tell me then, oh tell me — what is that fair work which the the gods do by the help of our ministrations?

Euth. Many and fair, Socrates, are the works which they do.

14   *Soc.* Why, my friend, and so are those of a general. But the sum of them is easily told. Would you not say that the sum of his works is victory in war?

Euth. Certainly.

Soc. Many and fair, too, are the works of the husbandman, if I am not mistaken; but their sum is the production of food from the earth?

Euth. Exactly.

Soc. And of the many and fair things done by the gods, what is the sum?

Euth. I have told you already, Socrates, that to learn all these things accurately will be very tiresome. Let me simply say that piety or holiness is learning how to please the gods in word and deed, by prayers and sacrifices. Such piety is the salvation of families and states, just as impiety, which is unpleasing to the gods, is their ruin and destruction.

Soc. I think that you could have answered in much fewer words the substance of my questions if you had chosen. But I see plainly that you are not disposed to instruct me — clearly not: else why, when we reached the point, did you turn aside? Had you only answered me I should have truly learned of you by this time the nature of piety. But I must follow you as a lover must follow the caprice of his beloved, and therefore can only ask again, what is the pious, and what is piety? Do you mean that they are a sort of science of praying and sacrificing?

Euth. Yes, I do.

Soc. And sacrificing is giving to the gods, and prayer is asking of the gods?

Euth. Yes, Socrates.

Soc. Upon this view, then, piety is a science of asking and giving?

Euth. You understand me capitally, Socrates.

Soc. Yes, my friend; the reason is that I am a votary of your science, and give my mind to it, and therefore nothing which you say will be thrown away upon me. Please then to tell me, what is the nature of this service to the gods? Do you mean that we prefer requests and give gifts to them?

Euth. Yes, I do.

Soc. Is not the right way of asking to ask of them what we want?

Euth. Certainly.

Soc. And the right way of giving is to give to them in return what they want of us. There would be no meaning in an art which gives to anyone that which he does not want.

Euth. Very true, Socrates.

Soc. Then piety, Euthyphro, is an art which gods and men have of trafficking with one another?

Euth. That is an expression which you may use, if you like.

Soc. But I have no particular liking for anything but the truth. I wish, however, that you would tell me what benefit accrues to the gods from our gifts. There is no doubt about what they give to us, for there is no good thing which they do not give; but how they get any benefit from our gifts to them, is far from being equally clear. If they give everything and get from us nothing, that must be a traffic in which we have very greatly the advantage of them.

Euth. And do you imagine, Socrates, that any benefit accrues to the gods from our gifts?

Soc. But if not, Euthyphro, what is the meaning of the gifts we offer to the gods?

Euth. What else but tributes of honour; and, as I was just now saying, what pleases them?

Soc. Piety, then, is pleasing to the gods, but not beneficial or dear to them?

Euth. I should say that nothing could be dearer.

Soc. Then once more the assertion is repeated that piety is that which is dear to the gods?

Euth. Certainly.

Soc. And when you say this, can you wonder at your words not standing firm, but walking away? Will you accuse me of being the Daedalus who makes them walk away, not perceiving that there is another and far greater artist than Daedalus who makes things that go round in a circle, and he is yourself; for the argument, as you will perceive, comes round to the same point. Were we not saying that the holy or pious was not the same with that which is loved of the gods? Have you forgotten?

Euth. I quite remember.

Soc. And are you not now saying that what is dear to the gods is holy; and is not this the same as what is loved of them — do you see?

Euth. True.

Soc. Then either we were wrong in our former assertion; or, if we were right then, we are wrong now.

Euth. It appears so.

Soc. Then we must begin again and ask, What is piety? That is an inquiry which I shall never be weary of pursuing as far as in me lies; and I entreat you not to scorn me, but to apply your mind to the utmost, and tell me the truth. For, if any man knows, you are he; and therefore I must hold you fast, like Proteus, until you tell. If you had not certainly known the nature of piety and impiety, I am confident that you would never, on behalf of a serf, have charged your aged father with murder. You would not have run such a risk of doing wrong in the sight of the gods, and you would have had too much respect for the opinions of men. I am sure, therefore, that you know the nature of piety and impiety. Speak out then, my dear Euthyphro, and do not hide your knowledge.

Euth. Another time, Socrates; for I am in a hurry, and must go now.

Soc. Alas! my friend, and will you leave me in despair? I was hoping that you would instruct me in the nature of piety and impiety; 16 and then I might have cleared myself of Meletus and his indictment. I would have told him that I had been enlightened by Euthyphro, and had given up rash innovations and speculations in which I had indulged only through ignorance, and that now I am about to lead a better life.

Apology

∽§ The *Apology* is perhaps of all the Platonic writings, excepting
the last few pages of the *Phaedo*, the most deeply felt, by reader
and writer both. Every word of it is transparent and what shines
through is a man of immense moral stature, whom the last few words
of the *Phaedo* have finely characterized.

The *Apology* is not a tape-recording of an actual speech made by
the defendant Socrates charged with "atheism" and with "corrupting
the youth." Neither is it the baseless fabric of a Platonic dream.
It has a touch of each, in the sense that a gifted portrait painter may
present us with a good surface likeness of an actual man, while at the
same time transcending the "good surface-likeness" principle to present an interpretation of the living spirit within.

The contents of the speech have been sufficiently indicated in our
Introduction. Worth noting is the form, which will bear the closest
scrutiny in point of rhetorical structure and felicity of style. The
speech is a quite elaborate construction which manages by various
devices of rhetorical art to retain so great an appearance of extempore
spontaneity that for centuries readers have felt themselves present
and participating in this most moving occasion.

Socrates is represented as addressing his judges in court:

How you, O Athenians, have been affected by my accusers, I 17
cannot tell; but I know that they almost made me forget who I was
— so persuasively did they speak; and yet they have hardly uttered a
word of truth. But of the many falsehoods told by them, there was
one which quite amazed me; — I mean when they said that you
should be upon your guard and not allow yourselves to be deceived
by the force of my eloquence. To say this, when they were certain
to be detected as soon as I opened my lips and proved myself to be
anything but a great speaker, did indeed appear to me most shameless
— unless by the force of eloquence they mean the force of truth; for if
such is their meaning, I admit that I am eloquent. But in how different a way from theirs! Well, as I was saying, they have scarcely
spoken the truth at all; from me you shall hear the whole truth, but
not delivered after their manner in a set oration duly ornamented with
fine words and phrases. No, by heaven! I shall use the words and
arguments which occur to me at the moment, for I am confident in the
justice of my cause: at my time of life I ought not to be appearing
before you, O men of Athens, in the character of a boy inventing
falsehoods — let no one expect it of me. And I must particularly beg

19

of you to grant me this favour: — If I defend myself in my accustomed manner, and you hear me using the words which many of you have heard me using habitually in the agora, at the tables of the money-changers, and elsewhere, I would ask you not to be surprised, and not to interrupt me on this account. For I am more than seventy years of age, and appearing now for the first time before a court of law, I am quite a stranger to the language of the place; and therefore I would have you regard me as if I were really a stranger, whom you would 18 excuse if he spoke in his native tongue, and after the fashion of his country: — Am I making an unfair request of you? Never mind the manner, which may or may not be good; but think only of the truth of my words, and give heed to that: let the speaker speak truly and the judge decide justly.

And first, I have to reply to the older charges and to my first accusers, and then I will go on to the later ones. For of old I have had many accusers, who have accused me falsely to you during many years; and I am more afraid of them than of Anytus and his associates, who are dangerous, too, in their own way. But far more dangerous are the others, who began when most of you were children, and took possession of your minds with their falsehoods, telling of one Socrates, a wise man, who speculated about the heaven above, and searched into the earth beneath, and made the worse appear the better cause. The men who have besmeared me with this tale are the accusers whom I dread; for their hearers are apt to fancy that such inquirers do not believe in the existence of the gods. And they are many, and their charges against me are of ancient date, and they were made by them in the days when some of you were more impressible than you are now — in childhood, or it may have been in youth — and the cause went by default, for there was none to answer. And hardest of all, I do not know and cannot tell the names of my accusers; unless in the chance case of a comic poet. All who from envy and malice have persuaded you — some of them having first convinced themselves — all this class of men are most difficult to deal with; for I cannot have them up here, and cross-examine them, and therefore I must simply fight with shadows in my own defence, and argue when there is no one who answers. I will ask you then to take it from me that my opponents are of two kinds; one recent, the other ancient: and I hope that you will see the propriety of my answering the latter first, for these accusations you heard long before the others, and much oftener. 19 Well, then, I must make my defence, and endeavour to remove from your minds in a short time, a slander which you have had a long time to take in. May I succeed, if to succeed be for my good and yours, or likely to avail me in my cause! The task is not an easy one; I quite understand the nature of it. And so leaving the event with God, in obedience to the law I will now make my defence.

I will begin at the beginning, and ask what is the accusation which has given rise to the slander of me, and in fact has encouraged Meletus to prefer this charge against me. Well, what do the slanderers say? They shall be my prosecutors, and this is the information they swear against me: 'Socrates is an evildoer; a meddler who searches into things under the earth and in heaven, and makes the worse appear the better cause, and teaches the aforesaid practices to others.' Such is the nature of the accusation: it is just what you have yourselves seen in the comedy of Aristophanes,[1] who has introduced a man whom he calls Socrates, swinging about and saying that he walks on air, and talking a deal of nonsense concerning matters of which I do not pretend to know either much or little — not that I mean to speak disparagingly of anyone who is a student of natural philosophy. May Meletus never bring so many charges against me as to make me do that! But the simple truth is, O Athenians, that I have nothing to do with physical speculations. Most of those here present are witnesses to the truth of this, and to them I appeal. Speak then, you who have heard me, and tell your neighbours whether any of you have ever known me hold forth in few words or in many upon such matters. . . . You hear their answer. And from what they say of this part of the charge you will be able to judge of the truth of the rest.

As little foundation is there for the report that I am a teacher, and take money; this accusation has no more truth in it than the other. Although, if a man were really able to instruct mankind, this too would, in my opinion, be an honour to him. There is Gorgias of Leontium, and Prodicus of Ceos, and Hippias of Elis, who go the round of the cities, and are able to persuade the young men to leave their own citizens by whom they might be taught for nothing, and come to them whom they not only pay, but are thankful if they may be allowed to pay them. There is at this time a Parian philosopher residing in Athens, of whom I have heard; and I came to hear of him in this way: — I came across a man who has spent more money on the sophists than the rest of the world put together, Callias, the son of Hipponicus, and knowing that he had sons, I asked him: 'Callias,' I said, 'if your two sons were foals or calves, there would be no difficulty in finding someone to put over them; we should hire a trainer of horses, or a farmer probably, who would improve and perfect them in the appropriate virtue and excellence; but as they are human beings, whom are you thinking of placing over them? Is there anyone who understands human and civic virtue? You must have thought about the matter, for you have sons; is there anyone?' 'There is,' he said. 'Who is he?' said I; 'and of what country? and what does he charge?' 'Evenus the Parian,' he replied; 'he is the man, and his

[1] Aristoph. *Clouds*, 225 foll.

charge is five minas.' Happy is Evenus, I said to myself, if he really has this wisdom, and teaches at such a moderate charge. Had I the same, I should have been very proud and conceited; but the truth is that I have no knowledge of the kind.

I dare say, Athenians, that someone among you will reply, 'Yes, Socrates, but what *is* your occupation? What is the origin of these accusations which are brought against you; there must have been something strange which you have been doing? All these rumours and this talk about you would never have arisen if you had been like other men: tell us, then, what is the cause of them, for we should be sorry to judge hastily of you.' Now I regard this as a fair challenge, and I will endeavour to explain to you the reason why I am called wise and have such an evil fame. Please to attend then. And although some of you may think that I am joking, I declare that I will tell you the entire truth. Men of Athens, this reputation of mine has come of a certain sort of wisdom which I possess. If you ask me what kind of wisdom, I reply, wisdom such as may perhaps be attained by man, for to that extent I am inclined to believe that I am wise; whereas the persons of whom I was speaking have a kind of superhuman wisdom, which I know not how to describe, because I have it not myself; and he who says that I have, speaks falsely, and is taking away my character. And here, O men of Athens, I must beg you not to interrupt me, even if I seem to say something extravagant. For the word which I will speak is not mine. I will refer you to a witness who is worthy of credit; that witness shall be the god of Delphi — he will tell you about my wisdom, if I have any, and of what sort it is. You

21 must have known Chaerephon; he was early a friend of mine, and also a friend of yours, for he shared in the recent exile of the people, and returned with you. Well, Chaerephon, as you know, was very impetuous in all his doings, and he went to Delphi and boldly asked the oracle to tell him whether — as I was saying, I must beg you not to interrupt — he actually asked the oracle to tell him whether anyone was wiser than I was, and the Pythian prophetess answered that there was no man wiser. Chaerephon is dead himself; but his brother, who is in court, will confirm the truth of what I am saying.

Why do I mention this? Because I am going to explain to you why I have such an evil name. When I heard the answer, I said to myself, What can the god mean? and what is the interpretation of his riddle? for I know that I have no wisdom, small or great. What then can he mean when he says that I am the wisest of men? And yet he is a god, and cannot lie; that would be against his nature. After long perplexity, I thought of a method of trying the question. I reflected that if I could only find a man wiser than myself, then I might go to the god with a refutation in my hand. I should say to him, 'Here is a man who is wiser than I am; but you said that I was the wisest.' Accordingly I went to one who had the reputation of wisdom, and observed him — his name I need not mention, he was a politician; and in the process of examining him and talking with him, this, men of Athens, was what I found. I could not help thinking that he was not really wise, although he was thought wise by many, and still wiser by himself; and thereupon I tried to explain to him that he thought himself wise, but was not really wise; and the consequence was that he hated me, and his enmity was shared by several who were present and heard me. So I left him, saying to myself as I went away: Well, although I do not suppose that either of us knows anything really worth knowing, I am at least wiser than this fellow — for he knows nothing, and thinks that he knows; I neither know nor think that I know. In this one little point, then, I seem to have the advantage of him. Then I went to another who had still higher pretensions to wisdom, and my conclusion was exactly the same. Whereupon I made another enemy of him, and of many others besides him.

Then I went to one man after another, being not unconscious of the enmity which I provoked, and I lamented and feared this: but necessity was laid upon me, — the word of God, I thought, ought to be considered first. And I said to myself, Go I must to all who appear to know, and find out the meaning of the oracle. And I swear to you, 22 Athenians, — for I must tell you the truth — the result of my mission was just this: I found that the men most in repute were nearly the most foolish; and that others less esteemed were really closer to wisdom. I will tell you the tale of my wanderings and of the 'Herculean' labours, as I may call them, which I endured only to find at last the oracle irrefutable. After the politicians, I went to the poets; tragic, dithyrambic, and all sorts. And there, I said to myself, you will be instantly detected; now you will find out that you are more ignorant than they are. Accordingly, I took them some of the most elaborate passages in their own writings, and asked what was the meaning of them — thinking that they would teach me something. Will you believe me? I am ashamed to confess the truth, but I must say that there is hardly a person present who would not have talked better about their poetry than they did themselves. So I learnt that not by wisdom do poets write poetry, but by a sort of genius and inspiration; they are like diviners or soothsayers who also say many fine things, but do not understand the meaning of them. The poets appeared to me to be much in the same case; and I further observed that upon the strength of their poetry they believed themselves to be the wisest of men in other things in which they were not wise. So I departed, conceiving myself to be superior to them for the same reason that I was superior to the politicians.

At last I went to the artisans, for I was conscious that I knew nothing at all, as I may say, and I was sure that they knew many fine things; and here I was not mistaken, for they did know many things of which I was ignorant, and in this they certainly were wiser than I was. But I observed that even the good artisans fell into the same error as the poets; — because they were good workmen they thought that they also knew all sorts of high matters, and this defect in them overshadowed their wisdom; and therefore I asked myself on behalf of the oracle, whether I would like to be as I was, neither having their knowledge nor their ignorance, or like them in both; and I made answer to myself and to the oracle that I was better off as I was.

23 This inquisition has led to my having many enemies of the worst and most dangerous kind, and has given rise also to many imputations, including the name of 'wise'; for my hearers always imagine that I myself possess the wisdom which I find wanting in others. But the truth is, O men of Athens, that God only is wise; and by his answer he intends to show that the wisdom of men is worth little or nothing; although speaking of Socrates, he is only using my name by way of illustration, as if he said, He, O men, is the wisest, who, like Socrates, knows that his wisdom is in truth worth nothing. And so I go about the world, obedient to the god, and search and make inquiry into the wisdom of anyone, whether citizen or stranger, who appears to be wise; and if he is not wise, then in vindication of the oracle I show him that he is not wise; and my occupation quite absorbs me, and I have had no time to do anything useful either in public affairs or in any concern of my own, but I am in utter poverty by reason of my devotion to the god.

There is another thing: — young men of the richer classes, who have not much to do, come about me of their own accord; they like to hear people examined, and they often imitate me, and proceed to do some examining themselves; there are plenty of persons, as they quickly discover, who think that they know something, but really know little or nothing; and then those who are examined by them instead of being angry with themselves are angry with me: This confounded Socrates, they say; this villainous misleader of youth! — and then if somebody asks them, Why, what evil does he practice or teach? they do not know, and cannot tell; but in order that they may not appear to be at a loss, they repeat the ready-made charges which are used against all philosophers about teaching things up in the clouds and under the earth, and having no gods, and making the worse appear the better cause; for they do not like to confess that their pretence of knowledge has been detected — which is the truth; and as they are numerous and ambitious and energetic, and speak vehemently with persuasive tongues, they have filled your ears with their loud and inveterate calumnies. And this is the reason why my three accusers, Meletus and Anytus and Lycon, have set upon me; Meletus, who has a quarrel with me on behalf of the poets; Anytus, on behalf of the craftsmen and politicians; Lycon, on behalf of the 24 rhetoricians: and as I said at the beginning, I cannot expect to get rid of such a mass of calumny all in a moment. And this, O men of Athens, is the truth and the whole truth; I have concealed nothing, I have dissembled nothing. And yet, I feel sure that my plainness of speech is fanning their hatred of me, and what is their hatred but a proof that I am speaking the truth? — Hence has arisen the prejudice against me; and this is the reason of it, as you will find out either in this or in any future inquiry.

I have said enough in my defence against the first class of my accusers; I turn to the second class. They are headed by Meletus, that good man and true lover of his country, as he calls himself. Against these, too, I must try to make a defence: — Let their affidavit be read: it contains something of this kind: It says that Socrates is a doer of evil, inasmuch as he corrupts the youth, and does not receive the gods whom the state receives, but has a new religion of his own. Such is the charge; and now let us examine the particular counts. He says that I am a doer of evil, and corrupt the youth; but I say, O men of Athens, that Meletus is a doer of evil, in that he is playing a solemn farce, recklessly bringing men to trial from a pretended zeal and interest about matters in which he really never had the smallest interest. And the truth of this I will endeavour to prove to you.

Come hither, Meletus, and let me ask a question of you. You attach great importance to the improvement of youth?

Yes, I do.

Tell the judges, then, who is their improver; for you must know, as you take such interest in the subject, and have discovered their corrupter, and are citing and accusing me in this court. Speak, then, and tell the judges who is the improver of youth: — Observe, Meletus, that you are silent, and have nothing to say. But is this not rather disgraceful, and a very considerable proof of what I was saying, that you have no interest in the matter? Speak up, friend, and tell us who their improver is.

The laws.

But that, my good sir, is not my question: Can you not name some person — whose first qualification will be that he knows the laws?

The judges, Socrates, who are present in court.

What, do you mean to say, Meletus, that they are able to instruct and improve youth?

Certainly they are.

What, all of them, or some only and not others?

All of them.

Truly, that is good news! There are plenty of improvers, then.
25 And what do you say of the audience, — do they improve them?

Yes, they do.

And the senators?

Yes, the senators improve them.

But perhaps the members of the assembly corrupt them? — or do they too improve them?

They improve them.

Then every Athenian improves and elevates them; all with the exception of myself; and I alone am their corrupter? Is that what you affirm?

That is what I stoutly affirm.

I am very unfortunate if you are right. But suppose I ask you a question: Is it the same with horses? Does one man do them harm and all the world good? Is not the exact opposite the truth? One man is able to do them good, or at least very few; — the trainer of horses, that is to say, does them good, but the ordinary man does them harm if he has to do with them? Is not that true, Meletus, of horses, or of any other animals? Most assuredly it is; whether you and Anytus say yes or no. Happy indeed would be the condition of youth if they had one corrupter only, and all the rest of the world were their benefactors. But you, Meletus, have sufficiently shown that you never had a thought about the young: your carelessness is plainly seen in your not caring about the very things which you bring against me.

And now, Meletus, I adjure you to answer me another question: Which is better, to live among bad citizens, or among good ones? Answer, friend, I say; the question is one which may be easily answered. Do not the good do their neighbours good, and the bad do them evil?

Certainly.

And is there anyone who would rather be injured than benefited by those who live with him? Answer, my good friend, the law requires you to answer — does anyone like to be injured?

Certainly not.

And when you accuse me of corrupting and deteriorating the youth, do you allege that I corrupt them intentionally or unintentionally?

Intentionally, I say.

But you have just admitted that the good do their neighbours good, and the evil do them evil. Now, is that a truth which your superior wisdom has recognized thus early in life, and am I, at my age, in such darkness and ignorance as not to know that if a man with whom I have to live is corrupted by me, I am very likely to be harmed by him; and yet I corrupt him, and intentionally, too — so you say, although neither I nor any other human being is ever likely to be convinced by you. But either I do not corrupt them, or I 26 corrupt them unintentionally; and on either view of the case you lie. If my offence is unintentional, the law has no cognizance of unintentional offences: you ought to have taken me privately, and warned and admonished me; for if I had had instruction, I should have left off doing what I only did unintentionally — beyond doubt I should; but you would have nothing to say to me and refused to teach me. And now you bring me up in this court, which is a place not of instruction, but of punishment.

It will be very clear to you, Athenians, as I was saying, that Meletus has never had any care, great or small, about the matter. But still I should like to know, Meletus, in what I am affirmed to corrupt the young. I suppose you mean, as I infer from your indictment, that I teach them not to acknowledge the gods which the state acknowledges, but some other new divinities or spiritual agencies in their stead. These are the lessons by which I corrupt the youth, as you say.

Yes, that I say emphatically.

Then, by the gods, Meletus, of whom we are speaking, tell me and the court, in somewhat plainer terms, what you mean! for I do not as yet understand whether you affirm that I teach other men to acknowledge some gods, and therefore that I do believe in gods, and am not an entire atheist — this you do not lay to my charge, — but only you say that they are not the same gods which the city recognizes — the charge is that they are different gods. Or, do you mean that I am an atheist simply, and a teacher of atheism?

I mean the latter — that you are a complete atheist.

What an extraordinary statement! Why do you think so, Meletus? Do you mean that I do not believe in the god-head of the sun or moon, like the rest of mankind?

I assure you, judges, that he does not: for he says that the sun is stone, and the moon earth.

Friend Meletus, do you think that you are accusing Anaxagoras? Have you such a low opinion of the judges, that you fancy them so illiterate as not to know that these doctrines are found in the books of Anaxagoras the Clazomenian, which are full of them? And so, forsooth, the youth are said to be taught them by Socrates, when they can be bought in the book-market for one drachma at most; and they might pay their money, and laugh at Socrates if he pretends to father these extraordinary views. And so, Meletus, you really think that I do not believe in any god?

I swear by Zeus that you verily believe in none at all.

Nobody will believe you, Meletus, and I am pretty sure that you do not believe yourself. I cannot help thinking, men of Athens, that Meletus is reckless and impudent, and that he has brought this indict-

27 ment in a spirit of mere wantonness and youthful bravado. Has he not compounded a riddle, thinking to try me? He said to himself: — I shall see whether the wise Socrates will discover my facetious self-contradiction, or whether I shall be able to deceive him and the rest of them. For he certainly does appear to me to contradict himself in the indictment as much as if he said that Socrates is guilty of not believing in the gods, and yet of believing in them — but this is not like a person who is in earnest.

I should like you, O men of Athens, to join me in examining what I conceive to be his inconsistency; and do you, Meletus, answer. And I must remind the audience of my request that they would not make a disturbance if I speak in my accustomed manner:

Did ever man, Meletus, believe in the existence of human things, and not of human beings? . . . I wish, men of Athens, that he would answer, and not be always trying to get up an interruption. Did ever any man believe in horsemanship, and not in horses? or in flute-playing, and not in flute-players? My friend, no man ever did; I answer to you and to the court, as you refuse to answer for yourself. But now please to answer the next question: Can a man believe in the existence of things spiritual and divine, and not in spirits or demigods?

He cannot.

How lucky I am to have extracted that answer, by the assistance of the court! But then you swear in the indictment that I teach and believe in divine or spiritual things (new or old, no matter for that); at any rate, I believe in spiritual things, — so you say and swear in the affidavit; and yet if I believe in them, how can I help believing in spirits or demigods; — must I not? To be sure I must; your silence gives consent. Now what are spirits or demigods? are they not either gods or the sons of gods?

Certainly they are.

But this is what I call the facetious riddle invented by you: the demigods or spirits are gods, and you say first that I do not believe in gods, and then again that I do believe in gods; that is, if I believe in demigods. For if the demigods are the illegitimate sons of gods, whether by nymphs, or by other mothers, as some are said to be — what human being will ever believe that there are no gods when there are sons of gods? You might as well affirm the existence of mules, and deny that of horses and asses. Such nonsense, Meletus, could only have been intended by you to make trial of me. You have put this into the indictment because you could think of nothing real of which to accuse me. But no one who has a particle of understanding will ever be convinced by you that a man can believe in the existence of things divine and superhuman, and the same man refuse to believe 28 in gods and demigods and heroes.

I have said enough in answer to the charge of Meletus: any elaborate defence is unnecessary. You know well the truth of my statement that I have incurred many violent enmities; and this is what will be my destruction if I am destroyed; — not Meletus, nor yet Anytus, but the envy and detraction of the world, which has been the death of many good men, and will probably be the death of many more; there is no danger of my being the last of them.

Someone will say: And are you not ashamed, Socrates, of a course of life which is likely to bring you to an untimely end? To him I may fairly answer: There you are mistaken: a man who is good for anything ought not to calculate the chance of living or dying; he ought only to consider whether in doing anything he is doing right or wrong — acting the part of a good man or of a bad. Whereas, upon your view, the heroes who fell at Troy were not good for much, and the son of Thetis above all, who altogether despised danger in comparison with disgrace; and when he was so eager to slay Hector, his goddess mother said to him that if he avenged his companion Patroclus, and slew Hector, he would die himself — 'Fate,' she said, in these or the like words, 'waits for you next after Hector;' he, receiving this warning, utterly despised danger and death, and instead of fearing them, feared rather to live in dishonour, and not to avenge his friend. 'Let me die forthwith,' he replies, 'and be avenged of my enemy, rather than abide here by the beaked ships, a laughing-stock and a burden of the earth.' Had Achilles any thought of death and danger? For wherever a man's place is, whether the place which he has chosen or that in which he has been placed by a commander, there he ought to remain in the hour of danger, taking no account of death or of anything else in comparison with disgrace. And this, O men of Athens, is a true saying.

Strange, indeed, would be my conduct, O men of Athens, if I who, when I was ordered by the generals whom you chose to command me at Potidaea and Amphipolis and Delium, remained where they placed me, like any other man, facing death — if now, when, as I conceive and imagine, God orders me to fulfil the philosopher's mission of searching into myself and other men, I were to desert my post through 29 fear of death, or any other fear; that would indeed be strange, and I might justly be arraigned in court for denying the existence of the gods, if I disobeyed the oracle because I was afraid of death, fancying that I was wise when I was not wise. For the fear of death is indeed the pretence of wisdom, and not real wisdom, being a pretence of knowing the unknown; and no one knows whether death, of which men are afraid because they apprehend it to be the greatest evil, may not be the greatest good. Is not this ignorance of a disgraceful sort, the ignorance which is the conceit that a man knows what he does not know? And in this respect only I believe myself to differ from men in general, and may perhaps claim to be wiser than they are: — that whereas I know but little of the world below, I do not suppose that I know: but I do know that injustice and disobedience to a better, whether God or man, is evil and dishonourable, and I will never fear or avoid a possible good rather than a certain evil. And therefore if you let me go now, and are not convinced by Anytus, who said that since I had been prosecuted I must be put to death; (or if not that I ought never to have been prosecuted at all); and that if I escape now, your sons will all be utterly ruined by practising what I teach — if you say to me, Socrates, this time we will not mind Anytus, and you shall be let off, but upon one condition, that you are not to inquire and speculate in this way any more, and that if you are caught doing so again you shall die; — if this was the condition on which you let me go, I should reply: Men of Athens, I honour and love you; but I shall obey God rather than you, and while I have life and strength I shall never cease from the practice and teaching of philosophy, exhorting any one of you whom I meet and saying to him after my manner: You, my friend, — a citizen of the great and mighty and wise city of Athens, — are you not ashamed of heaping up the largest amount of money and honour and reputation, and caring so little about wisdom and truth and the greatest improvement of the soul, which you never regard nor heed at all? And if the person with whom I am arguing, says: Yes, but I do care; then I shall not leave him nor let him go at once, but proceed to interrogate and examine and cross-examine him, and if I think that he has no virtue in him but only says 30 that he has, I shall reproach him with undervaluing the most precious, and overvaluing the less. And I shall repeat the same words to everyone whom I meet, young and old, citizen and alien, but especially to you citizens, inasmuch as you are my brethren. For know that this is the command of God; and I believe that no greater good has ever happened in the state than my service to the God. For I do nothing but go about persuading you all, old and young alike, not to take thought for your persons or your properties, but first and chiefly to care about the greatest improvement of the soul. I tell you that virtue is not given by money, but that from virtue comes money and every other good of man, public as well as private. This is my teaching, and if it corrupts the young, it is mischievous; but if anyone says that this is not my teaching, he is speaking an untruth. Wherefore, O men of Athens, I say to you, do as Anytus bids or not as Anytus bids, and either acquit me or not; but whichever you do, understand that I shall never alter my ways, not even if I have to die many times.

Men of Athens, do not interrupt, but hear me; I begged you before to listen to me without interruption, and I beg you now to hear me to the end. I have something more to say, at which you may be inclined to cry out; but I believe that to hear me will be good for you, and therefore I beseech you to restrain yourselves. I would have you know, that if you kill such an one as I am, you will injure yourselves more than you will injure me. Nothing will injure me, not Meletus nor yet Anytus — they cannot, for a bad man is not permitted to injure a better than himself. I do not deny that Anytus may, perhaps, kill him, or drive him into exile, or deprive him of civil rights; and he may imagine, and others may imagine, that he is inflicting a great injury upon him: but there I do not agree. For the evil of doing as he is doing — the evil of seeking unjustly to take the life of another — is greater far.

And now, Athenians, I am not going to argue for my own sake, as you may think, but for yours, that you may not sin against God by condemning me, who am his gift to you. For if you kill me you will not easily find a successor to me, who, if I may use such a ludicrous figure of speech, am a sort of gadfly, given to the state by God; and the state is a great and noble steed who is tardy in his motions owing to his very size, and requires to be stirred into life. I am that gadfly which God has attached to the state, and all day long and in all places am always fastening upon you, arousing and persuading and reproaching 31 you. You will not easily find another like me, and therefore I would advise you to spare me. I dare say that you may feel out of temper (like a person who is suddenly awakened from sleep), and you think that you might easily strike me dead as Anytus advises, and then you would sleep on for the remainder of your lives, unless God in his care of you sent you another gadfly. When I say that I am given to you by God, the proof of my mission is this: — if I had been like other men, I should not have neglected all my own concerns or patiently seen the neglect of them during all these years, and have been doing yours, coming to you individually like a father or elder brother, exhorting you to regard virtue; such conduct, I say, would be unlike human nature. If I gained anything, or if my exhortations were paid, there would be some sense in my doing so; but now, as you see for yourselves, not even the unfailing impudence of my accusers dares to say that I have ever exacted or sought pay of anyone; of that they can produce no witness. And I have a sufficient witness to the truth of what I say — my poverty.

Someone may wonder why I go about in private giving advice and busying myself with the concerns of others, but do not venture to come forward in public and advise the state. I will tell you why. You have heard me speak at sundry times and in divers places of a superhuman oracle or sign which comes to me, and is the divinity which Meletus ridicules in the indictment. This sign, which is a kind of voice, first began to come to me when I was a child; from time to time it forbids me to do something which I am going to do, but never commands anything. This is what deters me from being a politician. And rightly, as I think. For I am certain, O men of Athens, that if I had engaged in politics, I should have perished long ago, and done no good either to you or to myself. And do not be offended at my telling you the truth: for the truth is, that no man who sets himself firmly against you or any other multitude, honestly striving to keep the state from many lawless and unrighteous deeds, will save his life; he who will fight for the right, if he would live even for a brief space, must have a private station and not a public one.

I can give you convincing evidence of what I say, not words only, but what you value far more — actions. Let me relate to you a passage of my own life which will prove to you that to no man should I ever wrongly yield from fear of death, and that I should in fact be willing to perish for not yielding. I will tell you a tale of the courts, not very interesting perhaps, but nevertheless true. The only office of state which I ever held, O men of Athens, was that of senator: the tribe Antiochis, which is my tribe, had the presidency at the trial of the generals who had not taken up the bodies of the slain after the battle of Arginusae; and you proposed to try them in a body, contrary to law, as you all thought afterwards; but at the time I was the only one of the Prytanes who was opposed to the illegality, and I gave my vote against you; and when the orators threatened to impeach and arrest me, and you called and shouted, I made up my mind that I would run the risk, having law and justice with me, rather than take part in your injustice because I feared imprisonment and death. This happened in the days of the democracy. But when the oligarchy of the Thirty was in power, they sent for me and four others into the rotunda, and bade us bring Leon the Salaminian from Salamis, as they wanted to put him to death. This was a specimen of the sort of commands which they were always giving with the view of implicating as many as possible in their crimes; and then I showed again, not in word only but in deed, that, if I may be allowed to use such an expression, I care not a straw for death, and that my great and only care is lest I should do an unrighteous or unholy thing. For the strong arm of that oppressive power did not frighten me into doing wrong; and when we came out of the rotunda the other four went to Salamis and fetched Leon, but I went quietly home. For which I might have lost my life, had not the power of the Thirty shortly afterwards come to an end. And many will witness to my words.

Now do you really imagine that I could have survived all these years, if I had led a public life, supposing that like a good man I had always maintained the right and had made justice, as I ought, the first thing? No indeed, men of Athens, neither I nor any other man. But I have been always the same in all my actions, public as well as private, and never have I yielded any base compliance to those who are slanderously termed my disciples, or to any other. Not that I have ever had any regular disciples. But if anyone likes to come and hear me while I am pursuing my mission, whether he be young or old, he is not excluded. Nor do I converse only with those who pay; but anyone, whether he be rich or poor, may ask and answer me and listen to my words; and whether he turns out to be a bad man or a good one, neither result can be justly imputed to me; for I never taught nor professed to teach anything. And if anyone says that he has ever learned or heard anything from me in private which all the world has not heard, let me tell you that he is lying.

But I shall be asked, Why do people delight in continually conversing with you? I have told you already, Athenians, the whole truth about this matter: they like to hear the cross-examination of the pretenders to wisdom; there is amusement in it. Now this duty of cross-examining other men has been imposed upon me by God; and has been signified to me by oracles, dreams, and in every way in which the will of divine power was ever intimated to anyone. This is true, O Athenians; or, if not true, can easily be disproved. If I really am or have been corrupting the youth, those of them who are now grown up and have become sensible that I gave them bad advice in the days of their youth should of course come forward as accusers, and take their revenge; or if they do not like to come themselves, some of their relatives, fathers, brothers, or other kinsmen, should think of the evil their families have suffered at my hands. Now is their time. Many of them I see in the court. There is Crito, who is of the same age and of the same deme with myself, and there is Crito-bulus his son, whom I also see. Then again there is Lysanias of Sphettus, who is the father of Aeschines — he is present; and also there is Antiphon of Cephisus, who is the father of Epigenes; and there are the brothers of several who have associated with me. There is Nicostratus the son of Theodotides, and the brother of Theodotus (now Theodotus himself is dead, and therefore he, at any rate, will not to seek to stop him); and there is Paralus the son of Demodocus, who had a brother Theages; and Adeimantus the son of Ariston, whose brother Plato is present; and Aeantodorus, who is the brother of Apollodorus, whom I also see. I might mention a great many others, some of whom Meletus should have produced as witnesses in the course of his speech; and let him still produce them, if he has forgotten — I will make way for him. And let him say, if he has any testimony of the sort which he can produce. Nay, Athenians, the very opposite is the truth. For all these are ready to witness on behalf of the corrupter, of the injurer of their kindred, as Meletus and Anytus call me; not the corrupted youth only — there might have been a motive for that — but their uncorrupted elder relatives. Why should they too support me with their testimony? Why, indeed, except for the sake of truth and justice, and because they know that I am speaking the truth, and that Meletus is a liar.

Well, Athenians, this and the like of this is all the defence which I have to offer. Yet a word more. Perhaps there may be someone who is offended at me, when he calls to mind how he himself on a similar, or even a less serious occasion, prayed and entreated the judges with many tears, and how he produced his children in court to excite compassion, together with a host of relations and friends; whereas I, who am probably in danger of my life, will do none of these things. The contrast may occur to his mind, and he may be set against me, and vote in anger because he is displeased at me on this account. Now if there be such a person among you, — mind, I do not say that there is, — to him I may fairly reply: My friend, I am a man, and like other men, a creature of flesh and blood, and not 'of wood or stone', as Homer says; and I have a family, yes, and sons, O Athenians, three in number, one almost a man, and two others who are still young; and yet I will not bring any of them hither in order to petition you for an acquittal. And why not? Not from any self-assertion or want of respect for you. Whether I am or am not afraid of death is another question, of which I will not now speak. But when I think of my own good name, and yours, and that of the whole state, I feel that such conduct would be discreditable. One who has reached my years, and has the name I have, ought not to demean himself. Whether this opinion of me be deserved or not, at any rate the world 35 has decided that Socrates is in some way superior to other men. And if those among you who are said to be superior in wisdom or courage, or any other virtue, demean themselves in this way, how shameful is their conduct! I have seen men of reputation behaving in the strangest manner while they were being tried: they seemed to fancy that they were going to suffer something dreadful if they had to die, and that they would live for ever if you spared them; and I think that such are a dishonour to the state, and that any stranger coming in would have said of them that the most eminent men of Athens, to whom the Athenians themselves give office and honour, are no better than women. And I say that these things ought not to be done to you by those who have a reputation in any walk of life; and if they are done, you ought not to permit them; you ought rather to show that you are far more disposed to condemn the man who gets up a doleful scene and makes the city ridiculous, than him who holds his peace.

But, setting aside the question of honour, there seems to be something wrong in asking a favour of a judge, and thus procuring an acquittal, instead of informing and convincing him. For his duty is not to make a present of justice, but to give judgement; and he was sworn that he will judge according to the laws, and not according to his own good pleasure; and we ought not to encourage you, nor should you allow yourselves to be encouraged, in this habit of perjury — there can be no piety in that. Do not then require me to do what I consider dishonourable and impious and wrong, especially now, when I am being tried for impiety on the indictment of Meletus. For if, O men of Athens, by force of persuasion and entreaty I could overpower your oaths, then I should be teaching you to believe that there are no gods, and in defending should simply convict myself of the charge of not believing in them. But that is not so — far otherwise. For I do believe that there are gods, and in a sense higher than that in which any of my accusers believe in them. And to you and to God I commit my cause, to be determined as is best for you and me.

There are many reasons why I am not grieved, O men of Athens, at the vote of condemnation. I expected it, and am only surprised that the votes are so nearly equal; for I had thought that the majority against me would have been far larger; but now, had thirty votes gone over to the other side, I should have been acquitted, And I may say, I think, that I have escaped Meletus. I may say more; for without the assistance of Anytus and Lycon, anyone may see that he would not have had a fifth part of the votes, as the law requires, in which case he would have incurred a fine of a thousand drachmas.

And so he proposes death as the penalty. And what shall I propose on my part, O men of Athens? Clearly that which is my due. And what is my due? What ought I to have done to me, or to pay — a man who has never had the wit to keep quiet during his whole life; but has been careless of what the many care for — wealth, and family interests, and military offices, and speaking in the assembly, and magistracies, and plots, and parties. Reflecting that I was really too honest a man to be a politician and live, I did not go where I could do no good to you or to myself; but where I could do privately the greatest good (as I affirm it to be) to everyone of you, thither I went, and sought to persuade every man among you that he must look to himself, and seek virtue and wisdom before he looks to his private interests, and look to the state before he looks to the interests of the state; and that this should be the order which he observes in all his actions. What shall be done to such an one? Doubtless some good thing, O men of Athens, if he has his reward; and the good should be of a kind suitable to him. What would be a reward suitable to a poor man who is your benefactor, and who desires leisure that he

may instruct you? There can be no reward so fitting as maintenance in the Prytaneum, O men of Athens, a reward which he deserves far more than the citizen who has won the prize at Olympia in the horse or chariot race, whether the chariots were drawn by two horses or by many. For I am in want, and he has enough; and he only gives you
37 the appearance of happiness, and I give you the reality. And if I am to estimate the penalty fairly, I should say that maintenance in the Prytaneum is the just return.

Perhaps you think that I am braving you in what I am saying now, as in what I said before about the tears and prayers. But this is not so. I speak rather because I am convinced that I never intentionally wronged anyone, although I cannot convince you — the time has been too short; if there were a law at Athens, as there is in other cities, that a capital cause should not be decided in one day, then I believe that I should have convinced you. But I cannot in a moment refute great slanders; and, as I am convinced that I never wronged another, I will assuredly not wrong myself. I will not say of myself that I deserve any evil, nor propose any penalty. Why should I? Because I am afraid of the penalty of death which Meletus proposes? When I do not know whether death is a good or an evil, why should I propose a penalty which would certainly be an evil? Shall I say imprisonment? And why should I live in prison, and be the slave of the magistrates of the year — of the Eleven? Or shall the penalty be a fine, and imprisonment until the fine is paid? There is the same objection. I should have to lie in prison, for money I have none, and cannot pay. And if I say exile (and this may possibly be the penalty which you will affix), I must indeed be blinded by the love of life, if I am so irrational as to expect that when you, who are my own citizens, cannot endure my discourses and arguments, and have found them so grievous and odious that you will have no more of them, others are likely to endure them. No indeed, men of Athens, that is not very likely. And what a life should I lead, at my age, wandering from city to city, ever changing my place of exile, and always being driven out! For I am quite sure that wherever I go, there, as here, the young men will flock to listen to me; and if I drive them away, their elders will drive me out at their request; and if I let them come, their fathers and friends will drive me out for their sakes.

Someone will say: Yes, Socrates, but cannot you hold your tongue, and then you may go into a foreign city, and no one will interfere with you? Now I have great difficulty in making you understand my answer to this. For if I tell you that to do as you say would be a dis-
38 obedience to God, and therefore that I cannot hold my tongue, you will not believe that I am serious; and if I say again that daily to discourse about virtue, and of those other things about which you hear

me examining myself and others, is the greatest good of man, and that the unexamined life is no life for a human being, you are still less likely to believe me. Yet I say what is true, although a thing of which it is hard for me to persuade you. Also, I have never been accustomed to think that I deserve to suffer any harm. Had I money I might have estimated the offence at what I was able to pay, and not have been much the worse. But I have none, and therefore I must ask you to proportion the fine to my means. Well, perhaps I could afford a mina, and therefore I propose that penalty: Plato, Crito, Critobulus, and Apollodorus, my friends here, bid me say thirty minas, and they will be the sureties. Let thirty minas be the penalty; for which sum they will be ample security to you.

Not much time will be gained, O Athenians, in return for the evil name which you will get from the detractors of the city, who will say that you killed Socrates, a wise man; for they will call me wise, even although I am not wise, when they want to reproach you. If you had waited a little while, your desire would have been fulfilled in the course of nature. For I am far advanced in years, as you may perceive, and not far from death. I am speaking now not to all of you, but only to those who have condemned me to death. And I have another thing to say to them: You think that I was convicted because I had no words of the sort which would have procured my acquittal — I mean, if I had thought fit to leave nothing undone or unsaid. Not so; the deficiency which led to my conviction was not of words — certainly not. But I had not the boldness nor impudence nor inclination to address you as you would have liked me to do, weeping and wailing and lamenting, and saying and doing many things, such indeed as you have been accustomed to hear from others, but I maintain to be unworthy of myself. I thought at the time that I ought not to do anything common or mean when in danger: nor do I now repent of the style of my defence; I would rather die having spoken after my manner, than speak in your manner and live. For neither in war nor yet at law ought I or any man to use every way of escaping death. 39 Often in battle there can be no doubt that if a man will throw away his arms, and fall on his knees before his pursuers, he may escape death; and in other dangers there are other ways of escaping death, if a man has the hardihood to say and do anything. The difficulty, my friends, is not to avoid death, but to avoid unrighteousness; for that runs faster than death. I am old and move slowly, and the slower runner has overtaken me; my accusers are keen and quick, and the faster runner, who is wickedness, has overtaken them. And now I depart hence condemned by you to suffer the penalty of death, — they too go their ways condemned by the truth to suffer the penalty of villainy and wrong; and I must abide by my award — let them abide by theirs. I suppose that these things may be regarded as fated, — and I think that they are well.

And now, O men who have condemned me, I would fain prophesy to you; for I am about to die, and in the hour of death men are gifted with prophetic power. And I prophesy to you who are my murderers, that immediately after my departure punishment far heavier than you have inflicted on me surely awaits you. Me you have killed because you wanted to escape the accuser, and not to give an account of your lives. But that will not be as you suppose: far otherwise. For I say that there will be more accusers of you than there are now; accusers whom hitherto I have restrained: and as they are younger they will be more severe with you, and you will be more offended at them. If you think that by killing men you will stop all censure of your evil lives, you are mistaken; that is not a way of escape which is either very possible, or honourable; the easiest and the noblest way is not to be disabling others, but to be improving yourselves. This is the prophecy which I utter before my departure to the judges who have condemned me.

Friends, who would have acquitted me, I would like also to talk with you about the thing which has come to pass, while the magistrates are busy, and before I go to the place at which I must die. 40 Stay then a little, for we may as well talk with one another while there is time. You are my friends, and I should like to show you the meaning of this event which has happened to me. O my judges — for you I may truly call judges — I should like to tell you of a wonderful circumstance. Hitherto the divine faculty of which the internal oracle is the source has constantly been in the habit of opposing me even about trifles, if I was going to make a slip or error in any matter; and now as you see there has come upon me that which may be thought, and is generally believed to be, the last and worst evil. But the oracle made no sign of opposition, either when I was leaving my house in the morning, or when I was on my way to the court, or while I was speaking, at anything which I was going to say; and yet I have often been stopped in the middle of a speech, but now in nothing I either said or did touching the matter in hand has the oracle opposed me. What do I take to be the explanation of this silence? I will tell you. It is an intimation that what has happened to me is a good, and therefore those of us who think that death is an evil must be in error. I have this conclusive proof; the customary sign would surely have opposed me had I been going to evil and not to good.

Let us reflect in another way, and we shall see that there is great reason to hope that death is a good; for one of two things — either death is a state of nothingness and utter unconsciousness, or, as men say, there is a change and migration of the soul from this world to another. Now if you suppose that there is no consciousness, but a sleep like the sleep of him who is undisturbed even by dreams, death will be an unspeakable gain. For if a person were to select the night in which his sleep was undisturbed even by dreams, and were to compare with this the other days and nights of his life, and then were to tell us how many days and nights he had passed in the course of his life better and more pleasantly than this one, I think that any man, I will not say a private man, but even the great king will not find many such days or nights, when compared with the others. Now if death be of such a nature, I say that to die is gain; for eternity is then only a single night. But if death is the journey to another place, and there, as men say, all the dead abide, what good, O my friends and 41 judges, can be greater than this? If indeed when the pilgrim arrives in the world below, he is delivered from our earthly professors of justice, and finds the true judges who are said to give judgement there, Minos and Rhadamanthus and Aeacus and Triptolemus, and other sons of God who are righteous in their own life, that pilgrimage will be worth making. What would not a man give if he might converse with Orpheus and Musaeus and Hesiod and Homer? Nay, if this be true, let me die again and again. I myself, too, shall find a wonderful interest in there meeting and conversing with Palamedes, and Ajax the son of Telamon, and any other ancient hero who has suffered death through an unjust judgement; and there will be no small pleasure, as I think, in comparing my own experience with theirs. Above all, I shall then be able to continue my search into true and false knowledge, as in this world, so also in the next; and I shall find out who is wise, and who pretends to be wise, and is not. What would not a man give, O judges, to be able to examine the leader of the great Trojan expedition; or Odysseus or Sisyphus, or numberless others, men and women too! What infinite delight would there be in conversing with them and asking them questions! In another world they do not put a man to death for asking questions: assuredly not. For besides being happier than we are, they will be immortal, if what is said is true.

Wherefore, O judges, be of good cheer about death, and know of a certainty that no evil can happen to a good man, either in life or after death, and that he and his are not neglected by the gods. Nor has my own approaching end happened by mere chance; I see clearly that the time had arrived when it was better for me to die and be released from trouble; therefore the oracle gave no sign, and therefore also I am not at all angry with my condemners, or with my accusers. But although they have done me no harm, they intended it; and for this I may properly blame them.

Still I have a favour to ask of them. When my sons are grown up,
I would ask you, O my friends, to punish them; I would have you
trouble them, as I have troubled you, if they seem to care about
riches, or anything, more than about virtue; or if they pretend to be
something when they are really nothing, — then reprove them, as I
have reproved you, for not caring about that for which they ought to
42 care, and thinking that they are something when they are really
nothing. And if you do this, I shall have received justice at your
hands, and so will my sons.

The hour of departure has arrived, and we go our ways — I to die,
and you to live. Which is better God only knows.

Crito

Persons of the Dialogue

SOCRATES   CRITO

Scene: The prison of Socrates

⋖§ A worthy sequel to the *Apology* is this "duologue," as we may
call it, between Socrates and his faithful and rather plodding friend,
Crito. In it the ideals affirmed in the *Apology* are, in a manner, put
to the proof and validated in the moral conduct of their affirmer,
Socrates.

Crito has arranged a means of opening prison doors and of smug-
gling Socrates across frontiers into a safety zone such as Thessaly.
It is upon the quality of the reasons that motivate Socrates' refusal
to accept freedom, on the terms offered him by Crito, that the moral
grandeur of this dialogue depends. This it is that prompts us, by
parity of reasoning, to think in this connection of such men as Thoreau
and Mahatma Gandhi.

The reader's special attention is directed to the passage near the end
of the dialogue in which Socrates imagines that he is addressed by
the personified Laws of Athens, who solemnly adjure him to remember his debt of obedience to them, who have given him life and
nurture. This personification, as Burnet well remarks, "allows Socrates
to invest the declaration of his principles with a certain emotion. It
thus fulfills the same function as the myths of the more elaborate
dialogues."[1]

Socrates. Why have you come at this hour, Crito? it must be quite **43**
early?

Crito. Yes, certainly.

Soc. What is the exact time?

Cr. The dawn is about to break.

Soc. I wonder that the keeper of the prison would let you in.

Cr. He knows me, because I often come, Socrates; moreover, I
have done him a kindness.

Soc. And are you only just arrived?

Cr. No, I came some time ago.

[1] John Burnet, *Plato's* Euthyphro, Apology of Socrates, *and* Crito (Oxford:
Clarendon Press, 1924), pp. 199–200. (L)

Soc. Then why did you sit and say nothing, instead of at once awakening me?

Cr. Awaken you, Socrates? Certainly not! I wish I were not myself so sleepless and full of sorrow. I have been watching with amazement your peaceful slumbers; and I deliberately refrained from awaking you, because I wished time to pass for you as happily as might be. Often before during the course of your life I have thought you fortunate in your disposition; but never did I see anything like the easy, tranquil manner in which you bear this calamity.

Soc. Why, Crito, when a man has reached my age he ought not to be repining at the approach of death.

Cr. And yet other old men find themselves in similar misfortunes, and age does not prevent them from repining.

Soc. That is true. But you do not say why you come so early.

Cr. I come to bring you a painful message; not, as I believe, to yourself, but painful and grievous to all of us who are your friends, and most grievous of all to me.

Soc. What? Has the ship come from Delos, on the arrival of which I am to die?

Cr. No, the ship has not actually arrived, but she will probably be here today, as persons who have come from Sunium tell me that they left her there; and therefore tomorrow, Socrates, must be the last day of your life.

Soc. Very well, Crito; if such is the will of God, I am willing; but my belief is that there will be a delay of a day.

44   *Cr.* Why do you think so?

Soc. I will tell you. I am to die on the day after the arrival of the ship.

Cr. Yes; that is what the authorities say.

Soc. But I do not think that the ship will be here until tomorrow; this I infer from a vision which I had last night, or rather only just now, when you fortunately allowed me to sleep.

Cr. And what was the nature of the vision?

Soc. There appeared to me the likeness of a woman, fair and comely, clothed in bright raiment, who called to me and said: 'O Socrates,

> The third day hence to fertile Phthia shalt thou come.'

Cr. What a singular dream, Socrates!

Soc. There can be no doubt about the meaning, Crito, I think.

Cr. Yes; the meaning is only too clear. But, oh! my beloved Socrates, let me entreat you once more to take my advice and escape. For if you die I shall not only lose a friend who can never be replaced, but there is another evil: people who do not know you and me will believe that I might have saved you if I had been willing to spend money, but that I did not care. Now, can there be a worse disgrace than this — that I should be thought to value money more than the life of a friend? For the many will not be persuaded that I wanted you to escape, and that you refused.

Soc. But why, my dear Crito, should we care about the opinion of the many? The best men, and they are the only persons who are worth considering, will think of these things truly as they occurred.

Cr. But you see, Socrates, that the opinion of the many must be regarded, for what is now happening shows of itself that they can do the greatest evil to anyone who has lost their good opinion.

Soc. I only wish it were so, Crito, and that the many could do the greatest evil; for then they would also be able to do the greatest good — and what a fine thing this would be! But in reality they can do neither; for they cannot make a man either wise or foolish, and they do not care what they make of him.

Cr. Well, I will not dispute with you; but please to tell me Socrates, whether you are not acting out of regard to me and your other friends: are you not afraid that if you escape from prison we may get into trouble with the informers for having stolen you away, and lose either the whole or a great part of our property; or that even a worse evil may happen to us? Now, if you fear on our account, be at ease; for in order to save you, we ought surely to run this, or even a greater risk; be persuaded, then, and do as I say.

Soc. Yes, Crito, that is one fear which you mention, but by no means the only one.

Cr. Fear not — there are persons who are willing to get you out of prison at no great cost; and as for the informers, you know that they are far from being exorbitant in their demands — a little money will satisfy them. My means, which are certainly ample, are at your service, and if out of regard for my interests you have a scruple about spending my money, here are strangers who will give you the use of theirs; and one of them, Simmias the Theban, has brought a large sum for this very purpose; and Cebes and many others are prepared to spend their money in helping you to escape. I say, therefore, do not shirk the effort on our account, and do not say, as you did in the court, that you will have a difficulty in knowing what to do with yourself anywhere else. For men will love you in other places to which you may go, and not in Athens only; there are friends of mine in Thessaly, if you like to go to them, who will value and protect you, and no Thessalian will give you any trouble. Nor can I think that you are at all justified, Socrates, in betraying your own life when you might be saved; in acting thus you are working to bring on yourself the very fate which your enemies would and did work to bring on you, your

own destruction. And further I should say that you are deserting
your own children; for you might bring them up and educate them;
instead of which you go away and leave them, and they will have to
take their chance; and if they do not meet with the usual fate of
orphans, there will be small thanks to you. No man should bring
children into the world who is unwilling to persevere to the end in
their nurture and education. But you appear to be choosing the easier
part, not the better and manlier, which would have been more
becoming in one who professes to care for virtue in all his life, like
yourself. And indeed, I am ashamed not only of you, but of us who
are your friends, when I reflect that the whole business may be attributed entirely to our want of courage. The trial need never have come
on, or might have been managed differently; and this last opportunity
will seem (crowning futility of it all) to have escaped us through our
46 own incompetence and cowardice, who might have saved you if we
had been good for anything, and you might have saved yourself; for
there was no difficulty at all. See now, Socrates, how discreditable as
well as disastrous are the consequences, both to us and you. Make
up your mind then, or rather have your mind already made up, for the
time of deliberation is over, and there is only one thing to be done,
which must be done this very night, and if we delay at all will be no
longer practicable or possible; I beseech you therefore, Socrates, be
persuaded by me, and do not say me nay.

Soc. Dear Crito, your zeal is invaluable, if a right one; but if
wrong, the greater the zeal the greater the danger; and therefore we
ought to consider whether I shall or shall not do as you say. For I am
and always have been one of those natures who must be guided by
reason, whatever the reason may be which upon reflection appears to
me to be the best; and now that this chance has befallen me, I cannot
repudiate my own doctrines, which seem to me as sound as ever: the
principles which I have hitherto honoured and revered I still honour,
and unless we can at once find other and better principles, I am certain not to agree with you; no, not even if the power of the multitude
could let loose upon us many more imprisonments, confiscations,
deaths, frightening us like children with hob-goblin terrors. What
will be the fairest way of considering the question? Shall I return to
your old argument about the opinions of men? — we were saying
that some of them are to be regarded, and others not. Now were we
right in maintaining this before I was condemned? And has the argument which was once good now proved to be talk for the sake of talking — mere childish nonsense? That is what I want to consider with
your help, Crito: — whether, under my present circumstances, the
argument will appear to me in any way different or not; and whether
we shall dismiss or accept it. That argument, which, as I believe, is
maintained by many persons of authority, was to the effect, as I was

saying, that the opinions of some men are to be regarded, and of other men not to be regarded. Now you, Crito, are not going to die 47 tomorrow — at least, there is no human probability of this — and therefore you are disinterested and not liable to be deceived by the circumstances in which you are placed. Tell me then, I beg you, whether I am right in saying that some opinions, and the opinions of some men only, are to be valued, and that others are to be disregarded. Is not this true?

Cr. Certainly.

Soc. The good opinions are to be regarded, and not the bad?

Cr. Yes.

Soc. And the opinions of the wise are good, and the opinions of the unwise are evil?

Cr. Certainly.

Soc. And what was said about another matter? Does the pupil who devotes himself to the practice of gymnastics attend to the praise and blame and opinion of any and every man, or of one man only — his physician or trainer, whoever he may be?

Cr. Of one man only.

Soc. And he ought to fear the censure and welcome the praise of that one only, and not of the many?

Cr. Clearly so.

Soc. And he ought to act and train, and eat and drink in the way which seems good to his single master who has understanding, rather than according to the opinion of all other men put together?

Cr. True.

Soc. And if he disobeys and disregards the opinion and approval of the one, and regards the opinion of the many who have no understanding, will he not suffer evil?

Cr. Certainly he will.

Soc. And what will the evil be, whither tending and what affecting, in the disobedient person?

Cr. Clearly, affecting the body; that is what is ruined by the evil.

Soc. Very good; and is not this true, Crito, of other things which we need not separately enumerate? In questions of just and unjust, fair and foul, good and evil, which are the subjects of our present consultation, ought we to follow the opinion of the many and to fear them; or the opinion of the one man who has understanding? ought we not to fear and reverence him more than all the rest of the world, and if we desert him shall we not corrupt and outrage that principle in us which may be assumed to be improved by justice and deteriorated by injustice? — there is such a principle?

Cr. Certainly there is, Socrates.

Soc. Take a parallel instance: — if, acting against the advice of those who have understanding, we ruin that which is improved by health and is corrupted by disease, would life be worth having? And that which has been corrupted is — the body?

Cr. Yes.

Soc. Is our life worth living, with an evil and corrupted body?

Cr. Certainly not.

Soc. And will it be worth living, if that higher part of man be corrupted which is improved by justice and depraved by injustice? Do we suppose that principle, whatever it may be in man, which has to do with justice and injustice, to be inferior to the body?

Cr. Certainly not.

Soc. More honourable than the body?

Cr. Far more.

Soc. Then, my friend, we must not particularly regard what the many say of us: but what he, the one man who has understanding of just and unjust, will say, and what the truth will say. And therefore you begin in error when you advise that we should regard the opinion of the many about just and unjust, good and evil, honourable and dishonourable. — 'Well,' someone will say, 'but the many can kill us.'

Cr. That will clearly be the answer, Socrates; you are right there.

Soc. But still, my excellent friend, I find that the old argument is unshaken as ever. And I should like to know whether I may say the same of another proposition — that not life, but a good life, is to be chiefly valued?

Cr. Yes, that also remains unshaken.

Soc. And a good life is equivalent to a just and honourable one — that holds also?

Cr. Yes, it does.

Soc. From these premises I proceed to argue the question whether it is or is not right for me to try and escape without the consent of the Athenians: and if it is clearly right, then I will make the attempt; but if not, I will abstain. The other considerations which you mention, of money and loss of character and the duty of educating one's children, are, I fear, only the doctrines of the multitude, who would restore people to life, if they were able, as thoughtlessly as they put them to death — and with as little reason. But now, since the argument has carried us thus far, the only question which remains to be considered is, whether we shall do rightly, I by escaping and you by helping me, and by paying the agents of my escape in money and thanks; or whether in reality we shall not do rightly; and if the latter, then death or any other calamity which may ensue on my remaining quietly here must not be allowed to enter into the calculation.

Cr. I think that you are right, Socrates; how then shall we proceed?

Soc. Let us consider the matter together, and do you either refute me if you can, and I will be convinced; or else cease, my dear friend, from repeating to me that I ought to escape against the wishes of the Athenians: for I am very eager that what I do should be done with your approval. And now please to consider my first position, and try how you can best answer me. 49

Cr. I will.

Soc. Are we to say that we are never intentionally to do wrong, or that in one way we ought and in another way we ought not to do wrong, or is doing wrong always evil and dishonourable, as has already been often acknowledged by us? Are all the admissions we have made within these last few days to be thrown over? And have we, at our age, been earnestly discoursing with one another all our life long only to discover that we are no better than children? Or, in spite of the opinion of the many, and in spite of all consequences whether for the better or the worse, shall we insist on the truth of what was then said, that injustice is always an evil and dishonour to him who acts unjustly? Shall we say so or not?

Cr. Yes.

Soc. Then we must do no wrong?

Cr. Certainly not.

Soc. Nor when injured injure in return, as the many imagine; for we must injure no one at all?

Cr. Clearly not.

Soc. Again, Crito, may we do evil?

Cr. Surely not, Socrates.

Soc. And what of doing evil in return for evil, which is the morality of the many — is that just or not?

Cr. Not just.

Soc. For doing evil to another is the same as injuring him?

Cr. Very true.

Soc. Then we ought not to retaliate or render evil for evil to anyone, whatever evil we may have suffered from him. But I would have you consider, Crito, whether you really mean what you are saying. For this opinion has never been held, and never will be held, by any considerable number of persons; and those who are agreed and those who are not agreed upon this point have no common ground, and can only despise one another when they see how widely they differ. Tell me, then, whether you agree with and assent to my first principle, that neither injury nor retaliation nor warding off evil by evil is ever right. And shall that be the premiss of our argument? Or do you decline and dissent from this? For so I have ever thought, and continue to think; but, if you are of another opinion, let me hear what you have to say. If, however, you remain of the same mind as formerly, I will proceed to the next step.

Cr. You may proceed, for I have not changed my mind.

Soc. Then I will go on to the next point, which may be put in the form of a question: — Ought a man to do what he admits to be right, or ought he to betray the right?

Cr. He ought to do what he thinks right.

50 *Soc.* But if this is true, what is the application? In leaving the prison against the will of the Athenians, do I wrong any? or rather do I not wrong those whom I ought least to wrong? Do I not desert the principles which were acknowledged by us to be just — what do you say?

Cr. I cannot answer your question, Socrates; for I do not understand it.

Soc. Then consider the matter in this way: — Imagine that I am about to run away (you may call the proceeding by any name which you like), and the laws and the state appear to me and interrogate me: 'Tell us, Socrates,' they say; 'what are you about? are you not going by an act of yours to bring us to ruin — the laws, and the whole state, as far as in you lies? Do you imagine that a state can subsist and not be overthrown, in which the decisions of laws have no power, but are set aside and trampled upon by individuals?' What will be our answer, Crito, to these and the like words? Anyone, and especially a rhetorician, will have a good deal to say against the subversion of the law which requires a sentence to be carried out. Shall we reply, 'Yes; but the state has injured us and given an unjust sentence.' Suppose we say that?

Cr. Very good, Socrates.

Soc. 'And was that our agreement with you?' the law would answer; 'or were you to abide by the sentence of the state?' And if we were to express our astonishment at their words, the law would probably add: 'Answer, Socrates, instead of opening your eyes — you are in the habit of asking and answering questions. Tell us, — What complaint have you to make against us which justifies you in attempting to ruin us and the state? In the first place did we not bring you into existence? Your father married your mother by our aid and begat you. Say whether you have any objection to urge against those of us who regulate marriage?' None, I should reply. 'Or against those of us who after birth regulate the nurture and education of children, in which you also were trained? Were not the laws, which have the charge of education, right in commanding your father to train you in music and gymnastic?' Right, I should reply. 'Well then, since you were brought into the world and nurtured and educated by us, can you deny in the first place that you are our child and slave, as your fathers were before you? And if this is true you cannot suppose that you are on equal terms with us in matters of right

and wrong, or think that you have a right to do to us what we are
doing to you. Would you have any right to strike or revile or do any
other evil to your father or your master, if you had one, because you
have been struck or reviled by him, or received some other evil at   51
his hands? — you would not say this? And because we think right to
destroy you, do you think that you have any right to destroy us in
return, and your country as far as in you lies? Will you, O professor
of true virtue, pretend that you are justified in this? Has a philosopher like you failed to discover that our country is more precious
and higher and holier far than mother or father or any ancestor, and
more to be regarded in the eyes of the gods and of men of understanding? also to be soothed, and gently and reverently entreated
when angry, even more than a father, and either to be persuaded, or
if not persuaded, to be obeyed? And when we are punished by her,
whether with imprisonment or stripes, the punishment is to be endured in silence; and if she lead us to wounds or death in battle,
thither we follow as is right; neither may anyone yield or retreat or
leave his rank, but whether in battle or in a court of law, or in any
other place, he must do what his city and his country order him; or
he must change their view of what is just: and if he may do no
violence to his father or mother, much less may he do violence to
his country.' What answer shall we make to this, Crito? Do the
laws speak truly, or do they not?

Cr. I think that they do.

Soc. Then the laws will say: 'Consider, Socrates, if we are speaking
truly that in your present attempt you are going to do us a wrong.
For, having brought you into the world, and nurtured and educated
you, and given you and every other citizen a share in every good
which we had to give, we further proclaim to any Athenian by the
liberty which we allow him, that if he does not like us, the laws, when
he has become of age and has seen the ways of the city, and made
our acquaintance, he may go where he pleases and take his goods
with him. None of us laws will forbid him or interfere with anyone
who does not like us and the city, and who wants to emigrate to a
colony or to any other city; he may go where he likes, with his
property. But he who has experience of the manner in which we
order justice and administer the state, and still remains, has by so
doing entered into an implied contract that he will do as we command
him. And he who disobeys us is, as we maintain, thrice wrong; first,
because in disobeying us he is disobeying his parents; secondly, because we are the authors of his education; thirdly, because having
made an agreement with us that he will duly obey our commands,
he neither obeys them nor convinces us that our commands are unjust;   52

although we do not roughly require unquestioning obedience, but give
him the alternative of obeying or convincing us; — that is what we
offer, and he does neither.

'These are the sort of accusations to which, as we were saying, you,
Socrates, will be exposed if you accomplish your intentions; you,
above all other Athenians.' Suppose now I ask, why I rather than
anybody else? no doubt they will justly retort upon me that I above
all other Athenians have acknowledged the agreement. 'There is clear
proof,' they will say, 'Socrates, that we and the city were not displeasing to you. Of all Athenians you have been the most constant
resident in the city, which, as you never leave, you may be supposed
to love. For you never went out of the city either to see the games,
except once when you went to the Isthmus, or to any other place
unless when you were on military service; nor did you travel as other
men do. Nor had you any curiosity to know other states or their laws:
your affections did not go beyond us and our state; we were your
special favourites, and you acquiesced in our government of you;
and here in this city you begat your children, which is a proof of
your satisfaction. Moreover, you might in the course of the trial, if
you had liked, have fixed the penalty at banishment; you might then
have done with the state's assent what you are now setting out to do
without it. But you pretended that you preferred death to exile, and
that you were not unwilling to die. And now you have forgotten these
fine sentiments, and pay no respect to us the laws, of whom you are
the destroyer; and are doing what only a miserable slave would do,
running away and turning your back upon the compacts and agreements of your citizenship which you made with us. And first of all
answer this very question: Are we right in saying that you agreed to
live under our government in deed, and not in word only? Is that true
or not?' How shall we answer, Crito? Must we not assent?

Cr. We cannot help it, Socrates.

Soc. Then will they not say: 'You, Socrates, are breaking the
covenants and agreements which you made with us at your leisure,
not under any compulsion or deception or in enforced haste, but
after you have had seventy years to think of them, during which
time you were at liberty to leave the city, if we were not to your mind
or if our covenants appeared to you to be unfair. You had your
choice, and might have gone either to Lacedaemon or Crete, both
which states are often praised by you for their good government, or
to some other Hellenic or foreign state. Whereas you, above all other
Athenians, seemed to be so fond of the state, and obviously therefore
of us her laws (for who would care about a state without its laws?),
that you never stirred out of her; the halt, the blind, the maimed were
not more stationary in her than you were. And now you refuse to

abide by your agreements. Not so, Socrates, if you will take our advice; do not make yourself ridiculous by leaving the city.

'For just consider, if you transgress and err in this sort of way, what good will you do either to yourself or to your friends? That your friends will be in danger of being driven into exile and deprived of citizenship, or of losing their property, is tolerably certain; and you yourself, if you fly to one of the neighbouring cities, as, for example, Thebes or Megara, both of which are well governed, will come to them as an enemy of their government and all patriotic citizens will look askance at you as a subverter of the laws, and you will confirm in the minds of the judges the justice of their own condemnation of you. For he who is a corrupter of the laws is more than likely to be a corrupter of the young and foolish portion of mankind. Will you then flee from well-ordered cities and virtuous men? and is existence worth having on these terms? Or will you go to them without shame, and talk to them, saying — what will you say to them? What you say here about virtue and justice and institutions and laws being the best things among men? Would that be decent of Socrates? Surely not. But if you go away from well-governed states to Crito's friends in Thessaly, where there is great disorder and licence, they will be charmed to hear the tale of your escape from prison, set off with ludicrous particulars of the manner in which you were wrapped in a goatskin or some other disguise, and metamorphosed as the manner is of runaways; but will there be no one to remind you that in your old age, when little time was left to you, you were not ashamed to violate the most sacred laws from a greedy desire of life? Perhaps not, if you keep them in a good temper; but if they are out of temper you will hear many degrading things. You will live, but how? — fawning upon all men, and the servant of all men; and doing what? — faring sumptuously in Thessaly, having gone abroad in order that you may get a dinner. And where will be your fine sentiments about justice and virtue? Say that you wish to live for the sake of your 54 children — you want to bring them up and educate them — will you take them into Thessaly and deprive them of Athenian citizenship? Is this the benefit which you will confer upon them? Or are you under the impression that they will be better cared for and educated here if you are still alive, although absent from them; for your friends will take care of them? Do you fancy that if you have left Athens for Thessaly they will take care of them, but if you have left it for the other world that they will not take care of them? Nay; but if they who call themselves friends are good for anything, they will — to be sure they will.

'Listen, then, Socrates, to us who have brought you up. Think not of life and children first, and of justice afterwards, but of justice first, that you may so vindicate yourself before the princes of the world below. For neither will you nor any that belong to you be happier or holier or juster in this life, or happier in another, if you do as Crito bids. Now you depart, if it must be so, in innocence, a sufferer and not a doer of evil; a victim, not of the laws but of men. But if you leave the city, basely returning evil for evil and injury for injury, breaking the covenants and agreements which you have made with us, and wronging those whom you ought least of all to wrong, that is to say, yourself, your friends, your country, and us, we shall be angry with you while you live, and our brethren, the laws in the world below, will give you no friendly welcome; for they will know that you have done your best to destroy us. Listen, then, to us and not to Crito.'

This, dear Crito, is the voice which I seem to hear murmuring in my ears, like the sound of the flute in the ears of the mystic; that voice, I say, is humming in my ears, and prevents me from hearing any other. Be assured, then, that anything more which you may say to shake this my faith will be said in vain. Yet speak, if you have anything to say.

Cr. I have nothing to say.

Soc. It is enough then, Crito. Let us fulfil the will of God, and follow whither He leads.

Phaedo

Persons of the Dialogue

PHAEDO, who narrates to Echecrates, a fellow
disciple, the events of the master's last day

APOLLODORUS   SOCRATES

SIMMIAS   CEBES   CRITO

ATTENDANT OF THE PRISON

Scene: The prison of Socrates

◄§ In our Introduction we compared the sequence, *Apology, Crito,
Phaedo,* to a dramatic trilogy. There is no good reason why the
Phaedo should not be read in this literary-dramatic fashion. But there
are indeed good reasons against reading it only as literature and failing
to mark the many fruitful philosophical ideas that throng its pages.

The doctrine of Recollection was mentioned in our inquiry into
the meaning of Plato's Theory of Ideas. This doctrine, the view that
the soul has acquired knowledge of the Ideas before birth and hence
is able to recognize their partial embodiments in the material world,
appears in the *Phaedo*. That Socrates the man probably did not regard the soul as immortal we have already explained; what we have
here, then, is an early statement of Plato's own position. Similarly
Plato's Theory of Ideas is here expounded, ascribed by the pupil to
the master. The dialogue's conception of "misology" (in analogy with
"misanthropy") is the distrust of reasoning which may result from
believing too trustfully and later experiencing the collapse of the
cherished beliefs. The historian of psychology finds at Stephanus
page 73d the earliest known statement of theory of the "association of
ideas."

An important and recurrent feature of Plato's literary and dramatic
art makes its appearance in the *Phaedo*. This is the so-called "Platonic
myth." After death, Socrates avers toward the end of the dialogue,
a new life opens for the soul in which she faces judgment upon her
earthly conduct, good or bad, and she brings nothing with her save
nurture and enlightenment. As he speaks (107 ff.), and as the discussion proceeds, we cannot fail to notice a decided change of tone
and a heightening of style. There is also a significant shift from
argument and reasoned proof to poetic suggestion and the majesty of
prophetic utterance. Nor does Socrates scruple to speak of matters
beyond the furthest reach of Reason to decide, having abandoned
the marketplace for the Cosmos.

53

The myth in the *Phaedo* is only one of many. The interested reader will find several others included in this volume: the Myth of the Charioteer (*Phaedrus,* 246 ff.); the Myth of the Spherical Men and the Myth of Eros (*Symposium,* 189 ff., 202 ff.); the Myth of the Metals and the Myth of Er (*Republic,* 414, 614 ff.); and the Myth of Atlantis (*Timaeus,* 21 ff.). The main body of the *Timaeus* may also be seen as the Myth of Creation. The harmonious blending of reasoned with imagined truth is the distinguishing mark of the Platonic myth.

The dialogue, which now begins, opens shortly after the death of Socrates. Two devoted followers meet and converse:

57 *Echecrates*. Were you yourself, Phaedo, in the prison with Socrates on the day when he drank the poison?

Phaedo. Yes, Echecrates, I was.

Ech. I should so like to know what he said during his last hours, and the manner of his death. No Phliasian goes much to Athens now, and it is a long time since any stranger has come from there who could give us a trustworthy account. We heard that he died by taking poison: but that was all.

58 *Phaed*. Did you hear of the proceedings at the trial?

Ech. Yes; someone told us about the trial, and we could not understand why, having been condemned, he should have been put to death, not at the time, but long afterwards. What was the reason of this?

Phaed. An accident, Echecrates: the stern of the ship which the Athenians send to Delos happened to have been crowned on the day before he was tried.

Ech. What is this ship?

Phaed. It is the ship in which, according to Athenian tradition, Theseus went to Crete when he took with him 'the fourteen', and was the saviour of them and of himself. And they are said to have vowed to Apollo at the time, that if they were saved they would send a yearly mission to Delos. Well, the custom has continued without a break to this day, and the whole period of the voyage to and from Delos, beginning when the priest of Apollo crowns the stern of the ship, is a holy season, during which it is strictly forbidden to pollute the city by executions; and when the vessel is detained by contrary winds, the time spent in going and returning is very considerable. As I was saying, the ship was crowned on the day before the trial, and this was the reason why Socrates lay in prison and was not put to death until long after he was condemned.

Ech. What was the manner of his death, Phaedo? What was said or done? And which of his friends were with him? Or would the authorities forbid them to be present — so that he had no friends near him when he died?

Phaed. No; there were some with him, in fact a good many.

Ech. If you have nothing else to do, I wish that you would tell me what passed, as exactly as you can.

Phaed. I have nothing at all to do, and will try to give you the facts. To be reminded of Socrates is always the greatest delight to me, whether I speak myself or hear another speak of him.

Ech. You will have listeners who are of the same mind with you; just try to relate everything as precisely as possible.

Phaed. I had a singular feeling at being in his company. For I could hardly believe that I was present at the death of a friend, and therefore I did not pity him, Echecrates; he died so fearlessly, and his words and bearing were so noble and gracious, that to me he appeared blessed. I realized that even in going to the other world he could not be without a divine call, and that he would be happy, if any man ever was, when he arrived there; and therefore no feeling of pity for him entered my mind, as might have seemed natural at such an hour. Nor on the other hand did I feel pleasure that we were occupied as usual with philosophy (that was the theme of our conversation). My state of mind was curious, a strange compound of pleasure and pain, as I reflected that he was soon to die; and this double feeling was shared by us all; we were laughing and weeping by turns, especially the excitable Apollodorus — you know what kind of man he is?

Ech. Yes.

Phaed. He was quite beside himself; and I and all of us were greatly moved.

Ech. Who were present?

Phaed. Of native Athenians there were, besides Apollodorus, Critobulus and his father, Hermogenes, Epigenes, Aeschines, Antisthenes; likewise Ctesippus of the deme of Paeania, Menexenus, and some others; Plato, if I am not mistaken, was ill.

Ech. Were there any strangers?

Phaed. Yes, there were; Simmias the Theban, and Cebes, and Phaedondes; Euclides and Terpsion, who came from Megara.

Ech. And was Aristippus there, and Cleombrotus?

Phaed. No, they were said to be in Aegina.

Ech. Anyone else?

Phaed. I feel fairly sure that these were all.

Ech. Well, and what did you talk about?

Phaed. I will begin at the beginning, and endeavour to repeat the entire conversation. During the whole time we had all been used to visit Socrates daily, assembling early in the morning at the court in

which the trial took place as it was not far from the prison. There we would wait talking with one another until the opening of the doors (for they were not opened very early); then we went in and generally passed the day with Socrates. On the last morning we assembled sooner than usual, having heard on the day before when we quitted the prison in the evening that the sacred ship had come from Delos; and so we arranged to meet very early at the accustomed place. On our arrival the jailer who answered the door, instead of admitting us, came out and told us to wait until he called us. 'For the Eleven' he said, 'are now with Socrates; they are taking off his chains, and giving
60 orders that he is to die today.' He soon returned and said that we might come in. On entering we found Socrates just released from chains, and Xanthippe, whom you know, sitting by him, and holding his child in her arms. When she saw us she uttered a cry and burst out in true feminine fashion: 'O Socrates, this is the last time that you will converse with your friends, and they with you.' Socrates turned to Crito and said: 'Crito, let someone take her home.' Some of Crito's people accordingly led her away, crying out and beating her breast. When she was gone, Socrates, sitting up on the couch, bent and rubbed his leg, saying, as he was rubbing: How singular is the thing mankind call pleasure, and how curiously related to pain, which might be thought to be the opposite of it; for they are never present to a man at the same instant, and yet he who pursues and gets either is generally compelled to get the other; their bodies are two, but they are joined by a single head. And I cannot help thinking that if Aesop had remembered them, he would have made a fable about God trying to reconcile their strife, and how, when he could not, he fastened their heads together; and this is the reason why when one comes the other follows: as I know by my own experience now, when after the pain in my leg which was caused by the chain pleasure, it seems, has succeeded.

Upon this Cebes said: I am glad, Socrates, that you have mentioned the name of Aesop. For it reminds me of a question which has been asked by many, and was asked of me only the day before yesterday by Evenus — he will be sure to ask it again, and therefore if you would like me to have an answer ready for him, you may as well tell me what I should say to him: — he wanted to know for what conceivable reason you, who never before wrote a line of poetry, now that you are in prison are turning Aesop's fables into verse, and also composing that hymn in honour of Apollo.

Tell him, Cebes, he replied, what is the truth — that I had no idea of rivalling him or his poems; to do so, as I knew, would be no easy task. But I wanted to see whether I could satisfy my conscience on a scruple which I felt about the meaning of certain dreams. In the course of my life I have often had intimations in dreams 'that I should make music'. The same dream came to me sometimes in one form, and sometimes in another, but always saying the same or nearly the same words: 'Set to work and make music', said the dream. And hitherto I had imagined that this was only intended to exhort and encourage me in the study of philosophy, which has been the pursuit of my life, and is the noblest and best of music. The 61 dream was bidding me do what I was already doing, in the same way that the competitor in a race is bidden by the spectators to run when he is already running. But I was not certain of this; for the dream might have meant music in the popular sense of the word, and being under sentence of death, and the festival giving me a respite, I thought that it would be safer for me to satisfy the scruple, and, in obedience to the dream, to compose a few verses before I departed. And first I made a hymn in honour of the god of the festival, and then considering that a poet, if he is really to be a poet, should not only put together words, but should invent stories, and that I have no invention, I took some fables of Aesop, which I had ready at hand and knew by heart — the first that occurred to me — and turned them into verse. Tell this to Evenus, Cebes, and bid him farewell from me; say that I would have him come after me if he be a wise man, and not tarry; and that today I am likely to be going, for the Athenians say that I must.

Simmias said: What a message for such a man! Having been a frequent companion of his I should say that, as far as I know him, he will never take your advice unless he is obliged.

Why, said Socrates, — is not Evenus a philosopher?

I think that he is, said Simmias.

Then he, or any man who has the spirit of philosophy, will be willing to die; but he will not take his own life, I conceive, for that is held to be unlawful.

Here he changed his position, and put his legs off the couch on to the ground, and during the rest of the conversation he remained sitting.

Why do you say, inquired Cebes, that a man ought not to take his own life, but that the philosopher will be ready to follow one who is dying?

Socrates replied: and have you, Cebes and Simmias, who are the disciples of Philolaus, never heard him speak of this?

Yes, but his language was indefinite, Socrates.

My words, too, are only an echo; but there is no reason why I should hesitate to repeat what I have heard: and indeed, when a man is going to the other world, it seems highly proper for him to reason and speculate about the nature of our sojourn there. What could one do better in the interval between this and the setting of the sun?

Then tell me, Socrates, why is suicide held to be unlawful? as I have certainly heard Philolaus, about whom you were just now asking, affirm when he was staying with us at Thebes; and there are others who say the same, although I have never heard anybody give a definite reason.

62 Do not lose heart, replied Socrates, and the day may come when you will hear one. I suppose that you wonder why, when other things which are evil may be good at certain times and to certain persons, death is to be the only exception, and why, when a man is better dead, he is not permitted to be his own benefactor, but must wait for the kindness of another.

Fery true, said Cebes, laughing gently and speaking in his native Boeotian.

I admit the appearance of inconsistency in what I am saying; but there may not be any real inconsistency after all. There is a doctrine whispered in secret that man is a prisoner who has no right to open the door and run away; this is a great mystery, not to be easily apprehended. Yet I too believe that the gods are our guardians, and that we men are a chattel of theirs. Do you not agree?

Yes, I quite agree, said Cebes.

And if one of your own chattels, an ox or an ass, for example, took the liberty of putting itself out of the way when you had given no intimation of your wish that it should die, would you not be angry with it, and would you not punish it if you could?

Certainly, replied Cebes.

Then, if we look at the matter thus, there may be reason in saying that a man should wait, and not take his own life unless God sends some constraint such as that which has now come upon me.

Yes, Socrates, said Cebes, there seems to be truth in what you say. And yet how can you reconcile this seemingly true belief that God is our guardian and we his chattels, with the uncomplaining willingness to die which you were just now attributing to the philosopher? That the wisest of men should leave without reluctance a service in which they are ruled by the gods, who are the best of rulers, is not reasonable; for surely no wise man thinks that when set at liberty he will be able to take better care of himself. A fool may perhaps think so — he may argue that he had better run away from his master, not considering that he ought not to run away from the good but to cling to it, and that there would therefore be no sense in his running away. The wise man will want to be ever with him who is better than himself. Now this, Socrates, looks like the reverse of what was

just now said; upon this view the wise man should sorrow and the
fool rejoice at passing out of life.

The earnestness of Cebes seemed to please Socrates. Here, said **63**
he, turning to us, is a man who is always inquiring, and is not so
easily convinced by the first thing which he hears.

And to me too, added Simmias, the objection which he is now
making does appear to have some force. For what can be the meaning of a truly wise man wanting to fly away and lightly leave a master
who is better than himself? And I rather imagine that Cebes is referring to you; he thinks that you are too ready to leave us, and too
ready to leave the gods whom you acknowledge to be our good
masters.

Yes, replied Socrates; there is justice in what you say. And so
you think that I ought to answer your indictment as if I were in a
court?

We should like you to do so, said Simmias.

Then I must try to make a more successful defence before you
than I did before the judges. For I am quite ready to admit, Simmias
and Cebes, that in meeting death without resentment I should be
doing wrong, if I were not persuaded in the first place that I am
going to other gods who are wise and good (of which I am as certain
as I can be of any such matters), and secondly (though I am not so
sure of this last) to men departed, better than those whom I leave
behind; and therefore I do not resent it as I might have done, for I
have good hope that there is yet something remaining for the dead,
and as has been said of old, some far better thing for the good than
for the evil.

But do you mean to take away your thoughts with you, Socrates?
said Simmias. Will you not impart them to us? — for they are a
benefit in which we too are entitled to share. Moreover, if you succeed in convincing us, that will be the answer to the charge against
yourself.

I will do my best, replied Socrates. But you must first let me hear
what Crito wants; he has long been wishing to say something to me.

Only this, Socrates, replied Crito: — the attendant who is to give
you the poison has been telling me, and he wants me to tell you, that
you are not to talk much; talking, he says, increases heat, and this is
apt to interfere with the action of the poison; persons who excite
themselves are sometimes obliged to take a second or even a third
dose.

Never mind him, said Socrates, let him be prepared to give the
poison twice or even thrice if necessary; that is all.

I knew quite well what you would say, replied Crito; but he has
been worrying me about it for some time.

Never mind him, he repeated; and went on. Now, O my judges, I desire to prove to you that the real philosopher has reason to be of good cheer when he is about to die, and that after death he may hope to obtain the greatest good in the other world. And how this may be, Simmias and Cebes, I will endeavour to explain. For I deem that the true votary of philosophy is likely to be misunderstood by other men; they do not perceive that of his own accord he is always engaged in the pursuit of dying and death; and if this be so, and he has had the desire of death all his life long, why when his time comes should he repine at that which he has been always pursuing and desiring?

Simmias said laughingly: Though I am not altogether in a laughing humour, you have made me laugh, Socrates; for I cannot help thinking that the many when they hear your words will say how truly you have described philosophers, and our people at home will likewise say that philosophers are in reality moribund, and that they have found them out to be deserving of the death which they desire.

And they are right, Simmias, in thinking so, with the exception of the words 'they have found them out'; for they have not found out either in what sense the true philosopher is moribund and deserves death, or what manner of death he deserves. But enough of them: — let us discuss the matter among ourselves. Do we attach a definite meaning to the word 'death'?

To be sure, replied Simmias.

Is it not just the separation of soul and body? And to be dead is the completion of this; when the soul exists by herself and is released from the body, and the body is released from the soul. This, I presume, is what is meant by death?

Just so, he replied.

There is another question, which will probably throw light on our present inquiry if you and I can agree about it: — Ought the philosopher to care about such pleasures — if they are to be called pleasures — as those of eating and drinking?

Certainly not, answered Simmias.

And what about the pleasures of love — should he care for them? By no means.

And will he think much of the other ways of indulging the body, for example, the acquisition of costly raiment or sandals, or other adornments of the body? Instead of caring about them, does he not rather despise anything more than nature needs? What do you say?

I should say that the true philosopher would despise them.

Would you not say that he is entirely concerned with the soul and not with the body? He would like, as far as he can, to get away from the body and to turn to the soul.

Quite true.

First, therefore, in matters of this sort philosophers, above all other men, may be observed in every sort of way to dissever the soul from the communion of the body.

Very true.

Whereas, Simmias, the rest of the world are of opinion that to him who has no taste for bodily pleasures and no part in them, life is not worth having; and that he who is indifferent about them is as good as dead.

Perfectly true.

What again shall we say of the actual acquirement of knowledge? — is the body, if invited to share in the inquiry, a hindrance or a help? I mean to say, have sight and hearing, as found in man, any truth in them? Are they not, as the poets are always repeating, inaccurate witnesses? and yet, if even they are inaccurate and indistinct, what is to be said of the other senses? — for you will allow that they are the best of them?

Certainly, he replied.

Then when does the soul attain truth? — for in attempting to consider anything in company with the body she is obviously deceived by it.

True.

Then must not true reality be revealed to her in thought, if at all?

Yes.

And thought is best when the mind is gathered into herself and none of these things trouble her — neither sounds nor sights nor pain, nor again any pleasure, — when she takes leave of the body, and has as little as possible to do with it, when she has no bodily sense or desire, but is aspiring after true being?

Certainly.

And here again it is characteristic of the philosopher to despise the body; his soul runs away from his body and desires to be alone and by herself?

That is true.

Well, but there is another thing, Simmias: Is there or is there not an absolute justice?

Assuredly there is.

And an absolute beauty and absolute good?

Of course.

But did you ever behold any of them with your eyes?

Certainly not.

Or did you ever reach them with any other bodily sense? — and I speak not of these alone, but of absolute greatness, and health, and strength, and, in short, of the reality or true nature of everything. Is the truth of them ever perceived through the bodily organs? or rather, is not the nearest approach to the knowledge of their several natures made by him who so orders his intellectual vision as to have the most exact conception of the essence of each thing which he considers?

Certainly.

And he attains to the purest knowledge of them who goes to each with the intellect alone, not introducing or intruding in the act of
66 thought sight or any other sense together with reason, but with the intellect in its own purity searches into the truth of each thing in its purity; he who has got rid, as far as he can, of eyes and ears and, so to speak, of the whole body, these being in his opinion distracting elements which when they associate with the soul hinder her from acquiring truth and knowledge — who, if not he, is likely to attain to the knowledge of true being?

What you say has a wonderful truth in it, Socrates, replied Simmias.

And when real philosophers consider all these things, will they not be led to make a reflection which they will express in words something like the following? 'Have we not found', they will say, 'a path of thought which seems to bring us and our argument to the conclusion, that while we are in the body, and while the soul is mixed with the evils of the body, our desire will not be satisfied? and our desire is of the truth. For the body is a source of countless distractions by reason of the mere requirement of food, and is liable also to diseases which overtake and impede us in the pursuit of truth: it fills us full of loves, and lusts, and fears, and fancies of all kinds, and endless foolery, and in very truth, as men say, takes away from us the power of thinking at all. Whence come wars, and fightings, and factions? whence but from the body and the lusts of the body? All wars are occasioned by the love of money, and money has to be acquired for the sake of the body and in slavish ministration to it; and by reason of all these impediments we have no time to give to philosophy; and, last and worst of all, even if the body allows us leisure and we betake ourselves to some speculation, it is always breaking in upon us, causing turmoil and confusion in our inquiries, and so amazing us that we are prevented from seeing the truth. It has been proved to us by experience that if we would have pure knowledge of anything we must be quit of the body — the soul by herself must behold things by themselves: and then we shall attain that which we desire, and of which we say that we are lovers — wisdom; not while we live, but, as the argument shows, only after death; for if while in company with the body the soul cannot have pure knowledge, one of two things follows — either knowledge is not to be

attained at all, or, if at all, after death. For then, and not till then,
the soul will be parted from the body and exist by herself alone. In
this present life, we think that we make the nearest approach to
knowledge when we have the least possible intercourse or communion with the body, and do not suffer the contagion of the bodily
nature, but keep ourselves pure until the hour when God himself is
pleased to release us. And thus getting rid of the foolishness of the
body we may expect to be pure and hold converse with the pure,
and to know of ourselves all that exists in perfection unalloyed, which,
I take it, is no other than the truth. For the impure are not permitted
to lay hold of the pure.' These are the sort of words, Simmias, which
the true lovers of knowledge cannot help saying to one another, and
thinking. You would agree; would you not?

Undoubtedly, Socrates.

But, O my friend, if this be true, there is great reason to hope that,
going whither I go, when I have come to the end of my journey I
shall fully attain that which has been the pursuit of our lives. And
therefore I accept with good hope this change of abode which is now
enjoined upon me, and not I only, but every other man who believes
that his mind has been made ready and that he is in a manner
purified.

Certainly, replied Simmias.

And does it not follow that purification is nothing but that separation of the soul from the body, which has for some time been the
subject of our argument; the habit of the soul gathering and collecting herself into herself from all sides out of the body; the dwelling in
her own place alone, as in another life, so also in this, as far as she
can; — the release of the soul from the chains of the body?

Very true, he said.

And this separation and release of the soul from the body is termed
death?

To be sure, he said.

And the true philosophers, and they only, are ever seeking to
release the soul. Is not the separation and release of the soul from
the body their especial study?

That is true.

And, as I was saying at first, there would be a ridiculous contradiction in men studying to live as nearly as they can in a state like that
of death, and yet repining when death comes upon them.

Clearly.

In fact, the true philosophers, Simmias, are always occupied in
the practice of dying, wherefore also to them least of all men is death
terrible. Look at the matter thus: — if they have been in every way
estranged from the body, and are wanting to be alone with the soul,

when this desire of theirs is being granted, how inconsistent would they be if they trembled and repined, instead of rejoicing at their departure to that place where, when they arrive, they hope to gain that which in life they desired — and their desire was for wisdom — and at the same time to be rid of the company of their enemy. Many a man who has lost by death an earthly love, or wife, or son, has been willing to go in quest of them to the world below, animated by the hope of seeing them there and of being with those for whom he yearned. And will he who is a true lover of wisdom, and is strongly persuaded in like manner that only in the world below he can worthily enjoy her, still repine at death? Will he not depart with joy? Surely he will, O my friend, if he be a true philosopher. For he will have a firm conviction that there, and there only, he can find wisdom in her purity. And if this be true, he would be very absurd, as I was saying, if he were afraid of death.

He would indeed, replied Simmias.

And when you see a man who is repining at the approach of death, is not his reluctance a sufficient proof that after all he is not a lover of wisdom, but a lover of the body, and probably at the same time a lover of either money or power, or both?

Quite so, he replied.

And then, Simmias, is not the quality we term courage most characteristic of the philosopher?

Certainly.

There is temperance again — I mean the quality which the vulgar also call by that name, the calm disdain and control of the passions — is not temperance a virtue belonging to those only who disdain the body, and who pass their lives in philosophy?

Most assuredly.

For the courage and temperance of other men, if you care to consider them, are really a paradox.

How so?

Well, he said, you are aware that death is regarded by men in general as a great evil.

Very true, he said.

And do not courageous men face death because they are afraid of yet greater evils?

That is quite true.

Then all but the philosophers are courageous only from fear, and because they are afraid; and yet that a man should be courageous from fear, and because he is a coward, is surely a strange thing.

Very true.

And are not the self-restrained exactly in the same case? They are temperate because in a sense they are intemperate — which might seem to be impossible, but is nevertheless the sort of thing which happens with this fatuous temperance. For there are pleasures which they are afraid of losing; and in their desire to keep them, they abstain from some pleasures because they are overcome by others; and although to be conquered by pleasure is called by men intemperance, to them the conquest of pleasure consists in being conquered by pleasure. And that is what I mean by saying that, in a sense, they are made temperate through intemperance.

Such appears to be the case.

Yet perhaps the exchange of one fear or pleasure or pain for another fear or pleasure or pain, of the greater for the less as if they were coins, is not the right exchange by the standard of virtue. O my dear Simmias, is there not one true coin for which all these ought to be exchanged? — and that is wisdom; and only in company with this do we attain real courage or temperance or justice. In a word, is not all true virtue the companion of wisdom, no matter what fears or pleasures or other similar goods or evils may or may not attend her? But the virtue which is made up of these goods, when they are severed from wisdom and exchanged with one another, is perhaps a mere facade of virtue, a slavish quality, wholly false and unsound; the truth is far different — temperance and justice and courage are in reality a purging away of all these things, and wisdom herself may be a kind of baptism into that purity. The founders of the mysteries would appear to have had a real meaning, and were not devoid of sense when they intimated in a figure long ago that he who passes unsanctified and uninitiated into the world below will lie in a slough, but that he who arrives there after initiation and purification will dwell with the gods. For 'many', as they say in the mysteries, 'are the thyrsus-bearers, but few are the mystics', — meaning, as I interpret the words, 'the true philosophers'. In the number of whom, during my whole life, I have been seeking, according to my ability, to find a place; — whether I have sought in a right way or not, and whether we have succeeded, we shall know for certain in a little while, if God will, when we arrive in the other world — such is my belief. And therefore I answer that I am right, Simmias and Cebes, in not grieving or repining at parting from you and my masters in this world, for I believe that I shall equally find good masters and friends in another world. If now I succeed in convincing you by my defence better than I did the Athenian judges, it will be well.

When Socrates had finished, Cebes began to speak: I agree, Socrates, in the greater part of what you say. But in what concerns the soul, men are apt to be incredulous; they fear that when she has left the body her place may be nowhere, and that on the very day of death she may perish and come to an end immediately on her release from the body, issuing forth like smoke or breath, dispersing and vanishing away into nothingness in her flight. If she could only be collected into herself after she has obtained release from the evils of which you were speaking, there would be much reason for the goodly hope, Socrates, that what you say is true. But surely it requires a great deal of persuasion and proof to show that when the man is dead his soul yet exists, and has any force or intelligence.

True, Cebes, said Socrates; and shall I suggest that we speculate a little together concerning the probabilities of these things?

For my part, said Cebes, I should greatly like to know your opinion about them.

I reckon, said Socrates, that no one who heard me now, not even if he were one of my old enemies, the comic poets, could accuse me of idle talking about matters in which I have no concern: — If you please, then, we will proceed with the inquiry.

Suppose we consider the question whether the souls of men after death are or are not in the world below. There comes into my mind an ancient doctrine which affirms that they are there after they leave our world, and returning hither, are born again from the dead. Now if it be true that the living come from the dead, then our souls must exist in the other world, for if not, how could they have been born again? And this would be conclusive, if it were established that the living are born from the dead and have no other origin; but if this is not so, then other arguments will have to be adduced.

Very true, replied Cebes.

Then let us consider the whole question, not in relation to man only, but in relation to animals generally, and to plants, and to everything of which there is generation, and the proof will be easier. Are not all things which have opposites generated out of their opposites? I mean such things as the beautiful and the ugly, the just and the unjust — and there are innumerable other cases. Let us consider therefore whether it is necessary that a thing should come to be from its own opposite, if it has one, and from no other source: for example, anything which becomes greater must become greater after being less?

True.

71　And that which becomes less must have been once greater and then have become less?

Yes.

And the weaker is generated from the stronger, and the swifter from the slower?

Very true.

And the worse is from the better, and the more just is from the more unjust?

Of course.

And is this true of all opposites? and are we convinced that all of them are generated out of opposites?

Yes.

And in this universal opposition of all things, are there not also two intermediate processes which are ever going on, from one to the other opposite, and back again; for example, where there is a greater and a less there is also the intermediate process of increase and diminution, and so a thing is said to increase or to diminish?

Yes, he said.

And there are many other processes, such as analysis and combination, cooling and heating, which equally involve a passage into and out of one another. And this necessarily holds of all opposites, even though not always expressed in words — they are really generated out of one another, and there is a passing or process from one to the other of them?

Very true, he replied.

Well, and is there not an opposite of being alive, as sleep is the opposite of being awake?

True, he said.

And what is it?

Being dead, he answered.

And these, if they are opposites, are generated the one from the other, and have their two intermediate processes also?

Of course.

Now, said Socrates, I will analyse one of the two pairs of opposites which I have mentioned to you, and also its intermediate processes, and you shall analyse the other to me. The two members of the first pair are sleep and waking. The state of sleep is opposed to the state of waking, and out of sleeping waking is generated, and out of waking, sleeping; and the process of generation is in the one case falling asleep, and in the other waking up. Do you agree?

I entirely agree.

Then, suppose that you analyse life and death to me in the same manner. Is not the state of death opposed to that of life?

Yes.

And they are generated one from the other?

Yes.

What is generated from the living?

The dead.

And what from the dead?

I can only say in answer — the living.

Then the living, whether things or persons, Cebes, are generated from the dead?

So it would seem, he replied.

Then the inference is that our souls exist in the world below?

It appears so.

And one of the two processes or generations is visible — for surely the act of dying is visible?

Surely, he said.

What then is to be the result? Shall we exclude the opposite process? and shall we suppose nature to be lame in this respect? Must we not rather assign to the act of dying some corresponding process of generation?

Certainly, he replied.

And what is that?

Return to life.

72   And return to life, if there be such a thing, is the birth of the dead into the number of the living?

Quite true.

Then here is a new way by which we arrive at the conclusion that the living come from the dead, just as the dead come from the living; and we agreed that this, if true, would be adequate proof that the souls of the dead must exist in some place out of which they come again.

Yes, Socrates, he said; the conclusion seems to flow necessarily out of our previous admissions.

And that these admissions were not wrong, Cebes, he said, may be shown, I think, as follows: If generation were in a straight line only, and there were no compensation or circle in nature, no turn or return of elements into their opposites, then you know that all things would at last have the same form and suffer the same fate, and there would be no more generation of them.

What do you mean? he said.

A simple thing enough, which I will illustrate by the case of sleep, he replied. You know that if there were no alternation of sleeping and waking, the tale of the sleeping Endymion would in the end have no point, because all other things would be asleep too, and he would not be distinguishable from the rest. Or if there were combination only, and no analysis of substances, then we should soon have the chaos of Anaxagoras where 'all things were together'. And in like manner, my dear Cebes, if all things which partook of life were to die, and after they were dead remained in the form of death, and did not come to life again, all would at last be dead, and nothing would be alive — what other result could there be? For if living things had some other origin, and living things died, must not all things at last be swallowed up in death?

There is no escape, Socrates, said Cebes; and to me your argument seems to be absolutely true.

Yes, he said, Cebes, it is and must be so, in my opinion, and we have not been deluded in making these admissions; but I am confident that there truly is such a thing as living again, and that the living spring from the dead, and that the souls of the dead are in existence.

Yes, said Cebes interposing, your favourite doctrine, Socrates, that our learning is simply recollection, if true, also necessarily implies a previous time in which we have learned that which we now recollect. But this would be impossible unless our soul had been somewhere 73 before existing in this form of man; here then is another proof of the soul's immortality.

But tell me, Cebes, interrupted Simmias, what arguments are urged in favour of this doctrine of recollection. I am not very sure at the moment that I remember them.

One excellent proof, said Cebes, is afforded by questions. If you put a question to a person properly, he will give a true answer of himself, but how could he do this unless there were knowledge and a right account of the matter already in him? Again, this is most clearly shown when he is taken to a diagram or to anything of that sort.

But if, said Socrates, you are still incredulous, Simmias, I would ask you whether you may not agree with me when you look at the matter in another way; — I mean, if you are still incredulous as to whether what is called learning is recollection?

Incredulous I am not, said Simmias; but I want to have this doctrine of recollection brought to my own recollection, and, from what Cebes has started to say, I am beginning to recollect and be convinced; but I should still like to hear you develop your own argument.

This is what I would say, he replied: — We should agree, if I am not mistaken, that what a man is to recollect he must have known at some previous time.

Very true.

And do we also agree that knowledge obtained in the way I am about to describe is recollection? I mean to ask, Whether a person who, having seen or heard or in any way perceived anything, knows not only that, but also thinks of something else which is the subject not of the same but of some other kind of knowledge, may not be fairly said to recollect that of which he thinks?

How do you mean?

I mean what I may illustrate by the following instance: — The knowledge of a lyre is not the same as the knowledge of a man?

Of course not.

And yet what is the feeling of lovers when they recognize a lyre, or a cloak, or anything else which the beloved has been in the habit of using? Do not they, from knowing the lyre, form in the mind's eye an image of the youth to whom the lyre belongs? And this is recollection. In like manner anyone who sees Simmias may often remember Cebes; and there are endless examples of the same thing.

Endless, indeed, replied Simmias.

And is not this sort of thing a kind of recollection — though the word is most commonly applied to a process of recovering that which has been already forgotten through time and inattention?

Very true, he said.

Well; and may you not also from seeing the picture of a horse or a lyre recollect a man? and from the picture of Simmias, you may be led to recollect Cebes?

True.

Or you may also be led to the recollection of Simmias himself?

74 Quite so.

And in all these cases, the recollection may be derived from things either like or unlike?

It may be.

And when the recollection is derived from like things, then another consideration is sure to arise, which is — whether the likeness in any degree falls short or not of that which is recollected?

Certainly, he said.

Now consider this question. We affirm, do we not, that there is such a thing as equality, not of one piece of wood or stone or similar material thing with another, but that, over and above this, there is absolute equality? Shall we say so?

Say so, yes, replied Simmias, and swear to it, with all the confidence in life.

And do we know the nature of this absolute existence?

To be sure, he said.

And whence did we obtain our knowledge? Did we not see equalities of material things, such as pieces of wood and stones, and conceive from them the idea of an equality which is different from them? For you will acknowledge that there is a difference? Or look at the matter in another way: — Do not the same pieces of wood or stone appear to one man equal, and to another unequal?

That is certain.

But did pure equals ever appear to you unequal? or equality the same as inequality?

Never, Socrates.

Then these equal objects are not the same with the idea of equality?

I should say, clearly not, Socrates.

And yet from these equals, although differing from the idea of equality, you obtained the knowledge of that idea?

Very true, he said.

Which might be like, or might be unlike them?

Yes.

But that makes no difference: so long as from seeing one thing you conceive another, whether like or unlike, there must surely have been an act of recollection?

Very true.

But what would you say of equal portions of wood or other material equals? and what is the impression produced by them? Are they equals in the same sense in which absolute equality is equal? or do they fall short of this perfect equality in a measure?

Yes, he said, in a very great measure too.

And must we not allow, that when a man, looking at any object, reflects 'the thing which I see aims at being like some other thing, but falls short of and cannot be like that other thing, and is inferior', he who so reflects must have had a previous knowledge of that to which the other, although similar, was inferior?

Certainly.

And has not this been our own case in the matter of equals and of absolute equality?

Precisely.

Then we must have known equality previously to the time when 75 we first saw the material equals, and reflected that they all strive to attain absolute equality, but fall short of it?

Very true.

And we recognize also that we have only derived this conception of absolute equality, and can only derive it, from sight or touch, or from some other of the senses, which are all alike in this respect?

Yes, Socrates, for the purposes of the present argument, one of them is the same as the other.

From the senses then is derived the conception that all sensible equals aim at an absolute equality of which they fall short?

Yes.

Then before we began to see or hear or perceive in any way, we must have had a knowledge of absolute equality, or we could not have referred to that standard the equals which are derived from the senses? — for to that they all aspire, and of that they fall short.

No other inference can be drawn from the previous statements.

And did we not begin to see and hear and have the use of our other senses as soon as we were born?

Certainly.

Then we must have acquired the knowledge of equality at some previous time?

Yes.

That is to say, before we were born, I suppose?

It seems so.

And if we acquired this knowledge before we were born, and were born having the use of it, then we also knew before we were born and at the instant of birth not only the equal or the greater or the less, but all other such ideas; for we are not speaking only of equality, but of beauty, goodness, justice, holiness, and of all which we stamp with the name of absolute being in the dialectical process, both when we ask and when we answer questions. Of all this we affirm with certainty that we acquired the knowledge before birth?

We do.

But if, after having acquired, we have not on each occasion forgotten what we acquired, then we must always come into life having this knowledge, and shall have it always as long as life lasts — for knowing is the acquiring and retaining knowledge and not losing it. Is not the loss of knowledge, Simmias, just what we call forgetting?

Quite true, Socrates.

But if this knowledge which we acquired before birth was lost by us at birth, and if afterwards by the use of the senses we recovered what we previously knew, will not the process which we call learning be a recovering of knowledge which is natural to us, and may not this be rightly termed recollection?

Very true.

76 So much is clear — that when we perceive something, either by the help of sight, or hearing, or some other sense, that perception can lead us to think of some other thing like or unlike which is associated with it but has been forgotten. Whence, as I was saying, one of two alternatives follows: — either we all have this knowledge at birth, and continue to know through life; or, after birth, those who are said to learn only recollect, and learning is simply recollection.

Yes, that is quite true, Socrates.

And which alternative, Simmias, do you prefer? Have we the knowledge at our birth, or do we recollect afterwards things which we knew previously to our birth?

I cannot decide at the moment.

At any rate you can decide whether he who has knowledge will or will not be able to render an account of his knowledge? What do you say?

Certainly, he will.

But do you think that every man is able to give an account of the matters about which we were speaking a moment ago?

Would that they could, Socrates, but I much rather fear that to-morrow, at this time, there will no longer be anyone alive who is able to give an account of them such as ought to be given.

Then you are not of opinion, Simmias, that all men know these things?

Certainly not.

They are in process of recollecting that which they learned before?

Certainly.

But when did our souls acquire this knowledge? — clearly not since we were born as men?

Certainly not.

And therefore, previously?

Yes.

Then, Simmias, our souls must also have existed without bodies before they were in the form of man, and must have had intelligence.

Unless indeed you suppose, Socrates, that all such knowledge is given us at the very moment of birth; for this is the only time which remains.

Yes, my friend, but if so, when, pray, do we lose it? For it is not in us when we are born — that is admitted. Do we lose it at the moment of receiving it, or if not at what other time?

No, Socrates, I perceive that I am unconsciously talking nonsense.

Then may we not say, Simmias, that if there do exist these things of which we are always talking, absolute beauty and goodness, and all that class of realities; and if to this we refer all our sensations and with this compare them, finding the realities to be pre-existent and our own possession — then just as surely as these exist, so surely must our souls have existed before our birth? Otherwise our whole argument would be worthless. By an equal compulsion we must believe both that these realities exist, and that our souls existed before our birth; and if not the realities, then not the souls.

Yes, Socrates; I am convinced that there is precisely the same necessity for the one as for the other; and the argument finds a safe **77** refuge in the position that the existence of the soul before birth cannot be separated from the existence of the reality of which you speak. For there is nothing which to my mind is so patent as that beauty, goodness, and the other realities of which you were just now speaking, exist in the fullest possible measure; and I am satisfied with the proof.

Well, but is Cebes satisfied? for I must convince him too.

I think, said Simmias, that Cebes is satisfied: although he is the most incredulous of mortals, yet I believe that he is sufficiently convinced of the existence of the soul before birth. But that after death the soul will continue to exist is not yet proven even to my own satisfaction. I cannot get rid of the objection to which Cebes was referring — the common fear that at the moment when the man dies the soul is dispersed, and that this may be the end of her. For admitting that she may have come into being and been framed out of some unknown other elements, and was in existence before entering the human body, why after having entered in and gone out again may she not herself be destroyed and come to an end?

Very true, Simmias, said Cebes; it appears that about half of what was required has been proven; to wit, that our souls existed before we were born; — that the soul will exist after death as well as before birth is the other half of which the proof is still wanting, and has to be supplied; when that is given the demonstration will be complete.

But that proof, Simmias and Cebes, has been already given, said Socrates, if you put the two arguments together — I mean this and the former one, in which we agreed that everything living is born of the dead. For if the soul exists before birth, and in coming to life and being born can be born only from death and the state of death, must she not after death continue to exist, since she has to be born again? — Surely the proof which you desire has been already furnished. Still I suspect that you and Simmias would be glad to probe the argument further. Like children, you are haunted with a fear that when the soul leaves the body, the wind may really blow her away and scatter her; especially if a man should happen to die in a great storm and not when the weather is calm.

Cebes answered with a smile: Then, Socrates, you must argue us out of our fears — and yet, strictly speaking, they are not our fears, but perhaps even in us men there is a child to whom death is a sort of hobgoblin: him too we must persuade not to be afraid.

Socrates said: Let the voice of the charmer be applied daily until you have charmed away the fear.

78 And where shall we find a good charmer of our fears, Socrates, now that you are abandoning us?

Hellas, he replied, is a large place, Cebes, and has good men, and there are barbarous races not a few: seek for him among them all, far and wide, sparing neither pains nor money; for there is no better way of spending your money. And you must seek yourselves too, along with one another; for perhaps you will not easily find others better able to do it.

The search, replied Cebes, shall certainly be made. And now, if you please, let us return to the point of the argument at which we digressed.

By all means, replied Socrates; what else should I please?

Very good.

Must we not, said Socrates, ask ourselves what kind of thing that is which is liable to be scattered, and for what kind of thing we ought to fear that fate? and what is that for which we need have no fear? And then we may proceed further to inquire to which of the two classes soul belongs — our hopes and fears as to our own souls will turn upon the answers to these questions.

Very true, he said.

Now that which is compounded and is by nature composite may be supposed to be therefore capable, as of being compounded, so also of being dissolved; but that which is not composite, and that only, must be, if anything is, indissoluble.

Yes; I should imagine so, said Cebes.

And the non-composite may be assumed to be the same and unchanging, whereas the composite is always changing and never the same.

I agree, he said.

Then now let us return to the previous discussion. Is that reality of whose being we give account in the dialectical process — whether equality, beauty, or anything else — are these realities, I say, liable at times to some degree of change? or are they each of them always what they are, having the same uniform self-existent and unchanging natures, not admitting of variation at all, or in any way, or at any time?

They must be always the same, Socrates, replied Cebes.

And what would you say of the many beautiful, for instance, men or horses or garments or any other such things, or of the many equal, or generally of all the things which are named by the same names as the realities — are they the same always? May they not rather be described in exactly opposite terms, as almost always changing and hardly ever the same either with themselves or with one another?

The latter, replied Cebes; they are always in a state of change.

And these you can touch and see and perceive with the senses, **79** but the unchanging things you can only grasp with the mind — they are invisible and are not seen?

That is very true, he said.

Well then, added Socrates, let us suppose that there are two sorts of existences — one seen, the other unseen.

Let us suppose them.

The seen is the changing, and the unseen is the unchanging?

That may be also supposed.

And, further, of ourselves is not one part body, another part soul?

To be sure.

And to which class is the body more alike and akin?

Clearly to the seen — no one can doubt that.

And is the soul seen or not seen?

Not by man, Socrates.

And what we mean by 'seen' and 'not seen' is that which is or is not visible to the eye of man?

Yes, to the eye of man.

And is the soul seen or not seen?

Not seen.

Unseen then?

Yes.

Then the soul is more like to the unseen, and the body to the seen?

That follows necessarily, Socrates.

And were we not saying some time ago that the soul when using the body as an instrument of perception, that is to say, when using the sense of sight or hearing or some other sense (for the meaning of perceiving through the body is perceiving through the senses) — were we not saying that the soul too is then dragged by the body into the region of the changeable, and wanders and is confused; the world spins round her, and she is like a drunkard, when she touches change?

Very true.

But when returning into herself she reflects, then she passes into the other world, the region of purity, and eternity, and immortality, and unchangeableness, which are her kindred, and with them she ever lives, when she is by herself and is not let or hindered; then she ceases from her wandering, and being in contact with things unchanging is unchanging in relation to them. And this state of the soul is called wisdom?

That is well and truly said, Socrates, he replied.

And to which class is the soul more nearly alike and akin, as far as may be inferred from this argument, as well as from the preceding one?

I think, Socrates, that, in the opinion of everyone who follows the argument, the soul will be infinitely more like the unchangeable — even the most stupid person will not deny that.

And the body is more like the changing?

Yes.

80 Yet once more consider the matter in another light: When the soul and the body are united, then nature orders the soul to rule and govern, and the body to obey and serve. Now which of these two functions is like to the divine? and which to the mortal? Does not the divine appear to you to be that which is formed to govern and command, and the mortal to be that which is by its nature subject and servant?

True.

And which does the soul resemble?

The soul resembles the divine, and the body the mortal — there can be no doubt of that, Socrates.

Then reflect, Cebes: of all which has been said is not this the conclusion? — that the soul is in the very likeness of the divine, and immortal, and rational, and uniform, and indissoluble, and unchangeable; and that the body is in the very likeness of the human, and mortal, and irrational, and multiform, and dissoluble, and changeable.

Can we, my dear Cebes, find any possible ground for rejecting this conclusion?

We cannot.

But if it be true, then is not the body liable to speedy dissolution? and is not the soul almost or altogether indissoluble?

Certainly.

And do you further observe, that after a man is dead, the body, or visible part of him, which is lying in the visible world, and is called a corpse, and would naturally be dissolved and decomposed and dissipated, is not dissolved or decomposed at once, but may remain for some time, nay even for a long time, if the constitution be sound at the time of death, and the season of the year favourable? For the body when shrunk and embalmed, as the manner is in Egypt, may remain almost entire for a prodigious time; and even in decay, there are still some portions, such as the bones and ligaments, which are practically indestructible: — Do you agree?

Yes.

And is it likely that the soul, which is invisible, in passing to the place of the true Hades, which like her is invisible, and pure, and noble, and on her way to the good and wise God, whither, if God will, my soul is also soon to go, — that the soul, I repeat, if this be her nature, is blown away and destroyed immediately on quitting the body, as the many say? That can never be, my dear Simmias and Cebes. The truth rather is that the soul which is pure at departing and draws after her no bodily taint, having never voluntarily during life had connexion with the body, which she is ever avoiding, herself gathered into herself, and making such abstraction her perpetual study — all this means that she has been a true disciple of philosophy; and therefore has in fact been always practising how to die without complaint. For is not such a life the practice of death? 81

Certainly.

That soul, I say, herself invisible, departs to the invisible world — to the divine and immortal and rational: thither arriving, she is secure of bliss and is released from the error and folly of men, their fears and wild passions and all other human ills, and for ever dwells, as they say of the initiated, in company with the gods. Is not this true, Cebes?

Yes, said Cebes, beyond a doubt.

But the soul which has been polluted, and is impure at the time of her departure, and is the companion and servant of the body always, and is in love with and bewitched by the body and by the desires and pleasures of the body, until she is led to believe that the truth only exists in a bodily form, which a man may touch and see, and drink and eat, and use for the purposes of his lusts, — the soul, I mean, accustomed to hate and fear and avoid that which to the bodily eye is dark and invisible, but is the object of mind and can be attained by philosophy; — do you suppose that such a soul will depart pure and unalloyed?

Impossible, he replied.

She is intermixed with the corporeal, which the continual association and constant care of the body have wrought into her nature.

Very true.

And this corporeal element, my friend, is burdensome and weighty and earthy, and is visible; a soul thus hampered is depressed and dragged down again into the visible world, because she is afraid of the invisible and of the other world — prowling about tombs and sepulchres, near which, as they tell us, are seen certain ghostly apparitions of souls, spectres emanating from souls which have not departed pure, but still retain something of the visible element: which is why they can be seen.[1]

That is very likely, Socrates.

Yes, that is very likely, Cebes; and these must be the souls, not of the good, but of the evil, which are compelled to wander about such places in payment of the penalty of their former evil way of life; and they continue to wander until through the craving after their constant associate, the corporeal, they are imprisoned finally in another body. And they may be supposed to find their prisons in natures of the same character as they have cultivated in their former lives.

What natures do you mean, Socrates?

What I mean is that men who have followed after gluttony, and wantonness, and drunkenness, and have had no thought of avoiding them, would pass into asses and animals of that sort. What do you think?

I think such an opinion to be exceedingly probable.

And those who have chosen the portion of injustice, and tyranny, and violence, will pass into wolves, or into hawks and kites; — whither else can we suppose them to go?

---

[1] Compare Milton, *Comus*, 463 foll.: —

> But when lust,
> By unchaste looks, loose gestures, and foul talk,
> But most by lewd and lavish act of sin,
> Lets in defilement to the inward parts,
> The soul grows clotted by contagion,
> Imbodies, and imbrutes, till she quite lose,
> The divine property of her first being.
> Such are those thick and gloomy shadows damp
> Oft seen in charnel vaults and sepulchres,
> Lingering, and sitting by a new made grave,
> As loath to leave the body that it lov'd,
> And linked itself by carnal sensuality
> To a degenerate and degraded state.

Yes, said Cebes; into such creatures, beyond question.

And there is no difficulty, he said, in assigning to each class of them places answering to their several natures and propensities?

There is not, he said.

Even among these, some are happier than others; and the happiest both in themselves and in the place to which they go are those who have practised the virtues of the populace, the social virtues which are called by them temperance and justice, and are acquired by habit and practice without philosophy and mind.

Why are they the happiest?

Because they may be expected to pass into some gentle and social kind which is like their own, such as bees or wasps or ants, or back again into the form of man, and worthy men may be supposed to spring from them.

Very likely.

But to the company of the gods no one who has not studied philosophy and who is not entirely pure at the time of his departure is admitted, save only the lover of knowledge. And this is the reason, Simmias and Cebes, why the true votaries of philosophy abstain from all fleshly lusts, and hold out against them and refuse to give themselves up to them, — not because they fear poverty or the ruin of their families, like the lovers of money, and the world in general; nor like the lovers of power and honour, because they dread the dishonour or disgrace of evil deeds.

No, Socrates, that would not become them, said Cebes.

No indeed, he replied; and therefore they who have any care of their own souls, and do not merely live for the body and its fashioning, say farewell to all this; they will not walk in the ways of the blind: and when philosophy offers them purification and release from evil, they feel that they ought not to resist her influence, and whither she leads they turn and follow.

What do you mean, Socrates?

I will tell you, he said. The lovers of knowledge are conscious that the soul was simply fastened and glued to the body — until philosophy took her in hand, she could only view real existence through the bars of a prison, not in and through herself, and she was wallowing in the mire of every sort of ignorance. This was her original state; and then, as I was saying, and as the lovers of knowledge are well aware, philosophy saw the ingenuity of her prison — a prison built by lust so that a captive might be the principal accomplice in his own captivity — and took her in hand, and gently comforted her and sought to release her, pointing out that the eye and the ear and the other senses are full of deception, and persuading her to retire from them, and abstain from all but the necessary use of them, and be gathered 83 up and collected into herself, bidding her trust only in herself and her own pure apprehension of pure existence, and to mistrust whatever comes to her through other channels and is subject to variation; for such things are sensible and visible, but what she sees in her own nature is of the mind and invisible. And the soul of the true philosopher thinks that she ought not to resist this deliverance, and therefore abstains from pleasures and desires and pains, as far as she is able; reflecting that when a man has great joys or fears or desires, he suffers from them not merely the sort of evil which might be anticipated — as for example, the loss of his health or property which he has sacrificed to his lusts — but an evil greater far, which is the greatest and worst of all evils, and one of which he never thinks.

What is it, Socrates? said Cebes.

The evil is that when the feeling of pleasure or pain is most intense, every soul of man imagines the objects of this intense feeling to be then plainest and truest, though they are not so. And the things of sight are the chief of these objects, are they not?

Yes.

And is not this the state in which the soul becomes most firmly gripped by the body?

How so?

Why, because each pleasure and pain is a sort of nail which nails and rivets the soul to the body, until she becomes like the body, and believes that to be true which the body affirms to be true; and from agreeing with the body and having the same delights she is obliged to have the same habits and haunts, and is not likely ever to be pure at her departure to the world below, but is always infected by the body; and so she sinks into another body and there germinates and grows, and has therefore no part in the communion of the divine and pure and simple.

Most true, Socrates, answered Cebes.

And this, Cebes, is the reason why the true lovers of knowledge are temperate and brave; and not for the reason which the world gives.

84 Certainly not.

Certainly not! The soul of a philosopher will reason in quite another way; she will not ask philosophy to release her in order that in the very process of release she may deliver herself up again to the thraldom of pleasures and pains, doing a work only to be undone again, weaving and in turn unweaving her Penelope's web. But she will calm passion, and follow reason, and dwell always with her, contemplating the true and the divine and that which is beyond appearance and opinion, and thence deriving nourishment. Thus she seeks to live while she lives, and after death she hopes to go to her own kindred and to that which is like her, and to be freed from human ills. Thus nurtured, Simmias and Cebes, a soul will never fear that at her departure from the body she will be scattered and blown away by the winds and be nowhere and nothing.

When Socrates had done speaking, for a considerable time there was silence; he himself appeared to be meditating, as most of us were, on what had been said; only Cebes and Simmias spoke a few words to one another. And Socrates observing them asked what they thought of the argument, and whether there was anything wanting? For, said he, there are many points still open to suspicion and attack, if anyone were disposed to sift the matter thoroughly. Should you be considering some other matter I say no more, but if you feel any doubt on the present subject do not hesitate either to give us your own thoughts if you have any improvement to suggest, or, if you think that you will make more progress with my assistance, allow me to help you.

Simmias said: I must confess, Socrates, that doubts do arise in our minds, and each of us has for some time been urging and inciting the other to put the question which we wanted to have answered but which neither of us liked to ask, fearing that our importunity might be troublesome at such a time.

Socrates replied with a smile: O Simmias, what are you saying? I am not very likely to persuade other men that I do not regard my present situation as a misfortune if I cannot even persuade you, and find you afraid that I may be more irritable than I used to be. Will you not allow that I have as much of the spirit of prophecy in me as the swans? For they, when they perceive that they must die, having sung at times during their life, do then sing a longer and lovelier song than ever, rejoicing in the thought that they are about to go away to the god whose ministers they are. But men, because they are themselves afraid of death, slanderously affirm of the swans that they sing a lament at the last, a cry of woe, not considering that no bird sings when cold, or hungry, or in pain, not even the nightingale, nor the swallow, nor yet the hoopoe; which are said indeed to tune a woeful lay, although I do not believe this to be true of them any more than of the swans. But because they are sacred to Apollo, they have the gift of prophecy, and anticipate the good things of another world; wherefore they sing and rejoice in that day more than ever they did before. And I too, believing myself to be the consecrated servant of the same god, and the fellow servant of the swans, and thinking that I have received from my master gifts of prophecy which are not inferior to theirs, would not go out of life less merrily than the swans.

85

Never mind then, if this be your only objection, but speak and ask anything which you like, while the eleven magistrates of Athens allow.

Very good, Socrates, said Simmias; then I will tell you my difficulty, and Cebes will tell you his. I feel myself (and I dare say that you have the same feeling) that it is impossible or at least very hard to attain any certainty about questions such as these in the present life. And yet I should deem him a coward who did not prove what is said about them to the uttermost, not desisting until he had examined them on every side. For he should persevere until he has achieved one of these things: either he should discover, or be taught the truth about them; or, if this be impossible, I would have him take the best and most irrefragable of human theories, and let this be the raft upon which he sails through life — not without risk, as I admit, if he cannot find some word of God which will more surely and safely carry him. And now, as you bid me, I will venture to question you, and then I shall not have to reproach myself hereafter with not having said at the time what I think. For when I consider the matter, either alone or with Cebes, the argument does certainly appear to me, Socrates, to be not sufficient.

Socrates answered: I dare say, my friend, that you may be right, but I should like to know in what respect the argument is insufficient.

In this respect, replied Simmias: — Suppose a person to use the same argument about harmony and the lyre — might he not say that

86 harmony is a thing invisible, incorporeal, perfect, divine, existing in the lyre which is harmonized, but that the lyre and the strings are matter and material, composite, earthy, and akin to mortality? And when someone breaks the lyre, or cuts and rends the strings, then he who takes this view would argue as you do, and on the same analogy, that the harmony survives, and has not perished — you cannot imagine, he would say, that the lyre without the strings, and the broken strings themselves which are mortal remain, and yet that the harmony, which is of heavenly and immortal nature and kindred, has perished — perished before the mortal. The harmony must still be somewhere, and the wood and strings will decay before anything can happen to that. The thought, Socrates, must have occurred to your own mind that such is our conception of the soul; and that when the body is in a manner strung and held together by the elements of hot and cold, wet and dry, then the soul is the harmony or due proportionate admixture of them. But if so, whenever the strings of the body are unduly loosened or overstrained through disease or other injury, then the soul, though most divine, like other harmonies of music or of works of art, of course perishes at once; although the material remains of the body may last for a considerable time, until they are

either decayed or burnt. And if any one maintains that the soul, being an admixture of the elements of the body, is first to perish in that which is called death, how shall we answer him?

Socrates looked fixedly at us as his manner was, and said with a smile: Simmias has reason on his side; and why does not some one of you who is better able than myself answer him? for there is force in his line of argument. But perhaps, before we answer him, we had better also hear what Cebes has to say that we may gain time for reflection, and when they have both spoken, we may either assent to them, if there is truth in their concord, or if not, then we must fight our case. Please to tell me then, Cebes, he said, what was the difficulty which troubled you?

Cebes said: I will tell you. My feeling is that the argument is where it was, and open to the same objections which were urged **87** before; for I am ready to admit that the existence of the soul before entering into the bodily form has been very ingeniously, and, if I may say so, quite sufficiently proven; but the existence of the soul after death is in my judgement unproven. Now in spite of Simmias' objections I am not disposed to deny that the soul is stronger and more lasting than the body, being of opinion that in all such respects the soul very far excels the body. Well then, says the argument to me, why do you remain unconvinced? — When you see that the weaker continues in existence after the man is dead, will you not admit that the more lasting must also survive during the same period of time? Now I will ask you to consider whether the objection, which I think I must, like Simmias, express in a figure, is of any weight. The analogy which I will adduce is that of an old weaver, who dies, and after his death somebody says: — He is not dead, he must be alive somewhere; — see, there is the coat which he himself wove and wore, surviving whole and unruined. And then he proceeds to ask of someone who is incredulous, whether a man lasts longer, or the coat which is in use and wear; and when he is answered that a man lasts far longer, thinks that he has thus certainly demonstrated the survival of the man, inasmuch as the less lasting has not perished. But that, Simmias, as I would beg you to remark, is a mistake; anyone would retort that he who talks thus is talking nonsense. For the truth is that the weaver aforesaid, having woven and worn many such coats, outlived several of them, but was outlived by the last; yet a man is not therefore proved to be slighter and weaker than a coat. Now the relation of the body to the soul may be expressed in a similar figure; and anyone may very fairly say in like manner that the soul is lasting, and the body weak and shortlived in comparison. He may argue that every soul wears out many bodies, especially if a man live many years. While he is alive the body deliquesces and decays, and the soul always weaves another garment and repairs the waste. But of course, whenever the soul perishes, she must have on her last garment, and this will survive her; and then at length, when the soul is dead, the body will show its native weakness, and quickly decompose and pass away. I would therefore rather not rely on the argument from superior strength to prove the continued existence of the soul after death. For granting even more than you affirm to be possible, and acknowledging not only that the soul existed before birth, but also that the souls of some exist and will continue to exist after death, and will be born and die again and again, and that there is a natural strength in the soul by which she will hold out and be born many times — nevertheless, we may be still inclined to think that she will weary in the labours of successive births, and may at last succumb in one of her deaths and utterly perish; and this death and dissolution of the body which brings destruction to the soul may be unknown to any of us, for no one of us can have had any experience of it: and if so, then I maintain that he who is confident about death can have but a foolish confidence, unless he is able to prove that the soul is altogether immortal and imperishable. But if he cannot prove the soul's immortality, he who is about to die will always have reason to fear that when the body is disunited, the soul also may utterly perish.

All of us, as we afterwards remarked to one another, had an unpleasant feeling at hearing what they said. When we had been so firmly convinced before, now to have our faith shaken seemed to introduce a confusion and uncertainty, not only into the previous argument, but into any future one; either we were but poor judges, or the subject itself might prove to be such that certainly was impossible.

Ech. There I feel with you — by heaven I do, Phaedo, and when you were speaking, I was moved to ask myself the same question: What argument can I ever trust again? For what could be more convincing than the argument of Socrates, which has now fallen into discredit? That the soul is a kind of harmony is a doctrine which has always had a wonderful hold upon me, and, when mentioned, came back to me at once, as my own original conviction. And now I must begin again and find another argument which will assure me that when the man is dead the soul survives. Tell me, I implore you, how did Socrates pursue the argument? Did he appear to share the unpleasant feeling which you mention? or did he calmly meet the attack? And did he succeed in meeting it, or fail? Narrate what passed as exactly as you can.

Phaed. Often, Echecrates, I have wondered at Socrates, but never more than on that occasion. That he should be able to answer was perhaps nothing, but what astonished me was, first, the gentle and pleasant and approving manner in which he received the words of the young men, and then his quick sense of the wound which had been inflicted on us by the argument, and the readiness with which he healed it. He might be compared to a general rallying his defeated and broken army, urging them to follow his lead and return to the field.

Ech. What followed?

Phaed. You shall hear, for I was close to him on his right hand, seated on a sort of stool, and he on a couch which was a good deal higher. He stroked my head, and pressed the hair upon my neck — he had a way of teasing me about my hair; and then he said: Tomorrow, Phaedo, I suppose that these fair locks of yours will be severed.

Yes, Socrates, I suppose that they will, I replied.

Not so, if you will take my advice.

What shall I do with them? I said.

Today, he replied, and not tomorrow, if this argument dies and we cannot bring it to life again, you and I will both cut off our hair: and if I were you, and the argument got away from me, and I could not hold my ground against Simmias and Cebes, I would myself take an oath, like the Argives, not to let my hair grow any more until I had renewed the conflict and defeated them.

Yes, I said; but Heracles himself is said not to be a match for two.

Summon me then, he said, and I will be your Iolaus until the sun goes down.

I summon you rather, I rejoined, not as Heracles summoning Iolaus, but as Iolaus might summon Heracles.

That will do as well, he said. But first let us take care that we avoid a danger.

Of what nature? I said.

Lest we become misologists, he replied: no worse thing can happen to a man than this. For as there are misanthropists or haters of mankind, there are also misologists or haters of argument, and both spring from the same cause, which is ignorance of the world. Misanthropy arises out of the too great confidence of inexperience; — you trust a man and think him altogether true and sound and faithful, and then in a little while he turns out to be false and knavish; and then another and another, and when this has happened several times to a man, especially when it happens among those whom he deems to be his own most trusted and familiar friends, after many disappointments he at last hates all men, and believes that no one has any good in him at all. You must have observed this process?

I have.

And is it not discreditable? Is it not obvious that such a one was attempting to deal with other men before he had acquired the art of human relationships? This art would have taught him the true state

90 of the case, that few are the good and few the evil, and that the great majority are in the interval between them.

What do you mean? I said.

I mean, he replied, as you might say of the very large and very small — that nothing is more uncommon than a very large or very small man; and this applies generally to all extremes, whether of great and small, or swift and slow, or fair and foul, or black and white: and whether the instances you select be men or dogs or anything else, very few are the extremes, but in the mean between them there is a countless multitude. Did you never observe this?

Yes, I said, I have.

And do you not imagine, he said, that if there were a competition in evil, even there the pre-eminent would be found to be very few?

That is very likely, I said.

Yes, that is very likely, he replied; although in this respect arguments are unlike men — there I was led on by you to say more than I had intended. The point of comparison was, that when a simple man who has no skill in dialectics believes an argument to be true which he afterwards imagines to be false, whether really false or not, and then another and another, — and those especially who have devoted themselves to the study of antinomies come, as you know, to think at last that they have grown to be the wisest of mankind, and that they alone perceive how unsound and unstable are things themselves and all our arguments about them, and how all existence, like the currents in the Euripus, hurries up and down in never-ceasing ebb and flow.

That is quite true, I said.

Yes, Phaedo, he replied, and if there be such a thing as truth or certainty or possibility of knowledge, how melancholy that a man should have lighted upon some argument or other which at first seemed true and then turned out to be false, and instead of blaming himself and his own want of wit, should at last out of sheer annoyance be only too glad to transfer the blame from himself to arguments in general: and for ever afterwards should hate and revile them, and lose truth and the knowledge of realities.

Yes, indeed, I said; that would be most melancholy.

Let us then, in the first place, he said, be careful of allowing or of admitting into our souls the notion that there may be no health or soundness in any arguments at all. Rather say that we have not yet attained to soundness in ourselves, and that we must struggle manfully and do our best to gain it — you and all other men having

91 regard to the whole of your future life, and I myself in the prospect of death. For at this moment I fear that I have not the temper of a philosopher; like the vulgar, I am only a partisan. Now the partisan,

when he is engaged in a dispute, cares nothing about the rights of the question, but is anxious only to convince his hearers of his own assertions. And the difference between him and me at the present moment is merely this — that whereas he seeks to convince his hearers that what he says is true, I am rather seeking to convince myself; to convince my hearers is a secondary matter with me. And do but see how I stand to gain either way by the argument. For if what I say is true, then I do well to be persuaded of the truth; but if there be nothing after death, still, during the short time that remains, I shall not distress my friends with lamentations, and my folly will not last, but will die very soon, and therefore no harm will be done. This is the state of mind, Simmias and Cebes, in which I approach the argument. And I would ask you to be thinking of the truth and not of Socrates: agree with me, if I seem to you to be speaking the truth; or if not, withstand me might and main, that I may not deceive you as well as myself in my enthusiasm, and like the bee leave my sting in you before I die.

And now let us proceed, he said. And first of all let me be sure that I have in my mind what you were saying. Simmias, if I remember rightly, has fears and misgivings whether the soul, although a fairer and diviner thing than the body, being as she is in the form of harmony may not perish first. On the other hand, Cebes appeared to grant that the soul was more lasting than the body, but he said that no one could know whether the soul, after having worn out many bodies, might not perish herself and leave her last body behind her; and that this might be death, the destruction not of the body but of the soul, for in the body the work of destruction is ever going on. Are not these, Simmias and Cebes, the points which we have to consider?

They both agreed to this statement of them.

He proceeded: And did you deny the force of the whole preceding argument, or of a part only?

Of a part only, they replied.

And what did you think, he said, of that part of the argument in which we said that learning was recollection, and hence inferred that the soul must have previously existed somewhere else before she was **92** imprisoned in the body?

Cebes said that he had been wonderfully impressed by that part of the argument, and that his conviction remained absolutely unshaken. Simmias agreed, and added that he himself could hardly imagine the possibility of his ever thinking differently.

But, rejoined Socrates, you will have to think differently, my Theban friend, if you still maintain that harmony is a composite thing, and that the soul is a harmony which is made out of strings set in the frame of the body; for you will surely never allow yourself to say that a harmony is composed and exists prior to the elements necessary to its composition.

Never, Socrates.

But do you not see that this is what you imply when you say both that the soul existed before she took the form and body of man, and that she was made up of elements which as yet had no existence? For harmony is not like that to which you are comparing it; but first the lyre, and the strings, and the sounds exist in a state of discord, and then harmony is made last of all, and perishes first. And how can such an account of the soul as this be in concord with your former statement?

Not at all, replied Simmias.

And yet, he said, there surely ought to be harmony in a discourse of which harmony is the theme?

There ought, replied Simmias.

But there is no harmony, he said, in the two propositions that learning is recollection, and that the soul is a harmony. Which of them will you retain?

I think, he replied, that I have a much stronger faith, Socrates, in the first of the two; of the latter I have had no demonstration at all, but derived it only from a specious analogy, which has commended it to most of its adherents. I know too well that these arguments from analogies are impostors, and unless great caution is observed in the use of them, they are very deceptive — in geometry, and in other things too. But the doctrine of learning and recollection derives its proof from a satisfactory postulate: and the proof was that the soul must have existed before she came into the body, because to her belongs the reality of which the very name signifies existence. Having, as I am convinced, rightly accepted this postulate, and on sufficient grounds, I must, as I suppose, cease to argue or allow others to argue that the soul is a harmony.

Let me put the matter, Simmias, he said, in another point of view:
93 Do you imagine that a harmony or any other composition can be in a state other than that of the elements out of which it is compounded?

Certainly not.

Or do or suffer anything other than they do or suffer?

He agreed.

Then a harmony does not, properly speaking, lead the parts or elements which make up the harmony, but only follows them.

He assented.

So it is far from being possible that a harmony can have any motion, or sound, or other quality which is opposed to that of its parts.

Far indeed, he replied.

And does not the nature of every harmony depend upon the manner in which the elements are harmonized?

I do not undrestand you, he said.

I mean to say that a harmony is more of a harmony, and more completely a harmony, when more truly and fully harmonized, supposing such a thing is possible; and less of a harmony, and less completely a harmony, when less truly and fully harmonized.

True.

Now does the soul admit of degrees? or is one soul in the very least degree more or less, or more or less completely, a soul than another?

Not in the least.

Yet surely of two souls, one is said to have intelligence and virtue, and to be good, and the other to have folly and vice, and to be an evil soul: and this is said truly?

Yes, truly.

But what will those who maintain the soul to be a harmony say of this presence of virtue and vice in the soul? — will they say that here is another harmony, and another discord, and that the virtuous soul is harmonized, and herself being a harmony has another harmony within her, and that the vicious soul is both herself inharmonical and has no other harmony within her?

I cannot tell, replied Simmias; but clearly something of the sort would be asserted by those who say that the soul is a harmony.

And we have already admitted that no soul is more a soul than another; which means admitting that one harmony is not more or less harmony, or more or less completely a harmony, than another?

Quite true.

And that which is not more or less a harmony is not more or less harmonized?

True.

And that which is not more or less harmonized cannot have more or less harmony, but only an equal harmony?

Yes, an equal harmony.

Then one soul not being more or less completely a soul than another, is not more or less harmonized?

Exactly.

And therefore has neither more nor less of discord, nor yet of harmony?

She has not.

And having neither more nor less of harmony or of discord, one soul has no more vice or virtue than another, if vice be discord and virtue harmony?

Not at all more.

94   Or speaking more correctly, Simmias, the soul, if she is a harmony, will never have any vice; because a harmony, being entirely harmony, can have no part in the inharmonical.

No.

Nor, I presume, could a soul, being entirely soul, have any part in vice?

How can she have, if the previous argument holds?

Then, if all souls are equally by their nature souls, all souls of all living creatures will be equally good?

I agree with you, Socrates, he said.

Well, can all this be true, think you? he said; and would such consequences have followed if the assumption that the soul is a harmony were correct?

It cannot be true.

Once more, he said, what ruler is there of the elements of human nature other than the soul, and especially the wise soul? Do you know of any?

Indeed, I do not.

And is the soul in agreement with the affections of the body? or is she at variance with them? For example, when the body is hot and thirsty, does not the soul pull us away from drinking? and when the body is hungry, away from eating? And this is only one instance out of ten thousand of the opposition of the soul to the things of the body.

Very true.

But we have already acknowledged that the soul, if she were a harmony, could never utter a note at variance with the tensions and relaxations and percussions and other affections of the strings out of which she is composed; she could only follow, she could not lead them?

It must be so, he replied.

And yet do we not now discover the soul to be doing the exact opposite — leading the elements of which she is believed to be composed; almost always opposing and coercing them in all sorts of ways throughout life, sometimes more violently with the pains of medicine and gymnastic; then again more gently; now threatening, now admonishing, the desires, passions, fears, as if talking to a thing which is not herself, as Homer in the Odyssey represents Odysseus doing in the words —

> He beat his breast, and thus reproached his heart:
> Endure, my heart; far worse hast thou endured!

Do you think that Homer wrote this under the idea that the soul is a harmony destined to be led by the affections of the body, and not rather of a nature which should lead and master them — herself far too divine a thing to be compared with any harmony?

Yes, Socrates, I quite think so.

Then, my friend, we can never be right in saying that the soul is 95 a kind of harmony, for we should apparently contradict the divine Homer, and contradict ourselves.

True, he said.

Thus much, said Socrates, of Harmonia, your Theban goddess, who has graciously yielded to us; but what shall I say, Cebes, to her husband Cadmus, and how shall I make peace with him?

I think that you will discover a way of propitiating him, said Cebes; I am sure that you have put the argument with Harmonia in a manner that I could never have expected. For when Simmias was mentioning his difficulty, I quite imagined that no answer could be given to him, and therefore I was surprised at finding that his argument could not sustain the first onset of yours, and not impossibly the other, whom you call Cadmus, may share a similar fate.

Nay, my good friend, said Socrates, do not boast, lest some evil eye should blight the growing argument. That, however, may be left in the hands of those above; while we draw near the foe in Homeric fashion, and try the mettle of your words. Here lies the point: — You want to have it proven to you that the soul is imperishable and immortal, for otherwise the philosopher, who meets death confidently in the belief that he will fare better in the world below than if he had led another sort of life, must be the dupe of a vain and foolish confidence: and you say that the demonstration of the strength and divinity of the soul, and of her existence prior to our becoming men, does not necessarily imply her immortality, but only that she is long-lived, and has known and done much in a former state of immense duration. Still she is not on that account immortal; and her entrance into the human form may itself be a sort of disease which is the beginning of dissolution, and she may be sorely vexed during her earthly life, and sooner or later perish in that which is called death. And whether the soul enters into the body once only or many times, does not, so you say, make any difference in the fears of individuals. For any man who is not devoid of sense must fear, if he has no knowledge and can give no account of the soul's immortality. This, or something like this, I suspect to be your view, Cebes; and I have designedly repeated it more than once in order that nothing may escape us, and that you may, if you wish, add or subtract anything.

But, said Cebes, as far as I see at present, I have nothing to add or subtract; I mean what you say that I mean.

Socrates paused for a long while, and seemed to be absorbed in reflection. At length he said: You are raising a tremendous question,

96 Cebes, involving the whole nature and cause of coming into being and ceasing to be, about which, if you like, I will give you my own experience; and if anything which I say seems helpful to you, you may use it to overcome your difficulty.

I should very much like, said Cebes, to hear what you have to say.

Then I will tell you, said Socrates. When I was young, Cebes, I had a prodigious desire to know that department of philosophy which is called the investigation of nature; to know the causes of things, and why a thing is and is created or destroyed, appeared to me to be a lofty profession; and I was always agitating myself with the consideration of questions such as these: — Is the growth of animals the result of some putrefaction which the hot and the cold principle suffer, as some have said? Is the blood the element with which we think, or the air, or the fire? or perhaps nothing of the kind — but the brain may be the originating power of the perceptions of hearing and sight and smell, and memory and opinion may come from them, and knowledge from memory and opinion when they have attained fixity. And then I went on to examine the corruptions of them, and then to the things of heaven and earth, and at last I concluded myself to be utterly and absolutely incapable of these inquiries, as I will satisfactorily prove to you. For I was fascinated by them to such a degree that my eyes grew blind to things which I had seemed to myself, and also to others, to know quite well; I unlearned what I had before thought self-evident truths; e.g. such a fact as that the growth of man is the result of eating and drinking; for when by the digestion of food flesh is added to flesh and bone to bone, and when by the same process each tissue has received its appropriate accretion, then the lesser bulk becomes larger and so the small man becomes big. Was not that a reasonable notion?

Yes, said Cebes, I think so.

Well; but let me tell you something more. There was a time when I thought that I understood the meaning of greater and less pretty well; and when I saw a big man standing by a little one, I fancied that one was taller than the other just by the head, and similarly with horses: and still more clearly did I seem to perceive that ten is more than eight because it has two additional units, and that two cubits are more than one because it is larger by a half of itself.

And what is now your notion of such matters? said Cebes.

I should be far enough from imagining, he replied, that I knew the cause of any of them, by heaven I should; for I cannot satisfy
97 myself that, when one is added to one, either the one to which the addition is made or the one which is added becomes two, or that the two units added together make two by reason of the addition. I cannot understand how, when separated from the other, each of them was

one and not two, and now, when they are brought together, the mere juxtaposition or meeting of them should be the cause of their becoming two. Neither can I believe that the division of one is the way to make two; for then an opposite cause would produce the same effect, — as in the former instance the addition and juxtaposition of one to one was the cause of two, in this the separation and subtraction of one from the other would be the cause. Nor am I any longer satisfied that I understand how the unit comes into being at all, or in short how anything else is either generated or destroyed or exists, so long as this is the method of approach; but I have in my mind some confused notion of a new method, and can never admit the other.

Then I heard someone reading, as he said, from a book of Anaxagoras, that mind was the disposer and cause of all, and I was delighted at this notion, which appeared quite admirable, and I said to myself: If mind is the disposer, mind will dispose all for the best, and put each particular in the best place; and I argued that if anyone desired to find out the cause of the generation or destruction or existence of anything, he must find out what state of being or doing or suffering was best for that thing, and therefore a man had only to consider what was best and most desirable both for the thing itself and for other things, and then he must necessarily also know the worse, since the same science comprehended both. Arguing in this way, I rejoiced to think that I had found in Anaxagoras a teacher of the causes of existence such as I desired, and I imagined that he would tell me first whether the earth is flat or round; and after telling me this, he would proceed to explain the cause and the necessity of this being so, starting from the greater good, and demonstrating that it is better for the earth to be such as it is; and if he said that the earth was in the centre, he would further explain that this position was the better, and I should be satisfied with the explanation given, and not want any other sort of cause. And I thought that I would then go on and ask him about the sun and moon and stars, and that he would explain to me their comparative swiftness, and their returnings and various states, active and passive, and in what way all of them were for the best. For I could not imagine that when he spoke of mind as the disposer of them, he would give any other account of their being as they are, except that this was best; and I thought that while explaining to me in detail the cause of each and the cause of all, he would also explain to me what was best for each and what was good for all. These hopes I would not have sold for a large sum of money, and I seized the books and started to read them as fast as I could in my eagerness to know the best and the worse.

How high were my hopes, and how quickly were they lost to me!

As I proceeded, I found my philosopher altogether forsaking mind and making no appeal to any other principle of order, but having recourse to air, and ether, and water, and many other eccentricities. I might compare him to a person who began by maintaining generally that mind is the cause of the actions of Socrates, but who, when he endeavoured to explain the causes of my several actions in detail, went on to show that I sit here because my body is made up of bones and muscles; and the bones, as he would say, are hard and have joints which divide them, and the muscles are elastic, and they cover the bones, which have also a covering or environment of flesh and skin which contains them; and as the bones swing in their sockets, through the contraction or relaxation of the muscles I am able to bend my limbs, and this is why I am sitting here in a curved posture — that is what he would say; and he would have a similar explanation of my talking to you, which he would attribute to sound, and air, and hearing, and he would assign ten thousand other causes of the same sort, forgetting to mention the true cause, which is, that the Athenians have thought it better to condemn me, and accordingly I have thought it better and more right to remain here and undergo my sentence; for 99 I strongly suspect that these muscles and bones of mine would long ago have been in Megara or Boeotia, borne there by their own idea of what was best, if I did not think it more right and honourable to endure any penalty ordered by the state, instead of running away into exile. There is surely a strange confusion of causes and conditions in all this. It may be said, indeed, that without bones and muscles and the other parts of the body I cannot execute my purposes. But to say at the same time that I act from mind, and that I do as I do because of them and not from the choice of the best, is a very careless and idle mode of speaking. I wonder that they cannot distinguish the cause from the condition without which the cause would never be the cause; it is the latter, I think, which the many, feeling about in the dark, are always mistaking and misnaming 'cause'. And thus one man sets the earth within a cosmic whirling, and steadies it by the heaven; another gives the air as a support to the earth, which is a sort of broad trough. They never look for the power which in arranging them as they are arranges them for the best; and instead of ascribing to it any superhuman strength, they rather expect to discover another Atlas who is stronger and more everlasting than this earthly Atlas, and better able to hold all things together. That it is really the good and the right which holds and binds things together, they never reflect. Such then is the principle of causation which I would fain learn if anyone would teach me. But as I have failed either to discover it myself, or to learn it of anyone else, I will exhibit to you, if you like, the method I have followed as the second best mode of inquiring into the cause.

I should very much like to hear, he replied.

Socrates proceeded: — I thought that as I had failed in the study of material things, I ought to be careful that I did not lose the eye of my soul; as people may injure their bodily eye by observing and gazing on the sun during an eclipse, unless they take the precaution of only looking at the image reflected in the water, or in some similar medium. So in my own case, I was afraid that my soul might be blinded altogether if I looked at things with my eyes or tried to apprehend them by the help of particular senses. And I thought that I had better retreat to the domain of reasoning and seek there the truth of existence. I dare say that the simile is not perfect — for I do not quite 100 agree that he who contemplates things through the medium of thought, sees them only 'through a glass darkly', more so than he who considers them in their material existence. However, this was the method which I adopted; I first assumed some proposition, which I judged to be the strongest, and then I affirmed as true whatever seemed to agree with this, whether relating to causation or to anything else; and that which disagreed I regarded as untrue. But I should like to explain my meaning more clearly, as I do not think that you as yet understand me.

No indeed, replied Cebes, not very well.

There is nothing new, he said, in what I am about to tell you; but only what I have been always and everywhere repeating in the previous discussion and on other occasions: I shall try to show you the sort of causation which has occupied my thoughts. I shall have to go back to those familiar theories which are in the mouth of everyone, and first of all assume that there is an absolute beauty and goodness and greatness, and the like; grant me these and admit that they exist, and I hope to be able to show you the nature of cause, and to prove the immortality of the soul.

Cebes said: You may proceed at once with the proof, for I grant you this.

Well, he said, then I should like to know whether you agree with me in the next step; for I cannot help thinking that if there be anything beautiful other than absolute beauty it is beautiful only in so far as it partakes of absolute beauty — and I should say the same of everything. Do you agree in this notion of the cause?

Yes, he said, I agree.

He proceeded: I no longer look for, nor can I understand, those other ingenious causes which are alleged; and if a person says to me that the bloom of colour, or form, or any such thing is a source of beauty, I dismiss all that, which is only confusing to me, and simply and singly, and perhaps foolishly, hold and am assured in my own mind that nothing makes a thing beautiful but the presence or participation of beauty in whatever way or manner obtained; for as to the manner I am uncertain, but I stoutly contend that by beauty all beautiful things become beautiful. This appears to me to be the safest answer which I can give, either to myself or to another, and to this I cling, in the persuasion that this principle will never be overthrown, and that to myself or to anyone who asks the question, I may safely reply, That by beauty beautiful things become beautiful. Do you not agree with me?

I do.

And that by greatness great things become great and greater greater, and by smallness the less become less?

True.

Then if a person were to remark that A is taller by a head than B, **101** and B less by a head than A, you would refuse to admit his statement, and would stoutly contend that what you mean is only that the greater is greater by, and by reason of, greatness, and the less is less only by, and by reason of, smallness. I imagine you would be afraid of a counter-argument that if the greater is greater and the less less by the head, then, first, the greater is greater and the less less by the same thing; and, secondly, the greater man is greater by the head which is itself small, and so you get the monstrous absurdity that a man is great by something small. You would be afraid of this, would you not?

Indeed I should, said Cebes, laughing.

In like manner you would think it dangerous to say that ten exceeded eight by, and by reason of, two; but would say by, and by reason of, number; or you would say that two cubits exceed one cubit not by a half, but by magnitude? — for there is the same danger in all these cases.

Very true, he said.

Again, would you not be cautious of affirming that the addition of one to one, or the division of one, is the cause of two? And you would loudly asseverate that you know of no way in which anything comes into existence except by participation in the distinctive reality of that in which it participates, and consequently, as far as you know, the only cause of two is the participation in duality — this is the way to make two, and the participation in unity is the way to make one. You would say: 'I will let alone all subleties like these of division and addition — wiser heads than mine may answer them; inexperienced as I am, and ready to start, as the proverb says, at my own shadow, I cannot afford to give up the sure ground of the original postulate.' And if anyone fastens on you there, you would not mind him, or answer him until you could see whether the consquences which follow agree with one another or not, and when you are further required to give an account of this postulate, you would give it in the same way, assuming some higher postulate which seemed to you to be the best founded, until you arrived at a satisfactory resting-place; but you would not jumble together the fundamental principle and the consequences in your reasoning, like the eristics — at least if you wanted to discover real existence. Not that this confusion signifies to them, who probably never care or think about the matter at all, for they have the wit to be well pleased with themselves however thorough may be the muddle of their ideas. But you, if you are a philosopher, will certainly do as I say. 102

What you say is most true, said Simmias and Cebes, both speaking at once.

Ech. Yes, Phaedo; and I do not wonder at their assenting. Anyone who has the least sense will acknowledge the wonderful clearness of Socrates' reasoning.

Phaed. Certainly, Echecrates; and such was the feeling of the whole company at the time.

Ech. Yes, and equally of ourselves, who were not of the company, and are now listening to your recital. But what followed?

Phaed. After all this had been admitted, and they had agreed, that the forms exist individually, and that other things participate in them and derive their names from them, Socrates, if I remember rightly, said: —

This is your way of speaking; and yet when you say that Simmias is greater than Socrates and less than Phaedo, do you not predicate of Simmias both greatness and smallness?

Yes, I do.

But still, he continued, you allow that Simmias does not in fact exceed Socrates, as the words may seem to imply, essentially because he is Simmias, but by reason of the size which he happens to have; exactly as on the other hand he does not exceed Socrates because Socrates is Socrates, but because Socrates has smallness when compared with the greatness of Simmias?

True.

And if Phaedo exceeds him in size, this is not because Phaedo is Phaedo, but because Phaedo has greatness relatively to Simmias, who is comparatively smaller?

That is true.

And therefore Simmias is said to be small, and is also said to be great, because he is in a mean between them, submitting his smallness to be exceeded by the greatness of the one, and presenting his greatness to the other to exceed that other's smallness. He added, laughing, I am speaking like a book, but I believe that what I am saying is true.

Simmias assented.

I speak as I do because I want you to agree with me in thinking, not only that absolute greatness will never be simultaneously great and small, but also that the greatness in us will never admit the small or consent to be exceeded; instead of this, one of two things will happen, either it will fly and retire before its opposite, the small, or at the approach of its opposite it has already ceased to exist; but it refuses to become other than what it was by staying and receiving smallness. For instance, I having received and admitted smallness remain as I was, and am the same person and small: but greatness has not condescended to become small. In like manner the smallness in us refuses to 103 be or become great; nor can any other opposite which remains the same ever be or become its own opposite, but either goes away or perishes in the change.

That, replied Cebes, is quite my notion.

Hereupon one of the company, though I do not exactly remember which of them, said: In heaven's name, is not this the direct contrary of what was admitted before — that out of the greater came the less and out of the less the greater, and that opposites were simply generated from opposites; but now this principle seems to be utterly denied.

Socrates turned his head to the speaker and listened. I like your courage, he said, in reminding us of this. But you do not observe that there is a difference in the two cases. For then we were saying that an opposite thing comes into being from its opposite; now, however, speaking of bare opposites, and taking them either as they are realized in us or as they exist in themselves, we say that one of them can never become the other: then, my friend, we were speaking of things in which opposites are inherent and which are called after them, but now about the opposites which are inherent in them and which give their name to them; and these essential opposites will never, as we maintain, admit of generation into or out of one another. At the same time, turning to Cebes, he said: Are you at all disconcerted, Cebes, at our friend's objection?

No, not by this one, said Cebes; and yet I cannot deny that I am often disturbed by objections.

Then we are agreed after all, said Socrates, that the opposite will never in any case be opposed to itself?

To that we are quite agreed, he replied.

Yet once more let me ask you to consider the question from another point of view, and see whether you agree with me: — There is a thing which you term heat, and another thing which you term cold?

Certainly.

But are they the same as fire and snow?

Most assuredly not.

Heat is a thing different from fire, and cold is not the same with snow?

Yes.

And yet I fancy you agree that when snow receives heat (to use our previous phraseology), they will not remain snow and heat; but at the advance of the heat, the snow will either retire or perish?

Very true, he replied.

And the fire too at the advance of the cold will either retire or perish; but it will never receive the cold, and yet insist upon remaining what it was, and so be at once fire and cold.

That is true, he said.

And in some cases the name of the form is attached not only to the form in an eternal connexion; but something else which, not being the form, yet never exists without it, is also entitled to be called by that name. I will try to make this clearer by an example: — The odd number is always called by the name of odd?

Very true.

But is this the only thing which is called odd? Here is my point. **104** Are there not other things which have their own name and yet must be called odd, because, although not the same as oddness, they are essentially never without oddness? I mean such a case as that of the number three, and there are many other examples. Take that case. Would you not say that three may be called by its proper name, and also be called odd, which is not the same with three? and this may be said not only of three but also of five, and of every alternate number — each of them without being oddness is odd; and in the same way two and four, and the other series of alternate numbers, has every number even, without being evenness. Do you agree?

Of course.

Then now mark the point at which I am aiming: — not only do essential opposites seem to exclude one another, but also concrete things, which, although not in themselves opposed, contain opposites; these, I say, likewise reject the form opposed to that which is contained in them, and when it approaches them they either perish or withdraw. For example; Will not the number three endure annihilation or anything sooner than be converted into an even number, while remaining three?

Very true, said Cebes.

And yet, he said, the number two is certainly not opposed to the number three?

It is not.

Then not only do opposite forms repel the advance of one another, but also there are other things which withdraw before the approach of opposites.

Very true, he said.

Suppose, he said, that we endeavour, if possible, to determine what these are.

By all means.

Are they not, Cebes, such as compel anything of which they have possession, not only to take their own form, but also the form of an opposite?

What do you mean?

I mean, as I was just now saying, and as I am sure that you know, that those things which are possessed by the form of the number three must not only be three in number, but must also be odd.

Quite true.

And such things will never suffer the intrusion of the form opposite to that which gives this impress?

No.

And this impress was given by the form of the odd?

Yes.

And to the odd is opposed the even?

True.

Then the form of the even number will never intrude on three?

No.

Then three has no part in the even?

None.

Then the triad or number three is uneven?

Very true.

To return then to my definition of things which are not opposite to one of a pair of opposites, and yet do not admit that opposite — as, in the instance given, three, although not opposed to the even, does not any the more admit of the even, but always brings the opposite
105 into play on the other side; or as two does not receive the odd, or fire the cold — from these examples (and there are many more of them) perhaps you may be able to arrive at the general conclusion, that not only opposites will not receive opposites, but also that nothing which brings an opposite will admit the opposite of that which it brings, in that to which it is brought. And here let me recapitulate — for there is no harm in repetition. The number five will not admit the form of the even, any more than ten, which is the double of five, will admit the form of the odd. The double has itself a different opposite, but nevertheless rejects the odd altogether. Nor similarly will parts in the ratio 3:2 admit the form of the whole, nor will the half or the one-third, or any such fraction: You will agree?

Yes, he said, I entirely agree and go along with you in that.

And now, he said, let us begin again; and do not you answer my question in the words in which I ask it, but follow my example: let me have not the old safe answer of which I spoke at first, but another equally safe, of which the truth will be inferred by you from what has been just said. If you ask me 'what that is, of which the inherence makes the body hot', I shall reply not heat (this is what I call the safe and stupid answer), but fire, a far superior answer, which we are now in a condition to give. Or if you ask me 'why a body is diseased', I shall not say from disease, but from fever; and instead of saying that oddness is the cause of odd numbers, I shall say that the monad is the cause of them: and so of things in general, as I dare say that you will understand sufficiently without my adducing any further examples.

Yes, he said, I quite understand you.

Tell me, then, what is that of which the inherence will render the body alive?

The soul, he replied.

And is this always the case?

Yes, he said, of course.

Then whatever the soul occupies, to that she comes bearing life?

Yes, certainly.

And is there any opposite to life?

There is, he said.

And what is that?

Death.

Then from our previous conclusion it follows that the soul will never admit the opposite of what she always brings.

Impossible, replied Cebes.

And now, he said, what did we just now call that which does not admit the form of the even?

Uneven.

And that which does not admit the musical or the just?

The unmusical, he said, and the unjust.

And what do we call that which does not admit death?

The immortal, he said.

And does the soul admit of death?

No.

Then the soul is immortal?

Yes, he said.

And may we say that this has been proven?

Yes, abundantly proven, Socrates, he replied.

Supposing that the odd were necessarily imperishable, must not 106 three be imperishable?

Of course.

And if that which is cold were necessarily imperishable, when heat came attacking the snow, must not the snow have retired whole and unmelted — for it could never have perished, nor again could it have remained and admitted the heat?

True, he said.

Again, if that which cannot be cooled were imperishable, the fire when assailed by cold would not have perished or have been extinguished, but would have gone away unaffected?

Certainly, he said.

And the same may be said of the immortal: if the immortal is also imperishable, the soul when attacked by death cannot perish; for the preceding argument shows that the soul will not admit death, or exist as dead, any more than three or the odd number will exist as even, or fire, or the heat in the fire, will be cold. Yet a person may say: 'But although the odd will not become even at the approach of the even, why may not the odd perish and the even take the place of the odd?' Now to him who makes this objection, we cannot answer that the odd is imperishable; for this is not the fact. If we had accepted it as a fact, there would have been no difficulty in contending that at the approach of the even the odd and the number three took their departure; and the same argument would have held good of fire and heat and any other thing.

Very true.

And the same may be said of the immortal: if we agree that the immortal is also imperishable, then the soul will be imperishable as well as immortal; but if not, some other proof of her imperishableness will have to be given.

No other proof is needed, he said; for if the immortal, being eternal, is liable to perish, then nothing is imperishable.

Yes, replied Socrates, and all men, I think, will agree that God, and the essential form of life, and the immortal in general, will never perish.

Yes, all men, he said — that is true; and what is more, gods, if I am not mistaken, as well as men.

Seeing then that the immortal is indestructible, must not the soul, if she is immortal, be also imperishable?

Most certainly.

Then when death attacks a man, the mortal portion of him may be supposed to die, but the immortal retires at the approach of death and is preserved safe and indestructible?

Yes.

107   Then, Cebes, beyond question, the soul is immortal and imperishable, and our souls will truly exist in another world!

I am convinced, Socrates, said Cebes, and have nothing more to object; but if my friend Simmias, or anyone else, has any further objection to make, he had better speak out, and not keep silence, since I do not know to what other season he can defer the discussion if there is anything which he wants to say or to have said.

But I too, replied Simmias, can give no reason for doubting the result of the argument. It is when I think of the greatness of the subject and feebleness of man that I still feel and cannot help feeling uncertain in my own mind.

Yes, Simmias, replied Socrates, that is well said: and I may add that our first principles, even if they appear to you certain, should be closely examined; and when they are satisfactorily analysed, then you will, I imagine, follow up the argument as far as is humanly possible; and if you make sure you have done so, there will be no need for any further inquiry.

Very true.

But then, O my friends, he said, if the soul is really immortal, what care should be taken of her, not only in respect of the portion of time allowed to what is called life, but of eternity! And the danger of neglecting her from this point of view does indeed now appear to be awful. If death had only been the end of all, dying would have been a godsend to the wicked, for they would have been happily quit not only of their body, but of their own evil together with their souls. But now, inasmuch as the soul is manifestly immortal, there is for her no release or salvation from evil except the attainment of the highest virtue and wisdom. For the soul when on her progress to the world below takes nothing with her but nurture and education; and these are said greatly to benefit or greatly to injure the departed, at the very beginning of his journey thither.

For after death, as they say, each individual is led by the genius to whom he had been allotted in life to a certain place in which the dead are gathered together, whence after submitting to judgement they pass into the world below, following the guide who is appointed to conduct them from this world to the other: and when they have received their due and remained their time, another guide brings them back again after many revolutions of ages. Now this way to the other world is not, as Aeschylus says in the *Telephus*, a single and straight path — if that were so no guide would be needed, for no one could miss it; but there are many partings of the road, and windings, as I infer from the rites and sacrifices which are offered to the gods below in places where three ways meet on earth. The wise and orderly soul follows her appointed guide and knows her surroundings; but the soul which desires the body, and which, as I was relating before, has long been fluttering about the lifeless frame and the world of sight, is after many struggles and many sufferings hardly and with violence carried away by her attendant genius; and when she arrives at the place where the other souls are gathered, if she be impure and have done impure deeds, whether foul murders or other crimes which are the brothers of these, and the works of brothers in crime — from that soul everyone flees and turns away; no one will be her companion, no one her guide, but alone she wanders in extremity of distress until certain times are fulfilled, and when they are fulfilled, she is borne irresistibly to her own fitting habitation; as every pure and just soul which has passed through life in the company and under the guidance of the gods has also her own proper home.

Now the earth has divers wonderful regions, and is indeed in nature

and extent very unlike the notions of geographers, as I believe on the
authority of one who shall be nameless.

What do you mean, Socrates? said Simmias. I have myself heard
many descriptions of the earth, but I do not know, and I should very
much like to hear the account in which you put faith.

Well, Simmias, replied Socrates, it scarcely needs the art of Glaucus
to give you a description; although I know not that the art of Glaucus
could prove the truth of my tale, which I myself should perhaps
never be able to prove, and even if I could, I fear, Simmias, that my
life would come to an end before the argument was completed. I
may describe to you, however, the form and regions of the earth
according to my conception of them.

That, said Simmias, will be enough.

Well then, he said, my conviction is, that the earth is a round
109 body in the centre of the heavens, and therefore has no need of air
or of any similar force to be a support, but is kept there and hindered
from falling or inclining any way by the equability of the surrounding
heaven and by her own equipoise. For that which, being in equipoise,
is in the centre of that which is equably diffused, will not incline any
way in any degree, but being similarly related to every extreme will
remain unmoving, and not deviate. And this is my first belief.

Which is surely a correct one, said Simmias.

Also I believe that the earth is very vast, and that we who dwell
in the region extending from the River Phasis to the Pillars of Heracles inhabit a small portion only about the sea, like ants and frogs
about a marsh, and that there are many other inhabitants of many
other like places; for everywhere on the surface of the earth there are
hollows of various forms and sizes, into which the water and the mist
and the lower air have collected. But the true earth is pure and situated in the pure heaven — there are the stars also; and it is the heaven
which is commonly spoken of by most authorities as the ether, and of
which those other things are the sediment gathering in the hollows
beneath. We who live in these hollows are deceived into the notion
that we are dwelling above on the surface of the earth; which is just
as if a creature who lived at the bottom of the sea were to fancy that
he was living on the surface of the water, and that the sea was the
heaven through which he saw the sun and the other stars, he having
never come to the surface by reason of his feebleness and sluggishness,
and having never lifted up his head and seen, nor ever heard from one
who had seen, how much purer and fairer the world above is than his
own. And such is exactly our case. We are dwelling in a hollow of
the earth, and fancy that we are on the surface; and the air we call the
heaven, in which we imagine that the stars move. But the fact is that
owing to our feebleness and sluggishness we are prevented from reach-

ing the surface of the air: for if any man could arrive at the exterior limit, or take the wings of a bird and come to the top, then, like a fish who puts his head out of the water and sees this world, he would see a world beyond; and, if the nature of man could sustain the sight, he would acknowledge that this other world was the place of the true heaven and the true light and the true earth. For our earth, and the 110 stones, and the entire region which surrounds us, are spoilt and corroded, as in the sea all things are corroded by the brine, neither has the sea any notable or perfect growth, but even where it meets earth it has only caverns, and sand, and an endless slough of mud — in no wise to be compared to the fairer sights of our world. And still less is this our world to be compared with the other. If a myth is not to be despised, Simmias, I can tell you one that is well worth hearing about that upper earth which is under the heaven.

And we, Socrates, replied Simmias, shall be charmed to listen to your myth.

The tale, my friend, he said, is as follows: — In the first place, the true earth, when looked at from above, is in appearance like one of those balls which are made of twelve pieces of leather; it is variegated, a patchwork of different colours of which the colours used by painters on our earth are in a manner samples. But there the whole earth is made up of them, and they are brighter far and clearer than ours; there is a purple of wonderful lustre, also the radiance of gold, and the white which is in the earth is whiter than any chalk or snow. Of these and other colours the earth is made up, and they are more in number and fairer than the eye of man has ever seen; the very hollows (of which I was speaking) filled with air and water have a colour of their own, and are seen like light gleaming amid the diversity of the other colours, so that the whole presents a single and continuous appearance of variety in unity. And in this fair region all things which grow — trees, and flowers, and fruits — are in a like degree fairer than any here; and there are hills, having stones in them in a like degree smoother, and more transparent, and fairer in colour than our highly valued emeralds and cornelians and jaspers and other gems, which are but minute fragments of them: for there all the stones are like our precious stones, and fairer still. The reason is that they are pure, and not, like our precious stones, corroded or defiled by the confluence of corrupt briny elements which breed foulness and disease both in earth and stones, as well as in animals and plants. They are the jewels of the upper earth, which also shines with gold and silver 111 and the like, and they are set in the light of day and are large and abundant and in all places, making the earth a sight to gladden the beholder's eye. And there are many animals and also men, some living inland, others dwelling about the air as we dwell about the sea;

others in islands which the air flows round, near the mainland; and in a word, the air is used by them as the water and the sea are by us, and the ether is to them what the air is to us. Moreover, the temperament of their seasons is such that they have no disease, and live much longer than we do, and have sight and hearing and intelligence and all the other faculties in far greater perfection, in the same proportion that air is purer than water or the ether than air. Also they have temples and sacred places in which the gods really dwell, and they hear their voices and receive their answers, and are conscious of them and hold converse with them face to face; and they see the sun, moon, and stars as they truly are, and their other blessedness is of a piece with this.

Such is the nature of the whole earth, and of the things which are around the earth; and there are divers regions in the hollows on the face of the globe everywhere, some of them deeper and more extended than that which we inhabit, others deeper but narrower, and some are shallower and also wider. All have numerous perforations, and there are passages broad and narrow in the interior of the earth, connecting them with one another; and there flows out of and into them, as into basins, a vast tide of water, and huge subterranean streams of perennial rivers, and springs hot and cold, and a great fire, and great rivers of fire, and streams of liquid mud, thin or thick (like the rivers of mud in Sicily, and the lava streams which follow them), and the regions about which they happen to flow are filled up with them. And there is a swinging or see-saw in the interior of the earth which moves all this up and down, and is due to the fol-

112 lowing cause: — There is a chasm which is the vastest of them all, and pierces right through the whole earth; this is that chasm which Homer describes in the words, —

Far off, where is the inmost depth beneath the earth;

and which he in other places, and many other poets, have called Tartarus. And the see-saw is caused by the streams flowing into and out of this chasm, and they each have the nature of the soil through which they flow. And the reason why the streams are always flowing in and out, is that the watery element has no bed or bottom, but is swinging and surging up and down, and the surrounding wind and air do the same; they follow the water up and down, towards the further side of the earth and back again; and just as in the act of respiration the air is always in process of inhalation and exhalation, so the wind swinging with the water in and out produces fearful and irresistible blasts: when the waters retire into the regions below, as they are called, they flow into the streams on the further side of the earth, and fill them up like water raised by a pump, and then when they leave those regions and rush back hither, they again fill the streams here, and these being filled flow through subterranean channels and find their way to their appointed places, forming seas, and lakes, and rivers, and springs. Thence they again enter the earth, some of them making a long circuit into many lands, others going to a few places and not so distant; and again fall into Tartarus, some at a point a good deal lower than that at which they rose, and others not much lower, but all in some degree lower than the point from which they came; and some fall in on the opposite side, and some on the same side. Some wind round the earth with one or many folds like the coils of a serpent, and after descending as far as they can fall again into the chasm. The rivers flowing in either direction can descend only to the centre and no further, for on either side of it their course would be uphill.

Now these rivers are many, and mighty, and diverse, and there are four principal ones, of which the greatest and outermost is that called Oceanus, which flows round in a circle; and diametrically opposite to it is Acheron, which flows in the opposite direction and **113** passes through desert places and under the earth into the Acherusian lake: this is the lake to the shores of which the souls of the many go when they are dead, and after waiting an appointed time, which is to some a longer and to some a shorter time, they are sent back to be born again as animals. The third river passes out between the two, and near the place of outlet pours into a vast region of fire, and forms a lake larger than the Mediterranean Sea, boiling with water and mud; and proceeding muddy and turbid, and coiling round inside the earth, comes, among other places, to the extremities of the Acherusian lake, but mingles not with the waters of the lake, and after making many coils about the earth plunges into Tartarus at a deeper level. This is that Pyriphlegethon, as the stream is called, which throws up jets of lava in different parts of the earth. The fourth river goes out on the opposite side, and falls first of all, it is said, into a savage and frightful region, which is all of a blue-grey colour, like lapis lazuli; and this is that region which is called the Stygian, and the lake which the river forms by its influx is called Styx. After falling into the lake and receiving strange powers in the waters, it passes under the earth, winding round in the opposite direction to Pyriphlegethon, and meets it at the Acherusian lake from the opposite side. And the water of this river too mingles with no other, but flows round in a circle and falls into Tartarus over against Pyriphlegethon; and the name of the river, as the poets say, is Cocytus.

Such is the nature of the other world; and when the dead arrive at the place to which the genius of each severally guides them, first of all, they submit themselves to judgement, as they have lived well and piously or not. And those who appear to have lived neither well nor ill, go to the river Acheron, and embarking in the vessels which we may imagine they find there, are carried in them to the lake, and there they dwell and are purified of their evil deeds, and having suffered the penalty of the wrongs which they have done to others, they are absolved, and receive the rewards of their good deeds, each of them according to his deserts. But those who appear to be incurable by reason of the greatness of their crimes — who have committed many and terrible deeds of sacrilege, many murders foul and violent, or the like — such are hurled into Tartarus which is their fitting destiny, and they never come out. Those again who have committed crimes, which, although great, are not irremediable — who in a 114 moment of anger, for example, have done some violence to a father or a mother, and have repented for the remainder of their lives, or who have taken the life of another under the like extenuating circumstances — these are plunged into Tartarus, the pains of which they are compelled to undergo for a year, but at the end of the year the wave casts them forth — mere homicides by way of Cocytus, parricides and matricides by Pyriphlegethon — and they are borne to the Acherusian lake, and there they lift up their voices and call upon the victims whom they have slain or wronged, to have pity on them, and to be kind to them, and let them come out into the lake. And if they prevail, then they come forth and cease from their troubles; but if not, they are carried back again into Tartarus and from thence into the rivers unceasingly, until they obtain mercy from those whom they have wronged: for that is the sentence inflicted upon them by their judges. But those who have been pre-eminent for holiness of life are released from this earthly prison, and go to their pure home which is above, and dwell on the true earth; and of these, such as have duly purified themselves with philosophy live henceforth altogether without the body, in mansions fairer still, which are not easily to be described, and of which the time now fails me to tell.

Wherefore, Simmias, seeing all these things, what ought not we to do that we may obtain virtue and wisdom in this life? Fair is the prize, and the hope great!

A man of sense ought not to assert that the description which I have given of the soul and her mansions is exactly true. But I do say that, inasmuch as the soul is shown to be immortal, he may venture to think, not improperly or unworthily, that something of the kind is true. The venture is a glorious one, and he ought to comfort himself with words of power like these, which is the reason why I lengthen out the tale. Wherefore, I say, let a man be of good cheer about his soul, who having cast away the pleasures and ornaments of the body as alien to him and working harm rather than good, has sought after the pleasures of knowledge; and has arrayed the soul, not in some foreign attire, but in her own proper jewels, temperance, and justice, and courage, and nobility, and truth — in these adorned she is ready to go on her journey to the world below. You, Simmias and Cebes, and you others, will depart at some time or other. Me already, as a tragic poet would say, the voice of fate calls. Soon I must drink the poison; and I think that I had better repair to the bath first, in order that the women may not have the trouble of washing my body after I am dead.

When he had done speaking, Crito said: And have you any commands for us, Socrates — anything to say about your children, or any other matter in which we can serve you?

Nothing particular, Crito, he replied: only, as I have always told you, take care of yourselves; that is a service which you may be ever rendering to me and mine and to yourselves, whether you promise to do so or not. But if you have no thought for yourselves, and care not to walk in the path of life which I have shown you, not now for the first time, then however much and however earnestly you may promise at the moment, it will be of no avail.

We will do our best, said Crito: And in what way shall we bury you?

In any way that you like; but you must first get hold of me, and take care that I do not run away from you. Then he turned to us, and added with a smile: — I cannot make Crito believe that I am the same Socrates who have been talking and conducting the argument; he fancies that I am the other Socrates whom he will soon see, a dead body — and indeed he asks, How shall he bury me? And though I have spoken many words in the endeavour to show that when I have drunk the poison I shall leave you and go to the joys of the blessed, — these words of mine, with which I was comforting you and myself, have had, as I perceive, no effect upon Crito. And therefore I want you to be surety for me to him now, as at the trial he was surety to the judges for me: but let the promise be of another sort; for he was surety for me to the judges that I would remain, and you must be my surety to him that I shall not remain, but go away and depart; and then he will suffer less at my death, and not be grieved when he sees my body being burned or buried. I would not have him sorrow at my hard lot, or say at the burial, Thus we lay out Socrates, or, Thus we follow him to the grave or bury him; for be well assured, my dear Crito, that false words are not only evil in themselves, but they infect the soul with evil. Be of good cheer then and say that you are burying my body only, and do with that whatever is usual, and what you think best.

When he had spoken these words, he arose and went into a chamber to bathe; Crito followed him and told us to wait. So we remained behind, talking and thinking of the subject of discourse, and also of the greatness of our loss; he was like a father of whom we were being bereaved, and we were about to pass the rest of our lives as orphans. When he had taken the bath his children were brought to him — (he had two young sons and an elder one); and the women of his family also came, and he talked to them and gave them a few directions in the presence of Crito; then he dismissed them and returned to us.

Now the hour of sunset was near, for a good deal of time had passed while he was within. When he came out, he sat down with us again after his bath, but not much was said. Soon the jailer, who was the servant of the Eleven, entered and stood by him, saying: — To you, Socrates, whom after your time here I know to be the noblest and gentlest and best of all who ever came to this place, I will not impute the angry feelings of other men, who rage and swear at me, when, in obedience to the authorities, I bid them drink the poison — indeed, I am sure that you are not angry with me; for others, as you are aware, and not I, are to blame. And so fare you well, and try to bear lightly what must needs be — you know my errand. Then bursting into tears he turned and started on his way out.

Socrates looked up at him and said: I return your good wishes, and will do as you bid. Then turning to us, he said, How charming the man is: since I have been in prison he has always been coming to see me, and at times he would talk to me, and was as good to me as could be, and now see how generously he sorrows on my account. We must do as he says, Crito; and therefore let the cup be brought, if the poison is prepared: if not, let the attendant prepare some.

But, said Crito, the sun is still upon the hill-tops, and is not yet set. I know that many a one takes the draught quite a long time after the announcement has been made to him, when he has eaten and drunk to his satisfaction and enjoyed the society of his chosen friends; do not hurry — there is time enough.

Socrates said: Yes, Crito, and therein they of whom you speak act logically, for they think that they will be gainers by the delay; but I likewise act logically in not following their example, for I do not think that I should gain anything by drinking the poison a little later; I should only be ridiculous in my own eyes for sparing and saving a life which is already down to its dregs. Please then to do as I say, and not to refuse me.

Crito made a sign to the servant, who was standing by; and he went out, and having been absent for some time, returned with the jailer carrying the cup of poison. Socrates said: You, my good friend, who are experienced in these matters, shall give me directions how I am to proceed. The man answered: You have only to walk about until your legs are heavy, and then to lie down, and the poison will act. At the same time he handed the cup to Socrates, who in the easiest and gentlest manner, without the least fear or change of colour or feature, and looking at the man sideways with that droll glance of his, took the cup and said: What do you say about making a libation out of this cup to any god? May I, or not? The man answered: We only prepare, Socrates, just so much as we deem enough. I understand, he said: but a prayer to the gods I may and must offer, that they will prosper my journey from this to the other world — even so — and so be it according to my prayer. Then he held his breath and drank off the poison quite readily and cheerfully. And hitherto most of us had been fairly able to control our sorrow; but now when we saw him drinking, and saw too that he had finished the draught, we could no longer forbear, and in spite of myself my own tears were flowing fast; so that I covered my face and wept, not indeed for him, but at the thought of my own calamity in having to part from such a friend. Nor was I the first; for Crito, when he found himself unable to restrain his tears, had got up, and I followed; and at that moment, Apollodorus, who had been weeping all the time, burst out in a loud and passionate cry which broke us all down. Socrates alone retained his calmness: What is this strange outcry? he said. I sent away the women mainly in order that they might not misbehave in this fashion, for I have been told that a man should die in peace. Be quiet then, and bear yourselves with fortitude. When we heard his words we were ashamed, and refrained our tears; and he walked about until, as he said, his legs began to fail, and then he lay on his back, according to the directions, and the man who gave him the poison now and then looked at his feet and legs; and after a while he pressed his foot hard, and asked him if he could feel; and he said, No; and then his leg, and so upwards and upwards, and showed us that he was becoming cold and stiff. And he felt them himself, and said: When the poison reaches the heart, that will be the end. He was beginning to grow cold about the groin, when he uncovered his face, for he had covered himself up, and said — they were his last words — he said: Crito, I owe a cock to Aesculapius; will you remember to pay the debt? The debt shall be paid, said Crito; is there anything else? There was no answer to this question; but in a minute or two a movement was heard, and the attendant uncovered him; his eyes were set, and Crito closed his eyes and mouth. 118

Such was the end, Echecrates, of our friend; concerning whom we may truly say that of all the men of his time whom we have known, he was the wisest and justest and best.

Symposium

Persons of the Dialogue

APOLLODORUS, who repeats to his companions the
dialogue which he had heard from Aristodemus,
and had already once narrated to Glaucon

PHAEDRUS	AGATHON
PAUSANIAS	SOCRATES
ERYXIMACHUS	ALCIBIADES
ARISTOPHANES	A TROOP OF REVELLERS

Scene: The house of Agathon

⋘ Before reading the dialogue to which Plato gave the name
"Symposium," one might well ask whether Plato's meaning of the
term is the same as our meaning today; and if not, whether anything
of importance remains that is common to both.

The etymology of "symposium" — a "together-drinking" — must be
supplemented by cultural history, from which we learn that the
Greeks long before Plato's day had given form and content to their
"drinking together," turning it into a literary and musical institution
of genuine educational worth. What Plato did, according to the late
Werner Jaeger, was to carry the cultural component still further,
dismissing the flute-girls in favor of reasoned speech, giving each
man in turn his right and duty to contribute to the collective understanding of the topic under view. It is not difficult to see how, from
the level thus achieved, the modern meaning developed of a "group
of experts, each from the standpoint of his own specialty discussing
a single theme."

But the symposium before us is no plodding sequence of professional papers. It is rather one of those two dialogues (the other is
the *Phaedrus*) which we have described in our Introduction, Theme 4,
as treating of love and beauty, and from which the sixteenth- and
seventeenth-century poets caught the flame of the Platonic love of
beauty. The reader can, if he will, mount with them to the heights.

The dialogue opens quietly (in two Stephanus pages which we
omit) with the request of an unnamed person that Apollodorus, a
friend of Socrates, will relate to him the speeches in praise of love
spoken at the dinner given by Agathon, the dramatic poet, on the
occasion when he had first won the prize for the best tragedy in the
annual competition. Apollodorus had not been present at the dinner
but had heard a verbatim report of the conversation from another

Socratic admirer, Aristodemus, and is quite willing to repeat it. Apollodorus begins:

Apoll. Well, the tale of love was on this wise: — But perhaps I had better begin at the beginning, and endeavour to give you the exact words of Aristodemus:

He said that he met Socrates fresh from the bath and sandalled; and as the sight of the sandals was unusual, he asked him whither he was going that he had been converted into such a beau: —

To a banquet at Agathon's, he replied, whose invitation to his sacrifice of victory I refused yesterday, fearing a crowd, but promising that I would come today instead; and so I have put on my finery, because he is such a fine man. What say you to going with me unasked?

I will do as you bid me, I replied.

Follow then, he said, and let us demolish the proverb: —

To the feasts of inferior men the good unbidden go;

instead of which our proverb will run: —

To the feasts of the good the good unbidden go;

and this alteration may be supported by the authority of Homer himself, who not only demolishes but literally outrages the proverb. For, after picturing Agamemnon as the most valiant of men, he makes Menelaus, who is 'a faint-hearted warrior', come unbidden to the banquet of Agamemnon, who is feasting and offering sacrifices; not the better going to the worse, but the worse to the better.

I rather fear, Socrates, said Aristodemus, lest this may still be my case; and that, like Menelaus in Homer, I shall be the inferior person, who

To the feasts of the wise unbidden goes.

But I shall say that I was bidden of you; so have your excuse ready.

Two going together,

he replied, in Homeric fashion, one or other of us will invent an excuse by the way. Come: let us start.

As they went along after a conversation of this style, Socrates dropped behind in a fit of abstraction, and desired Aristodemus, who was waiting, to go on before him. When he reached the house of Agathon he found the doors wide open, and a comical thing happened. A servant coming out met him, and led him at once into the banqueting-hall in which the guests were reclining, for the banquet was about to begin. Welcome, Aristodemus, said Agathon, as soon as he ap-

peared — you are just in time to sup with us; if you come on any
other matter put it off, and make one of us, as I was looking for you
yesterday and meant to have asked you, if I could have found you.
But what have you done with Socrates?

I turned round, but Socrates was nowhere to be seen; and I had
to explain that he had been with me a moment before, and that I
came by his invitation to the supper.

You were quite right in coming, said Agathon; but where is he
himself?

175   He was behind me just now, as I entered, he said, and I cannot
think what has become of him.

Go and look for him, boy, said Agathon, and bring him in; and
do you, Aristodemus, meanwhile take the place by Eryximachus.

The servant then assisted him to wash, and he lay down, and
presently another servant came in and reported that our friend
Socrates had retired into the portico of the neighbouring house.
'There he is fixed,' said he, 'and when I call to him he will not stir.'

How strange, said Agathon; then you must call him again, and
keep calling him.

Let him alone, said my informant; he has a way of going off sometimes by himself, and standing still anywhere he happens to be. I
believe that he will soon appear; do not therefore disturb him.

Well, if you think so, I will leave him, said Agathon. And then,
turning to the servants, he added, 'Let us have supper without waiting for him. Serve up whatever you please, for there is no one to give
you orders; hitherto I have never left you to yourselves. But on this
occasion imagine that you are our hosts, and that I and the company
are your guests; treat us well, and then we shall commend you.'
After this, supper was served, but still no Socrates; and during the
meal Agathon several times expressed a wish to send for him, but
Aristodemus objected; and at last when the feast was about half over
— for the fit, as usual, was not of long duration — Socrates entered.
Agathon, who was reclining alone at the end of the table, begged that
he would take the place next to him; that 'I may touch you', he said,
'and have the benefit of that wise thought which came into your mind
in the portico, and is now in your possession; for I am certain that you
would not have come away until you had found what you sought.'

How I wish, said Socrates, taking his place as he was desired, that
wisdom could be infused by touch, out of the fuller into the emptier
man, as water runs through wool out of a fuller cup into an emptier
one; if that were so, how greatly should I value the privilege of reclining at your side! For you would have filled me full with a stream
of wisdom plenteous and fair; whereas my own is of a very mean and

questionable sort, no better than a dream. But yours is bright and full of promise, and was manifested forth in all the splendour of your youth the day before yesterday, in the presence of more than thirty thousand Hellenes.

You are mocking, Socrates, said Agathon, and ere long you and I will have to determine who bears off the palm of wisdom — of this Dionysus shall be the judge; but at present you are better occupied with supper.

Socrates took his place on the couch, and supped with the rest; 176 and then libations were offered, and after a hymn had been sung to the god, and there had been the usual ceremonies, they were about to commence drinking, when Pausanias said, And now, my friends, how can we drink with least injury to ourselves? I can assure you that I feel severely the effect of yesterday's potations, and must have time to recover; and I suspect that most of you are in the same predicament, for you were of the party yesterday. Consider then: How can the drinking be made easiest?

I entirely agree, said Aristophanes, that we should, by all means, avoid hard drinking, for I was myself one of those who were deeply dipped yesterday.

I think that you are right, said Eryximachus, the son of Acumenus; but I should still like to hear one other person speak: Is Agathon able to drink hard?

I am not equal to it, said Agathon.

It is a blessing, said Eryximachus, for the weak heads like myself, Aristodemus, Phaedrus, and others who never can drink, to find that the stronger ones are not in a drinking mood. (I do not include Socrates, who is able either to drink or to abstain, and will not mind, whichever we do.) Well, as none of the company seem disposed to drink much, I may be forgiven for speaking the truth about deep drinking. My experience as a physician has convinced me that it is a bad practice, which I never follow, if I can help, and certainly do not recommend to another, least of all to anyone who still feels the effects of yesterday's carouse.

I always do what you advise, and especially what you prescribe as a physician, rejoined Phaedrus the Myrrhinusian, and the rest of the company, if they are wise, will do the same.

It was agreed that heavy drinking was not to be the order of the day, but that they were all to drink only so much as they pleased.

Then, said Eryximachus, as you are all agreed that drinking is to be voluntary, and that there is to be no compulsion, I move, in the next place, that the flute-girl, who has just made her appearance, be told to go away and play to herself, or, if she likes, to the women who are within. Today let us have conversation instead; and, if you allow

177 me, I will tell you what sort of conversation. This proposal having been welcomed unanimously, Eryximachus proceeded as follows: —

I will begin, he said, after the manner of Melanippe in Euripides:

Not mine the word

which I am about to speak, but that of Phaedrus here. For he is always saying to me in an indignant tone: — 'What a strange thing it is, Eryximachus, that, whereas other gods have poems and hymns made in their honour, the ancient and mighty god, Love, has never had a single encomiast among all the poets who are so many. There are the worthy sophists too — the excellent Prodicus for example — who have descanted in prose on the virtues of Heracles and other heroes; which after all is not so extraordinary, considering that I have come across a philosophical work in which the utility of salt has been made the theme of an eloquent discourse; and many other like things have had a like honour bestowed upon them. And only to think that there should have been an eager interest created about them, and yet that to this day no one has ever dared worthily to hymn Love's praises! So entirely has this great deity been neglected.' Now in this Phaedrus seems to me to be quite right, and therefore I want to offer him a contribution; also I think that at the present moment we who are here assembled cannot do better than honour the god Love. If you agree with me, there will be no lack of conversation; for I mean to propose that each of us in turn, going from left to right, shall make a speech in honour of Love. Let him give us the best which he can; and Phaedrus, because he is sitting first on the left hand, and because he is the father of the theme, shall begin.

No one will vote against you, Eryximachus, said Socrates. How can I oppose your motion, who profess to understand nothing but matters of love; nor, I presume, will Agathon and Pausanias; and there can be no doubt of Aristophanes, whose whole concern is with Dionysus and Aphrodite; nor will any one disagree of those whom I see around me. The proposal, as I am aware, may seem rather hard upon us whose place is last; but we shall be contented if we hear some good speeches first. Let Phaedrus begin the praise of Love, and good luck to him. All the company expressed their assent, and desired him to

178 do as Socrates bade him.

Aristodemus did not recollect all the individual speeches, nor do I recollect all that he related to me; but I will tell you what I thought most worthy of remembrance, and what the chief speakers said.

Phaedrus began by affirming that Love is a mighty god, and wonderful among gods and men on many accounts, but especially wonderful in his birth. For he is the eldest of the gods, which is an honour to him; and a proof of his claim to this honour is, that of his parents there is no memorial; neither poet nor prose-writer has ever affirmed that he had any. As Hesiod says: —

> First Chaos came, and then broad-bosomed Earth,
> The everlasting seat of all that is,
> And Love.

In other words, after Chaos, the Earth and Love, these two, came into being. Also Parmenides sings of Generation:

> First in the train of gods, she fashioned Love.

And Acusilaus agrees with Hesiod. Thus numerous are the authorities who acknowledge Love to be the eldest of the gods. And not only is he the eldest, he is also the source of the greatest benefits to us. For I know not any greater blessing to a young man who is beginning life than a virtuous lover, or to the lover than a beloved youth. For the principle which ought to be the guide of men who would nobly live — that principle, I say, neither kindred, nor honour, nor wealth, nor any other influence is able to impart so well as love. Of what am I speaking? Of the sense of honour and dishonour, without which neither states nor individuals ever do any good or great work. And I say that a lover who is detected in doing any dishonourable act, or submitting through cowardice when any dishonour is done to him by another, will be more pained at being detected by his beloved than at being seen by his father, or by his companions, or by anyone else. The beloved too, when he is found in any disgraceful situation, has the same feeling about his lover. And if there were only some way of contriving that a state or an army should be made up of lovers and their loves, they would be the very best governors of their own city, abstaining from all dishonour, and emulating one another in honour; and it is scarcely an exaggeration to say that when **179** fighting at each other's side, although a mere handful, they would overcome the world. For what lover would not choose rather to be seen by all mankind than by his beloved, either when abandoning his post or throwing away his arms? He would be ready to die a thousand deaths rather than endure this. Or who would desert his beloved or fail him in the hour of danger? The veriest coward would become an inspired hero, equal to the bravest, at such a time; Love would inspire him. That courage which, as Homer says, the god breathes into the souls of some heroes, Love of his own bounty infuses into the lover.

Love will make men dare to die for their beloved — love alone; and women as well as men. Of this, Alcestis, the daughter of Pelias, is a monument to all Hellas; for she was willing to lay down her life

on behalf of her husband, when no one else would, although he had a
father and mother; but the tenderness of her love so far exceeded
theirs, that she made them seem to be strangers in blood to their own
son, and in name only related to him; and so noble did this action of
hers appear to the gods, as well as to men, that among the many who
have done virtuously she is one of the very few to whom, in admiration
of her noble action, they have granted the privilege of returning alive
to earth; such exceeding honour is paid by the gods to the devotion
and virtue of love. But Orpheus, the son of Oeagrus, the harper, they
sent empty away, having presented to him an apparition only of her
whom he sought, but herself they would not relinquish, because he
showed no spirit; he was only a harp-player, and did not dare like
Alcestis to die for love, but was contriving how he might enter Hades
alive; therefore they afterwards caused him to suffer death at the hands
of women, as the punishment of his cowardliness. Very different was
the reward of the true love of Achilles towards his lover Patroclus —
his lover and not his love (the notion that Patroclus was the beloved
one is a foolish error into which Aeschylus has fallen, for Achilles was
the fairer of the two, fairer also than all the other heroes; and, as
180 Homer informs us, he was still beardless, and younger far). And
greatly as the gods honour the virtue of love, still the return of love on
the part of the beloved to the lover is more admired and valued and
rewarded by them; for the lover is more divine, because he is inspired
by God. Now Achilles was quite aware, for he had been told by his
mother, that he might avoid death and return home, and live to a good
old age, if he abstained from slaying Hector. Nevertheless he gave his
life to revenge his friend, and dared to die for him, not only in his
defence, but after he was dead. Wherefore the gods honoured him
even above Alcestis, and sent him to the Islands of the Blest. These
are my reasons for affirming that Love is the eldest and noblest and
mightiest of the gods, and the chiefest author and giver of virtue and
happiness, alike in life and after death.

This, or something like this, was the speech of Phaedrus; and some
other speeches followed which Aristodemus did not remember; the
next which he repeated was that of Pausanias. Phaedrus, he said, the
argument has not been set before us, I think, quite in the right
form; — we should not be called upon to praise Love in such an indiscriminate manner. If there were only one Love, then what you said
would be well enough; but since there are more Loves than one,
you should have begun by determining which of them was to be the
theme of our praises. I will try to amend this defect; and first of all
I will tell you which Love is deserving of praise, and then try to
hymn the praiseworthy one in a manner worthy of him. For we all
know that Love is inseparable from Aphrodite, and if there were

only one Aphrodite there would be only one Love; but as there are
two goddesses there must be two Loves. And am I not right in asserting that there are two goddesses? The elder one, having no mother,
who is called the heavenly Aphrodite — she is the daughter of Uranus; the younger, who is the daughter of Zeus and Dione — her
we call common; and the Love who is her fellow-worker is rightly
named common, as the other Love is called heavenly. All the gods
ought to have praise given to them, but not without distinction of
their natures; and therefore I must try to distinguish the characters
of the two Loves. Now actions vary according to the manner of
their performance. Take, for example, that which we are now doing,   181
drinking, singing, and talking — these actions are not in themselves
either good or evil, but they turn out in this or that way according
to the mode of performing them; and when well done they are good,
and when wrongly done they are evil; and in like manner not every
kind of loving nor every Love is noble and worthy of praise, but only
that which inspires men to love nobly. The Love who is the offspring
of the common Aphrodite is essentially common, and has no discrimi-
nation, being such as moves the meaner sort of men. They are apt
to love women as well as youths, and the body rather than the soul
— the most foolish beings they can find are the objects of this love
which desires only to gain an end, but never thinks of accomplishing
the end nobly, and therefore does good and evil quite indiscriminately. The goddess who is the mother of this love is far younger
than the other, and she was born of the union of the male and female, and partakes of both. But the offspring of the heavenly Aphrodite is derived from a mother in whose birth the female has no part,
— she is from the male only; this is that love which is of youths, and
the goddess being older, there is nothing of wantonness in her.
Those who are inspired by this love turn to the male, and delight
in him who is the more valiant and intelligent nature; anyone may
recognize the pure enthusiasts in the very character of their attachments. For they love not boys, but intelligent beings whose reason
is beginning to be developed, much about the time at which their
beards begin to grow. And starting from such a choice, they are
ready, I apprehend, to be faithful to their companions, and pass
their whole life with them, not to take them in their inexperience,
and deceive them, and make fools of them, and then run away to
others of them. But the love of young boys should be forbidden by
law, because their future is uncertain; they may turn out good or
bad, either in body or soul, and much noble enthusiasm may be
thrown away upon them. The good impose this law upon themselves
of their own free will; and the coarser sort of lovers ought to be
restrained by force, as we restrain or attempt to restrain them from

182 fixing their affections on women of free birth. These are the persons who bring such reproach on love that seeing their impropriety and evil some people go so far as to hold up such attachments to shame; for surely nothing that is decorously and lawfully done can justly be censured. Now here and in Lacedaemon the rules about love are perplexing, but in most cities they are simple and easily intelligible. In Elis and Boeotia, and in countries having no gifts of eloquence, they are very straightforward; the law is simply in favour of these connexions, and no one, whether young or old, has anything to say to their discredit; the reason being, as I suppose, that they are men of few words in those parts, and therefore the lovers do not like the trouble of pleading their suit. In Ionia and other places, and generally in countries which are subject to the barbarians, the custom is held to be dishonourable; because of their despotic governments, loves of youths share the evil repute in which philosophy and gymnastics are held, for the interests of the rulers require, I suppose, that their subjects should be poor in spirit, and that there should be no strong bond of friendship or society among them, which love, above all other motives, is likely to inspire — a lesson that our Athenian tyrants learned by experience, since the love of Aristogeiton and the constancy of Harmodius had a strength which undid their power. And, therefore, the ill repute into which these attachments have fallen is to be ascribed to the evil condition of those who make them to be ill reputed, that is to say, to the self-seeking of the governors and the cowardice of the governed; on the other hand, the indiscriminate honour which is given to them in some countries is attributable to the mental laziness of those who hold this opinion of them. In our own country a far better principle prevails, but, as I was saying, the explanation of it is not easy to grasp. For, observe that open loves are held to be more honourable than secret ones, and that the love of the noblest and highest, even if their persons are less beautiful than others, is especially honourable. Consider, too, how great is the encouragement which all the world gives to the lover, not treating him as though he were doing something dishonourable; but if he succeeds he is praised, and if he fails he is blamed. And in the pursuit of his love the custom of mankind allows him to do many strange things, which philosophy would

183 bitterly censure if they were done from any other interest or motive, such as the desire for money or office or some other kind of power. He may pray, and entreat, and supplicate, and vow upon oath, and lie on a mat at the door, and endure a slavery worse than that of any slave — in any other case friends and enemies would be equally ready to prevent him, but now there is no friend who will be ashamed of him and admonish him, and no enemy will charge

him with meanness or flattery; the actions of a lover have a grace which ennobles them; and custom has decided that they are open to no reproach, because they have a noble purpose: and, what is strangest of all, he only may swear and forswear himself (so men say), and the gods will forgive his transgression, for there is no such thing as a lover's oath. Such is the entire liberty which gods and men have allowed the lover, according to the custom which prevails in our part of the world — from this point of view a man might fairly argue that in Athens to love and to be loved is held to be a most honourable thing. But when parents forbid their sons to talk with their lovers, and place them under a tutor's care who is instructed to that effect, and their companions and equals cast in their teeth anything of the sort which they may observe, and their elders refuse to silence the reprovers and do not rebuke this mistaken censure, — anyone who reflects on all this will, on the contrary, think that we hold these practices to be most disgraceful. But the truth as I imagine is, that judgement on such practices cannot be absolute; in themselves they are neither honourable nor dishonourable, as was said at the beginning; they are honourable to him who follows them honourably, dishonourable to him who follows them dishonourably. There is dishonour in yielding to the evil, or in an evil manner; but there is honour in yielding to the good, or in an honourable manner. Evil is the vulgar lover who loves the body rather than the soul, inasmuch as he is not even stable, because he loves a thing which is in itself unstable, and therefore when the bloom of youth which he was desiring is over, he takes wing and flies away, dishonouring all his words and promises; whereas the love of the noble disposition is lifelong, for it becomes one with the perdurable. The custom of our **184** country would have both of them proven well and truly, and would have us yield to the one sort of lover and avoid the other; and therefore encourages some to pursue, and others to fly, testing both the lover and beloved in contests and trials, until they show to which of the two classes they respectively belong. And this is the reason why, in the first place, a hasty attachment is held to be dishonourable, because time is the true test of this as of most other things; and secondly there is dishonour in being overcome by the love of money or political power, whether one is frightened into surrender by much hardship or, living in enjoyment of the advantages they offer, is unable to rise above their seductions. For none of these things are of a permanent or lasting nature; not to mention that no generous friendship ever sprang from them. There remains, then, only one road of honourable attachment which our custom allows the beloved to follow; for it is our rule that as any menial service which the lover does to him is not to be accounted flattery or a reproach to himself, so the beloved has one way only of voluntary service which is not open to reproach, and this is service directed to virtue.

For you know it is our custom that anyone who does service to another under the idea that he will be improved by him either in wisdom, or in some other particular of virtue — such a voluntary service, I say, is not to be regarded as a dishonour, and is not open to the charge of flattery. And these two customs, one the love of youth, and the other the practice of philosophy and virtue in general, ought to meet in one, and then the beloved may honourably indulge the lover. For when the lover and beloved come together, having each of them an inner law, the lover thinking that he is right in doing any service which he can to his gracious love, and the other that he is right in showing any kindness which he can to him who is making him wise and good; the one capable of communicating understanding and virtue, the other seeking to acquire them with a view to education and wisdom; when the two laws of love are fulfilled and meet in one — then, and then only, may the beloved yield with honour to the lover. Nor when love is of this disinterested sort is there any disgrace in being deceived, but in every other case there
185 is equal disgrace in being or not being deceived. For he who is gracious to his lover under the impression that he is rich, and is disappointed of all gain because he turns out to be poor, is disgraced all the same: for he has done his best to show that he would give himself up to anyone's 'uses base' for the sake of money; but this is not honourable. And on the same principle he who gives himself to a lover because he is a good man and in the hope that he will be improved by his company, shows himself to be virtuous, even though the object of his affection turn out to be a villain, and to have no virtue; and though he is deceived he has commited a noble error. For he has proved that for his part he will do anything for anybody with a view to virtue and improvement, than which there can be nothing nobler. Thus noble in every case is the acceptance of another, if it be for the sake of virtue. This is that love which comes from the heavenly goddess, and is heavenly, and of great price to individuals and cities, making the lover and the beloved alike eager in the work of their own improvement. But all other loves are the offspring of the other, who is the common goddess. To you, Phaedrus, I offer this my contribution in praise of love, which is as good as I could make extempore.

Pāusănĭās cāme tŏ ă pāuse — this is the balanced way in which I have been taught by the wise to speak; and Aristodemus said that the turn of Aristophanes was next, but either he had eaten too much, or from some other cause he had the hiccough, and was unable to speak. So he turned to Eryximachus the physician, who was reclining on the couch below him, and said, 'Eryximachus, you ought either to stop my hiccough, or to speak in my turn until I have left off.'

I will do both, said Eryximachus: I will speak in your turn, and do you speak in mine; and while I am speaking let me recommend you to hold your breath, and if after you have done so for some time the hiccough is no better, then gargle with a little water; and if it is still violent, tickle your nose with something and sneeze; if you sneeze once or twice, even the most violent hiccough is sure to stop. I will do as you prescribe, said Aristophanes, and now get on.

Eryximachus spoke as follows: Seeing that Pausanias made a fair beginning, and but a lame ending, I must endeavour to supply his deficiency. I think that he has rightly distinguished two kinds of love. But my art further informs me that the double love is not merely an affection of the soul of man towards human beauty, but is an affection directed to many other objects, and is to be found in other things, in the bodies of all animals and in productions of the earth, and I may say in all that is; such is the conclusion which I seem to have gathered from my own art of medicine, whence I learn how great and wonderful and universal is the deity of love, whose empire extends over all things, divine as well as human. And from medicine I will begin that I may do honour to my art. In the body there are by its nature these two kinds of love; the state of bodily health and the state of sickness are confessedly different and unlike, and being unlike, they have loves and desires which are unlike; so the desire of the healthy is one, and the desire of the diseased is another. As Pausanias was just now saying, to indulge good men is honourable, and bad men dishonourable; so it is with the body. In each body it is right and proper to favour the good and healthy elements (and this is what is called the practice of medicine), and the bad elements and the elements of disease are not to be indulged, but discouraged. This is what the physician has to do, and in this the art of medicine consists: for medicine may be briefly described as the knowledge of the loves and desires of the body, and how to satisfy them or mortify them; and the best physician is he who is able to separate fair love from foul, or to convert one into the other; and he who knows how to eradicate and how to implant love, whichever is required, and can reconcile the most hostile elements in the constitution and make them loving friends, is a skilful practitioner. Now the most hostile are the most opposite, such as hot and cold, bitter and sweet, moist and dry, and the like. And our father, Aesculapius, knowing how to implant friendship and accord in these elements, was the creator of our art, as our friends the poets here tell us, and I believe them; and not only medicine in every branch, but the arts of gymnastic and husbandry

186

187 are likewise under his dominion. Anyone who pays the least attention
to the subject will also perceive that in music there is the same reconciliation of opposites; and I suppose that this must have been the
meaning of Heracleitus, although his words are not accurate; for he
says that the One is united by disunion, like the harmony of the bow
and the lyre. Now it is the height of absurdity to say that harmony
is discord or is composed of elements which are still in a state of discord. But what he probably meant was, that harmony is attained
through the art of music by the reconciliation of differing notes of
higher or lower pitch which once disagreed; for if the higher and
lower notes still disagreed, there could be no harmony, — clearly not.
For harmony is a symphony, and symphony is a kind of agreement;
but an agreement of disagreements while they disagree there cannot
be; you cannot, I repeat, harmonize that which disagrees. In like
manner rhythm is compounded of elements short and long, once
differing and now in accord; which accordance, as in the former
instance medicine, so in all these other cases music implants, making
love and concord to grow up among them; and thus music, too, is a
science of the phenomena of love in their application to harmony and
rhythm. Again, in the constitution of a harmony as of a rhythm there
is no difficulty in discerning love, and as yet there is no sign of its
duality. But when you want to use them in actual life, either in the
kind of composition to which the term 'lyrical' is applied or in the
correct employment of airs or metres composed already, which latter
is called education, then indeed the difficulty begins, and the good
artist is needed. Then the old tale has to be repeated of fair and
heavenly love — the love that comes from Urania the fair and
heavenly muse — and of the duty of gratifying the temperate, and
those who are as yet intemperate only that they may become temperate, and of preserving their love; and again, of the common love
that comes from Polyhymnia, that must be used with circumspection
in order that the pleasure be enjoyed, but may not generate licentiousness; just as in our own art it is a great matter so to regulate the
desires of the epicure that he may attain his pleasure without the
attendant evil of disease. Whence I infer that in music, in medicine,
188 in all other things human as well as divine, both loves ought to be
watched as far as may be, for they are both present.

The course of the seasons is also full of both these principles; and
when, as I was saying, the elements of hot and cold, moist and dry,
attain the temperate love of one another and blend in chastened harmony, they bring to men, animals, and plants health and plenty, and
do them no harm; whereas the wanton love, getting the upper hand
and affecting the seasons of the year, is very destructive and injurious,
being the source of pestilence, and bringing many different kinds of

diseases on animals and plants; and also hoar-frost and hail and blight are wont to spring from the mutual disproportions and disorders caused by this love, which to know in relation to the revolutions of the heavenly bodies and the seasons of the year is termed astronomy. Moreover all sacrifices and the activities that are the province of divination, which constitute the communion between gods and men — these, I say, are concerned only with the preservation of the good and the cure of the evil love. For all manner of impiety is likely to ensue if, instead of gratifying and honouring and reverencing the temperate love in all his actions, a man honours the other love, whether in his relations with gods or parents, with the living or the dead. Wherefore the business of divination is to watch over these lovers and to heal them, and divination is the peacemaker between gods and men, working by a knowledge of the tendencies to religion and piety which exist in human loves. Such is the great and mighty, or rather omnipotent, force of love in general. And the love, more especially, which is concerned with the good and which is perfected in company with temperance and justice, whether among gods or men, has the greatest power, and is the source of all our happiness, and gives us communion and friendship with the gods who are above us, and with one another. I dare say that I, too, have omitted much that might be said in praise of Love, but this was not intentional, and you, Aristophanes, may now supply the omission or take some other line of commendation; for I perceive that you are rid of the hiccough.

Yes, said Aristophanes, who followed, the hiccough is gone; not, 189 however, until I applied the sneezing; and I wonder whether the orderly system of the body has a love of such noises and ticklings, for I no sooner applied the sneezing than I was cured.

Eryximachus said: Beware, friend Aristophanes; although you are going to speak, you are making fun of me; and I shall have to watch and see whether I cannot have a laugh at your expense, when you might speak in peace.

You are quite right, said Aristophanes, laughing, and I unsay my words. But do you please not to watch me, as I fear that in the speech which I am about to make, instead of others laughing with me, which is the natural work of our muse and would be satisfactory, I shall only be laughed at by them.

Do you expect to shoot your bolt and escape, Aristophanes? Well, perhaps if you are very careful and bear in mind that you will be called to account, I may be induced to let you off.

Aristophanes professed to open another vein of discourse; he had a mind to praise Love in another way, unlike that of either Pausanias or Eryximachus. Mankind, he said, judging by their neglect of him, have never, as I think, at all understood the power of Love. For if

they had understood him they would surely have built noble temples
and altars, and offered solemn sacrifices in his honour; but this is not
done, and most certainly ought to be done: since of all the gods he is
the best friend of men, the helper and the healer of the ills which
are the great impediment to the happiness of the race. I will try to
describe his power to you, and you shall teach the rest of the world
what I am teaching you. In the first place, let me treat of the nature
of man and what has happened to it. The original human nature was
not like the present, but different. The sexes were not two as they
are now, but originally three in number; there was man, woman, and
the union of the two, of which the name survives but nothing else.
Once it was a distinct kind, with a bodily shape and a name of its
own, constituted by the union of the male and the female: but now
only the word 'androgynous' is preserved, and that as a term of reproach. In the second place, the primeval man was round, his back
and sides forming a circle; and he had four hands and the same num-
190   ber of feet, one head with two faces, looking opposite ways, set on a
round neck and precisely alike; also four ears, two privy members,
and the remainder to correspond. He could walk upright as men now
do, backwards or forwards as he pleased, and he could also roll over
and over at a great pace, turning on his four hands and four feet,
eight in all, like tumblers going over and over with their legs in the
air; this was when he wanted to run fast. Now the sexes were three,
and such as I have described them; because the sun, moon, and earth
are three; and the man was originally the child of the sun, the woman
of the earth, and the man-woman of the moon, which is made up of
sun and earth, and they were all round and moved round and round
because they resembled their parents. Terrible was their might and
strength, and the thoughts of their hearts were great, and they made
an attack upon the gods; of them is told the tale of Otys and Ephialtes
who, as Homer says, attempted to scale heaven, and would have laid
hands upon the gods. Doubt reigned in the celestial councils. Should
they kill them and annihilate the race with thunderbolts, as they had
done the giants, then there would be an end of the sacrifices and worship which men offered to them; but, on the other hand, the gods
could not suffer their insolence to be unrestrained. At last, after a
good deal of reflection, Zeus discovered a way. He said: 'Methinks
I have a plan which will enfeeble their strength and so extinguish
their turbulence; men shall continue to exist, but I will cut them in
two and then they will be diminished in strength and increased in
numbers; this will have the advantage of making them more profitable
to us. They shall walk upright on two legs, and if they continue
insolent and will not be quiet, I will split them again and they shall
hop about on a single leg.' He spoke and cut men in two, like a

sorb-apple which is halved for pickling, or as you might divide an egg with a hair; and as he cut them one after another, he bade Apollo give the face and the half of the neck a turn in order that man might contemplate the section of himself: he would thus learn a lesson of humility. Apollo was also bidden to heal their wounds and compose their forms. So he gave a turn to the face and pulled the skin from the sides all over that which in our language is called the belly, like the purses which draw tight, and he made one mouth at the centre, which he fastened in a knot(the same which is called the navel); he also moulded the breast and took out most of the wrinkles, much as **191** a shoemaker might smooth leather upon a last; he left a few, however, in the region of the belly and navel, as a memorial of the primeval state. After the division the two parts of man, each desiring his other half, came together, and throwing their arms about one another, entwined in mutual embraces, longing to grow into one, they began to die from hunger and self-neglect, because they did not like to do anything apart; and when one of the halves died and the other survived, the survivor sought another mate, man or woman as we call them, — being the sections of entire men or women, — and clung to that. Thus they were being destroyed, when Zeus in pity invented a new plan: he turned the parts of generation round to the front, for this had not been always their position, and they sowed the seed no longer as hitherto like grasshoppers in the ground, but in one another; and after the transposition the male generated in the female in order that by the mutual embraces of man and woman they might breed, and the race might continue; or if man came to man they might be satisfied, and rest, and go their ways to the business of life. So ancient is the desire of one another which is implanted in us, reuniting our original nature, seeking to make one of two, and to heal the state of man. Each of us when separated, having one side only, like a flat fish, is but the tally-half of a man, and he is always looking for his other half. Men who are a section of that double nature which was once called androgynous are lovers of women; adulterers are generally of this breed, and also adulterous women who lust after men. The women who are a section of the woman do not care for men, but have female attachments; the female companions are of this sort. But they who are a section of the male follow the male, and while they are young, being slices of the original man, they have affection for men and embrace them, and these are the best of boys and youths, be- **192** cause they have the most manly nature. Some indeed assert that they are shameless, but this is not true; for they do not act thus from any want of shame, but because they are valiant and manly, and have a manly countenance, and they embrace that which is like them. And these when they grow up become our statesmen, and

these only, which is a great proof of the truth of what I am saying.
When they reach manhood they are lovers of youth, and are not
naturally inclined to marry or beget children, — if at all, they do so
only in obedience to custom; but they are satisfied if they may be
allowed to live with one another unwedded; and such a nature is
prone to love and ready to return love, always embracing that which
is akin to him. And when one of them meets with his other half, the
actual half of himself, whether he be a lover of youth or a lover of
another sort, the pair are lost in an amazement of love and friendship
and intimacy, and one will not be out of the other's sight, as I may
say, even for a moment: these are the people who pass their whole
lives together, and yet they could not explain what they desire of
one another. For the intense yearning which each of them has towards the other does not appear to be the desire of lover's intercourse, but of something else which the soul of either evidently desires and cannot tell, and of which she has only a dark and doubtful
presentiment. Suppose Hephaestus, with his instruments, to come to
the pair who are lying side by side and to say to them, 'What do you
mortals want of one another?' they would be unable to explain. And
suppose further, that when he saw their perplexity he said: 'Do you
desire to be wholly one; always day and night in one another's company? for if this is what you desire, I am ready to melt and fuse you
together, so that being two you shall become one, and while you live
a common life as if you were a single man, and after your death
in the world below still be one departed soul, instead of two — I ask
whether this is what you lovingly desire and whether you are satisfied
to attain this?' — there is not a man of them who when he heard the
proposal would deny or would not acknowledge that this meeting and
melting into one another, this becoming one instead of two, was the
very expression of his ancient need. And the reason is that human
193 nature was originally one and we were a whole, and the desire and
pursuit of the whole is called love. There was a time, I say, when
we were one, but now because of the wickedness of mankind God
has dispersed us, as the Arcadians were dispersed into villages by the
Lacedaemonians. And if we are not obedient to the gods, there is a
danger that we shall be split up again and go about in basso-relievo,
like the profile figures showing only one half the nose which are
sculptured on monuments, and that we shall be like tallies. Wherefore
let us exhort all men to piety in all things, that we may avoid evil
and obtain the good, taking Love for our leader and commander.
Let no one oppose him — he is the enemy of the gods who opposes
him. For if we are friends of God and at peace with him we shall
find our own true loves, which rarely happens in this world at
present. I am serious, and therefore I must beg Eryximachus not to
make fun or to find any allusion in what I am saying to Pausanias and

Agathon, who, as I suspect, are both of the manly nature, and belong to the class which I have been describing. But my words have a wider application — they include men and women everywhere; and I believe that if our loves were perfectly accomplished, and each one returning to his primeval nature had his original true love, then our race would be happy. And if this would be best of all, the best in the next degree must in present circumstances be the nearest approach to such a union; and that will be the attainment of a congenial love. Wherefore, if we would praise him who has given to us the benefit, we must praise the god Love, who is our greatest benefactor, both leading us in this life back to our own nature, and giving us high hopes for the future, for he promises that if we are pious, he will restore us to our original state, and heal us and make us happy and blessed. This, Eryximachus, is my discourse of love, which, although different to yours, I must beg you to leave unassailed by the shafts of your ridicule, in order that each may have his turn; each, or rather either, for Agathon and Socrates are the only ones left.

Indeed, I am not going to attack you, said Eryximachus, for I thought your speech charming, and did I not know that Agathon and Socrates are masters in the art of love, I should be really afraid that they would have nothing to say, after the world of things which have been said already. But, for all that, I am not without hopes.

Socrates said: You played your part well, Eryximachus; but if you were as I am now, or rather as I shall be when Agathon has added another fine discourse, you would indeed be frightened out of your wits. **194**

You want to cast a spell over me, Socrates, said Agathon, in the hope that I may be disconcerted by the idea that the audience confidently expect a fine discourse from me.

I should be strangely forgetful, Agathon, replied Socrates, of the courage and strength of mind which you showed when your own compositions were about to be exhibited, and you came upon the stage with the actors and faced the vast theatre altogether undismayed, if I thought that your nerves could be fluttered at a small party of friends.

Do you think, Socrates, said Agathon, that my head is so full of the theatre as not to know how much more formidable to a man of sense a few intelligent men are than many fools?

Nay, replied Socrates, I should be very wrong in attributing to you, Agathon, that or any other want of perception; I am quite aware that if you happened to meet with any whom you thought wise, you would care for their opinion much more than for that of the many. But then we, having been a part of the foolish many in the theatre, cannot be regarded as the select wise; and I fancy that if you chanced to be in the presence, not of one of ourselves, but of some really wise man,

you would be ashamed of disgracing yourself before him — would
you not?

Yes, said Agathon.

But before the many you would not be ashamed, if you thought
that you were doing something disgraceful?

Here Phaedrus interrupted them, saying: Do not answer him, my
dear Agathon; for if he can only get a partner with whom he can
talk, especially a good-looking one, he will no longer care what happens about the completion of our plan. Now I love to hear him talk;
but just at present I must not forget the encomium on Love which I
ought to receive from him and from everyone. When you and he
have paid your tribute to the god, then you may talk.

Very good, Phaedrus, said Agathon; I see no reason why I should
not proceed with my speech, as I shall have many opportunities of
conversing with Socrates. Let me say first how I ought to speak, and
then speak: —

195   The previous speakers, instead of praising the god Love, and unfolding his nature, appear to have congratulated mankind on the
benefits which he confers upon them. But I would rather praise the
god first, and then speak of his gifts; this is always the right way of
praising everything. May I say without impiety or offence, that of
all the blessed gods he is the most blessed because he is the fairest
and best? And he is the fairest: for, in the first place, he is the youngest, and of his youth he is himself the witness, fleeing out of the way
of age, who is swift enough, coming indeed to us more swiftly than
we like: — Love has a natural hatred for him and will not come near
him; but youth and love live and have their being together — like to
like, as the ancient proverb says. Many things were said by Phaedrus
about Love in which I agree with him, but I cannot agree that he is
older than Iapetus and Cronos: — not so; I maintain him to be the
youngest of the gods, and youthful ever. The ancient doings among
the gods of which Hesiod and Parmenides spoke, if the tradition of
them be true, were done of Necessity and not of Love; had Love been
in those days, there would have been no chaining or mutilation of
the gods, or other violence, but peace and sweetness, as there is now
in heaven since the rule of Love began. Love then is young, and he
is also tender; he ought to have a poet like Homer to describe his
tenderness, as Homer says of Ate that she is a goddess and tender, at
least her feet are tender: —

> Her feet are tender, for she sets her steps,
> Not on the ground but on the heads of men:

herein is an excellent proof of her tenderness, — that she walks not
upon the hard but upon the soft. Let us adduce a similar proof of

the tenderness of Love; for he walks not upon the earth, nor yet upon the skulls of men, which are not so very soft, but in the hearts and souls of both gods and men, which are of all things the softest: in them he walks and dwells and makes his home. Not in every soul without exception, for where there is hardness he departs, where there is softness there he takes up his abode; and nestling always with his feet and in all manner of ways in the softest of soft places, how can he be other than the most tender of all things? Of a truth he is the tenderest as well as the youngest and also he is of flexile form; for if he were hard and without flexure he could not enfold all things, or wind his way into and out of every soul of man undiscovered. And a proof of his flexibility and symmetry of form is his grace, which is universally admitted to be in an especial manner the attribute of Love; ungracefulness and love are always at war with one another. The beauty of his complexion is revealed by his habitation among the flowers; for he dwells not amid bloomless or fading charms, whether of body or soul or aught else, but in the place of flowers and scents, there he sits and abides. Concerning the beauty of the god I have said enough; and yet there remains much more which I might say. Of his virtue I have now to speak: his greatest glory is that he can neither do nor suffer wrong to or from any god or any man. For he suffers not by force if he suffers — force comes not near him — neither when he acts does he act by force; for all men in all things serve him of their own free will, and where there is voluntary agreement, there, as the laws which are the lords of the city say, is justice. And not only is he just but exceedingly temperate, for Temperance is the acknowledged ruler of the pleasures and desires, and no pleasure ever masters Love; he is their master and they are his servants; and if he conquers them he must be temperate indeed. As to courage, even the god of war stands not up against him; he is the captive and Love is the lord, for love, the love of Aphrodite, masters him, as the tale runs; and the master is stronger than the servant. And if he conquers the bravest of all others, he must be himself the bravest. Of his courage and justice and temperance I have spoken, but I have yet to speak of his wisdom; and according to the measure of my ability I must try to rise to the height of my theme. In the first place he is a poet (and here, like Eryximachus, I magnify my art), and he is also the source of poesy in others, which he could not be if he were not himself a poet. And at the touch of him every one becomes a poet, 'even though he had no music in him before'; this we may properly take as a proof that Love is a good poet and, speaking summarily, accomplished in all the fine arts; for no one can give to another that which he has not himself, or teach that of which he has no knowledge. Who will deny that all living beings are of his creation? Are they not 197 all the works of his wisdom, born and begotten of him? And as to the artists, do we not know that he only who has love for his instructor emerges into the light of fame? — he whom Love touches not walks in darkness. The arts of medicine and archery and divination were discovered by Apollo under the guidance of love and desire; so that he too is a disciple of Love. Likewise the arts of the Muses, the metallurgy of Hephaestus, the weaving of Athene, the governance of Zeus over gods and men, are all due to the teaching of Love. And so, you see, Love set in order the empire of the gods — the love of beauty, as is evident, for with deformity Love has no concern. In the days of old, as I began by saying, dreadful deeds were done among the gods, for they were ruled by Necessity; but now since the birth of Love, and from the love of the beautiful, has sprung every good in heaven and earth. Therefore, Phaedrus, I say of Love that he is first the fairest and best in himself, and then the cause of what is fairest and best in all other things. And there comes into my mind a line of poetry in which he is said to be the god who

> Gives peace on earth and calms the stormy deep,
> Who stills the winds and bids the sufferer sleep.

This is he who empties men of disaffection and fills them with affection, who makes them to meet together at gatherings such as sacrifices, feasts, dances, where he is our lord — who sends courtesy and sends away discourtesy, who gives kindness ever and never gives unkindness; gracious and good, the wonder of the wise, the amazement of the gods; desired by those who have no part in him, and precious to those who have the better part in him; parent of delicacy, luxury, desire, fondness, softness, grace; regardful of the good, regardless of the evil: in every word, labour, wish, fear — saviour, pilot, comrade, warrior, glory of gods and men, leader best and brightest: in whose footsteps let every man follow, sweetly singing in his honour and joining in that sweet strain with which love charms the souls of gods and men alike. Such is the speech, Phaedrus, half-playful, yet having a certain measure of seriousness according to my ability, which I dedicate to the god.

198   When Agathon had done speaking, Aristodemus said that there was a general cheer; the young man was thought to have spoken in a manner worthy of himself, and of the god. And Socrates, looking at Eryximachus, said: Tell me, son of Acumenus, was there not reason in my fears? and was I not a true prophet when I said that Agathon would make a wonderful oration, and that I should be in a strait?

The part of the prophecy which concerns Agathon, replied Eryximachus, appears to me to be true; but not the other part — that you will be in a strait.

Why, my dear friend, said Socrates, must not I or anyone be in a

strait who has to speak after he has heard such a rich and varied
discourse? It culminated in the beautiful diction and style of the
concluding words — who could listen to them without amazement?
When I reflected on the immeasurable inferiority of my powers, I
was ready to run away for shame, if there had been a possibility of
escape. For I was reminded of Gorgias, and at the end of his speech
I fancied in my terror that Agathon was shaking at me the Gorginian
or Gorgonian head of the great master of rhetoric, which was simply
to turn me and my speech into stone, as Homer says, and strike me
dumb. And then I perceived how foolish I had been in consenting
to take my turn with you in praising love, and saying that I too was
an expert on love, when I really had no conception how anything
whatever ought to be praised. For in my simplicity I imagined that
the substance of praise should be truth, and that this being presup-
posed, the speaker was to choose the best topics and set them forth
in the best manner. And I felt quite proud, thinking that I knew the
true nature of all praise, and should speak well. Whereas I now see
that, on the contrary, in order to pay a goodly tribute of praise to
anything, you must attribute to it every species of greatness and
glory, without regard to truth or falsehood — that doesn't matter;
it looks as if the original proposal was not that each of us should
really praise Love, but only that we should appear to praise him. And
so, I suggest, you attribute to Love every imaginable form of praise
which can be gathered anywhere, and you say that 'he is all this',
and 'the cause of all that', making him appear a paragon of beauty   199
and excellence to those who know him not, for you cannot impose
upon those who know him. And a noble and solemn hymn of praise
have you rehearsed. But as I misunderstood the nature of this praise
when I said that I would take my turn, I must beg to be absolved
from the promise which I made in ignorance; it was (as Euripides
would say) a promise of the lips and not of the mind. Farewell then
to such a strain, for I do not praise in that way; no, indeed, I cannot.
But if you like to hear the truth about love, I am ready to speak in
my own manner, though I will not make myself ridiculous by entering into any rivalry with you. Say then, Phaedrus, whether you
would like to have the truth about love, spoken in any words and in
any order which may happen to come into my mind at the time.
Will that be agreeable to you?

Aristodemus said that Phaedrus and the company bid him speak
in any manner which he thought best. Then, he added, let me have
your permission first to ask Agathon a few questions, in order that I
may take what he accepts as the premisses of my discourse.

I grant the permission, said Phaedrus: put your questions. Socrates
then proceeded as follows: —

In your oration, my dear Agathon, I think that you were certainly right in proposing to speak of the nature of Love first and afterwards of his works — that is a way of beginning which I very much approve. And as you have set forth his nature with such stately eloquence, may I ask you further, Whether Love is by his nature the love of something or of nothing? And here I must explain myself: I do not want you to say that Love is the love of a father or the love of a mother — that would be ridiculous; but to answer as you would, if I asked, Is a father a father of something? to which you would find no difficulty in replying, of a son or daughter: and the answer would be right.

Very true, said Agathon.

And you would say the same of a mother?

He assented.

Yet let me ask you one more question in order to illustrate my meaning: Is not a brother to be regarded essentially as a brother of something?

Certainly, he replied.

That is, of a brother or sister?

Yes, he said.

And now, said Socrates, I will ask about Love: — Is Love of something or of nothing?

200   Of something, surely, he replied.

Keep in mind what this is, and tell me what I want to know — whether Love desires that of which love is.

Yes, surely.

And does he possess, or does he not possess, that which he loves and desires?

Probably not, I should say.

Nay, replied Socrates, I would have you consider whether 'necessarily' is not rather the word. The inference that he who desires something is lacking in that thing, and that he who does not desire a thing is not in lack of it, is in my judgement, Agathon, absolutely and necessarily true. What do you think?

I agree with you, said Agathon.

Very good. Would he who is great, desire to be great, or he who is strong, desire to be strong?

That would be inconsistent with our previous admissions.

True. For he who has those qualities cannot be lacking in them?

Very true.

Suppose that a man being strong desired to be strong, or being swift desired to be swift, or being healthy desired to be healthy, — since in that case he might be thought to desire something which he already has or is, I refer to the point in order that we may not be led astray — you will see on reflection that the possessors of those qualities must have their respective advantages at the time, whether they choose or not; and who can desire that which he has? Therefore, when a person says, I am well and wish to be well, or I am rich and wish to be rich, and I desire to have exactly what I have — to him we shall reply: 'You, my friend, having wealth and health and strength, want to have the continuance of them; for at this moment, whether you choose or no, you have them. And when you say, I desire that which I have and nothing else, is not your meaning that you want to have in the future what you have at present?' He must agree with us — must he not?

He must, replied Agathon.

Then, said Socrates, he desires that what he has at present may be preserved to him in the future, which is equivalent to saying that he desires something which is non-existent to him, and which as yet he has not got?

Very true, he said.

Then he and everyone who desires, desires that which he has not already, and which is future and not present, and which he has not, and is not, and which he lacks; — these are the sort of things which love and desire seek?

Very true, he said.

Then now, said Socrates, let us recapitulate the argument. First, is not love of something, and of something too which is wanting to a man?

Yes, he replied.

Remember further what you said in your speech, or if you like I will remind you: you said that the love of the beautiful set in order the empire of the gods, for that of deformed things there is no love — did you not say something of that kind?

Yes, said Agathon.

Yes, my friend, and the remark was a just one. And if this is true, love is the love of beauty and not of deformity?

He assented.

And the admission has been already made that love is of something which one lacks and has not?

True, he said.

Then Love lacks and has not beauty?

Certainly, he replied.

And would you call that beautiful which lacks beauty and does not possess it in any way?

Certainly not.

Then would you still say that Love is beautiful?

Agathon replied: I fear that I said what I did without understanding.

Indeed, you made a very good speech, Agathon, replied Socrates; but there is yet one small question which I would fain ask: — Is not the good also the beautiful?

Yes.

Then in lacking the beautiful, love lacks also the good?

I cannot refute you, Socrates, said Agathon: — Be it as you say.

Say rather, beloved Agathon, that you cannot refute the truth; for Socrates is easily refuted.

And now, taking my leave of you, I will rehearse a tale of love which I heard from Diotima of Mantinea, a woman wise in this and many other kinds of knowledge, who in the days of old, when the Athenians offered sacrifice before the coming of the plague, delayed the disease ten years. She was my instructress in the art of love, and I shall try to repeat to you what she said to me, beginning with the propositions on which Agathon and I are agreed; I will do the best I can do without any help. As you, Agathon, suggested, it is proper to speak first of the being and nature of Love, and then of his works. (I think it will be easiest for me if in recounting my conversation with the wise woman I follow its actual course of question and answer.) First I said to her in nearly the same words which he used to me, that Love was a mighty god, and likewise fair; and she proved to me, as I proved to him, that by my own showing Love was neither fair nor good. 'What do you mean, Diotima,' I said, 'is Love then evil and 202 foul?' 'Hush,' she cried; 'must that be foul which is not fair?' 'Certainly,' I said. 'And is that which is not wise, ignorant? do you not see that there is a mean between wisdom and ignorance?' 'And what may that be?' I said. 'Right opinion,' she replied; 'which, as you know, being incapable of giving a reason, is not knowledge (for how can knowledge be devoid of reason?) nor again ignorance (for neither can ignorance attain the truth), but is clearly something which is a mean between ignorance and wisdom.' 'Quite true,' I replied. 'Do not then insist,' she said, 'that what is not fair is of necessity foul, or what is not good evil; or infer that because Love is not fair and good he is therefore foul and evil; for he is in a mean between them.' 'Well,' I said, 'Love is surely admitted by all to be a great god.' 'By those who know or by those who do not know?' 'By all.' 'And how, Socrates,' she said with a smile, 'can Love be acknowledged to be a great god by those who say that he is not a god at all?' 'And who are they?' I said. 'You and I are two of them,' she replied. 'How can that be?' I said. 'It is quite intelligible,' she replied; 'for you yourself would acknowledge that the gods are happy and fair — of course you would — would you dare to say that any god was not?' 'Certainly not,' I replied. 'And you mean by the happy, those who are the possessors of things good and things fair?' 'Yes.' 'And you admitted that Love, because he was in want, desires those good and fair things of which he is in want?' 'Yes, I did.' 'But how can he be a god who has no portion in what is good and fair?' 'Impossible.' 'Then you see that you also deny the divinity of Love.'

'What then is Love?' I asked; 'Is he mortal?' 'No.' 'What then?' 'As in the former instance, he is neither mortal nor immortal, but in a mean between the two.' 'What is he, Diotima?' 'He is a great spirit ($\delta\alpha\acute{\iota}\mu\omega\nu$) [*daimōn*], and like all spirits he is intermediate between the divine and the mortal.' 'And what,' I said, 'is his power?' 'He interprets between gods and men, conveying and taking across to the gods the prayers and sacrifices of men, and to men the commands of the gods and the benefits they return; he is the mediator who spans the chasm which divides them, and therefore by him the universe is bound together, and through him the arts of the prophet and the priest, their sacrifices and mysteries and charms, and all prophecy and incantation, find their way. For God mingles not with man; but through Love all the intercourse and converse of gods with men, whether they be awake or asleep, is carried on. The wisdom which understands this is spiritual; all other wisdom, such as that of arts and handicrafts, is mean and vulgar. Now these spirits or intermediate powers are many and diverse, and one of them is Love.' 'And who,' I said, 'was his father, and who his mother?' 'The tale,' she said, 'will take time; nevertheless I will tell you. On the day when Aphrodite was born there was a feast of all the gods, among them the god Poros or Plenty, who is the son of Metis or Sagacity. When the feast was over, Penia or Poverty, as the manner is on such occasions, came about the doors to beg. Now Plenty, who was the worse for nectar (there was no wine in those days), went into the garden of Zeus and fell into a heavy sleep; and Poverty considering that for her there was no plenty, plotted to have a child by him, and accordingly she lay down at his side and conceived Love, who partly because he is naturally a lover of the beautiful, and because Aphrodite is herself beautiful, and also because he was begotten during her birthday feast, is her follower and attendant. And as his parentage is, so also are his fortunes. In the first place he is always poor, and anything but tender and fair, as the many imagine him; and he is rough and squalid, and has no shoes, nor a house to dwell in; on the bare earth exposed he lies under the open heaven, in the streets, or at the doors of houses, taking his rest; and like his mother he is always in distress. Like his father too, whom he also partly resembles, he is always plotting against the fair and good; he is bold, enterprising, strong, a mighty hunter, always weaving some intrigue or other, keen in the pursuit of wisdom, fertile in resources; a philosopher at all times, terrible as an enchanter, sorcerer, sophist. He is by nature neither mortal

203

nor immortal, but alive and flourishing at one moment when he is in plenty, and dead at another moment in the same day, and again alive by reason of his father's nature. But that which is always flowing in is always flowing out, and so he is never in want and never in 204 wealth; and, further, he is in a mean between ignorance and knowledge. The truth of the matter is this: No god is a philosopher or seeker after wisdom, for he is wise already; nor does any man who is wise seek after wisdom. Neither do the ignorant seek after wisdom; for herein is the evil of ignorance, that he who is neither a man of honour nor wise is nevertheless satisfied with himself: there is no desire when there is no feeling of want.' 'But who then, Diotima,' I said, 'are the lovers of wisdom, if they are neither the wise nor the foolish?' 'A child may answer that question,' she replied; 'they are those who are in a mean between the two; Love is one of them. For wisdom is a most beautiful thing, and Love is of the beautiful; and therefore Love is also a philosopher or lover of wisdom, and being a lover of wisdom is in a mean between the wise and the ignorant. And of this, too, his birth is the cause; for his father is wealthy and wise, and his mother poor and foolish. Such, my dear Socrates, is the nature of the spirit Love. The error in your conception of him was very natural; from what you say yourself, I infer that it arose because you thought that Love is that which is loved, not that which loves; and for that reason, I think, Love appeared to you supremely beautiful. For the beloved is the truly beautiful, and delicate, and perfect, and blessed; but the active principle of love is of another nature, and is such as I have described.'

I said: 'O thou stranger woman, thou sayest well; but, assuming Love to be such as you say, what is the use of him to men?' 'That, Socrates,' she replied, 'I will attempt to unfold: of his nature and birth I have already spoken; and you acknowledge that love is of the beautiful. But someone will say: What does it consist in, Socrates and Diotima? — or rather let me put the question more clearly, and ask: When a man loves the beautiful, what does his love desire?' I answered her 'That the beautiful may be his.' 'Still,' she said, 'the answer suggests a further question: What is given by the possession of beauty?' 'To what you have asked,' I replied, 'I have no answer ready.' 'Then,' she said, 'let me put the word "good" in the place of the beautiful, and repeat the question once more: If he who loves loves the good, what is it then that he loves?' 'The possession of the good.' 'And what does he gain who possesses the good?' 'Happiness,' 205 I replied; 'there is less difficulty in answering that question.' 'Yes,' she said, 'the happy are made happy by the acquisition of good things. Nor is there any need to ask why a man desires happiness; the answer is already final.' 'You are right,' I said. 'And is this wish and this desire common to all? and do all men always desire their own good, or only some men? — what say you?' 'All men,' I replied; 'the desire is common to all.' 'Why, then,' she rejoined, 'are not all men, Socrates, said to love, but only some of them? whereas you say that all men are always loving the same things.' 'I myself wonder,' I said, 'why this is.' 'There is nothing to wonder at,' she replied; 'the reason is that one part of love is separated off and receives the name of the whole, but the other parts have other names.' 'Give an illustration,' I said. She answered me as follows: 'There is creative activity which, as you know, is complex and manifold. All that causes the passage of non-being into being is a "poesy" or creation, and the processes of all art are creative; and the masters of arts are all poets or creators.' 'Very true.' 'Still,' she said, 'you know that they are not called poets, but have other names; only that one portion of creative activity is separated off from the rest, and is concerned with music and metre, is called by the name of the whole and is termed poetry, and they who possess poetry in this sense of the word are called poets.' 'Very true,' I said. 'And the same holds of love. For you may say generally that all desire of good and happiness is only the great and subtle power of love; but they who are drawn towards him by any other path, whether the path of money-making or gymnastics or philosophy, are not called lovers — the name of the whole is appropriated to those whose desire takes one form only — they alone are said to love, or to be lovers.' 'I dare say,' I replied, 'that you are right.' 'Yes,' she added, 'and you hear people say that lovers are seeking for their other half; but I say that they are seeking neither for the half of themselves, nor for the whole, unless the half or the whole be also a good; men will cut off their own hands and feet and cast them away, if they think them evil. They do not, I imagine, each cling to what is his own, unless perchance there be someone who calls what belongs to him the good, and what belongs to another the evil; for there is nothing which men love but the good. Is there anything?' 'Certainly, I should say, that there is nothing.' 'Then,' she said, 'the simple truth is, that men love the good.' 'Yes,' I said. 'To which must be added that they love the possession of the good?' 'Yes, that must be added.' 'And not only the possession, but the everlasting possession of the good?' 'That must be added too.' 'Then love,' she said, 'may be described generally as the love of the everlasting possession of the good?' 'That is most true.'

'Then if this be always the nature of love, can you tell me further,' she went on, 'what is the manner of the pursuit? what are they doing who show all this eagerness and heat which is called love? and what is the object which they have in view? Answer me.' 'Nay, Diotima,' I replied, 'if I knew, I should not be wondering at your wisdom,

neither should I come to learn from you about this very matter.'
'Well,' she said, 'I will teach you: — The object which they have in
view is birth in beauty, whether of body or soul.' 'I do not understand you,' I said; 'the oracle requires an explanation.' 'I will make
my meaning clearer,' she replied. 'I mean to say, that all men are
bringing to the birth in their bodies and in their souls. There is a
certain age at which human nature is desirous of procreation —
procreation which must be in beauty and not in deformity. The union
of man and woman is a procreation; it is a divine thing, for conception and generation are an immortal principle in the mortal creature,
and in the inharmonious they can never be. But the deformed is
inharmonious with all divinity, and the beautiful harmonious. Beauty,
then, is the destiny or goddess of parturition who presides at birth,
and therefore, when approaching beauty, the procreating power is
propitious, and expansive, and benign, and bears and produces fruit:
at the sight of ugliness she frowns and contracts and has a sense of
pain, and turns away, and shrivels up, and not without a pang refrains from procreation. And this is the reason why, when the
hour of procreation comes, and the teeming nature is full, there is
such a flutter and ecstasy about beauty whose approach is the allevia-
tion of the bitter pain of travail. For love, Socrates, is not, as you
imagine, the love of the beautiful only.' 'What then?' 'The love of
generation and of birth in beauty.' 'Yes,' I said. 'Yes, indeed,' she
replied. 'But why of generation? Because to the mortal creature,
generation is a sort of eternity and immortality, and if, as has been
already admitted, love is of the everlasting possession of the good,
all men will necessarily desire immortality together with good:
whence it must follow that love is of immortality.'

All this she taught me at various times when she spoke of love.
And I remember her once saying to me, 'What is the cause, Socrates,
of love, and the attendant desire? See you not how all animals, birds
as well as beasts, in their desire of procreation, are in agony when
they take the infection of love, which begins with the desire of union
and then passes to the care of offspring, on whose behalf the weakest
are ready to battle against the strongest even to the uttermost, and to
die for them, and will let themselves be tormented with hunger, or
make any other sacrifice, in order to maintain their young. Man may
be supposed to act thus from reason; but why should animals have
these passionate feelings? Can you tell me why?' Again I replied
that I did not know. She said to me: 'And do you expect ever to
become a master in the art of love, if you do not know this?' 'But I
have told you already, Diotima, that my ignorance is the reason why
I come to you, for I am conscious that I want a teacher; tell me then
the cause of this and of the other mysteries of love.' 'Marvel not,' she

207

said, 'if you believe that love is of the immortal, as we have several times acknowledged; for here again, and on the same principle too, the mortal nature is seeking as far as is possible to be everlasting and immortal: and this is only to be attained by generation, because generation always leaves behind a new and different existence in the place of the old. Nay, even in the life of the same individual there is succession and not absolute uniformity: a man is called the same, and yet in the interval between youth and age, during which every animal is said to have life and identity, he is undergoing a perpetual process of loss and reparation — hair, flesh, bones, blood, and the whole body are always changing. Which is true not only of the body, but also of the soul, whose habits, tempers, opinions, desires, pleasures, pains, fears, never remain the same in any one of us, but are always coming and going. What is still more surprising, it is equally true of science; not only do some of the sciences come to life in our minds, and others die away, so that we are never the same in regard to them either: but the same fate happens to each of them individually. For what is implied in the word "recollection", but the departure of knowledge, which is ever being forgotten, and is renewed and preserved by recollection, and appears to be the same although in reality new, according to that law by which all mortal things are preserved, not absolutely the same, but by substitution, the old worn-out mortality leaving another new and similar existence behind — unlike the divine, which is wholly and eternally the same? And in this way, Socrates, the mortal body, or mortal anything, partakes of immortality; but the immortal in another way. Marvel not then at the love which all men have of their offspring; for that universal love and interest is for the sake of immortality.'

I was astonished at her words, and said: 'Is this really true, O most wise Diotima?' And she answered with all the authority of an accomplished sophist: 'Of that, Socrates, you may be assured; — think only of the ambition of men, and you will wonder at the senselessness of their ways, unless you consider how they are stirred by the passionate love of fame. They are ready to run all risks, even greater than they would have run for their children, and to pour out money and undergo any sort of toil, and even to die, "if so they leave an everlasting name". Do you imagine that Alcestis would have died to save Admetus, or Achilles to avenge Patroclus, or your own Codrus in order to preserve the kingdom for his sons, if they had not imagined that the memory of their virtues, which still survives among us, would be immortal? Nay,' she said, 'I am persuaded that all men do all things, and the better they are the more they do them, in hope of the glorious fame of immortal virtue; for they desire the immortal.

'Those who are pregnant in the body only, betake themselves to

208

women and beget children — this is the character of their love; their offspring, as they hope, will preserve their memory and give 209 them the blessedness and immortality which they desire for all future time. But souls which are pregnant — for there certainly are men who are more creative in their souls than in their bodies, creative of that which is proper for the soul to conceive and bring forth; and if you ask me what are these conceptions, I answer, wisdom, and virtue in general — among such souls are all creative poets and all artists who are deserving of the name inventor. But the greatest and fairest sort of wisdom by far is that which is concerned with the ordering of states and families, and which is called temperance and justice. And he who in youth has the seed of these implanted in his soul, when he grows up and comes to maturity desires to beget and generate. He wanders about seeking beauty that he may get offspring — for from deformity he will beget nothing — and naturally embraces the beautiful rather than the deformed body; above all, when he finds a fair and noble and well-nurtured soul, he embraces the two in one person, and to such a one he is full of speech about virtue and the nature and pursuits of a good man, and he tries to educate him. At the touch and in the society of the beautiful which is ever present to his memory, even when absent, he brings forth that which he had conceived long before, and in company with him tends that which he brings forth; and they are married by a far nearer tie and have a closer friendship that those who beget mortal children, for the children who are their common offspring are fairer and more immortal. Who, when he thinks of Homer and Hesiod and other great poets, would not rather have their children than ordinary human ones? Who would not emulate them in the creation of children such as theirs, which have preserved their memory and given them everlasting glory? Or who would not have such children as Lycurgus left behind him to be the saviours, not only of Lacedaemon, but of Hellas, as one may say? There is Solon, too, who is the revered father of Athenian laws; and many others there are in many other places, both among Hellenes and barbarians, who have given to the world many noble works, and have been the parents of virtue of every kind; and many temples have been raised in their honour for the sake of children such as theirs; which were never raised in honour of anyone, for the sake of his mortal children.

'These are the lesser mysteries of love, into which even you, Soc- 210 rates, may enter; to the greater and more hidden ones which are the crown of these, and to which, if you pursue them in a right spirit, they will lead, I know not whether you will be able to attain. But I will do my utmost to inform you, and do you follow if you can. For he who would proceed aright in this matter should begin in youth to seek the company of corporeal beauty; and first, if he be guided by his instructor aright, to love one beautiful body only — out of that he should create fair thoughts; and soon he will of himself perceive that the beauty of one body is akin to the beauty of another; and then if beauty of form in general is his pursuit, how foolish would he be not to recognize that the beauty in every body is one and the same! And when he perceives this he will abate his violent love of the one, which he will despise and deem a small thing, and will become a steadfast lover of all beautiful bodies. In the next stage he will consider that the beauty of the soul is more precious than the beauty of the outward form; so that if a virtuous soul have but a little comeliness, he will be content to love and tend him, and will search out and bring to the birth thoughts which may improve the young, until he is compelled next to contemplate and see the beauty in institutions and laws, and to understand that the beauty of them all is of one family, and that personal beauty is a trifle; and after institutions his guide will lead him on to the sciences, in order that, beholding the wide region already occupied by beauty, he may cease to be like a servant in love with one beauty only, that of a particular youth or man or institution, himself a slave mean and narrow-minded; but drawing towards and contemplating the vast sea of beauty, he will create many fair and noble thoughts and discourses in boundless love of wisdom, until on that shore he grows and waxes strong, and at last the vision is revealed to him of a single science, which is the science of beauty everywhere. To this I will proceed; please to give me your very best attention;

'He who has been instructed thus far in the things of love, and who has learned to see the beautiful in due order and succession, when he comes toward the end will suddenly perceive a nature of wondrous beauty (and this, Socrates, is the final cause of all our 211 former toils) — a nature which in the first place is everlasting, knowing not birth or death, growth or decay; secondly, not fair in one point of view and foul in another, or at one time or in one relation or at one place fair, at another time or in another relation or at another place foul, as if fair to some and foul to others, or in the likeness of a face or hands or any other part of the bodily frame, or in any form of speech or knowledge, or existing in any individual being, as for example, in a living creature, whether in heaven, or in earth, or anywhere else; but beauty absolute, separate, simple, and everlasting, which is imparted to the ever growing and perishing beauties of all other beautiful things, without itself suffering diminution, or increase, or any change. He who, ascending from these earthly things under the influence of true love, begins to perceive that beauty, is not far from the end. And the true order of going, or being led by another,

to the things of love, is to begin from the beauties of earth and mount
upwards for the sake of that other beauty, using these as steps only,
and from one going on to two, and from two to all fair bodily forms,
and from fair bodily forms to fair practices, and from fair practices
to fair sciences, until from fair sciences he arrives at the science of
which I have spoken, the science which has no other object than
absolute beauty, and at last knows that which is beautiful by itself
alone. This, my dear Socrates,' said the stranger of Mantinea, 'is that
life above all others which man should live, in the contemplation of
beauty absolute; a beauty which if you once beheld, you would see
not to be after the measure of gold, and garments, and fair boys and
youths, whose presence now entrances you; and you and many a one
would be content to live seeing them only and conversing with them
without meat or drink, if that were possible — you only want to
look at them and to be with them. But what if a man had eyes to
see the true beauty — the divine beauty, I mean, pure and clear and
unalloyed, not infected with the pollutions of the flesh and all the
colours and vanities of mortal life — thither looking, and holding
212 converse with the true beauty simple and divine? Remember how
in that communion only, beholding beauty with that by which it can
be beheld, he will be enabled to bring forth, not images of beauty,
but realities (for he has hold not of an image but of a reality), and
bringing forth and nourishing true virtue will properly become the
friend of God and be immortal, if mortal man may. Would that be
an ignoble life?'

Such, Phaedrus — and I speak not only to you, but to all of you —
were the words of Diotima; and I am persuaded of their truth. And
being persuaded of them, I try to persuade others, that in the attainment of this end human nature will not easily find a helper better
than Love. And therefore, also, I say that every man ought to honour him as I myself honour him and walk in his ways, and exhort
others to do the same, and praise the power and spirit of Love according to the measure of my ability now and ever.

The words which I have spoken, you, Phaedrus, may call an encomium of Love, or anything else which you please.

When Socrates had done speaking, the company applauded, and
Aristophanes was beginning to say something in answer to the allusion which Socrates had made to his own speech, when suddenly
there was a great knocking at the door of the house, as of revellers,
and the sound of a flute-girl was heard. Agathon told the attendants
to go and see who were the intruders. 'If they are friends of ours,'
he said, 'invite them in, but if not, say that the drinking is over.' A
little while afterwards they heard the voice of Alcibiades resounding
in the court; he was in a great state of intoxication, and kept roaring

and shouting 'Where is Agathon? Lead me to Agathon,' and at length, supported by the flute-girl and some of his attendants, he found his way to them. 'Hail, friends,' he said, appearing at the door crowned with a massive garland of ivy and violets, his head flowing with ribands. 'Will you have a very drunken man as a companion of your revels? Or shall I crown Agathon, which was my intention in coming, and go away? For I was unable to come yesterday, and therefore I am here today, carrying on my head these ribands, that taking them from my own head, I may crown the head of this fairest and wisest of men, as I may be allowed to call him. Will you laugh at me because I am drunk? Yet I know very well that I am speaking the truth, although you may laugh. Come now, I have stated my terms: am I to come in or not? Yes or no, will you drink with me?'

213

The company were vociferous in begging that he would take his place among them, and Agathon specially invited him. Thereupon he was led in by the people who were with him; and as he was being led, intending to crown Agathon, he took the ribands from his own head and held them in front of his eyes; he was thus prevented from seeing Socrates, who made way for him, and Alcibiades took the vacant place between Agathon and Socrates, and in taking the place he embraced Agathon and crowned him. Take off his sandals, said Agathon, and let him make a third on the same couch.

By all means; but who makes the third partner in our revels? said Alcibiades, turning around and starting up as he caught sight of Socrates. Good heavens, he said, what is this? Why, it is Socrates! Here you are, always laying an ambush for me, and always, as your way is, pouncing out upon me at all sorts of unsuspected places: and now, what have you to say for yourself, and why are you lying here, where I perceive that you have contrived to find a place, not by a joker or lover of jokes like Aristophanes, but by the fairest of the company?

Socrates turned to Agathon and said: I must ask you to protect me, Agathon; for my passion for this man has grown quite a serious matter to me. Since I became his admirer I have never been allowed to speak to any other beauty, or so much as to look at them. If I do, he goes wild with envy and jealousy, and not only abuses me but can hardly keep his hands off me, and at this moment he may do me some harm. Please to see to this, and either reconcile me to him, or, if he attempts violence, protect me, as I am in bodily fear of his mad and passionate attempts.

There can never be reconciliation between you and me, said Alcibiades; but for what you have just said, I will chastise you some other time. At the moment, Agathon, I must beg you to give me some of the ribands that I may crown his head, his marvellous head

— I would not have him complain of me for crowning you, and neglecting him, who in his eloquence is the conqueror of all mankind; and this not only once, as you were the day before yesterday, but always. Whereupon, taking some of the ribands, he crowned Socrates, and again reclined.

Then he said: You seem, my friends, to be sober, which is a thing not to be endured; you must drink — for that was the agreement under which I was admitted — and I elect myself master of the feast until you have drunk an adequate amount. Let us have a large goblet, Agathon, if there is one; or rather, he said, addressing the attendant, bring me that wine-cooler. The wine-cooler which had caught 214 his eye was a vessel holding more than two quarts — this he filled and emptied, and bade the attendant fill it again for Socrates. Observe, my friends, said Alcibiades, that this ingenious trick of mine will have no effect on Socrates, for he can drink any quantity of wine and not be at all nearer being drunk. Socrates drank the cup which the attendant filled for him.

Eryximachus said: What is this, Alcibiades? Are we to have neither conversation nor singing over our cups; but simply to drink as if we were thirsty?

Alcibiades replied: Hail, worthy son of a most wise and worthy sire!

The same to you, said Eryximachus; but what shall we do?

That I leave to you, said Alcibiades.

The wise physician worth a thousand men

ought to prescribe and we to obey. What do you want?

Well, said Eryximachus, before you appeared we had passed a resolution that each one of us in turn should make a speech in praise of love, and as good a one as he could: the turn was passed round from left to right; and as all of us have spoken, and you have not spoken but have well drunken, you ought to speak, and then impose upon Socrates any task which you please, and he on his right hand neighbour, and so on.

That is good, Eryximachus, said Alcibiades; and yet the comparison of a drunken man's speech with those of sober men is hardly fair. Also I should like to know, sweet friend, whether you really believe what Socrates was just now saying; for I can assure you that the very reverse is the fact, and that if I praise anyone but himself in his presence, whether god or man, he will hardly keep his hands off me.

For shame, said Socrates.

Hold your tongue, said Alcibiades, for I swear there is no one else whom I will praise when you are of the company.

Well then, said Eryximachus, if you like praise Socrates.

What do you think, Eryximachus? said Alicibiades: shall I attack him and inflict the punishment before you all?

What are you about? said Socrates; are you going to raise more laughter, at my expense? Is that the meaning of your praise?

I am going to speak the truth, if you will permit me.

I not only permit, but exhort you to speak the truth.

Then I will begin at once, said Alcibiades, and if I say anything which is not true, you may interrupt me if you will, and say 'that is a lie', though my intention is to speak the truth. But you must not 215 wonder if I speak anyhow as things come into my mind; for the fluent and orderly enumeration of all your singularities is not a task which is easy to a man in my condition.

And now, my boys, I shall praise Socrates in a figure which will appear to him to be a caricature, and yet I speak, not to make fun of him, but only for the truth's sake. I say, that he is exactly like the busts of Silenus, which are set up in the statuaries' shops, holding pipes or flutes in their mouths; and they are made to open in the middle, and have images of gods inside them. I say also that he is like Marsyas the satyr. You yourself will not deny, Socrates, that your face is like that of a satyr. Aye, and there is a resemblance in other points too. For example, you are a bully, as I can prove by witnesses, if you will not confess. And are you not a flute-player? That you are, and a performer far more wonderful than Marsyas. He indeed with instruments used to charm the souls of men by the power of his breath, and the players of his music do so still: for the melodies of Olympus are derived from Marsyas who taught them, and these, whether they are played by a great master or by a miserable flute-girl, have a power which no others have; they alone possess the soul and reveal the wants of those who have need of gods and mysteries, because they are divine. But you produce the same effect with your words only, and do not require the flute: that is the difference between you and him. When we hear any other speaker, even a very good one, he produces absolutely no effect upon us, or not much, whereas the mere fragments of you and your words, even at second hand, and however imperfectly repeated, amaze and possess the souls of every man, woman, and child who comes within hearing of them. And if I were not afraid that you would think me hopelessly drunk, I would have sworn as well as spoken to the influence which they have always had and still have over me. For my heart leaps within me more than that of any Corybantian reveller, and my eyes rain tears when I hear them. And I observe that very many others are affected in the same manner. I have heard Pericles and other great orators, and I thought that they spoke well, but I never had any similar feeling; my soul was not shaken by them, nor was I

angry at the thought of my own slavish state. But this Marsyas has
often brought me to such a pass, that I have felt as if I could not
endure the life which I am leading (this, Socrates, you will admit);
and at this very moment I am conscious that if I did not shut my
ears against him, and fly as from the voice of the siren, I could not
hold out against him, and my fate would be like that of others, —
he would pin me down, and I should grow old sitting at his feet.
For he makes me confess that I ought not to live as I do, neglecting
the many wants of my own soul and busying myself with the concerns of the Athenians; therefore I hold my ears and tear myself
away from him. And he is the only person who ever made me
ashamed, which you might think not to be in my nature, and there is
no one else who does the same. For I know that I cannot answer
him or say that I ought not to do as he bids, but when I leave his
presence the love of popularity gets the better of me. And therefore
I steal away and fly from him, and when I see him I am ashamed of
what I have confessed to him. Many a time have I wished that he
were dead, and yet I know that I should be much more sorry than
glad if he were to die: so that I am at my wit's end what to do about
the fellow.

And this is what I and many others have suffered from the flute-
playing of this satyr. Yet hear me once more while I show you how
exact the image is, and how marvellous his power. For be assured of
this, none of you know him; but I will reveal him to you, since, having begun, I must go on. See you how fond he is of the fair? He is
always with them and is always being smitten by them, and then
again he knows nothing and is ignorant of all things — such is the
appearance which he puts on. Is he not like a Silenus in this? To
be sure he is: his outer mask is the carved head of the Silenus; but,
O my companions in drink, when he is opened, what temperance
there is residing within! Know you that beauty and wealth and all
the other blessings which in popular opinion bring felicity, are of no
account with him, and are utterly despised by him: he regards not at
all the persons who are gifted with them, nor us ourselves — this is
fact; but he spends all his life in teasing mankind, and hiding his true
intent. When, however, I opened him, and looked within at his
serious purpose, I saw in him divine and golden images of such
fascinating beauty that I was ready to do in a moment whatever Socrates commanded: they may have escaped the observation of others,
but I saw them. Now I fancied that he was seriously enamoured of
my beauty, and I thought it a marvellous piece of luck; I had the
means of persuading him to tell me everything that he knew, for I
had a wonderful opinion of the attractions of my youth. In the prosecution of this design, when I next went to him, I sent away the

attendant who usually accompanied me (I will confess the whole truth, and beg you to listen; and if I speak falsely, do you, Socrates, expose the falsehood). Well, he and I were alone together, and I thought that when there was nobody with us, I should hear him speak the language which lovers use to their loves when they are by themselves, and I was delighted. Nothing of the sort; he conversed as usual, and spent the day with me and then went away. Afterwards I challenged him to the palaestra; and he wrestled and closed with me several times when there was no one present; I fancied that I might succeed in this manner. Not a bit; I made no way with him. Lastly, as I had failed hitherto, I thought that I must take stronger measures and attack him boldly, and, as I had begun, not give him up, but see how matters stood between him and me. So I invited him to sup with me, just as if he were a fair youth, and I a designing lover. He was not easily persuaded to come; he did, however, after a while accept the invitation, and when he came the first time, he wanted to go away at once as soon as supper was over, and I had not the face to detain him. The second time, still in pursuance of my design, after we had supped, I went on conversing far into the night, and when he wanted to go away, I pretended that the hour was late and compelled him to remain. So he lay down on the couch next to me, on which he had reclined at supper, and there was no one but ourselves sleeping in the apartment. All this may be told without shame to anyone, but what follows I could hardly tell you if I were sober; yet as the proverb says, *In vino veritas*, whether there are also the mouths of children or not;[1] and therefore I may speak. Nor should I be justified in concealing a resplendent action of Socrates when I have set out to praise him. Moreover I have felt the serpent's sting; and he who has suffered, as they say, is willing to tell only his fellow sufferers as they alone will be likely to under- 218
stand him, and will not be extreme in judging of the sayings or doings which have been wrung from his agony. For I have been bitten by a worse than a viper's tooth; I have known in my soul, or in my heart, or however else it ought to be described, that worst of pangs, more violent in ingenuous youth than any serpent's tooth, the pang of philosophy, which will make a man say or do anything. And you whom I see around me, Phaedrus and Agathon and Eryximachus and Pausanias and Aristodemus and Aristophanes, all of you, and I need not say Socrates himself, and multitudes of others, have had experience of the same dionysiac madness and passion of philosophy. Therefore listen and excuse my doings then and my

[1] In allusion to the two proverbs, *οἶνος καὶ παῖδες ἀληθεῖς*, and *οἶνος καὶ ἀλήθεια*. (JOWETT) The proverbs mean, respectively, "Wine and children speak truth," and "Wine and truth go together." (L)

sayings now. But let the attendants and other profane and unmannered persons close tightly the doors of their ears.

When the lamp was put out and the servants had gone away, I thought that I must be plain with him and have no more ambiguity. So I gave him a shake, and I said: 'Socrates, are you asleep?' 'No,' he said. 'Do you know what I am thinking?' 'What is it?' he said. 'I think,' I replied, 'that of all the lovers whom I have ever had you are the only one who is worthy of me, and you appear to be too modest to speak. Now I feel that I should be a fool to refuse you this or any other favour, and therefore I come to lay at your feet all that I have and all that my friends have, in the hope that you will assist me in the way of virtue, which I desire above all things, and in which I believe that you can help me better than anyone else. And I should certainly have more reason to be ashamed of what wise men would say if I were to refuse my favour to such as you, than of what the world, who are mostly fools, would say of me if I granted it.' To these words he replied in the ironical manner which is so characteristic of him: — 'Alcibiades, my friend, you have indeed an elevated aim if what you say is true, and if there really is in me any power by which you may become better; truly you must see in me some rare beauty of a kind infinitely higher than the comeliness which I see in you. And therefore, if you mean to share with me and to exchange beauty for beauty, you will have greatly the advantage of me; you will gain true beauty in return for appearance — like Diomede, gold in exchange for brass. But look again, sweet friend, and see whether you are not deceived in me. The mind begins to grow critical when the bodily eye fails, and you are still a long way from that point.' Hearing this, I said; 'I have told you my own thoughts, saying exactly what I mean; and now it is for you to consider what you think best for you and me.' 'That is good,' he said; 'at some other time then we will consider and act as seems best about this and about other matters.' After this interchange, I imagined that he was wounded by my shafts, and so without waiting to hear more I got up, and throwing my coat about him crept under his threadbare cloak, as the time of year was winter, and there I lay during the whole night having this truly superhuman wonder in my arms. This again, Socrates, will not be denied by you. And yet, notwithstanding all, he was so superior to my solicitations, so contemptuous and derisive and disdainful of my beauty — which really, as I fancied, had some attractions — hear, O judges; for judges you shall be of the haughty virtue of Socrates — nothing more happened, but in the morning when I awoke (let all the gods and goddesses be my witnesses) I arose as from the couch of a father or an elder brother.

What do you suppose must have been my feelings, after this rejection, at the thought of my own dishonour? And yet I could not help wondering at his natural temperance and self-restraint and manliness. I never imagined that I could have met with a man such as he is in wisdom and endurance. And therefore, I could not be angry with him or renounce his company, any more than I could find a way to win him. For I well knew that if Ajax could not be wounded by steel, much less he by money; and he had escaped me when I tried the only means by which I thought I might captivate him. So I was at my wit's end; no one was ever more hopelessly enslaved by another. All this happened before he and I went on the expedition to Potidaea; there we messed together, and I had the opportunity of observing his extraordinary power of sustaining fatigue. His endurance was simply marvellous when, being cut off from our supplies, we were compelled to go without food — on such occasions, which often happen in time of war, he was superior not only to me but 220 to everybody; there was on one to be compared to him. Yet at a festival he had no equal in his power of enjoyment; though not willing to drink, he could if compelled beat us all at that, — wonderful to relate! no human being had ever seen Socrates drunk; and his powers, if I am not mistaken, will be tested before long. His fortitude in enduring cold was also surprising. There was a most severe frost, for the winter in that region is really tremendous, and everybody else either remained indoors, or if they went out had on an amazing quantity of clothes, and were all shod, and had their feet swathed in felt and fleeces: in the midst of this, Socrates with his bare feet on the ice and in his ordinary dress marched better than the other soldiers who had shoes, and they looked daggers at him because he seemed to despise them.

I have told you one tale, and now I must tell you another, which is worth hearing,

Of the doings and sufferings of the enduring man

while he was on the expedition. One morning he was thinking about something which he could not resolve; he would not give it up, but continued thinking from early dawn until noon — there he stood fixed in thought; and at noon attention was drawn to him, and the rumour ran through the wondering crowd that Socrates had been standing and thinking about something ever since the break of day. At last, in the evening after supper, some Ionians out of curiosity (I should explain that this was not in winter but in summer), brought out their mats and slept in the open air that they might watch him and see whether he would stand all night. There he stood until the following morning; and with the return of light he offered up a prayer to the sun, and went his way. I will also tell, if you please —

and indeed I am bound to tell — of his courage in battle; for who but he saved my life? Now this was the engagement in which I received the prize of valour: I was wounded and he would not leave me, but rescued both me and my arms; and he ought to have received the prize of valour which the generals wanted to confer on me on account of my rank, and I told them so (this, again, Socrates will not impeach or deny), but he was more eager than the generals that I and not he should have the prize. There was another occasion on 221 which his behaviour was very remarkable — in the flight of the army after the battle of Delium, where he served among the heavy-armed, — I had a better opportunity of seeing him than at Potidaea, for I was myself on horseback, and therefore comparatively out of danger. The troops were scattered in flight and he was retreating in company with Laches; I happened to meet them and told them not to be discouraged, and promised to remain with them; and there you might see him, Aristophanes, as you describe, just as he is in the streets of Athens, stalking like a pelican and rolling his eyes, calmly contemplating enemies as well as friends, and making very intelligible to anybody, even a great way off, that whoever attacked him would be likely to meet with a stout resistance; and in this way he and his companion escaped — for this is the sort of man who is never touched in war; those only are pursued who are running away headlong. I particularly observed how superior he was to Laches in presence of mind. Much else that is extraordinary might be said in praise of Socrates; some of his ways might perhaps be paralleled in another man, but yet his absolute unlikeness to any human being that is or ever has been is perfectly astonishing. You may imagine Brasidas and others to have been like Achilles, or you may imagine Nestor and Antenor to have been like Pericles, and the same may be said of other famous men; but of this strange being, and of his words, you will never be able to find any likeness, however remote, either in the present or in past generations — other than that which I have already suggested of Silenus and the satyrs; and they may represent not only himself, but his words. For, although I forgot to mention this to you before, his discourses are like the images of Silenus which open; they are ridiculous when you first hear them; they are enveloped in words and phrases that are like the skin of the wanton satyr — for his talk is of pack-asses and smiths and cobblers and curriers, and he is always repeating the same things in the same words, so that any stupid or inexperienced person might feel disposed to laugh at 222 him. But he who sees the bust opening and looks into its interior, will find that they are the only words which have a meaning in them, and also are most divine, abounding in fair images of virtue, and of the widest comprehension, or rather comprehending everything which a man should bear in mind if he is to become a man of honour.

This, friends, is my praise of Socrates. I have added my blame of him for his ill treatment of me; and he has ill treated not only me, but Charmides the son of Glaucon, and Euthydemus the son of Diocles, and many others in the same way — beginning as their lover, the deceiver has ended by making them pay their addresses to him. Wherefore I say to you, Agathon, 'Be not deceived by him; learn from me and take warning, and do not be a fool and learn by experience, as the proverb says.'

When Alcibiades had finished, there was a laugh at his outspokenness; for he seemed to be still in love with Socrates. You are sober, Alcibiades, said Socrates, or you would never have gone so far about to hide the purpose of your satyr's praises, for all this long story is only an ingenious circumlocution, of which the point comes in by the way at the end; you want to get up a quarrel between me and Agathon, and your notion is that I ought to love you and nobody else, and that you and you only ought to love Agathon. But the plot of this Satyric or Silenic drama has been detected, and you must not allow him, Agathon, to score a success, and set us at variance.

I believe you are right, said Agathon; so I infer from the way in which he has placed himself between you and me with the intention of dividing us; but he shall gain nothing by that move, for I will go and lie on the couch next to you.

Yes, yes, replied Socrates, by all means come here and lie on the couch below me.

Alas, said Alcibiades, how the fellow goes on persecuting me; he is determined to get the better of me at every turn. I do beseech you, at least allow Agathon to lie between us.

Certainly not, said Socrates; as you praised me, and I in turn ought to praise my neighbour on the right, he will be out of order in praising me again when he ought rather to be praised by me, and I must entreat you to consent to this, and not be jealous, for I have 223 a great desire to praise the youth.

Hurrah! cried Agathon, I cannot possibly stay here, Alcibiades; I must move instantly, that I may be praised by Socrates.

The usual way, said Alcibiades; where Socrates is, no one else has any chance with beauty; and now how readily has he invented a specious reason for attracting Agathon to himself.

Agathon arose in order that he might take his place on the couch by Socrates, when suddenly a large band of revellers entered, and spoiled the order of the banquet. Someone who was going out having left the door open, they had found their way in, and made themselves at home; great confusion ensued, and everyone was compelled to drink large quantities of wine. Aristodemus said that Eryximachus, Phaedrus, and others went away — he himself fell asleep, and as the nights were long took a good rest: he was awakened towards daybreak by a crowing of cocks, and when he awoke, the others were either asleep, or had gone away; there remained only Socrates, Aristophanes, and Agathon, who were drinking out of a large goblet which they passed round, and Socrates was discoursing to them. Aristodemus was only half awake, and he did not hear the beginning of the discourse; the chief thing which he remembered was Socrates compelling the other two to acknowledge that the genius of comedy was the same with that of tragedy, and that the true artist in tragedy was an artist in comedy also. To this they were constrained to assent, being drowsy, and not quite following the argument. And first of all Aristophanes dropped off, then, when the day was already dawning, Agathon. Socrates, having laid them to sleep, rose to depart; Aristodemus, as his manner was, following him. At the Lyceum he took a bath, and passed the day as usual. In the evening he retired to rest at his own home.

Phaedrus

Persons of the Dialogue

SOCRATES   PHAEDRUS

Scene: Under a plane-tree, by the banks of the Ilissus

◄§ The *Phaedrus*, like the *Symposium*, has been discussed in our Introduction, Theme 4. Its first part, which alone is given here, deals directly with the Platonic conception of ideal love. The character Phaedrus is the same whom we have met in the *Symposium*.

In order to heighten the ideality of the commended type of love, the dialogue opens with a defense of the very opposite type, put forward in the purported speech of the orator Lysias. Let us not fall into the error of supposing as we read it that it represents Plato's views. These will appear in due course in the speeches of Socrates. The opening speech is interesting also as illustrating the love of skill in argument for its own sake and the delight in paradox which were so prevalent in the Athens of the later fifth century.

The dialogue opens with a chance encounter, probably in the streets of Athens, between Socrates and Phaedrus:

Socrates. My dear Phaedrus, whence come you, and whither are 227 you going?

Phaedrus. I have come from the house of Lysias the son of Cephalus, and I am going to take a walk outside the wall, for I have been sitting with him the whole morning; and following the advice of our common friend Acumenus I take my walk along the road rather than around the race-tracks; he says it is less tiring.

Soc. There he is right. Lysias then, I suppose, was in the town?

Phaedr. Yes, he was staying with Epicrates, here at the house of Morychus; that house which is near the temple of Olympian Zeus.

Soc. And how did he entertain you? Can I be wrong in supposing that Lysias gave you a feast of discourse?

Phaedr. You shall hear, if you can spare time to accompany me.

Soc. Do you doubt that I should deem the conversation of you and Lysias 'a thing of higher import', as I may say in the words of Pindar, 'than any business'?

Phaedr. Will you go on?

Soc. And will you go on with the narration?

Phaedr. My tale, Socrates, is one of your sort, for love was the theme which occupied us — love after a fashion: Lysias has been writing about a fair youth who was being tempted, but not by a lover; and this was the point: he ingeniously proved that the non-lover should be accepted rather than the lover.

Soc. O that is noble of him! I wish that he would say the poor man rather than the rich, and the old man rather than the young one; — then he would meet the case of me and of many a man; his words would be quite refreshing, and he would be a public benefactor. For my part, I do so long to hear his speech, that if you walk all the way to Megara, and when you have reached the wall come back, as Herodicus recommends, without going in, I will keep you company.

228 *Phaedr.* What do you mean, my good Socrates? How can you imagine that my unpractised memory can do justice to an elaborate work, which the greatest rhetorician of the age spent a long time in composing. Indeed, I cannot; I would prefer such a talent to a large sum of money.

Soc. I believe that I know Phaedrus about as well as I know myself, and I am very sure that the speech of Lysias was repeated to him, not once only, but again and again: — he insisted on hearing it many times over and Lysias was very willing to gratify him; at last, when nothing else would do, he got hold of the book, and looked at what he most wanted to see, — this occupied him during the whole morning; — and then when he was tired with sitting, he went out to take a walk, not until, by the dog, as I believe, he had simply learned by heart the entire discourse, unless it was unusually long, and he started on a walk outside the wall that he might practise his lesson. There he saw a certain lover of discourse who had a similar weakness; — he saw and rejoiced; now thought he, 'I shall have a partner in my revels'. And he invited him to lead on. But when the lover of discourse begged that he would repeat the tale, he gave himself airs and said, 'No I cannot', as if he were not longing to do so; although, if the hearer had refused, he would sooner or later have been compelled by him to listen whether he would or no. Therefore, Phaedrus, bid him do at once what he will soon do whether bidden or not.

Phaedr. I see that you will by no means let me off until I speak in some fashion or other; and, in truth, my best plan is to speak as I best can.

Soc. You judge my intention correctly.

Phaedr. I will do as I say; but believe me, Socrates, I did not learn the very words — O no; nevertheless I have a general notion of what he said, and will give you a summary of the points in which the lover differed from the non-lover. Let me begin at the beginning.

Soc. Yes, my sweet one; but you must first of all show what you have in your left hand under your cloak, for that roll, as I suspect, is the actual discourse. Now, much as I love you, I would not have you suppose that I am going to have your memory exercised at my expense, if you have Lysias himself here.

Phaedr. Enough; I see that I have no hope of practising my art upon you. But if I am to read, where would you please to sit?   229

Soc. Let us turn aside and go by the Ilissus; we will sit down at some quiet spot.

Phaedr. I am fortunate in not having my sandals, and as you never have any, I think that we may go along the brook and cool our feet in the water; this will be the easiest way, and at midday and in the summer is far from being unpleasant.

Soc. Lead on, and look out for a place in which we can sit down.

Phaedr. Do you see that tallest plane-tree in the distance?

Soc. Yes.

Phaedr. There are shade and gentle breezes, and grass on which we may either sit or lie down.

Soc. Move forward.

Phaedr. I should like to know, Socrates, whether the place is not somewhere here at which Boreas is said to have carried off Orithyia from the banks of the Ilissus?

Soc. Such is the tradition.

Phaedr. And is this the exact spot? The little stream is delightfully clear and bright; I can fancy that there might be maidens playing near.

Soc. I believe that the spot is not exactly here, but about a quarter of a mile lower down, where you cross to the shrine of Agra, and there is, I think, some sort of an altar of Boreas at the place.

Phaedr. I have never noticed it; but I beseech you to tell me, Socrates, do you believe this tale?

Soc. The wise are doubtful, and I should not be singular if, like them, I too doubted. I might have a rational explanation that Orithyia was playing with Pharmacia, when a northern gust carried her over the neighbouring rocks; and this being the manner of her death, she was said to have been carried away by Boreas. There is a discrepancy, however, about the locality; according to another version of the story she was taken from the Areopagus, and not from this place. Now I quite acknowledge that these allegories are very nice, but he is not to be envied who has to invent them; much labour and ingenuity will be required of him; and when he has once begun, he must go on and rehabilitate Hippocentaurs and chimeras dire. Gorgons and winged steeds flow in apace, and numberless other inconceivable and portentous natures. And if he is sceptical about

them, and would fain reduce them one after another to the rules
of probability, this sort of crude philosophy will take up a great
deal of time. Now I have no leisure for such inquiries; shall I tell
230 you why? I must first know myself, as the Delphian inscription says;
to be curious about that which is not my concern, while I am still in
ignorance of my own self, would be ridiculous. And therefore I bid
farewell to all this; the common opinion is enough for me. For, as I
was saying, I want to know not about this, but about myself: am I
a monster more complicated and swollen with passion than Typho,
or a creature of a gentler and simpler sort, possessing, by divine
grace, a nature devoid of pride. But meanwhile let me ask you,
friend: have we not reached the plane-tree to which you were
conducting us?

Phaedr. Yes, this is the tree.

Soc. By Hera, a fair resting-place, full of summer sounds and
scents. Here is this lofty and spreading plane-tree, and the agnus
castus high and clustering, in the fullest blossom and the greatest
fragrance; and the stream which flows beneath the plane-tree is
deliciously cold to the feet. Judging from the ornaments and images,
this must be a spot sacred to Achelous and the Nymphs. How delightful is the breeze: — so very sweet; and there is a sound in the
air shrill and summerlike which makes answer to the chorus of the
cicadae. But the greatest charm of all is the grass, like a pillow
gently sloping to the head. My dear Phaedrus, you have been an
admirable guide.

Phaedr. What an incomprehensible being you are, Socrates: when
you are in the country, as you say, you really are like some stranger
who is led about by a guide. Do you ever cross the border? I rather
think that you never venture even outside the gates.

Soc. I must ask your forgiveness, my good friend. I am a lover
of knowledge, and the men who dwell in the city are my teachers,
and not the trees or the country. Though I do indeed believe that
you have found a spell with which to draw me out of the city into
the country, like a hungry animal before whom a bough or a bunch of
fruit is waved. For only hold up before me in like manner a book,
and you may lead me all round Attica, and over the wide world.
And now having arrived, I intend to lie down, and do you choose
any posture in which you can read best. Begin.

231 *Phaedr.* Listen. 'You know how matters stand with me; and how,
as I conceive, this affair may be arranged for the advantage of both
of us. And I maintain that I ought not to fail in my suit, because I am
not your lover: for lovers repent of the kindnesses which they have
shown when their passion ceases, but to the non-lovers who are free
and not under any compulsion, no time of repentance ever comes; for

they confer their benefits according to the measure of their ability, in the way which is most conducive to their own interest. Then again, lovers consider how by reason of their love they have neglected their own concerns and rendered service to others: and when to these benefits conferred they add on the troubles which they have endured, they think that they have long ago made to the beloved a very ample return. But the non-lover has no such tormenting recollections; he has never neglected his affairs or quarrelled with his relations; he has no troubles to add up or excuses to invent; and being well rid of all these evils, why should he not freely do what, as he supposes, will gratify the beloved? If you say that the lover is more to be esteemed, because his love is thought to be greater; for he is willing to say and do what is hateful to other men, in order to please his beloved; — that, if true, is only a proof that he will prefer any future love to his present, and will injure his old love at the pleasure of the new. And how, in a matter of such infinite importance, can a man be right in trusting himself to one who is afflicted with a malady which no experienced person would attempt to cure, for the patient himself admits that he is not in his right mind, and acknowledges that he is wrong in his mind, but says that he is unable to control himself? And if he came to his right mind, would he ever imagine that the desires were good which he conceived when in his wrong mind? Once more, there are many more non-lovers than lovers; and if you choose the best of the lovers, you will not have many to choose from; but if you choose the most congenial of the non-lovers, the choice will be larger, and you will be far more likely to find among them a person who is worthy of your friendship. If public opinion be your dread, and you would avoid discovery and reproach, in all probability the lover, who is always thinking that other men are 232 as emulous of him as he is of them, will boast to some one of his successes, and make a show of them openly in the pride of his heart; — he wants others to know that his labour has not been lost; but the non-lover is more his own master, and is desirous of solid good, and not of the opinion of mankind. Again, the lover may be generally noted or seen following the beloved (this is his regular occupation), and whenever they are observed to exchange two words they are supposed to meet about some affair of love either past or in contemplation; but when non-lovers meet, no one asks the reason why, because people know that talking to another is natural, whether friendship or mere pleasure be the motive. Once more, if you fear the fickleness of friendship, consider that in any other case a quarrel might be a mutual calamity; but now, when you have given up what is most precious to you, you will be the greater loser, and therefore, you will have more reason in being afraid of the lover, for his vexations are many, and he is always fancying that every one is leagued against him. Wherefore also he debars his beloved from the society of others; he will not have you intimate with the wealthy, lest they should outbid him by their wealth, or with men of education, lest they should vanquish him by their understanding; and he is equally afraid of anybody's influence who has any other advantage over himself. If he can persuade you to make yourself hateful to them, you are left without a friend in the world; or if, out of a regard to your own interest, you have more sense than to comply with his desire, you will have to quarrel with him. But those who are non-lovers, and whose success in love is the reward of their merit, will not be jealous of the companions of their beloved, and will rather hate those who refuse to be his associates, thinking that their favourite is slighted by the latter and benefited by the former; so that the affair is, in this case, likely to bring him much more love than hatred. Many lovers too have loved the person of a youth before they knew his character or obtained experience of his circumstances; so that they can not be sure whether, when their passion has passed away,

233 they will continue to be his friends; whereas, in the case of non-lovers who were always friends, the friendship is not lessened by the favours granted; but the recollection of these remains with them, and is an earnest of good things to come. Further, I say you are likely to be more improved by me than by a lover. For they praise your words and actions in a wrong way; partly, because they are afraid of offending you, and also, their judgement is weakened by passion. Such are the feats which love exhibits; he makes things painful to the disappointed which give no pain to others; he compels the successful lover to praise what ought not to give him pleasure, and therefore the beloved is to be pitied rather than envied. But if you listen to me, in the first place, I, in my intercourse with you, shall not merely regard present enjoyment, but also future advantage, being not mastered by love, but my own master; nor for small causes taking violent dislikes, but even when the cause is great, slowly laying up little wrath — unintentional offences I shall forgive, and intentional ones I shall try to prevent; for these are the marks of a friendship which will last. Do you think that a lover only can be a firm friend? reflect: — if this were true, we should set small value on sons, or fathers, or mothers; nor should we ever have loyal friends, for our love of them arises not from passion, but from other associations. Further, if we ought to shower favours on those who are the most eager suitors, — on that principle, we ought always to do good, not to the most virtuous, but to the most needy; for they are the persons who will be most relieved, and will therefore be the most grateful; and when you make a feast you should invite not your friend, but the beggar and the empty soul; for they

will love you, and attend you, and come about your doors, and will be the best pleased, and the most grateful, and will invoke many a blessing on your head. Yet surely you ought not to be granting favours to those who besiege you with prayer, but to those who are best able to reward you; nor to the lover only, but to those who are worthy of love; nor to those who will enjoy the bloom of your youth, but 234 to those who will share their possessions with you as you grow older; nor to those who, having succeeded, will glory in their success to others, but to those who will be modest and tell no tales; nor to those who care about you for a moment only, but to those who will continue your friends through life; nor to those who, when their passion is over, will pick a quarrel with you, but rather to those who, when the charm of youth has left you, will show their own virtue. Remember what I have said; and consider yet this further point: friends admonish the lover under the idea that his way of life is bad, but no one of his kindred ever yet censured the non-lover, or thought that he was ill advised about his own interests.

'Perhaps you will ask me whether I propose that you should indulge every non-lover. To which I reply that not even the lover would advise you to be so disposed towards all lovers, for the indiscriminate favour is less esteemed by the rational recipient, and less easily hidden by him who would escape the censure of the world. Now love ought to be for the advantage of both parties, and for the injury of neither.

'I believe that I have said enough; but if there is anything more which you desire or which in your opinion needs to be supplied, ask and I will answer.'

Now, Socrates, what do you think? Is not the discourse excellent, more especially in the matter of the language?

Soc. Yes, quite admirable; the effect on me was ravishing. And this I owe to you, Phaedrus, for I observed you while reading to be in an ecstasy, and thinking that you are more experienced in these matters than I am, I followed your example, and, like you, my divine darling, I became inspired with a phrenzy.

Phaedr. Indeed, you are pleased to be merry.

Soc. Do you mean that I am not in earnest?

Phaedr. Now don't talk in that way, Socrates, but let me have your real opinion; I adjure you, by Zeus, the god of friendship, to tell me whether you think that any Hellene could have said more or spoken better on the same subject.

Soc. Well, but are you and I expected to praise the sentiments of the author, or only the clearness, and roundness, and finish, and tournure of the language? As to the first I willingly submit to your 235 better judgement, for I am not worthy to form an opinion, having only attended to the rhetorical manner; and I was doubting whether this could have been defended even by Lysias himself; I thought, though I speak under correction, that he repeated himself two or three times, either from want of fluency in speaking at length on a single topic, or from want of interest in such a subject; and also, he appeared to me ostentatiously to exult in showing how well he could say the same thing in two different ways.

Phaedr. Nonsense, Socrates; what you call repetition was the especial merit of the speech; for he omitted no topic of which the subject rightly allowed, and I do not think that anyone could have spoken better or more exhaustively.

Soc. There I cannot go along with you. Ancient sages, men and women, who have spoken and written of these things, would rise up in judgement against me, if out of complaisance I assented to you.

Phaedr. Who are they, and where did you hear anything better than this?

Soc. I am sure that I must have heard; but at this moment I do not remember from whom; perhaps from Sappho the fair, or Anacreon the wise; or, possibly, from a prose writer. What ground have I for saying so? Why, because I perceive that my bosom is full, and that I could make another speech as good as that of Lysias, and different. Now I am certain that this is not an invention of my own, who am well aware that I know nothing, and therefore I can only infer that I have been filled through the ears, like a pitcher, from the waters of another, though I have actually forgotten in my stupidity how this occurred, and who was my informant.

Phaedr. That is grand: — but never mind how you heard the discourse or from whom; let that be a mystery not to be divulged even at my earnest desire. Only, as you say, promise to make another and better oration, equal in length and entirely new, on the same subject; and I, like the nine Archons, will promise to set up a golden image at Delphi, not only of myself, but of you and as large as life.

Soc. You are a dear friend, of golden disposition indeed, if you suppose me to mean that Lysias has altogether missed the mark, and that I can make a speech from which all his arguments are to be excluded. The worst of authors will say something which is to the 236 point. Who, for example, could speak on this thesis of yours without praising the discretion of the non-lover and blaming the indiscretion of the lover? These are the commonplaces of the subject which must come in (for what else is there to be said?) and must be allowed and excused; the only merit is in the arrangement of them, for there can be none in the invention; but when you leave the commonplaces, then there may be some originality.

Phaedr. I admit that there is reason in what you say, and I too will be reasonable, and will allow you to start with the premiss that the lover is more disordered in his wits than the non-lover; if in what remains you make a longer and better speech than Lysias, and use other arguments, then I say again, that a statue you shall have of beaten gold, and take your place by the colossal offerings of the Cypselids at Olympia.

Soc. How profoundly in earnest is the lover, because to tease him I lay a finger upon his love! And so, Phaedrus, you really imagine that I am going to improve upon the ingenuity of Lysias?

Phaedr. There I have you as you had me, and you must just speak 'as you best can.' Do not let us exchange *tu quoque* as in a farce, or compel me to say to you as you said to me, 'I know Socrates as well as I know myself, and he was wanting to speak, but he gave himself airs.' Rather I would have you consider that from this place we stir not until you have unbosomed yourself of the speech; for here are we all alone, and I am stronger, remember, and younger than you: — Wherefore perpend, and do not compel me to use violence.

Soc. But, my sweet Phaedrus, how ridiculous it would be of me to compete with Lysias in an extempore speech! He is a master in his art and I am an untaught man.

Phaedr. You see how matters stand; and therefore let there be no more pretences; for, indeed, I know the word that is irresistible.

Soc. Then don't say it.

Phaedr. Yes, but I will; and my word shall be an oath. 'I say, or rather swear' — but what god will be the witness of my oath? — 'By this plane-tree I swear, that unless you repeat the discourse here in the face of this very plane-tree, I will never again either recite or report to you any speech by any author.'

Soc. Villain! I am conquered; the poor lover of discourse has no more to say.

Phaedr. Then why are you still at your tricks?

Soc. I am not going to play tricks now that you have taken the oath, for I cannot allow myself to be starved.

Phaedr. Proceed.

Soc. Shall I tell you what I will do?

Phaedr. What?

Soc. I will veil my face and gallop through the discourse as fast as I can, for if I see you I shall feel ashamed and not know what to say.

Phaedr. Only go on and you may do anything else which you please.

Soc. Come, O ye Muses, whether you have received your name Ligeiai [clear-toned] from the character of your strains, or because the Ligurians are a musical race, help, O help me in the tale which my good friend here desires me to rehearse, in order that his friend whom he always deemed wise may seem to him to be wiser now than ever.

Once upon a time there was a fair boy, or, more properly speaking, a youth; he was very fair and had a great many lovers; and there was one special cunning one, who had persuaded the youth that he did not love him, but he really loved him more than any; and one day when he was paying his addresses to him, he used this very argument — that he ought to accept the non-lover rather than the lover; his words were as follows: —

'All good counsel begins in the same way; a man should know what he is advising about, or his counsel will all come to nought. But most people are not aware of their ignorance of a thing's essential nature, and, not having come to an understanding at first because they think that they know, they end, as might be expected, in contradicting one another and themselves. Now you and I must not be guilty of this fundamental error which we condemn in others; but as our question is whether the lover or non-lover is to be preferred, let us first of all agree in defining the nature and powers of love, and then, keeping our eyes upon the definition and to this appealing, let us further inquire whether love brings advantage or disadvantage.

'Every one sees that love is a desire, and we know that even non-lovers desire the beautiful. Now in what way is the lover to be distinguished from the non-lover? Let us note that in every one of us there are two guiding and ruling principles which lead us whither they will; one is the natural desire of pleasure, the other is an acquired opinion which aspires after the best; and these two are sometimes in harmony and then again at war, and sometimes the one, sometimes the other conquers. When opinion by the help of reason leads us to 238 the best, and proves superior, its government is called temperance; but when desire, which is devoid of reason, rules in us and drags us to pleasure, that power of misrule is called excess (*hubris*). Now excess has many names, being composed of many members, and many forms, and any of these forms when very marked gives its own name to the possessor, a name neither honourable nor creditable. The desire of eating, for example, which gets the better of the higher reason and the other desires, is called gluttony, and he who has it is called a glutton; the tyrannical desire of drink, which inclines the possessor of the desire to drink, has a name which is only too obvious, and there can be as little doubt by what name any other appetite of the same family would be called; — it will be the name of that which happens to be dominant. And now I think that you will perceive the drift of my discourse; but as every spoken word is in a manner plainer than the unspoken, I had better say further that the irrational desire which overcomes the tendency of opinion towards right, and is led away to the enjoyment of beauty, and especially of personal beauty, by the desires which are her own kindred — that supreme desire, I say, which by leading conquers and by the force of passion is reinforced, from this very force, receiving a name, is called love (ἐρρωμένως ἔρως) [*errōmenōs erōs*].'

And now, dear Phaedrus, I shall pause for an instant to ask whether you do not think me, as I appear to myself, inspired?

Phaedr. Yes, Socrates, you seem to have a very unusual flow of words.

Soc. Listen to me, then, in silence; for surely the place is holy; so that you must not wonder, if, as I proceed, I appear to be in a divine fury, for already I am getting into dithyrambics.

Phaedr. Nothing can be truer.

Soc. The responsibility rests with you. But hear what follows, and perhaps the fit may be averted; all is in their hands above. I will go on talking to my youth. Listen: —

Thus, my friend, we have declared and defined the nature of the subject. Keeping the definition in view, let us now inquire what advantage or disadvantage is likely to ensue from the lover or the non-lover to him who accepts their advances.

He who is the victim of his passions and the slave of pleasure will of course desire to make his beloved as agreeable to himself as possible. Now to him who has a mind diseased anything is agreeable which is not opposed to him; but that which is equal or superior is hateful; and therefore the lover will not brook any superiority or equality on the part of his beloved; he is always employed in reducing him to inferiority. And the ignorant is the inferior of the wise, the coward of the brave, the slow of speech of the speaker, the dull of the clever. Such, or even graver than these, are the mental defects in which a lover will necessarily delight when they are implanted by nature; and which otherwise he must contrive to implant, if he would not be deprived of his fleeting joy. But then he cannot help being jealous, and will debar his beloved from the advantages of society which would most tend to make a man of him, doing him great harm; and especially harmful is it to withdraw him from that society which would have given him wisdom. That is to say, in his excessive fear lest he should come to be despised in his eyes he will be compelled to banish from him divine philosophy; and there is no greater injury which he can inflict upon him than this. He will contrive that his beloved shall be wholly ignorant, and in everything shall look to him; he is to be the delight of the lover's heart, and a curse to himself. Verily, a lover is a profitable guardian and associate for him in all that relates to his mind.

Let us next see how his master, whose law of life is pleasure and not good, will keep and train the body of his servant. Will he not choose a beloved who is delicate rather than sturdy and strong? One brought up in shady bowers and not in the bright sun, a stranger to manly exercises and the sweat of toil, accustomed only to a soft and luxurious diet, instead of the hues of health having the colours of paint and ornament, and the rest of a piece? — such a life as any one can imagine and which I need not detail at length. But I may sum up all that I have to say in a word, and pass on. Such a person in war, or in any of the great crises of life, will be the anxiety of his friends and also of his lover, and certainly not the terror of his enemies.

Leaving this obvious point, let us tell what advantage or disadvantage the beloved will receive from the guardianship and society of his lover in the matter of his property; this is the next point to be considered. The lover will be the first to see what, indeed, will be sufficiently evident to all men, that he desires above all things to deprive his beloved of those dearest and most kindly disposed to him, and of his dearest and holiest possessions; father, mother, kindred, friends, — he would be glad to see him deprived of all who he thinks may be hinderers or reprovers of their most sweet converse; he will even cast a jealous eye upon his gold and silver or other property, because these make him a less easy prey, and when caught less manageable; hence a lover is of necessity displeased at his possession of them and rejoices at their loss; and he would like him to be wifeless, childless, homeless, as well; and the longer the better, for what he desires is to continue his selfish fruition for as long as possible.

There are some sort of animals, such as flatterers, who are dangerous and mischievous enough, and yet nature has mingled a temporary pleasure and grace in their composition. You may say that a courtesan is hurtful, and disapprove of many such creatures and practices, and yet for the time they are very pleasant. But the lover is not only hurtful to his love; he is also an extremely disagreeable companion. The old proverb says that 'birds of a feather flock together'; I suppose that equality of years inclines them to the same pleasures, and similarity begets friendship; yet you may have more than enough even of this. Constraint, also, is said to be grievous to all men at all times. But the relation between the lover and his beloved, apart from their unlikeness, is as constrained as possible. For he is old and his love is young, and neither day nor night will he leave him if he can help; necessity and the sting of desire drive him on, and allure him with the pleasure which he receives from seeing, hearing, touching, perceiving him in every way. And therefore he is delighted to fasten upon him and to minister to him. But what pleasure or consolation can the beloved be receiving all this time? Must he not feel the extremity of disgust when he looks at a face from which youthful charm has faded, as indeed it has from the whole person of the lover? If the mention of such things is disagreeable, much worse is it to be forced into daily contact with them; for he is jealously watched and guarded against everything and everybody, and has to hear misplaced and exaggerated praises of himself, and censures equally inappropriate, which are intolerable when the man is sober, and, when he is drunk, become disgusting, as well as intolerable, in their wearisome and unrestrained frankness.

And not only while his love continues is he mischievous and unpleasant, but when his love ceases he becomes a perfidious enemy of him on whom he showered his oaths and prayers and promises, and yet could hardly prevail upon him to tolerate the tedium of his company even from motives of interest. The hour of payment arrives, and now he is the servant of another master; instead of love and infatuation, wisdom and temperance are his bosom's lords, but the beloved has not discovered the change which has taken place in him; when he asks for a return and recalls to his recollection former sayings and doings, he believes himself to be speaking to the same person, and the other, not having the courage to confess the truth, and not knowing how to fulfil the oaths and promises which he made when under the dominion of folly, and having now grown wise and temperate, does not want to do as he did or to be as he was before. And so he runs away and is constrained to be a defaulter; the oyster-shell[1] has fallen with the other side uppermost — he changes pursuit into flight, while the other is compelled to follow him with passion and imprecation, not knowing that he ought never from the first to have accepted a demented lover instead of a sensible non-lover; and that in making such a choice he was giving himself up to a faithless, morose, envious, disagreeable being, hurtful to his estate, hurtful to his bodily health, and still more hurtful to the cultivation of his mind, than which there neither is nor ever will be anything more honoured in the eyes both of gods and men. Consider this, fair youth, and know that in the friendship of the lover there is no real kindness; he has an appetite and wants to feed upon you:

> As wolves love lambs so lovers love their loves.

But I told you so, I am speaking in verse, and therefore I had better make an end; enough.

Phaedr. I thought that you were only half-way and were going to make a similar speech about all the advantages of accepting the non-lover. Why do you not proceed?

---

[1] In allusion to a game in which two parties fled or pursued according as an oyster-shell which was thrown into the air fell with the dark or light side uppermost.

Soc. Does not your simplicity observe that I have got out of dithyrambics into heroics, when only uttering a censure on the lover? And if I am to add the praises of the non-lover what will become of me? Do you not perceive that my wits are plainly overpowered by the Nymphs to whom you have mischievously exposed me? And therefore I will only add that the non-lover has all the advantages in which the lover is accused of being deficient. And now I will say no more; there has been enough of both of them. Leaving the tale to its fate, I will cross the river and make the best of my way home, lest a worse thing be inflicted upon me by you.

242

Phaedr. Not yet, Socrates; not until the heat of the day has passed; do you not see that the hour is almost noon? there is the midday sun standing still, as people say, in the meridian. Let us rather stay and talk over what has been said, and then return in the cool.

Soc. Your love of discourse, Phaedrus, is superhuman, simply marvellous, and I do not believe that there is any one of your contemporaries who has either made or in one way or another has compelled others to make an equal number of speeches. I would except Simmias the Theban, but all the rest are far behind you. And now I do verily believe that you have been the cause of another, which I have to pronounce.

Phaedr. That is good news. But what do you mean?

Soc. I mean to say that as I was about to cross the stream the usual sign was given to me, — that sign which always forbids, but never bids, me to do anything which I am going to do; and I thought that I heard a voice saying in my ear that I had been guilty of impiety, and that I must not go away until I had made an atonement. Now I am a diviner, though not a very good one, but I have enough religion for my own use, as you might say of a bad speller — his spelling is good enough for him; and I now clearly perceive my error. O my friend, how prophetic is the human soul! Some time ago, while I was still speaking, I had a sort of misgiving, and, like Ibycus, 'I was troubled; I feared that I might be buying honour from men at the price of sinning against the gods.' Now I recognize my error.

Phaedr. What error?

Soc. That was a dreadful speech which you brought with you, and you made me utter one as bad.

Phaedr. How so?

Soc. It was foolish, I say, — to a certain extent, impious; can anything be more dreadful?

Phaedr. Nothing, if the speech was really such as you describe.

Soc. Well, and is not Eros the son of Aphrodite, and a god?

Phaedr. So men say.

Soc. But that was not acknowledged by Lysias in his speech, nor by you in that other speech which you by a charm drew from my lips. For if love be, as he surely is, a divinity, he cannot be evil. Yet this was the error of both the speeches. There was also a simplicity about them which was refreshing; having no truth or honesty in them, nevertheless they pretended to be something, hoping to succeed in deceiving the manikins of earth and gain celebrity among them. Wherefore I must have a purgation. And I bethink me of an ancient purgation of mythological error which was devised, not by Homer, for he never had the wit to discover why he was blind, but by Stesichorus, who was a philosopher and knew the reason why; and therefore, when he lost his eyes, for that was the penalty which was inflicted upon him for reviling the lovely Helen, he at once purged himself. And the purgation was a recantation, which began thus, —

> False is that word of mine — the truth is that thou didst not
> embark in well-benched ships, nor ever go to the citadel of Troy;

and when he had completed his poem, which is called 'the recantation', immediately his sight returned to him. Now I will be wiser than either Stesichorus or Homer, in that I am going to make my recantation for reviling love before I suffer; and this I will attempt, not as before, veiled and ashamed, but with forehead bold and bare.

Phaedr. Nothing could be more agreeable to me than to hear you say so.

Soc. Only think, my good Phaedrus, what an utter want of delicacy was shown in the two discourses; I mean, in my own and in that which you recited out of the book. Would not any one who was himself of a noble and gentle nature, and who loved or ever had loved a nature like his own, when we tell of the petty causes of lovers' jealousies, and of their exceeding animosities, and of the injuries which they do to their beloved, have imagined that our ideas of love were taken from some haunt of sailors to which good manners were unknown — he would certainly never have admitted the justice of our censure?

Phaedr. I dare say not, Socrates.

Soc. Therefore, because I blush at the thought of this person, and also because I am afraid of Love himself, I desire to wash the brine out of my ears with water from the spring; and I would counsel Lysias not to delay, but to write another discourse, which shall prove that *ceteris paribus* the lover ought to be accepted rather than the non-lover.

Phaedr. Be assured that he shall. You shall speak the praises of the lover, and Lysias shall be compelled by me to write another discourse on the same theme.

Soc. You will be true to your nature in that, and therefore I believe you.

Phaedr. Speak, and fear not.

Soc. But where is the fair youth whom I was addressing before, and who ought to listen now; lest, if he hear me not, he should accept a non-lover before he knows what he is doing?

Phaedr. He is close at hand, and always at your service.

Soc. Know then, fair youth, that the former discourse was the word of Phaedrus, the son of Pythocles, of the deme Myrrhina. And this which I am about to utter is the recantation of Stesichorus the son of Euphemus, who comes from the town of Himera, and is to the following effect: 'False was that word of mine' that the beloved ought to accept the non-lover when he might have the lover, because the one is sane, and the other mad. It might be so if madness were simply an evil; but there is also a madness which is a divine gift, and the source of the chiefest blessings granted to men. For prophecy is a madness, and the prophetess at Delphi and the priestesses at Dodona when out of their senses have conferred great benefits on Hellas, both in public and private life, but when in their senses few or none. And I might also tell you how the Sibyl and other inspired persons have given to many an one many an intimation of the future which has saved them from falling. But it would be tedious to speak of what every one knows.

There will be more reason in appealing to the ancient inventors of names, who would never have connected prophecy (μαντική) [*mantikē*], which foretells the future and is the noblest of arts, with madness (μανική) [*manikē*], or called them both by the same name, if they had deemed madness to be a disgrace or dishonour; — they must have thought that there was an inspired madness which was a noble thing; for the two words, μαντική [*mantikē*] and μανική [*manikē*], are really the same, and the letter τ [*t*] is only a modern and tasteless insertion. And this is confirmed by the name which was given by them to the rational investigation of futurity, whether made by the help of birds or other signs — this, for as much as it is an art which supplies from the reasoning faculty mind (νοῦς) [*nous*] and information (ἱστορία) [*historia*] to human thought (οἴησις) [*oiēsis*], they originally termed οἰονοιστική [*oionoistikē*], but the word has been lately altered and made sonorous by the modern introduction of the letter Omega (οἰονοιστική [*oionoistikē*] and οἰωνιστική [*oiōnistikē*]), and in proportion as prophecy (μαντική) [*mantikē*] is more perfect and august than augury, both in name and fact, in the same proportion, as the ancients testify, is madness superior to a sane mind (σωφροσύνη) [*sōphrosynē*], for the one is only of human, but the other of divine, origin. Again, where plagues and mightiest woes have bred in certain families, owing to some ancient bloodguiltiness, there madness, inspiring and taking possession of those whom destiny has appointed, has found deliverance, having recourse to prayers and religious rites. And learning thence the use of purifications and mysteries, it has sheltered from evil, future as well as present, the man who has some part in this gift, and has afforded a release from his present calamity to one who is truly possessed, and duly out of his mind. The third kind is the madness of those who are possessed by the Muses; which taking hold of·a delicate and virgin soul, and there inspiring frenzy, awakens lyrical and all other numbers; with these adorning the myriad actions of ancient heroes for the instruction of posterity. But he who, having no touch of the Muses' madness in his soul, comes to the door and thinks that he will get into the temple by the help of art — he, I say, and his poetry are not admitted; the sane man disappears and is nowhere when he enters into rivalry with the madman.

I might tell of many other noble deeds which have sprung from inspired madness. And therefore, let not the mere thought of this frighten us, and let us not be scared and confused by an argument which says that the temperate friend is to be chosen rather than the inspired, but let him further show that love is not sent by the gods for any good to lover or beloved; if he can do so we will allow him to carry off the palm. And we, on our part, must prove in answer to him that the madness of love is the greatest of heaven's blessings, and the proof shall be one which the wise will receive, and the witling disbelieve. But first of all, let us view the affections and actions of the soul divine and human, and try to ascertain the truth about them. The beginning of our proof is as follows: —

The soul through all her being is immortal, for that which is ever in motion is immortal; but that which moves another and is moved by another, in ceasing to move ceases also to live. Only the self-moving, since it cannot depart from itself, never ceases to move, and is the fountain and beginning of motion to all that moves besides. Now, the beginning is unbegotten, for that which is begotten must have a beginning; but this itself cannot be begotten of anything, for if it were dependent upon something, then the begotten would not come from a *beginning*. But since it is unbegotten, it must also be indestructible. For surely if a beginning were destroyed, then it could neither come into being itself from any source, nor serve as the beginning of other things, if it be true that all things must have a beginning. Thus it is proved that the self-moving is the beginning of motion; and this can neither be destroyed nor begotten, else the whole heavens and all creation would collapse and stand still, and, lacking all power of motion, never again have birth. But whereas

245

the self-moving is proved to be immortal, he who affirms that this is
the very meaning and essence of the soul will not be put to confusion. For every body which is moved from without is soul-less,
but that which is self-moved from within is animate, and our usage
246 makes it plain what is the nature of the soul. But if this be true, that
the soul is identical with the self-moving, it must follow of necessity
that the soul is unbegotten and immortal. Enough of her immortality:
let us pass to the description of her form.

To show her true nature would be a theme of large and more than
mortal discourse, but an image of it may be given in a briefer discourse within the scope of man; in this way, then, let us speak. Let
the soul be compared to a pair of winged horses and charioteer joined
in natural union. Now the horses and the charioteers of the gods are
all of them noble and of noble descent, but those of other races are
mixed. First, you must know that the human charioteer drives a pair;
and next, that one of his horses is noble and of noble breed, and the
other is ignoble and of ignoble breed; so that the management of the
human chariot cannot but be a difficult and anxious task. I will endeavour to explain to you in what way the mortal differs from the
immortal creature. The soul in her totality has the care of inanimate
being everywhere, and traverses the whole heaven in divers forms
appearing; — when perfect and fully winged she soars upward, and
orders the whole world; whereas the imperfect soul, losing her wings
and drooping in her flight at last settles on the solid ground — there,
finding a home, she receives an earthly frame which appears to be
self-moved, but is really moved by her power; and this composition
of soul and body is called a living and mortal creature. For immortal
no such union can be reasonably believed to be; although fancy, not
having seen nor surely known the nature of God, may imagine an
immortal creature having both a body and also a soul which are united
throughout all time. Let that, however, be as God wills, and be
spoken of acceptably to him. And now let us ask the reason why the
soul loses her wings!

The wing is the corporeal element which is most akin to the divine,
and which by nature tends to soar aloft and carry that which gravi-
tates downwards into the upper region, which is the habitation of
the gods. The divine is beauty, wisdom, goodness, and the like; and
by these the wing of the soul is nourished, and grows apace; but
when fed upon evil and foulness and the opposite of good, wastes
and falls away. Zeus, the mighty lord, holding the reins of a winged
chariot, leads the way in heaven, ordering all and taking care of all;
247 and there follows him the array of gods and demi-gods, marshalled
in eleven bands; Hestia alone abides at home in the house of heaven;
of the rest they who are reckoned among the princely twelve march

in their appointed order. They see many blessed sights in the inner heaven, and there are many ways to and fro, along which the blessed gods are passing, every one doing his own work; he may follow who will and can, for jealousy has no place in the celestial choir. But when they go to banquet and festival, then they move up the steep to the top of the vault of heaven. The chariots of the gods in even poise, obeying the rein, glide rapidly; but the others labour, for the vicious steed goes heavily, weighing down the charioteer to the earth when his steed has not been thoroughly trained: — and this is the hour of agony and extremest conflict for the soul. For the immortals, when they are at the end of their course, go forth and stand upon the outside of heaven; its revolution carries them round, and they behold the things beyond. But of the heaven which is above the heavens, what earthly poet ever did or ever will sing worthily? It is such as I will describe; for I must dare to speak the truth, when truth is my theme. There abides the very being with which true knowledge is concerned; the colourless, formless, intangible essence, visible only to mind, the pilot of the soul. The divine intelligence, being nurtured upon mind and pure knowledge, and the intelligence of every soul which is capable of receiving the food proper to it, rejoices at beholding reality once more, after so long a time, and gazing upon truth, is replenished and made glad, until the revolution of the world brings her round again to the same place. In the revolution she beholds justice, and temperance, and knowledge absolute, not that to which becoming belongs, nor that which is found, in varying forms, in one or other of those regions which we men call *real*, but real knowledge really present where true being is. And beholding the other true existences in like manner, and feasting upon them, she passes down into the interior of the heavens and returns home; and there the charioteer putting up his horses at the stall, gives them ambrosia to eat and nectar to drink.

Such is the life of the gods; but of other souls, that which follows 248 God best and is likest to him lifts the head of the charioteer into the outer world, and is carried round in the revolution, troubled indeed by the steeds, and with difficulty beholding true being; while another only rises and falls, and sees, and again fails to see by reason of the unruliness of the steeds. The rest of the souls are also longing after the upper world and they all follow, but not being strong enough they are carried round below the surface, plunging, treading on one another, each striving to be first; and there is confusion and perspiration and the extremity of effort; and many of them are lamed or have their wings broken through the ill driving of the charioteers; and all of them after a fruitless toil, not having attained to the mysteries of true being, go away, and feed upon opinion [or appearance]. The reason why the souls exhibit this exceeding eagerness to behold the Plain of Truth is that pasturage is found there, which is suited to the highest part of the soul; and the wing on which the soul soars is nourished with this. And there is a law of Destiny, that the soul which attains any vision of truth in company with a god is preserved from harm until the next period, and if attaining always is always unharmed. But when she is unable to follow, and fails to behold the truth, and through some ill-hap sinks beneath the double load of forgetfulness and vice, and her wings fall from her and she drops to the ground, then the law ordains that this soul shall at her first birth pass, not into any other animal, but only into man; and the soul which has seen most of truth shall be placed in the seed from which a philosopher, or artist, or some musical and loving nature will spring; that which has seen truth in the second degree shall be some righteous king or warrior chief; the soul which is of the third class shall be a politician, or economist, or trader; the fourth shall be a lover of gymnastic toils, or a physician; the fifth shall lead the life of a prophet or hierophant; to the sixth the character of a poet or some other imitative artist will be assigned; to the seventh the life of an artisan or husbandman; to the eighth that of a sophist or demagogue; to the ninth that of a tyrant; — all these are states of probation, in which he who does righteously improves, and he who does unrighteously deteriorates, his lot.

Ten thousand years must elapse before the soul of each one can
249 return to the place from whence she came, for she cannot grow her wings in less, save only the soul of a philosopher, guileless and true, or of a lover, who has been guided by philosophy. And these when the third period comes round, if they have chosen this life three times in succession, have wings given them, and go away at the end of three thousand years. But the others receive judgement when they have completed their first life, and after the judgement they go, some of them to the houses of correction which are under the earth, and are punished; others to some place in heaven whither they are lightly borne by justice, and there they live in a manner worthy of the life which they led here when in the form of men. And in the thousandth year, both arrive at a place where they must draw lots and choose their second life, and they may take any which they please. And now the soul of a man may pass into the life of a beast, or that which has once been a man return again from the beast into human form. But the soul which has never seen the truth will not pass into the human form. For a man must have intelligence by what is called the Idea, a unity gathered together by reason from the many particulars of sense. This is the recollection of those things which our soul once saw while following God — when regardless of that which we now call being

she raised her head up towards the true being. And therefore the mind of the philosopher alone has wings; and this is just, for he is always, according to the measure of his abilities, clinging in recollection to those things in which God abides, and in beholding which He is what He is. And he who employs aright these memories is ever being initiated into perfect mysteries and alone becomes truly perfect. But, as he forgets earthly interests and is rapt in the divine, the vulgar deem him mad, and rebuke him; they do not see that he is inspired.

Thus far I have been speaking of the fourth and last kind of madness, which is imputed to him who, when he sees the beauty of earth, is transported with the recollection of the true beauty; he would like to fly away, but he cannot; he is like a bird fluttering and looking upward and careless of the world below; and he is therefore thought to be mad. And I have shown this of all inspirations to be the noblest and highest and the offspring of the highest to him who has or shares in it, and that he who loves the beautiful is called a lover because he partakes of it. For, as has been already said, every soul of man has in the way of nature beheld true being; this was the condition of her passing into the form of man. But all souls do not 250 easily recall the things of the other world; they may have seen them for a short time only, or they may have been unfortunate in their earthly lot, and, having had their hearts turned to unrighteousness through some corrupting influence, they may have lost the memory of the holy things which once they saw. Few only retain an adequate remembrance of them; and they, when they behold here any image of that other world, are rapt in amazement; but they are ignorant of what this rapture means, because they do not clearly perceive. For there is no radiance in our earthly copies of justice or temperance or those other things which are precious to souls: they are seen through a glass dimly; and there are few who, going to the images, behold in them the realities, and these only with difficulty. But beauty could be seen, brightly shining, by all who were with that happy band, — we philosophers following in the train of Zeus, others in company with other gods; at which time we beheld the beatific vision and were initiated into a mystery which may be truly called most blessed, celebrated by us in our state of innocence, before we had any experience of evils to come, when we were admitted to the sight of apparitions innocent and simple and calm and happy, which we beheld shining in pure light, pure ourselves and not enshrined in that living tomb which we carry about, now that we are imprisoned in the body, like an oyster in his shell. Let me linger over the memory of scenes which have passed away.

But of beauty, I repeat that we saw her there shining in company with the celestial forms; and coming to earth we find her here too, shining in clearness through the clearest aperture of sense. For sight is the most piercing of our bodily senses; though not by that is wisdom seen; her loveliness would have been transporting if there had been a visible image of her, and the other ideas, if they had visible counterparts, would be equally lovely. But this is the privilege of beauty, that being the loveliest she is also the most palpable to sight. Now he who is not newly initiated or who has become corrupted, does not easily rise out of this world to the sight of true beauty in the other, when he contemplates her earthly namesake, and instead of being awed at the sight of her, he is given over to pleasure, and like a brutish beast he rushes on to enjoy and beget; he consorts with wantonness, and is not afraid or ashamed of pursuing pleasure in violation of nature. But he whose initiation is recent, and who has been the spectator of many glories in the other world, is amazed when he sees anyone having a godlike face or form, which is the expression of divine beauty; and at first a shudder runs through him, and again the old awe steals over him; then looking upon the face of his beloved as of a god he reverences him, and if he were not afraid of being thought a downright madman, he would sacrifice to his beloved as to the image of a god; then while he gazes on him there is a sort of reaction, and the shudder passes into an unusual heat and perspiration; for, as he receives the effluence of beauty through the eyes, the wing moistens and he warms. And as he warms, the parts out of which the wing grew, and which had been hitherto closed and rigid, and had prevented the wing from shooting forth, are melted, and as nourishment streams upon him, the lower end of the wing begins to swell and grow from the root upwards; and the growth extends under the whole soul — for once the whole was winged. During this process the whole soul is all in a state of ebullition and effervescence, — which may be compared to the irritation and uneasiness in the gums at the time of cutting teeth, — bubbles up, and has a feeling of uneasiness and tickling; but when in like manner the soul is beginning to grow wings, the beauty of the beloved meets her eye and she receives the sensible warm motion of particles which flow towards her, therefore called emotion (ἵμερος) [*himeros*], and is refreshed and warmed by them, and then she ceases from her pain with joy. But when she is parted from her beloved and her moisture fails, then the orifices of the passage out of which the wing shoots dry up and close, and intercept the germ of the wing; which, being shut up with the emotion, throbbing as with the pulsations of an artery, pricks the aperture which is nearest, until at length the entire soul is pierced and maddened and pained, and at the recollection of beauty is again delighted. And from both of them together the soul is oppressed at the strangeness of her condition, and is in a great strait and excitement, and in her madness can neither sleep by night nor abide in her place by day. And wherever she thinks that she will behold the beautiful one, thither in her desire she runs. And when she has seen him, and bathed herself in the waters of beauty, her constraint is loosened, and she is refreshed, and has no more pangs and pains; and this is the sweetest of all pleasures at the time, and is 252 the reason why the soul of the lover will never forsake his beautiful one, whom he esteems above all; he has forgotten mother and brethren and companions, and he thinks nothing of the neglect and loss of his property; the rules and proprieties of life, on which he formerly prided himself, he now despises, and is ready to sleep like a servant, wherever he is allowed, as near as he can to his desired one, who is the object of his worship, and the physician who can alone assuage the greatness of his pain. And this state, my dear imaginary youth to whom I am talking, is by men called love, and among the gods has a name at which you, in your simplicity, may be inclined to mock; there are two lines in the apocryphal writings of Homer in which the name occurs. One of them is rather outrageous, and not altogether metrical. They are as follows: —

> Mortals call him fluttering love,
> But the immortals call him winged one,
> Because the growing of wings is a necessity to him.

You may believe this, but not unless you like. At any rate the plight of lovers and its cause are such as I have described.

Now the lover who is taken to be the attendant of Zeus is better able to bear the winged god, and can endure a heavier burden; but the attendants and companions of Ares, who made the circuit in his company, when under the influence of love they fancy that they have been at all wronged, are ready to kill and put an end to themselves and their beloved. And he who followed in the train of any other god, while he is unspoiled and the impression lasts, honours and imitates him, as far as he is able; and after the manner of his god he behaves in his intercourse with his beloved and with the rest of the world during the first period of his earthly existence. Every one chooses his love from the ranks of beauty according to his character, and this he makes his god, and fashions and adorns as a sort of image which he is to fall down and worship. The followers of Zeus desire that their beloved should have a soul like him; and therefore they seek out someone of a philosophical and imperial nature, and when they have found him and loved him, they do all they can to confirm such a nature in him, and if they have no experience of such a disposition hitherto, they learn of anyone who can teach them, and themselves follow in the same way. And they have the less difficulty 253 in finding the nature of their own god in themselves, because they

have been compelled to gaze intensely on him; their recollection clings
to him, and they become possessed of him, and receive from him
their character and disposition, so far as man can participate in God.
The qualities of their god they attribute to the beloved, wherefore
they love him all the more, and if, like the Bacchic Nymphs, they
draw inspiration from Zeus, they pour out their own fountain upon
him, wanting to make him as like as possible to their own god. But
those who were the followers of Hera seek a royal love, and when
they have found him they do just the same with him; and in like
manner the followers of Apollo and of every other god, walking in the
ways of their god, seek a love who is to be made like him whom
they serve, and when they have found him, they themselves imitate
their god, and persuade their love to do the same, and educate him
into the manner and nature of the god as far as they each can; for
no feelings of envy or jealousy are entertained by them towards
their beloved, but they do their utmost to create in him the greatest
likeness of themselves and of the god whom they honour. Thus fair
and blissful to the beloved is the desire of the inspired lover, and
the initiation of which I speak into the mysteries of true love, if he
be captured by the lover and their purpose is effected. Now the
beloved is taken captive in the following manner: —

At the beginning of this tale, I divided each soul into three parts
— two having the form of horses and the third being like a charioteer;
the division may remain. I have said that one horse was good, the
other bad, but I have not yet explained in what the goodness or
badness of either consists, and to that I will now proceed. The
right-hand horse is upright and cleanly made; he has a lofty neck and
an aquiline nose; his colour is white, and his eyes dark; he is one who
loves honour with modesty and temperance, and the follower of true
opinion; he needs no touch of the whip, but is guided by word and
admonition only. The other is a crooked, lumbering animal, put together anyhow; he has a short, thick neck; he is flat-faced and of a
dark colour, with grey eyes and blood-red complexion; the mate of
insolence and pride, shag-eared and deaf, hardly yielding to whip
and spur. Now when the charioteer beholds the vision of love, and has
his whole soul warmed through sense, and is full of the prickings and
254 ticklings of desire, the obedient steed, then as always under the government of shame, refrains from leaping on the beloved; but the
other, heedless of the pricks and of the blows of the whip, plunges
and runs away, giving all manner of trouble to his companion and
the charioteer, whom he forces to approach the beloved and to
remember the joys of love. They at first indignantly oppose him and
will not be urged on to do terrible and unlawful deeds; but at last,
when he persists in plaguing them, they yield and agree to do as he

bids them. And now they are at the spot and behold the flashing beauty of the beloved; which when the charioteer sees, his memory is carried to the true beauty, whom he beholds in company with Modesty like an image placed upon a holy pedestal. He sees her, but he is afraid and falls backwards in adoration, and by his fall is compelled to pull back the reins with such violence as to bring both the steeds on their haunches, the one willing and unresisting, the unruly one very unwilling; and when they have gone back a little, the one is overcome with shame and wonder, and his whole soul is bathed in perspiration; the other, when the pain is over which the bridle and the fall had given him, having with difficulty taken breath, is full of wrath and reproaches, which he heaps upon the charioteer and his fellow steed, for want of courage and manhood, declaring that they have been false to their agreement and guilty of desertion. Again they refuse, and again he urges them on, and will scarce yield to their prayer that he would wait until another time. When the appointed hour comes, they make as if they had forgotten, and he reminds them, fighting and neighing and dragging them on, until at length he, on the same thoughts intent, forces them to draw near again. And when they are near he stoops his head and puts up his tail, and takes the bit in his teeth and pulls shamelessly. Then the charioteer is worse off than ever; he falls back like a racer at the barrier, and with a still more violent wrench drags the bit out of the teeth of the wild steed and covers his abusive tongue and jaws with blood, and forces his legs and haunches to the ground and punishes him sorely. And when this has happened several times and the villain has ceased from his wanton way, he is tamed and humbled, and follows the will of the charioteer, and when he sees the beautiful one he is ready to die of fear. And from that time forward the soul of the lover follows the beloved in modesty and holy fear.

And so the beloved who, like a god, has received every true and loyal service from his lover, not in pretence but in reality, being also himself of a nature friendly to his admirer, if in former days he has blushed to own his passion and turned away his lover, because his youthful companions or others slanderously told him that he would be disgraced, now as years advance, at the appointed age and time, is led to receive him into communion. For fate which has ordained that there shall be no friendship among the evil has also ordained that there shall ever be friendship among the good. And the beloved when he has received him into communion and intimacy, is quite amazed at the good will of the lover; he recognizes that the inspired friend is worth all other friends or kinsmen; they have nothing of friendship in them worthy to be compared with his. And when this feeling continues and he is nearer to him and embraces him, in gym-

255

nastic exercises and at other times of meeting, then the fountain of
that stream, which Zeus when he was in love with Ganymede named
Desire, overflows upon the lover, and some enters into his soul, and
some when he is filled flows out again; and as a breeze or an echo
rebounds from the smooth rocks and returns whence it came, so does
the stream of beauty, passing through the eyes which are the win-
dows of the soul, come back to the beautiful one; there arriving and
quickening the passages of the wings, watering them and inclining
them to grow, and filling the soul of the beloved also with love.
And thus he loves, but he knows not what; he does not understand
and cannot explain his own state; he appears to have caught the
infection of blindness from another; the lover is his mirror in whom
he is beholding himself, but he is not aware of this. When he is with
the lover, both cease from their pain, but when he is away then he
longs as he is longed for, and has love's image, love for love [Anteros]
lodging in his breast, which he calls and believes to be not love but
friendship only, and his desire is as the desire of the other, but
weaker; he wants to see him, touch him, kiss, embrace him, and
probably not long afterwards his desire is accomplished. When they
meet, the wanton steed of the lover has a word to say to the charioteer;
256 he would like to have a little pleasure in return for many pains, but
the wanton steed of the beloved says not a word, for he is bursting
with passion which he understands not; — he throws his arms round
the lover and embraces him as his dearest friend; and, when they are
side by side, he is not in a state in which he can refuse the lover
anything, if he ask him; although his fellow steed and the charioteer
oppose him with the arguments of shame and reason. After this
their happiness depends upon their self-control; if the better elements
of the mind which lead to order and philosophy prevail, then they
pass their life here in happiness and harmony — masters of themselves
and orderly — enslaving the vicious and emancipating the virtuous
elements of the soul; and when the end comes, they are light and
winged for flight, having conquered in one of the three heavenly or
truly Olympian victories; nor can human discipline or divine inspiration confer any greater blessing on man than this. If, on the other
hand, they leave philosophy and lead the lower life of ambition, then
probably, after wine or in some other careless hour, the two wanton
animals take the two souls when off their guard and bring them
together, and they accomplish that desire of their hearts which to
the many is bliss; and this having once enjoyed they continue to
enjoy, yet rarely, because they have not the approval of the whole
soul. They too are dear, but not so dear as the others; and it is for
each other that they live, throughout the time of their love and

afterwards. They consider that they have given and taken from each other the most sacred pledges, and they may not break them and fall into enmity. At last they pass out of the body, unwinged, but eager to soar, and thus obtain no mean reward of love and madness. For those who have once begun the heavenward pilgrimage may not go down again to darkness and the journey beneath the earth, but they live in light always; happy companions in their pilgrimage, and when the time comes at which they receive their wings they have the same plumage because of their love.

Thus great are the heavenly blessings which the friendship of a lover will confer upon you, my youth. Whereas the attachment of the non-lover, which is alloyed with a worldly prudence and has worldly and niggardly ways of doling out benefits, will breed in your soul those vulgar qualities which the populace applaud, will send you bowling round the earth during a period of nine thousand years, and leave you a fool in the world below. 257

And thus, dear Eros, I have made and paid my recantation, as well and as fairly as I could; more especially in the matter of the poetical figures which I was compelled to use, because Phaedrus would have them. And now forgive the past and accept the present, and be gracious and merciful to me, and do not in thine anger deprive me of sight, or take from me the art of love which thou hast given me, but grant that I may be yet more esteemed in the eyes of the fair. And if Phaedrus or I myself said anything rude in our first speeches, blame Lysias, who is the father of the brat, and let us have no more of his progeny; bid him study philosophy, like his brother Polemarchus; and then his lover Phaedrus will no longer halt between two opinions, but will dedicate himself wholly to love and to philosophical discourses.

◄§ Here begins the second half of the dialogue, which in a broad sense has as its function the development of the principles implied or stated in the first half, chiefly in the speeches of Socrates. Love and beauty, which have been the most prominent themes of the first part, reappear in the second in muted form. Love is seen as the basis of the relation between teacher and pupil; it is the selfless love of all beautiful souls of which we heard in the *Symposium,* and Socrates' bantering pose of being enamored of the fair Phaedrus is seen more truly as his wish to bring to birth in him the love of truth and the desire for his soul's betterment of which Socrates spoke in the *Apology.* The theme of rhetoric, or the art of speaking and writing, has also been present from the dialogue's beginning, and now becomes more centrally its topic. Rhetoric is divided into the rhetoric of appearance and the rhetoric of truth, the simple rhetoric suited to simple souls and the variegated form suited to the persuasion and teaching of the more complex souls. It is this rhetoric which the dialogue itself clearly exemplifies and which at the end is shown to coalesce with philosophical discussion and the search for truth.

Before leaving the spot beside the river, Socrates offers a final prayer, most apt to the occasion, to which Phaedrus assents. Here is the version made by the translator of the *Rubaiyat:* "O auspicious Pan, and ye other deities of this place, grant me to become beautiful inwardly, and that all my outward goods may prosper my inner soul. Grant that I may esteem wisdom the only riches, and that I may have so much gold as temperance can handsomely carry."

Republic

Persons of the Dialogue

SOCRATES, who is the narrator

GLAUCON	CEPHALUS
ADEIMANTUS	THRASYMACHUS
POLEMARCHUS	CLEITOPHON

and others who are mute auditors

The scene is laid in the house of Cephalus at the Peiraeus; and the whole dialogue is narrated by Socrates the day after it actually took place to persons who are never named.

◄§ Plato's most daring ventures in the arena of social reform, matched by some of his most daring epistemological and ontological flights, are expounded in the *Republic*. There he tells us, almost without regard to possibility, how he believes a city could harmoniously serve the needs of all, how the mind can climb from knowledge of particulars to abstract knowledge, and what to him seem the basic constituents of the universe. While we may not accept his solutions, we cannot but admire the nobility of his aims and salute his splendid intellectual vigor, his mind balanced between the poles of soaring idealism and logical precision of thought.

Now, from their very nature such ideas require wide room for their telling and are all but impossible to compress without serious loss. To achieve the necessary shortening, Books I and II have been replaced by brief summary-analyses and other omitted passages by shorter summaries.

Republic · Book I

◄§ The whole *Republic*, as indicated in the description of the scene, is a reported dialogue, supposedly repeated by Socrates himself on the day following its occurrence; we are probably intended to imagine that the listeners are the persons who constitute, with Socrates, the cast of the *Timaeus* (see our foreword to that dialogue). But in our summaries of the first two books, we shall tell the tale direct:

◄§ A sturdy Socrates still in middle life, companioned by a youth of noble bearing whom at second sight we recognize as Plato's older brother Glaucon, are just heading for home after attending a religious festival at the Peiraeus. The Peiraeus was (and is) the chief port of Athens, distant some six miles from the heart of town. Many wealthy businessmen and industrialists found it a convenient place of residence. Socrates and his young companion are halted and "captured" by Polemarchus, who with a playful show of violence insists that Socrates and his companion come home with him and his friends, dine, and enjoy the pleasures of the evening, among which is mentioned, as a great novelty, a torchlight relay race on horseback. And Polemarchus is clever enough to remember, as special bait for Socrates, the young men of the locale with whom Socrates will be able to converse to his heart's content. Polemarchus prevails and leads the way to the house of his father Cephalus, one of the industrialists just mentioned.

Arriving, Socrates is warmly greeted by his aged host, who "was seated on a cushioned chair, and had a garland on his head, for he had been sacrificing in the court."J Were it not for the weakness of old age, he assures his guest, he would take turn and turn about in arranging conversations with Socrates, for he finds that the decay of the bodily pleasures that accompanies old age is compensated for by an increase in the pleasures of reason and discourse.

"I take great interest in the very old," says Socrates, "for they have traveled and can tell us of a road that we too will one day travel, whether it is rough and difficult or easy and pleasant."[1]

Cephalus in reply presents a miniature "Apology for Old Age," which in a later age was to become the model for Cicero's more elaborate *De Senectute*. According to Cephalus, a man's old age is pretty much what he makes it, an unhappy old age being properly the consequence not of old age but of the character of the man himself. He will, however, admit that a rich man has a certain advantage here; wealth provides many consolations.

Cephalus is about to leave the party for the completion of his sacrifices, but Socrates submits a quiet little question which neverthe-

---

[1] Here, as often in this summary, I have employed paraphrase rather than strict translation. (L)

less contains the germ of all the discussion to come. Socrates asks Cephalus what he would regard as the greatest consolation he has enjoyed from his wealth. "As we grow older, Socrates," Cephalus replies, "the threats of punishment in the next world for wrongs done in this, once matter for jest, take on a fearsome shape. We ask, 'How if they be true?' and the man who is conscious of having done many unjust deeds starts often from his sleep, like a frightened child in the dark, and lives ever in fear and misboding. It is here that in the hands of a good man wealth can avail most." Cephalus puts it thus: "And the great blessing of riches . . . is that he [the rich man] has had no occasion to deceive or to defraud others, even without intention; and that when he departs to the world below he is not in any apprehension about offerings due to the gods or debts which he owes to men."ᴶ [331b]

"Excellent, Cephalus," says Socrates, "but paying one's debts to gods and men and telling the truth — are these actions justice pure and simple, always and everywhere? Or are there times and occasions when to follow them would be the exact opposite? As for example, would it be just to restore borrowed weapons to a friend when that friend has run roaring mad and demands them as his just due? Paying debts and telling the truth is not a definition of justice."

At this point Cephalus returns to his sacrificing, bequeathing the argument, as is jestingly said, to his son and heir Polemarchus.

We get now a kind of logical game comparable to that played by Socrates with Euthyphro in the dialogue of that name, and with other victims in other Socratic dialogues. Here Polemarchus undertakes to defend the questionable definition by appealing to the authority of the poet Simonides, a poet remembered today chiefly for the massive brevity and pathos of his epitaph on the 300 Spartans who fell at Thermopylae. In appealing to Simonides, Polemarchus was following the Greek custom of his day, by which the major poets — Homer, Hesiod, and others — were often treated as authorities in the domain of morals. He cites Simonides as declaring it just to pay one's debts, and is led to maintain that justice is repaying good to friends and evil to enemies. The result of the unequal combat between the novice Polemarchus and the master Socrates can readily be anticipated. By adroit maneuvers, trading on the ambiguities of language, Socrates soon reduces Polemarchus' definition to hilarious absurdity.

But at the end of the discussion Socrates gives the argument a noble turn, foreshadowing things to come: To say that justice approves and requires us to harm our enemies involves a contradiction comparable to asserting that heat cools. For as Polemarchus has conceded, justice presupposes goodness, and goodness is by its very nature incapable of harming any man.

No, Socrates concludes, it was not Simonides who fathered this definition; it must have been some rich tyrant (and he names some, Xerxes among others) who confused wealth with power. Our definition has failed. Whither shall we turn?

The sophist Thrasymachus, who had only with great difficulty been restrained from interrupting the discussion, now finds an opening. Disgusted with what he regards as childish drivel, he offers to present (cash prior to delivery) a definition of justice better than any yet heard: "I proclaim that justice is nothing else than the interest of the stronger."ᴶ This proclamation, as will later appear, is of the greatest negative importance to the argument. It constitutes in fact the complete antithesis to the ethical import of Plato's book.

Pressed by Socrates for clarification of his formula, Thrasymachus explains that every state, whether tyranny, democracy, or aristocracy, has a ruling class, which is "the stronger," and this class legislates always with an eye to its own "interest." To obey the laws and ordinances of one's own state is held to be just, to disobey them unlawful and unjust.

It follows that to be just is to serve the interest of the ruling class, i.e., to be their dupes, for there is no question here of open-eyed mutual amity. On this view, moral virtues, as we conceive them, vanish altogether or sink to a level of unimportance. Their place is taken by a crude form of what was later to become Nietzsche's "master morality"; there is abundant evidence that Nietzsche made early acquaintance with this passage and with a more extensive similar passage in the *Gorgias,* another Platonic dialogue (see the appendix to Dodd's edition of the *Gorgias*). This anti-moral doctrine is expounded by Thrasymachus (343e), who stuns the reader with his cynical conception of human nature and his willingness to accept on any terms the fruits of fraud and force. One begins to see more clearly in the light of negation what Plato will not sponsor in his remodeled state.

The remainder of Book I is a blow-by-blow report of the bout between Socrates and the sophist, interesting in itself but, as we shall soon see, not of major importance to the argument because Socrates will not build upon the conclusions therein reached.

And so the first book ends, like so many of the earlier Socratic dialogues (e.g., *Euthyphro*), with a confession of ignorance. Socrates is discontented with his debater's victory over Thrasymachus. Like a gourmand at a feast, he says, he has snatched greedily at every dish and has left no time for the full relish of any. Seeking a definition of justice, he has allowed himself to wander into the question of whether justice is virtue or vice, wisdom or folly. Result of the whole discussion: "That I [Socrates] know nothing at all."ᴶ

Republic · Book II

✑ Plato's brother Glaucon is also dissatisfied. He wishes to know what the nature of justice and injustice is apart from "their rewards and results, . . . to know what they are in themselves, and how they inwardly work in the soul."ᴶ And he wishes Socrates to show justice as belonging to that class of good things which we value not merely for themselves, e.g., harmless pleasure, and not merely for their consequences, e.g., gymnastics or going to the doctor, but for both, as for example intelligence and health. Thrasymachus gave up too soon, under the spell of the snake charmer Socrates. There is much more to be said in favor of the popular view that puts justice in the class of "goods which are to be pursued for the sake of rewards and of reputation, but in themselves [are] disagreeable and rather to be avoided."ᴶ

Accordingly, with Socrates' hearty consent, Glaucon will bring back to life the argument of Thrasymachus, reinforced by fresh evidence in behalf of injustice. After this shall have been duly considered, Socrates is besought to make a definitive refutation.

Glaucon will marshal his defense of injustice under three heads, as follows:

1. *Origin and nature of justice.* Justice arose when men discovered that being free to wrong others and being, in turn, liable to be wronged by others, was not in their interest; for only the few who were strong were able to benefit. Hence a compromise was sought and found: ". . . they began to establish laws and mutual covenants. And that which was ordained by law was termed by them lawful and just." Thus justice appears as a midpoint "between the best of all, which is to do injustice and not be punished, and the worst of all, which is to suffer injustice without the power of retaliation."ᴶ (No student of political theory will fail to recognize that Socrates is here alluding to what in modern parlance is called the "social contract.")

2. *Justice is never voluntary.* Glaucon now appeals to the experience of his auditors, through the medium of a tale that reminds one of the Arabian Nights, about a shepherd Gyges, a Lydian, who finds a magic ring that confers invisibility upon its owner. Thus equipped, he readily contrives to seduce the queen, and with her aid to kill the king and take over the kingdom. Now imagine yourself or any man in possession of such a ring. Could the just man remain just, or would the just and the unjust man collide on their way to commit the same crime?

3. *The unjust life is best.* The unjust man has shown his good sense in choosing injustice as his way of life. Seeming justice is a valuable asset to the unjust man but only its semblance is called for. Glaucon continues to contrast the happy life of the clever wrongdoer with the miserable condition of the morally good man. The climax of

his speech is reached in the two contrasting pictures, one showing the perfectly unjust man who nevertheless contrives to appear perfectly just. Set this picture beside that of its converse, the perfectly just man who appears perfectly unjust, and what do we see? We see the unjust man honored and admired, a veritable pillar of society; while his opposite, the inwardly just man, as the eulogists of injustice will tell you, will enjoy none of these advantages. On the contrary, he

361 will be scourged, racked, bound — will have his eyes burnt out; and at last, after suffering every kind of evil, he will be impaled: then he
362 will understand that he ought to seem only, and not to be, just; the words of Aeschylus may be more truly spoken of the unjust than the just. For the unjust, they will say, is in fact pursuing a reality; he does not live with a view to appearance — he wants to be really unjust and not to seem only: —

> 'His mind has a soil deep and fertile,
> Out of which spring his prudent counsels.'

In the first place, he is thought just, and therefore bears rule in the city; he can marry whom he will, and give in marriage to whom he will; also he can trade and deal where he likes, and always to his own advantage, because he has no misgivings about injustice; and at every contest, whether in public or in private, he gets the better of his antagonists, and gains at their expense, and is rich, and out of his gains he can benefit his friends, and harm his enemies; moreover, he can offer sacrifices, and dedicate gifts to the gods abundantly and magnificently, and can honour the gods or any man whom he wants to honour in a far better style than the just, and therefore he is likely to be dearer than they are to the gods. And thus, Socrates, they say that a better life is provided, by gods and men alike, for the unjust than for the just.

⌦ Glaucon has hardly finished his speech when his brother Adeimantus takes up the strain. In part, he will supplement the points made by Glaucon but much is new, and all bears the mark of integral conviction salted here and there with keen satire. "The Anatomy of Hypocrisy" might be its title. We are asked to consider the praises of justice that fathers utter in the presence of their sons and to note that what is getting praised is not justice but only the results of being just or thought just, which include the awards and prizes of which Glaucon spoke. And this outward shell of justice replaces religion or corrupts it. The belief arises that the gods shower blessings upon the heads of the just — "tickets to bliss,"[1] admitting them to a sensual paradise of perpetual intoxication — and for the unjust a "ticket to

---

[1] This vividly amusing terminology reached me from A. W. H. Adkins' *Merit and Responsibility* (Oxford: Clarendon Press, 1960), p. 147. (L)

mud," requiring the bearer to be immersed in a slough in Hades and to carry water in a sieve. But let not the wicked despair, if only they are rich:

And mendicant prophets go to rich men's doors and persuade them that they [the prophets] have a power committed to them by the gods of making an atonement for a man's own or his ancestor's sins by sacrifices or charms, with rejoicings and feasts; and they offer their services in harming an enemy, whether just or unjust, at a small cost; with magic arts and incantations binding heaven, as they say, to execute their will.

364

◄§ Gathering energy as it flows along, the speech of Adeimantus reaches its climax in an impassioned appeal to Socrates, the man who has given his life to such inquiry, to do what no one from the age of the heroes up to our own time has done: to define and to evaluate justice and injustice respectively and to show that although, like sight or hearing, justice is valuable for its results, it is far more so in its own right. You must, then, he urges "not only prove to us that justice is better than injustice, but show what they either of them do to the possessor of them, which makes the one to be a good and the other an evil, whether seen or unseen by gods and men."J

Socrates congratulates the two "godlike" sons of Ariston for their staunch resistance to the current view that injustice is superior to justice, and this in spite of their acquaintance with all the evidence to the contrary displayed in their respective speeches. As to himself, he is discouraged by the failure of his arguments against Thrasymachus to gain credence.

But just on the edge of total defeat, the moralist within the man Socrates steps forth and takes command. And the orders are "Forward in full strength," for it would be a great impiety to stand idly by when justice is under attack, and not defend her with all our might, so long as our power of speech remains.

The aid that Socrates will render takes the form of a clarifying shift in perspective. He is about to turn our gaze away for a while from individuals to a consideration of a whole society ("state," "city," and "society," in our usage, will function here as interchangeable terms), but he will not forget the principle he will later assert: the character of a state is determined by the character of the individuals who comprise it (Bk. VIII, 544d). Neither social group nor social unit will be forgotten, but at this point Plato has chosen to effect a transition to a consideration of the group.

The bridge by which the transition is effected is at once an analogy and a parable. Socrates asks us to imagine a number of persons whose visual powers, like his own mental vision, are not very great (*sic*). We are further to imagine that these people have been asked to read certain small letters some distance away. And now someone discovers that the selfsame letters are written elsewhere on a larger scale. What a help from Hermes, god of good fortune! Applied to the search for justice, the analogy suggests that our failure to read the small letters that spell justice in the individual, can be redeemed by the opportunity of reading the same "message" so much more legibly written across the face of society. And Socrates adds the plausible conviction, smacking of the modern "genetic method," that the spectacle of a city just coming into being in our discourse, should make the discovery of justice and injustice an easier quest.

What then is this thing called a city and what its contribution to the life of man? Socrates gives us a direct and unambiguous answer, a functional definition which, freely rendered, runs as follows: All men have many needs and wants which no man, taken individually, can satisfy. Hence men are drawn together into a relation of mutual aid, thereby creating the cooperative community that we name "city," or state.

As his point of departure Socrates takes the very smallest association of cooperants that could provide in sufficient measure the basic human needs of food, shelter, clothing, and the like, thus calling into being a farmer, a carpenter, a weaver, and a shoemaker. These men would soon discover the wisdom of the division of labor which Plato, in contrast to Adam Smith, bases upon the unlikenesses between one man and another. Under this system each worker must master his one and only productive art or craft. The consistent application of this principle will greatly increase the number of workers along with the number of occupations, for it will not permit the farmer, for example, to make his own plow or hoe. Then, too, by a further extension, the principle is applicable to the city as a whole and justifies imports and gives rise to the class of importers and exporters, which again entails shippers and skippers, a marketplace, currency, and retail shopkeepers who, in well-regulated cities, will be those whose physical infirmity unfits them for other tasks. And finally there are those with strong backs and weak minds, who sell the use of their strength for wages and serve to fill out the population of the state.

Has our city at last reached its full growth? Where then within it can we find justice and injustice? Adeimantus replies, "I cannot say unless it be in some need that the various constituents have of one another."

This shrewd surmise Socrates acknowledges and to it he will return, but first of all he wishes to depict the way of life of the citizens whom we have called into being:

372 Will they not work at the production of corn, and wine, and clothes, and shoes? . . . In summer they will . . . work stripped and barefoot. . . . They will feed on barleymeal and flour of wheat, . . . making noble cakes and loaves; these they will serve up on a mat of reeds or on clean leaves, themselves reclining the while upon beds strewn with yew or myrtle. And they and their children will feast,

drinking of the wine which they have made, wearing garlands on their heads, and hymning the praises of the gods, in happy converse with one another. And they will take care that their families do not exceed their means; having an eye to poverty or war.

◄§ This happy and idyllic scene, with its romantic nostalgia for a golden age, was later to appeal mightily to Rousseau and his followers. Not so, however, to the luxury-loving Glaucon, to whom such a diet seems fit only for pigs.

Half-reluctantly Socrates consents to Glaucon's demand for a more sophisticated city in which one eats in a civilized fashion, "dining off tables, and having sauces and sweets in the modern style."ᴶ This would entail enlarging the number of occupations in the city to include the luxury trades. There will be "sofas, and tables, . . . dainties, and perfumes, and incense, and courtezans, and cakes, . . . [and] the arts of the painter and the embroiderer will have to be set in motion, and gold and ivory . . . procured."ᴶ This, says Socrates, is a city at fever heat; but, from the point of view of our search, that is an advantage, "for by extending our inquiry to such a State we shall be more likely to see how political justice and injustice originate."ᴶ

This enlargement of population, he continues, inevitably will require us to extend our borders.

A slice of our neighbors' land will be wanted by us for pasture and tillage, and they will want a slice of ours, if like ourselves they exceed the limit of necessity and give themselves up to the unlimited accumulation of wealth. . . . And so we shall go to war, Glaucon. Shall we not? . . . And our State must once more enlarge; and this time the enlargement will be nothing short of a whole army, which will have to go out and fight with the invaders for all that we have. 373

◄§ Glaucon is mildly shocked: "What, can't our citizens defend themselves?" No, replies Socrates, if our earlier conclusion holds: that it is impossible for one man to practice successfully more than one art. War is an art, a very important and very difficult art, requiring native aptitude in addition to long preparation. "How then will he who takes up a shield [for the first time] or other implement of war become a good fighter all in a day?"ᴶ

Socrates, accordingly, proposes as a duty to our city, that we give serious attention to these "guardians," as they will continue to be called, to their selection and training for the vital function that they will perform. In short we are about to hear, through the channel of Socrates, Plato's educational ideals and techniques as applied to the soldier citizens of the city he is gradually constructing. Later, in Books V, VI, and VII, Plato will present his conception of an education higher still, a philosophical curriculum, reserved for the small number of guardians *par excellence* who alone administer the constitution and make the decisions of state.

What then are the qualities of a good guardian? Socrates suggests that there is a striking correspondence between a well-bred dog and a well-bred man of mettle: keen perception, speed in pursuit, and strength for use in close combat, are qualities common to both. We want our guardians to be brave, hence they must be high-spirited.

Here a difficulty is encountered, a dilemma: If the guardians are high-spirited and courageous, how can they fail to be savage toward each other and toward us? And if our guardians lack spirit and courage, how will they be able to defend our city from savage foes?

The answer comes from the very same creature that inspired the original comparison, for the dog shows that it is possible to combine in one and the same animate being the contrary qualities of gentleness to friends and fierceness to enemies. And in a lighter key Socrates attributes a touch of philosophy, that our guardians should share, to this creature who barks at the unknown and takes "known" and "unknown" as his only criterion for distinguishing friend from foe.

The kind of human material out of which the guardians are to be formed has been specified. Socrates turns now to the problem of how they should be reared and educated. Once again he reminds us of the central object of our quest, *viz.* the origin of justice and injustice in the state, and again defers our hope. Let us for a page or two "listen in."

Socrates is speaking:

376 Come then, and let us pass a leisure hour in story-telling, and our story shall be the education of our heroes.

By all means.

And what shall be their education? It would be hard, I think, to find a better than the traditional system, which has two divisions, gymnastic for the body, and music for the soul.

True.

Presumably we shall begin education with music, before gymnastic can begin.

By all means.

And when you speak of music, do you include literature or not?

I do.

And literature may be either true or false?

Yes.

377 Both have a part to play in education but we must begin with the false?

I do not understand your meaning, he said.

You know, I said, that we begin by telling children stories which, though not wholly destitute of truth, are in the main fictitious; and these stories are told them when they are not of an age for gymnastics.

Very true.

That was my meaning when I said that we must teach music before gymnastics.

Quite right, he said.

You know also that the beginning is the most important part of any work, especially in the case of a young and tender thing; for that is the time at which the character is being formed and the desired impression is more readily taken.

Quite true.

And shall we just carelessly allow children to hear any casual tales which may be devised by casual persons, and to receive into their minds ideas for the most part the very opposite of those which we shall wish them to have when they are grown up?

We cannot.

Then the first thing will be to establish a censorship of the writers of fiction, and let the censors receive any tale of fiction which is good, and reject the bad; and we will persuade mothers and nurses to tell their children the authorized ones only. Let them fashion the mind with such tales, even more fondly than they mould the body with their hands; but most of those which are now in use must be discarded.

Of what tales are you speaking? he said.

You may find a model of the lesser in the greater, I said; for they must both be of the same type, and the same spirit ought to be found in both of them.

Very likely, he replied; but I do not as yet know what you would term the greater.

Those, I said, which are narrated by Homer and Hesiod, and the rest of the poets, who have ever been the great story-tellers of mankind.

But which stories do you mean, he said; and what fault do you find with them?

A fault which is fundamental and most serious, I said; the fault of saying what is false, and doing so for no good purpose.

But when is this fault committed?

Whenever an erroneous representation is made of the nature of gods and heroes, — as when a painter paints a picture not having the shadow of a likeness to his subject.

Yes, he said, that sort of thing is certainly very blameable; but what are the stories which you mean?

First of all, I said, there was that greatest of all falsehoods on great subjects, which the misguided poet told about Uranus, — I mean what Hesiod says that Uranus did, and how Cronus retaliated on him.[1] The doings of Cronus, and the sufferings which in turn his son inflicted upon him, even if they were true, ought certainly

378

[1] According to Hesiod (*Theogony* 154 ff., 459 ff.) Uranus confined his children beneath the earth, and his son Cronus emasculated and dethroned him. Cronus devoured all of his sons except Zeus, and Zeus overcame and dethroned Cronus. (L)

not to be lightly told to young and thoughtless persons; if possible, they had better be buried in silence. But if there is an absolute necessity for their mention, a chosen few might hear them in a mystery, and they should sacrifice not a common [Eleusinian] pig,[1] but some huge and unprocurable victim, so that the number of the hearers may be very few indeed.

Why, yes, said he, those stories are extremely objectionable.

Yes, Adeimantus, they are stories not to be repeated in our State; the young man should not be told that in committing the worst of crimes he is far from doing anything outrageous; and that even if he chastises in savage fashion his father when he does wrong, he will only be following the example of the first and greatest among the gods.

I entirely agree with you, he said; in my opinion those stories are quite unfit to be repeated.

⊷⊱ Returning to our summary: These deplorable tales of divine misdoings, Socrates affirms, must not be given entrance to our State. To call them allegories is of no avail, since the very young cannot recognize such subtle distinctions. We are not poets ourselves but it is our task to indicate the limits within which the poets may properly work when treating of things divine.

Accordingly, by means of a little analysis of the concepts involved (e.g., good, evil, god), Socrates establishes the two norms, canons, or basic principles of theology, as follows:

1. *God is good and the author of good only.* Examples of the mistaken view of God are cited from Homer, e.g., the two jars of Zeus, one of goods, one of evils (*Iliad* XXIV, 527–9).

2. *The divine nature is incapable of change or deceit.* God is no juggling magician who palters with us in deceitful shapes, nor does he send lying dreams; we must condemn as slander Homer's account of the "false dream" sent to Agamemnon by Zeus himself (*Iliad* II, 1 ff.).

And with these norms firmly established, the long second book draws to a close.

---

[1] Pigs were sacrificed as part of the ritual celebration of the Eleusinian mysteries. (L)

Republic · Book III

From this point onward, with minor exceptions, the text of the *Republic* will be presented. It is to be remembered that Socrates himself is recounting the conversation; it is he who says, "I said." As the third book opens, Adeimantus is replying.

Then as far as the gods are concerned, I said, such tales are **386** to be told, and such others are not to be told to our disciples from their youth upwards, if we mean them to honour the gods and their parents, and to value friendship with one another.

Yes; and I think that our principles are right, he said.

But if they are to be courageous, must they not learn other lessons besides these, and lessons of such a kind as will take away the fear of death? Can any man be courageous who has the fear of death in him?

Certainly not, he said.

And can he be fearless of death, or will he chose death in battle rather than defeat and slavery, who believes the world below to be real and terrible?

Impossible.

Then we must assume a control over the narrators of this class of tales as well as over the others, and beg them not simply to revile, but rather to commend the world below, intimating to them that their descriptions are untrue, and will do harm to our future warriors.

That will be our duty, he said.

Then, I said, we shall have to obliterate many obnoxious passages, beginning with the verses.

'I would rather be a serf on the land of a poor and portionless man than rule over all the dead who have come to nought'.

We must also expunge the verse, which tells us how Pluto feared

'Lest the mansions grim and squalid which the gods abhor should be seen both of mortals and immortals' . . . .

Again: —

'The soul flying from the limbs had gone to Hades, lamenting her fate, leaving manhood and youth.' . . .

And we must beg Homer and the other poets not to be angry if **387** we strike out these and similar passages, not because they are

195

unpoetical, or unattractive to the popular ear, but because the greater
the poetical charm of them, the less are they meet for the ears of
boys and men who are meant to be free, and who should fear slavery
more than death.

Undoubtedly.

Also we shall have to reject all the terrible and appalling names
which describe the world below — Cocytus and Styx, ghosts under
the earth, and sapless shades, and any similar words of which the
very mention causes a shudder to pass through the inmost soul of
him who hears them. I do not say that these horrible stories may
not have a use of some kind; but there is a danger that our guardians
may be rendered too excitable and effeminate by them.

There is a real danger, he said.

Then we must have no more of them.

True.

Our poets must sing in another and a nobler strain.

Clearly.

And shall we proceed to get rid of the weepings and wailings of
famous men?

They will go with the rest.

But shall we be right in getting rid of them? Reflect: our principle
is that the good man will not consider death terrible to any other
good man who is his comrade.

Yes; that is our principle.

And therefore he will not sorrow for his departed friend as though
he had suffered anything terrible?

He will not.

Another thing which we should say of him is that he is the most
sufficient for himself and his own happiness, and therefore is least
in need of other men.

True, he said.

And for this reason the loss of a son or brother, or any deprivation
of fortune, is to him of all men least terrible.

Assuredly.

And therefore he will be least likely to lament, and will bear
with the greatest equanimity any misfortune of this sort which may
befall him.

Yes, he will feel such a misfortune far less than another.

Then we shall be right in getting rid of the lamentations of famous
388 men, and making them over to women (and not even to women
who are good for anything), or to men of a baser sort, that those
who are being educated by us to be the defenders of their country
may scorn to do the like.

That will be very right.

Then we will once more entreat Homer and the other poets not to depict Achilles, who is the son of a goddess, first lying on his side, then on his back, and then on his face; then starting up and sailing in a frenzy along the shores of the barren sea; now taking the sooty ashes in both hands and pouring them over his head, or weeping and wailing in the various modes which Homer has delineated . . . . But if he must introduce the gods, at any rate let him not dare so completely to misrepresent the greatest of the gods, as to make him say —

'O heavens! with my eyes verily I behold a dear friend of mine chased round and round the city, and my heart is sorrowful.' . . .

For if, my dear Adeimantus, our young men seriously listen to such unworthy representations of the gods, instead of laughing at them as they ought, hardly will any of them deem that he himself, being but a man, can be dishonoured by similar actions; neither will he rebuke any inclination which may arise in his mind to say and do the like. And instead of having any shame or endurance, he will be always whining and lamenting on slight occasions.

Yes, he said, that is most true.

Yes, I replied; but that surely is what ought not to be, as the argument has just proved to us; and by that proof we must abide until it is disproved by a better.

It ought not to be.

Neither ought our guardians to be given to laughter. For a fit of laughter which has been indulged to excess almost always demands a violent reaction.

So I believe.

Then persons of worth, even if only mortal men, must not be represented as overcome by laughter, and still less must such a representation of the gods be allowed.

Still less of the gods, as you say, he replied. . . .   389

Again, truth should be highly valued; if we were right in saying that falsehood is useless to the gods, and useful only as a medicine to men, then the use of such medicines should be restricted to physicians; private individuals have no business with them.

Clearly not, he said.

Then if anyone at all is to have the privilege of lying, the rulers of the State should be the persons; and they, in their dealings either with enemies or with their own citizens, may be allowed to lie for the public good. But nobody else should meddle with anything of the kind; and although the rulers have this privilege, for a private man to lie to them in return is to be deemed a more heinous fault than for the patient or the pupil of a gymnasium not to speak the truth about his own bodily illnesses to the physician or to the trainer, or for a sailor not to tell the captain what is happening about the ship and the rest of the crew, and how things are going with himself or his fellow sailors.

Most true, he said.

If, then, the ruler catches in a lie anybody beside himself in the State,

> 'Any of the craftsmen, whether he be priest or physician or carpenter',

he will punish him for introducing a practice which is equally subversive and destructive of ship or State.

Most certainly, he said, if our talk about the State is ever translated into action.

In the next place our youth must be temperate?

Certainly.

Are not the chief elements of temperance, speaking generally, obedience to commanders and command of oneself in the pleasures of eating and drinking, and of sexual relations?

True.

Then we shall approve such language as that of Diomede in Homer,

> 'Friend, sit still and obey my word',

and the verses which follow,

> 'The Greeks marched breathing prowess,
> . . . in silent awe of their leaders',

and other sentiments of the same kind.

We shall.

What of this line,

> 'O heavy with wine, who hast the eyes of a dog and the heart of a stag'

390 and of the words which follow? Would you say that these, or any similar impertinences which private individuals are supposed to address to their rulers, whether in verse or prose, are well or ill spoken?

They are ill spoken.

They may very possibly afford some amusement, but they do not conduce to temperance. And therefore they are likely to do harm to our young men — you would agree with me there?

Yes.

And then, again, to make the wisest of men say that nothing in his opinion is more glorious than

> 'When the tables are full of bread and meat, and the cup-bearer carries round wine which he draws from the bowl and pours into the cups';

is it fit or conducive to self-control for a young man to hear such words? Or the verse

> 'The saddest of fates is to die and meet destiny from hunger'?

What would you say again to the tale of Zeus, who, while other gods and men were asleep and he the only person awake, lay devising plans, but forgot them all in a moment through his lust, and was so completely overcome at the sight of Hera that he would not even go into the hut, but wanted to lie with her on the ground, declaring that he had never been in such a state of rapture before, even when they first used to meet one another

> 'Without the knowledge of their parents',

or that other tale of how Hephaestus, because of similar goings-on, cast a chain around Ares and Aphrodite? . . .

Socrates acknowledges, however, that even in Homer there are examples of a nobler sort, for example, the words of Odysseus:

> He smote his breast, and thus reproached his heart,
> Endure, my heart; far worse hast thou endured![J]

Such words are fully suitable for our youth to hear, but they are in the minority.

The list of deplorable actions falsely attributed to the gods and to the heroes akin to the gods continues in full flow, greed and bribery heading the list. Socrates proposes that the poets be ordered to choose one or the other of these two contradictory statements: (1) the tales they have told of the sons of the gods are false, or (2) if the tales they have told are true, then those of whom the tales were told were not the sons of gods.

We have now, Socrates remarks, indicated the kind of tale that can truly be told of gods, daemons, and heroes. Only man remains. And here arises a subtle logical difficulty. Should we undertake to describe the tales to be told of men, we would soon find ourselves needing to speak of justice and injustice in their relation to happiness and misery, and in so doing we would be prejudging the issue of our whole inquiry.

Accordingly, Socrates announces a transition. Thus far he has been dealing with the contents only of the tales pre- or proscribed for the guardians-to-be, i.e., with what "the fable teaches," and has told us nothing about their style or form. Socrates says:

394   I will ask you to remember also what I began by saying, that we had done with the subject and might proceed to the style.

Yes, I remember.

In saying this, I intended to imply that we must come to an understanding about the mimetic art, — whether the poets, in narrating their stories, are to be allowed by us to imitate, and if so, whether in whole or in part, and if the latter, in what parts; or should all imitation be prohibited?

You mean, I suspect, to ask whether tragedy and comedy shall be admitted into our State?

Perhaps, I said; but there may be more than this in question: I really do not know as yet, but whither the argument may blow, thither we go.

And go we will, he said.

Then, Adeimantus, let me ask you to consider whether our guardians should or should not be fond of imitation; or rather, has not this question been decided by the rule already laid down that one man can only do one thing well, and not many; and that one who grasps at many will altogether fail of gaining much reputation in any?

Certainly.

And this is equally true of imitation; no one man can imitate many things as well as he would imitate a single one?

He cannot.

395   Then the same person will hardly be able to play a serious part in life, and at the same time to be an imitator and imitate many other parts as well; for even when two species of imitation are nearly allied, the same persons cannot succeed in both, as, for example, the writers of tragedy and comedy — did you not just now call them imitations?

Yes, I did; and you are right in thinking that the same persons cannot succeed in both.

Any more than they can be rhapsodists and actors at once?

True.

Neither do comic and tragic writers employ the same actors; yet all these things are imitations.

They are so.

And human nature, Adeimantus, appears to have been coined into yet smaller pieces, and to be as incapable of imitating many things well, as of performing well the actions of which the imitations are copies.

Quite true, he replied.

If then we adhere to our original notion and bear in mind that our

guardians, released from every other business, are to dedicate themselves wholly to the maintenance of the freedom of the State, making
this their craft and engaging in no work which does not bear on this
end, then they ought not to practise or even imitate anything else;
if they imitate at all, they should imitate from youth upward only
those characters which are suitable to their profession — the courageous, temperate, holy, free, and the like; but they should not depict
or be skilful at imitating any kind of illiberality or baseness, lest the
fruit of imitation should be reality. Did you never observe how
imitations, beginning in early youth and continuing far into life, at
length grow into habits and become a second nature, affecting body,
voice, and mind?

Yes, certainly, he said.

Then, I said, we will not allow those for whom we profess a care
and of whom we say that they ought to be good men, to imitate a
woman, whether young or old, quarrelling with her husband, or striving and vaunting against the gods in conceit of her happiness, or
when she is in affliction, or sorrow, or weeping; and certainly not one
who is in sickness, love, or labour.

Very right, he said.

Neither must they represent slaves, male or female, performing the
offices of slaves?

They must not.

And surely not bad men, whether cowards or any others, who do
the reverse of what we have just been prescribing, who scold or
mock or revile one another in drink or out of drink, or who in any
other manner sin against themselves and their neighbours in word
or deed, as the manner of such is. Neither should they be trained to
imitate the action or speech of madmen; they must be able to recognize madness and vice in man or woman, but none of these things is
to be practised or imitated.

Very true, he replied.

Neither may they imitate smiths or other artificers, or oarsmen,
or boatswains, or the like?

How can they, he said, when they are not allowed to apply their
minds to the callings of any of these?

Nor may they imitate the neighing of horses, the bellowing of
bulls, the murmur of rivers and roll of the ocean, thunder, and all
that sort of thing?

Nay, he said, if madness be forbidden, neither may they copy the
behaviour of madmen.

You mean, I said, if I understand you aright, that there is one sort
of narrative style which is likely to be employed by an upright and

good man when he has anything to say, and another sort, very unlike it, which will be preferred by a man of an opposite character and education.

And which are these two sorts? he asked.

As for the man of orderly life, I answered, when the time comes to describe some saying or action of another good man, — I think he will be willing to personate him, and will not be ashamed of this sort of imitation; he will be most ready to play the part of the good man when he is acting firmly and wisely; less often and in a less degree when he is overtaken by illness or love or drink, or has met with any other disaster. But when he comes to a character which is unworthy of him, he will not seriously assume the likeness of his inferior, and will do so, if at all, for a moment only when he is performing some good action; at other times he will be ashamed, both because he is not trained in imitation of such characters, and because he disdains to fashion and frame himself after the baser models; he feels the employment of such an art, unless in jest, to be beneath him.

So I should expect, he replied.

Then he will adopt a mode of narration such as we have illustrated out of Homer, that is to say, his style will be both imitative and narrative; but there will be, in a long story, only a small proportion of the former. Do you agree?

397   Certainly, he said; that is the model which such a speaker must necessarily take.

But there is another sort of character who will narrate anything, and, the worse he is, the more unscrupulous he will be; nothing will be too bad for him: and he will be ready to imitate anything, in right good earnest, and before a large company. As I was just now saying, he will attempt to represent the roll of thunder, the noise of wind and hail, or the creaking of wheels, and pulleys, and the various sounds of flutes, pipes, trumpets, and all sorts of instruments: he will bark like a dog, bleat like a sheep, or crow like a cock; his entire art will consist in imitation of voice and gesture, or will be but slightly blended with narration.

That, he said, will be his mode of speaking.

These, then, are the two kinds of style I had in mind.

Yes.

And you would agree with me in saying that one of them is simple and has but slight changes; and that if an author expresses this style in fitting harmony and rhythm, he will find himself, if he does his work well, keeping pretty much within the limits of a single harmony (for the changes are not great), and in like manner he will make a similar choice of rhythm?

That is quite true, he said.

Whereas the other requires all sorts of harmonies and all sorts of rhythms if the music and the style are to correspond, because the style has all sorts of changes.

That is also perfectly true, he replied.

And do not the two styles, or the mixture of the two, comprehend all poetry and every form of expression in words? No one can say anything except in one or other of them or in both together.

They include all, he said.

And shall we receive into our State all the three styles, or one only of the two unmixed styles? or would you include the mixed?

I should prefer only to admit the pure imitator of virtue.

Yes, I said, Adeimantus; and yet the mixed style is also charming: and indeed the opposite style to that chosen by you is by far the most popular with children and their attendants, and with the masses.

I do not deny it.

But I suppose you would argue that such a style is unsuitable to our State, in which human nature is not twofold or manifold, for one man plays one part only?

Yes; quite unsuitable.

And this is the reason why in our State, and in our State only, we shall find a shoemaker to be a shoemaker and not a pilot also, and a husbandman to be a husbandman and not a dicast also, and a soldier a soldier and not a trader also, and the same throughout?

True, he said.

And therefore when any one of these pantomimic gentlemen, 398 who are so clever that they can imitate anything, comes to us and makes a proposal to exhibit himself and his poetry, we will fall down and worship him as a sacred, marvellous and delightful being; but we must also inform him that in our State such as he are not permitted to exist; the law will not allow them. And so when we have anointed him with myrrh, and set a garland of wool upon his head, we shall send him away to another city. For we mean to employ for our souls' health the rougher and severer poet or story-teller, who will imitate the style of the virtuous only, and will follow those models which we prescribed at first when we began the education of our soldiers.

We certainly will, he said, if we have the power.

Then now, my friend, I said, that part of music or literary education which relates to the story or myth may be considered to be finished; for the matter and manner have both been discusssed.

I think so too, he said.

Next in order will follow melody and song.

That is obvious.

Everyone now would be able to discover what we ought to say about them, if we are to be consistent with ourselves.

I fear, said Glaucon, laughing, that the word 'everyone' hardly includes me, for I cannot at the moment say what they should be, though I have a suspicion.

At any rate you are aware that a song or ode has three parts — the words, the melody, and the rhythm.

Yes, he said; so much as that I know.

And as for the words, there will surely be no difference between words which are and which are not set to music; both will conform to the same laws, and these have been already determined by us?

Yes.

And the melody and rhythm will be in conformity with the words?

Certainly.

We were saying, when we spoke of the subject-matter, that we had no need of lamentation and strains of sorrow?

True.

And which are the harmonies expressive of sorrow? You are musical, and can tell me.

The harmonies which you mean are the mixed or tenor Lydian, and the full-toned or bass Lydian, and such-like.

These then, I said, must be banished; even to women who have a character to maintain they are of no use, and much less to men.

Certainly.

In the next place, drunkenness and softness and indolence are utterly unbecoming the character of our guardians.

Utterly unbecoming.

And which are the soft and convivial harmonies?

The Ionian, he replied, and some of the Lydian which are termed 'relaxed'.

399   Well, and are these of any use for warlike men?

Quite the reverse, he replied; and if so the Dorian and the Phrygian are the only ones which you have left.

I answered: Of the harmonies I know nothing, but would have you leave me one which can render the note or accent which a brave man utters in warlike action and in stern resolve; and when his cause is failing, and he is going to wounds or death or is overtaken by disaster in some other form, at every such crisis he meets the blows of fortune with firm step and a determination to endure; and an opposite kind for times of peace and freedom of action, when there is no pressure of necessity, and he is seeking to persuade God by prayer, or man by instruction and admonition, or when on the other hand he is expressing his willingness to yield to the persuasion or entreaty or admonition of others. And when in this manner he has attained his end, I would have the music show him not carried away by his success, but acting moderately and wisely in all circumstances, and acquiescing in the event. These two harmonies I ask you to leave; the strain of necessity and the strain of freedom, the strain of the unfortunate and the strain of the fortunate, the strain of courage, and the strain of temperance; these, I say, leave.

And these, he replied, are the Dorian and Phrygian harmonies of which I was just now speaking.

Then, I said, if these and these only are to be used in our songs and melodies, we shall not want multiplicity of strings or a panharmonic scale?

I suppose not.

Then we shall not maintain the artificers of lyres with three corners and complex scales, or the makers of any other many-stringed, curiously harmonized instruments?

Certainly not.

But what do you say to flute-makers and flute-players? Would you admit them into our State when you reflect that in this composite use of harmony the flute is worse than any stringed instrument; even the panharmonic music is only an imitation of the flute?

Clearly not.

There remain then only the lyre and the harp for use in the city, and the shepherds in the country may have some kind of pipe.

That is surely the conclusion to be drawn from the argument.

The preferring of Apollo and his instruments to Marsyas and his instruments is not at all strange, I said.

Not at all, he replied.

And so, by the dog of Egypt, we have been unconsciously purging the State, which not long ago we termed luxurious.

And we have done wisely, he replied.

Then let us now finish the purgation, I said. Next in order to harmonies, rhythms will naturally follow, and they should be subject to the same rules, for we ought not to seek out complex systems of metre, and a variety of feet, but rather to discover what rhythms are the expressions of a courageous and harmonious life; and when we 400 have found them, we shall adapt the foot and the melody to words having a like spirit, not the words to the foot and melody. To say what these rhythms are will be your duty — you must teach me them, as you have already taught me the harmonics.

But, indeed, he replied, I cannot tell you. I know from observation that there are some three principles of rhythm out of which metrical systems are framed, just as in sounds there are four notes out of which all the harmonies are composed. But of what sort of lives they are severally the imitations I am unable to say.

Then, I said, we must take Damon into our counsels; and he will tell us what rhythms are expressive of meanness, or insolence, or fury, or other unworthiness, and what are to be reserved for the expression of opposite feelings. And I think that I have an indistinct recollection of his mentioning a complex Cretic rhythm; also a dactylic or heroic, and he arranged them in some manner which I do not quite understand, making the rhythms equal in the rise and fall of the foot, long and short alternating; and, unless I am mistaken, he spoke of an iambic as well as of a trochaic rhythm, and assigned to them short and long quantities. Also in some cases he appeared to praise or censure the movement of the foot quite as much as the rhythm; or perhaps a combination of the two; for I am not certain what he meant. These matters, however, as I was saying, had better be referred to Damon himself, for the analysis of the subject would be difficult, you know?

Rather so, I should say.

But it does not require much analysis to see that grace or the absence of grace accompanies good or bad rhythm.

None at all.

And also that good and bad rhythm naturally assimilate to a good and bad style; and that harmony and discord in like manner follow style; for our principle is that rhythm and harmony are regulated by the words, and not the words by them.

Just so, he said, they should follow the words.

And will not the words and the character of the style depend on the temper of the soul?

Yes.

And everything else on the style?

Yes.

Then beauty of style and harmony and grace and good rhythm depend on simplicity, — I mean the true simplicity of a rightly and nobly ordered mind and character, not that other simplicity which is only a euphemism for folly?

Very true, he replied.

And if our youth are to do their work in life, must they not make these graces and harmonies their perpetual aim?

They must.

401 And surely the art of the painter and every other creative and constructive art are full of them, — weaving, embroidery, architecture, and every kind of manufacture; also nature, animal and vegetable, — in all of them there is grace or the absence of grace. And ugliness and discord and inharmonious motion are nearly allied to ill words and ill nature, as grace and harmony are the twin sisters of goodness and self-restraint and bear their likeness.

That is quite true, he said.

But shall our superintendence go no further, and are the poets only to be required by us to express the image of the good in their works, on pain, if they do anything else, of expulsion from our State? Or is the same control to be extended to other artists, and are they also to be prohibited from exhibiting the opposite forms of vice and intemperance and meanness and deformity in sculpture and building and the other creative arts; and is he who cannot conform to this rule of ours to be prevented from practising his art in our State, lest the taste of our citizens be corrupted by him? We would not have our guardians grow up amid images of moral deformity, as in some noxious pasture, and there browse and feed upon many a baneful herb and flower day by day, little by little, until they silently gather a festering mass of corruption in their own soul. Let us rather search for artists who are gifted to discern the true nature of the beautiful and graceful; then will our youth dwell in a land of health, amid fair sights and sounds, and receive the good in everything; and beauty, the effluence of fair works, shall flow into the eye and ear, like a health-giving breeze from a purer region, and insensibly draw the soul from earliest years into likeness and sympathy with the beauty of reason.

There can be no nobler training than that, he replied.

And therefore, I said, Glaucon, musical training is a more potent instrument than any other, because rhythm and harmony find their way into the inward places of the soul, on which they mightily fasten, imparting grace, and making the soul of him who is rightly educated graceful, or of him who is ill-educated ungraceful; and also because he who has received this true education of the inner being will most shrewdly perceive omissions or faults in art and nature, and with a true taste, while he praises and rejoices over and receives into his soul 402 the good, and becomes noble and good, he will justly blame and hate the bad, now in the days of his youth, even before he is able to know the reason why; and when reason comes he will recognize and salute the friend with whom his education has made him long familiar.

Yes, he said, I quite agree with you in thinking that it is for such reasons that they should be trained in music.

Just as in learning to read, I said, we were satisfied when we knew the letters of the alphabet, few as they are, in all their recurring combinations; not slighting them as unimportant whether they occupy a space large or small, but everywhere eager to make them out, because we knew we should not be perfect in the art of reading until we could do so:

True —

And as we recognize the reflection of letters in water, or in a mirror, only when we know the letters themselves, the same art and study giving us the knowledge of both:

Exactly —

Even so, as I maintain, neither we nor the guardians, whom we say that we have to educate, can ever become musical until we and they know the essential forms of temperance, courage, liberality, magnanimity, and their kindred, as well as the contrary forms, in all their combinations, and can recognize them and their images wherever they are found, not slighting them either in small things or great, but believing them all to be within the sphere of one art and study.

Most assuredly.

And when nobility of soul is observed in harmonious union with beauty of form, and both are cast from the same mould, that will be the fairest of sights to him who has an eye to see it? . . .

◄§ Socrates now observes that the youths thus made beautiful in soul will be most lovable. But declaring that true love is temperate and orderly, he obtains Glaucon's assent to the rule that in their city, no intemperate love shall be allowed. He states again the austere ideal of *paiderastia* which we have seen him uphold in the *Phaedrus* and the *Symposium* (cf. Introduction, the section on "Love and Beauty"):

403   Then mad or intemperate pleasure must never be allowed to come near the lover and his beloved; neither of them can have any part in it if their love is of the right sort?

No, indeed, Socrates, it must never come near them.

Then I suppose that in the city which we are founding you would make a law to the effect that a friend should use no other familiarity to his love than a father would use to his son, and then only for a noble purpose, and he must first have the other's consent; and this rule is to limit him in all his intercourse, and he is never to be seen going further, or, if he exceeds, he is to be deemed guilty of coarseness and bad taste.

I quite agree, he said.

Thus much of music, and the ending is appropriate; for what should be the end of music if not the love of beauty?

I agree, he said.

After music comes gymnastic, in which our youth are next to be trained.

Certainly.

Gymnastic as well as music should begin in early years; the training in it should be careful and should continue through life. Now my belief is, — and this is a matter upon which I should like to have your opinion in confirmation of my own, but my own belief is, — not that the good body by any bodily excellence improves the soul, but, on the contrary, that the good soul by her own excellence improves the body as far as this may be possible. What do you say?

Yes, I agree.

Then, to the mind when adequately trained, we shall be right in handing over the more particular care of the body; and in order to avoid prolixity we will now only give the general outlines of the subject.

Very good.

That they must abstain from intoxication has been already remarked by us; for of all persons a guardian should be the last to get drunk and not know where in the world he is.

Yes, he said; that a guardian should require another guardian to take care of him is ridiculous indeed.

But next, what shall we say of their food; for the men are in training for the great contest of all — are they not?

Yes, he said.

And will the habit of body of our ordinary athletes be suited to them?   404

Why not?

I am afraid, I said, that a habit of body such as they have is but a sleepy sort of thing, and rather perilous to health. Do you not observe that these athletes sleep away their lives, and are liable to most dangerous illnesses if they depart in ever so slight a degree from their customary regimen?

Yes, I do.

Then, I said, a finer sort of training will be required for our warrior athletes, who are to be like wakeful dogs, and to see and hear with the utmost keenness; amid the many changes of water and also of food, of summer heat and winter cold, which they will have to endure when on a campaign, they must not be liable to break down in health.

That is my view.

The really excellent gymnastic is twin sister of that simple music which we were just now describing.

How so?

Why, I conceive that simplicity is the great virtue of gymnastic training, and particularly of military exercises. . . .

⋙ Socrates explains that in speaking of simplicity, he means that only plain and wholesome food, fit for soldiers, will be allowed; there are to be no "Syracusan dinners," no dealings, either, with a fair "Corinthian girl." Next he condemns litigiousness, and the recourse to medical treatment for ill-health brought on by luxurious living. He

describes the ideal physician, such as he says Asclepius was of old;
such a physician will treat only those persons who, if they are cured,
will be of good use to themselves and to the community, either by
doing practical work, by serving the state, or by improving themselves, as the guardians must do; the hopelessly unhealthy he will allow to die rather than eke out a useless death-in-life. Socrates declares
that the good physician will have suffered from many diseases, thus
coming to know well the ills of the body. In contrast, the good judge
will be far from having had personal knowledge of the ills of the soul.
He must be an older man who, through long experience with the evil
in others' souls, will recognize it; and those whom such judges condemn, the citizens will put to death.

410   And thus our youth, having been educated only in that simple
music which, as we said, inspires temperance, will be reluctant to
go to law.

Clearly.

And the musician, who, keeping to the same track, is content to
practise the simple gymnastic, will have nothing to do with medicine
unless in some extreme case.

That I quite believe.

The very exercises and toils which he undergoes are intended to
stimulate the spirited element of his nature, and not to increase his
strength; he will not, like common athletes, use exercise and regimen
to develop his muscles.

Very right, he said.

Neither are the two arts of music and gymnastic really designed,
as is often supposed, the one for the training of the soul, the other
for the training of the body.

What then is the real object of them?

I believe, I said, that the teachers of both have in view chiefly the
improvement of the soul.

How can that be? he asked.

Did you never observe, I said, the effect on the mind itself of
exclusive devotion to gymnastic, or the opposite effect of an exclusive
devotion to music?

In what way shown? he said.

The one producing a temper of hardness and ferocity, the other
of softness and effeminacy, I replied.

Yes, he said, I am quite aware that the mere athlete becomes too
much of a savage, and that the mere musician is melted and softened
beyond what is good for him.

Yet surely, I said, this ferocity only comes from spirit, which if
rightly educated would give courage, but if too much intensified is
liable to become hard and brutal.

That I quite think.

On the other hand the quality of gentleness must come from the philosophical part of human nature. And this also when too much indulged will turn to softness, but if educated rightly will be gentle and moderate.

True.

And in our opinion the guardians ought to have both these qualities.

Assuredly.

And both should be in harmony?

Beyond question.

And the harmonious soul is both temperate and courageous?   411

Yes.

And the inharmonious is cowardly and boorish?

Very true.

And, when a man allows music to play upon him and to pour into his soul through the funnel of his ears those sweet and soft and melancholy airs of which we were just now speaking, and his whole life is passed in warbling and the delights of song; in the first stage of the process the passion or spirit which is in him is tempered like iron, and made useful instead of brittle and useless. But if he carries on the softening and soothing process, in the next stage he begins to melt and waste his spirit, until he has wasted it away and cut out the sinews of his soul; and he becomes a feeble warrior.

Very true.

If the element of spirit is naturally weak in him the change is speedily accomplished, but if he have a good deal, then the power of music weakening the spirit renders him excitable; — on the least provocation he flames up at once, and is speedily extinguished; instead of having spirit he grows irritable and passionate and peevish.

Exactly.

And so again, if a man takes violent physical exercise and is a great feeder, but is disinclined for music and philosophy, at first the high condition of his body fills him with pride and spirit, and he becomes twice the man that he was.

Certainly.

And what happens? if he does nothing else, and holds no converse with the Muses, does not even that intelligence which there may be in him, having no taste of any sort of learning or inquiry or thought or culture, grow feeble and dull and blind, his mind never waking up or receiving nourishment, and his senses not being purged of their mists?

True, he said.

And he ends by becoming a hater of reason [or argument], uncivilized, never using the weapons of persuasion, — he is like a wild beast, all violence and fierceness, and knows no other way of dealing; and he lives in ignorance and stupidity, and has no sense of propriety and grace.

That is quite true, he said.

And as there are two principles of human nature, one the spirited and the other the philosophical, some god, as I should say, has given mankind two arts answering to them (and only indirectly to the soul and body), in order that these two principles (like the strings of an instrument) may be relaxed or drawn tighter until they are duly harmonized.

That appears to be the intention.

And he who mingles music with gymnastic in the fairest proportions and best attempers them to the soul, may be rightly called the true musician and harmonist in a far higher sense than the tuner of the strings.

You are quite right, Socrates.

And such a presiding genius will be always required in our State if the government is to last.

Yes, he will be absolutely necessary.

Such, then, are our principles of nurture and education: Where would be the use of going into further details about the dances of our citizens, or about their hunting and coursing, their gymnastic and equestrian contests? For these all follow the general principle, and having found that, we shall have no difficulty in discovering them.

I dare say that there will be no difficulty.

Very good, I said; then what is the next question? Must we not ask who are to be rulers and who subjects?

Certainly.

There can be no doubt that the elder must rule the younger.

Clearly.

And that the best of these must rule.

That is also clear.

Now, are the best husbandmen those who are most devoted to husbandry?

Yes.

And as we are to have the best of guardians for our city, must they not be those who have most the character of guardians?

Yes.

And to this end they ought to be wise and efficient, and to have a special care of the State?

True.

And a man will be most likely to care about that which he loves?

To be sure.

And he will be most likely to love that which he regards as having the same interests with himself, and that of which the good or evil fortune is supposed by him at any time most to affect his own?

Very true, he replied.

Then there must be a selection. Let us note among the guardians those who in their whole life show the greatest eagerness to do what they suppose to be for the good of their country, and the greatest repugnance to do what is against her interests.

Those are the right men.

And they will have to be watched at every age, in order that we may see whether they preserve their resolution, and never yield either to force or to enchantment, so as to forget or cast off their sense of duty to the State.

How cast off? he said.

I will explain to you, I replied. A resolution may go out of a man's mind either with his will or against his will; with his will when he gets rid of a falsehood and learns better, against his will whenever he is deprived of a truth. 413

I understand, he said, the willing loss of a resolution; the meaning of the unwilling I have yet to learn.

Why, I said, do you not see that men are unwillingly deprived of good, and willingly of evil? Is not to have lost the truth an evil, and to possess the truth a good? and you would agree that to conceive things as they are is to possess the truth?

Yes, he replied; I agree with you in thinking that mankind are deprived of truth against their will.

And is not this involuntary deprivation caused either by theft, or force, or enchantment?

Still, he replied, I do not understand you.

I must have been talking darkly, like the tragedians. As for theft, I only mean that some men are changed by persuasion and that others forget; argument steals away the beliefs of one class, and time of the other. Now you understand me?

Yes.

Those again who are forced, are those whom the violence of some pain or grief compels to change their opinion.

I understand, he said, and you are quite right.

And you would also acknowledge that the enchanted are those who change their minds either under the softer influence of pleasure, or the sterner shock of fear?

Yes, he said; everything that deceives may be said to enchant.

Therefore, as I was just now saying, we must inquire who are the best guardians of their own conviction that they should always do what they judge most advantageous to the State. We must watch them from their youth upwards, and make them perform actions in which they are most likely to forget or to be deceived, and he who remembers and is not deceived is to be selected, and he who fails in the trial is to be rejected. That will be the way?

Yes.

And there should also be toils and pains and conflicts prescribed for them, in which they will be made to give further proof of the same qualities.

Very right, he replied.

And then, I said, we must try them with enchantments — that is the third sort of test — and see what will be their behaviour: like those who take colts amid noise and tumult to see if they are of a timid nature, so must we take our youth amid terrors of some kind, and thence pass them into pleasures, and prove them more thoroughly than gold is proved in the furnace, that we may discover whether they are armed against all enchantments, and of a noble bearing always, good guardians of themselves and of the music which they have learned, and retaining under all circumstances a rhythmical and harmonious nature, such as will be most serviceable to themselves and to the State. And he who at every age, as boy and youth and in 414 mature life, has come out of the trial victorious and pure, shall be appointed a ruler and guardian of the State; he shall be honoured in life and death, and shall receive sepulture and other memorials of honour, the greatest that we have to give. But him who fails, we must reject. I am inclined to think that this is the sort of way in which our rulers and guardians should be chosen and appointed. I speak generally, and not with any pretension to exactness.

And, speaking generally, I agree with you, he said.

And perhaps the word 'guardian' in the fullest sense ought to be applied to this higher class only who both preserve us against foreign enemies and maintain peace among our citizens at home, that the one may not have the will, or the others the power, to harm us. The young men whom we before called guardians may be more properly designated auxiliaries and supporters of the principles of the rulers.

I agree with you, he said.

How then may we devise one of those needful falsehoods of which we lately spoke — just one royal lie which may deceive the rulers, if that be possible, and at any rate the rest of the city?

What sort of lie? he said.

Nothing new, I replied; only an old Phoenician tale of what has often occurred before now in other places (as the poets say, and have made the world believe), though not in our time, and I do not know whether such an event could ever happen again, or could now even be made to seem probable.

How your words seem to hesitate on your lips!

You will not wonder, I replied, at my hesitation when you have heard.

Speak, he said, and fear not.

Well then, I will speak, although I really know not how to look you in the face, or in what words to utter the audacious fiction, which I propose to communicate gradually, first to the rulers, then to the soldiers, and lastly to the people. They are to be told that the education and training which they seemed to receive from us in youth was but a dream; in reality during all that time they were being formed and fed in the womb of the earth, where they themselves and their arms and appurtenances were manufactured; when they were completed, the earth, their mother, sent them up; and so, their country being their mother and also their nurse, they are bound to advise for her good, and to defend her against attacks; and the other citizens they are to regard as children of the earth and their own brothers.

You had good reason, he said, to be ashamed of the lie which you were going to tell.

No doubt, I replied, but listen to the continuation of the tale. 415 Citizens, we shall say to them in our tale, you are brothers, yet God has framed you differently. Some of you have the power of command, and in the composition of these he has mingled gold, wherefore also they have the greatest honour; others he has made of silver, to be auxiliaries; others again who are to be husbandmen and craftsmen he has composed of brass and iron; and the species will generally be preserved in the children. But as all are of the same original stock, a golden parent will sometimes have a silver son, a silver parent a golden son, and so forth. And God proclaims as a first principle to the rulers, and above all else, that there is nothing which they should so anxiously guard, or of which they are to be such good guardians, as of the mixture of elements in the soul. First, if one of their own offspring has an admixture of brass or iron, they shall in no wise have pity on it, but give it the rank which is its due and send it down to the husbandmen or artisans. On the other hand, if there are sons of artisans who have an admixture of gold or silver in them, they will be raised to honour, and become guardians or auxiliaries. For an oracle says that when a man of brass or iron guards the State, it will be destroyed. Such is the tale; is there any possibility of making our citizens believe in it?

Not in the first generation, he replied; but their sons may be made to believe in the tale, and their sons' sons, and posterity after them.

I see the difficulty, I replied; yet the fostering of such a belief will make them care more for the city and for one another. Enough, however, of the fiction, which may now fly abroad upon the wings of rumour, while we arm our earth-born heroes, and lead them forth under the command of their rulers. Let them look round and select a spot whence they can best suppress insurrection, if any prove refractory within, and also defend themselves against enemies, who like wolves may come down on the fold from without; there let them encamp, and when they have encamped, let them sacrifice to the proper gods and prepare their lodging.

Just so, he said.

And this must be such as will shield them against the cold of winter and the heat of summer.

I suppose that you mean houses, he replied.

Yes, I said; but they must be the houses of soldiers, and not of shopkeepers.

416 What is the difference? he said.

That I will endeavour to explain, I replied. To keep watchdogs, who, from want of discipline or hunger, or some evil habit or other, would turn upon the sheep and worry them, and behave not like dogs but wolves, would be a foul and monstrous thing in a shepherd?

Truly monstrous, he said.

And therefore every care must be taken that our auxiliaries, being stronger than our citizens, may not behave in this fashion and become like savage tyrants instead of friends and allies?

Yes, great care should be taken.

And if they have really received a good education, will not that furnish the best safeguard?

But they have received it, he replied.

I cannot be so confident, my dear Glaucon, I said; but I believe the truth is as I said, that a sound education, whatever that may be, will have the greatest tendency to civilize and humanize them in their relations to one another, and to those who are under their protection.

Very true, he replied.

And not only their education, but their habitations, and all that belongs to them, should be such as will neither impair their virtue as guardians, nor tempt them to prey upon the other citizens. Any man of sense must acknowledge that.

He must.

Then now let us consider what will be their way of life, if they are to realize our idea of them. In the first place, none of them should have any property of his own beyond what is absolutely necessary; neither should they have a private house or store closed against any-one who has a mind to enter; their provisions should be only such as are required by trained warriors, who are men of temperance and courage; they should agree to receive from the citizens a fixed rate of pay, enough to meet the expenses of the year and no more; and they will go to mess and live together like soldiers in a camp. Gold and silver we will tell them that they have from God; the diviner metal is within them, and they have therefore no need of the dross which is current among men, and ought not to pollute the divine by any such earthly admixture; for that commoner metal has been the **417** sources of many unholy deeds, but their own is undefiled. And they alone of all the citizens may not touch or handle silver or gold, or be under the same roof with them, or wear them, or drink from them. And this will be their salvation, and they will be the saviours of the State. But should they ever acquire homes or lands or moneys of their own, they will become householders and husbandmen instead of guardians, enemies and tyrants instead of allies of the other citizens; hating and being hated, plotting and being plotted against, they will pass their whole life in much greater terror of internal than of external enemies, and the hour of ruin, both to themselves and to the rest of the State, will be at hand. For all which reasons may we not say that thus shall our State be ordered, and that these shall be the regulations appointed by us for our guardians concerning their lodging and all other matters?

Yes, said Glaucon.

Republic · Book IV

Here Adeimantus interposed a question: How would you answer, Socrates, said he, if a person were to say that you are not making these men very happy, and that they are themselves to blame; the city in fact belongs to them, but they reap no advantage from it; whereas other men acquire lands, and build large and handsome houses, and have everything handsome about them, offering sacrifices to the gods on their own account, and practising hospitality; moreover, they have the gold and silver which you have just mentioned, and all that is usual among the favourites of fortune; but our poor citizens are no better than mercenaries who are quartered in the city and are always mounting guard?

Yes, I said; and you may add that they are only fed, and not paid in addition to their food like other men; and therefore they cannot, if they would, take a private journey abroad; they have no money to spend on a mistress or any other luxurious fancy, which, as the world goes, is thought to be happiness; and many other accusations of the same nature might be added.

But, said he, let us suppose all this to be included in the charge.

You mean to ask, I said, what will be our answer?

Yes.

If we proceed along the old path, my belief, I said, is that we shall find the answer. And our answer will be that, even as they are, our guardians may very likely be the happiest of men; but that our aim in founding the State was not the disproportionate happiness of any one class, but the greatest happiness of the whole; we thought that in a State which is ordered with a view to the good of the whole we should be most likely to find justice, and in the worst-ordered State injustice: and, having found them, we might then decide upon the answer to our first question. At present, I take it, we are fashioning the happy State, not piecemeal, or with a view of making a few happy citizens, but as a whole; and by-and-by we will proceed to view the opposite kind of State. Suppose that we were painting a statue, and someone came up to us and said, Why do you not put the most beautiful colours on the most beautiful parts of the body — the eyes ought to be purple, but you have made them black — to him we might fairly answer, 'Sir, you would not surely have us beautify the eyes to such a degree that they are no longer eyes; consider rather whether, by giving this and the other features their due proportion, we make the whole beautiful.' And so I say to you, do not compel us to assign to the guardians a sort of happiness which

will make them no guardians at all; for we too can clothe our husbandmen in royal apparel, and set crowns of gold on their heads, and
bid them till the ground as much as they like, and no more. Our
potters also might be allowed to repose on couches, and feast by the
fireside, passing round the winecup, while their wheel is conveniently
at hand, so that they may make a few pots when they feel inclined;
in this way we might make every class happy — and then, as you
imagine, the whole State would be happy. But do not put this idea
into our heads; for, if we listen to you, the husbandman will be no 421
longer a husbandman, the potter will cease to be a potter, and no
one will have the character of any distinct class in the State. Now
this is not of much consequence where the corruption of society,
and pretension to be what you are not, is confined to cobblers; but
when the guardians of the laws and of the government are only
seeming and not real guardians, then see how they turn the State
upside down; and on the other hand they alone have the power
of giving order and happiness to the State. We mean our guardians
to be true saviours and not the destroyers of the State, whereas our
opponent is thinking of peasants at a festival, who are enjoying a life
of revelry, not of citizens who are doing their duty to the State. But,
if so, we mean different things, and he is speaking of something which
is not a State. And therefore we must consider whether in appointing
our guardians we look to their greatest happiness individually, or
whether our aim is not to ensure that happiness appears in the State
as a whole. What these guardians or auxiliaries must be compelled
or induced to do (and the same may be said of every other trade),
is to become as expert as possible in their professional work. And
thus the whole State will grow up in a noble order, and the several
classes will receive the proportion of happiness which nature assigns
to them.

I think that you are quite right.

I wonder whether you will agree with another remark which
occurs to me.

What may that be?

There seem to be two causes of the deterioration of the arts.

What are they?

Wealth, I said, and poverty.

How do they act?

The process is as follows: When a potter becomes rich, will he,
think you, any longer take the same pains with his art?

Certainly not.

He will grow more and more indolent and careless?

Very true.

And the result will be that he becomes a worse potter?

Yes; he greatly deteriorates.

But, on the other hand, if he has no money and cannot provide himself with tools or other requirements of his craft, his own work will not be equally good, and he will not teach his sons or apprentices to work equally well.

Certainly not.

Then, under the influence either of poverty or of wealth, workmen and their work are equally liable to degenerate?

That is evident.

Here then is a discovery of new evils, I said, against which the guardians will have to watch, or they will creep into the city unobserved.

What evils?

422 Wealth, I said, and poverty; the one is the parent of luxury and indolence, and the other of meanness and viciousness, and both of a revolutionary spirit.

That is very true, he replied; but still I should like to know, Socrates, how our city will be able to go to war, especially against an enemy who is rich and powerful, if deprived of the sinews of war.

Evidently it would be difficult, I replied, to wage war with one such enemy; but it will be easier where there are two of them.

How so? he asked.

In the first place, I said, if we have to fight, our side will be trained warriors fighting against an army of rich men.

That is true, he said.

And do you not suppose, Adeimantus, that a single boxer who was perfect in his art would easily be a match for two stout and well-to-do gentlemen who were not boxers?

Hardly, if they came upon him at once.

What, not, I said, if he were able to run away and then turn and strike at the one who first came up? And supposing he were to do this several times under the heat of a scorching sun, might he not, being an expert, overturn more than one stout personage?

Certainly, he said, there would be nothing wonderful in that.

And yet rich men probably have more instruction in the science and practise of boxing than they have in military science.

Likely enough.

Then we may assume that our athletes will be able to fight with two or three times their own number?

I will accept that, for I think you right.

And suppose that, before engaging, our citizens send an embassy to one of the two cities, telling them what is the truth: 'Silver and gold we neither have nor are permitted to have, but you may; do you therefore come and help us in war, and take the spoils of the other

city.' Who, on hearing these words, would choose to fight against
lean wiry dogs, rather than, with the dogs on their side, against fat
and tender sheep?

That is not likely; and yet there might be a danger to the poor
State if the wealth of many States were to be gathered into one.

But how simple of you to think that the term State is applicable at
all to any but our own!

Why so?

You ought to speak of other States in the plural number; not one
of them is a city, but many cities, as they say in the game. Each will
contain not less than two divisions, one the city of the poor, the other
of the rich, which are at war with one another; and within each there
are many smaller divisions. You would be altogether beside the mark
if you treated these as a single State; but if you deal with them as
many, and give the wealth or power or persons of the one to the
others, you will always have a great many friends and not many
enemies. And your State, while the wise order which has now been
prescribed continues to prevail in her, will be the greatest of States,
I do not mean to say in reputation or appearance, but in deed and
truth, though she number not more than a thousand defenders. A
single State of that size you will hardly find, either among Hellenes
or barbarians, though many that appear to be as great and many
times greater.

That is most true, he said.

Hence, I said, it can be seen what will be the best limit for our
rulers to fix when they are considering the size of the State and the
amount of territory which they are to include, and beyond which
they will not go.

What limit would you propose?

I would allow the State to increase so far as is consistent with
unity; that, I think, is the proper limit.

Very good, he said.

Here then, I said, is another order which will have to be conveyed
to our guardians: Let them guard against our city becoming small,
or great only in appearance. It must attain an adequate size, but
it must remain one.

And perhaps, said he, you do not think this is a very severe order?

And here is another, said I, which is lighter still, — I mean the
duty, of which some mention was made before, of degrading the
offspring of the guardians when inferior, and of elevating into the
rank of guardians the offspring of the lower classes, when naturally
superior. The intention was that, in the case of the citizens generally,
each individual should be put to the use for which nature intended
him, one to one work, and then every man would do his own busi-

423

ness, and become one and not many; and so the whole city would be one and not many.

Yes, he said; that is not so difficult.

The regulations which we are prescribing, my good Adeimantus, are not, as might be supposed, a number of great principles, but trifles all, if care be taken, as the saying is, of the one great thing, — a thing, however, which I would rather call, not great, but sufficient for our purpose.

What may that be? he asked.

Education, I said, and nurture: if our citizens are well educated, and grow into sensible men, they will easily see their way through all these, as well as other matters which I omit; such, for example, as 424 marriage, the possession of women and the procreation of children, which will all follow the general principle that friends have all things in common, as the proverb says.

That will be the best way of settling them.

Also, I said, the State, if once started well, moves with accumulating force like a wheel. For where good nurture and education are maintained, they implant good constitutions, and these good constitutions taking root in a good education improve more and more, and this improvement affects the breed in man as in other animals.

Very possibly, he said.

Then to sum up: This is the principle to which our rulers should cling throughout, taking care that neglect does not creep in — that music and gymnastic be preserved in their original form, and no innovation made. They must do their utmost to maintain them intact. And when anyone says that

'Mankind most regard the newest song which the singers have',

they will be afraid that he may be praising, not new songs, but a new kind of song; and this ought not to be praised, or conceived to be the meaning of the poet; for any musical innovation is to be shunned, as likely to bring danger to the whole State. So Damon tells me, and I can quite believe him; — he says that when modes of music change, the fundamental laws of the State always change with them.

Yes, said Adeimantus; and you may add my suffrage to Damon's and your own.

Then, I said, our guardians must lay the foundations of their fortress in music?

Yes, he said; the lawlessness of which you speak too easily steals in.

Yes, I replied, in the form of amusement, and as though it were harmless.

Why, yes, he said, and harmless it would be; were it not that little by little this spirit of licence, finding a home, imperceptibly penetrates into manners and customs; whence issuing with greater force it invades contracts between man and man, and from contracts goes on to laws and constitutions, in utter recklessness, ending at last, Socrates, by an overthrow of all rights, private as well as public.

Is that true? I said.

That is my belief, he replied.

Then, as I was saying, our boys should be trained from the first in a stricter system, for if childish amusement becomes lawless, it 425 will produce lawless children, who can never grow up into well-conducted and virtuous citizens.

Very true, he said.

And when boys who have made a good beginning in play, have later gained the habit of good order through music, then this habit accompanies them in all their actions and is a principle of growth to them, and is able to correct anything in the State which had been allowed to lapse. It is the reverse of the picture I have just drawn.

Very true, he said.

Thus educated, they will discover for themselves any lesser rules which their predecessors have altogether neglected.

What do you mean?

I mean such things as these: — when the young are to be silent before their elders; how they are to show respect to them by standing and making them sit; what honour is due to parents; what garments or shoes are to be worn; the mode of dressing the hair; deportment and manners in general. You would agree with me?

Yes.

But there is, I think, small wisdom in legislating about such matters, — precise written enactments cannot create these observances, and are not likely to make them lasting.

Impossible.

It would seem, Adeimantus, that the direction in which education starts a man will determine his future life. Does not like always attract like?

To be sure.

Until some one grand result is reached which may be good, and may be the reverse of good?

That is not to be denied.

And for this reason, I said, I, for my part, should not attempt to extend legislation to such details.

Naturally enough, he replied.

Well, and about the business of the agora, and the ordinary dealings between man and man, or again about agreements with artisans; about insult and injury, or the commencement of actions, and the appointment of juries, what would you say? there may also arise questions about any impositions and exactions of market and harbour dues which may be required, and in general about the regulations of markets, police, harbours, and the like. But, oh heavens! shall we condescend to legislate on any of these particulars?

No, he said, it is unseemly to impose laws about them on good men; what regulations are necessary they will find out soon enough for themselves.

Yes, I said, my friends, if God will only preserve to them the laws which we have given them.

And without divine help, said Adeimantus, they will go on for ever making and mending their laws and their lives in the hope of attaining perfection.

You would compare them, I said, to those invalids who, having no self-restraint, will not leave off their habits of intemperance?

Exactly.

426   Yes, I said; and what a delightful life they lead! they are always doctoring their disorders, with no result except to increase and complicate them, and always fancying that they will be cured by any nostrum which anybody advises them to try.

Such cases are very common, he said, with invalids of this sort.

Yes, I replied; and the charming thing is that they deem him their worst enemy who tells them the truth, which is simply that, unless they give up gorging and drinking and wenching and idling, neither drug nor cautery nor amputation nor spell nor amulet nor any other remedy will avail.

Charming? he replied. I see nothing charming in going into a passion with a man who tells you what is right.

These gentlemen, I said, do not seem to be in your good graces.

Assuredly not.

Nor would you approve if a whole State behaves in this way, and that brings me back to my point. For when, in certain ill-ordered States, the citizens are forbidden under pain of death to alter the constitution; and yet he who most sweetly courts those who live under this régime and indulges them and fawns upon them and is skilful in anticipating and gratifying their humours is honoured as a great and good statesman — do not these States resemble the persons whom I was describing?

Yes, he said; the fault is the same; and I am very far from approving it.

But what of these ready and eager ministers of political corruption? I said. Do you not admire their coolness and dexterity?

Yes, he said, I do; but not of all of them, for there are some whom the applause of the multitude has deluded into the belief that they are really statesmen.

What do you mean? I said; you should have more feeling for them. When a man cannot measure, and a great many others who cannot measure declare that he is four cubits high, can he help believing what they say?

Nay, he said, certainly not in that case.

Well, then, do not be angry with them; for are they not as good as a play, trying their hand at paltry reforms such as I was describing; they are always fancying that by legislation they will make an end of frauds in contracts, and the other rascalities which I was mentioning, not knowing that they are in reality cutting off the heads of a hydra?

Yes, he said; that is just what they are doing.

427

I conceive, I said, that the true legislator will not trouble himself with this class of enactments whether concerning laws or the constitution either in an ill-ordered or in a well-ordered State; for in the former they are quite useless, and in the latter they will either be of a kind which anyone can devise, or will naturally flow out of our previous regulations.

What, then, he said, is still remaining to us of the work of legislation?

Nothing to us, I replied; but to Apollo, the god of Delphi, there remains the ordering of the greatest and noblest and chiefest things of all.

Which are they? he said.

The institution of temples and sacrifices, and the entire service of gods, demigods, and heroes; also the ordering of the repositories of the dead, and the rites which have to be observed by him who would propitiate the inhabitants of the world below. These are matters of which we are ignorant ourselves, and as founders of a city we should be unwise in trusting them to any interpreter but the ancestral one. For it is Apollo who, sitting at the navel of the earth, is the ancestral interpreter of such observances to all mankind.

You are right, and we will do as you propose.

So now the foundation of your city, son of Ariston, is finished. What comes next? Provide yourself with a bright light and search, and get your brother and Polemarchus and the rest of our friends to help, and let us see where in it we can discover justice and where injustice, and in what they differ from one another, and which of them the man who would be happy should have for his portion, whether seen or unseen by gods and men.

Nonsense, said Glaucon: did you not promise to search yourself, saying that for you not to help justice in her need would be an impiety?

Your reminder is true, and I will be as good as my word; but you must join.

We will, he replied.

Well, then, I hope to make the discovery in this way: I mean to begin with the assumption that our State, if rightly ordered, is perfect.

That is most certain.

And being perfect, is therefore wise and valiant and temperate and just.

That is likewise clear.

And whichever of these qualities we first find in the State, the one which is not yet found will be the residue?

428   Very good.

If in some other instance there were four things, in one of which we were most interested, the one sought for might come to light first, and there would be no further trouble; or if we came to know the other three first, we should thereby attain the object of our search, for it must clearly be the part remaining.

Very true, he said.

And is not a similar method to be pursued about the virtues, which are also four in number?

Clearly.

First among the virtues found in the State, wisdom comes into view, and in this I detect a certain peculiarity.

What is that?

The State which we have been describing has, I think, true wisdom. You would agree that it is good in counsel?

Yes.

And this good counsel is clearly a kind of knowledge, for not by ignorance, but by knowledge, do men counsel well?

Clearly. . . .

    ◆§ Socrates enumerates several types of knowledge belonging to workmen and obtains Glaucon's agreement that it is not these which make the city wise.

428   Well, I said, and is there any knowledge in our recently founded State among any of the citizens which advises not about any particular thing in the State, but about the whole, and considers how it can best conduct itself in relation with itself and with other States?

There certainly is.

And what is this knowledge, and among whom is it found? I asked.

It is the knowledge of guarding, he replied, and is found in those rulers whom we were just now describing as perfect guardians.

And what is the name which the city derives from the possession of this sort of knowledge?

The name of good in counsel and truly wise.

And will there be in our city more of these true guardians or more smiths?

The smiths, he replied, will be far more numerous.

Will not the guardians probably be the smallest of all the classes who receive a name from the profession of some kind of knowledge?

Much the smallest.

And so by reason of the smallest part or class, and of the knowledge which resides in this presiding and ruling part of itself, the whole State, being thus constituted according to nature, will be wise; and this, which can claim a share in the only knowledge worthy to be called wisdom, has been ordained by nature to be of all classes the least.

Most true.

Thus, then, I said, the nature and place in the State of one of the four virtues has somehow or other been discovered.

And, in my humble opinion, very satisfactorily discovered, he replied.

Again, I said, there is no difficulty in seeing the nature of courage, and in what part that quality resides which gives the name of courageous to the State.

How do you mean?

Why, I said, everyone who calls any State courageous or cowardly, will be thinking of the part which fights and goes out to war on the State's behalf.

No one, he replied, would ever think of any other.

The rest of the citizens may be courageous or may be cowardly, but their courage or cowardice will not, as I conceive, have the effect of making the city either the one or the other.

No.

The city will be courageous also by one part of herself, in which resides the power to preserve under all circumstances that opinion about the nature and description of things to be feared in which our legislator educated them; and this is what you term courage.

I should like to hear what you are saying once more, for I do not think that I perfectly understand you.

I mean that courage is a kind of preservation.

Preservation of what kind?

Of the opinion respecting things to be feared, what they are and of what nature, which the law implants through education; and I mean by the words 'under all circumstances' to intimate that in pleasure or in pain, or under the influence of desire or fear, a man preserves and does not lose this opinion. Shall I give you an illustration?

If you please.

You know, I said, that dyers, when they want to dye wool for making the true sea-purple, begin by choosing the white from among all the colours available; this they prepare and dress with much care and pains, in order that the white ground may take the purple hue in full perfection. The dyeing then proceeds; and whatever is dyed in this manner becomes a fast colour, and no washing either with lyes or without them can take away the bloom. But, when the ground has not been duly prepared, you will have noticed how poor is the look either of purple or of any other colour.

Yes, he said; I know that they have a washed-out and ridiculous appearance.

430　　Then now, I said, you will understand that our object in selecting our soldiers, and educating them in music and gymnastic, was very similar; we were contriving influences which would prepare them to take the dye of the laws in perfection, and the colour of their opinion about dangers and of every other opinion was to be indelibly fixed by their nurture and training, not to be washed away by such potent lyes as pleasure — mightier agent far in washing the soul than any soda or lye — or by sorrow, fear, and desire, the mightiest of all other solvents. And this sort of universal saving power of true opinion in conformity with law about real and false dangers I call and maintain to be courage, unless you disagree.

But I agree, he replied; for I suppose that you mean to exclude mere right belief about dangers when it has grown up without instruction, such as that of a wild beast or of a slave — this, in your opinion, is something not quite in accordance with law, which in any case should have another name than courage.

Most certainly.

Then I concede courage to be such as you describe.

Excellent, said I, and if you add the words 'of a citizen', you will not be far wrong; — hereafter, if you agree, we will carry the examination of courage further, but at present we are seeking not for courage but justice; and for the purpose of our inquiry we have said enough.

You are right, he replied.

Two virtues remain to be discovered in the State — first, temperance, and then justice which is the end of our search.

Very true.

Now, can we find justice without troubling ourselves about temperance?

I do not know how that can be accomplished, he said, nor do I desire that justice be brought to light and temperance lost sight of; and therefore I wish that you would do me the favour of considering temperance first.

Certainly, I replied, I should not be justified in refusing your request.

Then consider, he said.

Yes, I replied; I will; and as far as I can at present see, temperance has more of the nature of harmony and symphony than have the preceding virtues.

How so? he asked.

Temperance, I replied, is the ordering or controlling of certain pleasures and desires; this is curiously enough implied in the saying of 'a man being his own master'; and other traces of the same notion may be found in language, may they not?

No doubt, he said.

There is something ridiculous in the expression 'master of himself'; 431 for the master must also be the servant and the servant the master, since in all these modes of speaking the same person is denoted.

Certainly.

The meaning of this expression is, I believe, that there is within the man's own soul a better and also a worse principle; and when the better has the worse under control, then he is said to be master of himself; and this is a term of praise: but when, owing to evil education or association, the better principle, which is also the smaller, is overwhelmed by the greater mass of the worse — in this case he is blamed and is called the slave of self and dissolute.

Yes, there is reason in that.

And now, I said, look at our newly created State, and there you will find one of these two conditions realized; for the State, as you will acknowledge, may be justly called master of itself, if the words 'temperance' and 'self-mastery' truly express the rule of the better part over the worse.

On looking, he said, I see that what you say is true.

Let me further note that the manifold and complex pleasures and desires and pains are generally found in children and women and servants, and in the freemen so called who are of the lowest and more numerous class.

Certainly, he said.

Whereas the simple and moderate desires, which follow reason and are under the guidance of mind and true opinion, are to be found only in a few, and those the best born and best educated.

Very true.

These too, as you may perceive, have a place in your State; and the meaner desires of the many are held down by the desires and wisdom of the more virtuous few.

That I perceive, he said.

Then if there be any city which may be described as master of its own pleasures and desires, and master of itself, ours may claim such a designation?

Certainly, he replied.

It may also for all these reasons be called temperate?

Yes.

And if there be any State in which rulers and subjects will be agreed as to the question who are to rule, that again will be our State? Do you think so?

I do, emphatically.

And the citizens being thus agreed among themselves, in which class will temperance be found — in the rulers or in the subjects?

In both, as I should imagine, he replied.

Do you observe that we were not badly inspired in our guess that temperance bore some resemblance to harmony?

Why so?

432 Why, because temperance is unlike courage and wisdom, each of which resides in a part only, the one making the State wise and the other valiant; not so temperance, which extends to the whole, and runs through all the notes of the scale, and produces a unison of the weaker and the stronger and the middle class, whether you suppose them to be stronger or weaker in wisdom or power or numbers or wealth, or anything else you please. Most truly then may we deem this unity of mind to be temperance, an agreement of the naturally superior and inferior as to the right to rule of either both in states and individuals.

I entirely agree with you.

And so, I said, we may consider three out of the four virtues to have been discovered in our State. What remainder is there of qualities which make a state virtuous? For this, it is evident, must be justice.

The inference is obvious. . . .

⮜ Socrates now heightens the suspense by proposing that he and Glaucon, like hunters, surround the covert where their prey lurks. He teases Glaucon by pretending first to be baffled and then to see the track of the quarry, which he still, however, does not identify. He exclaims that really they have been talking of justice for a long time unawares. Glaucon demands that Socrates cease his clowning, and Socrates replies:

433 Well then, tell me, I said, whether I am right or not: You remember the original principle which we laid down at the foundation of the State; we decided, and more than once insisted, that one man should practise one occupation only, that to which his nature was best adapted; — now justice, in my view, either is this principle or is some form of it.

Yes, we did.

Further, we affirmed that justice was doing one's own business, and not being a busybody; we said so again and again, and many others have said the same to us.

Yes, we said so.

Then to attend to one's own business, in some form or another, may be assumed to be justice. Do you know my evidence for this?

No, but I should like to be told.

Because I think that this is the virtuous quality which remains in the State when the other virtues of temperance and courage and wisdom are abstracted; and that this not only made it possible for them to appear, but is also their preservative as long as they remain; and we were saying that if the three were discovered by us, justice would be the fourth or remaining one.

That follows of necessity.

If we are asked to determine which of these four qualities by its presence will contribute most to the excellence of our State, whether the agreement of rulers and subjects, or the preservation in the soldiers of the opinion which the law ordains about the true nature of dangers, or wisdom and watchfulness in the rulers, or this other which is found in children and women, slave and freeman, artisan, ruler, subject (I mean the quality of every one doing his own work, and not being a busybody), the decision is not so easy.

Certainly, he replied, there would be a difficulty in saying which.

Then the attention of each individual to his own work appears to be a quality rivalling wisdom, temperance, and courage, with reference to the excellence of the State.

Yes, he said.

And the only virtue which, from that point of view, is of equal importance with them, is justice?

Exactly.

Let us look at the question also in this way: Are not the rulers in a State those to whom you would entrust the office of determining suits at law?

Certainly.

In the decision of such suits will any principle be prior to this, that a man may neither take what is another's nor be deprived of what is his own?

No.

Because it is a just principle?

Yes.

Then on this view also justice will be admitted to be the having 434 and doing what is a man's own, and belongs to him?

Very true.

Think, now, and say whether you agree with me or not. Suppose

a carpenter sets out to do the business of a cobbler, or a cobbler
that of a carpenter; and suppose them to exchange their implements
or social position, or the same person to try to undertake the work
of both, or whatever be the change; do you think that any great harm
would result to the State?

Not much.

But when the cobbler or any other man whom nature designed to
be a trader, having his heart lifted up by wealth or strength or the
number of his followers or any like advantage, attempts to force his
way into the class of warriors, or a warrior into that of legislators and
guardians, to which he ought not to aspire, and when these exchange
their implements and their social position with those above them; or
when one man would be trader, legislator, and warrior all in one, then
I think you will agree with me in saying that this interchange and
this meddling of one with another is the ruin of the State.

Most true.

Seeing then, I said, that there are three distinct classes, any meddling of one with another, or the change of one into another, is the
greatest harm to the State, and may be most justly termed evil-doing?

Precisely.

And the greatest degree of evil-doing to one's own city would be
termed by you injustice?

Certainly.

This then is injustice; and on the other hand when the three main
classes, traders, auxiliaries, and guardians, each do their own business,
that is justice, and will make the city just.

I agree with you. . . .

⤝ Socrates says that the nature of justice is not yet fully determined;
first, he says, we must inquire whether the same quality that has
been identified as justice in the state is also justice in the individual.
From the admission that the just state and the just man are alike in
respect to justice he concludes, with some apology for his use of a
short-cut method, that the individual soul has within it three principles — love of knowledge, spirit or passion, and the love of gain —
analogous to the three classes in the state. He continues:

436   But the question is not quite so easy when we proceed to ask
whether these principles are three or one; whether, that is to say,
we learn with one part of our nature, are angry with another, and
with a third part desire the satisfaction of our natural appetites; or
whether the whole soul comes into play in each sort of action — to
determine that is the difficulty.

Yes, he said; there lies the difficulty.

Then let us now try and determine whether they are the same or
different.

How?

Clearly the same thing cannot act or be acted upon in the same part or in relation to the same thing at the same time, in contrary ways; and therefore whenever this contradiction occurs in things apparently the same, we know that they are really not the same, but different.

Good.

For example, I said, can the same thing be at rest and in motion at the same time in the same part?

Impossible. . . .

◄§ Socrates illustrates his just-enunciated principle by the example of a man who stands still but moves his hands and his head. He obtains consent to the proposition that desire and repulsion are contraries or opposites. Next he proposes a principle in the logic of relations and illustrates it by the statement that thirst in general is related to drink in general, while thirst of a particular kind is related to drink of a particular kind. He now concludes that if a man is thirsty, yet something in his soul pulls him away from drink, two different parts (desire and reason) must be operating within him. Similarly if a man is angry at the violent desires he feels within himself and struggles against them, again two parts (desire and spirit) are entailed. Spirit obeys reason and is reason's ally or auxiliary. Yet spirit is not the same as reason: spirit appears in young children, who are as yet without reason, and in animals. Socrates sums up:

And so, after much tossing, we have reached land, and are fairly   441
agreed that the same principles which exist in the State exist also in the individual, and that they are three in number.

Exactly.

Must we not then infer that the individual is wise in the same way and in virtue of the same quality which makes the State wise?

Certainly.

Also that the State is brave in the same way and by the same quality as an individual is brave, and that there is the same correspondence in regard to the other virtues?

Assuredly.

Therefore the individual will be acknowledged by us to be just in the same way in which the State has been found just?

That follows of course.

We cannot but remember that the justice of the State consisted in each of the three classes doing the work of its own class?

I do not think we have forgotten, he said.

We must now record in our memory that the individual in whom the several components of his nature do their own work will be just, and will do his own work?

Yes, he said, we must record that important fact.

First, it is proper for the rational principle, which is wise, and has the care of the whole soul, to rule, and for the spirit to be the subject and ally?

Certainly.

And, as we were saying, the blending of music and gymnastic will
442 bring them into accord, nerving and sustaining the reason with noble words and lessons, and moderating and soothing and civilizing the wildness of passion by harmony and rhythm?

Quite true, he said.

And these two, thus nurtured and educated, and having learned truly to know their own functions, will rule over the concupiscent, which in each of us is the largest part of the soul and by nature most insatiable of gain; over this they will keep guard, lest, waxing great and strong with the fullness of bodily pleasures, as they are termed, the concupiscent soul, no longer confined to her own sphere, should attempt to enslave and rule those who are not her natural-born subjects, and overturn the whole life of man?

Very true, he said.

Both together will they not be the best defenders of the whole soul and the whole body against attacks from without; the one counselling, and the other going out to fight as the leader directs, and courageously executing his commands and counsels?

True.

Likewise it is by reference to spirit that an individual man is deemed courageous, because his spirit retains in pleasure and in pain the commands of reason about what he ought or ought not to fear?

Right, he replied.

And we call him wise on account of that little part which rules, and which proclaims these commands; the part in which is situated the knowledge of what is for the interest of each of the three parts and of the whole?

Assuredly.

And would you not say that he is temperate who has these same elements in friendly harmony, in whom the one ruling principle of reason, and the two subject ones of spirit and desire, are equally agreed that reason ought to rule, and do not rebel?

Certainly, he said, that is a precise account of temperance whether in the State or individual.

And, finally, I said, a man will be just in that way and by that quality which we have often mentioned.

That is very certain.

And is justice dimmer in the individual, and is her form different, or is she the same which we found her to be in the State?

There is no difference in my opinion, he said.

Because, if any doubt is still lingering in our minds, a few commonplace instances will satisfy us of the truth of what I am saying.

What sort of instances do you mean?

If the case is put to us, must we not admit that the just State, or the man of similar nature who has been trained in the principles of such a State, will be less likely than the unjust to make away with a deposit of gold or silver? Would any one deny this? 443

No one, he replied.

Will such a man ever be involved in sacrilege or theft, or treachery either to his friends or to his country?

Never.

Neither will he ever, for any reason, break faith where there have been oaths or agreements?

Impossible.

No one will be less likely to commit adultery, neglect his father and mother, or fail in his religious duties?

No one.

And the reason for all this is that each part of him is doing its own business, whether in ruling or being ruled?

Exactly so.

Are you satisfied then that the quality which makes such men and such states is justice, or do you hope to discover some other?

Not I, indeed.

Then our dream has been realized, and the suspicion which we expressed that, at the beginning of our work of construction, some divine power must have conducted us to a primary form of justice, has now been verified?

Yes, certainly.

And the division of labour which required the carpenter and the shoemaker and the rest of them to devote himself to the work for which he is naturally fitted, and to do nothing else, was a shadow of justice, and for that reason it was of use?

Clearly.

And in reality justice was such as we were describing, being concerned however, not with a man's external affairs, but with an inner relationship in which he himself is more truly concerned; for the just man does not permit the several elements within him to interfere with one another, or any of them to do the work of others, — he sets in order his own inner life, and is his own master and his own law, and at peace with himself; and when he has bound together the three principles within him, which may be compared to the higher, lower, and middle notes of the scale, and any that are intermediate between them — when he has bound all these together, and is no longer many, but has become one entirely temperate and perfectly adjusted nature, then he proceeds to act, if he has to act, whether in a matter of property, or in the treatment of the body, or in some affair of politics or private business; always thinking and calling that which preserves and co-operates with this harmonious condition, just and good action, and the knowledge which presides over it, wisdom, **444** and that which at any time impairs this condition, he will call unjust action, and the opinion which presides over it ignorance.

You have said the exact truth, Socrates.

Very good; and if we were to affirm that we had discovered the just man and the just State, and the nature of justice in each of them, we should not be far from the truth?

Most certainly not.

May we say so, then?

Let us say so.

And now, I said, injustice has to be considered.

Clearly.

Must not injustice be a strife which arises among the same three principles — a meddlesomeness, and interference, and rising up of a part of the soul against the whole, an assertion of unlawful authority, which is made by a rebellious subject against a true prince, of whom he is the natural vassal, — what is all this confusion and delusion but injustice and intemperance and cowardice and ignorance, and, in short, every form of vice?

Exactly so.

And if the nature of justice and injustice is known, then the meaning of acting unjustly and being unjust, or again of acting justly, is now also perfectly clear?

How so? he said.

Why, I said, they are like disease and health; being in the soul just what disease and health are in the body.

How so? he said.

Why, I said, that which is healthy causes health, and that which is unhealthy causes disease.

Yes.

And just actions cause justice, and unjust actions cause injustice?

That is certain.

And the creation of health is the institution of a natural order and government of one by another in the parts of the body; and the creation of disease is the production of a state of things at variance with this natural order?

True.

And is not the creation of justice the institution of a natural order and government of one by another in the parts of the soul, and the creation of injustice the production of a state of things at variance with the natural order?

Exactly so, he said.

Then virtue is the health and beauty and well-being of the soul, and vice the disease and weakness and deformity of the same?

True.

And how are virtue and vice acquired — is it not by good and evil practices?

Assuredly.

The time has come, then, to answer the final question of the 445 comparative advantage of justice and injustice: Which is the more profitable, to be just and act justly and honourably, whether one's character is or is not known, or to be unjust and act unjustly, if one is unpunished, that is to say unreformed?

In my judgement, Socrates, the question has now become ridiculous. We know that, when the bodily constitution is gone, life is no longer endurable, though pampered with all kinds of meats and drinks, and having all wealth and all power; and shall we be told that when the natural health of our vital principle is undermined and corrupted, life is still worth having to a man, if only he be allowed to do whatever he likes, except to take steps to acquire justice and virtue and escape from injustice and vice; assuming them both to be such as we have described?

Yes, I said, the question is, as you say, ridiculous. Still, as we are near the spot at which we may see the truth in the clearest manner with our own eyes, let us not faint by the way.

Certainly not, he replied.

Come here, then, I said, and behold the various forms of vice, those of them, I mean, which are worth looking at.

I am following you, he replied: proceed.

I said, The argument seems to have reached a height from which, as from some tower of speculation, a man may look down and see that virtue is one, but that the forms of vice are innumerable; there being four special ones which are deserving of note.

What do you mean? he said.

I mean, I replied, that there appear to be as many forms of the soul as there are distinct forms of the State.

How many?

There are five of the State, and five of the soul, I said.

What are they?

The first, I said, is that which we have been describing, and which may be given either of two names, monarchy or aristocracy, according as rule is exercised by one man distinguished among the ruling class or by more.

True, he replied.

But I regard the two names as describing one form only; for whether the government is in the hands of one or many, if the governors have been bred and trained in the manner which we have supposed, the fundamental laws of the State will not be disturbed.

Probably not, he replied.

Republic · Book V

Such is the city and constitution which I call good and true, and
the good and true man is of the same pattern; and if this is true,
every other is faulty and wrong; and whether we have regard to the
ordering of States, or to the regulation of the individual soul, four
kinds of wrongness are to be observed.

What are they? he said.

I was proceeding to tell the order in which the four wrong forms
appeared to me to succeed one another, when Polemarchus, who was
sitting a little way off, just beyond Adeimantus, stretched forth his
hand, and took hold of the upper part of his coat by the shoulder,
and drew him towards him, leaning forward himself and saying
something in his ear, of which I only caught the words, 'Shall we let
it go, or what shall we do?'...

 ◄§ Adeimantus banteringly accuses Socrates of laziness in having
failed to explain his earlier airy statement that the guardians in his
state will have the women and children in common, and demands
that he now describe how children will be born and reared. To this
the whole company agrees, Glaucon adding that the care of young
children before school age seems to him the chief stumbling block
in such a scheme. Socrates pretends to have feared the outcry that
his radical program will arouse and then adds in all seriousness that
he himself is uncertain of the wisdom of what he is about to propose
and fearful of misleading his friends. When Glaucon assures him of
absolution, he resumes:

Well, I replied, I suppose that I must retrace my steps and say
what I perhaps ought to have said before in the proper place. The
drama of the men has been played out, and now properly enough
comes the turn of the women, especially in view of your challenge.

For men born and educated like our citizens there can, in my
opinion, be no right possession and use of women and children unless
they follow the path on which we sent them forth. We proposed, as
you know, to treat them as watchdogs of the herd.

True.

Let us abide by that comparison in our account of their birth and
breeding, and let us see whether the result accords with our design.

What do you mean?

What I mean may be put into the form of a question, I said: Are
female sheepdogs expected to keep watch together with the males,
and to go hunting with them and share in their other activities? or
do we entrust to the males the entire and exclusive care of the flocks,

while we leave the females at home, because we think that the bearing and suckling their puppies is labour enough for them?

No, he said, they share alike; the only difference between them is that the males are regarded as stronger and the females as weaker.

But can you use different animals for the same purpose, unless they are bred and fed in the same way?

You cannot.

452　Then if women are to have the same duties as men, they must have the same education?

Yes.

The education which was assigned to the men was music and gymnastic.

Yes.

Then women also must be taught music and gymnastic and military exercises, and they must be treated like the men?

That is the inference, I suppose.

I fully expect, I said, that our proposals, if they are carried out, being unusual, may in many respects appear ridiculous.

No doubt of it.

Yes, and the most ridiculous thing of all will be the sight of women naked in the palaestra, exercising with the men, even when they are no longer young; they certainly will not be a vision of beauty, any more than the enthusiastic old men who in spite of wrinkles and ugliness continue to frequent the gymnasia.

Yes, indeed, he said: according to present notions the proposal would be thought ridiculous.

But then, I said, as we have determined to speak our minds, we must not fear the jests of the wits which will be directed against this sort of innovation; how they will talk of women's attainments both in music and gymnastic, and above all about their wearing armour and riding upon horseback.

Very true, he replied.

Yet having begun we must go forward to the rough places of the law; at the same time begging of these gentlemen for once in their life to be serious. Not long ago, as we shall remind them, the Hellenes were of the opinion, which is still generally received among the barbarians, that the sight of a naked man was ridiculous and improper; and when first the Cretans and then the Lacedaemonians introduced the custom of stripping for exercise, the wits of that day might equally have ridiculed the innovation.

No doubt.

But no doubt when experience showed that to let all things be uncovered was far better than to cover them up, the ludicrous effect to the outward eye vanished before what reason had proved to be best, and the man was perceived to be a fool who directs the shafts of his ridicule at any other sight but that of folly and vice, or seriously inclines to weigh the beautiful by any other standard but that of the good.

Very true, he replied.

First, then, let us come to an understanding whether the course 453 we propose is possible or not: let us admit any arguments put forward by comedians or persons more seriously inclined, and tending to show whether in the human race the female is able to take part in all the occupations of the male, or in some of them only, or in none; and to which class the art of war belongs. That will be the best way of commencing the inquiry, and will probably lead to the soundest conclusion.

That will be much the best way.

Shall we take the other side first and begin by arguing against ourselves; in this manner the adversary's position will not be undefended.

Why not? he said.

Then let us put a speech into the mouths of our opponents. They will say: "Socrates and Glaucon, no adversary is needed to convict you, for you yourselves, at the first foundation of the State, admitted the principle that everybody was to do the one work suited to his own nature.' And certainly, if I am not mistaken, such an admission was made by us. 'And do not the natures of men and women differ very much indeed?' And we shall reply: Of course they do. Then we shall be asked, 'Whether the tasks assigned to men and to women should not be different, and such as are agreeable to their different natures?' Certainly they should. 'But if so, have you not fallen into a serious inconsistency in saying that men and women, whose natures are so entirely different, ought to perform the same actions?' — What defence will you make for us, my good sir, against these objections?

That is not an easy question to answer when asked suddenly; and I shall and I do beg of you to draw out the case on our side.

These are the objections, Glaucon, and there are many others of a like kind, which I foresaw long ago; they made me afraid and reluctant to take in hand any law about the possession and nurture of women and children.

By Zeus, he said, the problem to be solved is anything but easy.

Why yes, I said, but the fact is that when a man is out of his depth, whether he has fallen into a little swimming-bath or into mid ocean, he has to swim all the same.

Very true.

And must not we swim and try to reach the shore, while hoping that Arion's dolphin or some other miraculous help may save us?

I suppose so, he said.

Well then, let us see if any way of escape can be found. We acknowledged — did we not? — that different natures ought to have different pursuits, and that men's and women's natures are different. And now what are we saying? that different natures ought to have the same pursuits, — this is the inconsistency which is charged upon us.

Precisely.

454   Verily, Glaucon, I said, glorious is the power of the art of disputation!

Why do you say so?

Because I think that many a man falls into the practice against his will. When he thinks that he is reasoning he is really disputing, just because he does not know how to inquire into a subject by distinguishing its various aspects, but pursues some verbal opposition in the statement which has been made. That is the difference between the spirit of contention and that of fair discussion.

Yes, he replied, that is a fairly common failing, but does it apply at present to us?

Yes, indeed; for there is a danger of our getting unintentionally into verbal contradiction.

In what way?

Why, we valiantly and pugnaciously insist upon the verbal truth that different natures ought to have different pursuits, but we never considered at all what was the meaning of sameness or difference of nature, or with what intention we distinguished them when we assigned different pursuits to different natures and the same to the same natures.

Why, no, he said, that was never considered by us.

I said: Yet it seems that we should be entitled to ask ourselves whether there is not an opposition in nature between bald men and hairy men; and if this is admitted by us, then, if bald men are cobblers, we should forbid the hairy men to be cobblers, and conversely?

That would be a jest, he said.

Yes, I said, a jest; and why? because we were not previously speaking of sameness or difference in *any* sense; we were concerned with one *form* of difference or similarity, namely that which would affect the pursuit in which a man is engaged; we should have argued, for example, that a physician and one who is in mind a physician may be said to have the same nature.

True.

Whereas the physician and the carpenter have different natures?

Certainly.

And if, I said, the male and female sex appear to differ in their fitness for any art or pursuit, we should say that such pursuit or art ought to be assigned to one or the other of them; but if the difference consists only in women bearing and men begetting children, this does not amount to a proof that a woman differs from a man in respect of the sort of education she should receive; and we shall therefore continue to maintain that our guardians and their wives ought to have the same pursuits.

Quite rightly, he said.

Only then shall we ask our opponent to inform us with reference to which of the pursuits or arts of civic life the nature of a woman differs from that of a man?

That will be quite fair.

And perhaps he, like yourself a moment ago, will reply that to give a sufficient answer on the instant is not easy; but that given time for reflection there is no difficulty.

Yes, perhaps.

Suppose then that we invite such an objector to accompany us in the argument, in the hope of showing him that there is no occupation peculiar to women which need be considered in the administration of the State.

By all means.

Let us say to him: Come now, and we will ask you a question: — when you spoke of a nature gifted or not gifted in any respect, did you mean to say that one man will acquire a thing easily, another with difficulty? the first, after brief instruction, is able to discover a great deal more for himself, whereas the other, after much teaching and application, cannot even preserve what he has learnt; or again, did you mean that the one has a body which is a good servant to his mind, while the body of the other is a hindrance to him? Would not these be the sort of differences which distinguish the man gifted by nature from the one who is ungifted?

No one will deny that.

And can you mention any pursuit of mankind in which the male sex has not all these gifts and qualities in a higher degree than the female? Need I waste time in speaking of the art of weaving, and the preparation of pancakes and preserves in which womankind is generally thought to have some skill, and in which for her to be beaten by a man is of all things the most absurd?

You are quite right, he replied, in maintaining that one sex greatly excels the other in almost every field. Although many women are in many things superior to many men, yet on the whole what you say is true.

And if so, my friend, I said, there is no special faculty of administration in a state which a woman has because she is a woman, or which a man has by virtue of his sex, but the gifts of nature are alike diffused in both; all the pursuits of men can naturally be assigned to women also, but in all of them a woman is weaker than a man.

Very true.

Then are we to impose all our enactments on men and none of them on women?

That will never do.

Because we shall say that a woman too may, or may not, have the gift of healing; and that one is a musician, and another has no music in her nature?

Very true.

456 And it can hardly be denied that one woman has a turn for gymnastic and military exercises, and another is unwarlike and hates gymnastics?

I think not.

And one woman is a philosopher, and another is an enemy of philosophy; one has spirit, and another is without spirit?

That is also true.

Then one woman will have the temper of a guardian, and another not. For these, as you remember, were the natural gifts for which we looked in the selection of the male guardians.

Yes.

Men and women alike possess the qualities which make a guardian; they differ only in their comparative strength or weakness.

Obviously.

Therefore those women who have such qualities are to be selected as the companions and colleagues of men who also have them and whom they resemble in capacity and in character?

Very true.

But ought not the same natures to be trained in the same pursuits?

They ought.

Then we have come round to the previous point that there is nothing unnatural in assigning music and gymnastic to the guardian women.

Certainly not.

The law which we then enacted was agreeable to nature, and therefore not an impossibility or mere aspiration; it is rather the contrary practice, which prevails at present, that is a violation of nature.

That appears to be true.

We had to consider, first, whether our proposals were possible, and secondly whether they were the most beneficial?

Yes.

And the possibility has been acknowledged?

Yes.

The very great benefit has next to be established?

Quite so.

You will admit that the same education which makes a man a good guardian will make a woman a good guardian; especially if the original nature of both is the same?

Yes.

I should like to ask you a question.

What is it?

Is it your opinion that one man is better than another? Or do you think them all equal?

Not at all.

And in the commonwealth which we were founding do you conceive the guardians who have been brought up on our model system to be more perfect men, or the cobblers whose education has been cobbling?

What a ridiculous question!

You have answered me, I replied: in fact, our guardians are the best of all our citizens?

By far the best.

And will not the guardian women be the best women?

Yes, by far the best.

And can there be anything better for the interests of the State than that the men and women of a State should be as good as possible?

There can be nothing better.

And this is what the arts of music and gymnastic, when present 457 in such manner as we have described, will accomplish?

Certainly.

Then we have made an enactment not only possible but in the highest degree beneficial to the State?

True.

Then let the guardian women strip, for their virtue will be their robe, and let them share in the toils of war and the defence of their country; only in the distribution of labours the lighter are to be assigned to the women, who are the weaker natures, but in other respects their duties are to be the same. And as for the man who laughs at naked women exercising their bodies from the best of motives, in his laughter he is plucking

A fruit of unripe wisdom,

and he himself is ignorant of what he is laughing at, or what he is about; — for that is, and ever will be, the best of sayings, *That the useful is noble and the hurtful is base.*

Very true.

Here, then, is one difficulty in our law about women, which we may say that we have now escaped; the wave has not swallowed us up alive for enacting that the guardians of either sex should have all their pursuits in common; to the utility and also to the possibility of this arrangement the consistency of the argument with itself bears witness.

Yes, that was a mighty wave which you have escaped.

Yes, I said, but you may not think it so impressive when you see the next.

Go on; let me see.

The law, I said, which is the sequel of this and of all that has preceded, is to the following effect, — 'that all these women are to be common to all the men of the same class, none living privately together; and, moreover, that their children are to be common, and no parent is to know his own child, nor any child his parent.'

Yes, he said, you will find it much harder to convince anyone either of the possibility or of the usefulness of such a law.

I do not think, I said, that there can be any dispute about the very great utility of having both women and children in common; the possibility is quite another matter, and will, no doubt, be very much disputed.

Both points are sure to be warmly disputed.

You imply that the two questions must be combined, I replied. I hoped that you would admit that the proposal was useful, and so I should escape from at least one of them, and then there would remain only the possibility.

But that attempt to escape is detected, and therefore you will please to give a defence of both.

Well, I said, I submit to my fate. Yet grant me a little favour: 458 let me feast my mind with the dream as day-dreamers are in the habit of feasting themselves when they are walking alone; for before they have discovered any means of effecting their wishes — that is a matter which never troubles them; they would rather not tire themselves by thinking about possibilities — but assuming that what they desire is already granted to them, they proceed with their plan, and delight in detailing what they mean to do when their wish has come true — a recreation which tends to make an idle mind still idler. Now I myself am beginning to lose heart, and I should like, with your permission, to pass over the question of possibility at present. Assuming therefore the possibility of the proposal, I shall now proceed to inquire how the rulers will carry out these arrangements, and I shall demonstrate that our plan, if executed, will be of the greatest possible benefit both to the State and to the guardians. First of all, then, if you have no objection, I will endeavour with your help to consider the advantages of the measure; and hereafter the question of possibility.

I have no objection; proceed.

First, I think that if our rulers and their auxiliaries are to be worthy of the name which they bear, there must be the power of command in the one and willingness to obey in the other; the guardians must themselves obey the laws, and they must also imitate the spirit of them in any details which are entrusted to their care.

That is right, he said.

You, I said, who are their legislator, having selected the men, will now select the women and give them to them; . . .

§ Socrates now declares that the prospective women guardians are to be chosen as having the same abilities to govern and be governed as the men, and are to live with the men and share all their activities. Inevitably, he says, men and women will be drawn to desire sexual union, but no licentiousness is to be permitted. "Sacred marriages" — by which, he explains, he means beneficial ones — will be arranged in such a way as to breed most often from the best. To accomplish this, brides and bridegrooms will be chosen by a pretended lottery, and in addition the brave will be more frequently chosen. There will be periodic festivals at which these unions will occur, solemnized by religious ceremonies, and the number of weddings will be planned so as to preserve the proper number of citizens. The sound children of the better parents will be reared, but deformed children of the better parents and offspring of the worse parents will be secretly put away. Socrates justifies the use of deceit in these matters on the part of the rulers by appealing to the earlier announced principle of the "medicinal lie" (*Republic* 382c, 414b), and says that here it is designed to prevent dissension arising from the resentment of those who are less frequently chosen for marriage or whose children are not reared.

Officers of the state will take the infants who are to be reared to the "fold," as Plato calls the nurseries, and there the mothers will come to nurse them, but no mother is to know which is her own child, and non-guardian nurses are to assume the main burden of care.

Marriages are to be limited to guardians of the most favorable ages, twenty to forty for women and twenty-five to fifty-five for men. The begetting of children before the proper ages or outside of marriage will be condemned as unholy and unrighteous; after the proper ages for marriage, sexual relations will be unrestricted (with one exception), but any children that result will not be reared. The exception is that sexual unions between presumed parents and children will be forbidden, and the presumption will be based on the child's having been born in the proper month following a given marriage festival. Those born in the same birth period after such a festival will be regarded as brothers and sisters, and these may marry if the Pythian oracle approves.

Having described the arrangements, Socrates proceeds to justify his proposal as good. He first obtains assent to the principle that community of interest among citizens and common feelings of joy or grief constitute the greatest good for a state. He then declares that in the ideal city all groups will call each other by such names as "saviors" and "helpers," "maintainers" and "supporters," and that the guardians will call each other by family names such as "brother" and "son"; nor will these be empty words, since the voice of public opinion will enjoin filial reverence and parental concern. Thus community of feeling will be obtained, and will result from the sharing of women and children. Socrates observes that unity of feeling will be a consequence also of the communal living and renunciation of property prescribed for the guardians. There will be no lawsuits among them arising from property or private family interests. Neither will there be suits for assault, since guardians of like age will be required to defend themselves against each other and the elder may rightfully chastise the younger, while the younger will be restrained by shame and fear from striking the elder. Thus there will be peace among the guardians and in consequence in the whole city, and the guardians despite their poverty will lead noble and blessed lives, honored while living and after death. But any who utterly ceases to be a guardian, and tries to seize the wealth of the city, will find it not to his advantage.

That such a plan is possible, and in what way, is now to be shown. The children of the guardians will be prepared for their task by being taken out to observe war, but only on relatively safe expeditions, under careful guidance, and mounted on swift horses. The bravery of the soldiers will be encouraged by many devices: the demotion of cowards to the rank of common citizen, the abandonment of those who allow themselves to be captured, above all by honors and privileges given the brave. They will be crowned and greeted by all their comrades, and — Socrates adds, at Glaucon's suggestion — they will be allowed to kiss whom they please on that particular expedition; they will be feasted. Those who die bravely will be ceremonially buried and honored after death as heroes; so also will those who show superlative excellence in other ways.

Socrates now lays down the restraints which his guardians are to exercise in their conduct of war. Being Greeks, they will not enslave other Greeks or despoil the dead or hinder their burial, nor will they dedicate in temples the arms of the vanquished, especially of fellow Greeks. They will not devastate the territory of Greeks or blame whole populations, or in fact conduct war in the full sense, but will fight like those who look forward to eventual reconciliation; though with non-Greeks they will truly be at war.

At this point Glaucon interrupts, objecting:

471   But still I must say, Socrates, that if you are allowed to go on in this way you will entirely forget the other question which at the commencement of this discussion you thrust aside: — Is such an

order of things possible, and how, if at all? For I am quite ready to acknowledge that the plan which you propose, if only feasible, would do all sorts of good to the State. I will add, what you have omitted, that your citizens will be the bravest of warriors and will never leave their ranks, for they will all know one another, and each will call the other father, brother, son; and if you suppose the women to join their armies, whether in the same rank or in the rear, either as a terror to the enemy or as auxiliaries in case of need, I know that they will then be absolutely invincible; and there are, as I can see, many domestic advantages which might also be mentioned: but, as I admit all these advantages and as many more as you please, if only this State of yours were to come into existence, you need not proceed with your description of it. What we have next to do is to convince ourselves that it is possible, and show how it is so — the rest may be left.

If I loiter for a moment, you instantly make a raid upon me, I said, **472** and have no mercy; I have hardly escaped the first and second waves, and you seem not to be aware that you are now bringing upon me the third, which is the greatest and heaviest. When you have seen and heard the third wave, I think you will be more considerate and will acknowledge that some fear and hesitation was natural respecting a proposal so extraordinary as that which I have now to state and investigate.

The more appeals of this sort which you make, he said, the more determined are we that you shall tell us how such a State is possible: speak out and at once.

Let me begin by reminding you that we found our way hither in the search after justice and injustice.

True, he replied; but what of that?

I was only going to ask whether, if we have discovered them, we are to require that the just man should in nothing fail of absolute justice; or may we be satisfied with an approximation, and the attainment in him of a higher degree of justice than is to be found in other men?

The approximation will be enough.

It was in order to have an ideal that we were inquiring into the nature of absolute justice and into the character of the supposed perfectly just man, and into injustice and the perfectly unjust man. We were to look at these two extremes in order that we might judge of our own happiness and unhappiness according to the standard of happiness and misery which they exhibited and the degree in which we resembled them, but not with any view of showing that they could exist in fact.

True, he said.

Would a painter, in your view, be less expert because, after having delineated with consummate art an ideal of a perfectly beautiful man, he was unable to show that any such man could ever have existed?

No, indeed.

Well, and were we not creating an ideal of a perfect State?

To be sure.

And is our theory a worse theory because we are unable to prove the possibility of a city being ordered in the manner described?

Surely not, he replied.

That is the truth, I said. But if, at your request, I am to try and show how and under what conditions the possibility is highest, I must ask you, having this in view, to repeat your former admissions.

What admissions?

473   I want to know whether a conception is ever fully realized in action? Must not action, whatever a man think, always, in the nature of things, have less hold upon the truth than words? What do you say?

I agree.

Then you must not insist on my proving that the actual State will in every respect coincide with the ideal: if we are only able to discover how a city may be governed nearly as we proposed, you will admit that we have discovered the possibility which you demand; and will be contented. I am sure that I should be contented — will not you?

Yes, I will.

Let me next endeavour to show what is that fault in States which is the cause of their present maladministration, and what is the least change which will enable a State to pass into the truer form; and let the change, if possible, be of one thing only, or, if not, of two; at any rate, let the changes be as few and slight as possible.

Certainly, he replied.

I think, I said, that there might be a reform of the State if only one change were made, which is not a slight or easy though still a possible one.

What is it? he said.

Now then, I said, I am faced with that which I likened to the greatest of the waves; yet shall the word be spoken, even though the wave break and drown me in laughter and discredit; and do you mark my words.

Proceed.

I said: Until philosophers are kings in their cities, or the kings and princes of this world have the spirit and power of philosophy, and political greatness and wisdom meet in one, and those commoner natures who pursue either to the exclusion of the other are compelled to stand aside, cities will never have rest from their evils, — no, nor the human race, as I believe, — and then only will this our ideal State have a possibility of life and behold the light of day. Such was the thought, my dear Glaucon, which I would fain have uttered if it had not seemed too extravagant; for to be convinced that in no other State can there be happiness private or public is indeed a hard thing.

Socrates, what do you mean? I would have you consider that the word which you have uttered is one at which numerous persons, and very respectable persons too, in a figure pulling off their coats all in 474 a moment and seizing any weapon that comes to hand, will run at you might and main before you know where you are, intending to do heaven knows what; and if you don't prepare an answer and make good your escape, you will be 'pared by their fine wits', and no mistake.

You got me into the scrape, I said.

And I was quite right; however, I will do all I can to protect you; but I can only give you goodwill and good advice, and, perhaps, I may be able to fit answers to your questions better than another — that is all. And now, having such an auxiliary, you must do your best to show the unbelievers that you are right.

I ought to try, I said, since you offer me such invaluable assistance. And I think that, if there is to be a chance of our escaping, we must explain to them whom we mean when we say that philosophers are to rule in the State; having brought them to light, our defence will be that there are some natures who ought to study philosophy and to be leaders in the State; and others who are not born to be philosophers, and are meant to be followers rather than leaders.

Then now for a definition, he said.

Follow me, I said, and I hope that I may in some way or other be able to give you a satisfactory explanation.

Proceed.

I dare say that you remember, and therefore I need not remind you, that a lover, if he is worthy of the name, ought to show his love, not to some one part of that which he loves, but to the whole.

Apparently you must remind me, for I have not fully understood.

Another person, I said, might fairly reply as you do; but a lover like yourself ought to be well aware that all who are in the flower of youth do somehow or other raise a pang or emotion in a lover's breast, and are thought by him to be worthy of his affectionate regards. Is not this a way which you have with the fair: one has a snub nose, and you praise his charming face; the hook-nose of another has, you say, a royal look; while he who is neither snub nor hooked has the grace of regularity: the dark visage is manly, the fair are children of the gods; and as to the sweet 'honey-pale', as they are called, what is the very name but the invention of a lover who talks in diminutives, and is not averse to paleness if appearing on the cheek of youth? In a word, there is no excuse which you will not make, and nothing which you will not say, in order not to lose a single flower that blooms in the spring-time of youth.

If you make me an authority in matters of love, for the sake of the argument, I assent.

And what do you say of lovers of wine? Do you not see them doing the same? They are glad of any pretext of drinking any wine.

Very glad.

And the same is true, you must have noticed, of ambitious men; if they cannot command an army, they are willing to command a platoon; and if they cannot be honoured by really great and important persons, they are glad to be honoured by lesser and meaner people, — for honour of some kind they must have.

Exactly.

Once more let me ask: Does he who is said to desire something, desire the whole class to which it belongs, or a part only?

The whole.

Thus we shall say of the philosopher that he is a lover, not of a part of wisdom only, but of the whole?

True.

And he who dislikes learning, especially in youth, when he has no power of judging what is good and what is not, such a one we maintain not to be a philosopher or a lover of knowledge, just as he who refuses his food is not hungry, and may be said to have a bad appetite and not a good one?

Very true, he said.

Whereas he who has a taste for every sort of knowledge and who is curious to learn and is never satisfied, may be justly termed a philosopher? Am I not right?

Glaucon said: If curiosity makes a philosopher, you will find many a strange being will have a title to the name. All the lovers of sights have a delight in learning, and must therefore be included. Musical amateurs, too, are a folk strangely out of place among philosophers, for they are the last persons in the world who would come to anything like a philosophical discussion if they could help; while they run about at the Dionysiac festivals as if they had let out their ears for the season to hear every chorus, and miss no performance either in town or country. Now are we to maintain that all these and any who have similar tastes, as well as the professors of quite minor arts, are philosophers?

Certainly not, I replied; they are only an imitation.

He said: Who then are the true philosophers?

Those, I said, who are lovers of the vision of truth.

That is also good, he said; but I should like to know what you mean?

To another, I replied, I might have a difficulty in explaining; but I am sure that you will admit a proposition which I am about to make.

What is the proposition?

That since beauty is the opposite of ugliness, they are two?

Certainly.

And inasmuch as they are two, each of them is one?

True again.

And of just and unjust, good and evil, and of every other form, the same remark holds: taken singly, each of them is one; but from the various combinations of them with actions and bodies and with one another, they are seen in all sorts of lights and appear many?

Very true.

And this is the distinction which I draw between the sight-loving, art-loving, practical class which you have mentioned, and those of whom I am speaking, and who are alone worthy of the name of philosophers.

How do you distinguish them? he said.

The lovers of sounds and sights, I replied, are, as I conceive, fond of fine tones and colours and forms and all the artificial products that are made out of them, but their mind is incapable of seeing or loving absolute beauty.

The fact is plain, he replied.

Few are they who are able to attain to this ideal beauty and contemplate it.

Very true.

And he who, having a sense of beautiful things, has no sense of absolute beauty, or who, if another lead him to a knowledge of that beauty, is unable to follow — of such a one I ask, Is he awake or in a dream only? Reflect: is not the dreamer, sleeping or waking, one who likens dissimilar things, who puts the copy in the place of the real object?

I should certainly say that such a one was dreaming.

But he who, on the contrary, recognizes the existence of absolute beauty and is able to contemplate both the Idea and the objects which participate in it, neither putting the objects in the place of the Idea nor the Idea in the place of the objects — is he a dreamer, or is he awake?

He is wide awake.

And since he knows, it would be right to describe his state of mind as knowledge, and the state of mind of the other, who opines only, as opinion?

Certainly.

But suppose that the latter should quarrel with us and dispute our statement, can we administer any soothing cordial or advice to him, without revealing to him that there is sad disorder in his wits?

We must certainly offer him some good advice, he replied.

Come, then, and let us think of something to say to him. Shall we begin by assuring him that he is welcome to any knowledge which he may have, and that we are rejoiced at his having it? But we should like to ask him a question: Does he who has knowledge know something or nothing? (You must answer for him.)

I answer that he knows something.

Something that is or is not?

477 Something that is; for how can that which is not ever be known?

And are we assured, after looking at the matter from many points of view, that the fully real is or may be fully known, but that the utterly unreal is utterly unknown?

Nothing can be more certain.

Good. But if there be anything which is of such a nature as to be and not to be, that will have a place intermediate between pure being [reality] and the absolute negation of being?

Yes, between them.

And, as knowledge corresponded to being and ignorance must obviously correspond to not-being, we have now to discover, for this intermediate between being and not-being, a corresponding intermediate between ignorance and knowledge, if there be such?

Certainly.

Do we admit the existence of opinion?

Undoubtedly.

As being the same faculty as knowledge, or another?

Another.

Then opinion and knowledge have to do with different things, each according to its faculty?

Yes.

And knowledge is relative to being and knows being as it is. But before I proceed further I shall have to make a division.

What division?

I will begin by placing faculties in a class by themselves: they are powers in us, and in all other things, by which we do as we do. Sight and hearing, for example, I should call faculties. Have I clearly explained the class which I mean?

Yes, I quite understand.

Then let me tell you my view about them. I do not perceive that a faculty has colour or figure, or any of those marks which enable me, in numerous cases, to differentiate one thing from another. In speaking of a faculty I think only of its sphere and its result; and that which has the same sphere and the same result I call the same faculty, but that which has another sphere and another result I call different. Would that be your way of speaking?

Yes.

And will you be so very good as to answer one more question? Would you say that knowledge is a faculty, or in what class would you place it?

Certainly knowledge is a faculty, and the mightiest of all faculties.

And is opinion also a faculty? Or is it to be ranked in another class?

No, he said; opinion is just that faculty whereby we are able to form an opinion.

But now you were acknowledging a little while ago that knowledge is not the same as opinion?

Why, yes, he said: how can any reasonable man ever identify that which is infallible with that which errs?

An excellent answer, proving, I said, that we are quite conscious 478 of a distinction between them.

Yes.

Then knowledge and opinion, having distinct powers, are meant to operate in distinct spheres?

That is certain.

Being is the sphere of knowledge, and the function of knowledge is to know the nature of being?

Yes.

And that of opinion is to form an opinion?

Yes.

About the same object which is known to knowledge? and will the same thing be both known and opined? Or is that not possible?

Nay, he replied, that has been already disproven; if difference in faculty implies difference in the sphere, and if, as we say, opinion and knowledge are distinct faculties, then the sphere of knowledge and of opinion cannot be the same.

Then if being is the sphere of knowledge, something other than being must be the sphere of opinion?

Yes, something else.

Well then, is not-being the sphere of opinion? or, rather, how can there be even an opinion about that which is not? Reflect: when a man has an opinion, does he not refer it to something? Can he have an opinion which is an opinion about nothing?

Impossible.

He who has an opinion has an opinion about some one thing?
Yes.
And not-being is not one thing but, properly speaking, nothing?
True.
Of not-being, ignorance was assumed to be the necessary correlative; of being, knowledge?
And rightly, he said.
Then opinion is not concerned either with being or with not-being?
Not with either.
And can therefore neither be ignorance nor knowledge?
That seems to be true.
But is opinion to be sought without and beyond either of them, in a greater clearness than knowledge, or in a greater darkness than ignorance?
In neither.
Then I suppose that opinion appears to you to be darker than knowledge, but lighter than ignorance?
Both; and in no small degree.
And also to be within and between them?
Yes.
Then you would infer that opinion is intermediate?
No question.
But have we not said before, that if anything appeared to be of a sort which is and is not at the same time, that sort of thing would appear also to lie in the interval between pure being and absolute not-being; and that the corresponding faculty would be neither knowledge nor ignorance, but will be found in the interval between them?
True.
And in that interval there has now been discovered something which we call opinion?
There has.
Then what remains to be discovered is the object which partakes equally of the nature of being and not-being, and cannot rightly be termed either, pure and simple; this unknown term, when discovered, we may truly call the subject of opinion and assign each to their proper faculty, — the extremes to the faculties of the extremes and the mean to the faculty of the mean.
True.
479   This being premised, I would ask the gentleman who is of opinion that there is no absolute or unchangeable Idea of beauty, but only a number of beautiful things — he, I say, your lover of beautiful sights, who cannot bear to be told that the beautiful is one, and the just is one, or that anything is one — to him I would appeal, saying,

Will you be so very kind, sir, as to tell us whether, of all these beautiful things, there is one which will not be found ugly; or of the just, which will not be found unjust; or of the holy, which will not also seem unholy?

No, he replied; these things must, from different points of view, be found both beautiful and ugly; and the same is true of the rest.

And do not the many which are doubles appear no less plainly to be halves?

Quite true.

And things great and small, heavy and light, will not be denoted by the names which we happen to use first any more than by the opposite names?

True; both names will always attach to all of them.

If so, can any one of those many things be said to be, rather than not to be, that which we happen to have termed it?

He replied: They are like the punning riddles which are asked at feasts or the children's puzzle about the eunuch aiming at the bat, with what he hit him, as they say in the puzzle, and upon what the bat was sitting. The individual objects of which I am speaking are also a riddle, and have a double sense: nor can you fix them in your mind, either as being or not-being, or both, or neither.

Then what will you do with them? I said. Can they have a better place than between being and not-being? For they are clearly not in greater darkness or negation than not-being, or more full of light and existence than being.

That is quite true, he said.

Thus then we seem to have discovered that the many notions which the multitude entertain about the beautiful and about all other things are tossing about in some region which is half-way between pure being and pure not-being?

We have.

Yes; and we had before agreed that anything of this kind which we might find was to be described as matter of opinion, and not as matter of knowledge; being the intermediate flux which is caught and detained by the intermediate faculty.

Quite true.

Then those who gaze on many beautiful things, and who yet neither see absolute beauty, nor can follow any guide who points the way thither; who see instances of justice, but not absolute justice, and the like, — such persons may be said in all their pronouncements to have opinion but not knowledge?

That is certain.

But those who in everything look to the absolute and eternal and immutable may be said to know, and not to have opinion only?

Neither can that be denied.

480 The one love and embrace the subjects of knowledge, the other those of opinion? The latter are the same, as I dare say you will remember, who listened to sweet sounds and gazed upon fair colours, but would not tolerate the existence of absolute beauty.

Yes, I remember.

Shall we then be guilty of any impropriety in calling them lovers of opinion rather than lovers of wisdom, and will they be very angry with us for thus describing them?

Not if they will listen to me; no man should be angry at what is true.

But those who love the truth in each thing are to be called lovers of wisdom and not lovers of opinion.

Assuredly.

Republic · Book VI

And thus, Glaucon, after the argument has gone a weary way, ⁴⁸⁴ the true and the false philosophers have at length appeared in view.

I do not think, he said, that the way could have been shortened.

I suppose not, I said; and yet I believe that we might have had a better view of both of them if the discussion could have been confined to this one subject, and if there were not many other questions which must be resolved before we can see in what respect the life of the just differs from that of the unjust.

And what is the next question? he asked.

Surely, I said, the one which follows next in order. Inasmuch as philosophers only are able to grasp the eternal and unchangeable, and those who wander in the region of the many and variable are not philosophers, I must ask you which of the two classes should be the rulers of our State?

And how can we rightly answer that question?

Whichever of the two seem best able to guard the laws and institutions of our State — let them be appointed guardians.

Very good.

Neither, I said, can there be any question that the watcher who is to guard anything should have eyes rather than no eyes?

There can be no question of that.

And are not those who are verily and indeed wanting in the knowledge of the true being of each thing, and who have in their souls no clear pattern, and are unable to look like painters at the absolute truth and to that original to repair, and having perfect vision thereof to frame laws about beauty, goodness, and justice, if not already framed, or to guard and preserve order where it exists — are not such persons, I ask, simply blind?

Truly, he replied, they are much in that condition.

And shall they be our guardians when there are others who, besides being their equals in experience and falling short of them in no particular of virtue, also know the very truth of each thing?

There can be no reason, he said, for choosing others, if it is true that our men are not inferior in other ways; for they excel in what is probably the most important point of all.

Suppose then, I said, that we determine how this union of knowl- ⁴⁸⁵ edge and experience in the same persons is to be achieved.

By all means.

In the first place, as we began by observing, the nature of the philosopher has to be ascertained. We must come to an under-

259

standing about him, and then we shall also, if I am not mistaken, acknowledge that such a union of qualities is possible, and that those in whom they are united, and those only, should be rulers in the State.

What do you mean?

Let us suppose it agreed that philosophical minds love any form of science which may give them a glimpse of an eternal reality not disturbed by generation and decay.

Agreed.

And further, I said, let us agree that they are lovers of all true being; there is no part whether greater or less, or more or less honourable, which they are willing to renounce; as we said before of the lover and the man of ambition.

True.

And if they are to be what we were describing, is there not another quality which they should also possess?

What quality?

Truthfulness: they will never intentionally receive into their mind falsehood, which is their detestation, and they will love the truth.

Yes, that may be safely affirmed of them.

'May be', my friend, I replied, is not the word; say rather, 'must be affirmed': for he whose nature is amorous of anything cannot help loving all that belongs or is akin to the object of his affections.

Right, he said.

And is there anything more akin to wisdom than truth?

How can there be?

Can the same nature be a lover of wisdom and a lover of falsehood?

Never.

The true lover of learning then must from his earliest youth, as far as in him lies, desire all truth?

Assuredly.

But then again, as we know by experience, he whose desires are strong in one direction will have them weaker in others; they will be like a stream which has been drawn off into another channel.

True.

He whose desires are drawn towards the sciences and other studies will be absorbed in the pleasures of the soul, and his eagerness for bodily pleasure will decline — I mean, if he be a true philosopher and not a sham one.

That is most certain.

Such a one is sure to be temperate and the reverse of covetous; for the motives which make another man desirous of wealth and lavish spending have no place in his character.

Very true.

Here is another criterion of the philosophical nature, which has **486**
also to be considered.

What is that?

There should be no secret corner of illiberality; nothing can be
more antagonistic than meanness to a soul which is ever longing
after the whole of things both divine and human.

Most true, he replied.

Then how can he who has magnificence of mind and is the
spectator of all time and all existence, think human life to be a great
thing?

He cannot.

Or can such a one account death fearful?

No indeed.

Then the cowardly and mean nature has no part in true philosophy?

Certainly not.

Or again: can he who is harmoniously constituted, who is not
covetous or mean, or a boaster, or a coward — can he, I say, ever
be unjust or hard in his dealings?

Impossible.

Then you have another sign which distinguishes even in youth
the philosophical nature from the unphilosophical; you will observe
whether a man is just and gentle, or rude and unsociable.

True.

There is another point which should be remarked.

What point?

Whether he has or has not facility in learning; for you must not
expect him to find entire satisfaction in a study which gives him
pain, and in which after much toil he makes little progress.

Certainly not.

And again, if he can retain nothing of what he learns, will he
not be full of forgetfulness and devoid of knowledge?

That is certain.

Labouring in vain, he must end in hating himself and his fruitless occupation?

Yes.

Then a forgetful soul can never be ranked among genuine philosophic natures; we must insist that the philosopher should have a
good memory?

Certainly.

And once more, the inharmonious and unseemly nature can only
tend to disproportion?

Undoubtedly.

And do you consider truth to be akin to proportion or to disproportion?

To proportion.

Then, besides other qualities, we must try to find a naturally well-proportioned and gracious mind, which will be easily led to the vision of the true being of everything.

Certainly.

I hope you do not doubt that all these qualities, which we have been enumerating, go together, and are necessary to a soul which is to have a full and perfect participation of being.

487   They are absolutely necessary, he replied.

And must not that be a blameless occupation which he only can pursue who has the gift of a good memory, and is quick to learn, — noble, gracious, the friend of truth, justice, courage, temperance, who are his kindred?

The god of jealousy himself, he said, could find no fault with such an occupation.

And to men like him, I said, when perfected by years and education, and to these only you will entrust the State.

Here Adeimantus interposed and said: To these statements, Socrates, no one can offer a reply; but whenever you talk in this way, a strange feeling passes over the minds of your hearers. They fancy that they are led astray a little at each step in the argument, owing to their own want of skill in asking and answering questions; these littles accumulate, and at the end of the discussion they are found to have sustained a mighty overthrow and their first opinion appears to be turned upside down. And as unskilful players of draughts are at last barred by their more skilful adversaries and have no piece to move, so they too find themselves barred at last; for they have nothing to say in this new game of which words are the pieces; and yet they are sure the truth is not on your side. I am speaking with reference to what is now occurring. For any one of us might say, that although in words he is not able to meet you at each step of the argument, he sees as a fact that the votaries of philosophy, when they carry on the study, not only in youth as a part of education, but as the pursuit of their maturer years, most of them become strange monsters, not to say utter rogues, and that those who may be considered the best of them are at least made useless to the world by this occupation which you extol.

Well, and do you think that those who say so are wrong?

I cannot tell, he replied; but I should like to know what is your opinion.

Hear my answer; I am of opinion that they are quite right.

Then how can we be justified in saying that cities will not cease from evil until philosophers rule in them, when we acknowledge that philosophers are useless to the State?

You ask a question, I said, to which a reply can only be given in a parable.

Yes, Socrates; and that is a way of speaking to which you are not at all accustomed, I suppose.

I perceive, I said, that you are vastly amused at having plunged me into such a hopeless discussion; but now hear the parable, and **488** then you will be still more amused at the meagreness of my imagination: for the manner in which the best men are treated in their own States is so grievous that no single thing on earth is comparable to it; and therefore, if I am to plead their cause, I must have recourse to fiction, and put together a figure made up of many things, like the fabulous unions of goats and stags which are found in pictures. Imagine then a fleet or a ship in which the owner is sailing, and he is taller and stronger than any of the crew, but he is a little deaf and has a similar infirmity in sight, and his knowledge of navigation is not much better. The sailors are quarrelling with one another about the steering — everyone is of opinion that he has a right to steer, though he has never learned the art of navigation and cannot tell who taught him or when he learned, and will further assert that it cannot be taught at all, and they are ready to cut in pieces anyone who says the contrary. They throng about the owner, begging and praying him to commit the helm to them; and if at any time they do not prevail, but others are preferred to them, they kill the others or throw them overboard, and having first chained up the excellent shipowner's senses with drink or some narcotic drug, they assume control of the ship and make free with the stores; thus, feasting and drinking, they proceed on their voyage in such manner as might be expected of them. Him who is their partisan and cleverly aids them in their plot for getting the ship out of the owner's hands whether by force or persuasion, they compliment with the name of sailor, pilot, able seaman, and abuse the other sort of man, saying that he is unfit for any service; but that the true pilot must pay attention to the year and seasons and sky and stars and winds, and whatever else belongs to his art, if he intends to be really qualified for the command of a ship, — this has never seriously entered into their thoughts; nor do they think it possible to learn some art, or obtain some experience, whereby a man will remain pilot whether the consent of other people has been granted or no. Yet such is the art of piloting. If all this should **489** occur, how do you suppose that the true pilot will be regarded by the voyagers who sail in such an ill-regulated ship? Will he not be called by them a prater, a star-gazer, a good-for-nothing?

Of course, said Adeimantus.

Then you will hardly need, I said, to hear the interpretation of the figure, which describes the true philosopher in his relation to the State; for you understand already.

Certainly.

Then suppose you now take this parable to the gentleman who is surprised at finding that philosophers have no honour in their cities; explain it to him and try to convince him that their having honour would be far more extraordinary.

I will.

Say to him that, in deeming the best votaries of philosophy to be useless to the rest of the world, he is right; but also tell him to attribute their uselessness to the fault of those who will not use them, and not to themselves. The pilot should not humbly beg the sailors to be commanded by him — that is not the order of nature; neither are 'the wise to go to the doors of the rich' — the ingenious author of this saying told a lie — but the truth is that when a man is ill, whether he be rich or poor, to the physician's door he must perforce go, and he who wants to be governed, to him who is able to govern. The ruler who is good for anything ought not beg his subjects to be ruled by him. However, the present governors of mankind are of a different stamp; they may be justly compared to the sailors in our story, and the true helmsmen to those who are called by them good-for-nothings and star-gazers.

Precisely so, he said.

For these reasons, and among men like these, the noblest occupation of all is not likely to be much esteemed by those who pursue an opposite course of life; but the greatest and most lasting scandal is brought upon philosophy by her own professing followers, the same of whom you suppose the accuser to say that the greater number of them are arrant rogues, and the best are useless; in which opinion I agreed.

Yes.

And the reason why the good are useless has now been explained?

True.

Then shall we proceed to show that the corruption of the majority is also unavoidable, and that this is not to be laid to the charge of philosophy any more than the other?

By all means.

Let us ask and answer in turn, first going back to the description
490 of the nature requisite for gentle and noble character. Truth, as you will remember, was his leader, whom he must follow always and in all things; failing in this, he was an impostor, and had no part or lot in true philosophy.

Yes, that was said.

Well, and is not this one quality, to mention no others, greatly at variance with present notions of him?

Certainly, he said.

And have we not a right to say in his defence that the true lover of knowledge is always striving after being — that is his nature; he will not rest in the multiplicity of individuals which is an appearance only, but will go on — the keen edge will not be blunted nor the force of his desire abate until he has attained the knowledge of the true nature of every essence by a sympathetic and kindred power in the soul, and by that power drawing near and mingling and becoming incorporate with very being, having begotten mind and truth, he will have knowledge and will truly live and grow; and then and not till then will he cease from his travail.

Nothing, he said, can be more just than such a description of him.

And will the love of a lie be any part of a philosopher's nature? Will he not utterly hate a lie?

He will.

And when truth is the captain, we cannot suspect any evil of the band which he leads?

Impossible.

Justice and health of mind will be of the company, and temperance will follow after?

True, he replied.

Neither is there any reason why I should again set in array the philosopher's virtues, as you will doubtless remember that courage, largeness of mind, quickness, memory, were his natural gifts. And you objected that, although no one could deny what I then said, still, if you leave words and look at the persons who are thus described, some of them are manifestly useless, and the greater number utterly depraved; we were then led to inquire into the grounds of these accusations, and have now arrived at the point of asking why are the majority bad, which question of necessity brought us again to the characteristics and definition of the true philosopher.

Exactly.

And we have next to consider the corruptions of this character, why so many are spoiled and so few escape spoiling — I am speaking of those who were said to be useless but not wicked — and, 491 when we have done with them, we will speak of other characters which imitate this and assume its way of life, what manner of men are they who aspire after a profession which is above them and of which they are unworthy, and then, by their manifold inconsistencies, bring upon philosophy, and upon all philosophers, that universal reprobation of which we speak.

What are these corruptions? he said.

I will see if I can explain them to you. Everyone will admit that a nature having in perfection all the qualities which we required in a philosopher, is a rare plant which is seldom seen among men.

Rare indeed.

And what numberless and powerful causes tend to destroy these rare natures!

What causes?

In the first place there are their own virtues, their courage, temperance, and the rest of them, every one of which praiseworthy qualities (and this is a most singular circumstance) destroys and distracts from philosophy the soul which is the possessor of them.

That is very singular, he replied.

Then there are all the ordinary goods of life — beauty, wealth, strength, rank, great connexions in the State, and so on — you understand the sort of things — these also have a corrupting and distracting effect.

I understand; but I should like to know more precisely what you mean about them.

Grasp the truth as a whole, I said, and in the right way; you will then see plainly what I mean, and the preceding remarks will no longer appear strange to you.

And how am I to do so? he asked.

Why, I said, we know that all germs or seeds, whether vegetable or animal, when they fail to meet with proper nutriment or climate or soil, in proportion to their vigour are all the more sensitive to the want of a suitable environment, for evil is a greater enemy to what is positively good than to what is neutral.

Very true.

There is reason, therefore, in supposing that the finest natures, when under alien conditions, receive more injury than the inferior.

Certainly.

And may we not say, Adeimantus, that the most gifted minds, when they are ill educated, become pre-eminently bad? Do not great crimes and the spirit of pure evil spring out of a vigorous nature ruined by education rather than from a feeble one? Weak natures are scarcely capable of any very great good or very great evil.

There I think that you are right.

492 And our philosopher follows the same analogy — he is like a plant which, having proper nurture, must necessarily grow and mature into all virtue, but, if sown and planted in an alien soil, becomes the most noxious of all weeds, unless he be preserved by some divine power. Do you really think, as people so often say, that our youth are corrupted by sophists, or that private teachers of the art corrupt them in any degree worth speaking of? Are not the public who say these things the greatest of all sophists? And do

they not educate to perfection young and old, men and women alike, and fashion them after their own hearts?

When is this accomplished? he said.

When they meet together, and the world sits down at an assembly, or in a court of law, or a theatre, or a camp, or in any other popular resort, and there is a great uproar, and they praise some things which are being said or done, and blame other things, equally exaggerating both, shouting and clapping their hands, and the echo of the rocks and the place in which they are assembled redoubles the sound of the praise or blame — at such a time what courage will be left, as they say, in a young man's heart? Will any private training enable him to stand firm against the overwhelming flood of popular praise or blame? or will he be carried away by the stream? Will he not assent to the notions of good and evil which the public in general have — practise what they practise, and be such as they are?

Yes, Socrates; necessity will compel him.

And yet, I said, there is a still greater necessity, which has not been mentioned.

What is that?

The gentle force of attainder or confiscation or death, which, as you are aware, these educators and sophists apply when their words are powerless.

Indeed they do; and in right good earnest.

Now what counsel from any other sophist, or from any private person, can be expected to overcome in such an unequal contest?

None, he replied.

No, indeed, I said, even to make the attempt is a great piece of folly; there neither is, nor has been, nor is ever likely to be, any different type of character which has had no other training in virtue but that which is supplied by public opinion — I speak, my friend, of human virtue only; what is more than human, as the proverb says, is not included: for I would not have you ignorant that, in the present evil state of governments, whatever is saved and comes to good is saved by the power of God, as we may truly say.   493

I quite assent, he replied.

Then let me crave your assent also to a further observation.

What are you going to say?

Why, that all those unofficial fee earners, whom the many call sophists and deem to be their rivals in business, do, in fact, teach nothing but the opinion of the many, that is to say, the opinions of their assemblies; and this is their wisdom. I might compare them to a man who should study the tempers and desires of a mighty strong beast who is fed by him — he would learn how to approach and handle him, also at what times and from what causes he is most dangerous or the reverse, and what is the meaning of his several cries, and by what sounds, when another utters them, he is soothed or infuriated; and you may suppose further that when, by continually attending upon him, he has become perfect in all this, he calls his knowledge wisdom, and makes of it a system or Art, which he proceeds to teach, although he has no notion which of these opinions and passions is really honourable or dishonourable, good or evil, or just or unjust; these are mere names which he allots in accordance with the tastes and tempers of the great brute. Good he pronounces to be that in which the beast delights and evil to be that which he dislikes; but he can give no further account of them. The just and noble he supposes to be the necessary, having never himself seen, and having no power of explaining to others, the nature of either, and the great and genuine difference between them. By heaven, would not such a one be a rare educator?

Indeed he would.

And in what way does he who thinks that wisdom is the discernment of the tempers and tastes of the motley multitude, whether in painting or music, or, finally, in politics, differ from him whom I have been describing? For when a man consorts with the many, and exhibits to them his poem or other work of art or the service which he has done the State, making them his judges when he is not obliged, the so-called necessity of Diomede will oblige him to produce whatever they praise. And yet the reasons are utterly ludicrous which they give in confirmation of their own notions about the honourable and good. Did you ever hear any of them which were not?

No, nor am I likely to hear.

Bearing all this, then, in mind, let me ask you to consider further whether the world will ever be induced to believe in the existence of absolute beauty rather than of the many beautiful, or of the absolute in each kind rather than of the many in each kind?

494

Certainly not.

Then the world cannot possibly be a philosopher?

Impossible.

And therefore philosophers must inevitably fall under the censure of the world?

They must.

And of individuals who consort with the mob and seek to please them?

That is evident.

Then, do you see any way in which the future philosopher can be preserved, and made to persist in his calling until he attains his full stature? and remember that he was to have quickness and memory and courage and largeness of mind — these were admitted by us to be the gifts of such a nature.

Yes.

Will not such a one from his early childhood be in all things first among all, especially if his bodily endowments are like his mental ones?

Certainly, he said.

And his friends and fellow citizens will want to use him as he gets older for their own purposes?

No question.

Falling at his feet, they will make requests to him and do him honour, because they want to get into their hands now, through flattery, the power which he will one day possess.

That often happens, he said.

And what will a man such as he is be likely to do under such circumstances, especially if he be a citizen of a great city, rich and noble, and a tall proper youth? Will he not be full of boundless aspirations, and fancy himself able to manage the affairs of Hellenes and of barbarians, and having got such notions into his head will he not dilate and elevate himself in the fullness of vain pomp and senseless pride?

To be sure he will.

Now, when he is in this state of mind, if someone gently comes to him and tells him what is true, that he is a fool and must get understanding, which can only be got by slaving for it, do you think that, under such adverse circumstances, he will be easily induced to listen?

Far otherwise.

And even if there be someone who through inherent goodness and natural reasonableness has had his eyes opened a little and is humbled and drawn towards philosophy, how will his friends behave when they think that they are likely to lose the advantage which they were hoping to reap from his companionship? Will they not do and say anything to prevent him from yielding to his better nature and to render his teacher powerless, using to this end private intrigues as well as public prosecutions?

It is inevitable.

And how can one who is thus circumstanced ever become a philosopher?

It is not easy.

Then were we not right in saying that even the very qualities which make a man a philosopher may, in the wrong environment, in some way tend to divert him from his calling, no less than the other so-called goods of life, riches and their accompaniments?

495

We were quite right.

Thus, my excellent friend, is brought about all that ruin and failure which I have been describing of the natures best adapted to the best of all pursuits; they are natures which we maintain to be rare at any time; and from this class come the men who are the authors both of the greatest evil to States and individuals, and also of the greatest good when the tide carries them in that direction; but a slight nature is never the doer of any great thing either to individuals or to States.

That is most true, he said.

And so philosophy is left desolate, with her marriage rite incomplete: for her own have fallen away and forsaken her, and while they are leading a false and unbecoming life, other unworthy persons, seeing that she has no kinsmen to be her protectors, enter in and dishonour her; and fasten upon her the reproaches which, as you say, her reprovers utter, who affirm of her votaries that some are good for nothing, and that the greater number deserve the severest punishment.

That is certainly what people say.

Yes; and what else would you expect, I said, when you think of the puny creatures who, seeing this land left unoccupied — a land well stocked with fair names and showy titles — like prisoners running out of prison into a sanctuary, take a leap out of their trades into philosophy; those who do so being probably the cleverest hands at their own miserable crafts? For, although philosophy be in this evil case, still there remains a dignity about her which is not to be found in the arts. And this is an attraction to many whose natures are imperfect and whose souls are cramped and maimed by their meannesses, as their bodies are by their trades and crafts. Is not this unavoidable?

Yes.

Are they not exactly like a bald little tinker who has just got out of durance and come into a fortune; he takes a bath and puts on a new coat, and is decked out as a bridegroom going to marry his master's daughter, who is left poor and desolate?

496　　A most exact parallel.

What will be the issue of such marriages? Will they not be vile and bastard?

There can be no question of it.

And when persons who are unworthy of education approach philosophy and make an alliance with her who is in a rank above them, what sort of ideas and opinions are likely to be generated? Will they not truly deserve to be called sophisms, having nothing in them genuine or akin to true wisdom?

No doubt, he said.

Then, Adeimantus, I said, the worthy disciples of philosophy will be but a very small remnant: perchance some noble and well-educated person, detained by exile in her service, who in the absence of corrupting influences remains devoted to her; or some lofty soul born in a mean city, the politics of which he contemns and neglects; and there may be a gifted few who leave the arts, which they justly despise, and come to her; — or peradventure there are some who are restrained by our friend Theages' bridle; for everything in the life of Theages conspired to divert him from philosophy: but the struggle against illness has always kept him away from politics. My own case of the internal sign is hardly worth mentioning, for rarely, if ever, has such a monitor been given to any other man. Those who belong to this small class have tasted how sweet and blessed a possession philosophy is, and have also seen enough of the madness of the multitude; and they know that, generally speaking, no politician is honest, nor is there any champion of justice at whose side they may fight and be saved. Such a one may be compared to a man who has fallen among wild beasts — he will not join in the wickedness of his fellows, but neither is he able singly to resist all their fierce natures, and therefore seeing that he would be of no use to the State or to his friends, and reflecting that he would have to throw away his life without doing any good either to himself or others, he holds his peace, and goes his own way. He is like one who, in the storm of dust and hail which the driving wind hurries along, retires under the shelter of a wall; and seeing the rest of mankind full of lawlessness, he is content, if only he can live his own life and be pure from unrighteousness and impious deeds, and take his departure from this life in peace and good-will, with bright hopes.

Yes, he said, and he will have done a great work before he departs.

A great work — yes; but not the greatest, unless he find a State 497 suitable to him; for in a State which is suitable to him, he will have a larger growth and be the saviour of his country, as well as of himself.

The causes why philosophy has received such an evil name have now been sufficiently explained: the injustice of the charges against her has been shown — is there anything more which you wish to say?

Nothing more on that subject, he replied; but I should like to know which of the governments now existing is in your opinion the one adapted to her.

Not any of them, I said; and that is precisely the accusation which I bring against them — not one existing constitution is worthy of the philosophic nature, and hence that nature is warped and estranged; — as the exotic seed which is sown in a foreign land is wont to be overpowered and to lose itself in the native form of the plant, even so this growth of philosophy at present cannot show its proper nature, but degenerates into another type. But if philosophy ever finds a State perfect as she herself is, then it will be seen that she is in truth divine, and that all other things, whether natures of men or institutions, are but human; — and now I know, that you are going to ask What that State is:

No, he said; there you are wrong, for I was going to ask another question — whether it is the State of which we are the founders and inventors, or some other?

Yes, I replied, ours in most respects; but you may remember my saying before, that some living authority would always be required in the State having the same idea of the constitution which guided you when as legislator you were laying down the laws.

That was said, he replied.

Yes, but not proved in a satisfactory manner; you frightened us by interposing objections, which certainly showed that the demonstration would be long and difficult; and what still remains is the reverse of easy.

What is there remaining?

The question how the study of philosophy may be so ordered as not to be the ruin of the State: All great attempts are attended with risk; 'hard is the good', as men say.

Still, he said, let the point be cleared up, and the demonstration will then be complete.

I shall not be hindered, I said, by any want of will, but, if at all, by a want of power: my zeal you may see for yourselves; and please to remark in what I am about to say how boldly and unhesitatingly I declare that States should pursue philosophy, not as they do now, but in a different spirit.

In what manner?

498 At present, I said, those who take up philosophy at all are quite young; when they are hardly past childhood, and have not yet begun money-making and house-keeping, they dally with the most difficult part of it, by which I mean the study of reasoning, and then pass on to other things. And it is these who are supposed to have most of the philosophic spirit. In after life when invited by someone else who is doing the same, they may, perhaps, go and hear a lecture, and about this they make much ado, for philosophy is not considered by them to be their proper business: at last, when they grow old, in most cases they are extinguished more truly than Heracleitus' sun, inasmuch as they never light up again.[1]

---

[1] Heracleitus said that the sun was extinguished every evening and relighted every morning.

But what ought to be their course?

Just the opposite. In childhood and youth their study, and what philosophy they learn, should be suited to their tender years: during this period while they are growing up towards manhood, the chief and special care should be given to their bodies that they may have them to use in the service of philosophy; as life advances and the intellect begins to mature, let them increase the gymnastics of the soul; but when the strength of our citizens fails and is past civil and military duties, then let them range at liberty and engage in no other labour except as a diversion, as we intend them to live happily here, and to crown this life with a similar happiness in another.

How truly in earnest you are, Socrates! he said; I am sure of that; and yet most of your hearers, if I am not mistaken, are likely to be still more earnest in their opposition to you, and will never be convinced; Thrasymachus least of all.

Do not make a quarrel, I said, between Thrasymachus and me, who have recently become friends, although, indeed, we were never enemies; for I shall go on striving to the utmost until I either convert him and other men, or do something which may profit them against the day when they live again, and hold the like discourse in another state of existence.

You are speaking of a time which is not very near.

Rather, I replied, of a time which is as nothing in comparison with eternity. Nevertheless, I do not wonder that the many refuse to believe; for they have never seen that of which we are now speaking realized; they have seen only a conventional imitation of philosophy, consisting of words artificially brought together, not like these of ours having a natural rhythm. But a human being who in word and work is perfectly moulded, as far as he can be, into the proportion and likeness of virtue — such a man ruling in a city which bears the same image, they have never yet seen, neither one nor many of them — do you think that they ever did?

No indeed.

No, my friend, and they have seldom, if ever, heard free and noble sentiments; such as men utter when they are earnestly and by every means in their power seeking after truth for the sake of knowledge, while they look coldly on the subtleties of controversy, of which the end is opinion and strife, whether they meet with them in the courts of law or in society.

They are strangers, he said, to the words of which you speak.

And this was what we foresaw, and this was the reason why truth forced us to admit, not without fear and hesitation, that neither cities nor States nor individuals will ever attain perfection until the small class of philosophers whom we termed useless but not corrupt are in consequence of some chance compelled, whether they will or not, to undertake the care of the State, and until a like necessity be laid on the State to obey them; or until kings, or if not kings, the sons of kings or princes, are divinely inspired with a true love of true philosophy. That either or both of these alternatives are impossible, I, at least, see no reason to affirm: if they were so, we might indeed be justly ridiculed as dreamers and visionaries. Am I not right?

Quite right.

If then, in the countless ages of the past, or at the present hour in some foreign clime which is far away and beyond our ken, the perfected philosopher is or has been or hereafter shall be compelled by a superior power to have the charge of the State, we are ready to assert to the death, that this our constitution has been, and is — yea, and will be whenever the Muse of Philosophy is queen. There is no impossibility in all this; that there is a difficulty, we acknowledge ourselves.

My opinion agrees with yours, he said.

But you mean to say once more that this is not the opinion of the multitude?

I should imagine not, he replied.

O my friend, I said, do not attack the multitude in such sweeping fashion: they will change their minds, if, not in an aggressive spirit, but gently and with the view of soothing them and removing their dislike of over-education, you show them your philosophers as they 500 really are and describe as you were just now doing their character and profession, so that they may no longer think you are speaking of such a person as they supposed — if they view him in this new light, they will surely change their notion of him, and answer in another strain. Who can be at enmity with one who loves them, who that is himself gentle and free from envy will be jealous of one in whom there is no jealousy? Nay, let me answer for you, that in a few this harsh temper may be found but not in the majority of mankind.

I quite agree with you, he said.

And do you not also think, as I do, that the harsh feeling which the many entertain towards philosophy originates in the pretenders, who have burst in uninvited, and are always abusing and finding fault with each other, and who make personalities the only theme of their conversation? and nothing can be more unbecoming in philosophers than this.

It is most unbecoming.

For he, Adeimantus, whose mind is fixed upon true being, has surely no time to look down upon the affairs of earth, or to be filled with malice and envy, contending against men; his eye is ever directed towards things fixed and immutable, which he sees neither injuring nor injured by one another, but all in order moving according to reason; these he imitates, and to these he will, as far as he can, conform himself. Can a man help imitating that with which he holds reverential converse?

Impossible.

And the philosopher, holding converse with the divine order, becomes orderly and divine as far as the nature of man allows; but like everyone else, he will suffer from detraction.

Of course.

And if a necessity be laid upon him of striving to transfer what he sees there to the characters of men, whether in States or individuals, instead of fashioning himself only: will he, think you, be an unskilful artificer of justice, temperance, and every civil virtue?

Anything but unskilful.

And if the world perceives that what we are saying about him is the truth, will they be angry with philosophy? Will they disbelieve us, when we tell them that no State can be happy which is not designed by artists who imitate the heavenly pattern?

They will not be angry if they understand, he said. But how will 501 they draw out the plan of which you are speaking?

They will begin by taking the State and the manners of men, from which, as from a tablet, they will rub out the picture, and leave a clean surface. This is no easy task. But whether easy or not, herein will lie the difference between them and every other legislator, — they will have nothing to do either with individual or State, and will inscribe no laws, until they have either received from others, or themselves made, a clean surface.

They will be very right, he said.

Having effected this, they will proceed to trace an outline of the constitution?

No doubt.

And when they are filling in the work, as I conceive, they will often turn their eyes upwards and downwards: I mean that they will first look at justice and beauty and temperance and all such things, as they are by nature, and again at the human copy; and will mingle and temper the various elements of life into the image of a man; and this they will conceive according to that other image, which, when existing among men, Homer calls the form and likeness of God.

Very true, he said.

And one feature they will erase, and another they will put in, until they have made the ways of men, as far as possible, agreeable to the ways of God?

Indeed, he said, in no way could they make a fairer picture.

And now, I said, are we beginning to persuade those whom you described as rushing at us with might and main, that the painter of constitutions is such a one as we were praising; at whom they were so very indignant because to his hands we committed the State; and are they growing a little calmer at what they have just heard?

Much calmer, if there is any sense in them.

Why, where can they still find any ground for objection? Will they doubt that the philosopher is a lover of truth and being?

They would not be so unreasonable.

Or that his nature, being such as we have delineated, is akin to the highest good?

Neither can they doubt this.

But again, will they tell us that such a nature, when suitably trained, will not be perfectly good and wise if any ever was? Or will they prefer those whom we have rejected?

Surely not.

Then will they still be angry at our saying that until philosophers bear rule, States and individuals will have no rest from evil, nor will this our imaginary State ever be realized?

I think that they will be less angry.

502 Shall we assume that they are not only less angry but quite gentle, and that they have been converted and for very shame, if for no other reason, cannot refuse to come to terms?

By all means, he said.

Then let us suppose that the reconciliation has been effected. Will anyone deny the other point, that there may be sons of kings or princes who are by nature philosophers?

Surely no man, he said.

And when they have come into being can anyone prove that they must of necessity be destroyed; that they can hardly be saved is not denied even by us; but that in the whole course of ages no single one of them can escape — who will venture to affirm this?

Who indeed!

But, said I, one is enough; let there be one man who has a city obedient to his will, and he might bring into existence everything about which the world is so incredulous.

Yes, one is enough.

And when the ruler imposes the laws and institutions which we have been describing, it is not impossible that the citizens will be willing to obey them?

By no means.

And that others should approve of what we approve, is no miracle or impossibility?

I think not.

But we have sufficiently shown, in what has preceded, that all this, if only possible, is assuredly for the best.

We have.

Then it seems that we may now conclude, not only that our laws, if they could be enacted, would be for the best, but also that the enactment of them, though difficult, is not impossible.

We may.

And so with pain and toil we have reached the end of one subject, but more remains to be discussed; — how and by what studies and pursuits will the saviours of the constitution be created, and at what ages are they to apply themselves to their several studies?

Certainly.

I omitted the troublesome business of the possession of women, and the procreation of children, and the appointment of the rulers, because I knew that the perfect State would be eyed with jealousy and was difficult of attainment; but that piece of cleverness was not of much service to me, for I had to discuss them all the same. The women and children are now disposed of, but the other question of the rulers must be investigated from the very beginning. We were say- 503 ing, as you will remember, that they were to be manifest lovers of their country, tried by the test of pleasures and pains, and neither in hardships, nor in dangers, nor at any other critical moment were to lose their conviction — he was to be rejected who failed, but he who always came forth pure, like gold tried in the refiner's fire, was to be made a ruler, and to receive honours and rewards in life and after death. This was the sort of thing which was being said, and then the argument turned aside and veiled her face; not liking to stir the question which has now arisen.

Most true, for I perfectly remember, he said.

Yes, my friend, I said, and I then shrank from hazarding the bold word; but now let me dare to say — that our perfect guardians must be philosophers.[1]

Yes, he said, let that be affirmed.

And do not suppose that there will be many of them; for the gifts which were deemed by us to be essential rarely grow together; they are mostly found in shreds and patches.

What do you mean? he said.

You are aware, I replied, that quick intelligence, memory, sagacity, cleverness, and similar qualities, do not often grow together, and that persons who possess them and are at the same time high-spirited and magnanimous are not so constituted by nature as to live in an orderly and peaceful and settled manner; they are driven any way by their impulses, and all solid principle goes out of them.

Very true, he said.

On the other hand, those stable and steadfast and, it seems, more

[1] [That is, the rulers selected from among the whole class of guardians as explained at iii 414b.]

trustworthy natures, which in a battle are impregnable to fear and immovable, are equally immovable when there is anything to be learned; they are always in a torpid state, and are apt to yawn and go to sleep over any intellectual toil.

Quite true.

And yet we declare that a right good share of both qualities is necessary in those to whom the higher education is to be imparted, and who are to share in any office or command.

Certainly, he said.

And will they be a class which is rarely found?

Yes, indeed.

Then the aspirant must not only be tested in those labours and dangers and pleasures which we mentioned before, but there is another kind of probation which we did not mention — he must be 504 exercised also in many kinds of knowledge, to see whether the soul will be able to endure the highest of all, or will faint under them, as men do in other studies and exercises.

Yes, he said, you are quite right in testing him. But what do you mean by the highest of all knowledge?

You may remember, I said, that we divided the soul into three parts; and, by relating them to each other, distinguished the several natures of justice, temperance, courage, and wisdom?

Indeed, he said, if I had forgotten, I should not deserve to hear more.

And do you remember the word of caution which preceded the discussion of them?

To what do you refer?

We were saying, if I am not mistaken, that he who wanted to see them in their perfect beauty must take a longer and more circuitous way, at the end of which they would appear; but that we could add on a popular exposition of them on a level with the discussion which had preceded. And you replied that such an exposition would be enough for you, and so the inquiry was continued in a manner which seemed to me to fall short of accuracy; whether you were satisfied or not, it is for you to say.

Yes, he said, I thought and the others thought that you gave us a fair measure of truth.

But, my friend, I said, a measure of such things which in any degree falls short of the whole truth is not fair measure; for nothing imperfect is the measure of anything, although persons are too apt to be contented and think that they need search no further.

Not an uncommon case when people are indolent.

Yes, I said; but a guardian of the State and of the laws is the last person who should show such indolence.

True.

The guardian then, I said, must be required to take the longer circuit, and toil in learning not less hard than in physical training, or he will never arrive at the highest knowledge which, as we were just now saying, most belongs to him.

What, he said, is there a knowledge still higher than this — higher than justice and the other virtues?

Yes, I said, there is. And of the virtues too we must behold not the outline merely, as at present — nothing short of the most finished picture should satisfy us. When things of little value are elaborated with an infinity of pains in order that they may appear in their full beauty and utmost clearness, how ridiculous that we should not think the highest truths worthy of the highest accuracy!

A right noble thought; but do you suppose that we shall refrain from asking you what you mean by this highest knowledge and what is its subject?

Nay, I said, ask if you will; but I am certain that you have heard the answer many times, and now you either do not understand me or, as I rather think, you are disposed to make trouble by holding me back; for you have often been told that the Idea of good is the highest knowledge, and that all other things, justice among them, become useful and advantageous only by their use of this. You can hardly be ignorant that this is what I am about to say, and moreover that our knowledge of the Idea of the good is inadequate. Yet you understand that without this knowledge, no other knowledge or possession of any kind will profit us at all. Do you think that the possession of all other things is of any value if it be not good? or a sort of wisdom which includes all else, but has no thought of the honourable or good?

Assuredly not.

You are further aware that most people affirm pleasure to be the good, but the finer sort of wits say it is knowledge?

Yes.

You are aware too that the latter cannot explain what knowledge they mean, but are obliged after all to say knowledge of the good?

True, and very ridiculous it is.

Yes, I said, that they should begin by reproaching us with our ignorance of the good, and then presume our knowledge of it — for the good they define to be knowledge of the good, just as if we understood them when they use the term 'good' — this is of course ridiculous.

Most true, he said.

What of those who make pleasure their good? are they not in equal perplexity? for they are compelled to admit that there are bad pleasures as well as good.

Certainly.

And therefore to acknowledge that the same things are both bad and good?

True.

Evidently, then, there are many great differences of opinion about the good.

Undoubtedly.

Is it not likewise evident that many are content to do or to have, or to seem to be, what is just and beautiful without the reality; but no one is satisfied with the appearance of good — the reality is what they seek; in the case of the good, appearance is despised by every one.

Very true, he said.

Of this then, which every soul of man pursues and makes the end of all his actions, having a presentiment that there is such an end, and yet hesitating because neither knowing the nature nor having the same assurance of this as of other things, and therefore losing whatever good there is in other things, — of a principle such and so great as this ought the best men in our State, to whom everything is entrusted, to be in the darkness of ignorance?

506

Certainly not, he said.

I am sure, I said, that he who does not know how the noble and the just are likewise good will be but a sorry guardian of them; and I suspect that no one who is ignorant of the good will have a true knowledge of them.

That, he said, is a shrewd suspicion of yours.

And if only we have a guardian who has this knowledge our State will be perfectly ordered?

Of course, he replied; but I wish that you would tell me whether you conceive this supreme principle of the good to be knowledge or pleasure, or different from either?

Sir, I said, I could see quite well all along that you would not be contented with the thoughts of other people about these matters.

True, Socrates; but I must say that one who like you has passed a lifetime in the study of philosophy should not be always repeating the opinions of others, and never telling his own.

Well, but has anyone a right to say positively what he does not know?

Not, he said, with the assurance of positive certainty; he has no right to do that: but he may say what he thinks, as a matter of opinion.

And have you not observed, I said, that all mere opinions are bad, and the best of them blind? You would not deny that those who have any true notion without intelligence are only like blind men who feel their way along the right road?

Very true.

And do you wish to behold what is blind and crooked and base, when others will tell you of brightness and beauty?

Still, I must implore you, Socrates, said Glaucon, not to turn away just as you are reaching the goal; if you will only give such an explanation of the good as you have already given of justice and temperance and the other virtues, we shall be satisfied.

Yes, my friend, and I shall be at least equally satisfied, but I cannot help fearing that I shall fail, and that my indiscreet zeal will bring ridicule upon me. No, sirs, let us not at present ask what is the actual nature of the good, for to reach what is now in my thoughts would be an effort too great for me. But of the child of the good who is likest him, I am ready to speak, if I could be sure that you wished to hear — otherwise, not.

By all means, he said, tell us about the child, and you shall remain in our debt for the account of the parent.

I do indeed wish, I replied, that I could pay, and you receive, 507 the account of the parent, and not, as now, of the offspring only; take, however, this latter by way of interest,[1] and at the same time have a care that I do not pay you in spurious coin, although I have no intention of deceiving you.

Yes, we will take all the care that we can: proceed.

Yes, I said, but I must first come to an understanding with you, and remind you of what I have mentioned in the course of this discussion, and at many other times.

What?

The old story, that there are many beautiful things and many good. And again there is a true beauty, a true good; and all other things to which the term *many* has been applied, are now brought under a single idea, and, assuming this unity, we speak of it in every case as *that which really is*.

Very true.

The many, as we say, are seen but not known, and the Ideas are known but not seen.

Exactly.

And what is the organ with which we see the visible things?

The sight, he said.

And with the hearing, I said, we hear, and with the other senses perceive the other objects of sense?

True.

But have you remarked that sight is by far the most costly and complex piece of workmanship which the artificer of the senses ever contrived?

Not exactly, he said.

---

[1] A play upon τόκος, which means both 'offspring' and 'interest.'

Then reflect: have the ear and voice need of any third or additional nature in order that the one may be able to hear and the other to be heard?

Nothing of the sort.

No, indeed, I replied; and the same is true of most, if not all, the other senses — you would not say that any of them requires such an addition?

Certainly not.

But you see that without the addition of some other nature there is no seeing or being seen?

How do you mean?

Sight being, as I conceive, in the eyes, and he who has eyes wanting to see; colour being also present in the objects, still unless there be a third nature specially adapted to the purpose, sight, as you know, will see nothing and the colours will be invisible.

Of what nature are you speaking?

Of that which you term light, I replied.

True, he said.

508 Then the bond which links together the sense of sight and the power of being seen, is of an evidently nobler nature than other such bonds — unless sight is an ignoble thing?

Nay, he said, the reverse of ignoble.

And which, I said, of the gods in heaven would you say was the lord of this element? Whose is that light which makes the eye to see perfectly and the visible to appear?

I should answer, as all men would, and as you plainly expect — the sun.

May not the relation of sight to this deity be described as follows? How?

Neither sight nor the organ in which it resides, which we call the eye, is the sun?

No.

Yet of all the organs of sense the eye is the most like the sun?

By far the most like.

And the power which the eye possesses is a sort of effluence which is dispensed from the sun?

Exactly.

Then the sun is not sight, but the author of sight who is recognized by sight?

True, he said.

And this, you must understand, is he whom I call the child of the good, whom the good begat in his own likeness, to be in the visible world, in relation to sight and the things of sight, what the good is in the intellectual world in relation to mind and the things of mind:

Will you be a little more explicit? he said.

Why, you know, I said, that the eyes, when a person directs them towards objects on which the light of day is no longer shining, but the moon and stars only, see dimly, and are nearly blind; they seem to have no clearness of vision in them?

Very true.

But when they are directed towards objects on which the sun shines, they see clearly and there is sight in them?

Certainly.

And the soul is like the eye: when resting upon that on which truth and being shine, the soul perceives and understands, and is radiant with intelligence; but when turned towards the twilight and to those things which come into being and perish, then she has opinion only, and goes blinking about, and is first of one opinion and then of another, and seems to have no intelligence?

Just so.

Now, that which imparts truth to the known and the power of knowing to the knower is, as I would have you say, the Idea of good, and this Idea, which is the cause of science and of truth, you are to conceive as being apprehended by knowledge, and yet, fair as both truth and knowledge are, you will be right to esteem it as 509 different from these and even fairer; and as in the previous instance light and sight may be truly said to be like the sun and yet not to be the sun, so in this other sphere science and truth may be deemed to be like the good, but it is wrong to think that they are the good; the good has a place of honour yet higher.

What a wonder of beauty that must be, he said, which is the author of science and truth, and yet surpasses them in beauty; for you surely cannot mean to say that pleasure is the good?

God forbid, I replied; but may I ask you to consider the image in another point of view?

In what point of view?

You would say, would you not, that the sun is not only the author of visibility in all visible things, but of generation and nourishment and growth, though he himself is not generation?

Certainly.

In like manner you must say that the good not only infuses the power of being known into all things known, but also bestows upon them their being and existence, and yet the good is not existence, but lies far beyond it in dignity and power.

Glaucon said, with a ludicrous earnestness: By the light of heaven, that is far beyond indeed!

Yes, I said, and the exaggeration may be set down to you; for you made me utter my fancies.

And pray continue to utter them; at any rate let us hear if there is anything more to be said about the similitude of the sun.

Yes, I said, there is a great deal more.

Then omit nothing, however slight.

I expect that I shall omit a great deal, I said, but shall not do so deliberately, as far as present circumstances permit.

I hope not, he said.

You have to imagine, then, that there are two ruling powers, and that one of them is set over the intellectual world, the other over the visible. I do not say heaven, lest you should fancy that I am playing upon the name (οὐρανός, ὁρατός) [*ouranos, horatos*]. May I suppose that you have this distinction of the visible and intelligible fixed in your mind?

I have.

Now take a line which has been cut into two unequal parts, and divide each of them again in the same proportion, and suppose the two main divisions to answer, one to the visible and the other to the intelligible, and then compare the subdivisions in respect of their clearness and want of clearness, and you will find that the first section 510 in the sphere of the visible consists of images. And by images I mean, in the first place, shadows, and in the second place, reflections in water and in solid, smooth and polished bodies and the like: Do you understand?

Yes, I understand.

Imagine, now, the other section, of which this is only the resemblance, to include the animals which we see, and every thing that grows or is made.

Very good.

Would you not admit that both the sections of this division have different degrees of truth, and that the copy is to the original as the sphere of opinion is to the sphere of knowledge?

Most undoubtedly.

Next proceed to consider the manner in which the sphere of the intellectual is to be divided.

In what manner?

Thus: — There are two subdivisions, in the lower of which the soul, using as images those things which themselves were reflected in the former division, is forced to base its enquiry upon hypotheses, proceeding not towards a principle but towards a conclusion; in the higher of the two, the soul proceeds *from* hypotheses, and goes up to a principle which is above hypotheses, making no use of images as in the former case, but proceeding only in and through the Ideas themselves.

I do not quite understand your meaning, he said.

Then I will try again; you will understand me better when I have made some preliminary remarks. You are aware that students of geometry, arithmetic, and the kindred sciences assume the odd and the even and the figures and three kinds of angles and the like in their several branches of science; these are their hypotheses, which they and everybody are supposed to know, and therefore they do not deign to give any account of them either to themselves or others; but they begin with them, and go on until they arrive at last, and in a consistent manner, at the solution which they set out to find?

Yes, he said, I know.

And do you not know also that although they make use of the visible forms and reason about them, they are thinking not of these, but of the ideals which they resemble; not of the figures which they draw, but of the absolute square and the absolute diameter, and so on — the forms which they draw or make, and which themselves have shadows and reflections in water, are in turn converted by them into images; for they are really seeking to behold the things themselves, which can only be seen with the eye of the mind?

That is true.

511

And this was what I meant by a subdivision of the intelligible, in the search after which the soul is compelled to use hypotheses; not ascending to a first principle, because she is unable to rise above the region of hypothesis, but employing now as images those objects from which the shadows below were derived, even these being deemed clear and distinct by comparison with the shadows.

I understand, he said, that you are speaking of the province of geometry and the sister arts.

And when I speak of the other division of the intelligible, you will understand me to speak of that other sort of knowledge which reason herself attains by the power of dialectic, using the hypotheses not as first principles, but literally as hypotheses — that is to say, as steps and points of departure into a world which is above hypotheses, in order that she may soar beyond them to the first principle of the whole; and clinging to this and then to that which depends on this, by successive steps she descends again without the aid of any sensible object, from Ideas, through Ideas, and in Ideas she ends.

I understand you, he replied; not perfectly, for you seem to me to be describing a task which is really tremendous; but, at any rate, I understand you to say that that part of intelligible Being, which the science of dialectic contemplates, is clearer than that which falls under the arts, as they are termed, which take hypotheses as their principles; and though the objects are of such a kind that they must be viewed by the understanding, and not by the senses, yet, because they start from hypotheses and do not ascend to a principle, those who contemplate them appear to you not to exercise the higher reason upon them, although when a first principle is added to them they are cognizable by the higher reason. And the habit which is concerned with geometry and the cognate sciences I suppose that you would term understanding and not reason, as being intermediate between opinion and reason.

You have quite conceived my meaning, I said; and now, corresponding to these four divisions, let there be four faculties in the soul — reason answering to the highest, understanding to the second, faith (or conviction) to the third, and perception of shadows to the last — and let there be a scale of them, and let us suppose that the several faculties have clearness in the same degree that their objects have truth.

I understand, he replied, and give my assent, and accept your arrangement.

Republic · Book VII

And now, I said, let me show in a figure how far our nature is 514 enlightened or unenlightened: — Behold! human beings housed in an underground cave, which has a long entrance open towards the light and as wide as the interior of the cave; here they have been from their childhood, and have their legs and necks chained, so that they cannot move and can only see before them, being prevented by the chains from turning round their heads. Above and behind them a fire is blazing at a distance, and between the fire and the prisoners there is a raised way; and you will see, if you look, a low wall built along the way, like the screen which marionette players have in front of them, over which they show the puppets.

I see.

And do you see, I said, men passing along the wall carrying all sorts of vessels, and statues and figures of animals made of wood and 515 stone and various materials, which appear over the wall? While carrying their burdens, some of them, as you would expect, are talking, others silent.

You have shown me a strange image, and they are strange prisoners.

Like ourselves, I replied; for in the first place do you think they have seen anything of themselves, and of one another, except the shadows which the fire throws on the opposite wall of the cave?

How could they do so, he asked, if throughout their lives they were never allowed to move their heads?

And of the objects which are being carried in like manner they would only see the shadows?

Yes, he said.

And if they were able to converse with one another, would they not suppose that the things they saw were the real things?

Very true.

And suppose further that the prison had an echo which came from the other side, would they not be sure to fancy when one of the passers-by spoke that the voice which they heard came from the passing shadow?

No question, he replied.

To them, I said, the truth would be literally nothing but the shadows of the images.

That is certain.

And now look again, and see in what manner they would be released from their bonds, and cured of their error, whether the process would naturally be as follows. At first, when any of them is liberated and compelled suddenly to stand up and turn his neck round and walk and look towards the light, he will suffer sharp pains; the glare will distress him, and he will be unable to see the realities of which in his former state he had seen the shadows; and then conceive someone saying to him that what he saw before was an illusion, but that now, when he is approaching nearer to being and his eye is turned towards more real existence, he has a clearer vision, — what will be his reply? And you may further imagine that his instructor is pointing to the objects as they pass and requiring him to name them, — will he not be perplexed? Will he not fancy that the shadows which he formerly saw are truer than the objects which are now shown to him?

Far truer.

And if he is compelled to look straight at the light, will he not have a pain in his eyes which will make him turn away to take refuge in the objects of vision which he can see, and which he will conceive to be in reality clearer than the things which are now being shown to him?

True, he said.

And suppose once more, that he is reluctantly dragged up that steep and rugged ascent, and held fast until he is forced into the
516 presence of the sun himself, is he not likely to be pained and irritated? When he approaches the light his eyes will be dazzled, and he will not be able to see anything at all of what are now called realities.

Not all in a moment, he said.

He will require to grow accustomed to the sight of the upper world. And first he will see the shadows best, next the reflections of men and other objects in the water, and then the objects themselves; and, when he turned to the heavenly bodies and the heaven itself, he would find it easier to gaze upon the light of the moon and the stars at night than to see the sun or the light of the sun by day?

Certainly.

Last of all he will be able to see the sun, not turning aside to the illusory reflections of him in the water, but gazing directly at him in his own proper place, and contemplating him as he is.

Certainly.

He will then proceed to argue that this is he who gives the seasons and the years, and is the guardian of all that is in the visible world, and in a certain way the cause of all things which he and his fellows have been accustomed to behold?

Clearly, he said, he would arrive at this conclusion after what he had seen.

And when he remembered his old habitation, and the wisdom of the cave and his fellow-prisoners, do you not suppose that he would felicitate himself on the change, and pity them?

Certainly, he would.

And if they were in the habit of conferring honours among themselves on those who were quickest to observe the passing shadows and to remark which of them went before and which followed after and which were together, and who were best able from these observations to divine the future, do you think that he would be eager for such honours and glories, or envy those who attained honour and sovereignty among those men? Would he not say with Homer,

'Better to be a serf, labouring for a landless master'.

and to endure anything, rather than think as they do and live after their manner?

Yes, he said, I think that he would consent to suffer anything rather than live in this miserable manner.

Imagine once more, I said, such a one coming down suddenly out of the sunlight, and being replaced in his old seat; would he not be certain to have his eyes full of darkness?

To be sure, he said.

And if there were a contest, and he had to compete in measuring the shadows with the prisoners who had never moved out of the 517 cave, while his sight was still weak, and before his eyes had become steady (and the time which would be needed to acquire this new habit of sight might be very considerable), would he not make himself ridiculous? Men would say of him that he had returned from the place above with his eyes ruined; and that it was better not even to think of ascending; and if anyone tried to loose another and lead him up to the light, let them only catch the offender, and they would put him to death.

No question, he said.

This entire allegory, I said, you may now append, dear Glaucon, to the previous argument; the prison-house is the world of sight, the light of fire is the power of the sun, and you will not misapprehend me if you interpret the journey upwards to be the ascent of the soul into the intellectual world according to my surmise, which, at your desire, I have expressed — whether rightly or wrongly God knows. But, whether true or false, my opinion is that in the world of knowledge the Idea of good appears last of all, and is seen only with an effort; although, when seen, it is inferred to be the universal author of all things beautiful and right, parent of light and of the lord of light in the visible world, and the immediate and supreme source of reason and truth in the intellectual; and that this is the power upon which he who would act rationally either in public or private life must have his eye fixed.

I agree, he said, as far as I am able to understand you.

Moreover, I said, you must agree once more, and not wonder that those who attain to this vision are unwilling to take any part in human affairs; for their souls are ever hastening into the upper world where they desire to dwell; which desire of theirs is very natural, if our allegory may be trusted.

Yes, very natural.

And is there anything surprising in one who passes from divine contemplations to the evil state of man, appearing grotesque and ridiculous; if, while his eyes are blinking and before he has become accustomed to the surrounding darkness, he is compelled to fight in courts of law, or in other places, about the images or the shadows of images of justice, and must strive against some rival about opinions of these things which are entertained by men who have never yet seen the true justice?

Anything but surprising, he replied.

518   Anyone who has common sense will remember that the bewilderments of the eyes are of two kinds and arise from two causes, either from coming out of the light or from going into the light, and, judging that the soul may be affected in the same way, will not give way to foolish laughter when he sees anyone whose vision is perplexed and weak; he will first ask whether that soul of man has come out of the brighter life and is unable to see because unaccustomed to the dark, or having turned from darkness to the day is dazzled by excess of light. And he will count the one happy in his condition and state of being, and he will pity the other; or, if he have a mind to laugh at the soul which comes from below into the light, this laughter will not be quite so laughable as that which greets the soul which returns from above out of the light into the cave.

That, he said, is a very just distinction.

But then, if I am right, certain professors of education must be wrong when they say that they can put a knowledge into the soul which was not there before, like sight into blind eyes.

They undoubtedly say this, he replied.

Whereas our argument shows that the power and capacity of learning exists in the soul already; and that just as if it were not possible to turn the eye from darkness to light without the whole body, so too the instrument of knowledge can only by the movement of the whole soul be turned from the world of becoming to that of being, and learn by degrees to endure the sight of being, and of the brightest and best of being, or in other words, of the good.

Very true.

And must there not be some art which will show how the conversion can be effected in the easiest and quickest manner; an art which
will not implant the faculty of sight, for that exists already, but will
set it straight when it has been turned in the wrong direction, and is
looking away from the truth?

Yes, he said, such an art may be presumed.

And whereas the other so-called virtues of the soul seem to be
akin to bodily qualities, for even when they are not originally innate
they can be implanted later by habit and exercise, the virtue of
wisdom more than anything else contains a divine element which
never loses its power, and by this conversion is rendered useful and
profitable; or, by conversion of another sort, hurtful and useless. 519
Did you never observe the narrow intelligence flashing from the keen
eye of a clever rogue — how eager he is, how clearly his paltry soul
sees the way to his end; he is the reverse of blind, but his keen
eye-sight is forced into the service of evil, and he is mischievous in
proportion to his cleverness?

Very true, he said.

But what if such natures had been gradually stripped, beginning
in childhood, of the leaden weights which sink them in the sea of
Becoming, and which, fastened upon the soul through gluttonous
indulgence in eating and other such pleasures, forcibly turn its vision
downwards — if, I say, they had been released from these impediments and turned in the opposite direction, the very same faculty
in them would have seen the truth as keenly as they see what their
eyes are turned to now.

Very likely.

Yes, I said; and there is another thing which is likely, or rather a
necessary inference from what has preceded, that neither the uneducated and uninformed of the truth, nor yet those who are suffered
to prolong their education without end, will be able ministers of
State; not the former, because they have no single aim of duty which
is the rule of all their actions, private as well as public; nor the
latter, because they will not act at all except upon compulsion, fancying that they are already dwelling apart in the islands of the blest.

Very true, he replied.

Then, I said, the business of us who are the founders of the State
will be to compel the best minds to attain that knowledge which we
have already shown to be the greatest of all, namely, the vision of
the good; they must make the ascent which we have described; but
when they have ascended and seen enough we must not allow them
to do as they do now.

What do you mean?

They are permitted to remain in the upper world, refusing to descend again among the prisoners in the cave, and partake of their labours and honours, whether they are worth having or not.

But is not this unjust? he said; ought we to give them a worse life, when they might have a better?

You have again forgotten, my friend, I said, the intention of our law, which does not aim at making any one class in the State happy above the rest; it seeks rather to spread happiness over the whole State, and to hold the citizens together by persuasion and necessity, 520 making each share with others any benefit which he can confer upon the State; and the law aims at producing such citizens, not that they may be left to please themselves, but that they may serve in binding the State together.

True, he said, I had forgotten.

Observe, Glaucon, that we shall do no wrong to our philosophers but rather make a just demand, when we oblige them to have a care and providence of others; we shall explain to them that in other States, men of their class are not obliged to share in the toils of politics: and this is reasonable, for they grow up spontaneously, against the will of the governments in their several States; and things which grow up of themselves, and are indebted to no one for their nurture, cannot fairly be expected to pay dues for a culture which they have never received. But we have brought you into the world to be rulers of the hive, kings of yourselves and of the other citizens, and have educated you far better and more perfectly than they have been educated, and you are better able to share in the double duty. Wherefore each of you, when his turn comes, must go down to rejoin his companions, and acquire with them the habit of seeing things in the dark. As you acquire that habit, you will see ten thousand times better than the inhabitants of the cave, and you will know what the several images are and what they represent, because you have seen the beautiful and just and good in their truth. And thus our State, which is also yours, will be a reality and not a dream only, and will be administered in a spirit unlike that of other States, in which men fight with one another about shadows only and are distracted in the struggle for power, which in their eyes is a great good. Whereas the truth is that the State in which those who are to govern have least ambition to do so is always the best and most quietly governed, and the State in which they are most eager, the worst.

Quite true, he replied.

And will our pupils, when they hear this, refuse to take their turn at the toils of State, when they are allowed to spend the greater part of their time with one another in the heavenly light?

Impossible, he answered; for they are just men, and the commands which we impose upon them are just. But there can be no doubt that every one of them will take office as a stern necessity, contrary to the spirit of our present rulers of State.

Yes, my friend, I said; and there lies the point. You must contrive 521 for your future rulers another and a better life than that of a ruler, and then you may have a well-ordered State; for only in the State which offers this, will they rule who are truly rich, not in gold, but in virtue and wisdom, which are the true blessings of life. Whereas if men who are destitute and starved of such personal goods go to the administration of public affairs, thinking to enrich themselves at the public expense, order there can never be; for they will be fighting about office, and the civil and domestic broils which thus arise will be the ruin of the rulers themselves and of the whole State.

Most true, he replied.

And the only life which looks down upon the life of political ambition is that of true philosophy. Do you know of any other?

Indeed, I do not, he said.

And those who govern should not 'make love to their employment'? For, if they do there will be rival lovers, and they will fight.

No question.

Whom, then, will you compel to become guardians of the State? Surely those who excel in judgement of the means by which a State is administered, and who at the same time have other honours and another and a better life than that of politics?

None but these, he replied.

And now shall we consider in what way such guardians will be produced, and how they are to be brought from darkness to light, — as some are said to have ascended from the world below to the gods?

By all means, he replied.

The process, I said, is not the turning over of an oyster-shell,[1] but the turning round of a soul passing from a day which is little better than night to the true day; an ascent towards reality, which we shall affirm to be true philosophy?

Quite so.

And should we not inquire what sort of knowledge has the power of effecting such a change?

Certainly.

What sort of knowledge is there, Glaucon, which would draw the soul from becoming to being? And I have in mind another consideration: You will remember that our young men are to be warrior athletes?

---

[1] In allusion to a game in which two parties fled or pursued according as an oyster-shell which was thrown into the air fell with the dark or light side uppermost.

Yes, that was said.

Then this new kind of knowledge must have an additional quality?

What quality?

It should not be useless to warriors.

Yes, if possible.

There were two parts in our former scheme of education, were there not?

Just so.

There was gymnastic which presided over the growth and decay of the body, and may therefore be regarded as having to do with generation and corruption?

True.

522   Then that is not the knowledge which we are seeking to discover?

No.

But what do you say of music, to the same extent as in our former scheme?

Music, he said, as you will remember, was the counterpart of gymnastic, and trained the guardians by the influences of habit, by harmony making them harmonious, by rhythm rhythmical, but not giving them science; and the words, whether fabulous or closer to the truth, were meant to impress upon them habits similar to these. But in music there was nothing which tended to that good which you are now seeking.

You are most accurate, I said, in your reminder; in music there certainly was nothing of the kind. But what branch of knowledge is there, my dear Glaucon, which is of the desired nature; since all the useful arts were reckoned mean by us?

Undoubtedly; and yet what study remains, distinct both from music and gymnastic and from the arts?

Well, I said, if nothing remains outside them, let us select something which is a common factor in all.

What may that be?

Something, for instance, which all arts and sciences and intelligences use in common, and which everyone has to learn among the first elements of education.

What is that?

The little matter of distinguishing one, two, and three — in a word, number and calculation: — do not all arts and sciences necessarily partake of them?

&ed; Glaucon agrees, and Socrates proceeds to show that arithmetic meets the two requirements laid down for the studies of the guardians. In ability to turn the soul toward reality, he says, it resembles certain contradictory sense perceptions, such as the perception of an object which is at the same time both big and small — big in relation to one thing, small in relation to another. Such a perception confuses us and awakens thought, requiring us to think of bigness and smallness in themselves as distinct entities. In the same way, the science of arithmetic accustoms the mind to deal with entities such as the mathematician's unit, which remains ever the same and ever one and not many, and which like other numbers can be grasped only by thought. Arithmetic will also be of practical use to our guardians in so far as they are military men, but its chief utility will be that of turning the minds of its students to the contemplation of true being, and beyond this, testing their abilities and sharpening their wits.

Socrates continues:

Let this then be adopted as one of our subjects of education. And 526 next, shall we inquire whether the kindred science also concerns us?

You mean geometry?

Exactly so.

Clearly, he said, we are concerned with that part of geometry which relates to war; for in pitching a camp, or taking up a position, or closing or extending the lines of an army, or any other military manoeuvre, whether in actual battle or on a march, it will make all the difference whether a general is or is not a geometrician.

Yes, I said, but for that purpose a very little of either geometry or calculation will be enough; the question relates rather to the greater and more advanced part of geometry — whether that tends in any degree to make more easy the vision of the Idea of good; and thither, as I was saying, all things tend which compel the soul to turn her gaze towards that place where is the full perfection of being, which she ought, by all means, to behold.

True, he said.

Then if geometry compels us to view being, it concerns us; if becoming only, it does not concern us?

Yes, that is what we assert. 527

Yet anybody who has the least acquaintance with geometry will not deny that such a conception of the science is in flat contradiction to the ordinary language of geometricians.

How so?

They speak, as you doubtless know, in terms redolent of the workshop. As if they were engaged in action, and had no other aim in view in all their reasoning, they talk of squaring, applying, extending and the like, whereas, I presume, the real object of the whole science is knowledge.

Certainly, he said.

Then must not a further admission be made?

What admission?

That the knowledge at which geometry aims is knowledge of

eternal being, and not of aught which at a particular time comes into being and perishes.

That, he replied, may be readily allowed, and is true.

Then, my noble friend, geometry will draw the soul towards truth, and create the spirit of philosophy, and raise up that which is now unhappily allowed to fall down.

Nothing will be more likely to have such an effect.

Then nothing should be more sternly laid down than that the inhabitants of your fair city should by no means remain unversed in geometry. Moreover the science has indirect effects, which are not small.

Of what kind? he said.

There are the military advantages of which you spoke, I said; and further, we know that for the better apprehension of any branch of knowledge, it makes all the difference whether a man has a grasp of geometry or not.

Yes indeed, he said, all the difference in the world.

Then shall we propose this as a second branch of knowledge which our youth will study?

Let us do so, he replied.

And suppose we make astronomy the third — what do you say?

I am strongly inclined to it, he said; the observation of the seasons and of months and years is as essential to the general as it is to the farmer or sailor.

I am amused, I said, at your fear of the world, lest you should appear as an ordainer of useless studies; and I quite admit that it is by no means easy to believe that in every man there is an eye of the soul which, when by other pursuits lost and dimmed, is purified and reillumined by these studies; and is more precious far than ten thousand bodily eyes, for by it alone is truth seen. Now there are two classes of persons: some who will agree with you and will take your words as a revelation; another class who have never perceived
528 this truth will probably find them unmeaning, for they see no notice-able profit which is to be obtained from them. And therefore you had better decide at once with which of the two you are proposing to argue. You will very likely say with neither, and that your chief aim in carrying on the argument is your own improvement, while at the same time you would not grudge to others any benefit which they may receive.

I should prefer, he said, to speak and inquire and answer mainly on my own behalf.

Then take a step backward, for we have gone wrong in the order of the sciences.

What was the mistake? he said.

After plane geometry, I said, we proceeded at once to solids in revolution, instead of taking solids in themselves; whereas after the second dimension the third, which is concerned with cubes and dimensions of depth, ought to have followed.

That is true, Socrates; but so little seems to have been discovered as yet about these subjects.

Why, yes, I said, and for two reasons: — in the first place, no government patronizes them; this leads to a want of energy in the pursuit of them, and they are difficult; in the second place, students cannot learn them unless they have a director. But then a director can hardly be found, and even if he could, as matters now stand, the students, who are very conceited, would not attend to him. That, however, would be otherwise if the whole State were to assist the director of these studies by giving honour to them; then disciples would show obedience, and there would be continuous and earnest search, and discoveries would be made; since even now, disregarded as they are by the world, and maimed of their fair proportions, because those engaged in the research have no conception of its use, still these studies force their way by their natural charm, and it would not be suprising if they should some day emerge into light.

Yes, he said, there is a remarkable charm in them. But I do not clearly understand the change in the order. By geometry, I suppose that you meant the theory of plane surfaces?

Yes, I said.

And you placed astronomy next, and then you made a step backward?

Yes, and my haste to cover the whole field has made me less speedy; the ludicrous state of research in solid geometry, which, in natural order, should have followed, made me pass over this branch and go on to astronomy, or motion of solids.

True, he said.

Then assuming that the science now omitted would come into existence if encouraged by the State, let us take astronomy as our fourth study.

The right order, he replied. And now, Socrates, as you rebuked the vulgar manner in which I praised astronomy before, my praise 529 shall be given in your own spirit. For everyone, as I think, must see that astronomy compels the soul to look upwards and leads us from this world to another.

Everyone but myself, I said; for I am not sure that it is so.

And what then would you say?

I should rather say that those who elevate astronomy into philosophy treat it in such a way as to make us look downwards and not upwards.

What do you mean? he asked.

You, I replied, have in your mind a truly sublime conception of our knowledge of the things above. And I dare say that if a person were to throw his head back and study the fretted ceiling, you would still think that his mind was the percipient, and not his eyes. And you are very likely right, and I may be a simpleton: but, in my opinion, that knowledge only which is concerned with true being and the unseen can make the soul look upwards, and whether a man gapes at the heavens or blinks on the ground, when seeking to learn some particular of sense, I would deny that he can learn, for nothing of that sort is matter of science; and I say that his soul is looking downwards, not upwards, even though, in the quest for knowledge he floats face upwards on the sea, or on the land.

I acknowledge, he said, the justice of your rebuke. Still, I should like to ascertain how astronomy can be learned in any manner more conducive than the present system to that knowledge of which we are speaking?

I will tell you, I said: The starry heaven which we behold is wrought upon a visible ground, and therefore, although the fairest and most perfect of visible things, must necessarily be deemed inferior far to the true motions with which the real swiftness and the real slowness move in their relation to each other, carrying with them that which is contained in them, in the true number and in true figures of every kind. Now, these are to be apprehended by reason and intelligence, but not by sight. Do you doubt that?

No, he replied.

The spangled heavens should be used as a pattern and with a view to that higher knowledge; they may be compared to diagrams which one might find excellently wrought by the hand of Daedalus, or some other great artist. For any geometrician who saw them would doubtless appreciate the exquisiteness of their workmanship, but he would never dream of thinking that in them he could find the true equal or 530 the true double, or the truth of any other proportion.

No, he replied, such an idea would be ridiculous.

And will not a true astronomer have the same feeling when he looks at the movements of the stars? Will he not think that heaven and the things in heaven are framed by the Craftsman who made them in the most perfect manner in which such things can be framed? But if he finds someone supposing that the proportions of night and day, or of both to the month, or of the month to the year, or of the stellar movements generally to these and to one another, being, as they are, embodied and visible, are eternal and unchanging, and never deviate in any direction, and that it is worth while to investigate their exact truth at any cost — will he not think him a queer fellow?

I quite agree, now that I hear it from you.

Then, I said, in astronomy, as in geometry, we should employ problems, and let the heavens alone if we would approach the subject in the right way and so make the natural gift of reason to be of any real use.

That, he said, is a work infinitely beyond our present astronomers.

Yes, I said; and I think we must prescribe the rest of our studies in the same spirit, if our legislation is to be of any value. But can you tell me of any other suitable study?

No, he said, not without thinking.

Motion, I said, has many forms, and not one only; a wise man will, perhaps, be able to name them all; but two of them are obvious enough even to wits no better than ours.

What are they?

There is a second, I said, which is the counterpart of the one already named.

And what may that be?

It appears, I said, that as the eyes are designed to look up at the stars, so are the ears to hear harmonious motions; and these are sister sciences — as the Pythagoreans say, and we, Glaucon, agree with them?

Yes, he replied.

But this, I said, is a laborious study, and therefore we shall inquire what they have to say on these points, or on any others. For our own part, we shall in all this preserve our own principle.

What is that?

There is a perfection which all knowledge ought to reach, and which our pupils ought also to attain, and not to fall short of, as I was saying that they did in astronomy. For in the science of harmony, 531 as you probably know, the same thing happens. The teachers of harmony compare only the sounds and consonances which are heard, and their labour, like that of the astronomers, is in vain.

Yes, by heaven! he said; and 'tis as good as a play to hear them talking about their close intervals, whatever they may be; they put their ears close alongside of the strings like persons catching a sound from their neighbour's wall — one set of them declaring that they distinguish an intermediate note and have found the least interval which should be the unit of measurement; the others insisting that the two sounds have passed into the same — either party setting their ears before their understanding.

You mean, I said, those gentlemen who tease and torture the strings and rack them on the pegs of the instrument: I might carry on the metaphor and speak after their manner of the blows which the plectrum gives, and of accusations against the strings, and of their reticence or forwardness; but this would be tedious, and therefore I will only say that these are not the men, and that I am referring to the Pythagoreans, of whom I was just now proposing to inquire about harmony. For they too are in error, like the astronomers; they investigate the numbers of the harmonies which are heard, but they never attain to problems — to inquiring which numbers are harmonious and which are not, and for what reason.

That, he said, is a thing of more than mortal knowledge.

A thing, I replied, which I would rather call useful; that is, if sought after with a view to the beautiful and good; but if pursued in any other spirit, useless.

Very true, he said.

Now, when all these studies reach the point of inter-communion and connexion with one another, and come to be considered in their mutual affinities, then, I think, but not till then, will the pursuit of them have a value for our objects; otherwise there is no profit in them.

I suspect so; but you are speaking, Socrates, of a vast work.

What do you mean? I said; the prelude or what? Do you not know that all these are but preludes to the actual strain which must be learnt? For you surely would not regard those skilled in these sciences as dialecticians?

Assuredly not, he said; apart from a very few whom I have met.

But do you imagine that men who are unable to give and take a 532 reason will have the knowledge which we require of them?

Neither can this be supposed.

And so, Glaucon, I said, we have at last arrived at the hymn of dialectic. This is that strain which is of the intellect only, but which the faculty of sight will nevertheless be found to imitate; for sight, as you may remember, was imagined by us after a while to behold the real animals and stars, and last of all the sun himself. And so with dialectic; when a person starts on the discovery of the real by the light of reason only, and without any assistance of sense, and perseveres until by pure intelligence he arrives at the perception of the absolute good, he at last finds himself at the end of the intellectual world, as in the case of sight at the end of the visible.

Exactly, he said.

Then this is the progress which you call dialectic?

True.

But the release of the prisoners from chains, and their turning from the shadows to the images and to the light, and the ascent from the underground cave to the sun, while in his presence they are vainly trying to look on animals and plants and the light of the sun, but are able to perceive even with their weak eyes images in the water which are divine, and are the shadows of true existence (not shadows of images cast by a light of fire, which compared with the sun is only an image) — this power of elevating the highest principle in the soul to the contemplation of that which is best in existence, with which we may compare the raising of that faculty which is the very light of the body to the sight of that which is brightest in the material and visible world — this power is given, as I was saying, by all that study and pursuit of the arts which has been described.

I agree in what you are saying, he replied, which may be hard to believe, yet from another point of view is harder still to deny. However, since this is not a theme to be treated of in passing only, but will have to be discussed again and again, let us assume that the present statement is true, and proceed at once from the prelude or preamble to the chief strain and describe that in like manner. Say, then, what is the nature and what are the divisions of the power of dialectic, and what are the paths which lead to our destination, where we can rest from the journey.

Dear Glaucon, I said, you will no longer be able to follow me here, 533 though I would do my best, and would endeavour to show you not an image only but the absolute truth, according to my notion. Whether that notion is or is not correct, it would not be right for me to affirm. But that it is something like this that you must see, of that I am confident.

Doubtless, he replied.

But I must also remind you, that the power of dialectic alone can reveal this, and only to one who is a disciple of the previous sciences.

Of that assertion you may be as confident as of the last.

And assuredly no one will argue that there is any other method of comprehending by any regular process all true existence or of ascertaining what each thing is in its own nature; for the arts in general are concerned with the desires or opinions of men, or with processes of growth and construction; or they have been cultivated in order to care for things grown and constructed; and as to the mathematical sciences which, as we were saying, have some apprehension of true being — geometry and the like — they only dream about being, but never can they behold the waking reality so long as they leave unmoved the hypotheses which they use, and are unable to give an account of them. For when a man knows not his own first principle, and when the conclusion and intermediate steps are also constructed out of he knows not what, how can he imagine that such a fabric of convention can ever become science?

Impossible, he said.

Then dialectic, and dialectic alone, goes directly to the first principle and is the only science which does away with hypotheses in

order to make her ground secure; the eye of the soul, which is
really buried in an outlandish slough, is by her gentle aid lifted upwards; and in this work she uses as hand-maids and helpers the
sciences which we have been discussing. We have often used the
customary name sciences, but they ought to have some other name,
implying greater clearness than opinion and less clearness than
science: and this, in our previous sketch, was called understanding.
But why should we dispute about names when we have realities of
such importance to consider?

Why indeed, he said, when any name will do which expresses the
thought of the mind with clearness?

At any rate, we are satisfied, as before, to have four divisions; two
for intellect and two for opinion, and to call the first division science,
the second understanding, the third belief, and the fourth perception
534 of shadows, opinion being concerned with becoming, and intellect
with being; and so to make a proportion: —

As being is to becoming, so is pure intellect to opinion.
And as intellect is to opinion, so is science to belief, and understanding to the perception of shadows.

But let us defer the further correlation and subdivision of the
objects of opinion and of intellect, for it will be a long inquiry, many
times longer than this has been.

Apart from that, then, he said, as far as I understand, I agree.

And do you also agree, I said, in describing the dialectician as one
who attains a conception of the essence of each thing? And he who
does not possess and is therefore unable to impart this conception,
in whatever degree he fails, may in that degree also be said to fail in
intelligence? Will you admit so much?

Yes, he said; how can I deny it?

And you would say the same of the conception of the good? Unless
the person is able to abstract from all else and define rationally the
Idea of good, and unless he can run the gauntlet of all objections,
and is keen to disprove them by appeals not to opinion but to
absolute truth, never faltering at any step of the argument — unless
he can do all this, you would say that he knows neither the Idea
of good nor any other good; he apprehends only a shadow, if anything at all, which is given by opinion and not by science; — dreaming and slumbering in this life, before he is well awake here, he
arrives at the world below, and has his final quietus.

In all that I should most certainly agree with you.

And surely you would not have the children of your imaginary
State, whom you are nurturing and educating — if your imagination
ever becomes a reality — you would not allow the future rulers to

be mere irrational quantities, and yet to be set in authority over the highest matters?

Certainly not.

Then you will make a law that they shall have such an education as will enable them to attain the greatest skill in asking and answering questions?

Yes, he said, you and I together will make it.

Dialectic, then, as you will agree, is the coping-stone of the sciences, and is set over them; no other study can rightly be built on and above this, and our treatment of the studies required has now reached its end?

I agree, he said.

But to whom we are to assign these studies, and in what way they are to be assigned, are questions which remain to be considered. 535

Yes, clearly.

You remember, I said, the character which was preferred in our former choice of rulers?

Certainly, he said.

I would have you think that, in other respects, the same natures must still be chosen, and the preference again given to the surest and the bravest, and, if possible, to the fairest; but now we must look for something more than a noble and virile temper; they should also have the natural gifts which accord with this higher education.

And what are these?

Such gifts as keenness and ready powers of acquisition; for the mind more often faints from the severity of study than from the severity of gymnastics: the toil is more entirely the mind's own, and is not shared with the body.

Very true, he replied.

Further, he of whom we are in search should have a good memory, and be an unwearied solid man who is a lover of labour in any line; or he will never be able, besides enduring some bodily exercise, to go through all the intellectual discipline and study which we require of him.

He will not, he said, unless he is gifted by nature in every way.

The mistake at present is that those who study philosophy have no vocation, and this, as I was before saying, is the reason why she has fallen into disrepute: her true sons should take her by the hand and not bastards.

What do you mean?

In the first place, her votary should not have a lame or halting industry — I mean, that he should not be half industrious and half idle: as, for example, when a man is a lover of gymnastic and hunting, and all other bodily exercises, but a hater rather than a

lover of the labour of learning or listening or inquiring. And
equally lame will be the man who has turned his love of work in the
opposite direction.

Certainly, he said.

And as to truth, I said, is not a soul equally to be deemed halt and
lame which hates voluntary falsehood and is extremely indignant at
herself and others when they tell lies, but is patient of involuntary
falsehood, and does not mind wallowing like a swinish beast in the
mire of ignorance, and has no shame at being detected?

To be sure.

536   And, again, in respect of temperance, courage, magnanimity, and
every other species of virtue, should we not carefully distinguish
between the true son and the bastard? for where there is no discernment of such qualities states and individuals unconsciously err;
and the state makes a ruler, and the individual a friend, of one who,
being defective in some part of virtue, is in a figure lame or a bastard.

That is very true, he said.

It is for us, then, to guard most carefully against all such dangers;
and if only those whom we introduce to this vast system of education
and training are sound in limb and in mind, justice herself will have
nothing to say against us, and we shall be the saviours of the constitution and of the State; but, if our pupils are men of another stamp,
the reverse will happen, and we shall pour a still greater flood of
ridicule on philosophy than she has to endure at present.

That would not be creditable.

Certainly not, I said; and yet perhaps, in thus turning jest into
earnest I am equally ridiculous.

In what respect?

I had forgotten, I said, that we were not serious, and spoke with
too much excitement. For when I saw philosophy so undeservedly
trampled under foot of men I could not help feeling a sort of
indignation at the authors of her disgrace: and my anger made me
too vehement.

Indeed! I was listening, and did not think so.

But I, who am the speaker, felt that I was. This, however, is the
point which we must not forget, that although in our former selection
we chose old men, we must not do so in this. Solon was under a
delusion when he said that a man when he grows old may learn many
things — for he can no more learn much than he can run much;
youth is the time for great and frequent toil.

Of course.

And, therefore, calculation and geometry and all the other elements
of instruction, which are to be a preparation for dialectic, should be

presented to the mind in childhood; not, however, under any notion of forcing our system of education.

Why not?

Because a freeman ought not to acquire knowledge of any kind like a slave. Bodily exercise, when compulsory, does no harm to the body; but knowledge which is acquired under compulsion obtains no hold on the mind.

Very true.

Then, my good friend, I said, do not use compulsion, but let early education be a sort of amusement; you will then also be better able to find out the natural bent. 537

There is reason in your remark, he said.

Do you remember that the children were even to be taken to see the battle on horseback; and that if there were no danger they were to be brought close up and, like young hounds, have a taste of blood given them?

Yes, I remember.

The same practice may be followed, I said, in all these things — labours, lessons, dangers — and he who is most at home in all of them ought to be enrolled in a select number.

At what age?

At the age when the necessary gymnastics are over: the period whether of two or three years which passes in this sort of training is useless for any other purpose, for sleep and tiring exercise are unpropitious to learning. Moreover the trial of their quality in gymnastic exercises is one of the most important tests to which our youth are subjected.

Certainly, he replied.

After that time those who are selected from the class of twenty years old will be promoted to higher honour than the rest, and the sciences which they learned without any order in their early education will now be brought together, and they will be able to see the natural relationship of them to one another and to true being.

Yes, he said, that is the only kind of knowledge which, in a few fortunate persons, takes lasting root.

Yes, I said; and the capacity for such knowledge is the great criterion of dialectical talent: the comprehensive mind is always the dialectical.

I agree with you, he said.

These, I said, are the points which you must consider; and those who have most of this comprehension, and who are most steadfast in their learning, and in their military and other appointed duties, when they pass the age of thirty will have to be chosen by you out

of the select class, and elevated to higher honour; and you will have
to prove them by the help of dialectic, in order to learn which of
them is able to give up the use of sight and the other senses, and in
company with truth to attain absolute being: And here, my friend,
great caution is required.

Why great caution?

Do you not remark, I said, how great is the evil which is associated
with dialectic today?

What evil? he said.

The students of the art are filled with lawlessness.

Quite true, he said.

Do you think that there is anything so very strange or inexcusable
in their case? or will you make allowance for them?

In what way make allowance?

I want you, I said, by way of parallel, to imagine a supposititious
538 son who is brought up in great wealth; he is one of a great and
numerous family, and has many flatterers. When he grows up to
manhood, he learns that his alleged are not his real parents; but
who the real are he is unable to discover. Can you guess how he
will be likely to behave towards his flatterers and his supposed
parents, first of all during the period when he is ignorant of the
false relation, and then again when he knows? Or shall I guess for
you?

If you please.

Then I should say that while he is ignorant of the truth he will
be likely to honour his father and his mother and his supposed
relations more than the flatterers; he will be less inclined to neglect
them when in need, or to do or say anything violent against them;
and he will be less willing to disobey them in any important matter.

Probably, he said.

But when he has made the discovery, I should imagine that he
would diminish his honour and regard for them, and would become
more devoted to the flatterers; their influence over him would greatly
increase; he would now live after their ways, and openly associate
with them, and, unless he were of an unusually good disposition, he
would trouble himself no more about his supposed parents or other
relations.

Well, all that is very probable. But how is the image applicable
to the disciples of philosophy?

In this way: you know that there are certain principles about
justice and honour which were taught us in childhood, and under
their parental authority we have been brought up, obeying and
honouring them.

That is true.

There are also habits of an opposite kind accompanied by pleasure, which flatter and attract the soul, but do not influence those of us who have any sense of right: these continue to obey and honour the maxims of their fathers.

True.

Now, when a man is in this state, and the questioning spirit asks what is fair or honourable, and he answers as the legislator has taught him, and then arguments many and diverse refute his words, until he is driven into believing that nothing is honourable any more than dishonourable, or just and good any more than the reverse, and so of all the notions which he most valued, how do you think he will behave? will he still honour and obey them?

It is impossible that he should either honour or obey them in the same way.

And when he ceases to think them honourable and natural as heretofore, and he fails to discover the true, can he be expected to pursue any life other than that which flatters his desires?   539

He cannot.

And from being a keeper of the law he will seem to have become a breaker of it?

Unquestionably.

Does not this show that the state of such students of philosophy as I have described, is very natural, and also, as I was just now saying, most excusable?

Yes, he said; and, I may add, pitiable.

Therefore, that your feelings may not be moved to pity about our citizens who are now thirty years of age, every care must be taken in introducing them to dialectic.

Certainly.

There is, surely, one great precaution, that they should not taste the dear delight too early; for youngsters, as you may have observed, when they first get the taste in their mouths, argue for amusement, and are always contradicting and refuting others in imitation of those who refute them; like puppy-dogs, they rejoice in pulling and tearing at all who come near them.

Yes, he said, there is nothing which they like better.

And when they have made many conquests and received defeats at the hands of many, they violently and speedily get into a way of not believing anything which they believed before, and hence not only they, but philosophy and all that relates to it is apt to have a bad name with the rest of the world.

Too true, he said.

But when a man begins to get older, he will no longer be guilty of such insanity; he will imitate the dialectician who is seeking for truth, and not the eristic who is contradicting for the sake of amusement; and he will not only attain greater moderation of character, but will increase instead of diminishing the honour of the pursuit.

Very true, he said.

And have not all our previous provisions been designed to avert this danger, when we said that those who are to be trained in reasoning must be orderly and steadfast, not, as now, any chance aspirant or intruder?

Very true.

Suppose, I said, the training in logic to be continued diligently and earnestly and exclusively for twice the number of years which were passed in equivalent bodily exercise — will that be enough?

Would you say six or four years? he asked.

Say five years, I replied; at the end of the time they must be sent down again into the cave and compelled to hold any military or other office which young men are qualified to hold, so that they may not be behind others in experience of life, and here again they must be tested, to show whether, when they are drawn all manner of ways by temptation, they will stand firm or flinch.

540 And how long is this stage of their lives to last?

Fifteen years, I answered; and when they have reached fifty years of age, then let those who still survive and have distinguished themselves in every action of their lives and in every branch of knowledge be brought at last to their consummation: the time has now arrived at which they must raise the eye of the soul to the universal light which lightens all things, and behold the absolute good; for that is the pattern according to which they are to order the State and the lives of individuals, and the remainder of their own lives also; making philosophy their chief pursuit, but, when their turn comes, toiling also at politics and ruling for the public good, not as though they were performing some heroic action, but simply as a necessity; and when they have brought up in each generation others like themselves and left them in their place to be governors of the State, then they will depart to the Islands of the Blest and dwell there; and the city will give them public memorials and sacrifices and honour them, if the Pythian oracle consent, as demigods, but if not, as in any case blessed and divine.

You are a sculptor, Socrates, and have wrought statues of our governors faultless in beauty.

Yes, I said, Glaucon, and of our governesses too; for you must not suppose that what I have been saying applies to men only and not to women as far as their natures can go.

There you are right, he said, since we have made them to share in all things like the men.

Well, I said, and you would agree (would you not?) that what has been said about the State and the government is not a mere dream, and although difficult not impossible, but only possible in the way which has been supposed; that is to say, when true philosophers are born in the reigning family in a State, one or more of them, despising the honours of this present world which they deem mean and worthless, esteeming above all things right and the honour that springs from right, and regarding justice as the greatest and most necessary of all things, whose ministers they are, and whose principles will be exalted by them when they set in order their own city?

How will they proceed?

They will begin by sending out into the country all the inhabitants of the city who are more than ten years old, and will take possession 541 of their children, who will be unaffected by the habits of their parents; these they will train in their own habits and laws, which will be such as we have described: and in this way the State and constitution of which we were speaking will soonest and most easily attain happiness, and the nation which has such a constitution will gain most.

Yes, that will be the best way. And I think, Socrates, that you have very well described how, if ever, such a constitution might come into being.

Enough then of the perfect State, and of the man who bears its image — there is no difficulty, I suppose, in seeing how we shall describe him also.

There is no difficulty, he replied; and I agree with you in thinking that nothing more need be said.

Republic · Book VIII

And so, Glaucon, we have arrived at the conclusion that in the perfect State wives and children are to be in common; and that all education and the pursuits of war and peace are also to be common, and that those who have proved to be both the best philosophers and the bravest warriors are to be their kings?

That, replied Glaucon, has been acknowledged.

Yes, I said; and we have further acknowledged that the governors, when appointed themselves, will take their soldiers and place them in houses such as we were describing, which are common to all, and contain nothing private or individual; and, apart from houses, you remember what sort of possessions we agreed to allow them?

Yes, I remember that no one was to have any of the ordinary possessions of mankind; they were to be warrior athletes and guardians, receiving from the other citizens, as their annual stipend, only the maintenance necessary for their duties, and they were to be responsible for themselves and for the whole State.

True, I said; and now that this division of our task is concluded, let us recall the point at which we digressed, that we may return into the old path.

There is no difficulty in returning; you implied, then as now, that you had finished the description of the State: you said that such a State as you had described was good, and the man was good who answered to it, although, as now appears, you had more excellent things to relate both of State and man. However that may be, you said that if this was the right form, then the others were wrong; and of the false forms, you said, as I remember, that four were worthy of notice, and that their defects, and the defects of the individuals corresponding to them, were worth examining. When we had seen all the individuals, and finally agreed as to who was the best and who was the worst of them, we were to consider whether the best was, or was not, also the happiest, and the worst the most miserable. I asked you what were the four forms of government of which you spoke, and then Polemarchus and Adeimantus put in their word; and you began again, and have found your way to the point at which we have now arrived.

Your recollection, I said, is most exact.

Then, like a wrestler, he replied, you must let me take my former hold; and let me ask the same questions, and do you give me the same answer which you were about to give me then.

Yes, if I can, I will, I said.

I shall particularly wish to hear what were the four constitutions of which you were speaking.

That question, I said, is easily answered: the four governments of which I spoke, so far as they have distinct names, are, first, this Cretan and Spartan kind, which is generally applauded; next, and second in order of approbation, comes what is termed oligarchy — a form of government which teems with evils: thirdly, the form which is antagonistic to this and succeeds it, democracy: and lastly comes tyranny, great and famous, which differs from them all, and is the fourth and worst disorder of a State. I do not know, do you? of any other constitution which can be said to have a distinct character. There are hereditary monarchies which are bought and sold, and principalities and some other intermediate forms of government. But these are nondescripts and may be found equally among Hellenes and among barbarians.

Yes, he replied, we certainly hear of many curious forms of government.

Do you know, I said, that governments vary as the dispositions of men vary, and that there must be as many of the one as there are of the other? Or do you suppose that States spring from 'oak and rock', and not from the human natures which are in them, and as it were, turn the scale and draw other things after them?

By no means, he said, they can spring from no other source.

Then if the constitutions of States are five, the dispositions of individual minds will also be five?

Certainly.

Him who answers to aristocracy, and whom we rightly call just 545 and good, we have already described.

We have.

Then let us now proceed to describe the inferior sort of natures, being the contentious and ambitious, who answer to the Spartan polity; also the oligarchical, democratical, and tyrannical, so that we may place the most just by the side of the most unjust, and so complete our comparison between pure justice and pure injustice, in respect of the happiness or misery which they bring to their possessor. And we shall know whether we ought to pursue injustice, as Thrasymachus advises, or in accordance with the argument which is now coming to light, to prefer justice.

Certainly, he replied, we must do as you say.

Shall we follow our old plan, which we adopted with a view to clearness, of taking the State first and then proceeding to the individual, and begin with the government based upon the love of honour? — I know of no name for such a government other than timocracy, or perhaps timarchy. We will compare with this the like character in the individual; and, after that, consider oligarchy and the oligarchical man; and then again we will turn our attention to democracy and the democratical man; and lastly, we will go and view the city of tyranny, and once more take a look into the tyrant's soul, and try to arrive at a satisfactory decision.

That way of viewing and judging of the matter will be very suitable.

First, then, I said, let us inquire how timocracy (the government of honour) would arise out of aristocracy (the government of the best). Clearly, all political changes originate in divisions of the actual governing power; a government which is united, however small, cannot be moved.

Very true, he said.

In what way, then, will our city be disturbed, and in what manner will the two classes of auxiliaries and rulers disagree among themselves or with one another? Shall we, after the manner of Homer, pray the Muses to tell us 'how discord first arose'? Shall we imagine them in solemn mockery to play and jest with us as if we were children, and to address us in a lofty tragic vein, making believe to be in earnest?

How would they address us?

546   After this manner: — A city which is thus constituted can hardly be shaken; but, seeing that everything which has a beginning has also an end, even a constitution such as yours will not last for ever, but will in time be dissolved. And this is the dissolution: — As in plants that grow in the earth, so in animals that move on the earth's surface, fertility and sterility of soul and body occur when the circumferences of the circles of each are completed, which in short-lived existences pass over a short space, and in long-lived ones over a long space. But to the knowledge of human fecundity and sterility all the wisdom and education of your rulers will not attain; the laws which regulate them will not be discovered by any blend of reasoning and sensation, but will escape them, and they will bring children into the world when they ought not. . . .

 ✑§ Socrates proceeds to describe in complicated language a number constructed by elaborate processes of squaring, cubing, adding, and multiplying, which, he says, the Muses declare to contain the period of human birth. About the meaning of this number, controversy has raged; but in my view it is intended by Plato only as part of his dramatic representation of the mocking Muses, and not as serious genetic doctrine. Socrates does not explain in any way how the number would be used in setting dates for marriages. He continues:

546 Now this number represents a geometrical figure which has control over the good and evil of births. For when your guardians are ignorant of the law of births and unite bride and bridegroom out of season, the children will not be goodly or fortunate. And though only the best of them will be appointed by their predecessors, still

they will be unworthy to hold their fathers' places, and when they
come into power as guardians, they will soon be found to fail in
taking care of us, the Muses, first by undervaluing music; which
neglect will soon extend to gymnastic; and hence the young men of
your State will be less cultivated. In the succeeding generation rulers
will be appointed who have lost the guardian power of testing the
metal of your different races, which, like Hesiod's, are of gold and   547
silver and brass and iron. And so iron will be mingled with silver,
and brass with gold, and hence there will arise dissimilarity and inequality and irregularity, which always and in all places are causes
of hatred and war. This the Muses affirm to be the stock from which
discord has sprung, wherever arising; and this is their answer to us.

Yes, and we may assume that they answer truly.

Why, yes, I said, of course they answer truly; how can the Muses
speak falsely?

And what do the Muses say next?

When discord arose, then the two races began to pull in opposite
directions — the iron and brass towards the acquisition of money
and land and houses and gold and silver; but the gold and silver
races, not wanting money but having the true riches in their own
natures, inclined towards virtue and the ancient order of things. There
was tension and opposition between them, and at last they came to
a compromise, agreeing to distribute their land and houses among
individual owners; and their friends and maintainers, whom they
had formerly protected in the condition of freemen, were to be enslaved and held as subjects and servants; and they themselves were
to keep watch against them, besides attending to warfare.

I believe that you have rightly conceived the origin of the change.

And the new government which thus arises will be of a form intermediate between oligarchy and aristocracy?

Very true.

Such will be the change, and after the change has been made,
what kind of life will they live? Clearly, the new State, being in
a mean between oligarchy and the perfect State, will partly follow
one and partly the other, and will also have some peculiarities.

True, he said.

In the honour given to rulers, in the abstinence of the warrior class
from agriculture, handicrafts, and trade in general, in the institution
of common meals, and in the attention paid to gymnastics and military
training — in all these respects this State will resemble the former.

True.

But in the fear of admitting philosophers to power, because such
men are no longer to be had simple and earnest, but are made up
of mixed elements; and in turning from them to passionate and less

548 complex characters, who are by nature fitted for war rather than peace; and in the value set by them upon military stratagems and contrivances, and in the waging of everlasting wars — this State will be for the most part peculiar.

Yes.

Yes, I said; and men of this stamp will be covetous of money, like those who live in oligarchies; they will have a fierce secret longing after gold and silver, which they will hoard in dark places, having magazines and treasuries of their own for the deposit and concealment of them; also castles which are just nests for their eggs, and in which they will spend large sums upon women, or on any others whom they please.

That is most true, he said.

And they are miserly because they have no means of openly acquiring the money which they prize; they will spend that which is another man's on the gratification of their desires, stealing their pleasures and running away like children from the law, their father: they have been schooled not by persuasion but by force, for they have neglected her who is the true Muse, the companion of reason and philosophy, and have honoured gymnastic more than music.

The form of government which you describe, he said, is a complete mixture of good and evil.

Why, there is a mixture, I said; but one thing, and one thing only, is predominantly seen, — the spirit of contention and ambition; and these are due to the prevalence of the passionate or spirited element.

Assuredly, he said.

Such is the origin and such the character of this State, which has been described in outline only; the more perfect execution was not required, for a sketch is enough to show the type of the most perfectly just and most perfectly unjust; and to go through all the States and all the characters of men, omitting no detail, would be an interminable labour.

Very true, he replied.

Now what man answers to this form of government — how did he come into being, and what is he like?

I think, said Adeimantus, that in the spirit of contention which characterizes him, he is not unlike our friend Glaucon.

Perhaps, I said, he may be like him in that one point; but there are other respects in which he is very different.

In what respects?

He should have more of self-assertion and be less cultivated, 549 though still a friend of culture; and a good listener, but no speaker. Such a person is apt to be rough with slaves, unlike the educated man, who esteems them beneath his notice; and he will also be courteous to freemen, and remarkably obedient to authority; he is a lover of power and a lover of honour; claiming to be a ruler, not because he is eloquent or on any ground of that sort, but because he is a soldier and has performed feats of arms; he is also a lover of gymnastic exercises and of the chase.

Yes, that is the type of character which answers to timocracy.

Such a one will despise riches so long as he is young; but as he gets older he will be more and more attracted to them, because he has a piece of the avaricious nature in him and is not single-minded towards virtue, having lost his best guardian.

Who was that? said Adeimantus.

Reason, I said, tempered with music, which alone, when established within a man, can maintain his excellence throughout life.

Good, he said.

Such, I said, is the timocratical youth, and he is like the timocratical State.

Exactly.

His origin is as follows: — He is often the young son of a brave father, who dwells in an ill-governed city, declining its honours and offices, and avoiding its lawsuits and other such business; and quite ready to waive his rights in order that he may escape trouble.

And how does the son come into being?

The character of the son begins to develop when he hears his mother complaining that her husband has no place in the government, of which the consequence is that she has no precedence among other women. Further, when she sees her husband not very eager about money, and instead of battling and railing in the law courts or assembly, taking whatever happens to him quietly; and when she observes that his thoughts always centre in himself, while he treats her with no special honour and no great disrespect, she is annoyed, and says to her son that his father is only half a man and far too easy-going: adding all the other complaints about her own ill-treatment which women are so fond of rehearsing.

Yes, said Adeimantus, they give us plenty of them, and their complaints are so like themselves.

And you know, I said, that the old servants also, who are supposed to be attached to the family, from time to time talk privately in the same strain to the son; and if they see anyone who owes money to his father or is wronging him in any way, and he fails to prosecute them, they tell the youth that when he grows up he must retaliate upon all people of this sort, and be more of a man than his father. He has only to walk abroad and he hears and sees the same sort of thing: those who mind their own business in the city are called simpletons and held in no esteem, while the busy-bodies are honoured and ap- 550 plauded. The result is that the young man, hearing and seeing all these things — hearing, too, the words of his father, and having a nearer view of his way of life, and making comparisons of him and others — is drawn opposite ways: while his father is watering and nourishing the rational principle in his soul, the others are encouraging the passionate and appetitive; and he being not originally of a bad nature, but having kept bad company, is at last brought by their joint influence to a middle point, and gives up the kingdom which is within him to the middle principle of contentiousness and passion, and, in his maturity, becomes arrogant and ambitious.

You seem to me to have described his origin perfectly.

Then we have now, I said, the second form of government and the second type of character?

We have.

Shall we, then, next look at another man who, as Aeschylus says,

> Is set over against another city;

or rather, as our plan requires, begin with the State?

By all means.

I believe that oligarchy follows next in order.

And what manner of government do you term oligarchy?

A government resting on a valuation of property, in which the rich have power and the poor man is deprived of it.

I understand, he replied.

Ought I not to begin by describing how the change from timocracy to oligarchy arises?

Yes.

Well, I said, no eyes are required in order to see how the one passes into the other.

How?

The accumulation of gold in the treasury of private individuals is the ruin of timocracy; for first, they invent for themselves new modes of expenditure and wrest the laws to allow of these; for what do they or their wives care about the law?

Yes, that is probable.

And then one, seeing another grow rich, seeks to rival him, and thus the great mass of the citizens become lovers of money.

Likely enough.

And so they grow richer and richer, and the more they think of making a fortune the less they honour virtue; for when riches and virtue are placed together in the scales of the balance, the one always rises as the other falls.

True.

551 Therefore, in proportion as riches and rich men are honoured in the State, virtue and the virtuous are dishonoured.

Clearly.

And what is honoured is practised, and that which has no honour is neglected.

That is obvious.

And so at last, instead of loving contention and glory, men become lovers of money and money-making; they honour and look up to the rich man, and promote him to high office, and dishonour the poor man.

They do so.

They next proceed to make a law which fixes a sum of money as the qualification of citizenship; the sum is higher in one place and lower in another, as the oligarchy is more or less exclusive; and they allow no one whose property falls below the amount fixed to have any share in the government. These changes in the constitution they effect by force of arms, if intimidation has not already done their work.

Very true.

And this, speaking generally, is the way in which oligarchy is established.

Yes, he said; but what are the characteristics of this form of government, and what are the defects in it of which we were speaking?

First of all, I said, consider the nature of the qualification. Just think what would happen if pilots were to be chosen according to a census of their property, and a poor man were refused permission to steer, even though he were a better pilot?

You mean that the voyage would be very unpleasant?

Yes; and is not this true of the government of anything?

I should imagine so.

Except a city? — or would you include a city?

Nay, he said, the case of a city is the strongest of all, inasmuch as the rule of a city is the greatest and most difficult of all.

This, then, will be the first great defect of oligarchy?

Clearly.

And here is another defect which is quite as bad.

What defect?

The inevitable division: such a State is not one, but two States, the one of poor, the other of rich men, living on the same spot and always conspiring against one another.

That, surely, is at least as bad.

Another discreditable feature is that, for a like reason, they are incapable of carrying on any war. Either they must arm the multitude, and then they are more afraid of them than of the enemy; or, if they do not call them out in the hour of battle, they are oligarchs indeed, few to fight as they are few to rule. And at the same time their fondness for money makes them unwilling to pay taxes.

Not a good thing.

552   And, under such a constitution there is the fault which we blamed long ago; the same persons have too many callings — they are husbandmen, tradesmen, warriors, all in one. Does that look well?

Anything but well.

There is another evil which is, perhaps, the greatest of all, and to which this State first begins to be liable.

What evil?

A man may sell all that he has, and another may acquire his property; yet after the sale he may dwell in the city of which he is no longer a part, and being neither trader, nor artisan, nor horseman, nor hoplite, is named a pauper, and destitute.

Yes, that is an evil which begins in this State.

The evil is certainly not prevented there; otherwise oligarchies would not show the extremes of great wealth and utter poverty.

True.

But think again: in his wealthy days, while he was spending his money, was a man of this sort a whit more good to the State for the purposes of which we were now speaking? Or did he only seem to be a member of the ruling body, although in truth he was neither ruler nor subject, but just a spendthrift?

As you say, he seemed to be a ruler, but was only a spendthrift.

May we not say that he is the drone who in his house is like the drone in its cell, and that the one is the plague of the city as the other is of the hive?

Just so, Socrates.

And God has made the flying drones, Adeimantus, all without stings, whereas of the walking drones he has made some, indeed, without stings but others with dreadful stings; of the stingless class are those who in their old age end as paupers; of the stingers come all the criminal class, as they are termed.

Most true, he said.

Clearly then, whenever you see paupers in a State, somewhere in that neighbourhood there are hidden away thieves and cut-purses and robbers of temples, and all sorts of malefactors.

Clearly.

Well, I said, and in oligarchical States do you not find paupers?

Yes, he said; nearly everybody is a pauper who is not a ruler.

And may we be so bold as to affirm that there are also many criminals to be found in them, rogues who have stings, and whom the authorities are careful to restrain by force?

Certainly, we may be so bold.

The existence of such persons is to be attributed to want of education, ill training, and an evil constitution of the State?

True.

Such, then, is the form and such are the evils of an oligarchical city; and there may be many other evils.

Very likely.

Then our picture of this form of government called oligarchy, in 553 which the rulers are elected for their wealth, may be regarded as complete. Let us next proceed to consider the nature and origin of the individual who answers to this State.

By all means.

Does not the timocratical man change into the oligarchical on this wise?

How?

A time arrives when the representative of timocracy has a son: at first he begins by emulating his father and walking in his footsteps, but presently he sees him of a sudden foundering against the State as upon a sunken reef, and he and all that he has is lost; he may have been a general or some other high officer who is brought to trial under a prejudice raised by informers, and either put to death, or exiled, or deprived of the privileges of a citizen, and all his property taken from him.

Nothing more likely.

And the son has seen and known all this — he is a ruined man, and his fear has taught him to knock ambition and passion headforemost from his bosom's throne; humbled by poverty he takes to money-making and by mean and miserly savings and hard work gets a fortune together. Is not such a one likely to seat the concupiscent and covetous element on the vacant throne and to suffer it to play the great king within him, girt with tiara and chain and scimitar?

Most true, he replied.

And when he has made reason and spirit sit down on the ground obediently on either side of their sovereign, and made them his slaves, he compels the one to think only of how lesser sums may be turned into larger ones, and will not allow the other to worship and admire anything but riches and rich men, or to be ambitious of anything so much as the possession of wealth and the means of acquiring it.

In no other way, he said, can the conversion of the ambitious youth into the avaricious one be so speedy and violent.

And the avaricious, I said, is the oligarchical youth?

Yes, he said; at any rate the individual out of whom he came is like the State out of which oligarchy came.

Let us then consider whether there is any likeness between them.

Very good. 554

First, then, they resemble one another in the supreme value which they set upon wealth?

Certainly.

Also in their penurious, laborious character; the individual only satisfies his necessary appetites, and confines his expenditure to them; his other desires he subdues, under the idea that they are unprofitable.

True.

He is a shabby fellow, who saves something out of everything and makes a purse for himself; and this is the sort of man whom the vulgar applaud. Is he not a true image of the State which he represents?

He appears to me to be so; at any rate money is highly valued by this type of man as well as by the State.

You see that he is not a man of cultivation, I said.

I imagine not, he said; had he been educated he would never have made a blind god director of his chorus, or given him chief honour.

Excellent! I said. Yet consider: Must we not further admit that owing to this want of cultivation there will be found in him drone-like desires as of pauper and rogue, which are forcibly kept down by his prudent habit of life?

True.

Do you know where you will have to look if you want to discover his rogueries?

Where must I look?

You should see him in some position which gives him complete liberty to act dishonestly, as in the guardianship of an orphan.

Aye.

Now does not this make it clear that in his ordinary dealings which give him a reputation for honesty he coerces his bad passions by an enforced virtue; not making them see that they are wrong, or taming them by reason, but by necessity and fear constraining them, because he trembles for his possessions?

To be sure.

Yes, indeed, my dear friend, but you will find that the natural desires of the drone commonly exist in him all the same whenever he has to spend what is not his own.

Yes, and they will be strong in him too.

Such a man, then, will not be at peace with himself; he will be two men, and not one; but, in general, his better desires will be found to prevail over his inferior ones.

True.

For these reasons such a one will be more respectable than many people; yet the true virtue of a unanimous and harmonious soul will flee far away and never come near him.

I should expect so.

555   And surely, the miser individually will be an ignoble competitor

in a State for any prize of victory, or other object of honourable ambition; he will not spend his money in the contest for glory; so afraid
is he of awakening his expensive appetites and inviting them to help
and join in the struggle; in true oligarchical fashion he fights with a
small part only of his resources, and the result commonly is that he
loses the prize and saves his money.

Very true.

Can we any longer doubt, then, that the miser and money-maker
answers to the oligarchical State?

There can be no doubt.

Next comes democracy; of this the origin and nature have still
to be considered by us; and then we will inquire into the ways of
the democratic man, and bring him up for judgement.

At any rate, he said, we shall then proceed consistently.

Well, I said, and how does the change from oligarchy into democracy arise? Is it not on this wise? — The good at which such a State
aims is to become as rich as possible, a desire which is insatiable?

What then?

The rulers, being aware that their power rests upon their wealth,
refuse to curtail by law the liberty of undisciplined young men to
spend and waste their money; wishing to buy up their estates or lend
money on them, and thus increase their own wealth and importance?

To be sure.

There can be no doubt that the love of wealth and the spirit of
moderation cannot exist together in citizens of the same state to any
considerable extent; one or the other will be disregarded.

That is tolerably clear.

And so in oligarchical States, where no one has troubled to check
self-indulgence, men of good family have often been reduced to
beggary?

Yes, often.

And still they remain in the city; there they are, ready to sting and
fully armed, either owing money, or having forfeited their citizenship,
or both; and they hate and conspire against those who have got their
property, and against everybody else, and are eager for revolution.

That is true.

On the other hand, the men of business, stooping as they walk,
and pretending not even to see those whom they have already ruined,
insert their sting — that is, their money — into some one else who is
not on his guard against them, and recover the parent sum many
times over multiplied into a family of children: and so they make 556
drone and pauper to abound in the State.

Yes, he said, there are plenty of them — that is certain.

The evil blazes up like a fire; and they will not extinguish it, either by restricting a man's use of his own property, or by another legal remedy for evils of this kind.

What other?

One which is the next best, and has the advantage of compelling the citizens to look to their characters: — Let there be a general rule that every one shall enter into voluntary contracts at his own risk, and there will be less of this scandalous moneymaking, and the evils of which we were speaking will be greatly lessened in the State.

Yes, they will be greatly lessened.

At present the governors, induced by the various motives which I have named, reduce their subjects to this condition; while as for themselves and their adherents, all the young men of the governing class are habituated to lead a life of luxury and idleness both of body and mind; they will not work, and have not the hardihood to resist either pleasure or pain.

Very true.

And they themselves care only for making money, and are as indifferent as the pauper to the cultivation of virtue.

Yes, quite as indifferent.

Such is the state of affairs which prevails among them. And often rulers and their subjects may come in one another's way, whether on a journey or on some other occasion of meeting, on a pilgrimage or a march, as fellow soldiers or fellow sailors; aye, and they may observe the behaviour of each other in the very moment of danger — for where danger is, there is no fear that the poor will be despised by the rich — and very likely the wiry sunburnt poor man may be placed in battle at the side of a wealthy one who has never spoilt his complexion and has plenty of superfluous flesh — when he sees such a one puffing and at his wit's end, how can he avoid drawing the conclusion that men like him are only rich because no one has the courage to despoil them? And when they meet in private will they not pass the word round, 'We have them in our power; they are good for nothing'?

Yes, he said, I am quite aware that this is their way of talking.

And, as in a body which is diseased the addition of a touch from without may bring on illness, and sometimes even when there is no external provocation a commotion may arise within — in the same way an enfeebled State may, upon some slight occasion (for instance if the one party introduce from without their oligarchical, or the other their democratical allies), fall sick, and be at war with herself; 557 and may be at times distracted, even when there is no external cause.

Yes, surely.

And then democracy comes into being after the poor have conquered their opponents, slaughtering some and banishing some, while to the remainder they give an equal share of freedom and power; and in this form of government the magistrates are commonly elected by lot.

Yes, he said, that is the genesis of democracy, whether the revolution has been effected by arms, or whether fear has caused the opposite party to withdraw.

And now what is their manner of life, and what sort of a government have they? for as the government is, such will be the man.

Clearly, he said.

In the first place, are they not free; and is not the city full of freedom and frankness — a man may say and do what he likes?

'Tis said so, he replied.

And where freedom is, the individual is clearly able to order for himself his own life as he pleases?

Clearly.

Then in this kind of State there will be the greatest variety of human natures?

There will.

This, then, seems likely to be the fairest of States, being like an embroidered robe which is spangled with every sort of flower. And just as women and children think a variety of colours to be of all things most charming, so there are many men to whom this State, which is spangled with the manners and characters of mankind, will appear to be the fairest of States.

Yes.

Yes, my good Sir, and there will be no better in which to look for a government.

Why?

Because, owing to the liberty which reigns there, it offers a complete assortment of constitutions; and he who has a mind to establish a State, as we have been doing, must go to a democratic city as he would to a bazaar at which they sell constitutions, and pick out the one that suits him; then, when he has made his choice, he may found his State.

He will be sure to find patterns enough.

And there being no necessity, I said, for you to govern in this State even if you have the capacity, or to be governed unless you like, or to go to war when the rest go to war, or to be at peace when others are at peace, unless you are so disposed — there being no necessity also, because some law forbids you to hold office or be a dicast, that you should not hold office or be a dicast, if you have a fancy — is not this a way of life which for the moment is supremely delightful?   558

For the moment, yes.

And is not their humanity to the condemned in some cases quite charming? Have you not observed how, in a democracy, many persons, although they have been sentenced to death or exile, just stay where they are and walk about the world — the gentleman parades like a hero, and nobody sees or cares?

Yes, he replied, many and many a one.

See too, I said, the forgiving spirit of democracy, and the 'don't care' about trifles, and the disregard which she shows of all the fine principles which we solemnly laid down at the foundation of the city — as when we said that, except in the case of some rarely gifted nature, there never will be a good man who has not from his childhood been used to play amid things of beauty and pursue only what is honourable — how grandly does she trample all these fine notions of ours under her feet, never giving a thought to the pursuits from which a man has come into political life, and promoting to honour anyone who professes to be the people's friend.

Yes, she is of a noble spirit.

These and other kindred characteristics are proper to democracy, which will be, so it seems, a charming form of government, full of variety and disorder, and dispensing a sort of equality to equals and unequals alike.

We know her well.

Consider now, I said, what manner of man the individual is, or should we first consider, as in the case of the State, how he comes into being?

Yes, he said.

Is not this the way — he is the son of the miserly and oligarchical father who has trained him in his own habits?

Exactly.

And, like his father, he keeps under by force the pleasures which are of the spending and not of the getting sort, being those which are called unnecessary?

Obviously.

Would you like, for the sake of clearness, to distinguish which are the necessary and which are the unnecessary pleasures?

I should.

May not those desires be rightly termed necessary, of which we cannot get rid, and of which the satisfaction is a benefit to us? For it is a necessity of our nature to desire both what is beneficial and what cannot be suppressed — is it not so?

559 True.

We shall not be wrong therefore in calling them necessary?

No.

And the desires of which a man may get rid, if he takes pains from his youth upwards — of which the presence, moreover, does no good, and in some cases the reverse of good — shall we not be right in saying that all these are unnecessary?

Yes, certainly.

Suppose we select an example of either kind, in order that we may have a general notion of them?

Very good.

Will not the desire of eating, that is, of simple food and condiments, in so far as they are required for health and strength, be of the necessary class?

That is what I should suppose.

The desire for simple food is necessary, both as beneficial, and because it is one which a man cannot check as long as he lives.

Yes.

But the condiments are only necessary in so far as they are good for health?

Certainly.

But what of the desire which goes beyond this, or extends to other kinds of food, which might generally be got rid of, if beaten down and trained in youth, and is hurtful to the body, and hurtful to the soul in the pursuit of wisdom and virtue? May this be rightly called unnecessary?

Very true.

May we not say that these desires spend, and that the others make money because they conduce to production?

Certainly.

And of the pleasures of love, and all other pleasures, the same holds good?

True.

And the drone of whom we spoke just now was, I suppose, meant to be one who was surfeited in pleasures and desires of this sort, and was the slave of the unnecessary desires, whereas he who was subject to the necessary only was miserly and oligarchical?

Very true.

Again, let us see how the democratical man grows out of the oligarchical: the following, as I suspect, is commonly the process.

What is the process?

When a young man who has been brought up as we were just now describing, in a vulgar and miserly way, has tasted drones' honey and has come to associate with fierce and crafty natures who are able to provide for him all sorts of refinements and varieties of pleasure — then, as you may imagine, the change will begin of the oligarchical principle within him into the democratical?

Inevitably.

And as in the city the change was effected by an alliance from without assisting one division of the citizens, like giving help to like, so too the young man is changed by a class of desires coming from without to assist the desires within him, to which they are akin and alike?

Certainly.

And if there be any ally which aids the oligarchical principle
560 within him, whether the influence of a father or of kindred advising
or rebuking him, then there arises in his soul a faction and an opposite faction, and so he comes to be at war with himself.

It must be so.

And there are times when the democratical principle gives way to
the oligarchical, and some of his desires die, and others are banished;
a spirit of reverence enters into the young man's soul and order is
restored.

Yes, he said, that sometimes happens.

And then, again, after the old desires have been driven out, fresh
ones spring up which are akin to them, and because he their father
does not know how to educate them, wax fierce and numerous.

Yes, he said, that is apt to be the way.

They draw him to his old associates, and holding secret intercourse
with them, breed and multiply in him.

Very true.

At length they seize upon the citadel of the young man's soul,
which they perceive to be void of all noble studies and pursuits and
principles, such as make their abode in the minds of men who are
dear to the gods, and are their best guardians and sentinels.

None better.

But now false and boastful conceits and phrases mount upwards and
take possession of the stronghold.

They are certain to do so.

And so the young man returns into the country of the lotus-eaters,
and takes up his dwelling there in the face of all men; and if any
help be sent by his friends to the economical part of him, the aforesaid vain conceits shut the gate of the king's fastness; and they will
neither allow his allies themselves to enter, nor if private advisers
offer the fatherly counsel of the aged will they listen to them or
receive them. There is a battle and they gain the day; the sense of
honour, which they call silliness, is ignominiously thrust into exile
by them, and temperance, which they nickname unmanliness, is
trampled in the mire and cast forth; they persuade men that moderation and orderly expenditure are vulgarity and meanness, and so, by
the help of a rabble of unprofitable appetites, they drive them beyond
the border.

Yes, with a will.

And when they have emptied and swept clean the soul of him who
is now in their power and who is being initiated by them in great
mysteries, the next thing is to bring back to their house insolence
and anarchy and waste and impudence in bright array having gar-

lands on their heads, and a great company with them; hymning their praises and calling them by sweet names, they term insolence breeding, and anarchy liberty, and waste magnificence, and impudence courage. Is it not thus that a man, while still young, passes out of his original nature, which was trained in the school of necessity, into the freedom and libertinism of useless and unnecessary pleasures?

Yes, he said, the change in him is visible enough.

After this he lives on, spending his money and labour and time on unnecessary pleasures quite as much as on necessary ones; but if he be fortunate and is not too much disordered in his wits, when years have elapsed and the heyday of passion is over — supposing that he then re-admits into the city some part of the exiled virtues, and does not wholly give himself up to their successors — in that case he balances his pleasures and lives in a sort of equilibrium, putting the government of himself into the hands of the one which comes first and wins the turn; and when he has had enough of that, then into the hands of another; he despises none of them but encourages them all equally.

Very true, he said.

Neither does he receive or let pass into the fortress any true word of advice; if any one says to him that some pleasures are the satisfactions of good and noble desires, and others of evil desires, and that he ought to use and honour some and chastise and master the others — whenever this is repeated to him he shakes his head and says that they are all alike, and that one is as good as another.

Yes, he said; that is the way with a man in this condition.

Yes, I said, he lives from day to day indulging the appetite of the hour; and sometimes he is lapped in drink and strains of the flute; then he becomes a water-drinker, and tries to get thin; then he takes a turn at gymnastics; sometimes idling and neglecting everything, then once more living the life of a philosopher; often he is busy with politics, and starts to his feet and says and does whatever comes into his head; and, if he is emulous of anyone who is a warrior, off he goes in that direction, or if of men of business, once more in that. His life has neither law nor order; and this distracted existence, which he terms joy and bliss and freedom, continues throughout his life.

You describe exactly, he replied, the life of one whose law is liberty and equality.

Yes, I said; his life is motley and manifold and an epitome of the lives of many; — he answers to the State which we described as fair and spangled. And many a man and many a woman will take him for their pattern, and many a constitution and many an example of manners is contained in him.

Just so.

562 Shall he then be set over against democracy, as one who may truly be called the democratic man?

Let that be his place, he said.

Last of all comes the most beautiful of all, man and State alike, tyranny and the tyrant; these we have now to consider.

Quite true, he said.

Say then, my friend, what do we find the character of tyranny to be? — that it has a democratic origin is evident.

Clearly.

And does not tyranny spring from democracy in the same manner, so to speak, as democracy from oligarchy?

How?

The good which oligarchy proposed to itself and the object for which it was established was wealth — am I not right?

Yes.

Thus, the insatiable desire of wealth and the neglect of all other things for the sake of money-getting was also the ruin of oligarchy?

True.

And democracy also is brought to dissolution by an insatiable desire for that which she designates as good?

What do you suppose that to be?

Freedom, I replied; which, as they tell you in a democracy, is the glory of the State — and that therefore in a democracy alone will the freeman of nature deign to dwell.

Yes; the saying is in everybody's mouth.

To return, then, to the question I was going to ask: is it true that the insatiable desire of this good, and the neglect of other things, introduces change in this constitution also, and occasions a demand for tyranny?

How so?

When a democracy which has begun to thirst for freedom has evil cup-bearers presiding over the feast, and has drunk too deeply of the strong wine of freedom, then, unless her rulers are very amenable and give a plentiful draught, she calls them to account and punishes them, and says that they are cursed oligarchs.

Yes, he replied, a very common occurrence.

Yes, I said; and men who obey their rulers are insultingly termed by her slaves who hug their chains and men of naught; she would have subjects who are like rulers, and rulers who are like subjects: these are men after her own heart, whom she praises and honours both in private and public. Now, in such a State, can there be anything to stop the progress of liberty?

Certainly not.

By degrees the anarchy must find a way into private houses, and end by getting among the animals and infecting them?

How do you mean?

I mean that the father grows accustomed to descend to the level of his sons and to fear them, and the son is on a level with his father; he shows no respect or reverence for either of his parents, such being his notion of freedom. And the metic is equal with the citizen and the citizen with the metic, and the stranger is quite as 563 good as either.

Yes, he said, that is the way.

And these are not the only evils, I said — there are several lesser ones: In such a state of society the master fears and flatters his scholars, and the scholars despise their masters and their tutors also; young and old are all alike; and the young man is on a level with the old, and is ready to compete with him in word or deed; and old men condescend to the young and are full of pleasantry and gaiety; they are loth to be thought morose and authoritative, and therefore they adopt the manners of the young.

Quite true, he said.

But the last extreme of popular liberty is when the slave bought with money, whether male or female, is just as free as his or her purchaser; nor must I forget to tell of the liberty and equality of the two sexes in relation to each other.

Why not, as Aeschylus says, utter the word which rises to our lips?

That is what I am doing, I replied; and I must add that no one who does not know would believe how much greater is the liberty which the animals who are under the dominion of man have in a democracy than in any other State: for truly, the she-dogs, as the proverb says, are as good as their she-mistresses, and the horses and asses have a way of marching along with all the rights and dignities of freemen; and they will run at any body who comes in their way if he does not leave the road clear for them: and all things are just ready to burst with liberty.

When I am on my way to the country, he said, I often experience what you describe. You and I have dreamed the same thing.

And above all, I said, and as the result of all, see how sensitive the citizens become; they chafe impatiently at the least touch of authority, and at length, as you know, they cease to care even for the laws, written or unwritten; they will have no master over them at all.

Yes, he said, I know it too well.

Such, my friend, I said, is the fair and glorious beginning out of which springs tyranny.

Glorious indeed, he said, But what is the next step?

The ruin of oligarchy is the ruin of democracy; the same disease magnified and intensified by liberty overmasters democracy — the truth being that the excessive increase of anything often causes a 564 reaction in the opposite direction; and this is the case not only in the seasons and in vegetable and animal life, but above all in forms of government.

True.

The excess of liberty, whether in States or individuals, seems only to pass into excess of slavery.

Yes, the natural order.

And so it is from democracy, and from no other source, that tyranny naturally arises, and the harshest and most complete form of tyranny and slavery out of the most extreme form of liberty?

As we might expect, he said.

That, however, was not, as I believe, your question — you rather desired to know what is that disorder which is generated alike in oligarchy and democracy, and is the ruin of both?

Just so, he said.

Well, I said, I meant to refer to the class of idle spendthrifts, of whom the more courageous are the leaders and the more timid the followers, the same whom we compare to drones, some stingless, and others having stings.

A very just comparison.

These two classes create disturbance in every city in which they are generated, being what phlegm and bile are to the body. And the good physician and lawgiver of the State ought, like the wise bee-master, to keep them at a distance and prevent, if possible, their ever coming in; and if they have anyhow found a way in, then he should have them and their cells cut out as speedily as possible.

Yes, by all means, he said.

Then, in order that we may obtain a more distinct view of our subject, let us imagine democracy to be divided, as indeed it is, into three classes; for in the first place freedom creates rather more drones in the democratic than there were in the oligarchical State.

That is true.

And in the democracy they are certainly more aggressive.

How so?

Because in the oligarchical State they are disqualified and driven from office, and therefore they cannot train or gather strength; whereas in a democracy they are almost the entire ruling power, and while the keener sort speak and act, the rest keep buzzing about the bema and do not suffer a word to be said on the other side; hence in democracies almost everything is managed by the drones.

Very true, he said.

Then there is another class which is always being severed from the mass.

What is that?

Those who are most orderly by nature — a class, which in a nation of traders is sure to be the richest.

Naturally so.

They are the most squeezable persons and yield the largest amount of honey to the drones.

Why, yes, he said, there is little to be squeezed out of people who have little.

And this is called the wealthy class, and is the food of the drones.

That is pretty much the case, he said.   565

The people are a third class, consisting of those who work with their own hands; they are not politicians, and have not much to live upon. This, when assembled, is the largest and most powerful class in a democracy.

True, he said; but then the multitude is seldom willing to congregate unless they get a little honey.

But then they do share, I said, in so far as their leaders can deprive the rich of their estates and distribute them among the people; at the same time taking care to reserve the larger part for themselves.

Why, yes, he said, to that extent the people do share.

And the persons whose property is taken from them are compelled to defend themselves by speech before the people and by action as they best can?

What else can they do?

And then, although they may have no desire of change, the others charge them with plotting against the people and being friends of oligarchy?

True.

And the end is that when they see the people, not of their own accord, but through ignorance and because they are deceived by informers, seeking to do them wrong, then at last they are forced to become oligarchs in reality; they do not wish to be, but the sting of the drones torments them and breeds revolution in them.

That is exactly the truth.

Then come impeachments and judgements and trials of one another.

True.

The people have always some champion whom they are wont to set over them and nurse into greatness.

Yes, that is their way.

So much then is clear, that whenever tyranny appears, the protectorship of the people is the root from which it springs.

Yes, that is quite clear.

How then does a protector begin to change into a tyrant? Clearly when he begins to do what the man is said to do in the tale of the Arcadian temple of Lycaean Zeus.

What tale?

The tale is that he who has tasted the entrails of a single human victim minced up with the entrails of other victims is destined to become a wolf. Did you never hear it?

O yes.

And the protector of the people is like him; having a mob entirely at his disposal, he is not restrained from shedding the blood of kinsmen; by the favourite method of false accusation he brings them into court and murders them, making the life of man to disappear, and with unholy tongue and lips tasting the blood of his fellow citizens; 566 some he kills and others he banishes, at the same time hinting at the abolition of debts and partition of lands: and after this, what will be his destiny? Must he not either perish at the hands of his enemies, or from being a man become a wolf — that is, a tyrant?

Inevitably.

This, I said, is he who forms a party against the owners of property.

The same.

After a while he is driven out, but comes back, in spite of his enemies, a tyrant full grown.

That is clear.

And if they are unable to expel him, or to get him condemned to death by a public accusation, they conspire to assassinate him secretly.

Yes, he said, that is their usual way.

Then comes the famous request for a body-guard, which is the device of all those who have got thus far in their tyrannical career — 'Let not the people's friend,' as they say, 'be lost to them.'

Exactly.

The people readily assent; probably because all their fears are for him — they have none for themselves.

Very true.

And when a man who is wealthy and is also accused of being an enemy of the people sees this, then, my friend, as the oracle said to Croesus,

> 'By pebbly Hermus' shore he flees and rests not, and is not ashamed to be a coward.'

And quite right too, said he, for if he were, he would never be ashamed again.

But if he is caught he dies.

Of course.

And he, the protector of whom we spoke, is to be seen, not 'larding the plain' with his bulk, but himself the overthrower of many, standing up in the chariot of State with the reins in his hand, no longer protector, but tyrant absolute.

No doubt, he said.

And now let us consider the happiness of the man, and also of the State in which a creature like him is generated.

Yes, he said, let us consider that.

At first, in the early days of his power, he is full of smiles, and he salutes every one whom he meets; — he to be called a tyrant, who is making promises in public and also in private! releasing men from their debts, and distributing land to the people and his followers, and professing to be so gracious and kind to every one!

Of course, he said.

But when he has disposed of foreign enemies by conquest or treaty, and there is nothing to fear from them, then he is always stirring up some war or other, in order that the people may require a leader.

To be sure.

Has he not also another object, which is that they may be im- **567** poverished by payment of taxes, and thus compelled to devote themselves to their daily wants and therefore less likely to conspire against him?

Clearly.

And if any of them are suspected by him of having such notions of freedom as may make them rebellious to his authority, he will have a good pretext for destroying them by placing them at the mercy of the enemy; and for all these reasons the tyrant must be always getting up a war.

He must.

Now he begins to grow unpopular.

A necessary result.

Then some of those who joined in setting him up, and who are in power, speak their minds to him and to one another, and the more courageous of them cast in his teeth what is being done.

Yes, that may be expected.

And the tyrant, if he means to rule, must get rid of them all; he cannot stop while he has a friend or an enemy who is good for anything.

He cannot.

And therefore he must look about him and see who is valiant, who is high-minded, who is wise, who is wealthy; happy man, he must be the enemy of them all, and must plot their destruction whether he will or no, until he has made a purgation of the State.

Yes, he said, and a rare purgation.

Yes, I said, not the sort of purgation which the physicians make of the body; for they take away the worse and leave the better part, but he does the reverse.

If he is to rule, I suppose that he cannot help himself.

What a blessed alternative, I said: — to be compelled to dwell only with the many bad and to be by them hated, or not to live at all!

Yes, that is the alternative.

And the more detestable such actions make him to the citizens the more satellites and the greater devotion in them will he require?

Certainly.

And who are the devoted band, and where will he procure them?

They will flock to him, he said, of their own accord, if he pays them.

By the dog! I said, you seem to foresee a new invasion of drones, of every sort and from every land.

Yes, he said, and I am right.

But whom will he enlist on the spot? Will he not be ready ——

To do what?

To rob the citizens of their slaves, and set them free and enrol them in his body-guard?

To be sure, he said; and he will be able to trust them best of all.

568   What a blessed creature, I said, must this tyrant be, if he has put to death the others and has these for his trusted friends.

Why, yes, he said; these are really the kind of men he employs.

Yes, I said, and these new citizens whom he has called into existence admire him and are his companions, while the good hate and avoid him.

Of course.

So it is not without reason that tragedy is reputed a wise thing and Euripides a great tragedian.

Why so?

Why, because he is the author of the pregnant saying,

'Tyrants are wise by living with the wise';

and he clearly meant to say that they are the wise whom the tyrant makes his companions.

Yes, he said, and he also praises tyranny as godlike; and many other things of the same kind are said by him and by the other poets.

And therefore, I said, the tragic poets being wise men will forgive us and any others who live after our manner if we do not receive them into our State, because they are the eulogists of tyranny.

Yes, he said, those who have the wit will doubtless forgive us.

But they will continue to go to other cities and attract mobs, and hire voices fair and loud and persuasive, and draw the cities over to tyrannies and democracies.

Very true.

Moreover, they are paid for this and receive honour — the greatest honour, as might be expected, from tyrants, and the next greatest from democracies; but the higher they ascend our constitution hill, the more their reputation fails, and seems unable from shortness of breath to proceed further.

True.

But we are wandering from the subject: let us therefore return and inquire how the tyrant will maintain that fair and numerous and various and ever-changing army of his.

Evidently, he said, if there are sacred treasures in the city, he will confiscate and spend them; and in so far as the fortunes of his victims may suffice, he will be able to diminish the taxes which he would otherwise have to impose upon the people.

And when these fail?

Why, clearly, he said, then he and his boon companions, whether male or female, will be maintained out of his father's estate.

You mean to say that the people, from whom he has derived his being, will maintain him and his companions?

Yes, he said; they will be obliged to do so.

But what if the people fly into a passion, and aver that a grown-up son ought not to be supported by his father, but that the father should be supported by the son? The father did not bring him into being, or settle him in life, in order that when his son became a man he should himself be the servant of his own servants and should support him and his rabble of slaves and companions; but that his son should protect him, and that by his help he might be emancipated from the government of the rich and aristocratic, as they are termed. And so he bids him and his companions depart, just as any other father might drive out of the house a riotous son and his undesirable associates. 569

By heaven, he said, then the parent will discover what a monster he has been fostering in his bosom; and, when he wants to drive him out, he will find that he is weak and his son strong.

Why, you do not mean to say that the tyrant will use violence? What! beat his father if he opposes him?

Yes, he will, having first disarmed him.

Then he is a parricide, and a cruel guardian of an aged parent; and this is real tyranny, about which there can be no longer a mistake; as the saying is, the people who would escape the smoke which is the slavery of freemen, has fallen into the fire which is the tyranny of slaves. And instead of that abundant and ill-timed liberty, it puts on the harshest and bitterest form of slavery, that is, slavery to slaves.

That, he said, is indeed what happens.

Very well; and may we not rightly say that we have sufficiently discussed the manner of the transition from democracy to tyranny? and the nature of tyranny when it has come into being.

Yes, quite enough, he said.

Republic · Book IX

Last of all comes the tyrannical man; about whom we have once more to ask, how is he formed out of the democratical? what is his character? and how does he live, in happiness or in misery?

Yes, he said, he is the only one remaining.

There is, however, I said, one thing which I still miss.

What is it?

I do not think that we have adequately determined the nature and number of the appetites, and until this is accomplished our inquiry will always be confused.

Well, he said, it is not too late to supply the omission.

Very true, I said; and observe the point which I want to understand: Certain of the unnecessary pleasures and appetites I conceive to be unlawful; everyone appears to have them, but in some persons they are controlled by the laws and by the better desires with the help of reason, and either they are wholly banished or they become few and weak; while in others they are stronger, and there are more of them.

Which appetites do you mean?

I mean those which wake when the rest of the soul — the reasoning and human and ruling power — is asleep; then the wild beast within us, gorged with meat or drink, starts up and having shaken off sleep goes forth to satisfy his desires; and you know that there is no action which at such a time, when he has parted company with all shame and sense, a man may not be ready to commit; for he does not, in his imagination, shrink from incest with his mother, or from any unnatural union with man, or god, or beast, or from parricide, or the eating of forbidden food. And in a word, no action is too irrational or indecent for him.

Most true, he said.

But when a man's pulse is healthy and temperate, and when before going to sleep he has awakened his rational powers, and fed them on noble thoughts and inquiries, collecting himself in meditation; after having first indulged his appetites neither too much nor too little, but just enough to lay them to sleep, and prevent them and their enjoyments and pains from interfering with the higher principle — which he leaves in the solitude of pure abstraction, free to contemplate and aspire to the knowledge of the unknown, whether in past, present, or future: when again he has allayed the passionate element, so that he does not go to sleep with his spirit still excited by anger against anyone — I say, when, after pacifying the two irrational principles,

he rouses up the third, in which resides reason, before he takes his
rest, then, as you know, he attains truth most nearly, and is least
likely to be the sport of fantastic and lawless visions.

I quite agree.

In saying this I have been running into a digression; but the point
which I desire to note is that in all of us, even the most highly respectable, there is a lawless wild-beast nature, which peers out in
sleep. Pray, consider whether I am right, and you agree with me.

Yes, I agree.

And now remember the character which we attributed to the
democratic man. He was supposed from his youth upwards to have
been trained under a miserly parent, who encouraged only the saving
appetites in him, but discountenanced the unnecessary, which aim
only at amusement and ornament?

True.

And then he got into the company of a more refined sort of people
who are full of the appetites we have just described, and taking to
all their wanton ways rushed into the opposite extreme from an ab-
horrence of his father's meanness. At last, being a better man than
his corruptors, he was drawn in both directions until he halted midway and led a life neither of the frugal nor of the anarchical kind, but
of what he deemed moderate indulgence in various pleasures. After
this manner the democrat was generated out of the oligarch.

Yes, he said, that was our view of him, and is so still.

And now, I said, years will have passed away, and you must conceive this man, in turn, to have a son, who is brought up in his
father's way of life.

I can imagine him.

Then you must further imagine the same thing to happen to the
son which has already happened to the father: — he is drawn into a
perfectly lawless life, which by his seducers is termed perfect liberty;
and his father and friends take part with his moderate desires, and
the opposite party assist the opposite ones. As soon as these dire
magicians and tyrant-makers find that they cannot keep their hold   573
on him otherwise, they contrive to implant in him a master passion,
to be the champion of his idle and spendthrift lusts — a sort of monstrous winged drone — that is the only image which will adequately
describe him.

Yes, he said, that is the only adequate image of him.

And when other lusts, amid clouds of incense and perfumes and
garlands and wines, and all the dissolute pleasures of such company
come buzzing around him; and when they implant in his drone-like
nature the sting of desire, while they fatten and nourish him, then at
last this lord of the soul, having Madness for the captain of his guard,

breaks out into a frenzy; and if he finds in the man such opinions or appetites as are deemed to be good, or still have the sense of shame about them, he kills them and casts them forth until he has purged away all temperance and brought in madness to the full.

Yes, he said, that is the way in which the tyrannical man is generated.

And is not this the reason why of old love has been called a tyrant?

I should not wonder.

Further, I said, has not a drunken man also the spirit of a tyrant?

He has.

And you know that a man who is deranged and not right in his mind, will fancy that he is able to rule, not only over men, but also over the gods?

That he will.

And the tyrannical man in the true sense of the word comes into being when, either under the influence of nature, or habit, or both, he becomes drunken, lustful, passionate? O my friend, is not that so?

Assuredly.

Such is the man and such is his origin. And next, how does he live?

Suppose, as people facetiously say, you were to tell me.

I imagine, I said, that at the next step in his progress there will be feasts and carousals and revellings and courtesans, and all that sort of thing; Love is the lord of the house within him, and orders all the concerns of his soul.

That is certain.

Yes; and every day and every night new offshoots of desire grow up many and formidable, and their demands are many.

They are indeed, he said.

His revenues, if he has any, are soon spent.

True.

Then comes borrowing and the cutting down of his capital.

Of course.

When he has nothing left, must not his desires, crowding in the nest like young ravens, be crying aloud for food; and he, goaded on by them, and especially by Love himself, who has all the other pas-574 sions for his body-guard, is in a frenzy, and would fain discover whom he can defraud or despoil of his property, in order that he may gratify them?

Yes, that is sure to be the case.

He must plunder, no matter how, if he is to escape horrid pains and pangs.

He must.

And as in himself there was a succession of pleasures, and the new got the better of the old and took away their rights, so he being younger will claim to have more than his father and his mother, and if he has spent his own share of the property, he will take a slice of theirs.

No doubt he will.

And if his parents will not give way, then he will try first of all to cheat and deceive them.

Very true.

And if he fails, then he will use force and plunder them.

Yes, probably.

And if the old man and woman fight for their own, what then, my friend? Will he feel any compunction or shrink from any act of a tyrant?

Nay, he said, I should not feel at all comfortable about his parents.

But, O heavens! Adeimantus, on account of some sudden fancy for a harlot, who is anything but a necessary connexion, can you believe that he would strike the mother who is his ancient friend and necessary to his very existence, and would place her under the authority of the other, when she is brought under the same roof with her; or that, under like circumstances, he would do the same to his withered old father, first and most indispensable of friends, for the sake of some newly found blooming youth who is the reverse of indispensable?

Yes, indeed, he said; I believe that he would.

Truly, then, I said, a tyrannical son is a blessing to his father and mother.

He is indeed, he replied.

But when the property of his father and mother has been spent, and pleasures are beginning to swarm in the hive of his soul, then he breaks into a house, or steals the garments of some nightly wayfarer; next he proceeds to clear a temple. Meanwhile the old opinions about good and evil, which he has had from childhood, and which have been accounted just, are overthrown by those others which were lately emancipated, and are now the body-guard of Love and share his empire. These in his democratic days, when he was still subject to the laws and to his father, were only let loose in the dreams of sleep. But now that he is under the dominion of Love, he becomes always and in waking reality what he was then very rarely and in a dream only; he will not abstain from the foulest murder, or from forbidden food, 575 or from any other horrid act. Love is his tyrant, and lives in him in complete anarchy and lawlessness, and being himself sole king leads him on, as a tyrant leads a State, to the performance of any reckless deed by which he can maintain himself and the rabble of his associates, whether those whom evil communications have brought in from without, or those whom he himself has allowed to break loose within him by reason of a similar evil nature in himself. Have we not here a picture of his way of life?

Yes, indeed, he said.

And if there are only a few of them in the State and the rest of the people are well disposed, they go away and become the body-guard of some other tyrant, or mercenary soldiers if there is war anywhere; and if they arise in time of peace and quiet, they stay at home and do many little pieces of mischief in the city.

What sort of mischief?

For example, they are the thieves, burglars, cut-purses, footpads, robbers of temples, man-stealers of the community; or if they are able to speak they turn informers, and bear false witness, and take bribes.

Such mischief is slight, perhaps, if the perpetrators are few in number.

Yes, I said; but small and great are comparative terms, and all these things, in the misery and evil which they inflict upon a State, do not come within a thousand miles of the tyrant; when this noxious class and their followers grow numerous and become conscious of their strength, it is they who, assisted by the infatuation of the people, create the tyrant, choosing from among themselves the one who has most of the tyrant in his own soul.

Naturally, he said, since he will be the most fit to be a tyrant.

If the people yield, well and good; but if they resist him, as he began by beating his own father and mother, so now, if he has the power, he beats them, and will keep his dear old fatherland, or motherland as the Cretans say, in subjection to his young retainers whom he has introduced to be their rulers and masters. And so such a man attains the end of his passions and desires.

Exactly in this way.

When such men are only private individuals and before they get power, this is their character; they associate entirely with their own flatterers or ready tools; or if they want anything from anybody, they in their turn are equally ready to bow down before them and perform
576 every gesture of friendship for them; but when they have gained their point they know them no more.

Yes, truly.

They are always either the masters or servants and never the friends of anybody; the tyrannical nature never tastes of true freedom or friendship.

Certainly not.

And may we not rightly call such men faithless?

No question.

Also they are utterly unjust, if we were right in our agreement as to the nature of justice?

Indeed, he said, we were perfectly right.

Let us then sum up in a word, I said, the character of the worst man: he is the waking reality of what we dreamed.

Most true.

And this is he who being by nature most of a tyrant bears rule, and the longer he lives the more of a tyrant he becomes.

That is certain, said Glaucon, taking his turn to answer.

And will not he who has been shown to be the wickedest, also be proved the most miserable? and he who has tyrannized longest and most, most continually and deeply miserable; although this may not be the opinion of men in general?

Yes, he said, inevitably.

And must not the tyrannical man be like the tyrannical State, and the democratical man like the democratical State; and the same of the others?

Certainly.

And as State is to State in virtue and happiness, so is man in relation to man?

To be sure.

Then comparing our original city, which was under a king, and the city which is under a tyrant, how do they stand as to virtue?

They are the opposite extremes, he said, for one is the very best and the other is the very worst.

I will not ask you, I said, which is which, for it is evident; but would you arrive at a similar decision about their relative happiness and misery? And here we must not allow ourselves to be panic-stricken at the apparition of the tyrant, who is only a unit and may perhaps have a few retainers about him; but let us go as we ought into every corner of the city and look all about, and then we will give our opinion.

A fair challenge, he replied; and every one must see that no city is more miserable than that which is governed by a tyrant, and none happier than that ruled by a king.

And in estimating the men too, may I not fairly offer a like challenge, that I should have a judge whose mind can enter into and see 577 through human nature? he must not be like a child who looks at the outside and is dazzled at the pompous aspect which the tyrannical nature assumes to the beholder, but let him be one who has a clear insight. May I suppose that the judgement is given in the hearing of us all by one who is able to judge, and has dwelt in the same place with him, and been present at his domestic life and known him in his family relations, where he may best be seen stripped of his tragedy attire, and again in the hour of public danger — he shall tell us about the happiness and misery of the tyrant when compared with other men?

That again, he said, is a very fair proposal.

Do you permit me, then, to assume that we ourselves are able and experienced judges who have before now met with such persons? We shall then have some one who will answer our inquiries.

By all means.

Let me ask you not to forget the parallel of the individual and the State; bearing this in mind, and glancing in turn from one to the other of them, will you tell me their respective conditions?

To what do you refer? he asked.

Beginning with the State, I replied, would you say that a city which is governed by a tyrant is free or enslaved?

No city, he said, can be more completely enslaved.

And yet, as you see, there are freemen as well as masters in such a State?

Yes, he said, I see that there are — a few; but the people, speaking generally, and the best of them are miserably degraded and enslaved.

Then if the man is like the State, I said, must not the same rule prevail? his soul is full of meanness and vulgarity — the best elements in him are enslaved; and he is despotically governed by that small part, which is also the worst and maddest.

Inevitably.

And would you say that the soul of such a one is the soul of a free-man, or of a slave?

He has the soul of a slave, in my opinion.

And the State which is enslaved under a tyrant is utterly incapable of acting as it desires?

Utterly incapable.

And also the soul which is under a tyrant (I am speaking of the soul taken as a whole) will be least capable of doing what she desires; there is a gadfly which goads her, and she will be full of confusion and remorse?

Certainly.

And is the city which is under a tyrant, of necessity rich or poor?

Poor.

578   Therefore, the tyrannical soul also must be always poor and insatiable?

True.

Again, must not such a State, and likewise such a man, be always full of fear?

Yes, indeed.

Is there any State in which you will find more of lamentation and mourning and groaning and pain?

Certainly not.

And is there any man in whom you will find more of this sort of misery than in this tyrannical man, who is maddened by his desires and passions?

Impossible.

Reflecting upon these and similar evils, you held the tyrannical State to be the most miserable of States?

Was I not right? he said.

Certainly, I said. And when you see the same evils in the tyrannical man, what do you say of him?

I say that he is by far the most miserable of all men.

There, I said, I think that you are beginning to go wrong.

What do you mean?

I do not think that he has as yet reached the utmost extreme of misery.

Then who is more miserable?

One of whom I am about to speak.

Who is that?

He who is of a tyrannical nature, and instead of leading a private life has been cursed with the further misfortune of becoming a public tyrant.

From what has been said, I gather that you are right.

Yes, I replied, but this high argument requires not mere belief, but earnest logical inquiry; for of all questions, this respecting a good or an evil life is the greatest.

Very true, he said.

Let me then offer you an illustration, which may, I think, throw a light upon this subject.

What is your illustration?

The case of rich individuals in cities who possess many slaves: for they have this in common with the tyrant, that they are masters of many; the only difference is that he is master of more.

Yes, that is the difference.

You know that they live securely and have nothing to apprehend from their servants?

What should they fear?

Nothing. But do you observe the reason of this?

Yes; the reason is, that the whole city is leagued together for the protection of each individual.

Very true, I said. But imagine one of these owners, the master say of some fifty slaves, or even more, together with his family and property and slaves, carried off by a god into the wilderness, where there are no freemen to help him — will he not be in an agony of fear lest he and his wife and children should be put to death by his slaves?

Yes, he said, he will be in the utmost fear.

579

The time has arrived when he will be compelled to fawn upon some of his slaves, and make large promises to them, and set them free, though he is under no obligation to do so, — he will find himself the flatterer of his own servants.

Yes, he said, that will be the only way of saving himself.

And suppose the same god, who carried him away, to surround him with neighbours who will not suffer one man to be the master of another, and who, if they could catch any offender, would inflict extreme punishment upon him?

His case will be still worse, if you suppose him to be everywhere surrounded and watched by enemies.

And is not this the sort of prison in which the tyrant will be bound — he who being by nature such as we have described, is full of all sorts of fears and lusts? His soul craves for pleasure and yet, alone of all men in the city, he is never allowed to go on a journey, or to see the things which other freemen desire to see, but he lives hidden in his house like a woman, and is jealous of any other citizen who goes into foreign parts and sees anything of interest.

Very true, he said.

So that these ills must be added to the account of the man, who is ill-governed in his own person — the tyrannical man, I mean, whom you just now decided to be the most miserable of all — when, instead of leading a private life, he is constrained by fortune to be a public tyrant? He has to be master of others when he is not master of himself: he is like a diseased or paralytic man who is compelled to pass his life, not in retirement, but fighting and combating with other men.

Yes, Socrates, he said, the similitude is most exact and true.

Is not his case utterly miserable, my dear Glaucon? and does not the actual tyrant lead a more grievous life than he whose life you determined to be the most grievous?

Certainly.

He who is the real tyrant, whatever men may think, is the real slave, and is obliged to practise the greatest adulation and servility, and to be the flatterer of the vilest of mankind. He has desires which he is utterly unable to satisfy, and has more wants than any one, and is truly poor, if you know how to inspect the whole soul of him: all his life long he is beset with fear and is full of convulsions and distractions, if his condition is like that of the State which he governs: and surely the resemblance holds?

Indeed it does, he said.

580　　Moreover, we have still to add to his score something which we have already mentioned, — that he is, and owing to his power steadily becomes, more jealous, more faithless, more unjust, more friendless, more impious, than he was at first; he is the purveyor and cherisher of every sort of vice, and the consequence is that he is supremely miserable, and that he makes his neighbours as miserable as himself.

No man of any sense will dispute your words.

Come then, I said, and as the final judge in a competition proclaims the result, do you also decide who in your opinion is first in the scale of happiness, and who second, and in what order the others follow:

there are five of them in all — they are the royal, timocratical, oligarchical, democratical, tyrannical.

The decision will be easily given, he replied; the order of the entrance of these choruses upon the stage is also their order of merit in respect of virtue and vice, happiness and misery.

Need we hire a herald, or shall I announce, that the son of Ariston [the best] has decided that the best and justest is also the happiest, and that this is he who is the most royal man and king over himself; and that the worst and most unjust man is also the most miserable, and that this is he who being the greatest tyrant of himself is also the greatest tyrant of his State?

You may make that proclamation, he said.

And shall I add, 'whether the character of each is seen or unseen by gods and men'?

Let the words be added.

Then this, I said, will be our first proof; now consider another, which may also have some weight. . . .

◄§ Socrates now proceeds to prove that the best and most just man is the happiest on the ground that he is better qualified to judge pleasures. He argues first that to the three parts of the soul there correspond three types of man, in each of whom one part of the soul is dominant. To each part of the soul and to each type of man there belong a peculiar love and a peculiar pleasure: to reason and to the philosopher, the love of learning and of knowledge, and the pleasures that accompany these; and similarly with the spirited and desirous parts of the soul and the men in whom these parts rule. To determine which life is pleasantest and noblest, appeal must be made to experience, intelligence, and reason, and in each the philosopher is superior. He alone of the three types has experience of all three kinds of pleasure, since he knows best his own pleasures and also knows what it is to receive honor and to enjoy bodily satisfactions. In intelligence and in reasoning he of course excels. Therefore he speaks with authority when he declares his own life the pleasantest; after that, the life of the lover of honor; and last, that of the lover of gain. So a second time the just man has been victorious.

A third proof is now advanced: the pleasures of the philosopher are more true and real. Socrates supports this assertion by several arguments, one of which is that soul, and also reason or knowledge, are more real and contain more of what is enduring and unchangeable than body and food, and therefore that the satisfaction of the soul's hunger by knowledge is more real and true than that of the body by food. He declares that the further a man is from being ruled by reason, the less genuine will be all his pleasures, and the tyrant is such a man. At the end he humorously calculates that the tyrant is 729 times less happy than the philosopher or the true king, and declares the life of the king to be immeasurably more noble and admirable.

Socrates then takes up a further point:

588 Well, I said, and now having arrived at this stage of the argument, we may revert to that earlier statement which caused us to set out on our journey hither: Was not some one saying that injustice was a gain to the perfectly unjust who was reputed to be just?

Yes, that was said.

Now then, having determined the power and quality of justice and injustice, let us have a little conversation with him.

What shall we say to him?

Let us make an image of the soul, that he may have his own words presented before his eyes.

Of what sort?

An image like the composite creations of ancient mythology, such as the Chimera or Scylla or Cerberus, and there are many others in which two or more different natures are said to grow into one.

There are said to have been such unions.

Then do you now model the form of a multitudinous, many-headed monster, having a ring of heads of all manner of beasts, tame and wild, which he is able to put forth and metamorphose at will.

You suppose marvellous powers in the artist; but as language is more pliable than wax or any similar substance, let there be such a model as you propose.

Suppose now that you make a second form as of a lion, and a third of a man; but let the first be far the largest, and the second next in size.

That, he said, is an easier task; and I have made them as you say.

And now join them into one, and let the three somehow grow together.

That has been accomplished.

Next fashion the outside of them into a single image, as of a man, so that he who is not able to look within, and sees only the outer case, may believe the beast to be a single human creature.

I have done so, he said.

And now, to him who maintains that it is profitable for this human creature to be unjust and unprofitable to be just, let us reply that, if he be right, it is profitable for this creature to feast the multitudinous
589 monster and strengthen the lion and the lion-like qualities, but to starve and weaken the man, who is consequently liable to be dragged about at the mercy of either of the other two; and he is not to attempt to familiarize or harmonize them with one another — he ought rather to suffer them to fight and bite and devour one another.

Certainly, he said; that is what the approver of injustice says.

To him the other, who says that justice is profitable, makes answer that one should ever so speak and act as to give to the man within the most complete mastery over the entire human creature, — to enable him to watch over the many-headed monster like a good hus-bandman, fostering and cultivating the gentle qualities, and preventing the wild ones from growing; and when he has made the lion-heart his ally, and in common care of them all has reconciled the several parts with one another and with himself, he will endeavour to preserve the whole.

Yes, he said, that is quite what the maintainer of justice will say.

And so from every point of view, whether of pleasure, honour, or advantage, the approver of justice is right and speaks the truth, and the disapprover who commends injustice is wrong and false and ig-norant of that which he blames?

Yes, from every point of view.

Come, now, and let us gently reason with the unjust, who is not intentionally in error. 'Good Sir,' we will say to him, 'what think you of things esteemed noble and ignoble? Is not the noble that which subjects the beast to the man, or rather to the god in man; and the ignoble that which subjects the tame to the savage?' He can hardly avoid saying Yes — can he now?

Not if he has any regard for my opinion.

Then, I said, if this be true, we may ask: Can it profit any man to receive gold, on the condition that he enslaves the noblest part of him to the worst? Since, if a man sold his son or daughter into slavery for money, especially if he sold them into the hands of fierce and evil men, no one would think him the gainer, however large might be the sum which he received, will any one say that he is not a miserable caitiff who remorselessly sells his own divine being to that which is most 590 godless and detestable? Eriphyle took the necklace as the price of her husband's life, but he is taking a bribe in order to compass a worse ruin.

Yes, said Glaucon, far worse — I will answer for him.

Has not intemperance been censured of old, because by such con-duct the huge multiform monster is allowed to be too much at large?

Clearly.

And men are blamed for self-will and bad temper when the lion and serpent element in them grows and is disproportionately excited?

Yes.

And luxury and softness are blamed, because they relax and weaken this same creature, and make a coward of him?

Very true.

And is not a man reproached for flattery and meanness who subor-dinates this spirited animal to the unruly monster, and habituates him in the days of his youth to be trampled in the mire for the sake of its insatiable greed, and from being a lion to become a monkey?

True, he said.

And why are mean employments and manual arts a reproach? Only because they imply such natural weakness of the higher principle that the individual is unable to control the creatures within him, but has to court them, and can learn nothing but ways of fawning upon them.

Such appears to be the reason.

And therefore, being desirous of placing him under a rule like that of the best, we say that he ought to be the servant of the best, in whom the Divine rules; not thinking that the servant ought to be ruled to his own disadvantage, as Thrasymachus thought that all subjects should, but because every one had better be ruled by divine wisdom dwelling within him; or, if this be impossible, then by an external authority, in order that we may be all, as far as possible, friends and equals under the same guiding power.

Quite right, he said.

And this is clearly seen to be the intention of law, which is the ally of the whole city; and is seen also in the authority which we exercise over children, and the refusal to let them be free until we **591** have established in them a principle analogous to the constitution of a state, and by cultivation of this higher element have set up in their hearts a guardian and ruler like our own, and when this is done we give them their freedom.

Yes, he said, the purpose is manifest.

From what point of view, then, and on what ground can we say that a man is profited by injustice or intemperance or other baseness, which will make him a worse man, even though he acquire money or power by his wickedness?

From no point of view at all.

What shall he profit, if his injustice be undetected and unpunished? He who is undetected only gets worse, whereas he who is detected and punished has the brutal part of his nature silenced and humanized; the gentler element in him is liberated, and his whole soul is perfected and ennobled by the acquirement of justice and temperance and wisdom, more than the body ever is by receiving gifts of beauty, strength and health, in proportion as the soul is more honourable than the body.

Certainly, he said.

To this nobler purpose the man of understanding will devote the energies of his life. And in the first place, he will honour the studies which impress these qualities on his soul, and will disregard others?

Clearly, he said.

In the next place, he will be so far from entrusting his bodily habit and sustenance to brutal and irrational pleasures and living with his face turned in that direction, that he will regard even health as quite a secondary matter; his first object will be not that he may be fair or strong or well, unless he is likely thereby to gain temperance, but he will always desire so to attemper the body as to preserve the harmony of the soul?

Certainly he will, if he has true music in him.

And again in the acquisition of wealth is there not a principle of order and harmony which he will observe? he will not allow himself to be dazzled by the foolish applause of the world, and heap up riches to his own infinite harm?

I think not, he said.

He will look at the city which is within him, and take heed that no disorder occur in it, such as might arise either from affluence or from want; and upon this principle he will regulate his property and gain or spend according to his means.

Very true.

And, for the same reason, he will gladly accept and enjoy such 592 honours as he deems likely to make him a better man; but those, whether private or public, which arc likely to disorder his life, he will avoid?

Then, if that is his motive, he will not be a statesman.

By the dog of Egypt, he will! in the city which is his own he certainly will, though in the land of his birth perhaps not, unless he have a divine call.

I understand; you mean that he will be a ruler in the city of which we are the founders, and which exists in idea only; for I do not believe that there is such an one anywhere on earth?

But perhaps, I replied, it is laid up as a pattern in heaven, which he who desires may behold, and beholding, may set his own house in order. But whether such a city exists or ever will exist in fact, is no matter; for he will live after the manner of that city, having nothing to do with any other.

I think so, he said.

Republic · Book X

◆ᢒ Book IX, as we have just seen, ends on a high, even a climactically high note. Is Socrates, or Plato his creator, fated for an anticlimactic fall? The question is not altogether rhetorical, for the reader may judge in the end that no equal height has been reached. But what we have first in Book X, this final book of the *Republic*, is a deliberate change of tone, a lessening of intensity in preparation for a further climax. The pattern resembles that of the latter part of the *Symposium*, where the speech of Diotima-Socrates with its celebration of the love of ideal Beauty is followed by the invasion of Alcibiades and his fellow revelers, and this in turn makes possible the praise of Socrates as the ideal practitioner of such love.

The book begins with the comment of Socrates that, in looking backward over the plan of the ideal city, he is especially pleased by the regulation banning the use of imitative or dramatic poetry other than that which imitates virtuous men. The forbidden poetry, he says, is harmful to any soul which does not already possess sound knowledge of virtue and vice. Now, in the light of our recognition of the three parts of the soul, we can see more clearly why this is so.

Socrates first establishes that there is an eternal Idea of every type of material thing and that the material thing itself, such as a bed, is only an imitation of this first bed. The painter in a sense can make a bed or any other material thing, yet he really makes only an imitation of the material thing, and, moreover, makes it only as the thing is seen from one standpoint, as from the side or front. Just so, a poet is only an imitator of imitations, and moreover imitates only aspects of such imitations. Though he may seem to show us all the arts and every kind of knowledge, he does not really possess them. Even Homer, who tells chiefly of the conduct of wars, of statecraft, and of the nurture of men, achieved no greatness in any of these arts, nor have the other poets. Since in fact the poet knows only the superficial aspects of the things and actions he depicts, and not their proper uses, he cannot know whether they are good or bad.

Socrates now argues that in the soul it is reason which enables us to avoid being misled by appearances or blinded by feelings. To follow reason's teaching we must not allow our griefs to determine our actions. But sorrows and other feelings such as mirth are the chief subject matter of the dramatic poet, and he seduces even the best of us into indulging in them as we listen. Thus poetry feeds the irrational part of the soul and in the end fosters our yielding to feeling and desire, and undermines reason's control. Therefore only hymns and praises of great men may be admitted to our state or to our souls, unless the banished poets can show us that they foster virtue. We must not be led astray by the beauty of poetry any more than by wealth and power.

350

He now proposes to show that the rewards of virtue are greater than has yet been claimed, since they extend beyond mortal life. For, he declares, the soul is immortal, as may be seen if we reflect that each thing has its own peculiar evil, such as rust for iron or disease for the body, and can be destroyed by no other evil. Therefore the soul cannot be destroyed by the ills of the body. But neither is it in fact destroyed by its own evil, which is injustice, intemperance, and the rest. Therefore all souls are deathless. Nor can further souls come into being, for they could arise only from what is mortal, and should this occur, all that is mortal would in time become immortal. The soul in her true nature is also simple and fair, and not as we know her, composite and incrusted with impurities from immersion in the sea of material existence.

At the beginning of our investigation, Socrates reminds Glaucon, you wished me to show that justice was good, not for its external results but in itself, for the soul in itself, and therefore I conceded that the just man might be believed by gods and men to be unjust and might suffer all penalties and misfortunes. Now that the case for justice in itself has been proved, you must let me revoke my admissions. The gods will surely recognize the man who strives to become like them and will bestow on him only good, except as he must suffer for his former wrongdoings, and this will be true though seeming evils befall him, for they will end in good, either in life or after death. And among men also the just man will in the end be acknowledged and will receive honors and rewards, while the unjust will receive due penalties.

Beyond this life, too, Socrates avers, blessings and punishments await each man according to his deserts; and Socrates will tell of them. What he says will be found later in this volume, under the title "The Myth of Er."

Cratylus

Persons of the Dialogue

SOCRATES HERMOGENES CRATYLUS

⊷§ We have already noted in our Introduction, Theme 7, the wide-spread contemporary interest in the nature of language and its influence on our perception and understanding of the world. Since language is the subject of the *Cratylus* and since also this dialogue is less widely available than most, large parts of it will be reproduced here.

It is now generally agreed that reality is grouped and articulated for us by language, and it is considered by some that differing world-views are implied by different languages, a possibility of which Plato seemingly was not aware; but whether we have any way of penetrating to the core of reality is still a moot question. Another topic still debated is how far there is objective likeness between certain vocal sounds and the qualities of objects. Plato is centrally concerned with both questions. Plato's thinking on many other points is recognizably like our own. He knows well that words are human in origin, not divine or natural; he sees their discriminative function, enabling us to distinguish and classify our experience; he is essentially a conventionalist, conceiving a word as a primarily arbitrary means of referring to what is meant; he recognizes and commends descriptive words compounded of meaningful parts. He shows us vividly some of the superstitious errors and thought-obstructing confusions prevalent in his day, and makes the logically irrefutable point that, if we are to judge the fitness of language, we must have some independent criterion of the nature of reality. If we let him, he will excite our own reflections on such topics.

In this dialogue many Greek words are brought into the discussion as illustrations. They will be presented here both in the Greek alphabet and in our own. For better following of the meaning, the reader may find it convenient to learn the sounds of the Greek letters given in Appendix B, on transliteration.

We begin our selections from the dialogue with the opening line.

383 *Hermogenes.* Suppose that we make Socrates a party to the argument?

Cratylus. If you please.

Her. I should explain to you, Socrates, that our friend Cratylus has been arguing about names; he says that they are natural and not

352

conventional; not a portion of the human voice which men agree to use; but that there is a truth or correctness in them, which is the same by nature for all, both Hellenes and barbarians. Whereupon I ask him whether his own name is truly Cratylus or not, and he answers, 'Yes.' And Socrates — is that a true name? 'Yes.' Then every man's name, as I tell him, is that which he is called. To this he replies — 'If all the world were to call you Hermogenes, that would not be your name.' And when I am anxious to have a further explanation he is ironical and mysterious, and seems to imply that he has a notion of his own about the matter if he would only tell, and could entirely convince me if he chose to be intelligible. Tell me, Socrates, what this oracle means; or rather tell me, if you will be so good, what is your own view of the truth or correctness of names, which I would far sooner hear. 384

Socrates. Son of Hipponicus, there is an ancient saying that 'hard is the knowledge of the good'. And the knowledge of names is a great part of knowledge. If I had not been poor, I might have heard the fifty-drachma course of the great Prodicus, which is a complete education in grammar and language — these are his own words — and then I should have been at once able to answer your question about the correctness of names. But, indeed, I have only heard the single-drachma course, and therefore I do not know the truth about such matters; I will, however, gladly assist you and Cratylus in the investigation of them. When he declared that your name is not really Hermogenes, I suspect that he is only making fun of you; he means to say that you are no true son of Hermes, because you are always looking for a fortune and never in luck. But, as I was saying, it is difficult to obtain certain knowledge of such things and therefore we had better inquire which view is better, yours or that of Cratylus, each of us contributing what he can.

Her. I have often talked over this matter, both with Cratylus and others, and cannot convince myself that there is any principle of correctness in names other than convention and agreement; any name which you give, in my opinion, is the right one, and if you change that and give another, the new name is as correct as the old — we frequently change the names of our slaves, and the newly imposed name is as good as the old: for there is no name given to anything by nature; all is convention and habit of the users; such is my view. But if I am mistaken I shall be happy to hear and learn of Cratylus, or of anyone else.

ই Socrates now assumes the role of questioner or chief investigator, and first elicits from Hermogenes the statement that on his view the right name of a thing is only whatever any individual or group of persons agree to call it, and for each user the name he gives is right. Obtaining Hermogenes' assent to each step, Socrates then proceeds to establish tentatively the following conclusions.

Speech can be true or false, and a name, as a part of speech, can also have these properties. There are men who are wise and others who are foolish; necessarily, therefore, things in general have objective properties or natures which are recognized by the wise, and Protagoras was wrong in asserting that all things are as they appear to each and every observer, nor are their properties imposed on them by the observer. Actions also have natures and may be done rightly or wrongly. Only if done in the natural way, by the use of the naturally right instrument, will actions, including naming, be rightly done.

As a shuttle is an instrument for separating the threads of warp and woof, so a name is an instrument for giving information and for making distinctions among things. As a shuttle must be made by a carpenter, so a name must be made by a "legislator" or "custom-establisher." A carpenter makes a shuttle with mind fixed on the ideal form of a shuttle, and produces always a shuttle, though he must also make different specific kinds of shuttles suited to different uses, and may use now one material, now another. Just so, a legislator must make names with mind fixed on the ideal form of a name, and by so doing will produce true names, though he must also adapt each name to its referent and may use as his material the sounds and syllables of different languages. Just as the best supervisor of the making of shuttles will be the skilled weaver, so the "dialectician" or skilled philosophical inquirer will best superintend the making of names. Names, therefore, cannot be casually bestowed, but must be made by one who looks to the ideal name for each thing and embodies its nature in letters and syllables.

Hermogenes replies that he cannot refute the arguments of Socrates, but might be more readily convinced if Socrates will explain what he has called the natural rightness of names.

Once again Socrates denies that he has the answer. We should, he ironically asserts, ask the experts in these matters, Protagoras and his fellow sophists. (He is remembering that the sophists often did this very thing, and that they found in the poets, by the application of Procrustean methods, whatever answers they chose.) Accordingly, Socrates professes now to prove that Homer possesses a "great and marvellous" knowledge of names. For example, he knew the very name by which the gods refer to the river that men call Xanthus, and he knew which of the two names given to Hector's son was more correct.

On further reflection Socrates finds that Hector's name means "holder," i.e., "defender," thus coinciding with his son's correct name, "Astyanax," i.e., "lord of the city." (The word play in these derivations is not translatable. It can be paralleled, however, by such popular etymologies as that of deriving "Samson" from "son of Sam," or "asparagus" from "sparrow grass.") On this showing, a name, if correct, indicates the essential character of its possessor, and normally reflects the nature of his parental stock. Socrates enlarges upon this theme, adding the assertion that deviates, such as the irreligious son of a religious father, should not inherit the father's name. He cites some examples of what he calls correct names from the heroic age: Orestes, "the man of mountain wildness," from ὄρος, *oros, mountain;* his father Agamemnon, "admirable for remaining," from ἀγαστός, *agastos, admirable,* and μονή, *monē, remaining;* and Tantalus, whose name truly proclaimed him both in this life and in the world below, "most miserable," from ταλάντατον, *talantaton,* which has this very meaning. Again, consider Tantalus' reputed father, Zeus. His name is really like a sentence, since some call him Zen (i.e., ζῆν, *zēn, to live*), while others call him Dia (i.e., the preposition διά, *dia,* meaning *through*). Putting the two parts together, we get the full name and nature of the god: *"through* whom all creatures always have *life."*

Hermogenes expresses his astonishment at all this prophetic and oracular wisdom, and Socrates explains:

Soc. Yes, Hermogenes, and I believe that I caught the inspiration from the great Euthyphro of the Prospaltian deme,[1] who gave me a long lecture which commenced at dawn: he talked and I listened, and his wisdom and enchanting ravishment has not only filled my ears but taken possession of my soul. I think that this will be the right course — today I shall let his superhuman power work and finish the investigation of names; but tomorrow, if you are so disposed, we will conjure him away, and make a purgation of him, if we can only find some priest or sophist who is skilled in purifications of this sort.

Hor. With all my heart; for I am very curious to hear the rest of the inquiry about names.

Soc. Then let us proceed; and where would you have us begin, now that we have got a sort of outline of the inquiry? . . . Ought we not to begin with the consideration of the gods, and show for what reason they are rightly so named?

Her. Yes, that will be well.

Soc. My notion would be something of this sort: — I suspect that the sun, moon, earth, stars, and heaven, which are still the gods of many barbarians, were the only gods known to the aboriginal Hellenes. Seeing that they were always moving and running, from their running nature they were called gods or runners (θεούς, θέοντας [*theous, theontas,* i.e., *gods, runners*]); and when men became acquainted with the other gods, they proceeded to apply the same name to them all. . . .

❧ Socrates, with the spirit of Euthyphro still working within him, continues to play the game of etymology, with a rapid fertility that astounds his listeners. There is method in his madness, however,

[1] Probably the same Euthyphro who appears in the dialogue of that name. (L)

or at least a clarity of expression and an unfailing order of development, and he covers an immense area: gods, daemons, men, soul, body, the proper names of gods, and at length sun, moon, and stars, by no means exhausting the list. The fourteen Stephanus pages within which this labor is accomplished are of interest to the special student of Greek mythology and religion; but the general reader, particularly if he has no Greek, will find therein more brambles than berries. Let us therefore proceed directly to Stephanus page 411a, where Socrates is about to introduce for discussion an interesting theory that the same basic meaning can be discerned in many names for moral and intellectual qualities, and that this meaning reveals the nature of the universe.

As we rejoin the dialogue, Hermogenes has a favor to ask:

411   *Her.* I should like very much to know, in the next place, how you would explain the names given to the virtues. What principle of correctness is there in those charming words — wisdom, understanding, justice, and the rest of them?

Soc. That is a tremendous class of names which you are disinterring; still, as I have put on the lion's skin, I must not be faint of heart; and I suppose that I must consider the meaning of wisdom (φρόνησις [*phronēsis*]) and understanding (σύνεσις [*synesis*]), and judgement (γνώμη [*gnōmē*]), and knowledge (ἐπιστήμη [*epistēmē*]), and all those other charming words, as you call them?

Her. Surely, we must not leave off until we find out their meaning.

Soc. By the dog of Egypt I believe that the notion which came into my head just now was not ill founded; that is, that the primeval givers of names were undoubtedly like too many of our modern philosophers, who, in their search after the nature of things, are always getting dizzy from constantly going round and round, and then they imagine that the world is going round and round and moving in all directions; and this appearance, which arises out of their own internal condition, they suppose to be a reality of nature; they think that there is nothing stable or permanent, but only flux and motion, and that the world is always full of every sort of motion and change. The consideration of the names which I mentioned has led me into making this reflection.

Her. How is that, Socrates?

Soc. Perhaps you did not observe that in the names which have just been cited, the motion or flux or generation of things is most surely indicated.

Her. No, indeed, I was hardly aware of it.

Soc. Take the first of those which you mentioned; clearly that is a name indicative of motion.

Her. What was the name?

Soc. Φρόνησις [*phronēsis*] (wisdom), which may signify φορᾶς καὶ ῥοῦ νόησις [*phoras kai rhou noēsis*] (perception of motion and flux), or perhaps φορᾶς ὄνησις [*phoras onēsis*] (the blessing of motion), but is at any rate connected with φέρεσθαι [*pheresthai*] (motion). . . .

◆§ Socrates continues in this fashion, and nearing the end of his list arrives at the word τέχνη (*technē, art* or *science*); in Plato's Greece, sculpture and cobbling were both called "arts." His dealings with this word are inspired by the satiric muse. He will show us how to bring *technē* into phonetic near-equivalence with what he conceives to be its proper meaning. It is a simple little trick: Strike off the initial consonant of *technē*, insert one *o* (*o*) between its χ (*ch*) and its ν (*n*), and another *o* (*o*) between its ν (*n*) and final η (*ē*). Result: ἐχονόη (*echonoē*), a near identity with ἔχειν νοῦν (*eichein noun, to have mind*).

This satire, as Jowett noted, anticipated the celebrated *mot* of Voltaire, when he defined etymology as "the science that makes little account of consonants and of vowels nothing at all." A broader version of the same is the story of a man named Middlebush, who claimed phonetic descent from Moses. Challenged for a proof he replied: "Nothing simpler; drop *iddlebush* and add *oses*."

Hermogenes protests, in the disparaging comment that follows:

Her. Your hunger for letters increases, Socrates.

Soc. Yes, my dear friend; but then you know that the original names have been long ago buried and disguised by people sticking on and stripping off letters for the sake of euphony, and twisting and bedizening them in all sorts of ways: and time too may have had a share in the change. Take, for example, the word κάτοπτρον [*katoptron*]; why is the letter ρ (*r*) inserted? This must surely be the addition of someone who cares nothing about the truth, but thinks only of putting the mouth into shape. And the additions are often such that at last no human being can possibly make out the original meaning of the word. . . .

Her. That is quite true, Socrates.

Soc. And yet, if you are permitted to put in and pull out any letters which you please, names will be too easily made, and any name may be adapted to any object.

◆§ Socrates returns to his appointed task of giving etymologies for words relating to moral qualities, ending with the explanation of the word *name* itself, and of *truth* and *falsehood*.

Hermogenes now introduces what will soon be seen to constitute a new topic: the origin of more basic words, such as those from which the words thus far treated have been said to be derived. It is in this connection that Socrates-Plato will set forth the dialogue's important and influential theory of the birth of speech.

414

421 *Her.* You have hammered away manfully, Socrates, at these names; but suppose that someone were to say to you, What of such words as ἰόν (*ion*) and ῥέον (*rheon*) and δοῦν (*doun*)? — show me their fitness.

Soc. You mean to say, how should I answer him?

Her. Yes.

Soc. One way of giving the appearance of an answer has already been suggested.

Her. What way?

Soc. To say that names which we do not understand are of foreign origin; and something of this kind may be true of many of them. In other cases the original forms of words may have been lost in the lapse of ages; names have been so twisted in all manner of ways, that we need not be surprised if the old language when compared with that now in use would appear to us to be a barbarous tongue.

Her. Very likely.

Soc. Yes, very likely. But still the inquiry demands our earnest attention and we must not flinch. For we should remember, that if a person goes on analysing names into words, and inquiring also into the elements out of which the words are formed, and keeps on always repeating this process, he who has to answer him must at last give up the inquiry in despair.

Her. Very true.

422 *Soc.* And at what point ought he to lose heart and give up the inquiry? Must he not stop when he comes to the names which are the elements of all other names and sentences? for these cannot fairly be supposed to be made up of other names. The word ἀγαθόν [*agathon*] (good), for example, is, as we were saying, a compound of ἀγαστός [*agastos*] (admirable) and θοός [*thoos*] (swift). And we should perhaps declare that θοός [*thoos*] is made up of other elements, and these again of others. But if, in the end, we obtain something which is incapable of further resolution, then we shall be right in saying that we have at last reached a primary element, which we are no longer obliged to resolve into other names.

Her. I believe you to be in the right.

Soc. And suppose the names about which you are now asking should turn out to be primary elements, must not their correctness be tested according to some new method?

Her. Very likely.

Soc. Quite so, Hermogenes; all that has preceded seems to converge upon this point. If this impression is correct, as I think it is, then I shall again say to you, come and help me, that I may not fall into some absurdity in stating the principle of primary names.

Her. Let me hear, and I will do my best to assist you.

Soc. I think that you will acknowledge with me, that one principle is applicable to all names, from the simplest to the most complex — when they are regarded simply as names, there is no difference in them.

Her. I will.

Soc. But now in the explanation which we have just completed, names were judged correct according to their power to show what each thing is like.

Her. Of course.

Soc. And that this is characteristic of the primary quite as much as of the secondary names, is implied in their being names.

Her. Surely.

Soc. But the secondary, as I conceive, derive their significance from the primary.

Her. So it seems.

Soc. Very good; but then how do the primary names which are not founded upon others show the natures of things, as far as they can be shown; which they must do, if they are to be real names? And here I will ask you a question: Suppose that we had no voice or tongue, and wanted to indicate objects to one another, should we not, like the deaf and dumb, make signs with the hands and head and the rest of the body?

Her. There would be no choice, Socrates.

Soc. We should imitate the nature of the thing; the elevation of our 423 hands to heaven would mean lightness and upwardness; heaviness and downwardness would be expressed by letting them drop to the ground; if we were describing the running of a horse, or any other animal, we should make our bodies and their gestures as like as we could to them.

Her. Yes, we should have been obliged to do as you say.

Soc. We should have had to take this course, I suppose, in order to indicate anything with the body; it must imitate the thing to which it would refer.

Her. Very true.

Soc. And so when we want to express something with the voice, or tongue, or mouth, the expression will be achieved by imitation, through one of these organs, of that which we want to express?

Her. It must be so, I think.

Soc. Then a name is, it seems, a vocal imitation of any object; and a man is said to *name* any object when he imitates it with the voice.

Her. I think so.

Soc. Nay, my friend, I am disposed to think that we have not reached the truth as yet.

Her. Why not?

Soc. Because if we have we shall be obliged to admit that the people who imitate sheep, or cocks, or other animals, name that which they imitate.

Her. Quite true.

Soc. Then could I have been right in what I was saying?

Her. In my opinion, no. But I wish that you would tell me, Socrates, what sort of an imitation is a name?

Soc. In the first place, I should reply, not a musical imitation, although that is also vocal; nor, again, an imitation of what music imitates; these, in my judgement, would not be naming. Let me put the matter as follows: All objects have sound and figure, and many have colour?

Her. Certainly.

Soc. But the art of naming appears not to be concerned with imitations of this kind; the arts which have to do with them are music and drawing?

Her. True.

Soc. Again, is there not in our opinion an essence of each thing, just as there is a colour, or sound? Firstly, is there not an essence of colour and sound themselves as well as of anything else?

Her. I should think so.

Soc. Well, and if anyone could express that essence of each thing in letters and syllables, would he not express the real nature of each thing?

424   *Her.* Quite so.

Soc. The musician and the painter were the two names which you gave to the two other imitators. What will this imitator be called?

Her. I imagine, Socrates, that he must be the namer, or name-giver, of whom we are in search.

Soc. If this is true, then I think that we are in a condition to consider the names ῥοή [*rhoē*] (stream), ἰέναι [*ienai*] (to go), σχέσις [*schesis*] (retention), about which you were asking; and we may see whether the namer has grasped the nature of them in letters and syllables in such a manner as to give a faithful rendering of the essence or not.

Her. Very good.

Soc. But are these the only primary names, or are there others?

Her. There must be others.

Soc. So I should expect. But from what kind of analysis does the imitator begin? Since it is assumed that he has to imitate the essence by syllables and letters, would it not be correct for him first to separate the letters, just as those who are propounding a theory of rhythm first distinguish the values of elementary, and then of compound sounds, and when they have done so, but not before, they proceed to the consideration of rhythms?

Her. Yes.

Soc. Must we not begin in the same way with letters? first separating the vowels, and then classifying the consonants and mutes, according to the received terminology of the learned; also the semivowels, which are neither vowels, nor yet mutes; and distinguishing into classes the vowels themselves. And having perfected this classification, we must turn our attention to all those existing things which are to receive names, and see whether, as in the case of letters, there are any classes to which they may be all referred; and hence we shall see their natures, and see, too, whether they have in them classes as there are in the letters; and when we have well considered all this, we must understand how to apply them to what they resemble — whether one letter is used to denote one thing, or whether there is to be an admixture of several of them; just as, in painting, the painter who wants to depict anything sometimes uses purple only, or any other colour, and sometimes mixes up several colours, as his method is when he has to paint flesh colour or anything of that kind — he uses his colours as his figures appear to require them; and so, too, we shall apply letters to the expression of objects, either single letters when required, or several letters; and so we shall form syllables, as they are called, and from a compound of syllables make nouns and verbs; and thus, at last, from the combinations of nouns and verbs arrive at language, large and fair and whole; and as the painter made a figure, even so shall we make speech by the art of the namer or the rhetorician, or however it should be termed. Not that I am literally speaking of ourselves, but I was carried away — meaning to say that this was the way in which (not we but) the ancients formed language, and what they put together we must take to pieces in like manner, if we are to attain a scientific view of the whole subject; and we must see whether the primary, and also whether the secondary elements are rightly given or not, for if they are not, the composition of them, my dear Hermogenes, will be a sorry piece of work, and in the wrong direction. 425

Her. That, Socrates, I can quite believe.

Soc. Well, but do you suppose that you will be able to analyse them in this way? for I am certain that I should not.

Her. Much less am I likely to be able.

Soc. Shall we leave them, then? or shall we seek to discover, if we can, something about them, according to the measure of our ability, saying by way of preface, as I said before of the Gods, that of the truth about them we know nothing, and do but entertain human notions of them. And in this present inquiry, let us say to ourselves, before we proceed, that the higher method is the one which we or others who would analyse language to any good purpose must follow; but under the circumstances, as men say, we must do as well as we can. What do you think?

Her. I very much approve.

Soc. That objects should be imitated in letters and syllables, and so find expression, may appear ridiculous, Hermogenes, but it cannot be avoided — there is no better principle to which we can look for the truth of first names. Deprived of this, we must have recourse to divine help, like the tragic poets, who in any perplexity have their gods waiting in the air; and must get out of our difficulty in like fashion, by saying that 'the Gods gave the first names, and therefore they are right'. Will this be the best contrivance — or should it be said that we have derived them from some barbarous people, and that the barbarians are older than we are? or that antiquity has 426 cast a veil over them, which is the same sort of excuse as the last? No! all these are not reasons but only ingenious excuses for failure to explain in what respect the primary names have been properly imposed. And yet any sort of ignorance of these names involves an ignorance of secondary words; for one would be reduced to explaining these from elements of which he knows nothing. Clearly then the professor of the science of language should be able to give a very lucid explanation of first names, or let him be assured he will only talk nonsense about the rest. Do you not suppose this to be true?

Her. Certainly, Socrates.

Soc. My first notions of original names are truly wild and ridiculous, though I have no objection to imparting them to you if you desire, and I hope that you will communicate to me in return anything better which you may have.

Her. Fear not; I will do my best.

Soc. In the first place, the letter ῥ [rh] appears to me to be the general instrument expressing all motion . . . the imposer of names . . . frequently uses the letter for this purpose: for example, in the actual words ῥεῖν [rhein] and ῥοή [rhoē] he represents motion by ῥ (rh); also in the words τρόμος [tromos] (trembling), τραχύς [trachys] (rugged); and again, in words such as κρούειν [krouein] (strike), θραύειν [thrauein] (crush), ἐρείκειν [ereikein] (bruise), θρύπτειν [thryptein] (break), κερματίζειν [kermatizein] (crumble), ῥυμβεῖν [rhymbein] (whirl): of all these sorts of movements he generally finds an expression in the letter R, because, as I imagine, he had observed that the tongue was most agitated and least at rest in the pronunciation of this letter, which he therefore used in order to express motion, just as by the letter ι (i) he expresses the subtle elements which pass through all things. This is 427 why he uses the letter ι (i), as imitative of motion, ἰέναι, ἴεσθαι [ienai, iesthai]. And there is another class of letters, φ (ph), ψ (ps), σ (s), and ζ (z), of which the pronunciation is accompanied by great expenditure of breath; these are used in the imitation of such notions as ψυχρόν [*psychron*] (shivering), ζέον [*zeon*] (seething), σείεσθαι [*seiesthai*] (to be shaken), σεισμός [*seismos*] (shock), and are always introduced by the giver of names when he wants to imitate what is φυσῶδες [*physōdes*] (windy). He seems to have thought that the closing and pressure of the tongue in the utterance of δ (*d*) and τ (*t*) was expressive of binding and rest in a place: he further observed the liquid movement of λ (*l*), in the pronunciation of which the tongue slips, and in this he found the expression of smoothness, as in λεῖος [*leios*] (level), and in the word ὀλισθάνειν [*olisthanein*] (to slip) itself, λιπαρόν [*liparon*] (sleek), in the word κολλῶδες [*kollōdes*] (gluey), and the like; the heavier sound of γ (*g*) detained the slipping tongue, and the union of the two gave the notion of a glutinous clammy nature, as in γλίσχρος, γλυκύς, γλοιῶδες [*glischros, glykys, gloiōdes*.] The ν (*n*) he observed to be sounded from within, and therefore to have a notion of inwardness; hence he introduced the sound in ἔνδον [*endon*], and ἐντός [*entos*] (within): α (*a*) he assigned to the expression of size, and η (*ē*) of length, because they are great letters: ο (*o*) was the sound of roundness, and therefore there is plenty of ο mixed up in the word γογγύλον [*gongylon*] (round). And, in general, by this kind of adaptation, sometimes of letters, and sometimes of whole syllables, the legislator seems to have created signs and names for every existing thing; and from these he proceeded to design compounds in order to perfect his imitation. That is my view, Hermogenes, of the truth of names; but I should like to hear what Cratylus has more to say.

Her. But, Socrates, as I was telling you before, Cratylus has often greatly mystified me: he says that there is a fitness of names, but he never explains what is this fitness, so that I cannot tell whether his obscurity whenever this subject is raised is intended or not. Tell me now, Cratylus, here in the presence of Socrates, do you agree in what Socrates has been saying about names, or have you something better of your own? and if you have, tell me what your view is, and then you will either learn of Socrates, or Socrates and I will learn of you.

Crat. Well, but surely, Hermogenes, you do not suppose that you can learn, or I explain, any subject of importance all in a moment; at any rate, not such a subject as language, which is, perhaps, the very greatest of all.

Her. No, indeed; but, as Hesiod says, and I agree with him, 'to add little to little' is worthwhile. And therefore, if you think that you can add anything at all, however small, to our knowledge, do not flinch, but oblige Socrates, and me too, who certainly have a claim upon you. **423**

Soc. I am by no means positive, Cratylus, in the view which Hermogenes and myself have worked out; and therefore do not hesitate to say what you think, which if it be better than my own view I shall gladly accept. And I should not be at all surprised to find that you have found some better notion. For you have evidently reflected on these matters and have had teachers, and if you have really a better theory of the truth of names, you may count me in the number of your disciples.

Crat. You are right, Socrates, in saying that I have made a study of these matters, and I might possibly convert you into a disciple. But I fear that the opposite is more probable, and I already find myself moved to say to you what Achilles in the 'Prayers' says to Ajax, —

Illustrious Ajax, son of Telamon, lord of the people,

You appear to have spoken in all things much to my mind.

And you, Socrates, appear to me to be an oracle, and to give answers much to my mind, whether you are inspired by Euthyphro, or whether some Muse may have long been an inhabitant of your breast, unconsciously to yourself.

Soc. Excellent Cratylus, I have long been wondering at my own wisdom, finding it beyond belief. And I think that I ought to stop and ask myself, What am I saying? for there is nothing worse than self-deception — when the deceiver is always at home and always with you — it is quite terrible, and therefore I ought often to retrace my steps and endeavour to 'look fore and aft', in the words of the aforesaid Homer. And now let me see; where are we? Have we not been saying that the correct name indicates the nature of the thing: — has this proposition been sufficiently proven?

Crat. Yes, Socrates, it has in my opinion been well established.

Soc. Names, then, are given in order to instruct?

Crat. Certainly.

Soc. And naming is an art, and has artificers?

Crat. Yes.

Soc. And who are they?

429 *Crat.* The legislators, as you declared at first.

Soc. And does this art grow up among men like other arts? Let me explain what I mean: of painters, some are better and some worse?

Crat. Yes.

Soc. The better painters execute their works, I mean their figures, better, and the worse execute them worse; and of builders also, the better sort build fairer houses, and the worse build them worse.

Crat. True.

Soc. And among legislators likewise, there are some who do their work better and some worse?

Crat. No; there I do not agree with you.

Soc. Then you do not think that some laws are better and others worse?

Crat. No, indeed.

Soc. Nor is one name, I suppose, in your opinion, more properly imposed than another?

Crat. Certainly not.

Soc. Then all names are rightly imposed?

Crat. Yes, if they are names at all.

Soc. Well, what do you say to the name of our friend Hermogenes, which was mentioned before: — assuming that he has nothing of the nature of Hermes in him, shall we say that this is a wrong name, or not his name at all?

Crat. I should reply that Hermogenes is not his name at all, but only appears to be his, and is really the name of somebody else, who has the nature which corresponds to it.

Soc. Must we not add that one who calls him Hermogenes, does not speak falsely? For there may well be a doubt whether you can call him Hermogenes, if he is not.

Crat. What do you mean?

Soc. Does your statement amount to this, that it is altogether impossible to speak falsely? For there are many who say this, my dear Cratylus, and there have been many in the past.

Crat. Why, Socrates, how can a man say that which is not? —say something and yet say nothing? For is not falsehood saying the thing which is not?

Soc. Your argument, friend, is too subtle for a man of my age. But I should like to know whether you are one of these philosophers who think that falsehood may be spoken but not said?

Crat. Neither spoken nor said.

Soc. Nor uttered nor addressed? For example: If a person, saluting you in a foreign country, were to take your hand and say: 'Hail, Athenian stranger, Hermogenes, son of Smicrion' — these words, whether spoken, said, uttered, or addressed, would have no application to you but only to our friend Hermogenes, or perhaps to nobody at all?

Crat. In my opinion, Socrates, the speaker would only be talking nonsense.

Soc. Well, but that will be quite enough for me, if you will tell 430 me whether the nonsense would be true or false, or partly true and partly false; for even that would be enough.

Crat. I should say that he would be putting himself in motion to no purpose; and that his words would be an unmeaning sound like the noise of hammering at a brazen pot.

Soc. But let us see, Cratylus, whether we cannot find a meeting-point, for you would admit that the name is not the same with the thing named?

Crat. I should.

Soc. And would you further acknowledge that the name is an imitation of the thing?

Crat. Certainly.

Soc. And you would say that pictures are also imitations of things, but in another way?

Crat. Yes.

Soc. I believe you may be right, but I do not rightly understand you. Please to say, then, whether both sorts of imitation (I mean both pictures or words) are not equally attributable and applicable to the things of which they are the imitation.

Crat. They are.

Soc. First look at the matter thus: one might attribute the likeness of the man to the man, and of the woman to the woman; and so on?

Crat. Certainly.

Soc. And conversely one might attribute the likeness of the man to the woman, and of the woman to the man?

Crat. Very true.

Soc. And are both modes of assigning them right, or only the first?

Crat. Only the first.

Soc. That is to say, the mode of assignment which attributes to each that which belongs to them and is like them?

Crat. That is my view.

Soc. Now then, as I am desirous that we being friends should have a good understanding about the argument, let me state my view to you: the first mode of assignment, whether applied to figures or to names, I call right, and when applied to names only, true as well as right; and the other mode, whereby that which is unlike is given or assigned, I call wrong, and in the case of names, false as well as wrong.

Crat. I suggest that may be true, Socrates, in the case of pictures; they may be wrongly assigned; but not in the case of names — they must necessarily be always right.

Soc. Why, what is the difference? May I not go to a man and say to him, 'This is your picture', showing him his own likeness, or perhaps the likeness of a woman; and when I say 'show', I mean bring before the sense of sight.

Crat. Certainly.

431   *Soc.* And may I not go to him again, and say, 'This is your name'? — for the name, like the picture, is an imitation. May I not say to him — 'This is your name'? and may I not then bring to his sense of hearing the imitation of himself, when I say, 'This is a man'; or of a female of the human species, when I say, 'This is a woman', as the case may be? Is not all that possible — does it not sometimes happen?

Crat. I would fain agree with you, Socrates; and therefore I say, Granted.

Soc. For that I am grateful, my friend, if the fact is true; it is hardly necessary to persist in the dispute at present. But if I can assign names as well as pictures to objects, the right assignment of them we may call truth, and the wrong assignment of them falsehood. Now if there be such a wrong assignment of names, there may also be a wrong or inappropriate assignment of verbs; and if of names and verbs then of the sentences, which are made up of them. What do say, Cratylus?

Crat. I agree; and think that what you say is very true.

Soc. And further, primitive nouns may be compared to pictures, and in pictures you may either render all the appropriate colours and figures, or you may not render them all — some may be wanting; or there may be too many or too much of them — may there not?

Crat. Very true.

Soc. And he who renders all gives a perfect picture and image; and he who takes away or adds also produces a picture or image, but not a good one.

Crat. Yes.

Soc. In like manner, he who by syllables and letters imitates the substance of things, if he renders all that is appropriate will produce a good image, or in other words a name; but if he subtracts or perhaps adds a little, he will make an image but not a good one; whence I infer that some names are well and others ill made.

Crat. Perhaps.

Soc. Perhaps then the artist of names may be sometimes good, or he may be bad?

Crat. Yes.

Soc. And this artist of names is called the legislator?

Crat. Yes.

Soc. Then like other artists the legislator may be good or he may be bad; it must surely be so if our former admissions hold good?

Crat. Very true, Socrates; but the case of language, you see, is different; for when by the help of grammar we assign the letters a [a] 432 or β [b], or any other letters to a certain name, then, if we add, or subtract, or misplace a letter, the name which is written is not only written wrongly, but not written at all; and in any of these cases at once becomes other than a name.

Soc. But I doubt whether your inference is altogether correct, Cratylus.

Crat. How so?

Soc. I believe that what you say may be true about these things which, if they are to be at all, must be composed of a certain number;

for example, the number ten at once becomes other than ten if a unit be added or subtracted, and so of any other number: but this does not apply to that which is qualitative or to anything which is represented under an image. I should say rather that the image, if expressing in every point the entire reality, would no longer be an image. Let us suppose the existence of two objects: one of them shall be Cratylus, and the other the image of Cratylus; and we will suppose, further, that some God makes not only a representation such as a painter would make of your outward form and colour, but also creates an inward organization like yours, having the same warmth and softness; and into this infuses motion, and soul, and mind, such as you have, and in a word copies all your qualities, and places them by you in another form; would you say that this was Cratylus and the image of Cratylus, or that there were two Cratyluses?

Crat. I should say that there were two Cratyluses.

Soc. Then you see, my friend, that we must find some different principle of truth in images, and in the other cases mentioned; and not insist that an image is no longer an image when something is added or subtracted. Do you not perceive that images are very far from having qualities which are the exact counterpart of the realities which they represent?

Crat. Yes, I see.

Soc. But then how ridiculous would be the effect of names on the things named, if they were always made like them in every way! Surely we should then have two of everything, and no one would be able to determine which were the names and which were the realities.

Crat. Quite true.

Soc. Then fear not, but have the courage to admit that one name may be correctly and another incorrectly given; and do not insist that the name shall include all the letters, so that it will be exactly the same with the thing; but allow the occasional substitution of a wrong letter, and if of a letter also of a noun in a sentence, and if of a noun in a sentence also of a sentence which is not appropriate to the matter, and acknowledge that the thing may be named, and described, so long as the general character of the thing which you are describing is retained; and this, as you will remember, was remarked by Hermogenes and myself in the particular instance of the names of the letters.

433

Crat. Yes, I remember.

Soc. Good; and when the general character is preserved, even if some of the proper letters are wanting, still the thing is signified; — well, if all the letters are given; not well, when only a few of them are given. I think that we had better admit this, lest we be punished like travellers in Aegina who wander about the street late at night: and be likewise told by truth herself that we have arrived too late; or if not, you must find out some new notion of correctness of names, and no longer maintain that a name is the expression of a thing in letters or syllables; for if you say both, you will be inconsistent with yourself.

Crat. I quite acknowledge, Socrates, what you say to be very reasonable.

Soc. Then as we are agreed thus far, let us ask ourselves whether a name rightly imposed ought not to have the proper letters.

Crat. Yes.

Soc. And the proper letters are those which are like the things?

Crat. Yes.

Soc. Enough then of names which are rightly given. And in names which are incorrectly given, the greater part may be supposed to be made up of proper and similar letters, or there would be no likeness; but there will be likewise a part which is improper and spoils the beauty and formation of the word: you would admit that?

Crat. There would be no use, Socrates, in my quarrelling with you, since I cannot be satisfied that a name which is incorrectly given is a name at all.

Soc. Do you admit a name to be the representation of a thing?

Crat. Yes, I do.

Soc. But do you not allow that some nouns are primitive, and some derived and compound?

Crat. Yes, I do.

Soc. Then if primitive or first nouns are meant to be representations of things, can you think of any better way of framing them than to assimilate them as closely as possible to those objects which they are to represent? or do you prefer the notion of Hermogenes and of many others, who say that names are conventional, and have a meaning to those who have agreed about them, and who have previous knowledge of the things intended by them, and that it is convention which makes a name right; and whether you abide by our present convention, or make a new and opposite one, according to which you call small great and great small — that, they would say, makes no difference, if you are only agreed. Which of these two notions do you prefer?

Crat. Representation by likeness, Socrates, is infinitely better than 434 representation by any chance sign.

Soc. Very good: but if the name is to be like the thing, the letters out of which the first names are composed must also have a natural resemblance to things. Returning to the image of the picture, I would ask, How could any one ever compose a picture which would be like anything at all, if there were not pigments in nature which resembled the things imitated by portraiture, and out of which the picture is composed?

Crat. Impossible.

Soc. No more could names ever resemble any actually existing thing, unless the elements of which they are compounded bore, from the first, some degree of resemblance to the objects of which the names are the imitation: And the original elements are letters?

Crat. Yes.

Soc. Let me now invite you to consider what Hermogenes and I were saying about sounds. Do you agree with me that the letter ῥ [r] is expressive of rapidity, motion, and hardness? Were we right or wrong in saying so?

Crat. I should say that you were right.

Soc. And that λ [l] was expressive of smoothness, and softness, and the like?

Crat. There again you were right.

Soc. And yet, as you are aware, that which is called by us σκληρότης [sklērotēs], is by the Eretrians called σκληρότηρ [sklērotēr].

Crat. Very true.

Soc. But are the letters ρ [r] and σ [s] similar to the same thing; and is there the same significance to them in the termination ρ [r], which there is to us in σ [s], or is there no significance to one of us?

Crat. Nay, surely there is a significance to both of us.

Soc. In as far as ρ [r] and σ [s] are like, or in as far as they are unlike?

Crat. In as far as they are like.

Soc. Are they altogether alike?

Crat. Yes; for the purpose of expressing motion.

Soc. And what do you say of the insertion of the λ [l]? for that is expressive not of hardness but of softness.

Crat. Why, perhaps the letter λ [l] is wrongly inserted, Socrates, and should be altered into ρ [r], as you were saying to Hermogenes, and in my opinion rightly, when you spoke of adding and subtracting letters upon occasion.

Soc. Good. But still the word is intelligible to both of us; when I say σκληρός [sklēros] (hard), you know what I mean.

Crat. Yes, my dear friend, and the explanation of that is custom.

Soc. And what is custom but convention? When I utter *this* sound, I have *that* thing in mind, and you know that I have it in mind; is not

435 this what you mean by 'custom'?

Crat. Yes.

Soc. And if when I speak you know my meaning, there is an indication given by me to you?

Crat. Yes.

Soc. This indication of my meaning may proceed from unlike as well as from like, for example, in the λ [l] of σκληρότης [sklērotēs]. But if this is true, then you have made a convention with yourself, and the correctness of a name turns out to be convention, since letters which are unlike are indicative equally with those which are like, if they are sanctioned by custom and convention. And even supposing that you distinguish custom from convention ever so much, still you must say that the signification of words is given by custom and not by likeness, for custom may indicate by the unlike as well as by the like. But as we are agreed thus far, Cratylus (for I shall assume that your silence gives consent), then custom and convention must be supposed to contribute to the indication of our thoughts; for suppose we take the instance of number, how can you ever imagine, my good friend, that you will find names resembling every individual number, unless you allow that which you term convention and agreement to have authority in determining the correctness of names? I quite agree with you that words should as far as possible resemble things; but I fear that this dragging in of resemblance, as Hermogenes says, is a kind of hunger, which has to be supplemented by the mechanical aid of convention with a view to correctness; for I believe that if we could always, or almost always, use expressions which are similar, and therefore appropriate, this would be the most perfect state of language; as the opposite is the most imperfect. But let me ask you, what is the force of names, and what is the use of them?

Crat. The use of names, Socrates, as I should imagine, is to inform: the simple truth is, that he who knows names knows also the things which are expressed by them.

Soc. I suppose you mean to say, Cratylus, that as the name is, so also is the thing, and that he knows the one will also know the other, because they are similars, and all similars fall under the same art or science; and therefore you would say that he who knows names will also know things.

Crat. That is precisely what I mean.

Soc. But let us consider what is the nature of this information about things which, according to you, is given us by names. Is it the best sort of information? or is there any other? What do you say?

Crat. I believe that to be both the only and the best sort of infor-   436
mation about them; there can be no other.

Soc. But do you believe that it is by the same process that things are discovered, and that he who discovers the names discovers also the things; or is this only the method of learning, and is there some other method of inquiry and discovery?

Crat. I certainly believe that the methods of inquiry and discovery are of the same nature as instruction.

Soc. Well, but do you not see, Cratylus, that he who follows names in the search after things, and analyses their meaning, is in great danger of being deceived?

Crat. How so?

Soc. Why clearly he who first gave names gave them according to his conception of the things which they signified — did he not?

Crat. True.

Soc. And if his conception was erroneous, and he gave names according to his conception, in what position shall we who are his followers find ourselves? Shall we not be deceived by him?

Crat. But, Socrates, perhaps no such case arises, because it is necessary that one who imposes names should have *knowledge*; or else, as I have long maintained, his names would not be names at all? And you have a clear proof that he has not missed the truth, and the proof is —that he is perfectly consistent. Did you not yourself make the remark that all the words which you utter have a common character and purpose?

Soc. But that, friend Cratylus, is no answer. For if he did begin in error, he may have forced the remainder into agreement with the original error and with himself; there would be nothing strange in this, any more than in geometrical diagrams, which have often a slight and invisible flaw in the first part of the process, and are consistently mistaken in the long deductions which follow. And this is the reason why every man should expend his chief thought and attention on the consideration of his first principles: — are they or are they not rightly laid down? and when he has duly sifted them, it is time to consider the consistency of the rest. Even so, I should be astonished to find that names are really consistent. And here let us revert to our former discussion: Were we not saying that our vocabulary indicates the essence of things on the assumption that all things are in motion and progress and flux? Do you not conceive that to be the meaning of them?

Crat. Yes; that is assuredly their meaning, and the true meaning.

437 *Soc.* Let us revert to ἐπιστήμη [epistēmē] (knowledge), and observe how ambiguous this word is, seeming rather to signify stopping the soul at things than going round with them; and therefore we should leave the beginning as at present, and not reject the ε (e) (cf. 412a), but make an insertion of an ι (i) instead of an ε (e), not πιστήμη [pistēmē], but ἐπιιστήμη [epiistēmē].

᪲᪲ By this derivation Socrates has transparently linked the word for knowledge with the Greek verb ἵστημι (histēmi), *stop* or *stand still*. He now gives a number of other examples of Greek words expressing notions of desirable moral and intellectual qualities and activities, such as the words for *sure, inquiry, faithful,* and *memory,* which by their similarity to Greek words expressing fixity of position, stopping, or remaining, suggest the opposite of motion, and a second set of words referring to undesirable qualities or happenings which seem to suggest motion, if the same process formerly applied to the words for virtues is applied to them. He concludes:

Thus the names which in these instances we find to have the worst sense, will turn out to be framed on the same principle as those which have the best. And anyone I believe who would take the trouble might find many other examples in which the giver of names indicates, not that things are in motion or progress, but that they are at rest; which is the opposite of motion.

Crat. Yes, Socrates, but observe; the greater number express motion.

Soc. What of that, Cratylus? Are we to count them like votes? and is correctness of names the voice of the majority? Are we to say of whichever sort there are most, those are the true ones?

Crat. No; that is not reasonable.

Soc. Certainly not. [But let us have done with this question and proceed to another, about which I should like to know whether you think with me. Were we not lately acknowledging that the first givers of names in states, both Hellenic and barbarous, were the legislators, and that the art which gave names was the art of the legislator?

Crat. Quite true.

Soc. Tell me, then, did the first legislators, who were the givers of the first names, know or not know the things which they named?

Crat. They must have known, Socrates.

Soc. Why, yes, friend Cratylus, they could hardly have been 438 ignorant.

Crat. I should say not.]¹

Soc. Let us return to the point from which we digressed. You were saying, if you remember, that he who gave names must have known the things which he named; are you still of that opinion?

Crat. I am.

Soc. And would you say that the giver of the first names had also a knowledge of the things which he named?

Crat. I should.

Soc. But how could he have learned or discovered things from names if the primitive names were not yet given? For, if we are correct in our view, the only way of learning and discovering things, is either to discover names for ourselves or to learn them from others.

Crat. I think that there is a good deal in what you say, Socrates.

Soc. But if things are only to be known through names, how can we suppose that the givers of names had knowledge, or were legisla-

---

¹ The Jowett editors have bracketed this passage as being of doubtful authenticity. (L)

tors, before there were names at all, and therefore before they could
have known them?

Crat. I believe, Socrates, the true account of the matter to be,
that a power more than human gave things their first names, and that
the names which are thus given are necessarily their true names.

Soc. Then how came the giver of the names, if he was an inspired
being or God, to contradict himself? For were we not saying just
now that he made some names expressive of rest and others of
motion? Were we mistaken?

Crat. But I suppose one of the two not to be names at all.

Soc. And which, then, did he make, my good friend; those which
are expressive of rest, or those which are expressive of motion? This
is a point which, as I said before, cannot be determined by counting
them.

Crat. No indeed, Socrates, that would be unfair.

Soc. But if this is a battle of names, some of them asserting that
they are like the truth, others contending that *they* are, how or by
what criterion are we to decide between them? For there are no
other names to which appeal can be made, but obviously recourse
must be had to another standard which, without employing names,
will make clear which of the two are right; and this must be a
standard which shows the truth of things.

Crat. I agree.

Soc. But if that is true, Cratylus, then I suppose that things may
be known without names?

Crat. Apparently.

Soc. But by what other device would you expect to know them?
What other way can there be of knowing them, except the true and
natural way, through their affinities, when they are akin to each
other, and through themselves? For that which is other and different
from them must signify something other and different from them.

Crat. What you are saying is, I think, true.

439   *Soc.* One moment! have we not several times acknowledged that
names rightly given are the likenesses and images of the things which
they name?

Crat. Yes.

Soc. Let us suppose that to any extent you please you can learn
things through the medium of names, and suppose also that you can
learn them from the things themselves — which is likely to be the
nobler and clearer way; to learn of the image, whether the image and
the truth of which the image is the expression have been rightly
conceived, or to learn of the truth whether the truth and the image
of it have been duly executed?

Crat. I should say that to learn of the truth must be the best way.

Soc. How real existence is to be studied or discovered is, I suspect, beyond you and me. We must rest content with the admission that the knowledge of things is not to be derived from names. No; they must rather be studied and investigated in their connexion with one another.

Crat. Clearly, Socrates.

Soc. There is another point. I should not like us to be imposed upon by the appearance of such a multitude of names, all tending in the same direction. I myself do not deny that the givers of names did really give them under the idea that all things were in motion and flux; which was their sincere but, I think, mistaken opinion. And having fallen into a kind of whirlpool themselves, they are carried round, and want to drag us in after them. There is a matter, master Cratylus, about which I often dream, and should like to ask your opinion: Tell me, whether there is or is not some permanent nature of goodness, beauty, and several other things.

Crat. Certainly, Socrates, I think so.

Soc. Then let us make the true beauty the object of our inquiry: not asking whether a face is fair, or anything of that sort, for all such things appear to be in a flux; but let us ask whether the true beauty does not always retain its essential quality.

Crat. Certainly.

Soc. And if it is continually escaping from our grasp, how can we properly apply to it the predicates *that* or *of such a kind?* Must it not rather become different, and retire, and no longer be 'thus', while the word is in our mouths?

Crat. Undoubtedly.

Soc. Then how can that be a real thing which is never in the same state? for if a thing remains for a moment in the same state, during that time at least it undergoes no change; whilst if it remains ever the same and in the same state, it is not a subject of motion or change at all, since it does not vary from its original form.

Crat. It is not.

Soc. Nor yet can the variable be known by anyone; for at the 440 moment that the observer approaches, it will become other and of another nature, so that you cannot get any further in knowing its nature or state, for no knowledge, I assume, can know that which is known to have no state.

Crat. True.

Soc. Nor can we reasonably say, Cratylus, that there is any knowing at all, if everything is in a state of transition and there is nothing abiding. For if this power of knowing does *not* vary and lose its identity, then knowing may continue always to abide and exist. But if the very nature of knowing is liable to change, then it will be transformed into something other than knowing, and knowing will thereby cease to exist; and if the transition is always going on, there will always be no knowing, and, according to this view, there will be no one to know and nothing to be known. But if that which knows and that which is known exists ever, and the beautiful exists and the good exists, and every other thing also exists, then I do not think that they can resemble a process or flux, as we were just now supposing. Whether there is this eternal nature in things, or whether the truth is what Heracleitus and his followers and many others say, is a question hard to determine; and no man of sense will like to put himself or the education of his mind in the power of names: neither will he so far trust names or the givers of names as to be confident in any knowledge which condemns himself and other existences to an unhealthy state of unreality; he will not believe that all things leak like a pot, or that the whole external world is afflicted with rheum and catarrh. This may be true, Cratylus, but is also very likely to be untrue; and therefore I would not have you be too easily persuaded of it. Reflect well and like a man, and do not easily accept such a doctrine; for you are young and of an age to learn. And when you have found the truth, come and share it with me.

Crat. I will do as you say, though I can assure you, Socrates, that I have been considering the matter already, and the result of a great deal of trouble and consideration is that I incline to Heracleitus.

Soc. Then, another day, my friend, when you come back, you shall give me a lesson; but at present, go into the country, as you are intending, and Hermogenes shall set you on your way.

Crat. Very good, Socrates; I hope, however, that you will continue to think about these things yourself.

Parmenides

Persons of the Dialogue

CEPHALUS	SOCRATES
ADEIMANTUS	ZENO
GLAUCON	PARMENIDES
ANTIPHON	ARISTOTELES
PYTHODORUS	

Cephalus rehearses a dialogue which is supposed to have been narrated in his presence by Antiphon, the half-brother of Adeimantus and Glaucon, to certain Clazomenians.

≈§ The dialogue opens with a little scene in which several of the persons listed as participants appear briefly. The main body of the dialogue, however, has as participants only the last five persons listed, and recounts a conversation which had supposedly taken place before Plato's birth, in the early manhood of Socrates. In the first part of the conversation, with which we shall be chiefly concerned, the speakers are Socrates and two distinguished visitors to Athens, the great philosopher Parmenides, who taught that "all is One" and that all change and multiplicity are mere illusions, and Parmenides' disciple Zeno, famous in his own right as the author of brain-teasing paradoxes proving the impossibility of motion.

Aside from the opening scene, the conversation falls into two neatly joined yet readily distinguishable parts. In part I the youthful Socrates voices an objection to one of the paradoxes in Zeno's treatise defending Parmenides' doctrine of the One, and employs the Platonic doctrine of Ideas as a solvent of this sort of pseudo-contradiction. To this challenge Parmenides replies by a devastating counterattack, a *reductio ad absurdum,* exposing the logical difficulties and contradictions that follow necessarily from the Ideal theory itself. It is shown that the Ideas, if they are as Socrates has described them, cannot be known by man, and finally that God and man are mutually unknown and unknowable.

There is a moment of despair. "What is to become of Philosophy? Whither shall we turn, if the Ideas are unknown?"

Here Father Parmenides (as Plato calls him elsewhere) shows himself truly paternal. "My dear boy," he says in effect, "don't be in a hurry and don't try to solve the last problems first. You have ability, plenty of it, but you are still untrained. You need something that Zeno has in stock." The ground is thus prepared for part II, in which Parmenides himself will present a specimen of that more rigorous dialectic he has prescribed for Socrates.

The following selection is from part I of the dialogue. The reader is asked to imagine that Cephalus of Clazomenae reports the conversation as it was repeated to him by Antiphon, Plato's older half-brother.

127 . . . At first he [Antiphon] was not very willing, and complained of the trouble, but at length he consented. He told us that Pythodorus had described to him the appearance of Parmenides and Zeno; they came to Athens, as he said, at the great Panathenaea. The former was, at the time of his visit, about 65 years old, very white with age, but well-favoured: Zeno was nearly 40 years of age, tall and fair to look upon; in the days of his youth he was reported to have been beloved by Parmenides. He said that they lodged with Pythodorus in the Cerameicus, outside the wall, whither Socrates, then a very young man, came to see them, and many others with him; they wanted to hear the writings of Zeno, which had been brought to Athens for the first time on the occasion of their visit. These Zeno himself read to them in the absence of Parmenides, and had very nearly finished when Pythodorus entered, and with him Parmenides and Aristoteles who was afterwards one of the Thirty, and heard the little that remained of the discourse. Pythodorus had heard Zeno repeat it before.

When the recitation was completed, Socrates requested that the first thesis of the first argument might be read over again, and this having been done, he said: What is your meaning, Zeno? Do you maintain that if being is many, it must be both like and unlike, and that this is impossible, for neither can the like be unlike, nor the unlike like — is that your position?

Just so, said Zeno.

And if the unlike cannot be like or the like unlike, then, according to you, being could not be many; for this would involve an impossibility. In all that you say have you any other purpose except to disprove the being of the many? and is not each division of your treatise intended to furnish a separate proof of this, there being in all as many proofs of the not-being of the many as you have composed arguments? Is that your meaning, or have I misunderstood you?

128 No, said Zeno; you have correctly understood my general purpose.

I see, Parmenides, said Socrates, that Zeno would like to be not only one with you in friendship but your second self in his writings too; he puts what you say in another way, and would fain make believe that he is telling us something which is new. For you in your poems say 'The All is one,' and of this you adduce excellent proofs; and he on the other hand says that it is not many, and on behalf of this he offers overwhelming evidence. You affirm unity, he denies plurality. And so you deceive the world into believing that you are saying different things when really you are saying much the same. This is a strain of art beyond the reach of most of us.

Yes, Socrates, said Zeno. But although you are as keen as a Spartan hound in pursuing the track, you do not fully apprehend the true motive of the composition, which is not really such an artificial work as you imagine; for what you speak of was an accident — there was no pretence of a great purpose, nor any serious intention of deceiving the world. The truth is, that these writings of mine were meant to protect the arguments of Parmenides against those who make fun of him and seek to show the many ridiculous and contradictory results which they suppose to follow from the affirmation of the one. My answer is addressed to the partisans of the many, whose attack I return with interest by retorting upon them that their hypothesis of the being of many, if followed out, appears to be still more ridiculous than the hypothesis of the being of one. Zeal for my master led me to write the book in the days of my youth, but someone stole the copy, and therefore I had no choice whether it should be published or not; the motive, however, of writing was not the ambition of an elder man, but the pugnacity of a young one. This you do not seem to see, Socrates; though in other respects, as I was saying, your notion is a very just one.

I understand, said Socrates, and quite accept your account. But tell me, Zeno, do you not further think that there is an idea of likeness, detached and existing by itself, and an opposite idea, which is the essence of unlikeness, and that in these two you and I and all other things to which we apply the term many participate — things which participate in likeness become in that degree and manner like; and so far as they participate in unlikeness become in that degree unlike; or again are both like and unlike in the degree in which they participate in both? And even though all things partake of both opposites, and be both like and unlike to themselves by reason of this participation, where is the wonder? Now if a person could prove the absolute like to become unlike, or the absolute unlike to become like, that, in my opinion, would indeed be a wonder; but there is nothing extraordinary, Zeno, in showing that the things which only partake of likeness and unlikeness experience both. Nor, again, if a person were to show that all is one by partaking of unity, and at the same time many by partaking of plurality, would that be very astonishing. But if he were to show me that the absolute one was many, or the absolute many one, I should be truly amazed. And so of all the rest: I should be surprised to hear that the natures or ideas themselves had these opposite qualities; but not if a person wanted to prove of me that I was many and also one. When he wanted to show I was many he would say that I have a right and a left side, and a front and a back, and an upper and a lower half, for I cannot deny that I partake of multitude; when, on the other hand, he wants to prove that I am one, he will say that we who are here assembled are seven, and that I am one man and partake of unity. In both instances he proves his case. So again, if a person sets out to show that such things as wood, stones, and the like, being many are also one, we shall say that he is proving that something is at once one and many, but not that unity is many, or plurality one; and that he is uttering not a paradox but a truism. If, however, someone were to begin by setting apart the ideas in such instances as I was just now mentioning — like, unlike, one, many, rest, motion, and all similar ideas — and then to show that these admit of admixture with and separation from one another, I should be very much astonished. This part of your argument appears to be treated by you, Zeno, in a very spirited man-

130 ner; but, as I was saying, I should be far more amazed if anyone found in the ideas themselves which are apprehended by reason, the same puzzle and entanglement which you have shown to exist in visible objects.

While Socrates was speaking, Pythodorus thought that Parmenides and Zeno were not altogether pleased at the successive steps of the argument; but still they gave the closest attention, and often looked at one another, and smiled as if in admiration of him. When he had finished, Parmenides expressed their feelings in the following words: —

Socrates, he said, I admire the bent of your mind towards philosophy; tell me now, was this your own distinction between ideas in themselves and the things which partake of them? and do you think that there is an idea of likeness apart from the likeness which we possess, and of the one and many, and of the other things which Zeno mentioned?

I think that there are such ideas, said Socrates.

Parmenides proceeded: And would you also make absolute ideas of the just and the beautiful and the good, and of all that class?

Yes, he said, I should.

And would you make an idea of man apart from us and from all other human creatures, or of fire and water?

I am often undecided, Parmenides, as to whether I ought to include them or not.

And would you feel equally undecided, Socrates, about things of which the mention may provoke a smile? — I mean such things as

hair, mud, dirt, or anything else which is vile and paltry; is it hard to decide whether each of these has an idea distinct from the actual objects with which we come into contact, or not?

Certainly not, said Socrates; visible things like these are such as they appear to us, and I am afraid that there would be an absurdity in assuming any idea of them, although I sometimes get disturbed, and begin to think that there is nothing without an idea; but then again, when I have taken up this position, I run away, because I am afraid that I may fall into a bottomless pit of nonsense, and perish; and so I return to the ideas of which I was just now speaking, and occupy myself with them.

Yes, Socrates, said Parmenides; that is because you are still young; the time will come, if I am not mistaken, when philosophy will have a firmer grasp of you, and then you will not despise even the meanest things; at your age, you are too much disposed to regard the opinions of men. But I should like to know whether you mean that there are certain ideas of which all other things partake, and from which they 131 derive their names; that similars, for example, become similar, because they partake of similarity; and great things become great, because they partake of greatness; and that just and beautiful things become just and beautiful, because they partake of justice and beauty?

Yes, certainly, said Socrates, that is my meaning.

Then each individual partakes either of the whole of the idea or else of a part of the idea? Can there be any other mode of participation?

There cannot be, he said.

Then do you think that the whole idea is one, and yet, being one, is in each one of the many?

What objection is there, Parmenides? said Socrates.

The result will be that one and the same thing will exist as a whole at the same time in many separate individuals, and will therefore be in a state of separation from itself.

Nay, but the idea may be like the day which is one, and the same in many places at once, and yet continuous with itself; in this way each idea may be one and the same in all at the same time.

I like your way, Socrates, of making one in many places at once. You mean to say, that if I were to spread out a sail and cover a number of men, there would be one whole including many — is not that your meaning?

I think so.

And would you say that the whole sail includes each man, or a part of it only, and different parts different men?

The latter.

Then, Socrates, the ideas themselves will be divisible, and things which participate in them will have a part of them only and not the whole idea existing in each of them?

That seems to follow.

Then would you like to say, Socrates, that the one idea is really divisible and yet remains one?

Certainly not, he said.

Suppose that you divide absolute greatness, and that of the many great things each one is great in virtue of a portion of greatness less than absolute greatness — is that conceivable?

No.

Or will each equal thing, if possessing some small portion of equality less than absolute equality, be equal to some other thing by virtue of that portion only?

Impossible.

Or suppose one of us to have a portion of smallness; this is but a part of the small, and therefore the absolutely small will be greater; while that to which the abstracted part of the small is added will be smaller and not greater than before.

That, indeed, can scarcely be.

Then in what way, Socrates, will all things participate in the ideas, if they are unable to participate in them either as parts or wholes?

Indeed, he said, you have asked a question which is not easily answered.

Well, said Parmenides, and what do you say of another question? What question?

132   I imagine that your reason for assuming one idea of each kind is as follows: — Whenever a number of objects appear to you to be great there doubtless seems to you to be one and the same idea (or nature) visible in them all; hence you conceive of greatness as one.

Very true, said Socrates.

But now, if you allow your mind in like manner to embrace in one view this real greatness and those other great things, will not one more greatness arise, being required to account for the semblance of greatness in all these?

It would seem so.

Then another idea of greatness now comes into view over and above absolute greatness and the individuals which partake of it; and then another, over and above all these, by virtue of which they will all be great, and so you will be left not with a single idea in every case, but with an infinite number.

But may not the ideas, asked Socrates, be thoughts only, and have no proper existence except in our minds, Parmenides? For in that case each idea may still be one, and not experience this infinite multiplication.

Tell me, then: can each thought have its own definite nature, and yet be a thought of nothing?

Impossible, he said.

The thought must be of something?

Yes.

Of something which is or which is not?

Of something which is.

Must it not be of a single something, which the thought recognizes as attaching to all, being a single form or nature?

Yes.

And will not the something, which is apprehended as one and the same in all, be an idea?

From that, again, there is no escape.

Then, said Parmenides, if you say that everything else must participate in the ideas, must you not say either that everything is made up of thoughts, and that all things think; or that they are thoughts but have no thought?

So this view, Parmenides, is no more rational than the previous one. In my opinion the ideas are, as it were, patterns fixed in nature, and other things are like them and resemblances of them — what is meant by the participation of other things in the ideas, is really assimilation to them.

But if, said he, the individual is like the idea, is it possible that the idea should not be like the copy, in so far as this has been fashioned in resemblance of the idea? That which is like, cannot be conceived of as other than the like of like.

Impossible.

And when two things are alike, must they not partake of the same idea?

They must.

And will not that, by partaking in which like things are alike, be the idea itself?

Certainly.

Then the idea cannot be like the individual, or the individual like the idea; for if they are alike, some further idea of likeness will 133 always be coming to light, and if that be like anything else, another; and new ideas will be always arising, if the idea resembles that which partakes of it?

Quite true.

The theory, then, that other things participate in the ideas by resemblance, has to be given up, and some other mode of participation devised?

It would seem so.

Do you see then, Socrates, how great is the difficulty of making this distinction of ideas (or classes) existing by themselves?

Yes, indeed.

And, further, let me say that as yet you only understand a small part of the difficulty which is involved if you make of each thing a single idea, parting it off from other things.

What difficulty? he said.

There are many, but the greatest of all is this: — If an opponent argues that these ideas, being such as we say they ought to be, must remain unknown, no one can prove to him that he is wrong, unless he who denies their existence be a man of great natural ability and experience, and is willing to follow a long and laborious demonstration; he will remain unconvinced, and still insist that they cannot be known.

What do you mean, Parmenides? said Socrates.

In the first place, I think, Socrates, that you, or anyone who maintains the existence of absolute essences, will admit that they cannot exist in us.

No, said Socrates; for then they would be no longer absolute.

True, he said; and therefore when ideas are what they are in relation to one another, their essence is determined by a relation among themselves, and has nothing to do with the resemblances, or whatever they are to be termed, which are in our sphere, and from which we receive this or that name when we partake of them. And the things which are within our sphere and have the same names with them, are likewise only relative to one another, and not to the ideas which have the same names with them, but belong to themselves and not to them.

What do you mean? said Socrates.

I may illustrate my meaning in this way, said Parmenides. Suppose a man to be a master or a slave — he is obviously not a slave of the abstract idea of a master, or a master of the abstract idea of a slave; the relation is one of man to man. The idea of mastership in the abstract must be defined by relation to the idea of slavery in the abstract, and vice versa. But the things familiar to us are not
134 empowered to act on those ideas, nor the ideas to act upon familiar things; but, as I have said, the ideas belong to and stand in relation to each other, as also do the things in our familiar world. Do you see my meaning?

Yes, said Socrates, I quite see your meaning.

And will not knowledge — I mean absolute knowledge — answer to absolute truth?

Certainly.

And each kind of absolute knowledge will answer to each kind of absolute being?

Yes.

But the knowledge which we have, will answer to the truth which we have; and again, each kind of knowledge which we have, will be a knowledge of each kind of being which we have?

Certainly.

But the ideas themselves, as you admit, we have not, and cannot have?

No, we cannot.

And the absolute natures or kinds are known severally by the absolute idea of knowledge?

Yes.

And we have not got the idea of knowledge?

No.

Then none of the ideas are known, at least by us, because we have no share in absolute knowledge?

I suppose not.

Then the nature of the beautiful in itself, and of the good in itself, and all other ideas which we suppose to exist absolutely, are unknown to us?

It would seem so.

Observe that there is a stranger consequence still.

What is it?

Would you, or would you not, say that absolute knowledge, if there is such a thing, must be a far more exact knowledge than our knowledge; and the same of beauty and of the rest?

Yes.

And no one is more likely than God to have this most exact knowledge, if other things can share in it at all?

Certainly.

But then, will God, having the true knowledge, also be capable of knowledge of human things?

Why not?

Because, Socrates, said Parmenides, we have admitted that the ideas are not valid in relation to human things; nor human things in relation to them; the relations of either are limited to their respective spheres.

Yes, that has been admitted.

And if God has this perfect authority and perfect knowledge, his authority cannot rule us, nor his knowledge know us or any human thing; just as our authority does not extend to the gods, nor our knowledge know anything which is divine, so by parity of reason they, being gods, are not our masters, neither do they know the things of men.

Yet, surely, said Socrates, to deprive God of knowledge is monstrous.

135   These, Socrates, said Parmenides, are a few and only a few of the difficulties in which we are involved if ideas really are and we determine each of them to be an absolute unity. He who hears what may be said against them will deny the very existence of them — and even if they do exist, he will say that they must of necessity be unknown to man; and he will seem to have reason on his side, and as we were remarking just now, will be very difficult to convince; a man must be gifted with very considerable ability before he can learn that everything has a class and an absolute essence; and still more remarkable will he be who discovers all these things for himself, and having thoroughly investigated them is able to teach them to others.

I agree with you, Parmenides, said Socrates; and what you say is very much to my mind.

And yet, Socrates, said Parmenides, if a man, fixing his attention on these and the like difficulties, does away with ideas of things and will not admit that every individual thing has its own determinate idea which is always one and the same, he will have nothing on which his mind can rest; and so he will utterly destroy the power of reasoning, as you seem to me to have particularly noted.

Very true, he said.

But then, what is to become of philosophy? Whither shall we turn, if the ideas are unknown?

I certainly do not see my way at present.

Yes, said Parmenides; and I think that this arises, Socrates, out of your attempting to define the beautiful, the just, the good, and the ideas generally, without sufficient previous training. I noticed your deficiency, when I heard you talking here with your friend Aristoteles, the day before yesterday. The impulse that carries you towards philosophy is assuredly noble and divine; but there is an art which is called by the vulgar idle talking, and which is often imagined to be useless; in that you must train and exercise yourself, now that you are young, or truth will elude your grasp.

ᐤᔾ The second part of the dialogue now begins. In it Parmenides recommends to Socrates that he practice the type of logical exercise which Zeno has demonstrated, and then himself gives a demonstration of such an exercise. He makes the assumption first that the One is, and second that the One is not, in each case giving the statement more than one sense, and in each case drawing out in detail the consequences, both for the One and for all the other things. He ends with the conclusion "that whether one is or is not, one and the others in relation to themselves and one another, all of them, in every way, are and are not, and appear to be and appear not to be."ᴶ

We shall not venture into the subtleties of this second part. Critics still disagree as to how Plato wished it to be understood. The Neo-Platonists discovered in it depths of mystical significance; one modern critic has gone so far as to call it an elaborate *jeu d'esprit*. More to the purpose are the words of Paul Shorey, which present an interpretation that seems inherently plausible and capable of being confirmed by following out the many clues that he has put into our hands: "Briefly then, I believe that the second part of the *Parmenides* is a conscious exercise in logic, a systematic exhibition of the fallacies that arise from the confusion of *is*, the copula,[1] with *is* referring to real existence, as well as incidentally of other metaphysical fallacies explained in the *Sophist* . . . and in the *Theaetetus,* and parodied in the *Euthydemus.* I hold that the illustration of these fallacies is too symmetrical and exhaustive to be unconscious . . . Plato knew what he was doing."[2]

---

[1] The verb *to be* used to express merely the relation between subject and predicate, with no implication that either exists, is called the copula. (L)

[2] Paul Shorey, *What Plato Said* (Chicago: University of Chicago Press, 1933), pp. 289–90. (L)

Theaetetus

Persons of the Dialogue

SOCRATES   THEODORUS   THEAETETUS

*Euclides and Terpsion meet in front of Euclides' house in Megara;
they enter the house, and the dialogue is read to them by a servant.*

◄§ This is the dialogue mentioned in our Introduction, Theme 7,
in which Plato discusses what knowledge is and finds no answer. Here
he is bent on showing that the definitions of knowledge advanced
by other thinkers are inadequate; he does not allow the Socrates of
the dialogue or Theaetetus, its namesake, to propose the solution closest
to Plato's heart, based on the Theory of Ideas. For reasons of space,
we shall present only that part of the dialogue in which test is made of
the first definition proposed: namely, that knowledge is sense perception, or judgment as to the nature of what is perceived. Here is the
opportunity for the philosophically serious reader to consider the arguments offered and decide how far he will go in accepting them, and he
should also note the fairness with which Plato presents his opponents'
views.

The dialogue deals centrally with the nature of knowledge but contains at least one more important motif. This is found in the so-called
"digression," beginning at 172a, a well-timed relief from the strain
of argument. Here a number of Plato's distinctive thoughts about the
true values of human life are set forth in two contrasting portraits of
the true philosopher and the shrewd vulgarian habitué of the court-
room. This is done in Plato's best style: satire and the grand manner
are mingled but never confused. Honorable mention must be made
also of several lively metaphors, e.g., "the mind a wax tablet," the
original of John Locke's "tabula rasa," and "Socrates a midwife of
the soul." There are others, but these two alone have achieved virtual
immortality.

Our selection from the dialogue begins with the opening lines:

142 *Euclides.* Have you only just arrived from the country, Terpsion?
Terpsion. No, I came some time ago: and I have been in the Agora
looking for you, and wondering that I could not find you.
Euc. But I was not in the city.
Terp. Where then?
Euc. As I was going down to the harbour, I met Theaetetus — he
was being carried up to Athens from the army at Corinth.
Terp. Was he alive or dead?

Euc. He was scarcely alive, for he has been badly wounded; but he was suffering even more from the sickness which has broken out in the army.

Terp. The dysentery, you mean?

Euc. Yes.

Terp. Alas! what a loss he will be!

Euc. Yes, Terpsion, he is a noble fellow; only today I heard some people highly praising his behaviour in this very battle.

Terp. No wonder; I should rather be surprised at hearing anything else of him. But why did he go on, instead of stopping at Megara?

Euc. He wanted to get home: although I entreated and advised him to remain, he would not listen to me; so I set him on his way, and turned back, and then I remembered what Socrates had said of him, and thought how remarkably this, like all his predictions, had been fulfilled. I believe that he had seen him a little before his own death, when Theaetetus was a youth, and he had a memorable conversation with him, which he repeated to me when I came to Athens; he was full of admiration of his genius, and said that he would most certainly be a great man, if he lived.

Terp. The prophecy has certainly been fulfilled; but what was the conversation? can you tell me?

Euc. No, indeed, not offhand; but I took notes of it as soon as I got home; these I filled up from memory, writing them out at leisure; and whenever I went to Athens, I asked Socrates about any point which I had forgotten, and on my return I made corrections; thus I have nearly the whole conversation written down.

Terp. I remember — you told me; and I have always been intending to ask you to show me the writing, but have put off doing so; and now, why should we not read it through? — having just come from the country, I should greatly like to rest.

Euc. I too shall be very glad of a rest, for I went with Theaetetus as far as Erineum. Let us go in, then, and while we are reposing, the servant shall read to us.

Terp. Very good.

Euc. Here is the roll, Terpsion; I may observe that I have introduced Socrates, not as narrating to me, but as actually conversing with the persons whom he mentioned — these were, Theodorus the geometrician (of Cyrene), and Theaetetus. I have omitted, for the sake of convenience, the interlocutory words 'I said', 'I remarked', which he used when he spoke of himself, and again, 'he agreed', or 'disagreed', in the answer, lest the repetition of them should be troublesome.

Terp. Quite right, Euclides,

Euc. And now, boy, you may take the roll and read.

Euclides' servant reads

Socrates. If I cared enough about the Cyrenians, Theodorus, I would ask you whether there are any rising geometricians or philosophers in that part of the world. But I am more interested in our own Athenian youth, and I would rather know who among them are likely to do well. I observe them as far as I can myself, and I inquire of any one whom they follow, and I see that a great many of them follow you, in which they are quite right, considering your eminence in geometry and in other ways. Tell me then, if you have met with any one who is at all remarkable.

Theodorus. Yes, Socrates, I have become acquainted with one very remarkable Athenian youth, whom I commend to you as well worthy of your attention. If he had been a beauty I should have been afraid to praise him, lest you should suppose that I was in love with him; but he is no beauty, and you must not be offended if I say that he is very like you; for he has a snub nose and projecting eyes, although these features are less marked in him than in you. Seeing, then, that he has no personal attractions, I may freely say, that in all my acquaintance, which is very large, I never knew any one who was his equal in natural gifts: for he has a quickness of apprehension which is almost unrivalled, and he is exceedingly gentle, and also the most courageous of men; there is a union of qualities in him such as I have never seen in any other, and should scarcely have thought possible; for those who, like him, have quick and ready and retentive wits, have generally also quick tempers; they are ships without ballast, and go darting about, and are mad rather than courageous; and the steadier sort, when they have to face study, prove stupid and cannot remember. Whereas he moves surely and smoothly and successfully in the path of knowledge and inquiry; and he is full of gentleness, flowing on silently like a river of oil; at his age, it is wonderful.

Soc. That is good news; whose son is he?

Theod. The name of his father I have forgotten, but the youth himself is the middle one of those who are approaching us; he and his companions have been anointing themselves in the outer court, and now they seem to have finished, and are coming towards us. Look and see whether you know him.

Soc. I know the youth, but I do not know his name; he is the son of Euphronius the Sunian, who was himself an eminent man, and such another as his son is according to your account of him; I believe that he left a considerable fortune.

Theod. Theaetetus, Socrates, is his name; but I rather think that the property disappeared in the hands of trustees; notwithstanding which he is wonderfully liberal.

Soc. He must be a fine fellow; tell him to come and sit by me.

Theod. I will. Come hither, Theaetetus, and sit by Socrates.

Soc. By all means, Theaetetus, in order that I may see the reflection of myself in your face, for Theodorus says that we are alike; and yet if each of us held in his hands a lyre, and he said that they were tuned alike, should we at once take his word, or should we ask whether he who said so was or was not a musician?

Theaetetus. We should ask.

Soc. And if we found that he was, we should take his word; and if not, not?

Theaet. True.

Soc. And if this supposed likeness of our faces is a matter of any interest to us, we should inquire whether he who says that we are alike is a painter or not?

Theaet. Certainly we should.

Soc. And is Theodorus a painter?

Theaet. I never heard that he was.

Soc. Is he a geometrician?

Theaet. Of course he is, Socrates.

Soc. And is he an astronomer and calculator and musician, and in general an educated man?

Theaet. I think so.

Soc. If, then, he remarks on a similarity in our persons, either by way of praise or blame, there is no particular reason why we should attend to him.

Theaet. I should say not.

Soc. But if he praises the virtue or wisdom which are the spiritual endowments of either of us, then he who hears the praises will naturally desire to examine him who is praised: and he again should be willing to exhibit himself.

Theaet. Very fine, Socrates.

Soc. Then now is the time, my dear Theaetetus, for me to examine, and for you to exhibit; since although Theodorus has praised many a citizen and stranger in my hearing, never did I hear him praise any one as he has been praising you.

Theaet. I am glad to hear it, Socrates; but what if he spoke only in jest?

Soc. Nay, Theodorus is not given to jesting; and I cannot allow you to retract your consent on any such pretence as that. If you do, he will have to swear to his words; and we are perfectly sure that no one will be found to impugn him. Do not be shy then, but stand to your word.

Theaet. I suppose I must, if you wish it.

Soc. In the first place, I should like to ask what you learn of

145

Theodorus: something of geometry, perhaps?

Theaet. Yes.

Soc. And astronomy and harmony and calculation?

Theaet. I am making an effort, at least.

Soc. And so am I, my friend, hoping to learn of him, or of anybody who seems to understand these things. And I get on pretty well in general; but there is a little difficulty which I want you and the company to aid me in investigating. Will you answer me a question: 'Is not learning growing wiser about that which you learn?'

Theaet. Of course.

Soc. And it is by wisdom, I suppose, that the wise are wise?

Theaet. Yes.

Soc. And is that different in any way from knowledge?

Theaet. What?

Soc. Wisdom; are not men wise in that which they know?

Theaet. Certainly they are.

Soc. Then wisdom and knowledge are the same?

Theaet. Yes.

146   *Soc.* Herein lies the difficulty which I can never solve to my satisfaction — What is knowledge? Can we answer that question? What say you? which of us will speak first? whoever misses shall sit down, as at a game of ball, and shall be donkey, as the boys say; he who lasts out his competitors in the game without missing, shall be our king, and shall have the right of putting to us any questions which he pleases. . . . Why is there no reply? I hope, Theodorus, that I am not betrayed into rudeness by my love of conversation? I only want to make us talk and be friendly and sociable.

Theod. The reverse of rudeness, Socrates: but I would rather that you would ask one of the young fellows; for the truth is, that I am unused to your method of discussion, and I am too old to learn; the young will be more suitable, and they will improve more than I shall, for it is a true saying that youth is the age for improvement. And so having made a beginning with Theaetetus, I would advise you to go on with him and not let him off.

Soc. Do you hear, Theaetetus, what Theodorus says? You would not, I think, like to disobey him, nor is it right for a younger man to disobey such a command from a wise man. Take courage, then, and nobly say what you think that knowledge is.

Theaet. Well, Socrates, I will answer as you and he bid me; and if I make a mistake, you will doubtless correct me.

Soc. We will, if we can.

Theaet. Then, I think that the sciences which I learn from Theodorus — geometry, and those which you just now mentioned — are knowledge; and I would include the art of the cobbler and other craftsmen; these, each and all of them, are just what is meant by knowledge.

Soc. Enough, my friend! the nobility and liberality of your nature make you give many and diverse things, when I am asking for one simple thing.

Theaet. What do you mean, Socrates?

Soc. Perhaps nothing. I will, however, say what I believe to be my meaning: When you speak of cobbling, you mean the knowledge of the making of shoes?

Theaet. Just so.

Soc. And when you speak of carpentering, you mean knowledge of the making of wooden implements?

Theaet. I do.

Soc. In both cases, then, it is the *subject known* that you are defining.

Theaet. True.

Soc. But that, Theaetetus, was not the point of my question: we did not ask about the subjects of knowledge, nor yet the number of its forms, for we were not going to count them, but we wanted to know the nature of knowledge in the abstract. Am I not right?

Theaet. Perfectly right.

Soc. Let me offer an illustration: Suppose that a person were to 147 ask about some very trivial and obvious thing — for example, What is clay? and we were to reply, that there is a clay of potters, there is a clay of oven-makers, there is a clay of brick-makers; would not the answer be ridiculous?

Theaet. Yes, perhaps.

Soc. In the first place, there would be an absurdity in assuming that he who asked the question would understand from our answer the meaning of 'clay', merely because we added 'of the image-makers', or of any other workers. How can a man understand the name of anything, when he does not know what the thing is?

Theaet. He cannot.

Soc. Likewise, a man who does not know what 'knowledge' stands for, cannot understand the phrase 'knowledge of shoemaking'?

Theaet. No, he cannot.

Soc. And therefore the same man will not understand the name 'cobbling', or the name of any other art?

Theaet. No.

Soc. And when a man is asked what knowledge is, to give in answer the name of some art is ridiculous; for his reply 'A knowledge of this or that' is no answer to the question that was asked.

Theaet. True.

Soc. Moreover, he might answer shortly and simply, but he makes an enormous circuit. For example, when asked about the clay, he might have given the simple and perhaps trivial answer that clay is moistened earth — what sort of clay is not to the point.

Theaet. Yes, Socrates, there is no difficulty as you put the question. You mean, if I am not mistaken, something like what occurred to me and to my friend here, your namesake Socrates, in a recent discussion.

Soc. What was that, Theaetetus?

Theaet. Theodorus was writing out for us something about roots, such as the sides of squares three or five feet in area, showing that they are incommensurable by the unit: he took the other examples up to seventeen, but there for some reason he stopped. Now as there are innumerable such roots, the notion occurred to us of attempting to find some common description which can be applied to them all.

Soc. And did you find any such thing?

Theaet. I think that we did; but I should like to have your opinion.

Soc. Let me hear.

Theaet. We divided all numbers into two classes: those which are made up of equal factors multiplying into one another, which we compared to square figures and called square or equilateral numbers; — that was one class.

Soc. Very good.

Theaet. The intermediate numbers, such as three and five, and
148 every other number which is made up of unequal factors, either of a greater multiplied by a less, or of a less multiplied by a greater, and, when regarded as a figure, is contained in unequal sides; — all these we compared to oblong figures, and called them oblong numbers.

Soc. Capital; and what followed?

Theaet. The lines, or sides, which have for their squares the equilateral plane numbers, were called by us lengths; and the lines whose squares are equal to the oblong numbers, were called powers or roots; the reason of this latter name being, that they are commensurable with the former not in linear measurement, but in the area of their squares. And a similar distinction was made among solids.

Soc. Excellent, my boys; I think that you fully justify the praises of Theodorus, and that he will not be found guilty of false witness.

Theaet. But I am unable, Socrates, to give you an answer about knowledge similar to this answer about the length and the power, which is what you appear to want; and therefore Theodorus is a deceiver after all.

Soc. Well, but if some one were to praise you for running, and to say that he never met your equal among boys, and afterwards you are beaten in a race by a grown-up man, who was a great runner — would the praise be any the less true?

Theaet. Certainly not.

Soc. And is the discovery of the nature of knowledge so small a matter, as I just now said? Is it not one which would task the powers of men perfect in every way?

Theaet. Yes, indeed, of men who were the cream of perfection!

Soc. Well, then, be of good cheer; do not say that Theodorus was mistaken about you, but do your best to ascertain the true nature of knowledge, as well as of other things.

Theaet. I am eager enough, Socrates, if that would bring to light the truth.

Soc. Come, then, you were on the right road just now; let your own answer about roots be your model, and as you comprehended them all in one class, try and bring the many sorts of knowledge under one definition.

Theaet. I can assure you, Socrates, that I have tried very often, when the report of questions asked by you was brought to me; but I can neither persuade myself that I have a satisfactory answer to give, nor hear of any one who answers as you would have him; and yet I cannot help being troubled by the problem.

Soc. These are the pangs of labour, my dear Theaetetus; you have something within you which you are bringing to the birth.

Theaet. I do not know, Socrates; I only say what I feel.

Soc. And have you never heard, simpleton, that I am the son of a midwife, brave and burly, whose name was Phaenarete? **149**

Theaet. Yes, I have.

Soc. And that I myself practise midwifery?

Theaet. No, never.

Soc. Let me tell you that I do though, my friend: but you must not reveal the secret, as the world in general have not found me out; and therefore they only say of me, that I am the strangest of mortals and drive men to their wits' end. Did you ever hear that too?

Theaet. Yes.

Soc. Shall I tell you the reason?

Theaet. By all means.

Soc. Bear in mind the whole business of the midwives, and then you will see my meaning better: — No woman, as you are probably aware, who is still able to conceive and bear, attends other women, but only those who are past bearing.

Theaet. Yes, I know.

Soc. It is said that Artemis was responsible for this, because though she is the goddess of childbirth, she is not herself a mother. She could not, indeed, allow the barren to be midwives, because human nature cannot know the mystery of an art without experience; but she assigned this office to those who are too old to bear, honouring their resemblance to herself.

Theaet. I dare say.

Soc. And I dare say too, or rather I am absolutely certain, that the midwives know better than others who is pregnant and who is not?

Theaet. Very true.

Soc. And by the use of potions and incantations they are able to arouse the pangs and to soothe them at will; they can make those bear who have a difficulty in bearing, and if they think fit they can smother the embryo in the womb.

Theaet. They can.

Soc. Did you ever remark that they are also most cunning match-makers, and have a thorough knowledge of what unions are likely to produce a brave brood?

Theaet. No, I cannot say that I knew it.

Soc. Then let me tell you that this is their greatest pride, more than cutting the umbilical cord. And if you reflect, you will see that the same art which cultivates and gathers in the fruits of the earth, will be most likely to know in what soils the several plants or seeds should be deposited.

Theaet. Yes, the same art.

Soc. And do you suppose that with women the arts of planting and of harvesting are different?

150　　*Theaet*. I should think not.

Soc. Certainly not; but midwives are respectable women who have a character to lose, and they avoid this department of their profession, because they are afraid of being called procuresses, which is a name given to those who join together man and woman in an unlawful and unscientific way; and yet the true midwife is also the true and only matchmaker.

Theaet. Clearly.

Soc. Such are the midwives, whose task is a very important one, but not so important as mine; for women do not bring into the world at one time real children, and at another time counterfeits which are with difficulty distinguished from them; if they did, then the discernment of the true and false birth would be the crowning achievement of the art of midwifery — you would think so?

Theaet. Indeed I should.

Soc. Well, my art of midwifery is in most respects like theirs; but differs, in that I attend men and not women, and I look after their souls when they are in labour, and not after their bodies: and the triumph of my art is in thoroughly examining whether the thought which the mind of the young man brings forth is false and lifeless, or fertile and true. And again I resemble the midwives in being barren of wisdom, and the reproach which is often made against me, that I ask questions of others and have not the wit to pronounce upon any subject myself, is very just — the reason is, that the god compels me to be a midwife, but has not allowed me to bring forth. I myself, then, am not particularly wise, nor have I anything to show which is the invention or birth of my own soul. But of those who converse with me, some at first appear utterly stupid; and all, as our acquaintance ripens, if the god is gracious to them, make astonishing progress; and this in the opinion of others as well as in their own. It is quite clear that they never learned anything from me; the many fine discoveries to which they give birth are of their own making. But to me and the god they owe their delivery. And the proof of my words is, that many of them, ignorantly taking all the credit to themselves, and despising me, have gone away too soon, either of their own accord or under the influence of others; and have not only lost the children of whom I had previously delivered them by an ill bringing up, but have stifled whatever else they had in them by evil communications, being fonder of lies and shams than of the truth; and they have at last ended by seeing themselves, as others see them, to be great fools. Aristeides, the son of Lysimachus, is one of them, and there are many others. The truants often return to me, and beg that I would consort with them again — they are ready to go to me on their knees — and then, if my divine sign allows, which is not always the case, I receive them, and they begin to improve again. Dire are the pangs which my art is able to arouse and to allay in those who consort with me, just like the pangs of women in childbirth; night and day they are full of perplexity and travail which is even worse than that of the women. So much for them. And there are others, Theaetetus, who come to me apparently not in a state of pregnancy; and as I know that they have no need of my art, I coax them into marrying some one, and by the grace of God I can generally tell who is likely to do them good. Many of them I have given away to Prodicus, and many to other inspired sages. I tell you this long story, friend Theaetetus, because I suspect, as indeed you seem to think yourself, that you are in labour — great with some conception. Come then to me, who am a midwife's son and myself a midwife, and do your best to answer the questions which I will ask you. And if I abstract and expose your first-born, because I discover upon inspection that the conception which you have formed is a vain shadow, do not quarrel with me on that account, as the manner of women is when their first children are taken from them. For I have actually known some who were ready to bite me when I deprived them of a darling folly; they did not perceive that I acted from goodwill, not knowing that no god is the enemy of man — that was not within the range of their ideas; neither am I their enemy in all this, but I hold it an impiety to admit falsehood, or to stifle the truth. Once more, then, Theaetetus, tell me from the beginning 'What is knowledge?' —

and do not say that you cannot answer; quit yourself like a man, and if God is willing you will be able to answer.

Theaet. At any rate, Socrates, after such an exhortation I should be ashamed of not trying to do my best. Now he who knows anything perceives what he knows, and, as far as I can see at present, knowledge is simply perception.

Soc. Bravely said, boy; that is the way in which you should express your opinion. And now, let us examine together this conception of yours, and see whether it is fertile or a mere wind-egg: — You say that knowledge is perception?

Theaet. Yes.

Soc. Well, you have delivered yourself of a very important
152 doctrine about knowledge; it is indeed the opinion of Protagoras, although he has another way of expressing the same view. Man, he says, 'is the measure of all things, of the existence of. things that are, and of the non-existence of things that are not': — You have read him?

Theaet. O yes, again and again.

Soc. Does he not say [or mean] that things are to you such as they appear to you, and to me such as they appear to me, and that you and I are men?

Theaet. Yes, he says so.

Soc. A wise man is not likely to talk nonsense. Let us try to understand him: the same wind is blowing, and yet one of us may be cold and the other not, or one may be slightly and the other very cold?

Theaet. Quite true.

Soc. Now at such a time is the wind, regarded not in relation to us but absolutely, cold or not; or are we to say, with Protagoras, that the wind is cold to him who is cold, and not to him who is not?

Theaet. I suppose the last.

Soc. And, moreover, it appears so to each of them?

Theaet. Yes.

Soc. And 'appears to him' means the same as 'he perceives'.

Theaet. True.

Soc. Then appearing and perceiving coincide in the case of hot and cold, and in similar instances. For we must presume that they really are for each man such as he perceives them to be.

Theaet. Yes.

Soc. Then perception is always of existence, and being the same as knowledge is unerring?

Theaet. Apparently.

Soc. In the name of the Graces, what an almighty wise man Protagoras must have been! He spoke these things in a parable to the common herd, like you and me, but told the truth, 'his Truth', in secret to his own disciples.

Theaet. What do you mean, Socrates?

Soc. I will explain, and tell you of a high argument, which proclaims that nothing in the world is by itself *one*, or can rightly be called *this* or *of this kind*; but if anything is termed great, it will appear to be also small, if heavy, light, and so forth. There is no *one thing*, no *this*, and no *such*. It is from motion, and change, and admixture with each other, that there *come to be* all those things which we declare to *be*, speaking incorrectly, for there is no being at all, but only perpetual becoming. The whole succession of philosophers with the exception of Parmenides may be supposed to agree with you in this — Protagoras, Heracleitus, Empedocles, and the rest. So may all the great masters of either kind of poetry — Epicharmus, the prince of Comedy, and Homer of Tragedy; when the latter sings of

Ocean whence sprang the gods, and mother Tethys,

does he not mean that all things are the offspring of flux and motion?

Theaet. I think so.

Soc. And who could take up arms against such a great army having Homer for its general, and not appear ridiculous? 153

Theaet. Who indeed, Socrates?

Soc. Yes, Theaetetus; for here are some other cogent proofs that motion is the source of what is called being and of becoming, and inactivity of not-being and of destruction. Firstly, fire and warmth, which are supposed to be the parent and guardian of all other things, are born of local movement and of friction, which are forms of movement in the wider sense. Are they not both the origin of fire?

Theaet. They are.

Soc. And again the race of animals is generated in the same way?

Theaet. Certainly.

Soc. And is not the bodily habit spoiled by rest and idleness, but preserved for a long time by motion and exercise?

Theaet. True.

Soc. And what of the mental habit? Is it not by study and attention (which are motions) that the soul both acquires and retains learning, and generally improves? while through rest, which, in the soul, means stupidity or want of mental exercise, she remains ignorant and is liable to forget whatever she has learned?

Theaet. True.

Soc. Then motion is a good, and rest an evil, to the soul as well as to the body?

Theaet. It seems so.

Soc. Need I go on to mention that breathless calm, stillness and the like waste and impair, while wind and storm preserve; and as the palmary argument of all, I may adduce the golden chain in Homer, by which he means the sun, thereby indicating that so long as the sun and the heavens go round in their orbits, all things human and divine are and are preserved, but if they were chained up and their motions ceased, then all things would be destroyed, and, as the saying is, turned upside down.

Theaet. I believe, Socrates, that you have truly explained his meaning.

Soc. Then let us apply his doctrine in this manner, my good friend, and first of all to vision; that which you call white colour is not in your eyes, and is not a distinct thing which exists out of them. And you must not assign any place to it: for if it had position it would be, and be at rest, and would not be in process of becoming.

Theaet. Then what is colour?

Soc. Let us carry out the principle which has just been affirmed, that there is nothing which, *per se*, *is* and *is one*, and then we shall see that white, black, and every other colour, arises out of the eye meeting the appropriate motion, and that the colour to which we attribute 'being' is in each case neither the active nor the passive element, but something which *comes to be* between them, and is peculiar to each percipient; for you would not affirm that the several colours appear to a dog or to any animal whatever as they appear to you?

Theaet. Far from it.

Soc. Or that anything appears the same to you as to another man? Are you so profoundly convinced of this? Rather would it not be true that it never appears exactly the same to you, because you are never exactly the same?

Theaet. The latter.

Soc. And if that with which I compare myself in size, or which I apprehend by touch, *were* great or white or hot, it could not have become different by mere contact with another subject, while its own nature is in no way changed; nor again, if the comparing or apprehending subject *were* great or white or hot, could this have been made different by any approximation or affection of any other thing, while its own nature is not affected. The fact is that in our ordinary way of speaking we allow ourselves to be driven into most ridiculous and wonderful contradictions, as Protagoras and all who take his line of argument would remark.

Theaet. How? and of what sort do you mean?

Soc. A little instance will sufficiently explain my meaning: When six dice are compared with four, we say that they are 'more' and 'one and a half times' as many; when compared with twelve, that they are 'fewer' and 'half'; and no other way of speaking is tolerable.

Theaet. Very true.

Soc. Well, then, suppose that Protagoras or some one asks whether anything can become greater or more if not by increasing, how would you answer him, Theaetetus?

Theaet. I should say 'No', Socrates, if I were to speak my mind in reference to this last question, but if I were thinking of my former answer, consistency would oblige me to say 'Yes'.

Soc. Capital! excellent! spoken like an oracle, my boy! And if you reply 'Yes', there will be a case for Euripides; for our tongue will be unconvinced, but not our mind.

Theaet. Very true.

Soc. The thoroughbred Sophists, who know all that can be known about the mind, and argue only out of the superfluity of their wits, would have had a regular sparring-match over this, and would have knocked their arguments together finely. But you and I, who have no professional aims, only desire to see what is the mutual relation of these principles, — whether they are consistent with each other or quite irreconcilable.

Theaet. Yes, that would certainly be my desire.

Soc. And mine too. But since this is our feeling, and there is plenty of time, why should we not calmly and patiently review our own thoughts, and thoroughly examine and see what these appearances in us really are? If I am not mistaken, they will be described by us as follows: — first, that nothing can become greater or less, either in size or number, while remaining equal to itself — you would agree?

Theaet. Yes.

Soc. Secondly, that without addition or subtraction there is no increase or diminution of anything, but only equality.

Theaet. Quite true.

Soc. Thirdly, it is surely clear that what was not before cannot be afterwards, without becoming and having become.

Theaet. Yes, so it seems.

Soc. These three axioms, if I am not mistaken, are fighting with one another in our minds in the case of the dice, or, again, in such a case as this — if I were to say that I, who am of a certain height and taller than you, who are still young, may within a year, without gaining or losing in height, be not so tall — not that I should have lost, but that you would have increased. In such a case, I am afterwards what I once was not, and yet I have not become; for I could not have become without becoming, neither could I have become less without losing somewhat of my height; and I could give you ten

thousand examples of similar contradictions, if we admit them at all.
I believe that you follow me, Theaetetus; for I suspect that you have
heard these questions raised before now.

Theaet. Yes, Socrates, and I am amazed when I think of them; by
the Gods I am! and I want to know what on earth they mean; and
there are times when my head quite swims with the contemplation of
them.

Soc. I see, my dear Theaetetus, that Theodorus had a true insight
into your nature when he said that you were a philosopher, for wonder
is the feeling of a philosopher, and philosophy begins in wonder. He
was not a bad genealogist who said that Iris [the messenger of
heaven] is the child of Thaumas [wonder]. But do you begin to see
what is the explanation of this perplexity on the hypothesis which
we attribute to Protagoras?

Theaet. Not as yet.

Soc. Then you will be obliged to me if I help you to unearth the
hidden 'truth' of a famous man or school.

Theaet. To be sure, I shall be very much obliged.

Soc. Take a look round, then, and see that none of the uninitiated
are listening. Now by the uninitiated I mean the people who think
that nothing *is* save what they can grasp in their hands, and who
will not allow that action or generation or anything invisible can have
real existence.

Theaet. Indeed, Socrates, they are themselves a very hard and
metallic sort of men.

156   *Soc.* Yes, my boy, outer barbarians. Far more ingenious are the
brethren whose mysteries I am about to reveal to you. Their first
principle is, that all is motion, and upon this all the affections of
which we were just now speaking are supposed to depend: all is
movement, and nothing else exists; a movement which has two forms,
one active and the other passive, both in endless number; and out
of the union and friction of them there is generated a progeny endless
in number, having twin forms, an object of sense, and a sensation
which always breaks forth together with it and is born at the same
moment. The senses are variously named, seeing, hearing, smelling,
and heat and cold; and then there are the senses of pleasure, pain,
desire, fear, and many more which have names, as well as innumerable others which are without them; each has its kindred sensible
object, — each variety of seeing has a corresponding variety of colour,
each kind of hearing a corresponding kind of sound, and there are
sensible objects adapted to all the types of sensation. Do you see,
Theaetetus, the bearings of this tale on the preceding argument?

Theaet. Indeed I do not.

Soc. Then attend, and I will try to finish the story. The purport

is that all these things are in motion, as I was saying, and that this
motion is of two kinds, a slower and a quicker; and the slower
elements have their motions in the same place and with reference
to things near them, and so they beget; but what is begotten is
swifter, for it is carried to and fro, and its motion is from place to
place. Apply this to sense: — When the eye and the appropriate
object meet together and give birth to whiteness and the sensation
connatural with it, which could not have been given by either of them
going elsewhere, then, while the sight is flowing from the eye, whiteness proceeds from the object which combines in producing the
colour; and so the eye is fulfilled with sight, and really sees, and
becomes, not sight, but a seeing eye; and the object which combined
to form the colour is fulfilled with whiteness, and becomes not
whiteness but a white thing, whether wood or stone or whatever the
object may be which happens to be coloured white. And this is true
of all sensible objects, hard, warm, and the like, which are similarly
to be regarded, as I was saying before, not as having any absolute   157
existence, but as being all of them of whatever kind generated by motion in their intercourse with one another; for of the agent and patient, as existing in separation, no trustworthy conception, as they
say, can be formed, for the agent has no existence until united with
the patient, and the patient has no existence until united with the
agent; and that which by uniting with something becomes an agent,
by meeting with some other thing is converted into a patient. And
from all these considerations, as I said at first, there arises a general
reflection, that there is no one self-existent thing, but everything is
becoming and in relation; and being must be altogether abolished, although from habit and ignorance we are compelled even in this
discussion to retain the use of the term. But these wise men tell us
that we are not to allow either the word 'something', or 'belonging to
something', or 'to me,' or 'this' or 'that', or any other name which
would bring things to a stand; but, as nature directs, we must speak
of them as becoming, being made, being destroyed, changing; he
who attempts to fix them is easily refuted. And this should be the
way of speaking, not only of particulars but of aggregates; such
aggregates as are expressed in the word 'man', or 'stone', or any
name of an animal or of a class. O Theaetetus, are not these speculations sweet as honey? And do you not like the taste of them in the
mouth?

Theaet. I do not know what to say, Socrates; for, indeed, I cannot
make out whether you are giving your own opinion or only wanting
to draw me out.

Soc. You forget, my friend, that I am ignorant, and claim none of
these theories as my own; you are the person who is in labour, I am

the barren midwife; and this is why I soothe you, and offer you one good thing after another, that you may taste them. And I hope that I may at last help to bring your own opinion into the light of day: when this has been accomplished, then we will determine whether what you have brought forth is only a wind-egg or a living truth. Therefore, keep up your spirits, and answer like a man what you think.

Theaet. Ask me.

Soc. Then once more: Is it your opinion that there is no such thing as being good and beautiful and so forth, only a becoming?

Theaet. When I hear you discoursing in this style, I think that there is a great deal in what you say, and I am very ready to assent.

Soc. Let us not leave the argument unfinished, then; for there still remains to be considered an objection which may be raised about dreams and diseases, in particular about madness, and the various illusions of hearing and sight, or of other senses. For you know that 158 in all these cases the theory which has been stated appears to be unmistakably refuted, since in dreams and illusions we certainly have false perceptions; and far from saying that everything is which appears to any man, we should rather say that nothing *is* which appears.

Theaet. Very true, Socrates.

Soc. But then, my boy, what argument is left for one who holds that knowledge is perception, or that the truth really is for every man such as it appears to him to be?

Theaet. I am afraid to say, Socrates, that I have nothing to answer, because you rebuked me just now for making this excuse; but I certainly cannot undertake to argue that madmen or dreamers do not think falsely, when they imagine, some of them that they are gods, and others that they can fly, and are flying in their sleep.

Soc. Do you see another question which can be raised about these phenomena, notably about dreaming and waking?

Theaet. What question?

Soc. A question which I think that you must often have heard persons ask: — How can you determine whether at this moment we are sleeping, and all our thoughts are a dream; or whether we are awake, and talking to one another in the waking state?

Theaet. Indeed, Socrates, I do not know how it could be determined, for in both cases the facts precisely correspond; and there is no difficulty in supposing that during all this discussion we have been talking to one another in a dream; and when in a dream we seem to be narrating dreams, the resemblance of the two states is quite astonishing.

Soc. You see, then, that a doubt about the reality of sense is easily raised, since there may even be a doubt whether we are awake or in a dream. And as our time is equally divided between sleeping and waking, in either sphere of existence the soul contends that the thoughts which are present to our minds at the time are true; and during one half of our lives we affirm the truth of the one, and, during the other half, of the other, and are equally confident of both.

Theaet. Most true.

Soc. And may not the same be said of madness and other disorders? the difference is only that the times are not equal.

Theaet. Certainly.

Soc. And is truth or falsehood to be determined by duration of time?

Theaet. That would be in many ways ridiculous.

Soc. But can you certainly determine by any other means which of these opinions is true?

Theaet. I do not think that I can.

Soc. Listen, then, to the explanation of the same facts which might be given by the champions of appearance. They would ask, as I imagine — When one thing is entirely different from another, can it have any power in common with that other thing? and observe, Theaetetus, that the word 'other' means not 'partially', but 'wholly other'.

Theaet. Certainly, putting the question as you do, that which 159 is wholly other cannot either in its power or in any other way be the same.

Soc. And must therefore be admitted to be unlike?

Theaet. True.

Soc. If, then, anything happens to become like or unlike itself or another, while it becomes like we shall say it is becoming the same, while unlike, other?

Theaet. Certainly.

Soc. Were we not saying that there are agents many and infinite, and patients many and infinite?

Theaet. Yes.

Soc. And also that each of these, with a different partner, will produce offspring which are not the same, but different?

Theaet. Certainly.

Soc. Let us take you and me, or anything as an example: — There is Socrates in health, and Socrates sick — Are they like or unlike?

Theaet. You mean to compare Socrates in health as a whole, and Socrates in sickness as a whole?

Soc. Exactly; that is my meaning.

Theaet. I answer, they are unlike.

Soc. And if unlike, they are so far other?

Theaet. Certainly.

Soc. And would you not say the same of Socrates sleeping and waking, or in any of the states which we were mentioning?

Theaet. I should.

Soc. It follows that everything which is by nature active, will find a different patient in Socrates, according as he is well or ill.

Theaet. Of course.

Soc. And I who am the patient, and that which is the agent, will engender something different in each of the two cases?

Theaet. Certainly.

Soc. The wine which I drink when I am in health, appears sweet and pleasant to me?

Theaet. True.

Soc. For, according to our acknowledged view, the patient and agent meet together and produce sweetness and a perception of sweetness, which are in simultaneous motion, and the perception which comes from the patient makes the tongue percipient, and the quality of sweetness which arises out of and is moving about the wine, makes the wine both to be and to appear sweet to the healthy tongue.

Theaet. Certainly; that has been already acknowledged.

Soc. But when I am sick, — firstly, the wine really acts upon another and a different person?

Theaet. Yes.

Soc. Once more, then, the combination of the draught of wine, and the Socrates who is sick, produces quite another result; which is the sensation of bitterness in the tongue, and the motion and creation of bitterness in and about the wine, which becomes not bitterness but something bitter; as I myself become not perception but percipient?

Theaet. True.

160 *Soc.* There is no other object of which I shall ever have the same perception, for another object would give another perception, and would make the percipient other and different; nor can that object which affects me, meeting another subject, produce the same, or become similar, for that too will produce another result from another subject, and become different.

Theaet. True.

Soc. Neither can I by myself have this sensation, nor the object by itself this quality.

Theaet. Certainly not.

Soc. It is necessary both that I, if I am to become percipient, must be related to an object — there can be no such thing as perceiving and perceiving nothing; and that the object, whether it becomes sweet, bitter, or of any quality, must have relation to a percipient; nothing can become sweet which is sweet to no one.

Theaet. Certainly not.

Soc. Then the inference is, that we [the agent and patient] are or become in relation to one another; there is a law which binds us one to the other, but not to any other existence, nor each of us to himself; and therefore we can only be bound to one another; so that whether a person prefers to say that a thing is or that it becomes, he must say that it is or becomes to or of or in relation to something else; but he must not say or allow any one else to say that anything is or becomes absolutely: — such is the conclusion of the view we have explained.

Theaet. Very true, Socrates.

Soc. Then, if that which acts upon me has relation to me and to no other, I and no other am the percipient of it?

Theaet. Of course.

Soc. Then my perception is true to me, being inseparable from my own 'being'; and, as Protagoras says, to myself I am judge of what is and is not to me.

Theaet. I suppose so.

Soc. How then, since I never err, and since my mind never trips in the conception of being or becoming, can I fail of knowing that which I perceive?

Theaet. You cannot.

Soc. Then you were quite right in affirming that knowledge is only perception; and the meaning turns out to be the same, whether with Homer and Heracleitus, and all that company, one says that all is motion and flux, or with the great sage Protagoras, that man is the measure of all things; or with Theaetetus, that, given these premises, perception is knowledge. Am I not right, Theaetetus, and may we compare this to a new-born child, to which you, with my assistance, have given birth? What say you?

Theaet. I cannot but agree, Socrates.

Soc. Then this is the child, however he may turn out, which you and I have with difficulty brought into the world. And now that he is born, we must run round the hearth with him, and see whether he is worth rearing, or is only a wind-egg and a sham. Is he to be reared in any case, and not exposed? or will you bear to see him examined, and not get into a passion if I take away your first-born? 161

Theod. Theaetetus will not be angry, for he is very good-natured. But tell me, Socrates, in heaven's name, what can be said in disproof of all this?

Soc. You, Theodorus, are a lover of theories, and now you innocently fancy that I am a bag full of them, and can easily pull one

out which will overthrow its predecessor. But you do not see that
in reality none of these theories come from me; they all come from
him who talks with me. I only know just enough to extract them
from the wisdom of another, and to receive them in a spirit of fairness. And now I shall say nothing myself, but shall endeavour to
elicit something from our young friend.

Theod. Do as you say, Socrates; you are quite right.

Soc. Shall I tell you, Theodorus, what amazes me in your
acquaintance Protagoras?

Theod. What is it?

Soc. I am charmed with his doctrine, that what appears is to each
one, but I wonder that he did not begin his book on Truth with a
declaration that a pig or a dog-faced baboon, or some other yet
stranger monster which has sensation, is the measure of all things;
then he might have shown a magnificent contempt for our opinion
of him by informing us at the outset that while we were reverencing
him like a God for his wisdom he was no more intelligent than a tad-
pole, not to speak of his fellow-men. Would you not say so,
Theodorus? If the judgement which each man forms through sensation is true for him, and no man can either discern another's feelings
better than he, or have any superior right to determine whether his
opinion is true or false, but each, as we have several times repeated,
is to himself the sole judge, and everything that he judges is true and
right, — why, my friend, should Protagoras be preferred to the place
of wisdom and instruction, and deserve to be well paid, and we poor
ignoramuses have to go to him, if each one is the measure of his own
wisdom? Must he not be flattering the public in all this? I say
nothing of the ridiculous predicament in which my own midwifery
and, I think, the whole art of dialectic is placed; for the attempt
to supervise or refute the notions or opinions of others would be a
tedious and enormous piece of folly, if to each man his own are right;
and this must be the case if Protagoras' Truth is the real truth, and
the philosopher is not merely amusing himself by giving oracles out
of the shrine of his book.

Theod. He was a friend of mine, Socrates, as you were saying,
and therefore I cannot have him refuted by my lips, nor can I oppose
you when I agree with you; please, then, to take Theaetetus again;
he seemed to answer very nicely.

Soc. If you were to go into a Lacedaemonian palestra, Theodorus,
would you have a right to look on at the naked wrestlers, some of
them making a poor figure, if you did not strip and give them an
opportunity of judging your own person?

Theod. Why not, Socrates, if they would allow me to remain as a
spectator, as I think you will, in consideration of my age and stiffness;

let some more supple youth try a fall with you, and do not drag me into the gymnasium.

Soc. What is dear to you, Theodorus, is not displeasing to me, as the proverb says, and therefore I will return to the sage Theaetetus: Tell me, Theaetetus, in reference to what I was saying, are you not lost in wonder, like myself, when you find that all of a sudden you are raised to the level of the wisest of men, or indeed of the gods? — for you would assume the measure of Protagoras to apply to the gods as well as men?

Theaet. Certainly I should, and I confess to you that I am lost in wonder. While we were working out the meaning of the theory that whatever appears to each man is true for him, I was quite satisfied, but now the face of things has changed.

Soc. Why, my dear boy, you are young, and therefore your ear is quickly caught and your mind influenced by popular arguments. Protagoras, or some one speaking on his behalf, will doubtless say in reply, — Good people, young and old, you meet and harangue, and bring in the gods, whose existence or non-existence I banish from writing and speech, or you talk about the reason of man being degraded to the level of the brutes, which is a telling argument with the multitude, but not one word of proof or demonstration do you offer. All is probability with you, and yet surely you and Theodorus had better reflect whether you are disposed to admit of probability **163** and plausible comparisons in matters of such importance. He or any other mathematician who argued from probability in geometry, would not be worth an ace.

Theaet. But neither you nor we, Socrates, would be satisfied with such arguments.

Soc. Then you and Theodorus mean to say that we must look at the matter in some other way?

Theaet. Yes, in quite another way.

Soc. And the way will be to ask whether perception is or is not the same as knowledge; for this was the real point of our argument, and with a view to this we raised (did we not?) those many strange questions.

Theaet. Certainly.

Soc. Shall we admit that we at once know whatever we perceive by sight or hearing? for example, shall we say that not having learned, we do not *hear* the language of foreigners when they speak to us? or shall we say that we hear and therefore know what they are saying? Or again, in looking at letters which we do not understand, shall we say that we do not *see* them? or shall we aver that, seeing them, we must know them?

Theaet. We shall say, Socrates, that we know what we actually see and hear of them — that is to say, we see, and hence know, the figure and colour of the letters, and we hear and know the elevation or depression of the sound; but we do not perceive by sight and hearing, and hence do not know, that which grammarians and interpreters teach about them.

Soc. Capital, Theaetetus; and about this there shall be no dispute, because I want you to grow; but look! there is another difficulty coming, and you must advise how we shall repulse it.

Theaet. What is it?

Soc. Some one will say, Can a man who has ever known anything, and still has and preserves a memory of that which he knows, not know that which he remembers at the time when he remembers? I have, I fear, a tedious way of putting a simple question, which is only, whether a man who has learned, and remembers, can fail to know?

Theaet. Impossible, Socrates; the supposition is monstrous.

Soc. Am I talking nonsense, then? Think: is not seeing perceiving, and is not sight perception?

Theaet. True.

Soc. And if our recent definition holds, every man knows that which he has seen?

Theaet. Yes.

Soc. And now, you would admit that there is such a thing as memory?

Theaet. Yes.

Soc. Is this memory of something or of nothing?

Theaet. Of something, surely.

Soc. Of things learned and perceived, that is?

Theaet. Certainly.

Soc. Often a man remembers that which he has seen?

Theaet. True.

Soc. Even if he closes his eyes? Or would he then forget?

Theaet. Who, Socrates, would dare to say so?

Soc. But we must say so, if the previous argument is to be maintained.

Theaet. What do you mean? I am not quite sure that I understand you, though I have a strong suspicion that you are right.

Soc. As thus: he who sees knows, as we say, that which he sees; for perception and sight and knowledge are admitted to be the same.

Theaet. Certainly.

Soc. But he who saw, and has knowledge of that which he saw, remembers, when he closes his eyes, that which he no longer sees.

Theaet. Yes.

Soc. But seeing is knowing, and therefore not-seeing is not-knowing?

Theaet. True.

Soc. Then the inference is, that a man who has attained the knowledge of something, though he still remembers this, may *not* know it since he does not see it; and this has been affirmed by us to be a monstrous supposition.

Theaet. Most true.

Soc. Thus, then, the assertion that knowledge and perception are one, seems to involve an impossible consequence.

Theaet. Yes.

Soc. Then they must be distinguished?

Theaet. I suppose that they must.

Soc. It seems that we must go back to our original question, What is knowledge? — But hold! Theaetetus, whatever are we proposing to do?

Theaet. About what?

Soc. Like a good-for-nothing cock, without having won the victory, we spring away from the argument and crow.

Theaet. How do you mean?

Soc. After the manner of disputers, we were satisfied with mere verbal consistency, and were well pleased if in this way we could gain an advantage. Although professing not to be mere eristics, but philosophers, I suspect that we have unconsciously fallen into the error of that ingenious class of persons.

Theaet. I do not as yet understand you.

Soc. Then I will try to explain myself: just now we asked the question, whether a man who had learned and remembered could fail to know, and we showed that a person who had seen might remember when he had his eyes shut and could not see, and then he would at the same time remember and not know. But this was an impossibility. And so the Protagorean fable came to nought, and yours also, who maintained that knowledge is the same as perception.

Theaet. So it seems.

Soc. And yet, my friend, I rather suspect that if Protagoras, who was the father of the first of the two brats, had been alive, he would have had a great deal to say on their behalf. But he is dead, and we insult over his orphan child; and even the guardians whom he left, and of whom our friend Theodorus is one, are unwilling to give any help, and therefore I suppose that we must take up his cause ourselves and see justice done?

Theod. Not I, Socrates, but rather Callias, the son of Hipponicus, 165 is his executor. For my part, I was too soon diverted from the abstractions of dialectic to geometry. Nevertheless, I shall be grateful to you if you assist him.

Soc. Very good, Theodorus; you shall see how I will come to the rescue. If a person does not attend to the meaning of terms as they are commonly used in argument, he may be involved even in greater paradoxes than these. Am I to explain this matter to you or to Theaetetus?

Theod. To both of us, and let the younger answer; he will incur less disgrace if he is discomfited.

Soc. Then now let me ask the awful question, which is this: — Can the same man know and also not know that which he knows?

Theod. How shall we answer, Theaetetus?

Theaet. He cannot, I should say.

Soc. He can, if you maintain that seeing is knowing. When you are imprisoned in a well, as the saying is, and the self-assured adversary closes one of your eyes with his hand, and asks whether you can see his cloak with the eye which he has closed, how will you answer the inevitable man?

Theaet. I should answer, 'Not with that eye but with the other'.

Soc. Then you see and do not see the same thing at the same time.

Theaet. Yes, in a certain sense.

Soc. None of that, he will reply; I do not ask or bid you answer in what sense you know, but only whether you know that which you do not know. You have been proved to see that which you do not see; and you have already admitted that seeing is knowing, and that not-seeing is not-knowing: I leave you to draw the inference.

Theaet. Yes; the inference is the contradictory of my assertion.

Soc. Yes, my marvel, and there might have been yet worse things in store for you, if an opponent had gone on to ask whether you can have a sharp and also a dull knowledge, and whether you can know near, but not at a distance, or know the same thing with more or less intensity, and so on without end. Such are the questions which might have been fired at you by a light-armed mercenary, who argued for pay. He would have lain in wait for you, and when you took up the position that sense and knowledge are the same, he would have made an assault upon hearing, smelling, and the other senses; he would have pressed the attack, until, in your envy and admiration of his wisdom, you were taken captive; and once he had got you into his net, you would not have escaped until you had come to an understanding about the sum to be paid for your release. Well, you ask, and how will Protagoras reinforce his position? Shall I answer for him?

Theaet. By all means.

Soc. He will repeat all those things which we have been urging 166 on his behalf, and then he will close with us in disdain, and say:— The worthy Socrates asks a little boy, whether the same man could at once remember and not know the same thing; and when the boy, because he is frightened and unable to see what is coming, says No, he thinks, it appears, that he has held me up to ridicule. The truth is, O slatternly Socrates, that when you ask questions about any assertion of mine, and the person asked is found tripping, if he has answered as I should have answered, then I am refuted, but if he answers something else, then he is refuted and not I. For firstly do you really suppose that any one would admit the memory which a man has of an impression which has passed away to be similar to that which he experienced at the time? Assuredly not. Or would he hesitate to acknowledge that the same man may know and not know the same thing? Or, if he is afraid of making this admission, would he ever grant that one who is becoming unlike is the same as before he became unlike? Or rather would he admit that a man is one at all, and not many and infinite as the changes which take place in him? But must we speak by the card in order to guard against precise criticism of each other's words? No, my good sir, he will say, examine my view itself in a more generous spirit; and either show, if you can, that our sensations are not private to each individual, or, if you admit them to be so, prove that this does not involve the consequence that the appearance becomes, or, if you will have the word, *is*, to the individual only. As to your talk about pigs and baboons, you are yourself behaving like a pig, and you teach your hearers to make sport of my writings in the same ignorant manner; but this is not to your credit. For I declare that the truth is as I have written, — that while each of us is a measure of existence and of non-existence, one man may be a thousand times better than another from the very fact that different things are and appear to him. And I am far from saying that wisdom and the wise man have no existence; but my definition of a wise man is, precisely, one who can take any of us to whom evil appears, and is, and by changing him make good appear and be to him instead. And once again I would beg you not to press my words in the letter, but to take the meaning of them as I will explain them. Remember what has been already said, — that to the sick man his food appears to be and is bitter, and to the man in health it is and appears the opposite. Now I cannot conceive that one of these men can be or ought to be made wiser than the other: 167 nor can you call the sick man foolish because he has one impression, and say that the healthy man because he has another is wise. But it can be said that the one state requires to be changed into the other, the worse into the better. So also in education, an improvement has to be effected, and the sophist accomplishes by words the change which the physician works by the aid of drugs. Not that any one ever made another think truly, who previously thought falsely. For no one can think what is not, or think anything different from

that which he feels; present feeling is always true. But when men of
inferior mind have thoughts of a kindred nature, I conceive that a
good mind has often caused them to have good thoughts; and these
appearances which the inexperienced call true, I maintain to be only
better, and not truer than others. And, O my dear Socrates, I do not
call wise men tadpoles: far from it; I call them 'physicians' and
'husbandmen' where the human body and plants are concerned — for
the husbandmen also take away the evil sensations of sickly plants,
and infuse into them good and healthy sensations; and the wise and
good rhetoricians make the good instead of the evil to seem just to
states; for whatever appears to each state to be just and fair, so long
as it is regarded as such, is just and fair to it; and what the wise man
does is to cause good to appear, and be real, for each of them instead
of evil. And in like manner the sophist who is able to train his pupils
in this spirit is a wise man, and deserves to be well paid by them.
And so I say both that some men are wiser than others, and that no
one thinks falsely, and you, whether you will or not, must endure to
be a measure. On these foundations the argument stands firm,
which you, Socrates, may, if you please, overthrow by an argument
proceeding from an opposite principle, or if you like you may put
questions to me — a method to which no intelligent person will
object, quite the reverse. But I must beg you to put fair questions:
for there is great inconsistency in saying that you have a zeal for
virtue, and yet giving a constant exhibition of injustice in argument.
Injustice it is when one does not converse differently in disputation
and in serious discussion: the disputer may trip up his opponent as
often as he likes, and make fun; but the dialectician will be in earnest,
and only correct his interlocutor when necessary, telling him the
errors into which he has fallen through his own fault, or that of the
168 company which he has previously kept. If you do so, your companion
will lay the blame of his own confusion and perplexity on himself,
and not on you. He will follow and love you, and will hate himself,
and escape from himself into philosophy, in order that he may
become different and be quit of his former self. But the other mode
of arguing, which is practised by the many, will have just the
opposite effect upon him; and as he grows older, instead of turning
philosopher, he will come to hate philosophy. I would recommend
you, therefore, as I said before, not to encourage yourself in this
polemical and controversial temper, but to find out, in a friendly and
congenial spirit, what we really mean when we say that all things are
in motion, and that to every individual and state what appears, is.
In this manner you will consider whether knowledge and sensation
are the same or different, but you will not argue, as you were just now
doing, from the customary use of names and words, which the vulgar

pervert in all sorts of ways, causing infinite perplexity to one another. Such, Theodorus, is the very slight help which I am able to offer to your old friend; had he been living, he would have helped himself in a far more gloriose style.

Theod. You are jesting, Socrates; indeed, your defence of him has been most valorous.

Soc. Thank you, friend; and I hope that you observed Protagoras bidding us be serious, as the text, 'Man is the measure of all things', was a solemn one; and he reproached us with making a boy the medium of discourse, and said that the boy's timidity was made to tell against his argument; he also declared that we made a joke of him.

Theod. How could I fail to observe all that, Socrates?

Soc. Well, and shall we do as he says?

Theod. By all means.

Soc. But if his wishes are to be regarded, you and I must take up the argument, and in all seriousness, and ask and answer one another, for you see that the rest of us are nothing but boys. In no other way can we escape the imputation, that in our analysis of his thesis we are making fun with boys.

Theod. Well, but is not Theaetetus better able to follow a philosophical inquiry than a great many men who have long beards?

Soc. Yes, Theodorus, but not better than you; and therefore please not to imagine that I am to defend by every means in my power your departed friend, and you not at all. At any rate, my good man, do not sheer off until we know whether you should be preferred as the measure of diagrams, or whether all men are judges equal to you, and sufficient for themselves, in astronomy and geometry, and the other branches of knowledge in which you are supposed to excel them. 169

Theod. He who is sitting by you, Socrates, will not easily avoid being drawn into an argument; and when I said just now that you would excuse me, and not, like the Lacedaemonians, compel me to strip and fight, I was talking nonsense — I should rather compare you to Sciron [who threw travellers from the rocks]; for the Lacedaemonian rule is 'strip or depart', but you seem to go about your work more after the fashion of Antaeus: you will not allow any one who approaches you to depart until you have stripped him, and he has been compelled to try a fall with you in argument.

Soc. There, Theodorus, you have hit off precisely the nature of my complaint; but I am even more pugnacious than the giants of old, for I have met with no end of heroes; many a Heracles, many a Theseus, mighty in words, has broken my head; nevertheless I am always at this rough exercise, which inspires me like a passion. Please, then, to try a fall with me, whereby you will do yourself good as well as me.

Theod. I consent; lead me whither you will, for I know that you are like destiny; no man can escape from any argument which you may weave for him. But I am not disposed to submit to your scrutiny farther than you suggest.

Soc. That will be enough; and now take particular care that we do not again unwittingly expose ourselves to the reproach of talking childishly.

Theod. I will do my best to avoid that error.

Soc. In the first place, let us return to our old objection, and see whether we were right in blaming and taking offence at the argument on the ground that it made every man self-sufficient in wisdom; upon which Protagoras admitted that there was a better and worse, and that in respect of this, some who as he said were the wise excelled others.

Theod. Very true.

Soc. Had Protagoras been living and answered for himself, instead of our answering for him, there would have been no need of our reviewing or reinforcing the argument. But as he is not here, and some one may accuse us of speaking without authority on his behalf, had we not better come to a clearer agreement about his meaning, for a great deal may be at stake?

Theod. True.

170 *Soc.* Then let us obtain, not through any third person, but from his own statement and in the fewest words possible, the basis of agreement.

Theod. In what way?

Soc. In this way: — His words are, 'What seems to a man, is to him.'

Theod. Yes, so he says.

Soc. And are not we, Protagoras, uttering the opinion of man, or rather of all mankind, when we say that every one thinks himself wiser than other men in some things, and their inferior in others? In the hour of danger, when they are in perils of war, or of the sea, or of sickness, do they not look up to those in authority as if they were gods, and expect salvation from them, only because they excel them in knowledge? Is not the world full of men who are looking for master-craftsmen and teachers and rulers of men and of the animals? and of others who think that they are able to teach and able to rule? Now, in all this is implied that ignorance and wisdom exist among them, at least in their own opinion.

Theod. Certainly.

Soc. And wisdom is assumed by them to be true thought, and ignorance to be false opinion.

Theod. Exactly.

Soc. How then, Protagoras, would you have us treat the argument? Shall we say that the opinions of men are always true, or sometimes true and sometimes false? In either case, the result is the same, and their opinions are not always true, but sometimes true and sometimes false. For tell me, Theodorus, do you suppose that you yourself, or any other follower of Protagoras, would contend that no one deems another ignorant or mistaken in his opinion?

Theod. The thing is incredible, Socrates.

Soc. And yet that absurdity is necessarily involved in the thesis which declares man to be the measure of all things.

Theod. How so?

Soc. Why, suppose that you determine in your own mind something to be true, and declare your opinion to me; let us assume, as he argues, that this is true to you. Now, if so, you must either say that the rest of us cannot be judges of this judgement of yours, or that we judge you always to have a true opinion. But are there not thousands upon thousands who, whenever you form a judgement, take up arms against you and are of an opposite judgement and opinion, deeming that you judge falsely?

Theod. Yes, indeed, Socrates, thousands and tens of thousands, as Homer says, who give me a world of trouble.

Soc. Well, but are we to assert that what you think is true to you and false to the ten thousand others?

Theod. No other inference seems to be possible.

Soc. And how about Protagoras himself? If neither he nor the multitude thought, as indeed they do not think, that man is the measure of all things, must it not follow that the Truth of which 171 Protagoras wrote would be true to no one? But if he himself thought this, while the multitude does not agree with him, you must begin by allowing that in whatever proportion the many are more than one, in that proportion his truth is more untrue than true.

Theod. That would follow if the truth is supposed to vary with individual opinion.

Soc. Moreover, the best of the joke is, that he acknowledges the truth of their opinion who believe his own opinion to be false; for he admits that the opinions of all men are true.

Theod. Certainly.

Soc. He should, then, allow that his own opinion is false, if he admits that the opinion of those who think him false is true?

Theod. Of course.

Soc. Whereas the other side do not admit that they speak falsely?

Theod. They do not.

Soc. And he, as may be inferred from his writings, agrees that this opinion is also true.

Theod. So it seems.

Soc. Then all mankind, beginning with Protagoras, will contend (or rather, I should say that he will *allow,* when he concedes that his adversary has a true opinion), Protagoras, I say, will himself allow that neither a dog nor any ordinary man is the measure of anything which he has not learned — am I not right?

Theod. Yes.

Soc. And the Truth of Protagoras being doubted by all, will be true neither to himself nor to any one else?

Theod. I think, Socrates, that we are running my old friend too hard.

Soc. But I do not know that we are going beyond the truth. Doubtless, as he is older, he may be expected to be wiser than we are. And if he could only just get his head out of the world below, he would have overthrown both of us again and again, me for talking nonsense and you for assenting to me, and have been off and underground in a trice. But as he is not within call, we must make the best use of our own faculties, such as they are, and speak out what appears to us to be true. And one thing which no one will deny is, that there are great differences in the understandings of men.

Theod. In that opinion I quite agree.

Soc. And is there not most likely to be firm ground in the distinction which we were indicating on behalf of Protagoras, viz. that most sensations, such as hot, dry, sweet, and all others of that class, are only such as they appear; if, however, superiority of opinion is to be allowed at all, surely we must allow it in respect of health or disease? for every woman, child, or living creature has not such a knowledge of what conduces to health as to enable them to cure themselves.

Theod. I quite agree.

172   *Soc.* Or again, in politics, while affirming that just and unjust, honourable and disgraceful, holy and unholy, are in reality to each state such as the state thinks and makes lawful, and that in determining these matters no individual or state is wiser than another, still the followers of Protagoras will not deny that in determining what is or is not *expedient* for the community one state is wiser and one counsellor better than another — they will scarcely venture to maintain, that what a city enacts in the belief that it is expedient will always be really expedient. But in the other case, I mean when they speak of justice and injustice, piety and impiety, they are confident that in nature these have no existence or essence of their own — the truth is that which is agreed on at the time of the agreement, and as long as the agreement lasts; and this is the philosophy of many who do not altogether go along with Protagoras. Here arises a new question, Theodorus, which threatens to be more serious than the last.

Theod. Well, Socrates, we have plenty of leisure.

Soc. That is true, and your remark recalls to my mind an observation which I have often made, that it is not surprising that those who have spent a long time upon any kind of philosophy are ridiculously at fault when they have to appear and speak in court.

Theod. What do you mean?

Soc. I mean to say, that those who have been trained in philosophy and liberal pursuits are as unlike those who from their youth upwards have been knocking about in the courts and such places, as a freeman is in breeding unlike a slave.

Theod. In what is the difference seen?

Soc. In the leisure spoken of by you, which a freeman can always command: he has his talk out in peace, and, like ourselves, he wanders at will from one subject to another, and from a second to a third, — if the fancy takes him, he begins again, as we are doing now, caring not whether his words are many or few; his only aim is to attain the truth. But the lawyer can never speak at leisure; there is the water of the clepsydra driving him on, and not allowing him to expatiate at will: and there is his adversary standing over him, and frequently glancing at an outline of points from which he is not allowed to deviate. He is a servant, and is continually disputing about a fellow servant before his master, who is seated, and has the cause in his hands; the trial is never about some indifferent matter, but always concerns himself; and often the race is for his life. The consequence 173 has been, that he has become keen and shrewd; he has learned how to flatter his master in word and indulge him in deed; but his soul is small and unrighteous. His condition, which has been that of a slave from his youth upwards, has deprived him of growth and uprightness and independence; dangers and fears, which were too much for his truth and honesty, came upon him in early years, when the tenderness of youth was unequal to them, and he has been driven into crooked ways; from the first he has practised deception and retaliation, and has become stunted and warped. And so he has passed out of youth into manhood, having no soundness in him; and is now, as he thinks, a master in wisdom. Such are these men, Theodorus. Will you have the companion picture of the philosopher, who is of our brotherhood; or shall we return to the argument? Do not let us abuse the freedom of digression which we claim.

Theod. Nay, Socrates, not until we have finished what we are about; for you truly said that we belong to a brotherhood which is free, and are not the servants of the argument; but the argument is our servant, and must wait our leisure. Who is our judge? Or where is the spectator having any right to censure or control us, as he might the poets?

Soc. Then, as this is your wish, I will describe the leaders; for there is no use in talking about those who pursue philosophy in a meaner spirit. In the first place, our leaders have never, from their youth upwards, known their way to the Agora, or the dicastery, or the council, or any other political assembly; they neither see nor hear the laws or decrees, as they are called, of the state written or recited; the eagerness of political societies in the attainment of offices — clubs, and banquets, and revels in the company of flute-girls, — do not enter even into their dreams. Whether someone in the city is of good or base birth, what disgrace may have descended to any one from his ancestors, male or female, are matters of which the philosopher no more knows than he can tell, as they say, how many pints are contained in the ocean. Neither is he conscious of his ignorance. For he does not hold aloof in order that he may gain a reputation; but the truth is, that the outer form of him only is in the city: his mind, regarding all these things with disdain as of slight or no worth, soars — to use the expression of Pindar — everywhere 'beneath the earth, and again beyond the sky', measuring the land, surveying the heavens, 174 and exploring the whole nature of the world and of every thing in its entirety, but not condescending to anything which is within reach.

Theod. What do you mean, Socrates?

Soc. I will illustrate my meaning, Theodorus, by the jest which the clever witty Thracian handmaid is said to have made about Thales, when he fell into a well as he was looking up at the stars. She said, that he was so eager to know what was going on in heaven, that he could not see what was before his feet. This is a jest which is equally applicable to all philosophers. For the philosopher is wholly unacquainted with his next-door neighbour; he is ignorant, not only of what he is doing, but he hardly knows whether he is a man or an animal; he is searching into the essence of man, and busy in inquiring what it is proper to such a nature to do or suffer different from any other; — I think that you understand me, Theodorus?

Theod. I do, and what you say is true.

Soc. And thus, my friend, on every occasion, private as well as public, as I said at first, when he appears in a law-court, or in any place in which he has to speak of things which are at his feet and before his eyes, he is the jest, not only of Thracian handmaids but of the general herd, tumbling into wells and every sort of disaster through his inexperience. His awkwardness is fearful, and gives the impression of imbecility. When he is reviled, he has nothing personal to say in answer to the civilities of his adversaries, for he knows no scandals of any one, and they do not interest him; and therefore he is laughed at for his sheepishness; and when others are being praised or glorifying themselves, his unaffected laughter, which he makes no attempt to conceal, causes him to be considered a downright idiot. When he hears a tyrant or king eulogized, he fancies that he is listening to the praises of some keeper of cattle — a swineherd, or shepherd, or perhaps a cowherd, who is congratulated on the quantity of milk which he squeezes from them; and he remarks that the creature whom they tend, and out of whom they squeeze the wealth, is of a less tractable and more insidious nature. Then, again, he observes that the great man is of necessity as ill mannered and uneducated as any shepherd — for he has no leisure, and he is surrounded by a wall, which is his mountain-pen. Hearing of enormous landed proprietors of ten thousand acres and more, our philosopher deems this to be a trifle, because he has been accustomed to think of the whole earth; and when they sing the praises of family, and say that some one is a gentleman because he can show seven generations of wealthy ancestors, he thinks that their sentiments only betray a dull and narrow **175** vision in those who utter them, and who are not educated enough to look always at the whole, nor to consider that every man has had thousands and ten thousands of progenitors, and among them have been rich and poor, kings and slaves, Hellenes and barbarians, innumerable. And when people pride themselves on having a pedigree of twenty-five ancestors, which goes back to Heracles, the son of Amphitryon, he cannot understand their poverty of ideas. Why are they unable to calculate that Amphitryon had a twenty-fifth ancestor, who might have been anybody, and was such as fortune made him, and he had a fiftieth, and so on? He amuses himself with the notion that they cannot count, and thinks that a little arithmetic would have got rid of their senseless vanity. Now, in all these cases our philosopher is derided by the vulgar, partly because he is thought to despise them, and also because he is ignorant of what is before him, and always at a loss.

Theod. That is very true, Socrates.

Soc. But, O my friend, when he draws the other into upper air, and gets him out of his pleas and rejoinders into the contemplation of justice and injustice in their own nature and in their difference from one another and from all other things; or from the commonplaces about the happiness of a king or of a rich man to the consideration of government, and of human happiness and misery in general — what they are, and how a man is to attain the one and avoid the other — when that narrow, keen, little legal mind is called to account about all this, he gives the philosopher his revenge; for dizzied by the height at which he is hanging, whence he looks down into space, which is a strange experience to him, he being dismayed, and lost, and stammering broken words, is laughed at, not by Thracian handmaidens or any other uneducated persons, for they have no eye for the situation, but by every man who has not been brought up a slave. Such are the two characters, Theodorus: the one of the freeman, who has been trained in liberty and leisure, whom you call the philosopher, — him we cannot blame because he appears simple and of no account when he has to perform some menial task, such as packing up bed-clothes, or flavouring a sauce or fawning speech; the other character is that of

176 the man who is able to do all this kind of service smartly and neatly, but knows not how to wear his cloak like a gentleman; still less with the music of discourse can he rightly hymn that life which is lived by immortals or men blessed of heaven.

Theod. If you could only persuade everybody, Socrates, as you do me, of the truth of your words, there would be more peace and fewer evils among men.

Soc. Evils, Theodorus, can never pass away; for there must always remain something which is antagonistic to good. Having no place among the gods in heaven, of necessity they hover around the mortal nature, and this earthly sphere. Wherefore we ought to fly away from earth to heaven as quickly as we can; and to fly away means to become like God, as far as this is possible; and to become like him, means to become holy, just, and wise. But, O my friend, you cannot easily convince mankind that they should pursue virtue or avoid vice, not merely in order that a man may seem to be good, which is the reason given by the world, and in my judgement is only a repetition of an old wives' fable. Whereas, the truth is that God is never in any way unrighteous — he is perfect righteousness; and he of us who is the most righteous is of all things most like him. Herein is seen the true cleverness of a man, and also his nothingness and want of manhood. For to know this is true wisdom and virtue, and ignorance of this is manifest folly and vice. All other kinds of what might seem wisdom or cleverness, such as the wisdom of politicians, or the wisdom of the arts, are coarse and vulgar. The unrighteous man, or the sayer and doer of unholy things, had far better not be encouraged in the illusion that his roguery is clever; for men glory in their shame — they fancy that they hear others saying of them, 'These are not mere good-for-nothing persons, mere burdens of the earth, but such as men should be who mean to dwell safely in a state.' Let us tell them that they are all the more truly what they do not think they are because they do not know it; for they do not know the penalty of injustice, which above all things they ought to know — not stripes and death, as they suppose, which evil-doers often escape, but a penalty which cannot be escaped.

Theod. What is that?

Soc. There are two patterns eternally set before them; the one divine and most happy, the other godless and most wretched: but

they do not see them, or perceive that in their utter folly and infatuation they are growing like the one and unlike the other, by reason of 177
their evil deeds; and the penalty is, that they lead a life answering
to the pattern which they are growing like. And if we tell them, that
unless they depart from their cunning, the place of innocence will not
receive them after death; and that here on earth, they will live ever
in the likeness of their own evil selves, and with evil friends — when
they hear this they in their superior cunning will seem to be listening
to the talk of idiots.

Theod. Very true, Socrates.

Soc. Too true, my friend, as I well know; there is, however, one
peculiarity in their case: when they begin to reason in private about
their dislike of philosophy, if they have the courage to hear the argument out, and do not run away, they grow at last strangely discontented with themselves; their rhetoric fades away, and they become
helpless as children. These however are digressions from which we
must now desist, or they will overflow, and drown the original argument; to which, if you please, we will now return.

Theod. For my part, Socrates, I would rather have the digressions,
for at my age I find them easier to follow; but if you wish, let us go
back to the argument.

Soc. Had we not reached the point at which the partisans of the
perpetual flux, who say that things are as they seem to each one,
were confidently maintaining that, as elsewhere, so in the special
instance of justice, the ordinances which the state commanded and
thought just, were just to the state which imposed them, while they
were in force; but as to the good, no one had any longer the hardihood to contend of any ordinances which the state enacted because it
thought them beneficial to itself, that these, while they were in force,
were really beneficial; — he who said so would be playing with the
name 'good', and would not touch the real question — it would be a
mockery, would it not?

Theod. Certainly it would.

Soc. He ought not to speak of the name, but contemplate the thing
for which it stands.

Theod. Right.

Soc. Whatever be the term used, the good or expedient is the aim
of legislation, and as far as it can have an opinion, the state imposes all
laws with a view to the greatest expediency; can legislation have
any other aim?

Theod. Certainly not. 178

Soc. But is the aim attained always? do not mistakes often happen?

Theod. Yes, I think that there are mistakes.

Soc. The possibility of error will be more distinctly recognized, if we put the question in reference to the whole class under which the expedient falls. That whole class has to do with the future, and laws are passed under the idea that they will be useful in after-time; which, in other words, is the future.

Theod. Very true.

Soc. Suppose now, that we ask Protagoras, or one of his disciples, a question: — O, Protagoras, we will say to him, Man is, as you declare, the measure of all things — white, heavy, light, and the whole class of such things; for he has the criterion of them in himself, and when he thinks that things are such as he experiences them to be, he thinks what is and is true to himself. Is it not so?

Theod. Yes.

Soc. What now of future events, Protagoras? we shall say. Has each man the criterion of these also within himself, so that they *will be* for him as he supposes that they will be? For example, take the case of heat: — When an ordinary man thinks that he is going to have a fever, and that this kind of heat is coming on, and another person, who is a physician, thinks the contrary, whose opinion about the future is likely to prove right? Or are they both right? — he will have both heat and fever in his own judgement, and neither in the physician's judgement?

Theod. That would be ridiculous.

Soc. And the vinegrower, if I am not mistaken, is a better judge of the sweetness or dryness of the vintage which is not yet gathered than the harp-player?

Theod. Certainly.

Soc. And in musical composition the musician will know better than the training master what the training master himself will hereafter think harmonious or the reverse?

Theod. Of course.

Soc. And the cook will be a better judge than the guest, who is not a cook, of the pleasure to be derived from the dinner which is in preparation; for of present or past pleasure we are not as yet arguing; the question is whether everyone is to himself the best judge of that which will seem to be and will be to him in the future? — nay, would not you, Protagoras, better guess which arguments in a court would convince any one of us than the ordinary man?

Theod. Certainly, Socrates, he used to profess in the strongest manner that he was the superior of all men in this respect.

179 *Soc.* To be sure, friend: who would have paid a large sum for the privilege of talking to him, if he had really persuaded his visitors that neither a prophet nor any other man was better able to judge what will be and seem to be in the future than everyone could for himself?

Theod. Who indeed?

Soc. But now legislation and expediency are all concerned with the future; and everyone will admit that states, in passing laws, must often fail of their highest interests?

Theod. Quite true.

Soc. Then we may fairly argue against your master, that he must admit one man to be wiser than another, and that the wiser is a measure: but I, who know nothing, am not at all obliged to accept the honour which the advocate of Protagoras was just now forcing upon me, whether I would or not, of being a measure of anything.

Theod. That is the best refutation of him, Socrates; although he is also caught when he ascribes truth to the opinions of others, who give the lie direct to his own opinion.

Soc. There are many ways, Theodorus, in which the doctrine that every opinion of every man is true may be refuted; but there is more difficulty in proving that states of feeling, which are present to a man, and out of which arise sensations and opinions in accordance with them, are sometimes not true. And very likely I have been talking nonsense about them; for they may be unassailable, and those who say that there is clear evidence of them, and that they are matters of knowledge, may probably be right; in which case our friend Theaetetus was not so far from the mark when he identified perception and knowledge. And therefore let us draw nearer, as the advocate of Protagoras desires, and give the truth of the universal flux a ring: is the theory sound or not? at any rate, no small war is raging about it, and there are combatants not a few.

Theod. No small war, indeed, for in Ionia the sect makes rapid strides; the disciples of Heracleitus are most energetic upholders of the doctrine.

Soc. Then we are the more bound, my dear Theodorus, to examine the question from the foundation as it is set forth by themselves.

Theod. Certainly we are. About these speculations of Heracleitus, which, as you say, are as old as Homer, or even older still, the Ephesians themselves, who profess to know them, are downright mad, and you cannot talk with them on the subject. For, in accordance with their text-books, they are always in motion; but as for dwelling upon an argument or a question, and quietly asking and answering in turn, they can no more do so than they can fly; or rather, the determination of these fellows not to have a particle of rest in them is more than the utmost powers of negation can express. If you ask any of them a question, he will produce, as from a quiver, sayings brief and dark, and shoot them at you; and if you inquire the reason of what he has said, you will be hit by some other new-fangled word, and will make no way with any of them, nor they with one another; their great care is, not to allow of any settled principle either in their arguments or

180

in their minds, conceiving, as I imagine, that any such principle would be stationary; for they are at war with the stationary, and do what they can to drive it out everywhere.

Soc. I suppose, Theodorus, that you have only seen them when they were fighting, and have never stayed with them in time of peace, for they are no friends of yours; and their peace doctrines are only communicated by them at leisure, as I imagine, to those disciples of theirs whom they want to make like themselves.

Theod. Disciples! my good sir, they have none; men of their sort are not one another's disciples, but they grow up at their own sweet will, and get their inspiration anywhere, each of them saying of his neighbour that he knows nothing. From these men, then, as I was going to remark, you will never get a reason, whether with their will or without their will; we must take the question out of their hands, and make the analysis ourselves, as if we were doing a geometrical problem.

Soc. Quite right too; but as touching the aforesaid problem, have we not heard from the ancients, who concealed their wisdom from the many in poetical figures, that Oceanus and Tethys, the origin of all things, are streams, and that nothing is at rest? And now the moderns, in their superior wisdom, have declared the same openly, that the cobbler too may hear and learn of them, and no longer foolishly imagine that some things are at rest and others in motion — having learned that all is motion, he will duly honour his teachers. But I had almost forgotten the opposite doctrine, Theodorus,

Alone Being remains unmoved, which is the name for the all.

This is the language of Parmenides, Melissus, and their followers, who stoutly maintain that all being is one and self-contained, and has no place in which to move. What shall we do, friend, with all these people; for, advancing step by step, we have imperceptibly got between the combatants, and, unless we can protect our retreat, we shall pay the penalty of our rashness — like the players in the palaestra who are caught upon the line, and are dragged different ways by the two parties. Therefore I think that we had better begin by considering those whom we first accosted, 'the river-gods,' and, if we find any truth in them, we will help them to pull us over, and try to get away from the others. But if the partisans of 'the whole' appear to speak more truly, we will fly off from the party which would move the immovable, to them. And if we find that neither of them have anything reasonable to say, we shall be in a ridiculous position, having so great a conceit of our own poor opinion and rejecting that of ancient and famous men. O Theodorus, do you think that there is any use in proceeding when the danger is so great?

Theod. Nay, Socrates, not to examine thoroughly what the two parties have to say would be quite intolerable.

Soc. Then examine we must, since you, who were so reluctant to begin, are so eager to proceed. The nature of motion appears to be the question with which we begin. What do they mean when they say that all things are in motion? That is to say, do they assert that there is only one kind of motion, or, as I think, two? I should like to have your opinion upon this point in addition to my own, that I may err, if I must err, in your company; tell me, then, when a thing changes from one place to another, or goes round in the same place, is not that what is called motion?

Theod. Yes.

Soc. Here then we have one kind of motion. But when a thing, remaining on the same spot, grows old, or becomes black from being white, or hard from being soft, or undergoes any other change, may not this be properly called motion of another kind?

Theod. I think it must be so called.

Soc. Of motion then there are these two kinds, 'change', and 'motion in place'.

Theod. You are right.

Soc. And now, having made this distinction, let us address ourselves to those who say that all is motion, and ask them whether all things according to them have the two kinds of motion, and are changed as well as move in place, or is one thing moved in both ways, and another in one only?

Theod. Indeed, I do not know what to answer; but I think they would say that all things are moved in both ways.

Soc. Yes, comrade; for, if not, they would have to say that the same things are in motion and at rest, and there would be no more truth in saying that all things are in motion, than that all things are at rest.

Theod. To be sure.

Soc. And if they are to be in motion, and nothing is to be devoid 182 of motion, all things must always have every sort of motion?

Theod. Most true.

Soc. Consider a further point: did we not understand them to explain the generation of heat, whiteness, or anything else, in some such manner as the following: — were they not saying that each of these is a movement which takes place at the time of perception between an agent and a patient, whereby the patient ceases to be a perceiving power and becomes a percipient, and the agent a quale instead of a quality? I suspect that quality may appear a strange and uncouth term to you, and that you do not understand the general expression. Then I will take particular instances: I mean to say that the producing power or agent becomes neither heat nor whiteness, but hot and white, and the like of other things. For I must repeat what I said before, that neither this agent and patient, nor anything else in the world, can exist in isolation, but when they come together and generate sensations and their objects, the one becomes a thing of a certain quality, and the other a percipient. You remember?

Theod. Of course.

Soc. We may leave the details of their theory unexamined, but we must not forget to ask them the only question with which we are concerned: Are all things in motion and flux?

Theod. Yes, they will reply.

Soc. And they are moved in both those ways which we distinguished; that is to say, they move in place and are also changed?

Theod. Of course, if the motion is to be perfect.

Soc. If they only moved in place and were not changed, we should be able to say what is the nature of the things which are in motion and flux?

Theod. Exactly.

Soc. But now, since not even white continues to flow white, and whiteness itself is a flux or change which is passing into another colour, and is never to be caught standing still, can the name of any colour be rightly used at all?

Theod. How is that possible, Socrates, either in the case of this or of any other quality — if while we are using the word the object is escaping in the flux?

Soc. And what would you say of perceptions, such as sight and hearing, or any other kind of perception? Is there any stopping in the act of seeing and hearing?

Theod. Certainly not, if all things are in motion.

Soc. Then we must not speak of seeing any more than of not-seeing, nor of any other perception more than of any non-perception, if all things partake of every kind of motion?

Theod. Certainly not.

Soc. Yet perception is knowledge: so at least Theaetetus and I were saying.

Theod. Very true.

Soc. Then when we were asked what is knowledge, we no more answered what is knowledge than what is not knowledge?

Theod. I suppose not.

183 *Soc.* Here, then, is a fine result: we corrected our first answer in our eagerness to prove that nothing is at rest and so save that answer. But now it is clear that if nothing is at rest, every answer upon whatever subject is equally right: you may say that a thing is or is not

thus; or, if you prefer, 'becomes' thus; and if we say 'becomes', we shall not then hamper them with words expressive of rest.

Theod. Quite true.

Soc. Yes, Theodorus, except in saying 'thus' and 'not thus'. But you ought not to use the word 'thus', for there is no motion in 'thus' or in 'not thus'. The maintainers of the doctrine have as yet no words in which to express themselves, and must get a new language. I might suggest to them the phrase 'no how', which being perfectly indefinite might suit them best.

Theod. Yes, that is a manner of speaking in which they will be quite at home.

Soc. And so, Theodorus, we have done with your friend without assenting to his doctrine, that every man is the measure of all things — a wise man only is a measure; neither can we allow that knowledge is perception, at least on the hypothesis of a perpetual flux; but perhaps our friend Theaetetus intends it in some other sense.

Theod. Very good, Socrates; and now that the argument about the doctrine of Protagoras has been completed, I am discharged from answering; for this was the agreement.

Theaet. Not, Theodorus, until you and Socrates have discussed the doctrine of those who say that all things are at rest, as you were proposing.

Theod. You, Theaetetus, who are a young rogue, must not instigate your elders to a breach of faith, but should prepare to answer Socrates in the remainder of the argument.

Theaet. Yes, if he wishes; but I would rather have heard about the doctrine of rest.

Theod. Invite Socrates to an argument — invite horsemen to the open plain; do but ask him, and he will answer.

Soc. Nevertheless, Theodorus, I am afraid that I shall not be able to comply with the request of Theaetetus.

Theod. Not comply! for what reason?

Soc. My reason is that I have a kind of reverence; not so much for Melissus and the others, who say that 'All is one and at rest', as for the great leader himself, Parmenides, venerable and awful, as in Homeric language he may be called; — him I should be ashamed to approach in a spirit unworthy of him. I met him when he was an old man, and I was a mere youth, and he appeared to me to have a 184 glorious depth of mind. And I am afraid that we may not understand his words, and may be still farther from understanding his meaning; above all I fear that the nature of knowledge, which is the main subject of our discussion, may be thrust out of sight by the unbidden guests who will come pouring in upon our feast of discourse, if we let them in — besides, the question which is now stirring is of immense extent, and will be treated unfairly if only considered by the way; or if treated adequately and at length, will put into the shade the other question of knowledge. Neither the one nor the other can be allowed; but I must try by my art of midwifery to deliver Theaetetus of his conceptions about knowledge.

Theaet. Very well; do so if you will.

Soc. Then now, Theaetetus, take another view of the subject: you answered that knowledge is perception?

Theaet. I did.

Soc. And if any one were to ask you: With what does a man see black and white colours? and with what does he hear high and low sounds? — you would say, if I am not mistaken, 'With the eyes and with the ears.'

Theaet. I should.

Soc. The free use of words and phrases, rather than minute precision, is generally characteristic of a liberal education, and the opposite is pedantic; but sometimes precision is necessary, and I believe that the answer which you have just given is open to the charge of incorrectness; for which is more correct, to say that we see or hear with the eyes and with the ears, or through the eyes and through the ears.

Theaet. I should say 'through', Socrates, rather than 'with'.

Soc. Yes, my boy, for no one can suppose that in each of us, as in a sort of Trojan horse, there are perched a number of unconnected senses, which do not all meet in some one nature, the soul or whatever we please to call it, of which they are the instruments, and with which through them we perceive objects of sense.

Theaet. I agree with you in that opinion.

Soc. The reason why I am thus precise is, because I want to know whether, when we perceive black and white through the eyes, and again, other qualities through other organs, we do not perceive them with one and the same part of ourselves; and whether, if you were asked, you could refer all such perceptions to the body. Perhaps, however, I had better allow you to answer for yourself and not interfere. Tell me, then, are not the organs through which you perceive warm and hard and light and sweet, organs of the body?

Theaet. Of the body, certainly.

185 *Soc.* And you would admit that what you perceive through one faculty you cannot perceive through another; the objects of hearing, for example, cannot be perceived through sight, or the objects of sight through hearing?

Theaet. Of course not.

Soc. If you have any thought about both of them, this common perception cannot come to you, either through the one or the other organ?

Theaet. It cannot.

Soc. How about sounds and colours: in the first place you may reflect that they both *exist*?

Theaet. Yes.

Soc. And that either of them is different from the other, and the same with itself?

Theaet. Certainly.

Soc. And that both are two and each of them one?

Theaet. Yes.

Soc. You can further observe whether they are like or unlike one another?

Theaet. I dare say.

Soc. But through what do you perceive all this about them? for neither through hearing nor yet through seeing can you apprehend that which they have in common. Let me give you an illustration of the point at issue: — If there were any meaning in asking whether sounds and colours are saline or not, you would be able to tell me what faculty would consider the question. It would not be sight or hearing, but some other.

Theaet. Certainly; the faculty of taste.

Soc. Very good; and now tell me what is the power which discerns, not only in sensible objects, but in all things, universal properties, such as those which are called being and not-being, and those others about which we were just asking — what organs will you assign for the perception of these by the appropriate power in us?

Theaet. You are thinking of being and not-being, likeness and unlikeness, sameness and difference, and also of unity and any other number which occurs in our judgement of objects. And evidently your question applies to odd and even numbers and other arithmetical conceptions — through what bodily organ the soul perceives them.

Soc. You follow me excellently, Theaetetus; that is precisely what I am asking.

Theaet. Indeed, Socrates, I cannot answer; my only notion is, that these, unlike objects of sense, have no separate organ, but that the mind, by a power of her own, contemplates such common properties in all things.

Soc. You are a beauty, Theaetetus, and not ugly, as Theodorus was saying; for he who utters the beautiful is himself beautiful and good. And besides being beautiful, you have done me a kindness in releasing me from a very long discussion, if you believe that the soul views some things by herself and others through the bodily organs. For that was my own opinion, and I wanted you to agree with me.

Theaet. Indeed, I do believe it.

186 *Soc.* And to which class would you refer being or essence; for this, of all our notions, is the most universal?

Theaet. I should say, to that class which the soul aspires to know of herself.

Soc. And would you say this also of like and unlike, same and other?

Theaet. Yes.

Soc. And would you say the same of the noble and base, and of good and evil?

Theaet. These also I conceive to be among the chief instances of those relative terms whose nature the soul perceives by comparing in herself things past and present with the future.

Soc. Hold! does she not perceive the hardness of that which is hard by the touch, and the softness of that which is soft equally by the touch?

Theaet. Yes.

Soc. But their *being*, I mean the fact that they are, and their opposition to one another, and the being (to repeat that term) of this opposition, the soul herself endeavours to decide for us by the review and comparison of them?

Theaet. Certainly.

Soc. The simple sensations which reach the soul through the body are given at birth to men and animals by nature, but their reflections on the being and use of them are slowly and hardly gained, if they are ever gained, by education and long experience.

Theaet. Assuredly.

Soc. And can a man attain truth who fails of attaining being?

Theaet. Impossible.

Soc. And can he who misses the truth of anything, have a knowledge of that thing?

Theaet. He cannot.

Soc. Then knowledge does not consist in impressions of sense, but in reasoning about them; in that only, and not in the mere impression, truth and being can be attained?

Theaet. Apparently.

Soc. And would you call the two processes by the same name, when there is so great a difference between them?

Theaet. That would certainly not be right.

Soc. And what name would you give to seeing, hearing, smelling, being cold and being hot?

Theaet. I should call all of them perceiving — what other name could be given to them?

Soc. Perception would be the collective name of them?

Theaet. Certainly.

Soc. Which, as we say, has no part in the attainment of truth, since it does not attain to being?

Theaet. Certainly not.

Soc. And therefore not in knowledge?

Theaet. No.

Soc. Then perception, Theaetetus, can never be the same as knowledge?

Theaet. Apparently not, Socrates; and knowledge has now been most distinctly proved to be different from perception.

❧ The claims of perception to be equated with knowledge have thus been finally dismissed. There follow some twenty Stephanus pages in which two other definitions of knowledge are considered. The first identifies knowledge with "true opinion," and there is a long discussion, but no general solution of the question, "How can false opinion exist?" In this section occurs Plato's famous image of the mind as a wax tablet upon which impressions are recorded, and another brilliant image of the mind as an aviary in which memories may be safely kept but fly about like birds and sometimes resist capture. True opinion is rejected as knowledge on the ground that it is capable of being derived from mere persuasion. There follows a subtle but fruitless attempt to prove knowledge the equivalent of "true opinion plus *logos* (explanation or definition)." But the ambiguity of the word *logos* leads the argument far afield and brings it finally to the tautology of asserting that "knowledge is right opinion plus a *knowledge* of some sort."

Omitting these pages we will be just in time to hear the conclusion of the whole matter, as voiced by the indefatigable son of a midwife who practices his mother's art:

Soc. And so, Theaetetus, knowledge is neither sensation nor true 210 opinion, nor yet definition and explanation accompanying and added to true opinion?

Theaet. I suppose not.

Soc. And are you still in labour and travail, my dear friend, or have you brought all that you have to say about knowledge to birth?

Theaet. I am sure, Socrates, that you have elicited from me a good deal more than ever was in me.

Soc. And does not my art show that you have brought forth wind, and that the offspring of your brain are not worth bringing up?

Theaet. Very true.

Soc. But if, Theaetetus, you should ever conceive afresh, you will be all the better for the present investigation, and if not, you will be soberer and humbler and gentler to other men, and will be too modest to fancy that you know what you do not know. These are the limits of my art; I can no further go, nor do I know aught of the things which great and famous men know or have known in this or former ages. The office of a midwife I, like my mother, have received from God; she delivered women, and I deliver men; but they must be young and noble and fair.

And now I have to go to the porch of the King Archon, where I am to meet Meletus and his indictment. Tomorrow morning, Theodorus, I shall hope to see you again at this place.

Sophist

Persons of the Dialogue

THEODORUS   **THEAETETUS**   **SOCRATES**

An ELEATIC STRANGER, whom Theodorus and Theaetetus bring
with them. The YOUNGER SOCRATES, who is a silent auditor.

❧ Written in Plato's later years, the *Sophist* is not acclaimed
as one of his more dramatic and inspiring works. It also displays
him seemingly attacking the whole group of those professional teachers
of well-to-do Athenians who were active in Plato's younger years.
Such an attack appears unfair, since these men included a number
who had important merit, and to some of whom Plato himself attributed a considerable measure of excellence. In this dialogue, in
fact, the so-called Sophist is no representative of a real group of men,
but an ideal of avoidance, the perfect charlatan in words, just as
Plato's guardians in the *Republic* are ideals of wisdom and justice.

Yet the dialogue can be read with interest as a well-contrived
argument, neatly organized, and it has sober logical excellences which
have been pointed out in our Introduction. Here we shall summarize
much of the argument; from the Platonic text we present only the
opening scene, the heart of the logical analysis, and the flourish of
demonstration at the end, in which Plato pretends to catch the elusive
Sophist in his net. This last short passage will serve also to illustrate
the method of definition by division. This method, not too felicitous
as it seems to us today, was evidently regarded by Plato as of great
worth, and was apparently used as an instructional device in the
Academy. We can see in it the early model from which Aristotle's
logical scheme of classification was derived.

The dialogue begins:

Theodorus. Here we are, Socrates, true to our agreement of yes- 216
terday; and we bring with us a stranger who is a native of Elea, and
a disciple of Parmenides and Zeno, a true philosopher.

Socrates. Is he not rather a god, Theodorus, who comes to us in
the disguise of a stranger? For Homer says that all the gods accompany such men as have any tinge of reverence and justice, and
that the god of hospitality, above all, takes note of men who disdain
or observe the law. And may not your companion be one of those
higher powers, a cross-examining deity, who has come to spy out
our weakness in argument, and to cross-examine us?

435

Theod. Nay, Socrates, he is not one of the disputatious sort — he is more reasonable. And, in my opinion, he is not a god at all; but divine he certainly is, for this is a title which I should give to all philosophers.

Soc. Capital, my friend! but I may add that you place him in a class which is almost as hard to discern as are the gods. For the true philosophers, and such as are not merely made up for the occasion, appear in various forms unrecognized by the ignorance of men, and they 'hover about cities', as Homer declares, looking from above upon human life; and some think nothing of them, and others can never think enough; and sometimes they appear as statesmen, and sometimes as sophists; and then, again, to many they seem to be no better than madmen. I should like to ask our Eleatic friend, if he would tell us, what is thought about them in Italy, and to whom the terms are applied?

Theod. What terms?

Soc. Sophist, statesman, philosopher.

Theod. What is your difficulty about them, and what made you ask?

Soc. I want to know whether by his countrymen they are regarded as one or two; or do they, as the names are three, distinguish also three kinds, and assign one to each name?

Theod. I dare say that the Stranger will not object to discuss the question. What do you say, Stranger?

Stranger. I am far from objecting, Theodorus, nor have I any difficulty in replying that by us they are regarded as three. But to define precisely the nature of each of them is by no means a slight or easy task.

&§ It is arranged that the inquiry shall be conducted by the method of question and answer, with Theaetetus providing the answers. Only the nature of the Sophist will be investigated at this time, and the attempt will be made to arrive at a detailed formula; for, the Stranger avers,

218 . . . at present we are only agreed about the name, but of the thing to which we both apply the name possibly you have one notion and I another; whereas we ought always to come to an understanding about the thing itself in terms of a definition, and not merely about the name minus the definition. Now the tribe of Sophists for which we propose now to go in search, is not the easiest of all to catch or define; and the world has long ago agreed, that in order to achieve success in some great exertion, it is best to practise in lesser and easier instances before we proceed to the greatest of all. And as we suspect that the tribe of Sophists is troublesome and hard to be caught, I should recommend

that we practise beforehand the method which is to be applied to them on some simple and smaller thing, unless you can suggest an easier way.

◄§ Theaetetus politely assures the visitor that he cannot and the Stranger proceeds. The "simple and smaller thing" turns out to be an angler; and the method, logical division. This method as here employed has some similarity to the old game of Animal, Vegetable, or Mineral. Instead, however, of gathering facts about the thing to be defined and then by induction establishing its identity, the present procedure consists in suggesting a highly general class to which the subject belongs and then in dividing and subdividing this class until a whole hierarchy of classes has been set up in all of which the subject has membership.

The Stranger first obtains Theaetetus' assent to the statement that the angler is a man possessing a skill or art. He then divides the arts into the productive, or creative, and the acquisitive; the angler's art is among the latter. The acquisitive arts are subdivided into two classes, purchasing and conquering; to this latter the angler is assigned. The process is continued, until finally after nine divisions the angler is reached. The Stranger sums up by listing in order all the characteristics that have been thus ascribed to the angler and claims thus to have fully identified him.

After this demonstration of the method, the Stranger applies it to the definition of the Sophist's art, with unexpected results: in short order, six definitions are produced, and the Sophist is credited with six different specific arts found in the subdivisions of hunting, importing, selling, producing, fighting, and separating. Such a result, the Stranger declares, indicates that an error has been made.

Making a new start, the Stranger points out as especially characteristic of the Sophist his claim to dispute successfully in every field and so to possess all arts. Such universal wisdom must be illusory. There is, however, an art which can, in a sense, do or make anything; this is the art of imitation, which includes the art of verbal imitation. The Sophist belongs here. Makers of images may produce true likenesses, or false appearances only. To which class shall the Sophist be assigned?

The Stranger pauses in dismay. The Sophist, he says, has taken refuge in a region where he and Theaetetus cannot follow. For the Sophist will deny that false images or even that falsehood in general can exist. There is indeed a problem here. For to assert that falsehood is, is seemingly to admit the being of not-being, and the great Parmenides long ago has warned us against such a delusion.

Plato is now beginning to approach the point of our special interest here, the problem of non- or not-being, to the solution of which he will bring his great powers of philosophical analysis. But first he will have the Stranger set forth some of the apparently formidable arguments current in his day against the possibility of making, saying, or thinking what is false. In presenting the arguments, Plato does not at all clarify the ambiguities on which they rest, and the reader must be content to let apparent proofs pass for the moment as valid, for the sake of their dramatic effect.

The Stranger asks first to what thing or things "not-being" may be attributed, or to what the term may be applied. He declares that plainly it cannot be applied to any being. Yet to speak of something apart from all being is impossible; we can speak only of some thing or some things. To say "not something," or to utter what is not, is not to speak at all. We must also, he says, assert that what is, cannot be attributed to not-being. Yet to speak of something which *is* not, or of things which *are* not, is to attribute number to not-being, and number undoubtedly exists. If we then admit that not-being is unspeakable and unthinkable, we again say that it is, and we again attribute number, since *is* is a singular verb.

Reverting to the Sophist, the Stranger says that unless some solution to these riddles can be found, our prey will escape us. For if we say that he is a maker of false images, or even of images, the Sophist will reply that a mere resemblance is not truly the thing itself, and so is not true or real. If we say that he makes us think falsely, he will say that this would be to make us think that what is, is not, or that what is not, is; and since we have ourselves admitted that being cannot be attributed to non-being or non-being to being, he will justly accuse us of self-contradiction.

Yet the Stranger is unwilling to surrender to such arguments. Instead, he says that, greatly daring, he will venture to test the chief tenet of his "father Parmenides," and will attempt to show that in a sense not-being is and that being is not.

The Stranger proposes now to show that it is not only about not-being that confusion of thought exists. Reviewing briefly the doctrines of the great philosophers of an earlier day and those of their contemporary followers and opponents, he shows that objections can be raised against all. If the universe is seen as arising out of two or more elements or kinds of being, such as the hot and the cold, which by their commingling are said to have created our world, then since both kinds are said to be, they coalesce into one, which is being. If it is held that all is One, as Parmenides maintained, it can be shown that there are at least two names, One and Being, and furthermore that if even one name exists, besides the One itself, multiplicity has been acknowledged; and if the One is a whole, that it has parts.

The materialists, he says, can be convicted of having admitted the existence of two kinds if they can be induced to admit, as they surely must, that any non-material thing such as justice exists and is real. The friends of the Ideas will assert that only the eternal, changeless Ideas are or compose being, and that the Ideas can neither affect anything nor be affected; they will say that change and motion belong only to becoming. But such views will imply that being is mindless and lifeless, and since it cannot be affected, that it cannot be known.

Such a conclusion is intolerable, the Stranger declares, and it will be necessary for him and Theaetetus to hold that both motion and rest exist; but such a doctrine will precipitate them into the difficulties of those earlier thinkers who saw the universe as arising from the hot and the cold: the two elements or kinds will coalesce into being.

Since, therefore, the current notions of being are as confused as those of not-being, the Stranger proposes now to attack directly the problem of being, in the hope of clarifying at the same time that of not-being. He establishes first that we may attribute to any one thing many qualities or characteristics, as when we say that a man is good or has any other attribute. In fact, no statement can be made without implying that one thing participates in another. Thus both motion and rest can be said to *be*, and thus to participate in being. But not all things participate in one another: motion cannot be at rest. Thus we must say that some classes intermingle and others do not. The person who has the science or knowledge which tells which classes intermingle, who can divide by classes and see one form pervading many lower forms and many lower forms contained in one higher form, while other forms exist only in separation, — such a person is the philosopher. But to find the Sophist we must continue our investigation of being.

The Stranger will now at last present Plato's proposed solution to the riddle of not-being:

Str. Since, then, we are agreed that some classes have a communion 254 with one another, and others not, and some have communion with a few and others with many, and that there is no reason why some should not have universal communion with all, let us now pursue the inquiry, as the argument suggests, not in relation to all Ideas, lest the multitude of them should confuse us, but let us select a few of those which are reckoned to be the principal ones, and consider their several natures and their capacity of communion with one another, in order that if we are not able to apprehend with perfect clearness the notions of being and not-being, we may at least not fall short in the consideration of them, so far as they come within the scope of the present inquiry, if peradventure we may be allowed to assert that there is something which really is not, and yet escape unscathed.

Theaet. We must do so.

Str. The most important of those genera which we have recently discussed are being itself and rest and motion.

Theaet. Yes, by far.

Str. And two of these are, as we affirm, incapable of communion with one another.

Theaet. Quite incapable.

Str. Whereas being surely has communion with both of them, for both of them are?

Theaet. Of course.

Str. That makes up three of them.

Theaet. To be sure.

Str. And each of them is other than the remaining two, but the same with itself.

Theaet. True.

Str. But then, what is the meaning of these two words, 'same' and 'other'? Are they two new kinds other than the three, and yet always of necessity intermingling with them, so that we must inquire into five kinds instead of three; or when we speak of the same and 255 other, are we unconsciously speaking of one of the three first kinds?

Theaet. Very likely we are.

Str. But, surely, motion and rest are neither the other nor the same.

Theaet. How is that?

Str. Whatever we attribute to motion and rest in common, cannot be either of them.

Theaet. Why not?

Str. Because motion would be at rest and rest in motion, for either of them, being predicated of both, will compel the other to change into the opposite of its own nature, because partaking of its opposite.

Theaet. Quite true.

Str. Yet they surely both partake of the same and of the other?

Theaet. Yes.

Str. Then we must not assert that motion, any more than rest, is either the same or the other.

Theaet. No; we must not.

Str. But are we to conceive that being and the same are identical?

Theaet. Possibly.

Str. But if 'being' and 'the same' in no way differ in meaning, then again in saying that motion and rest have being, we should also be saying that they are the same.

Theaet. Which surely cannot be.

Str. Then being and the same cannot be one.

Theaet. Scarcely.

Str. Then we may suppose the same to be a fourth class, which is now to be added to the three others.

Theaet. Quite true.

Str. And shall we call the other a fifth class? Or should we consider being and other to be two names of the same class?

Theaet. Very likely.

Str. But you would agree, if I am not mistaken, that there are two classes of things, some which exist in their own right, and others which are only said to *be* in relation to something else.

Theaet. Certainly.

Str. And other is one of those terms which are always relative to an other?

Theaet. True.

Str. But this would not be the case unless there were a vast difference between being and the other; for, if the other, like being, belonged to both classes, then there would have been a kind of other which was not other than other. As it is, we find simply that whatever is other must of necessity be what it is in relation to some other.

Theaet. That is the true state of the case.

Str. Then we must admit the other as the fifth of our selected classes.

Theaet. Yes.

Str. And we shall say that this is one which has penetrated all the remainder. For each severally is *other* than the rest, not by reason of its own nature, but because it has some share in the form of otherness.

Theaet. Quite true.

Str. Then let us now put the case with reference to each of the five.

Theaet. How?

Str. First there is motion, which we affirm to be absolutely 'other' than rest: what else can we say?

Theaet. It is so.

Str. And therefore is not rest.

Theaet. Certainly not.

Str. And yet is, because partaking of being.

Theaet. True.

Str. Again, motion is other than the same?

Theaet. Just so.

Str. And is therefore not the same.

Theaet. It is not.

Str. Yet, surely, motion was declared to be the same, because all things partake of sameness.

Theaet. Very true.

Str. Then we must admit, without grumbling, the statement that motion is the same and yet not the same; for when we apply these expressions to it, our point of view is different. We call it the same in relation to itself, because it partakes of sameness; whereas we call it not the same because, having communion with otherness, it is thereby severed from the same, and has become not that but other; so that it is with equal justice spoken of as 'not the same'.

Theaet. To be sure.

Str. Likewise if movement *per se* in any point of view partook of rest, there would be no absurdity in calling motion stationary.

256

Theaet. Quite right, — that is, on the supposition that some classes mingle with one another, and others not.

Str. That such a communion of kinds is according to nature, we had already proved before we arrived at this part of our discussion.

Theaet. Certainly.

Str. Let us proceed, then. May we not say that motion is other than the other, having been also proved by us to be other than the same and other than rest?

Theaet. That is certain.

Str. Then, according to this view, motion is other and also not other?

Theaet. True.

Str. What is the next step? Shall we say that motion is other than the three and not other than the fourth, — for we agreed that there are five classes about and in the sphere of which we proposed to make inquiry?

Theaet. Surely we cannot admit that the number is less than it appeared to be just now.

Str. Then we may without fear contend that motion is other than being?

Theaet. Without the least fear.

Str. The plain result is that motion, since it partakes of being, really is and also is not?

Theaet. Nothing can be plainer.

Str. Then not-being necessarily exists in the case of motion and of every class; for the nature of the other entering into them all makes each of them other than being, and so non-existent; and therefore of all of them, in like manner, we may truly say that they are not; and again, inasmuch as they partake of being, that they are and are existent.

Theaet. So we may assume.

Str. Every class, then, has plurality of being and infinity of not-being.

257 *Theaet.* So we must infer.

Str. And being itself may be said to be other than the other kinds.

Theaet. Certainly.

Str. Then we may infer that being is not, in respect of as many other things as there are; for not being these it is itself one, and is not the other things, which are infinite in number.

Theaet. That is not far from the truth.

Str. And we must not quarrel with this result, since it is of the nature of classes to have communion with one another; and if anyone denies our present statement [viz. that being is not, &c.], let him first argue with our former conclusion [i.e. respecting the communion of Ideas], and then he may proceed to argue with what follows.

Theaet. Nothing can be fairer.

◆§ The Stranger next brings arguments to support two further assertions. The first is that when a thing is said not to be something, as we may say it is not large, we do not assert that it is the opposite of that thing; it may not be small, but merely other than large. The second is that what is other than something has as much reality as that from which it differs; what is not beautiful is as real as what is beautiful.

He declares that he has now gone beyond Parmenides' prohibition, and sums up his findings:

Str. Let not anyone say, then, that the not-being, of which we venture to affirm the real existence, is the contrary of being. For as to whether there is an opposite of being, to that inquiry we have long said good-bye — it may or may not be, and may or may not be capable of definition. But as touching our present account of not-being, let a man either convince us of error, or, so long as he cannot, he too must say, as we are saying, that there is a communion of classes, and that being, and difference or other, traverse all things and mutually interpenetrate, so that the other partakes of being, and by reason of this participation *is*, and yet is not that of which it partakes, but other, and if it is other than being, it is clearly a necessity that it should be not-being. And again, being, through partaking of the other, becomes a class other than the remaining classes, and being other than all of them, is not each one of them, and is not all the rest, so that undoubtedly there are thousands upon thousands of cases in which being is not, and all other things, whether regarded individually or collectively, in many respects are, and in many respects are not.

◆§ Having shown that not-being is, the Stranger returns to the imagined assertions of the Sophist that images or imitations are unreal and hence cannot exist, and that false statements cannot be made or false beliefs entertained.

He exclaims that he and Theaetetus are fortunate in having established the fact that classes may intermingle, since reasoned discourse depends upon such admixture. They can also hope now to show that not-being mingles with language and thought.

He declares that all discourse consists of sentences, and further that every sentence must have at least a subject — a word denoting an agent, and a verb — a word denoting action. Some sentences assert about the subject what is, and as it is, and are true; an example is "Theaetetus sits." Others assert about the subject what is other than real, as if it were real, and are false; an example is "Theaetetus flies." Since there is much in relation to every subject which is other than real, false discourse is eminently possible.

Furthermore, opinion is nothing but unuttered speech, and imagination or perception is opinion presented to the mind by the help of the senses. Therefore these, too, can be false. Thus the Sophist's escape has been cut off, and the Stranger now confidently resumes the hunt.

264 *Str.* Then let us not be discouraged about the future; but now having made this discovery, let us go back to our previous classification.

Theaet. What classification?

Str. We divided image-making into two sorts; the one likeness-making, the other imaginative or phantastic.

Theaet. True.

Str. And we said that we were uncertain in which we should place the Sophist.

Theaet. We did say so.

Str. And our heads began to go round more and more when it was asserted that there is no such thing as an image or idol or appearance, because in no manner or time or place can there ever be such a thing as falsehood.

Theaet. True.

Str. But now, since there has been shown to be false speech and false opinion, there may be imitations of real existences, and out of this condition of the mind an art of deception may arise.

Theaet. Quite possible.

Str. And we have already admitted, in what preceded, that the Sophist was lurking in one of the divisions of the likeness-making art?

Theaet. Yes.

Str. Let us, then, renew the attempt, and in dividing any class, always take the part to the right, holding fast to that which holds the

265 Sophist, until we have stripped him of all his common properties, and reached his differentia or characteristic. Then we may exhibit him in his true nature, first to ourselves and then to kindred dialectical spirits.

Theaet. Very good.

Str. You may remember that all art was originally divided by us into creative and acquisitive.

Theaet. Yes.

Str. And the Sophist was flitting before us in the acquisitive class, in the subdivisions of hunting, contests, merchandise, and the like.

Theaet. Very true.

Str. But now that the imitative art has enclosed him, it is clear that we must begin by dividing the art of creation; for imitation is a kind of creation — of images, however, as we affirm, and not of real things.

Theaet. Quite true.

Str. In the first place, there are two kinds of creation.

Theaet. What are they?

Str. One of them is human and the other divine.

Theaet. I do not follow.

Str. Every power, as you may remember our saying originally, which causes things to exist, not previously existing, was defined by us as creative.

Theaet. I remember.

Str. Looking, now, at the world and all the animals and plants, at things which grow upon the earth from seeds and roots, as well as at inanimate substances which are formed within the earth, fusile or non-fusile, shall we say that they come into existence — not having existed previously — by the creation of God, or shall we agree with vulgar opinion about them?

Theaet. What is it?

Str. The opinion that nature brings them into being from some spontaneous and unintelligent cause. Or shall we say that they are created by a divine reason and a knowledge which comes from God?

Theaet. I myself, perhaps owing to my youth, often waver in my view, but now when I look at you and see that you incline to refer them to God, I defer to your authority.

Str. Nobly said, Theaetetus, and if I thought that you were one of those who would hereafter change your mind, I would have gently argued with you, and forced you to assent; but as I perceive that you will come of yourself and without any argument of mine, to that belief which, as you say, attracts you, I will not forestall the work of time. Let me suppose, then, that things which are said to be made by nature are the work of divine art, and that things which are composed by man out of these are works of human art. And so there are two kinds of making and production, the one human and the other divine.

Theaet. True.

Str. Then, now, subdivide each of the two sections which we have already.

Theaet. How do you mean?

Str. I mean to say that you should make a vertical division of 266 production or invention, as you have already made a lateral one.

Theaet. I have done so.

Str. Then, now, there are in all four parts or segments — two of them have reference to us and are human, and two of them have reference to the gods and are divine.

Theaet. True.

Str. And, again, in the division which was supposed to be made in the other way, one part in each subdivision is the making of the things themselves, but the two remaining parts may most properly be called the making of images; and so the productive art is again divided into two parts.

Theaet. Tell me the divisions once more.

Str. I suppose that we, and the other animals, and the elements out of which things are made — fire, water, and the like — are known by us to be each and all the creation and work of God.

Theaet. True.

Str. And there are images of them, which are not them, but which correspond to them; and these are also the creation of a wonderful skill.

Theaet. What are they?

Str. The appearances which spring up of themselves in sleep or by day, such as a shadow when darkness arises in a fire, or the reflection which is produced when the light in bright and smooth objects meets on their surface with an external light, and creates a perception the opposite of our ordinary sight.

Theaet. Yes; it is true that there are these two products of divine art, the object and the corresponding image.

Str. And what shall we say of human art? Do we not make one house by the art of building, and another by the art of drawing, which is a sort of dream created by man for those who are awake?

Theaet. Quite true.

Str. And other products of human creation are also twofold and go in pairs; there is the thing [with which the art of making the thing is concerned], and the image [with which imitation is concerned.]

Theaet. Now I begin to understand, and am ready to acknowledge that there are two kinds of production, and each of them twofold; in the lateral division there is both a divine and a human production; in the vertical there are realities and a creation of a kind of similitudes.

Str. And let us recall to mind that of the image-making class the one part was to have been likeness-making, and the other phantastic, if it could be shown that falsehood is a reality and belongs to the class of real being.

Theaet. Yes.

Str. And this appeared to be the case; and therefore now, without hesitation, we shall number the different kinds as two.

Theaet. True.

Str. Then, now, let us proceed to divide the phantastic art into two. 267

Theaet. Where shall we make the division?

Str. There is one kind which is produced by an instrument, and another in which the creator of the appearance is himself the instrument.

Theaet. What do you mean?

Str. When anyone, by the use of his own body, makes his figure or his voice appear to resemble yours, imitation is the usual name for this part of the phantastic art.

Theaet. Yes.

Str. Let this, then, be named the art of mimicry, and this the province assigned to it; as for the other division, we are weary and will give that up, leaving to someone else the duty of making the class and giving it a suitable name.

Theaet. Let us do as you say — assign a sphere to the one and leave the other.

Str. There is a further distinction, Theaetetus, which is worthy of our consideration, and for a reason which I will tell you.

Theaet. Let me hear.

Str. There are some who imitate, knowing what they imitate, and some who do not know. And what line of distinction can there possibly be greater than that which divides ignorance from knowledge?

Theaet. There can be no greater.

Str. Was not the sort of imitation of which we spoke just now the imitation of those who know? For he who would imitate you would surely know you and your figure?

Theaet. Naturally.

Str. And what would you say of the figure or form of justice or of virtue in general? Are we not well aware that many, having no knowledge of either, but only a sort of opinion, try hard to make it seem that they *have* the thing about which they hold this opinion, and zealously express it, as far as they can, in word and deed?

Theaet. Yes, that is very common.

Str. And do they always fail in their attempt to be thought just, when they are not? Or is not the very opposite true?

Theaet. The very opposite.

Str. Such a one, then, should be described as an imitator — to be distinguished from the other, as he who is ignorant is distinguished from him who knows?

Theaet. True.

Str. Can we find a suitable name for each of them? This is clearly not an easy task; for among the ancients, it would seem, there was some laziness and confusion of ideas, which prevented them from even making the attempt to divide genera into species; wherefore there is no great abundance of names. Yet, for the sake of distinctness, I will make bold to call the imitation which is accompanied by opinion, the imitation of appearance — that which is accompanied by knowledge, an 'historical'[1] sort of imitation.

Theaet. Granted.

Str. The former is our present concern, for the Sophist was classed with imitators indeed, but not among those who have knowledge.

Theaet. Very true.

Str. Let us, then, examine our imitator of appearance, and see whether he is sound, like a piece of iron, or whether there is still some crack in him.

Theaet. Let us examine him.

Str. Indeed there is a very considerable crack; for if you look, you find that one of the two classes of imitators is a simple creature, who thinks that he knows that which he only fancies; the other sort has knocked about among arguments, until he suspects and fears that he is ignorant of that which to others he pretends to know.

Theaet. There are certainly the two kinds which you describe.

Str. Shall we regard one as the simple imitator — the other as the dissembling or ironical imitator?

Theaet. Very suitable.

Str. And shall we further speak of this latter class as having one or two divisions?

Theaet. Answer yourself.

Str. Upon consideration, then, there appear to me to be two; there is the dissembler who harangues a multitude in public in a long speech, and the dissembler who in private and in short speeches compels the person who is conversing with him to contradict himself.

Theaet. What you say is most true.

Str. And what place shall we assign to the maker of the longer speeches? Is he the statesman or the popular orator?

Theaet. The latter.

Str. And what shall we call the other? Is he the philosopher or the Sophist?

Theaet. The philosopher he cannot be, for upon our view he is ignorant; but since he is an imitator of the wise he will have a name which is formed by an adaptation of the word σοφός [*sophos*, wise]. What shall we name him? I am pretty sure that I cannot be mistaken in terming him the true and very Sophist.

Str. Shall we bind up his name as we did before, making a chain from one end of his genealogy to the other?

---

1 [Plato connects the noun ἱστορία (*historia*), inquiry, with the adjective ἵστωρ (*histōr*), learned or knowing.]

Theaet. By all means.

Str. He, then, who traces the pedigree of his art as follows — who, belonging to the conscious or dissembling section of the art of causing self-contradiction, is an imitator of appearance, and is separated from the class of phantastic which is a branch of image-making into that further division of creation, the juggling of words, a creation human, and not divine — anyone who affirms the real Sophist to be of this blood and lineage will say the very truth.

Theaet. Undoubtedly.

Timaeus

Persons of the Dialogue

SOCRATES	CRITIAS
TIMAEUS	HERMOCRATES

◄§ Certain features of the *Timaeus,* in contrast with Plato's other writings, require initial notice. The metaphor which Jowett has used of it, if not taken as entailing radical changes in Plato's philosophical outlook, is a happy one. The *Timaeus* is, indeed, "a detached building in a different style, framed not after the Socratic, but after some Pythagorean model."[1] In point of fact it is not even a dialogue, save for the introduction making up one sixth of the whole. Its main body is the monologue spoken continuously by Timaeus (*alias* Plato, in a preponderantly Pythagorean mood). There is little in his discourse of argument, much of high solemn exposition akin to revelation. It is a fusion of science and symbolism, a hymn to the universe, and in it, in spite of its burden of sometimes tedious detail, Plato has achieved an unquestionable "persuasion" over the stubbornness of his materials; in this he resembles Lucretius, in a later age. The *Timaeus,* then, is a prose poem whose varied rhythms and balanced structure prompted Paul Shorey to liken it to the movement of a Pindaric ode.

There is, however, another theme (or sub-theme) which Plato has interwoven with his cosmology and with the social system of the *Republic,* to form a gigantic but, alas, never completed whole. This is the colorful and, through the centuries, much debated myth (or legend) of "the lost island" of Atlantis. The content and import of this myth, commonly regarded among scholars as a product of Plato's own historical and moral imagination, will be given brief consideration below, before we introduce the discourse of Timaeus.

Among the persons of the dialogue we find again Socrates. It would be an affront to the reader at this late time to offer him a definition of the bearer of this name in the Platonic dialogues, but it is worth considering how much of the historical "gadfly of Athens" is still audible here. Another figure is Critias, who is almost certainly not the leader of the Thirty Tyrants, mentioned in our introductory account of Plato's life, but rather his aging grandfather, bearer of the same name. Hermocrates, on good evidence, has been identified with the Sicilian statesman and victorious naval commander of whom the historian Thucydides has praiseful words to say. And Timaeus, the central figure? We hear nothing of him elsewhere, a fact most easily

[1] Introduction to *Timaeus,* Jowett, Fourth Edition, III, 633. (L)

explained by assuming that, in spite of Socrates' complimentations and Timaeus' own eloquent speech, he probably is only a brain-child of Plato.

From the opening pages of the dialogue we learn that on the previous day Socrates had "entertained" the same group of distinguished persons by an account of the social and political features of the *Republic*. It is now, he suggests, time for Critias and the others to "stand treat." He will tell them the form of entertainment that would please him most: he desires to see the citizens of his yesterday's discourse not at rest, as he had depicted them, but engaged in noble action, showing themselves, on the field of battle and in their parleying with other states, worthy of the education and nurture they have received. This portrayal, Socrates admits, is beyond his powers, but it is also beyond those of the poets past and present and of the wandering tribe of Sophists, the reason being in all three cases the same: the lack of capacity and experience in the joint fields of politics and philosophy. One class of men alone remains, he declares, that represented by the three men he is addressing, all of whom have effectively combined philosophy and politics.

Hermocrates, speaking for the first and last time in Plato's theater, proposes that Critias should submit to Socrates' approval a very old tale that Critias' grandfather, in his high age, had told him when a boy, having himself heard it from the lips of the wisest of the seven sages, the Athenian lawgiver and poet Solon. The tale runs thus:

In the Egyptian Delta, at the head of which the river Nile divides, 21 there is a certain district which is called the district of Sais, and the great city of the district is also called Sais, and is the city from which King Amasis came. The citizens have a deity for their foundress; she is called in the Egyptian tongue Neith, and is asserted by them to be the same whom the Hellenes call Athene; they are great lovers of the Athenians, and say that they are in some way related to them. To this city came Solon, and was received there with great 22 honour; he asked the priests who were most skilful in such matters about antiquity, and made the discovery that neither he nor any other Hellene knew anything worth mentioning about the times of old. On one occasion, wishing to draw them on to speak of antiquity, he began to tell about the most ancient things in our part of the world — about Phoroneus, who is called 'the first man', and about Niobe; and after the Deluge, of the survival of Deucalion and Pyrrha; and he traced the genealogy of their descendants, and reckoning up the dates, tried to compute how many years ago the events of which he was speaking happened. Thereupon one of the priests, who was of a very great age, said: O Solon, Solon, you Hellenes are never anything but children, and there is not an old man among you. Solon in return asked him what he meant. I mean to say, he replied, that in mind you are all young; there is no old opinion handed down among you by ancient tradition, nor any science which is hoary with age. And I will tell you why. There have been, and will be again, many destructions of mankind arising out of many causes; the greatest have been brought about by the agencies of fire and water, and other lesser ones by innumerable other causes. There is a story, which even you have preserved, that once upon a time Phaëthon, the son of Helios, having yoked the steeds in his father's chariot, because he was not able to drive them in the path of his father, burnt up all that was upon the earth, and was himself destroyed by a thunderbolt. Now this has the form of a myth, but really signifies a declination of the bodies moving in the heavens around the earth, and a great conflagration of things upon the earth, which recurs after long intervals; at such times those who live upon the mountains and in dry and lofty places are more liable to destruction than those who dwell by rivers or on the sea-shore. And from this calamity we are preserved by the liberation of the Nile, who is our never-failing saviour. When, on the other hand, the gods purge the earth with a deluge of water, the survivors in your country are herdsmen and shepherds who dwell on the mountains, but those who, like you, live in cities are carried by the rivers into the sea. Whereas in this land, neither then nor at any other time, does the water come down from above on the fields, having always a tendency to come up from below; for which reason the traditions preserved here are the most ancient. The fact is, that wherever the extremity of winter frost or of summer sun does not prevent, mankind exist, sometimes in

23 greater, sometimes in lesser numbers. And whatever happened either in your country or in ours, or in any other region of which we are informed — if there were any action noble or great or in any other way remarkable, they have all been written down by us of old, and are preserved in our temples. Whereas just when you and other nations are beginning to be provided with letters and the other requisites of civilized life, after the usual interval, the stream from heaven, like a pestilence, comes pouring down, and leaves only those of you who are destitute of letters and education; and so you have to begin all over again like children, and know nothing of what happened in ancient times, either among us or among yourselves. As for those genealogies of yours which you just now recounted to us, Solon, they are no better than the tales of children. In the first place you remember a single deluge only, but there were many previous ones; in the next place, you do not know that there formerly dwelt in your land the fairest and noblest race of men which ever lived, and that you and your whole city are descended from a small seed or remnant of them which survived. And this was unknown to you,

because, for many generations, the survivors of that destruction died, leaving no written word. For there was a time, Solon, before the great deluge of all, when the city which now is Athens was first in war and in every way the best governed of all cities, and is said to have performed the noblest deeds and to have had the fairest constitution of any of which tradition tells, under the face of heaven. Solon marvelled at his words, and earnestly requested the priests to inform him exactly and in order about these former citizens. You are welcome to hear about them, Solon, said the priest, both for your own sake and for that of your city, and above all, for the sake of the goddess who is the common patron and parent and educator of both our cities. She founded your city a thousand years before ours,[1] receiving from the Earth and Hephaestus the seed of your race, and afterwards she founded ours, of which the constitution is recorded in our sacred registers to be 8,000 years old. As touching your citizens of 9,000 years ago, I will briefly inform you of their laws and of their most famous action; the exact particulars of the whole we will here- 24 after go through at our leisure in the sacred registers themselves. If you compare these very laws with ours you will find that many of ours are the counterpart of yours as they were in the olden time. In the first place, there is the caste of priests, which is separated from all the others; next, there are the artificers, who ply their several crafts by themselves and do not intermix; and also there is the class of shepherds and of hunters, as well as that of husbandmen; and you will observe, too, that the warriors in Egypt are distinct from all the other classes, and are commanded by the law to devote themselves solely to military pursuits; moreover, the weapons which they carry are shields and spears, a style of equipment which the goddess taught of Asiatics first to us, as in your part of the world first to you. Then as to wisdom, do you observe how our law from the very first made a study of the whole order of things, extending even to prophecy and medicine which gives health; out of these divine elements deriving what was needful for human life, and adding every sort of knowledge which was akin to them. All this order and arrangement the goddess first imparted to you when establishing your city; and she chose the spot of earth in which you were born, because she saw that the happy temperament of the seasons in that land would produce the wisest of men. Wherefore the goddess, who was a lover both of war and of wisdom, selected and first of all settled that spot which was the most likely to produce men most like herself. And there you dwelt, having such laws as these and still better ones, and excelled all mankind in all virtue, as became the children and disciples of the gods.

[1] Observe that Plato gives the same date (9,000 years ago) for the foundation of Athens and for the repulse of the invasion from Atlantis. (*Crit.* 108c.)

Many great and wonderful deeds are recorded of your state in our histories. But one of them exceeds all the rest in greatness and valour. For these histories tell of a mighty power which unprovoked made an expedition against the whole of Europe and Asia, and to which your city put an end. This power came forth out of the Atlantic Ocean, for in those days the Atlantic was navigable; and there was an island situated in front of the straits which are by you 25 called the pillars of Heracles; the island was larger than Libya and Asia put together, and was the way to other islands, and from these you might pass to the whole of the opposite continent which surrounded the true ocean; for this sea which is within the Straits of Heracles is only a harbour, having a narrow entrance, but that other is a real sea, and the land surrounding it on every side may be most truly called a boundless continent. Now in this island of Atlantis there was a great and wonderful empire which had rule over the whole island and several others, and over parts of the continent, and, furthermore, the men of Atlantis had subjected the parts of Libya within the columns of Heracles as far as Egypt, and of Europe as far as Tyrrhenia. This vast power, gathered into one, endeavoured to subdue at a blow our country and yours and the whole of the region within the straits; and then, Solon, your country shone forth, in the excellence of her virtue and strength, among all mankind. She was pre-eminent in courage and military skill, and was the leader of the Hellenes. And when the rest fell off from her, being compelled to stand alone, after having undergone the very extremity of danger, she defeated and triumphed over the invaders, and preserved from slavery those who were not yet subjugated, and generously liberated all the rest of us who dwell within the pillars. But afterwards there occurred violent earthquakes and floods; and in a single day and night of misfortune all your warlike men in a body sank into the earth, and the island of Atlantis in like manner disappeared in the depths of the sea. For which reason the sea in those parts is impassable and impenetrable, because there is a shoal of mud in the way; and this was caused by the subsidence of the island. . . .

ᗖᔄ This tale, if approved, Critias is willing to narrate at full length and in detail, telling of the epic struggle between ancestral Athens and the island empire of Atlantis. And in so doing he proposes to "transfer to the world of reality" the city and citizens whom Socrates "yesterday [had] described . . . in fiction."ᴶ But in the interest of coherent order Critias' speech must wait, as he himself informs us:

27 Let me proceed to explain to you, Socrates, the order in which we have arranged our entertainment. Our intention is, that Timaeus, who is the most of an astronomer amongst us, and has made the

nature of the universe his special study, should speak first, beginning with the generation of the world and going down to the creation of man; next, I am to receive the men whom he has created, and of whom some will have profited by the excellent education which you have given them; and then, in accordance with the tale of Solon, and equally with his law, we will bring them into court and make them citizens, as if they were those very Athenians whom the sacred Egyptian record has recovered from oblivion, and thenceforward we will speak of them as Athenians and fellow citizens.

●§ Socrates is charmed. Reverting to his initial metaphor of "entertainment," he looks forward to the luxury of being the guest at the "feast of reason" that others will prepare. "And now, Timaeus, you, I suppose, should speak next, after duly calling upon the Gods."J And the *Timaeus* proper begins.

●§ It may be asked what will happen to Critias' narrative: Did Plato remember and keep his word? Let the truly interested reader possess himself of a translation of Plato's *Critias*. There he will meet Timaeus, who has just ended his discourse, and is more than willing to hand over the controls, as agreed, to Critias. (It is implied by Socrates that Hermocrates will make his contribution when Critias is done, but Plato has given us no hint of its content.) So now are we about to hear the detailed inside story for which we have waited so long? Well, the promise is at any rate kept to the extent of some sixteen Stephanus pages, in which we are given an account of the culture patterns of the two mighty rivals as of 9,000 years before Solon. We are told first of the glory that was ancestral Athens, leader of the Hellenes, "a just and famous race celebrated for their beauty and virtue all over Europe and Asia."J Then follows a vivid portrayal of Atlantis, its intricate plan of construction, its canals, harbors, docks, outer walls and magnificent palaces "flashing with the light of orichalcum," and "Poseidon's own temple which was covered with silver, and the pinnacles with gold."J We hear too of its equally intricate government: ten kings, each vested with absolute power within his own domain.

For many generations, we are told, the citizens of Atlantis were obedient to the precepts of their sponsoring god, Poseidon, but at last the divine element in their soul became diluted and they began, not yet with outward sign, to degenerate.

. . . being unable to bear their fortune, they behaved unseemly, and 121 to him who had an eye to see grew visibly debased, for they were losing the fairest of their precious gifts; but to those who had no eye to see the true happiness, they appeared glorious and blessed at the very time when they were becoming tainted with unrighteous ambition and power. Zeus, the god of gods, who rules according to law, and is able to see into such things, perceiving that an honourable race was in a woeful plight, and wanting to inflict punishment on them that they might be chastened and improve, collected all the gods into their most holy habitation, which, being placed in the centre of the world, beholds all created things. And when he called them together, he spake as follows: —

>≈ Here the *Critias* abruptly ends: it is a mere fragment, never completed. It would be an interesting flight of the controlled imagination to begin where Zeus left off and finish Plato's story. But we have delayed Timaeus and his account of the nature and origin of the universe for long enough.

>≈ Timaeus begins by addressing a prayer to God, and to gods and goddesses, to aid him in speaking acceptably, and goes on to distinguish two natures, first the eternal and changeless, which is apprehended by reason, and second that which is generated and perishes, but never really is, which is known only by opinion and by the senses. He says that the world, being visible and tangible, must be a created thing and that it is the fairest of created things; in framing it, "the father of this all" must have looked to an eternal pattern. But we cannot tell of the creation or the creature with certainty: being but men, speaking to men, we can tell only a probable tale.

Socrates accepts this preamble, and Timaeus continues:

29 Let me tell you then why the creator made this world of generation. He was good, and the good can never have any jealousy of anything.
30 And being free from jealousy, he desired that all things should be as like himself as they could be. This is in the truest sense the origin of creation and of the world, as we shall do well in believing on the testimony of wise men: God desired that all things should be good and nothing bad, so far as this was attainable. Wherefore also finding the whole visible sphere not at rest, but moving in an irregular and disorderly fashion, out of disorder he brought order, considering that this was in every way better than the other. Now the deeds of the best could never be or have been other than the fairest; and the creator, reflecting on the things which are by nature visible, found that no unintelligent creature taken as a whole could ever be fairer than the intelligent taken as a whole; and again that intelligence could not be present in anything which was devoid of soul. For which reason, when he was framing the universe, he put intelligence in soul, and soul in body, that he might be the creator of a work which was by nature fairest and best. On this wise, using the language of probability, we may say that the world came into being — a living creature truly endowed with soul and intelligence by the providence of God.

This being supposed, let us proceed to the next stage: In the likeness of what animal did the Creator make the world? It would be an unworthy thing to liken it to any nature which exists as a part only; for nothing can be beautiful which is like any imperfect thing; but let us suppose the world to be the very image of that whole of which all other animals both individually and in their tribes are portions. For the original of the universe contains in itself all intelligible beings, just as this world comprehends us and all other visible creatures. For the Deity, intending to make this world like the fairest and most perfect of intelligible beings, framed one visible animal comprehending within itself all other animals of a kindred nature. Are we right in saying that there is one world, or that they are many and infinite? There must be one only, if the created copy is to accord with the original. For that which includes all other intelligible creatures cannot have a second or companion; in that case there would be need of another living being which would include both, and of which they would be parts, and the likeness would be more truly said to resemble not them, but that other which included them. In order then that the world might be solitary, like the perfect animal, the creator made no two worlds or an infinite number of them; but there is and ever will be one only-begotten and created heaven. **31**

◄§ Timaeus next declares that God made the body of the universe out of fire and earth, as was necessary if it was to be visible and tangible, and added to these two elements two others, air and water. This he did in such a way that all were bound together in a continuing geometrical proportion such that as fire is to air, so air is to water, and as air is to water, so water is to earth. By establishing this proportion, God created the body of the world as a unity harmonized with itself, and therefore indissoluble save by the hand of its maker. Timaeus continues:

Now the creation took up the whole of each of the four elements; for the Creator compounded the world out of all the fire and all the water and all the air and all the earth, leaving no part of any of them nor any power of them outside. His intention was, in the first place, that the animal should be as far as possible a perfect whole and of perfect parts: secondly, that it should be one, leaving no remnants out of which another such world might be created; and also that it should be free from old age and unaffected by disease. Considering that if heat and cold and other powerful forces surround composite bodies and attack them from without, they decompose them before their time, and by bringing diseases and old age upon them, make them waste away — for this cause and on these grounds he made the world one whole, having every part entire, and being therefore perfect **32** **33**

and not liable to old age and disease. And he gave to the world the
figure which was suitable and also natural. Now to the animal which
was to comprehend all animals, that figure would be suitable which
comprehends within itself all other figures. Wherefore he made the
world in the form of a globe, round as from a lathe, having its
extremes in every direction equidistant from the centre, the most
perfect and the most like itself of all figures; for he considered that
the like is infinitely fairer than the unlike. This he finished off,
making the surface smooth all round for many reasons; in the first
place, because the living being had no need of eyes when there was
nothing remaining outside him to be seen; nor of ears when there was
nothing to be heard; and there was no surrounding atmosphere to be
breathed; nor would there have been any use of organs by the help
of which he might receive his food or get rid of what he had already
digested, since there was nothing which went from him or came into
him: for there was nothing beside him. Of design he was created
thus, his own waste providing his own food, and all that he did or
suffered taking place in and by himself; for the Creator conceived that
a being which was self-sufficient would be far more excellent than
one which lacked anything. And, as he had no need to take anything
or defend himself against anyone, the Creator did not think it neces-
34 sary to bestow upon him hands: nor had he any need of feet, nor of
the whole apparatus of walking; but the movement suited to his
spherical form was assigned to him, being of all the seven that which
is most appropriate to mind and intelligence; and he was made to
move in the same manner and on the same spot, within his own limits
revolving in a circle. All the other six motions were taken away
from him, and he was made not to partake of their deviations. And
as this circular movement required no feet, the universe was created
without legs and without feet.

Such was the whole plan of the eternal God about the god that
was to be; he made it smooth and even, having a surface in every
direction equidistant from the centre, a body entire and perfect, and
formed out of perfect bodies. And in the centre he put the soul,
which he diffused throughout the body, making it also to be the
exterior environment of it; and he made the universe a circle moving
in a circle, one and solitary, yet by reason of its excellence able to
converse with itself, and needing no other friendship or acquaintance.
Having these purposes in view he created the world a blessed god.

Now God did not make the soul after the body, although we are
speaking of them in this order; for when he put them together he
would never have allowed that the elder should be ruled by the
younger; but this is a random manner of speaking which we have,
because somehow we ourselves too are very much under the dominion

of chance. Whereas he made the soul in origin and excellence prior
to and older than the body, to be the ruler and mistress, of whom the
body was to be the subject. And he made her out of the following 35
elements and on this wise: From the being which is indivisible and
unchangeable, and from that kind of being which is distributed
among bodies, he compounded a third and intermediate kind of
being. He did likewise with the same and the different, blending
together the indivisible kind of each with that which is portioned
out in bodies. Then, taking the three new elements, he mingled them
all into one form, compressing by force the reluctant and unsociable
nature of the different into the same. When he had mingled them
with [the intermediate kind of] being and out of three made one, he
again divided this whole into as many portions as was fitting, each
portion being a compound of the same, the different, and being.

✍§ The preceding passage, difficult to comprehend, has been explained by Cornford in his book, *Plato's Cosmology*, a work which
the serious student of the *Timaeus* will find indispensable. There
follows a passage replete with mathematical expressions, which we
shall reproduce so that the reader may see how Plato makes use of
elaborate mathematical relations, which in this case represent musical
intervals, in expressing his attitude toward the universe. Their significance here lies in his wish to depict the World Soul as harmonious
and akin to reason.

And he proceeded to divide after this manner: — First of all, he 35
took away one part of the whole [1], and then he separated a second
part which was double the first [2], and then he took away a third
part which was half as much again as the second and three times as
much as the first [3], and then he took a fourth part which was twice
as much as the second [4], and a fifth part which was three times the
third [9], and a sixth part which was eight times the first [8], and a
seventh part which was twenty-seven times the first [27]. After this he
filled up the double intervals [i.e. between 1, 2, 4, 8] and the 36
triple [i.e. between 1, 3, 9, 27], cutting off yet other portions from the
mixture and placing them in the intervals, so that in each interval
there were two kinds of means, the one exceeding and exceeded by
equal parts of its extremes [as for example 1, $\frac{4}{3}$, 2, in which the
mean $\frac{4}{3}$ is one-third of 1 more than 1, and one-third of 2 less than 2],
the other being that kind of mean which exceeds and is exceeded by
an equal number.[1] Where there were intervals of $\frac{3}{2}$ and of $\frac{4}{3}$ and of

---

[1]
e.g.
$$\overline{1}, \tfrac{4}{3}, \tfrac{3}{2}, \overline{2}, \tfrac{8}{3}, 3, \overline{4}, \tfrac{16}{3}, 6, \overline{8}; \text{ and}$$

$$\overline{1}, \tfrac{3}{2}, 2, \overline{3}, \tfrac{9}{2}, 6, \overline{9}, \tfrac{27}{2}, 18, \overline{27}.$$

$\frac{9}{8}$, made by the connecting terms in the former intervals, he filled up all the intervals of $\frac{4}{3}$ with the interval of $\frac{9}{8}$, leaving a fraction over; and the interval which this fraction expressed was in the ratio of 256 to 243.[1] And thus the whole mixture out of which he cut these portions was all exhausted by him.

 ↩ In the passage which immediately follows, and which we shall also reproduce, Timaeus will talk of astronomy, describing the relation between the sidereal equator (the circle of the same) and the zodiac (circle of the other) and setting forth the motions of the heaven of fixed stars, the planets, and the other heavenly bodies, as Plato conceived them.

36 This entire compound[2] he divided lengthways into two parts which he joined to one another at the centre like the letter X, and bent them into a circular form, connecting them with themselves and each other at the point opposite to their original meeting-point; and, comprehending them in a uniform revolution upon the same axis, he made the one the outer and the other the inner circle. Now the motion of the outer circle he called the motion of the same, and the motion of the inner circle the motion of the other or diverse. The motion of the same he carried round by the side to the right, and the motion of the diverse diagonally to the left. And he gave dominion to the motion of the same and like, for that he left single and undivided; but the inner motion he divided in six places and made seven unequal circles having their intervals in ratios of two and three, three of each, and bade the orbits proceed in a direction opposite to one another; and three [Sun, Mercury, Venus] he made to move with equal swiftness, and the remaining four [Moon, Saturn, Mars, Jupiter] to move with unequal swiftness to the three and to one another, but in due proportion.

Now when the Creator had framed the soul according to his will, he formed within her the corporeal universe, and brought the two together, and united them centre to centre. The soul, interfused everywhere from the centre to the circumference of heaven, of which also she is the external envelopment, herself turning in herself, be-
37 gan a divine beginning of never-ceasing and rational life enduring throughout all time. The body of heaven is visible, but the soul is invisible, and partakes of reason and harmony, and being made by the best of intellectual and everlasting natures, is the best of things created. And because she is composed of the same and of the different

[1] e.g. 243 : 256 :: $\frac{81}{64}$: $\frac{4}{3}$ :: $\frac{243}{128}$: 2 :: $\frac{81}{32}$: $\frac{8}{3}$ :: $\frac{243}{64}$: 4 :: $\frac{81}{16}$: $\frac{16}{3}$ :: $\frac{243}{32}$: 8. (MARTIN)

[2] From which the World Soul is made. (L)

and of being, these three, and is divided and united in due proportion, and in her revolutions returns upon herself, the soul, when touching anything which has being, whether dispersed in parts or undivided, is stirred through all her powers, to declare the sameness or difference of that thing and some other. . . .

    ∻ Timaeus next describes how the World Soul, because of her composition and structure, judges equally surely the things of sense and those of reason. He continues:

When the father and creator saw the creature which he had made 37 moving and living, the created image of the eternal gods, he rejoiced, and in his joy determined to make the copy still more like the original; and as this was an eternal living being, he sought to make the universe eternal, so far as might be. Now the nature of the ideal being was everlasting, but to bestow this attribute in its fullness upon a creature was impossible. Wherefore he resolved to have a moving image of eternity, and when he set in order the heaven, he made this image eternal but moving according to number, while eternity itself rests in unity; and this image we call time. For there were no days and nights and months and years before the heaven was created, but when he constructed the heaven he created them also. . . .

Time, then, and the heaven came into being at the same instant 38 in order that, having been created together, if ever there was to be a dissolution of them, they might be dissolved together. It was framed after the pattern of the eternal nature, that it might resemble this as far as was possible; for the pattern exists from eternity, and the created heaven has been, and is, and will be, in all time. Such was the mind and thought of God in the creation of time. The sun and moon and five other stars, which are called the planets, were created by him in order to distinguish and preserve the numbers of time; and when he had made their several bodies, he placed them in the orbits in which the circle of the other was revolving [cf. 36d], — in seven orbits seven stars. . . .

Now, when each of the stars which were necessary to the creation of time had come to its proper orbit, and they had become living creatures having bodies fastened by vital chains, and learnt their appointed task, moving in the motion of the diverse, which is diag- 39 onal, and passes through and is governed by the motion of the same, they revolved, some in a larger and some in a lesser orbit.

    ∻ Timaeus describes the periods and apparent motions of the heavenly bodies, and tells how the moon and sun measure for mortal beings the month and year, making the universe intelligible. He continues:

39 Thus far and until the birth of time the created universe was made in the likeness of the original, but inasmuch as all animals were not yet comprehended therein, it was still unlike. Therefore the creator proceeded to fashion it after the nature of the pattern in this remaining point. Now as in the ideal animal the mind perceives ideas or species of a certain nature and number, he thought that this
40 created animal ought to have species of a like nature and number. There are four such; one of them is the heavenly race of the gods; another, the race of birds whose way is in the air; the third, the watery species; and the fourth, the pedestrian and land creatures. Of the heavenly and divine, he created the greater part out of fire, that they might be the brightest of all things and fairest to behold, and he fashioned them after the likeness of the universe in the figure of a circle, and made them follow the intelligent motion of the supreme, distributing them over the whole circumference of heaven, which was to be a true cosmos or glorious world spangled with them all over. And he gave to each of them two movements: the first, a movement on the same spot after the same manner, whereby they ever continue to think consistently the same thoughts about the same things, in the same respect; the second, a forward movement, in which they are controlled by the revolution of the same and the like; but by the other five motions they were unaffected [cf. 43b], in order that each of them might attain the highest perfection. And for this reason the fixed stars were created, to be divine and eternal animals, ever-abiding and revolving after the same manner and on the same spot; and the other stars which reverse their motion and are subject to deviations of this kind, were created in the manner already described. The earth, which is our nurse, clinging around the pole which is extended through the universe, he framed to be the guardian and artificer of night and day, first and eldest of gods that are in the interior of heaven. . . .

↝ The Greek participle describing the earth, which is here translated "clinging," can also be read as "circling" or as "winding." This doubt about the meaning raises a much debated point. Is Plato following the Pythagoreans and conceiving the earth as revolving in an orbit, as did his pupil at the Academy, Heracleides of Pontus? Modern scholars reject that view, for reasons expounded in Cornford, *Plato's Cosmology*.

Timaeus next declares that he will not recount the conjunctions and eclipses of the heavenly bodies, and having completed his account of the "created and visible gods,"ᴶ passes on:

40 To know or tell the origin of the other divinities is beyond us, and we must accept the traditions of the men of old time who affirm

themselves to be the offspring of the gods — that is what they say — and they must surely have known their own ancestors. How can we doubt the word of the children of the gods? Although they give no probable or certain proofs, still, as they declare that they are speaking of what took place in their own family, we must conform to custom and believe them. In this manner, then, according to them, the genealogy of these gods is to be received and set forth.

Oceanus and Tethys were the children of Earth and Heaven, and from these sprang Phorcys and Cronos and Rhea, and all that generation; and from Cronos and Rhea sprang Zeus and Hera, and 41 all those who are said to be their brethren, and others who were the children of these.

Now, when all of them, both those who visibly appear in their revolutions as well as those other gods who are of a more retiring nature, had come into being, the creator of the universe addressed them in these words: 'Gods, children of gods, who are my works, and of whom I am the artificer and father, my creations are indissoluble, if so I will. All that is bound may be undone, but only an evil being would wish to undo that which is harmonious and happy. Wherefore, since ye are but creatures, ye are not altogether immortal and indissoluble, but ye shall certainly not be dissolved, nor be liable to the fate of death, having in my will a greater and mightier bond than those with which ye were bound at the time of your birth. And now listen to my instructions: — Three tribes of mortal beings remain to be created — without them the universe will be incomplete, for it will not contain every kind of animal which it ought to contain, if it is to be perfect. On the other hand, if they were created by me and received life at my hands, they would be on an equality with the gods. In order then that they may be mortal, and that this universe may be truly universal, do ye, according to your natures, betake yourselves to the formation of animals, imitating the power which was shown by me in creating you. The part of them worthy of the name immortal, which is called divine and is the guiding principle of those who are willing to follow justice and you — of that divine part I will myself sow the seed, and having made a beginning, I will hand the work over to you. And do ye then interweave the mortal with the immortal, and make and beget living creatures, and give them food, and make them to grow, and receive them again in death.'

Thus he spake, and once more into the cup in which he had previously mingled the soul of the universe he poured the remains of the elements, and mingled them in much the same manner; they were not, however, pure as before, but diluted to the second and third degree. And having made it he divided the whole mixture into souls equal in number to the stars, and assigned each soul to a star; and having there placed them as in a chariot, he showed them the nature of the universe, and declared to them the laws of destiny, according to which their first birth would be one and the same for all, — no one should suffer a disadvantage at his hands; they were to be sown in the instruments of time severally adapted to them, and to come forth the most religious of animals; and as human nature was of two kinds, the superior race was of such-and-such a character, and would hereafter be called man. Now, when they should be implanted in bodies by necessity, and be always gaining or losing some part of their bodily substance, then in the first place it would be necessary that they should all have in them one and the same faculty of sensation, arising out of irresistible impressions; in the second place, they must have love, in which pleasure and pain mingle; also fear and anger, and the feelings which are akin or opposite to them; if they conquered these they would live righteously, and if they were conquered by them, unrighteously. He who lived well during his appointed time was to return and dwell in his native star, and there he would have a blessed and congenial existence. But if he failed in attaining this, at the second birth he would pass into a woman, and if, when in that state of being, he did not desist from evil, he would continually be changed into some brute who resembled him in the evil nature which he acquired, and would not cease from his toils and transformations until he helped the revolution of the same and the like within him to draw in its train the turbulent mob of later accretions, made up of fire and air and water and earth, and by this victory of reason over the irrational returned to the form of his first and better state. Having given all these laws to his creatures, that he might be guiltless of future evil in any of them, the creator sowed some of them in the earth, and some in the moon, and some in the other instruments of time; and when he had sown them he committed to the younger gods the fashioning of their mortal bodies, and desired them to furnish what was still lacking to the human soul, and having made all the suitable additions, to rule over them, and to pilot the mortal animal in the best and wisest manner which they could, and avert from him all but self-inflicted evils.

When the creator had made all these ordinances he remained in his own accustomed nature, and his children heard and were obedient to their father's word, and receiving from him the immortal principle of a mortal creature, in imitation of their own creator they borrowed portions of fire, and earth, and water, and air from the world, which were hereafter to be restored — these they took and welded them together, not with the indissoluble chains by which they were themselves bound, but with little pegs too small to be visible, making up out of all the four elements each separate body, and fastening the courses of the immortal soul in a body which was in a state of perpetual influx and efflux. Now these courses, detained as in a vast river, neither overcame nor were overcome; but were hurrying and hurried to and fro, so that the whole animal was moved and progressed, irregularly however and irrationally and anyhow, in all the six directions of motion, wandering backwards and forwards, and right and left, and up and down, and in all the six directions. For great as was the advancing and retiring flood which provided nourishment, the affections produced by external contact caused still greater tumult — when the body of anyone met and came into collision with some external fire, or with the solid earth or the gliding waters, or was caught in the tempest borne on the air, and the motions produced by any of these impulses were carried through the body to the soul. All such notions have consequently received the general name of 'sensations', which they still retain. . . .

&§ Timaeus describes how the flood of nutriment and tumult of sensations disturb the appointed motions of the mortal soul, which is compounded and patterned like the World Soul, having its own circles of the same and the other. The bodily influences at first completely stop the revolution of the soul's circle of the same and prevent it from governing, and disorder and break the circles of the other, and thus the soul cannot judge correctly. He continues:

And by reason of all these affections, the soul, when encased in 44 a mortal body, now, as in the beginning, is at first without intelligence; but when the flood of growth and nutriment abates, and the courses of the soul, calming down, go their own way and become steadier as time goes on, then the several circles return to their natural form, and their revolutions are corrected, and they call the same and the other by their right names, and make the possessor of them to become a rational being. And if these combine in him with any true nurture or education, he attains the fullness and health of the perfect man, and escapes the worst disease of all; but if he neglects education he walks lame to the end of his life, and returns imperfect and good for nothing to the world below. This however, is a later stage; at present we must treat more exactly the subject before us, which involves a preliminary inquiry into the generation of the body and its members, and how the soul was created, — for what reason and by what providence of the gods; and holding fast to probability, we must pursue our way.

First, then, the gods, imitating the spherical shape of the universe, enclosed the two divine courses in a spherical body, that, namely, which we now term the head, being the most divine part of us and

the lord of all that is in us: to this the gods, when they put together
the body, gave all the other members to be servants, considering that
it must partake of every sort of motion. In order then that it might
not tumble about among the high and deep places of the earth,
but might be able to get over the one and out of the other, they
provided the body to be its vehicle and means of locomotion; which
consequently had length and was furnished with four limbs extended
and flexible; these God contrived to be instruments of locomotion
45 with which it might take hold and find support, and so be able
to pass through all places, carrying on high the dwelling-place of the
most sacred and divine part of us. Such was the origin of legs and
hands, which for this reason were attached to every man; and the
gods, deeming the front part of man to be more honourable and
more fit to command than the hinder part, made us to move mostly
in a forward direction. Wherefore man must needs have his front
part unlike and distinguished from the rest of his body. And so in
the vessel of the head, they first of all put a face in which they inserted organs to minister in all things to the providence of the soul,
and they appointed this part, which has authority, to be the natural
front. And of the organs they first contrived the eyes to give light,
and the principle according to which they were inserted was as
follows: So much of fire as would not burn, but gave a gentle light,
they formed into a substance akin to the light of everyday life; and
the pure fire which is within us and related thereto they made to
flow through the eyes in a stream smooth and dense, compressing
the whole eye, and especially the centre part, so that it kept out
everything of a coarser nature, and allowed to pass only this pure
element. When the light of day surrounds the stream of vision, then
like falls upon like, and they coalesce, and one body is formed by
natural affinity in the line of vision, wherever the light that falls
from within meets with an external object. And the whole stream
of vision, being similarly affected in virtue of similarity, diffuses the
motions of what it touches or what touches it over the whole body,
until they reach the soul, causing that perception which we call sight.
But when night comes on and the external and kindred fire departs,
then the stream of vision is cut off; for going forth to an unlike element
it is changed and extinguished, being no longer of one nature with
the surrounding atmosphere which is now deprived of fire: . . .

46   All these are to be reckoned among the second and co-operative
causes which God, carrying into execution the idea of the best as
far as possible, uses as his ministers. They are thought by most men
not to be the second, but the prime causes of all things, because they
freeze and heat, and contract and dilate, and the like. But they are
not so, for they are incapable of reason or intellect; the only being

which can properly have mind is the invisible soul, whereas fire and water, and earth and air, are all of them visible bodies. The lover of intellect and knowledge ought to explore causes of intelligent nature first of all, and, secondly, of those things which, being moved by others, are compelled to move others. And this is what we too must do. Both kinds of causes should be acknowledged by us, but a distinction should be made between those which are endowed with mind and are the workers of things fair and good, and those which are deprived of intelligence and always produce chance effects without order or design. Of the second or co-operative causes of sight, which help to give to the eyes the power which they now possess, enough has been said. I will therefore now proceed to speak of the higher use and purpose for which God has given them to us. The sight in my opinion is the source of the greatest benefit to us, for had we never seen the stars, and the sun, and the heaven, none of the words which we have spoken about the universe would ever have been uttered. But now the sight of day and night, and the months and the revolutions of the years, have created number, and have given us a conception of time, and the power of inquiring about the nature of the universe; and from this source we have derived philosophy, than which no greater good ever was or will be given by the gods to mortal man. This is the greatest boon of sight: and of the lesser benefits why should I speak? even the ordinary man if he were deprived of them would bewail his loss, but in vain. Thus much let me say however: God invented and gave us sight to the end that we might behold the courses of intelligence in the heaven, and apply them to the courses of our own intelligence which are akin to them, the unperturbed to the perturbed; and that we, learning them and partaking of the natural truth of reason, might imitate the absolutely unerring courses of God and regulate our own vagaries. The same may be affirmed of speech and hearing: they have been given by the gods to the same end and for a like reason. For this is the principal end of speech, whereto it most contributes. Moreover, so much of music as is adapted to the sound of the voice and to the sense of hearing is granted to us for the sake of harmony; and harmony, which has motions akin to the revolutions of our souls, is not regarded by the intelligent votary of the Muses as given by them with a view to irrational pleasure, which is deemed to be the purpose of it in our day, but as meant to correct any discord which may have arisen in the courses of the soul, and to be our ally in bringing her into harmony and agreement with herself; and rhythm too was given by them for the same reason, on account of the irregular and graceless ways which prevail among mankind generally, and to help us against them.

47

Thus far in what we have been saying, with small exceptions, the works of intelligence have been set forth; and now we must place by the side of them in our discourse the things which come into being
48   through necessity — for the creation of this world is the combined work of necessity and mind. Mind, the ruling power, persuaded necessity to bring the greater part of created things to perfection; and thus and after this manner in the beginning, through necessity made subject to reason, this universe was created. But if a person will truly tell of the way in which the work was accomplished, he must include the variable cause as well, and explain its influence. Wherefore, we must return again and find another suitable beginning, as about the former matters, so also about these. To which end we must consider the nature of fire, and water, and air, and earth, such as they were prior to the creation of the heaven, and what was happening to them in this previous state. . . .

    ✍ Timaeus now makes a "new beginning" of his discussion. He names again the two kinds or principles which he laid down at the outset, the eternal and changeless and the generated and perishing, and now adds a third kind, called the "receptacle" or "nurse of generation." This we may conceive as a sort of space and at the same time, an indeterminate substance, in which and from which all sensible things are formed. From the beginning, Timaeus says, it was everywhere in confused motion, and in it were tossed about unformed traces of the four elements, but not yet the elements themselves. From these traces, God first formed the elements, shaping them from triangles into the shapes of regular solids; these Timaeus describes in painstaking geometrical detail, declaring that God, so far as Necessity yielded to his persuasion, gave them perfection and harmony.

    This done, Timaeus describes the transformations and movements which the elements may undergo, their various sizes, the manner in which they are constantly passing through and mixing with one another, their varieties, and the compounds they form. In this way he explains the many natural substances, and their physical and sensible properties; he comments on the meanings of "up" and "down," "heavy" and "light"; he describes the causes of pleasure and pain, and of the various tastes, odors, sounds, and colors. All this is done in terms of his theory of the elements, their shapes and motions. He sums up by repeating that these necessary causes have been accepted by God and made into his agents in achieving good, and declares that we men must do likewise.

    He now proposes to present the third section of his discourse, in which he will describe the cooperation of reason and necessity in the creation of mortal beings. He begins as follows:

69   As I said at first, when all things were in disorder God created in each thing in relation to itself, and in all things in relation to each

other, all the measures and harmonies which they could possibly receive. For in those days nothing had any proportion except by accident; nor was there anything deserving to be called by the names which we now use — as, for example, fire, water, and the rest of the elements. All these the creator first set in order, and out of them he constructed the universe, which was a single animal comprehending in itself all other animals, mortal and immortal. Now of the divine, he himself was the creator, but the creation of the mortal he committed to his offspring. And they, imitating him, received from him the immortal principle of the soul; and around this they proceeded to fashion a mortal body, and made it to be the vehicle of the soul, and constructed within the body a soul of another nature which was mortal, subject to terrible and irresistible affections, — first of all, pleasure, the greatest incitement to evil; then, pain, which deters from good; also rashness and fear, two foolish counsellors; anger hard to be appeased, and hope easily led astray; — these they mingled with irrational sense and with all-daring love according to necessary laws, and so framed man. Wherefore, fearing to pollute the divine any more than was absolutely unavoidable, they gave to the mortal nature a separate habitation in another part of the body, placing the neck between them to be the isthmus and boundary, which they constructed between the head and breast, to keep them apart. And in the breast, and in what is termed the thorax, they encased the mortal soul; and as the one part of this was superior and the other inferior they divided the cavity of the thorax into 70 two parts, as the women's and men's apartments are divided in houses, and placed the midriff to be a wall of partition between them. That part of the inferior soul which is endowed with courage and passion and loves contention they settled nearer the head, midway between the midriff and the neck, in order that being obedient to the rule of reason it might join with it in controlling and restraining the desires when they are no longer willing of their own accord to obey the word of command issuing from the citadel.

The heart, the knot of the veins and the fountain of the blood which races through all the limbs, was set in the place of guard, that when the might of passion was roused by reason making proclamation of any wrong assailing them from without or being perpetrated by the desires within, quickly the whole power of feeling in the body, perceiving these commands and threats, might obey and follow through every turn and alley, and thus allow the principle of the best to have the command in all of them. But the gods, foreknowing that the palpitation of the heart in the expectation of danger and excitement of passion must cause it to swell and become inflamed, formed and implanted as a supporter to the heart the lung, which was, in the first place, soft and bloodless, and also had within hollows like the pores of a sponge, in order that by receiving the breath and the drink, it might give coolness and the power of respiration and alleviate the heat. Wherefore they cut the air-channels leading to the lung, and placed the lung about the heart as a soft spring, that, when passion was rife within, the heart, beating against a yielding body, might be cooled and suffer less, and might thus become more ready to join with passion in the service of reason.

The part of the soul which desires meats and drinks and the other things of which it has need by reason of the bodily nature, they placed between the midriff and the boundary of the navel, contriving in all this region a sort of manger for the food of the body; and there they bound it down like a wild animal which was chained up with man, and must be nourished if man was to exist. They appointed this lower creation his place here in order that he might be always feeding at the manger, and have his dwelling as far as might be from the council-chamber, making as little noise and disturbance as possible, and permitting the best part to advise quietly for the good of the whole and the individual. And knowing that this lower principle in man would not comprehend reason, and even if attaining to some degree of perception would never naturally care for rational notions, but that it would be especially led by phantoms and visions night and day, — planning to make this very weakness serve a purpose, God combined with it the liver, and placed it in the house of the lower nature, contriving that it should be solid and smooth, and bright and sweet, and should also have a bitter quality, in order that the power of thought, which proceeds from the mind, might be reflected as in a mirror which receives likenesses of objects and gives back images of them to the sight; and so might strike terror into the desires, when, making use of the bitter part of the liver, to which it is akin, it comes threatening and invading, and diffusing this bitter element swiftly through the whole liver produces colours like bile, and contracting every part makes it wrinkled and rough; and twisting out of its right place and contorting the lobe and closing and shutting up the vessels and gates, causes pain and loathing. And the converse happens when some gentle inspiration of the understanding pictures images of an opposite character, and allays the bile and bitterness by refusing to stir or touch the nature opposed to itself, but by making use of the natural sweetness of the liver, corrects all things and makes them to be right and smooth and free, and renders the portion of the soul which resides about the liver happy and joyful, enabling it to pass the night in peace, and to practise divination in sleep, inasmuch as it has no share in mind and reason. For the authors of our being, remembering the command of their father

71

when he bade them create the human race as good as they could, that they might correct our inferior parts and make them to attain a measure of truth, placed in the liver the seat of divination. And herein is a proof that God has given the art of divination not to the wisdom, but to the foolishness of man. . . .

⌐§ Timaeus has thus described the making of the mortal parts of the soul and of the regions of the body in which they are lodged, showing their fitness for their tasks. We have presented this description as a sample of what in the dialogue follows for many pages: Timaeus' account of the anatomy and physiology of the body and related matters. It is a great compendium of the scientific knowledge and speculation current in Plato's day, selected and remodeled in accord with Plato's own judgment of what was the most probable account and what would best fit with his conception of the divine plan. Timaeus tells of the different organ systems and tissues of the body, among them the "marrow," which for him includes both the nervous tissue of the brain and spinal cord and the "seed" or semen. He describes processes such as respiration; diseases; disorders of the soul; and proper bodily regimen. In passing, he describes the nature of plants, created for our food and animated only by the lower of the two mortal kinds of soul. Ending his treatment of the living creature, soul and body, he proceeds to tell briefly of the proper training of the rational part of the soul.

I have often remarked that there are three kinds of soul located 89 within us, having each of them motions, and I must now repeat in the fewest words possible, that one part, if remaining inactive and ceasing from its natural motion, must necessarily become very weak, but that which is trained and exercised, very strong. Wherefore 90 we should take care that the movements of the different parts of the soul should be in due proportion.

And we should consider that God gave the sovereign part of the human soul to be the divinity of each one, being that part which, as we say, dwells at the top of the body, and inasmuch as we are a plant not of an earthly but of a heavenly growth, raises us from earth to our kindred who are in heaven. And in this we say truly; for the divine power suspends the head and root of us from that place where the generation of the soul first began, and thus makes the whole body upright. When a man is always occupied with the cravings of desire and ambition, and is eagerly striving to satisfy them, all his thoughts must be mortal, and, as far as it is possible altogether to become such, he must be mortal every whit, because he has cherished his mortal part. But he who has been earnest in the love of knowledge and of true wisdom, and has exercised his intellect more than any other part of him, must have thoughts immortal and divine, if he attain truth, and in so far as human nature is capable of sharing in immortality, he must altogether be immortal; and since he is ever cherishing the divine power, and has the divinity within him in perfect order, he will be singularly happy. Now there is only one way of taking care of things, and this is to give to each the food and motion which are natural to it. And the motions which are naturally akin to the divine principle within us are the thoughts and revolutions of the universe. These each man should follow, and by learning the harmonies and revolutions of the universe, should correct the courses of the head which were corrupted at our birth, and should assimilate the thinking being to the thought, renewing his original nature, so that having assimilated them he may attain to that best life which the gods have set before mankind, both for the present and the future.

Thus our original design of discoursing about the universe down to the creation of man is nearly completed. A brief mention may be made of the generation of other animals, so far as the subject admits of brevity; in this manner our argument will best attain a due proportion. On the subject of animals, then, the following remarks may be offered. Of the men who came into the world, those who were cowards or led unrighteous lives may with reason be supposed to have changed into the nature of women in the second generation. And this was the reason why at that time the gods created in us the desire of sexual intercourse, contriving in man one animated substance, and in woman another, which they formed respectively in the following manner. The outlet for drink by which liquids pass through the lung under the kidneys and into the bladder, which receives and then by the pressure of the air emits them, was so fashioned by them as to penetrate also into the body of the marrow, which passes from the head along the neck and through the back, and which in the preceding discourse we have named the seed. And the seed having life, and becoming endowed with respiration, produces in that part in which it respires a lively desire of emission, and thus creates in us the love of procreation. Wherefore also in men the organ of generation becoming rebellious and masterful, like an animal disobedient to reason, and maddened with the sting of lust, seeks to gain absolute sway; and the same is the case with the so-called womb or matrix of women; the animal within them is desirous of procreating children, and when remaining unfruitful long beyond its proper time, gets discontented and angry, and wandering in every direction through the body, closes up the passages of the breath, and, bv obstructing respiration, drives them to extremity, causing all varieties of disease, until at length the desire and love of the man and the woman, bringing them together and as it were plucking the fruit from the tree, sow in the womb, as in a field, animals unseen by reason of their smallness and without form; these again are separated and matured within; they are then finally brought out into the light, and thus the generation of animals is completed.

Thus were created women and the female sex in general. But the race of birds was created out of innocent lightminded men, who, although their minds were directed toward heaven, imagined, in their simplicity, that the clearest demonstration of the things above was to be obtained by sight; these were remodelled and transformed into birds, and they grew feathers instead of hair. The race of wild pedestrian animals, again, came from those who had no philosophy in any of their thoughts, and, never considered at all about the nature of the heavens, because they had ceased to use the courses of the head, but followed the guidance of those parts of the soul which are in the breast. In consequence of these habits of theirs they had their front legs and their heads resting upon the earth to which they were drawn by natural affinity; and the crowns of their heads were elongated and of all sorts of shapes, into which the courses of the soul were crushed by reason of disuse. And this was the reason why they were created 92 quadrupeds and polypods: God gave the more senseless of them the more support that they might be more attracted to the earth. And the most foolish of them, who trail their bodies entirely upon the ground and have no longer any need of feet, he made without feet to crawl upon the earth. The fourth class were the inhabitants of the water: these were made out of the most entirely senseless and ignorant of all, whom the transformers did not think any longer worthy of pure respiration, because they possessed a soul which was made impure by all sorts of transgression; and instead of the subtle and pure medium of air, they gave them the deep and muddy sea to be their element of respiration; and hence arose the race of fishes and oysters, and other aquatic animals, which have received the most remote habitations as a punishment of their outlandish ignorance. These are the laws by which all animals pass into one another, now, as in the beginning, changing as they lose or gain wisdom and folly.

We may now say that our discourse about the nature of the universe has an end. The world has received animals, mortal and immortal, and is fulfilled with them, and has become a visible animal containing the visible — the sensible God who is the image of the intellectual, the greatest, best, fairest, most perfect — the one only-begotten heaven.

Laws

•

Book X

Persons of the Dialogue

AN ATHENIAN STRANGER   CLEINIAS, a Cretan
MEGILLUS, a Lacedaemonian

◆§ At several points in our Introduction we had occasion to discuss the *Laws,* that great storehouse of Platonic political theory and of Plato's opinions and proposals, legal, social, educational, ethical, and metaphysical. In this work of his old age Plato for the second time has designed a Greek city-state, remodeled in closer conformity with his ideals, but this time intended to be more practicable than the city of the *Republic.* In discussing Plato's political and educational ideas we noted some of the more important differences between his city of the *Laws* and the actual Greek cities of his time, and pointed out the common features, as well as the divergent, of Plato's two cities. Also in our Theme 8, "The Cosmic Frame," we had much to say of the theology and cosmology of the *Laws.*

Of the twelve books of the dialogue, only the tenth is presented here. It sets forth what Plato regarded as the safest basis of social conformity and, in relation to this, his conception of the divine nature and the plan of the universe. For us, in this age of conflict between the authoritarian and the liberal, the high point of interest in the book is unquestionably what it tells us about the "crime" of atheism in its three forms and Plato's differential way of dealing with each.

While we can by no means accept Plato's position that it is proper to enforce conformity in the expression of religious beliefs, we can observe that Plato was unhappily in this respect a man of his own time.[1] His is a religion similar to that of Socrates in affirming the paramount importance of care for the soul and in asserting the reality of divine goodness and providence, but he went beyond Socrates in holding that such beliefs were for most men the necessary basis of civic virtue and therefore that denial of them must be prohibited. Plato's superiority to his intolerant contemporaries lies chiefly in the fact that he was not motivated by superstitious dread

[1] See especially Glenn R. Morrow, *Plato's Cretan City* (Princeton: Princeton University Press, 1960); and also Levinson, *In Defense of Plato* (Cambridge, Mass.: Harvard University Press, 1953). (L)

of divine retaliation if ritual requirements were not met, and that he at least hoped to convince rather than to coerce the unbeliever.

One further topic worked into the pattern of Book X deserves notice: the detailed analysis of the concept of motion which underlies the logical refutation of materialism, i.e., the denial of a divine element in the universe. We hear Plato speaking, as it were, *pro domo,* in valiant defense of what he regarded as the cornerstone of his philosophy.

The speakers in the *Laws* are the "Athenian Stranger," alias Plato, who like Socrates of the *Republic* provides the substance of the dialogue, and two very compliant and not at all original elderly men, one a Cretan and one a Spartan. As the tenth book opens, the Athenian Stranger continues his description of his proposed legislation for the new city:

And now having spoken of assaults, let us sum up all acts of **884** violence under a single law, which shall be as follows: — No one shall take or carry away any of his neighbour's goods, neither shall he use anything which is his neighbour's without the consent of the owner; for these are the offences which are and have been, and will ever be, the source of all the aforesaid evils. The greatest of them are excesses and insolences of youth, and are offences against the greatest when they are done against religion; and especially great **885** when in violation of public and holy rites, or of the partly common rites in which tribes and phratries share; and in the second degree great when they are committed against private rites and sepulchres, and in the third degree (not to repeat the acts formerly mentioned), when insults are offered to parents; the fourth kind of violence is when anyone, regardless of the authority of the rulers, takes or carries away or makes use of anything which belongs to them, not having their consent; and the fifth kind is when the violation of the civil rights of an individual demands reparation. There should be a common law embracing all these cases. For we have already said in general terms what shall be the punishment of sacrilege, whether fraudulent or violent, and now we have to determine what is to be the punishment of those who speak or act insolently toward the Gods. But first we must give them an admonition which may be in the following terms: — No one who in obedience to the laws believed that there were Gods, ever intentionally did any unholy act, or uttered any unlawful word; but he who did must have supposed one of three things, — either that they did not exist, — which is the first possibility, or secondly, that, if they did, they took no care of man, or thirdly, that they were easily appeased and turned aside from their purpose by sacrifices and prayers.

Cle. What shall we say or do to these persons?

Ath. My good friend, let us first hear the jests which I suspect that they in their superiority will utter against us.

Cle. What jests?

Ath. They will make some irreverent speech of this sort: — 'O inhabitants of Athens, and Sparta, and Cnosus', they will reply, 'in that you speak truly; for some of us deny the very existence of the Gods, while others, as you say, are of opinion that they do not care about us; and others that they are turned from their course by gifts. Now we have a right to claim, as you yourself allowed, in the matter of laws, that before you are hard upon us and threaten us, you should argue with us and convince us — you should first attempt to teach and persuade us that there are Gods by reasonable evidences, and also that they are too good to be propitiated, and turned from their course unrighteously by gifts. For when we hear such things said of them by those who are esteemed to be the best of poets, and orators, and prophets, and priests, and by innumerable others, the thoughts of most of us are not set upon abstaining from unrighteous acts, but upon doing them and atoning for them. When lawgivers profess that they are gentle and not stern, we think that they should first of all use persuasion to us, and show us the existence of Gods, if not in a better manner than other men, at any rate in a truer; and who knows but that we shall hearken to you? If then our request is a fair one, please to accept our challenge.'

Cle. But is there any difficulty in proving the existence of the Gods?

886 *Ath.* How would you prove it?

Cle. How? In the first place, the earth and the sun, and the stars and the universe, and the fair order of the seasons, and the division of them into years and months, furnish proofs of their existence; and also there is the fact that all Hellenes and barbarians believe in them.

Ath. I fear, my sweet friend, though I will not say that I much regard, the contempt with which the profane will be likely to assail us. For you do not understand the nature of their complaint, and you fancy that they rush into impiety only from a love of sensual pleasure.

Cle. Why, stranger, what other reason is there?

Ath. One which you who live in a different atmosphere would never guess.

Cle. What is it?

Ath. A very grievous sort of ignorance which is imagined to be the greatest wisdom.

Cle. What do you mean?

Ath. At Athens there are tales preserved in writing which the virtue of your state, as I am informed, refuses to admit. They speak of the Gods in prose as well as verse, and the oldest of them tell of the origin of the heavens and of the world, and not far from the beginning of their story they proceed to narrate the birth of the Gods, and how after they were born they behaved to one another. Whether these stories have in other ways a good or a bad influence, I should not like to be severe upon them, because they are ancient; but, looking at them with reference to the duties of children to their parents, I cannot praise them, or think that they are useful, or at all true. Of the words of the ancients I have nothing more to say; and I should wish to say of them only what is pleasing to the Gods. But as to our younger generation and their wisdom, I cannot let them off when they do mischief. For do but mark the effect of their words: when you and I argue for the existence of the Gods, and produce the sun, moon, stars, and earth, claiming for them a divine being, those who have been persuaded by the aforesaid philosophers will say that they are earth and stones only, which can have no care at all of human affairs, and that all religion is a cooking up of words and a make-believe.

Cle. One such teacher, O stranger, would be bad enough, and you imply that there are many of them, which is worse.

Ath. Well, then; what shall we say or do? — Shall we assume that some one is accusing us among unholy men, who say to us, as defendants in the matter of legislation: — How dreadful that you should legislate on the supposition that there are Gods! Shall we make a defence of ourselves? or shall we leave them and return to our laws, lest the prelude should become longer than the law? For the discourse will certainly extend to great length, if we are to treat the impiously disposed as they desire, partly demonstrating to them at some length the things of which they demand an explanation, partly making them afraid or dissatisfied, and then proceed to the requisite enactments.

Cle. Yes, stranger; but then how often have we repeated already that on the present occasion there is no reason why brevity should be preferred to length! for who is 'at our heels'? — as the saying goes — and it would be paltry and ridiculous to prefer the shorter to the better. It is a matter of no small consequence, in some way or other to give a convincing argument that there are Gods, and that they are good, and regard justice more than men do. The demonstration of this would be the best and noblest prelude of all our laws. And therefore, without impatience, and without hurry, let us unreservedly consider the whole matter, summoning up all the power of persuasion which we possess.

Ath. Seeing you thus in earnest, I would fain offer up a prayer that I may succeed: — but I must proceed at once. Who can be calm when he is called upon to prove the existence of the Gods? Who can avoid hating and abhorring the men who are and have been the cause of this argument; I speak of those who will not believe the tales which they have heard as babes and sucklings from their mothers and nurses, repeated by them both in jest and in earnest, like charms, who have also heard them in the sacrificial prayers, and seen sights accompanying them, — sights and sounds delightful to children, — and their parents during the sacrifices show-ing an intense earnestness on behalf of their children and of them-selves, and with eager interest talking to the Gods, and beseeching them, as though they were firmly convinced of their existence; who likewise see and hear the prostrations and invocations which are made by Hellenes and barbarians at the rising and setting of the sun and moon, in all the vicissitudes of life, not as if they thought that there were no Gods, but as if there could be no doubt of their existence, and no suspicion of their non-existence; when men, knowing all these things, despise them on no real grounds, as would be admitted by all who have any particle of intelligence, and when they force us to say what we are now saying, how can anyone in gentle terms remonstrate with the like of them, when he has to begin by proving to them the very existence of the Gods? Yet the attempt must be made; for it would be unseemly that one half of mankind should go mad in their lust of pleasure, and the other half in their indignation at such persons. Our address to these lost and perverted natures should not be spoken in passion; let us suppose ourselves to select some one of them, and gently reason with him, smothering our anger: — O my son, we will say to him, you are young, and the advance of time will make you reverse many of the opinions which you now hold. Wait awhile, and do not at-tempt to judge at present of the highest things; and that is the highest of which you now think nothing — to judge rightly about the Gods and so to live well, or the reverse. And in the first place let me indicate to you one point which is of great importance, and about which I cannot be deceived: — You and your friends are not the first who have held this opinion about the Gods. There have always been persons more or less numerous who have had the same disorder. I have known many of them, and can tell you that no one who had taken up in youth this opinion, that the Gods do not exist, ever continued in the same until he was old; the two other notions certainly do continue in some cases, but not in many; the notion, I mean, that the Gods exist, but take no heed of human things, and the other notion that they do take heed of them, but are

easily propitiated with sacrifices and prayers. As to the opinion about
the Gods which may some day become clear to you, I advise you to
wait and consider if it be true or not; ask of others, and above all
of the legislator. In the meantime take care that you do not
offend against the Gods. For the duty of the legislator is and always
will be to teach you the truth of these matters.

Cle. Our address, stranger, thus far, is excellent.

Ath. Quite true, Megillus and Cleinias, but I am afraid that we
have unconsciously lighted on a strange doctrine.

Cle. What doctrine do you mean?

Ath. The wisest of all doctrines, in the opinion of many.

Cle. I wish that you would speak plainer.

Ath. The doctrine that all things come into existence, or have
done or will do so, some by nature, some by art, and some by chance.

Cle. Is not that true?

Ath. Well, philosophers are probably right; at any rate we may   889
as well follow in their track, and examine what is the meaning of
them and their disciples.

Cle. By all means.

Ath. They say that the greatest and fairest things are the work
of nature and of chance, the lesser of art, which, receiving from
nature the greater and primeval creations, moulds and fashions
all those lesser works which are generally termed artificial.

Cle. How is that?

Ath. I will explain my meaning still more clearly. They say that
fire and water, and earth and air, all exist by nature and chance,
and none of them by art, and that as to the bodies which come
next in order, — earth, and sun, and moon, and stars, — they have
been created by means of these absolutely inanimate existences. The
elements are severally moved by chance and some inherent force
according to certain affinities among them — of hot with cold, or of
dry with moist, or of soft with hard, and according to all the other
accidental admixtures of opposites which have been formed by necessity. After this fashion and in this manner the whole heaven has
been created, and all that is in the heaven, as well as animals and
all plants, and all the seasons come from these elements, not by the
action of mind, as they say, or of any God, or from art, but as I was
saying, by nature and chance only. Art sprang up afterwards and
out of these, mortal and of mortal birth, and produced in play certain
images and very partial imitations of the truth, having an affinity to
one another, such as music and painting create and their companion
arts. And if there are other arts which achieve a serious purpose,
these co-operate with nature, such, for example, as medicine, and
husbandry, and gymnastic. And they say that politics co-operates

with nature, but very slightly, and has more of art; and so that legislation is entirely a work of art, and is based on assumptions which are not true.

Cle. How do you mean?

Ath. In the first place, my dear friend, these people would say that the Gods exist not by nature, but by art, and by the laws of states, which are different in different places, according to the agreement of those who make them; and that the honourable is one thing by nature and another thing by law, and that the principles of justice have no existence at all in nature, but that mankind are always disputing about them and altering them; and that the alterations which are made by art and by law have no basis in nature, but are of authority for the moment and at the time at which they are made. — These, my friends, are the sayings of wise men, poets and prose-writers, which find a way into the minds of youth. They are told by them that the highest right is might, and in this way the young fall into impieties, under the idea that the Gods are not such as the law bids them imagine; and hence arise factions, these philosophers inviting them to lead a true life according to nature, that is, to live in real dominion over others, and not in legal subjection to them.

Cle. What a dreadful picture, stranger, have you given, and how great is the injury which is thus inflicted on young men to the ruin of both of states and families!

Ath. True, Cleinias; but then what should the lawgiver do when this evil is of long standing? should he only rise up in the state and threaten all mankind, proclaiming that if they will not say and think that the Gods are such as the law ordains (and this may be extended generally to the honourable, the just, and to all the highest things, and to all that relates to virtue and vice; in all they must make their actions conform to the plan which the law gives them), — then he who refuses to obey the law shall die, or suffer stripes and bonds, or privation of citizenship, or in some cases be punished by loss of property and exile? Should he not rather, when he is making laws for men, at the same time infuse the spirit of persuasion into his words, and mitigate the severity of them as far as he can?

Cle. Why, stranger, if such persuasion be at all possible, then a legislator who has anything in him ought never to weary of persuading men; he ought to leave nothing unsaid in support of the ancient opinion that there are Gods, and of all those other truths which you were just now mentioning; he ought to support the law and also art, and acknowledge that both alike exist by nature, and no less than nature, if they are the creations of mind in accordance with right reason, as you appear to me to maintain, and I am disposed to agree with you in thinking.

Ath. Yes, my enthusiastic Cleinias; but are not these things when spoken to a multitude hard to be understood, not to mention that they take up a dismal length of time?

Cle. Why, stranger, shall we, whose patience failed not when drinking or music were the themes of discourse, weary now of discoursing about the Gods, and about divine things? This inquiry will be of the greatest help to rational legislation, since the laws when once written down are always at rest; they can be put to the test at any future time, and therefore, if on first hearing they seem difficult, there is no reason for apprehension about them, because any man however dull can go over them and consider them again and again; nor if they are tedious but useful, is there any reason or religion, as it seems to me, in any man refusing to maintain the principles of them to the utmost of his power. 891

Megillus. Stranger, I like what Cleinias is saying.

Ath. Yes, Megillus, and we should do as he proposes; for if impious discourses were not scattered, as I may say, throughout the world, there would have been no need for any vindication of the existence of the Gods — but seeing that they are spread far and wide, such arguments are needed; and who should come to the rescue of the greatest laws, when they are being undermined by bad men, but the legislator himself?

Meg. There is no more proper champion of them.

Ath. Well, then, tell me, Cleinias, — for I must ask you to be my partner, — does not he who talks in this way conceive fire and water and earth and air to be the first elements of all things? these he calls nature, and out of these he supposes the soul to be formed afterwards; and this is not a mere conjecture of ours about his meaning, but is what he really means.

Cle. Very true.

Ath. Then, by Heaven, we have discovered the source of this vain opinion of all those physical investigators; and I would have you examine their arguments with the utmost care, for it will make no small difference if it can be shown that those who traffic in impious arguments, and lead others astray, use an argument which is logically weak from the start. And in my opinion this is so.

Cle. You are right; but I should like to know how this happens.

Ath. I fear that the argument may seem singular.

Cle. Do not hesitate, stranger; I see that you are afraid of such a discussion carrying you beyond the limits of legislation. But if there be no other way of showing our agreement in the account of the Gods given by the existing law, let us take this way, my good sir.

Ath. Then I suppose that I must proceed with my unfamiliar argument. Those who manufacture the soul according to their own impious notions affirm that which is the first cause of the generation and destruction of all things, to be not first, but last, and that which is last to be first, and hence they have fallen into error about the true nature of the Gods.

892   *Cle.* Still I do not understand you.

Ath. Nearly all of them, my friends, seem to be ignorant of the nature and power of the soul, especially in what relates to her origin: they do not know that she is among the first of things, and before all bodies, and is the chief author of their changes and transpositions. And if this is true, and if the soul is older than the body, must not the things which are of the soul's kindred be of necessity prior to those which appertain to the body?

Cle. Certainly.

Ath. Then thought and attention and mind and art and law will be prior to that which is hard and soft and heavy and light; and the great and primordial works and actions will be works of art; they will be the first, and after them will come nature and works of nature, which however is a wrong term for men to apply to them; these will follow, and will be under the government of art and mind.

Cle. But why is the word 'nature' wrong?

Ath. Because those who use the term mean to say that nature is the first creative power; but if the soul turn out to be the primordial element, and not fire or air, then in the truest sense and beyond other things the soul may be said to exist by nature; and this would be true if you proved that the soul is older than the body, but not otherwise.

Cle. You are quite right.

Ath. Shall we, then, take this as the next point to which our attention should be directed?

Cle. By all means.

Ath. Let us be on our guard lest this most deceptive argument with its youthful looks, beguiling us old men, give us the slip and make a laughing-stock of us. Who knows but we may be aiming at the greater, and fail of attaining the lesser? Suppose that we three have to pass a rapid river, and I, being the youngest of the three and experienced in rivers, take upon me the duty of making the attempt first by myself; leaving you in safety on the bank, I am to examine whether the river is passable by older men like yourselves, and if such appears to be the case then I shall invite you to follow, and my experience will help to convey you across; but if the river is impassable by you, then there will have been no danger to anybody but myself, — would not that seem to be a very fair proposal? I mean to say that the argument in prospect is likely to be too much for you, out of your depth and beyond your strength, and

I should be afraid that the stream of my questions might create in 893
you who are not in the habit of answering, giddiness and confusion
of mind, and hence a feeling of unpleasantness and unsuitableness
might arise. I think therefore that I had better first ask the questions and then answer them myself while you listen in safety; in that
way I can carry on the argument until I have completed the proof
that the soul is prior to the body.

Cle. Excellent, stranger, and I hope that you will do as you
propose.

Ath. Come, then, and if ever we are to call upon the Gods, let
us call upon them now in all seriousness to come to the demonstration of their own existence. And so holding fast to the rope we
will venture the depths of the argument. When questions of this sort
are asked of me, my safest answer would appear to be as follows:
— Someone says to me, 'O stranger, are all things at rest and
nothing in motion, or is the exact opposite of this true, or are some
things in motion and others at rest?' — To this I shall reply that
some things are in motion and others at rest. 'And do not things
which move move in a place, and are not the things which are at
rest at rest in a place?' Certainly. 'And some move or rest in one
situation and some in more than one?' You mean to say, we shall
rejoin, that those things which rest at their centre move in one
situation, just as the circumference goes round of circles, which are
said to be at rest? 'Yes.' And we observe that, in the revolution,
the motion which carries round the larger and the lesser circle at
the same time is proportionally distributed to greater and smaller,
and is greater and smaller in a certain proportion. Here is a wonder
which might be thought an impossibility, that the same motion
should impart swiftness and slowness in due proportion to larger and
less circles. 'Very true.' And when you speak of bodies moving in
many situations, you seem to me to mean those which move from
one place to another, and sometimes have one centre of motion as
basis, and sometimes more than one because they turn upon their
axis; and whenever they meet anything, if it be stationary, they are
divided by it; but if they get in the midst between bodies which
are approaching and moving towards the same spot from opposite
directions, they unite with them. 'I admit the truth of what you are
saying.' Also when they unite they grow, and when they are divided
they waste away, — that is, supposing the constitution of each to
remain, or if that fails, then there is a second reason of their dissolution. 'And when are all things created and how?' Clearly, they 894
are created when the first principle receives increase and attains to
the second dimension, and from this arrives at the one which is
neighbour to this, and after reaching the third becomes perceptible

to sense. Everything which is thus changing and moving is in process of generation; only when at rest has it real existence; when it has passed from that into another state it is destroyed utterly. Have we not mentioned all motions that there are, and comprehended them under their kinds and numbered them with the exception, my friends, of two?

Cle. Which are they?

Ath. Just the two with which our present inquiry is concerned.

Cle. Speak plainer.

Ath. I suppose that our inquiry has reference to the soul?

Cle. Very true.

Ath. Let us assume that there is a motion able to move other things, but never to move itself; — that is one kind; and there is another kind which can always move itself as well as other things, working in composition and decomposition, by increase and diminution and generation and destruction, — that is also one of the many kinds of motion.

Cle. Granted.

Ath. And we will assume that which moves other, and is changed by other, to be the ninth, and that which changes itself and others, and is coincident with every action and every passion, and is the true principle of change and motion in all that is, — that we shall be inclined to call the tenth.

Cle. Certainly.

Ath. And which of these ten motions ought we to prefer as being the mightiest and most efficient?

Cle. I must say that the motion which is able to move itself is ten thousand times superior to all the others.

Ath. Very good; but may I make one or two corrections in what I have been saying?

Cle. What are they?

Ath. When I spoke of the tenth sort of motion, this was not quite correct.

Cle. What was the error?

Ath. According to the true order, the tenth was really the first in generation and power; then follows the second, which was strangely enough termed the ninth by us.

Cle. What do you mean?

Ath. I mean this: when one thing changes another, and that another, of such will there be any primary changing element? How can a thing which is moved by another ever be the beginning of change? Impossible. But when the self-moved changes other, and that again other, and thus thousands upon tens of thousands of bodies are set in motion, must not the beginning of all this motion be the change of the self-moving principle?

Cle. Very true, and I quite agree.

Ath. Or, to put the question in another way, making answer to ourselves: — If, as most of these philosophers have the audacity to affirm, all things were at rest in one mass, which of the above-mentioned principles of motion must necessarily be the first to spring up among them? Clearly the self-moving; for there could be no change in them arising out of any external cause; the change must first take place in themselves. Then we must say that self-motion being the origin of all motions, and the first which arises among things at rest as well as among things in motion, is the eldest and mightiest principle of change, and that which is changed by another and yet moves other is second.

Cle. Quite true.

Ath. At this stage of the argument let us put a question.

Cle. What question?

Ath. If we were to see this power existing in any earthy, watery, or fiery substance, simple or compound — how should we describe it?

Cle. You mean to ask whether we should call such a self-moving power life?

Ath. I do.

Cle. Certainly we should.

Ath. And when we see soul in anything, must we not do the same — must we not admit that this is life?

Cle. We must.

Ath. And now, I beseech you, reflect; — you would admit that we have a threefold knowledge of things?

Cle. What do you mean?

Ath. I mean that we know the essence, and that we know the definition of the essence, and the name, — these are the three; and there are two questions which may be raised about anything.

Cle. How two?

Ath. Sometimes a person may give the name and ask the definition; or he may give the definition and ask the name. I may illustrate what I mean in this way.

Cle. How?

Ath. Number like some other things is capable of being divided into equal parts; when thus divided, number is named 'even', and the definition of the name 'even' is 'number divisible into two equal parts'?

Cle. True.

Ath. I mean, that when we are asked about the definition and give the name, or when we are asked about the name and give the definition — in either case, whether we give name or definition, we speak of the same thing, calling 'even' the number which is divided into two equal parts.

Cle. Quite true.

Ath. And what is the definition of that which is named 'soul'? Can we conceive of any other than that which has been already given — the motion which can move itself?

Cle. You mean to say that the essence which is defined as the self-moved is the same with that which has the name soul?

Ath. Yes; and if this is true, do we still maintain that there is anything wanting in the proof that the soul is the first origin and moving power of all that is, or has become, or will be, and their contraries, when she has been clearly shown to be the source of change and motion in all things?

Cle. Certainly not; the soul as being the source of motion, has been most satisfactorily shown to be the oldest of all things.

Ath. And is not that motion which is produced in another, by reason of another, but never has any self-moving power at all, being in truth the change of an inanimate body, to be reckoned second, or by any lower number which you may prefer?

Cle. Exactly.

Ath. Then we are right, and speak the most perfect and absolute truth, when we say that soul is prior to body, and that body is second and comes afterwards, and is born to obey soul, which is the ruler?

Cle. Nothing can be more true.

Ath. Do you remember our old admission, that if soul was prior to body the things of soul were also prior to those of body?

Cle. Certainly.

Ath. Then characters and manners, and wishes and reasonings, and true opinions, and foresight, and recollection are prior to length and breadth and depth and strength of bodies, if soul is prior to body.

Cle. To be sure.

Ath. In the next place, must we not of necessity admit that the soul is the cause of good and evil, base and honourable, just and unjust, and of all other opposites, if we suppose her to be the cause of all things?

Cle. We must.

Ath. And as soul orders and inhabits all things that move, however moving, must we not say that she orders also the heavens?

Cle. Of course.

896

Ath. One soul or more? More than one — I will answer for you; at any rate, we must not suppose that there are less than two — one the author of good, and the other of evil.

Cle. Very true.

Ath. Yes, very true; soul then directs all things in heaven, and earth, and sea by her movements, and these are described by the terms — will, consideration, attention, deliberation, opinion true and false, joy and sorrow, confidence, fear, hatred, love, and other primary motions akin to these; which again receive the secondary motions of corporeal substances, and guide all things to growth and decay, to composition and decomposition, and to the qualities which accompany them, such as heat and cold, heaviness and lightness, hardness and softness, blackness and whiteness, bitterness and sweetness, and all those other qualities which the soul uses, herself a goddess, when truly receiving the divine mind she disciplines all things rightly to their happiness; but when she is the companion of folly, she does the very contrary of all this. Shall we assume so much, or do we still entertain doubts?

897

Cle. There is no room at all for doubt.

Ath. Shall we say then that it is the soul which controls heaven and earth, and the whole world? — that it is a principle of wisdom and virtue, or a principle which has neither wisdom nor virtue? Suppose that we make answer as follows: —

Cle. How would you answer?

Ath. If, my friend, we say that the whole path and movement of heaven, and of all that is therein, is by nature akin to the movement and revolution and calculation of mind, and proceeds by kindred laws, then, as is plain, we must say that the best soul takes care of the world and guides it along the good path.

Cle. True.

Ath. But if the world moves wildly and irregularly, then the evil soul guides it.

Cle. True again.

Ath. Of what nature is the movement of mind? — To this question it is not easy to give an intelligent answer; and therefore I ought to assist you in framing one.

Cle. Very good.

Ath. Then let us not answer as if we would look straight at the sun, making ourselves darkness at midday, — I mean as if we were under the impression that we could see with mortal eyes, or know, adequately the nature of mind; — it will be safer to look at the image only.

Cle. What do you mean?

Ath. Let us select of the ten motions the one which mind chiefly resembles; this I will bring to your recollection, and will then make the answer on behalf of us all.

Cle. That will be excellent.

Ath. You will surely remember our saying that all things were either at rest or in motion?

Cle. I do.

898   *Ath.* And that of things in motion some were moving in one place, and others in more than one?

Cle. Yes.

Ath. Of these two kinds of motion, that which moves in one place must move about a centre like wheels made in a lathe, and is most certainly akin and similar to the circular movement of mind.

Cle. What do you mean?

Ath. In saying that both mind and the motion which is in one place move in the same and like manner, in and about the same, and in relation to the same, and according to one proportion and order, and are like the motion of a globe, we invented a fair image, which does no discredit to our ingenuity.

Cle. It does us great credit.

Ath. And the motion of the other sort which is not after the same manner, nor in the same, nor about the same, nor in relation to the same, nor in one place, nor in order, nor according to any rule or proportion, may be said to be akin to senselessness and folly?

Cle. That is most true.

Ath. Then, after what has been said, there is no difficulty in distinctly stating, that since soul carries all things round, either the best soul or the contrary must of necessity carry round and order and arrange the revolution of the heaven.

Cle. And judging from what has been said, stranger, there would be impiety in asserting that any but the most perfect soul or souls carries round the heavens.

Ath. You have understood my meaning right well, Cleinias, and now let me ask you another question.

Cle. What are you going to ask?

Ath. If the soul carries round the sun and moon, and the other stars, does she not carry round each individual of them?

Cle. Certainly.

Ath. Then of one of them let us speak, and the same argument will apply to all.

Cle. Which will you take?

Ath. Everyone sees the body of the sun, but no one sees his soul, nor the soul of any other body living or dead; and yet there is great reason to believe that this nature, unperceived by any of our senses, is circumfused around them all, but is perceived only by mind; and therefore by mind and reflection only let us apprehend the following point.

Cle. What is that?

Ath. If the soul carries round the sun, we shall not be far wrong in supposing one of three alternatives.

Cle. What are they?

Ath. Either the soul which moves the sun this way and that, resides within the circular and visible body, like the soul which carries us about every way; or the soul provides herself with a body of fire or air, as some affirm, and from some point without violently propels body by body; or thirdly, she is without such a body, but guides the sun by some extraordinary and wonderful power.

899

Cle. Yes, certainly; the soul can only order all things in one of these three ways.

Ath. And this soul of the sun, which is therefore better than the sun, whether riding in the sun as in a chariot to give light to men, or acting from without, or in whatever way, ought by every man to be deemed a god.

Cle. Yes, by every man who has the least particle of sense.

Ath. And of the stars too, and of the moon, and of the years and months and seasons, must we not say in like manner, that since a soul or souls having every sort of excellence are the causes of all of them, those souls are gods, whether they are living beings and reside in bodies, and in this way order the whole heaven, or whatever be the place and mode of their existence; — and will anyone who admits all this tolerate the denial that all things are full of gods?

Cle. No one, stranger, would be such a madman.

Ath. And now, Megillus and Cleinias, let us offer terms to him who has hitherto denied the existence of the gods, and leave him.

Cle. What terms?

Ath. Either he shall teach us that we were wrong in saying that the soul is the original of all things, and arguing accordingly; or, if he be not able to say anything better, then he must yield to us and live for the remainder of his life in the belief that there are Gods. — Let us see, then, whether we have said enough or not enough to those who deny that there are Gods.

Cle. Certainly, — quite enough, stranger.

Ath. Then to them we will say no more. And now we are to address him who, believing that there are Gods, believes also that they take no heed of human affairs: To him we say, — O thou best of men, in believing that there are Gods you are led by some affinity to them, which attracts you towards your kindred and makes you honour and believe in them. But the fortunes of evil and unrighteous men in private as well as public life, which, though not really

happy, are wrongly counted happy in the judgement of men, and are celebrated both by poets and prose-writers — these draw you aside
900 from your natural piety. Perhaps you have seen impious men growing old and leaving their children's children in high offices, and their prosperity shakes your faith — you have known or heard or been yourself an eyewitness of many monstrous impieties, and have beheld men by such criminal means from small beginnings attaining to sovereignty and the pinnacle of greatness; and considering all these things you do not like to accuse the Gods of them, because they are your relatives; and so from some want of reasoning power, and also from an unwillingness to find fault with them, you have come to believe that they exist indeed, but have no thought or care of human things. Now, that your present evil opinion may not grow to still greater impiety, and that we may if possible use arguments which may conjure away the evil before it arrives, we will add another argument to that originally addressed to him who utterly denied the existence of the Gods. And do you, Megillus and Cleinias, answer for the young man as you did before; and if any impediment comes in our way, I will take the word out of your mouths, and carry you over the river as I did just now.

Cle. Very good; do as you say, and we will help you as well as we can.

Ath. There will probably be no difficulty in proving to him that the Gods care about the small things not less, but more than about the great. For he was present and heard what was said, that they are perfectly good, and that the care of all things is most entirely natural to them.

Cle. No doubt he heard that.

Ath. Let us consider together in the next place what we mean by this virtue which we ascribe to them. Surely we should say that to be temperate and to possess mind belongs to virtue, and the contrary to vice?

Cle. Certainly.

Ath. Yes; and courage is a part of virtue, and cowardice of vice?

Cle. True.

Ath. And the one is honourable, and the other dishonourable?

Cle. To be sure.

Ath. And the affinity of the baser kind, if it has any, is with human nature, but the Gods have no part in anything of the sort?

Cle. That again is what everybody will admit.

Ath. But do we imagine carelessness and idleness and luxury to be virtues? What do you think?

Cle. Decidedly not.

Ath. They rank under the opposite class?

Cle. Yes.

Ath. And their opposites, therefore, would fall under the opposite class?

Cle. Yes.

Ath. But are we to suppose that one who possesses all these good qualities will be luxurious and heedless and idle, like those whom the poet compares to stingless drones?

Cle. And the comparison is a most just one.

Ath. Surely God must not be supposed to have a nature which He Himself hates? — he who dares to say this sort of thing must not be tolerated for a moment.

Cle. Of course not. How could He have?

Ath. Should we not on any principle be entirely mistaken in praising anyone who has some special business entrusted to him, if he have a mind which takes care of great matters and no care of small ones? Reflect; he who acts in this way, whether he be God or man, must act from one of two principles.

Cle. What are they?

Ath. Either he must think that the neglect of the small matters is of no consequence to the whole, or if he knows that they are of consequence, and he neglects them, his neglect must be attributed to carelessness and indolence. Is there any other way in which his neglect can be explained? For surely, when it is impossible for him to take care of all, he is not negligent if he fails to attend to these things great or small, which a God or some inferior being might be wanting in strength or capacity to manage?

Cle. Certainly not.

Ath. Now, then, let us examine the offenders, who both alike confess that there are Gods, but with a difference, — the one saying that they may be appeased, and the other that they have no care of small matters: there are three of us and two of them, and we will say to them, — In the first place, you both acknowledge that the Gods hear and see and know all things, and that nothing can escape them which is matter of sense and knowledge: — do you admit this?

Cle. Yes.

Ath. And do you admit also that they have all power which mortals and immortals can have?

Cle. They will, of course, admit this also.

Ath. And surely we three and they two — five in all — have acknowledged that they are good and perfect?

Cle. Assuredly.

Ath. But, if they are such as we conceive them to be, can we possibly suppose that they ever act in the spirit of carelessness and indolence? For in us inactivity is the child of cowardice, and carelessness of inactivity and indolence.

Cle. Most true.

Ath. Then not from inactivity and carelessness is any God ever negligent; for there is no cowardice in them.

Cle. That is very true.

902   *Ath.* Then the alternative which remains is, that if the Gods neglect the lighter and lesser concerns of the universe, they neglect them because they know that they ought not to care about such matters — what other alternative is there but the opposite of their knowing?

Cle. There is none.

Ath. And, O most excellent and best of men, do I understand you to mean that they are careless because they are ignorant and do not know that they ought to take care, or that they know, and yet act like the meanest sort of men, who, it is said, knowing the better, choose the worse because they are overcome by pleasures and pains?

Cle. Impossible.

Ath. Do not all human things partake of the nature of soul? And is not man the most religious of all animals?

Cle. That is not to be denied.

Ath. And we acknowledge that all mortal creatures are the property of the Gods, to whom also the whole heaven belongs?

Cle. Certainly.

Ath. And, therefore, whether a person says that these things are to the Gods great or small — in either case it would not be natural for the Gods who own us, and who are the most careful and the best of owners, to neglect us. — There is also a further consideration.

Cle. What is it?

Ath. Sensation and power are in an inverse ratio to each other in respect to their ease and difficulty.

Cle. What do you mean?

Ath. I mean that there is greater difficulty in seeing and hearing the small than the great, but more facility in moving and controlling and taking care of small and unimportant things than of their opposites.

Cle. Far more.

Ath. Suppose a physician entrusted with the care of some living thing as a whole: if he is willing and able to attend to the main points, but neglects the parts and details, will the whole fare well at his hands?

Cle. Decidedly not well.

Ath. No better would be the result with pilots or generals, or householders or statesmen, or any other such class, if they neglected the small and regarded only the great; — as the builders say, the larger stones do not lie well without the lesser.

Cle. Of course not.

Ath. Let us not, then, deem God inferior to human workmen, who, in proportion to their skill, finish and perfect their works, small as well as great, by one and the same art; or that God, the wisest of beings, who is both willing and able to take care, is like a lazy good-for-nothing, or a coward, who turns his back upon labour and gives no thought to smaller and easier matters, but to the greater only. 903

Cle. Never, stranger, let us admit a supposition about the Gods which is both impious and false.

Ath. I think that we have now argued enough with him who delights to accuse the Gods of neglect.

Cle. Yes.

Ath. He has been forced to acknowledge that he is in error, but he still seems to me to need some words of consolation.

Cle. What consolation will you offer him?

Ath. Let us say to the youth: — The ruler of the universe has ordered all things with a view to the excellence and preservation of the whole, and each part, as far as may be, has an action and passion appropriate to it. Over these, down to the least fraction of them, ministers have been appointed to preside, who have wrought out their perfection with infinitesimal exactness. And one of these portions of the universe is thine own, unhappy man, which, however little, contributes to the whole; and you do not seem to be aware that this and every other creation is for the sake of the whole, and in order that the life of the whole may be blessed; and that you are created for the sake of the whole, and not the whole for the sake of you. For every physician and every skilled artist does all things for the sake of the whole, directing his effort towards the common good, executing the part for the sake of the whole, and not the whole for the sake of the part. And you are annoyed because you are ignorant how what is best for you in the universal scheme is also best for you singly, by the law of the common creation. Now, as the soul combining first with one body and then with another undergoes all sorts of changes, either of herself or through the influence of another soul, all that remains to the player of the game is that he should shift the pieces; sending the better nature to the better place, and the worse to the worse, and so assigning to them their proper portion.

Cle. In what way do you mean?

Ath. In a way which may be supposed to make the care of all things easy to the Gods. If anyone were to form or fashion all things without any regard to the whole, — if, for example, he formed a living element of water out of fire, instead of forming many things out of one or one out of many in regular order attaining to a first or second or third birth, the transmutation would have been infinite; but now the ruler of the world has a wonderfully easy task. 904

Cle. How so?

Ath. I will explain: — When the king saw that our actions had life, and that there was much virtue in them and much vice, and that the soul and body, although not, like the Gods of popular opinion, eternal, yet having once come into existence, were indestructible (for if either of them had been destroyed there would have been no generation of living beings); and when he observed that the good of the soul was ever by nature designed to profit men, and the evil to harm them — he, seeing all this, contrived so to place each of the parts that their position might in the easiest and best manner procure the victory of good and the defeat of evil in the whole. And he contrived a general plan by which a thing of a certain nature found a certain seat and room. But the formation of qualities he left to the wills of the individuals. For every one of us is made pretty much what he is by the bent of his desires and the nature of his soul.

Cle. Yes, that is probably true.

Ath. Then all things which have a soul change, and possess in themselves a principle of change, and in changing move according to law and to the order of destiny: natures which have undergone a lesser change move less and on the earth's surface, but those which have suffered more change and have become more criminal sink into the abyss, that is to say, into Hades and other places in the world below, of which the very names terrify men, and which they picture to themselves as in a dream, both while alive and when released from the body. And whenever the soul receives more of good or evil from her own energy and the strong influence of others — when she has communion with divine virtue and becomes divine, she is carried into another and better place, which is perfect in holiness; but when she has communion with evil, then she also changes the place of her life.

'This is the justice of the Gods who inhabit Olympus'

(O youth or young man, who fancy that you are neglected by the Gods), that if you become worse you shall go to the worse souls, or if better to the better, and in every succession of life and death you will do and suffer what like may fitly suffer at the hands of like. This is the justice of heaven, which neither you nor any other unfortunate will ever glory in escaping, and which the ordaining powers have specially ordained; take good heed thereof, for it will be sure to take heed of you. If you say: — I am small and will creep into the depths of the earth, or I am high and will fly up to heaven, you are not so small or so high but that you shall pay the fitting penalty, either here or in the world below or in some still more savage place whither you shall be conveyed. This is also the explanation of the fate of those whom you saw, who had done unholy and evil deeds, and from small beginnings had grown great, and you fancied that from being miserable they had become happy; and in their actions, as in a mirror, you seemed to see the universal neglect of the Gods, not knowing how they make all things work together and contribute to the great whole. And thinkest thou, bold man, that thou needest not to know this? — he who knows it not can never form any true idea of the happiness or unhappiness of life or hold any rational discourse respecting either. If Cleinias and this our reverend company succeed in proving to you that you know not what you say of the Gods, then will God help you; but should you desire to hear more, listen to what we say to the third opponent, if you have any understanding whatsoever. For I think that we have sufficiently proved the existence of the Gods, and that they care for men: — The other notion that they are appeased by the wicked, and take gifts, is what we must not concede to anyone, and what every man should disprove to the utmost of his power.

Cle. Very good; let us do as you say.

Ath. Well, then, by the Gods themselves I conjure you to tell me, — if they are to be propitiated, how are they to be propitiated? Who are they, and what is their nature? Must they not be at least rulers who have to order unceasingly the whole heaven?

Cle. True.

Ath. And to what earthly rulers can they be compared, or who to them? How in the less can we find an image of the greater? Are they charioteers of contending pairs of steeds, or pilots of vessels? Perhaps they might be compared to the generals of armies, or they might be likened to physicians providing against the diseases which 906 make war upon the body, or to husbandmen observing anxiously the effects of the seasons on the growth of plants; or perhaps to shepherds of flocks. For as we acknowledge the world to be full of many goods and also of evils, and of more evils than goods, there is, as we affirm, an immortal conflict going on among us, which requires marvellous watchfulness; and in that conflict the Gods and demigods are our allies, and we are their property. Injustice and insolence and folly are the destruction of us, and justice and temperance and wisdom are our salvation; and these latter reside in the living power of the Gods, although some vestige of them may occasionally be discerned among mankind. But upon this earth we know that there dwell souls possessing an unjust spirit, who may be compared to brute animals, which fawn upon their keepers, whether dogs or shepherds, or the best and most perfect masters; and try to persuade them that it is in their power to defraud other men and suffer no harm, by the use of flattering words or even of prayers and incantations; so the evil tale runs.

But we say that this sin, which is termed greed, is an evil of the same kind as what is termed disease in living bodies or pestilence in years or seasons of the year, and in cities and governments has another name, which is injustice.

Cle. Quite true.

Ath. Yet this is the argument of one who declares that the Gods are always lenient to the doers of unjust acts, if they divide the spoil with them. As if wolves were to toss a portion of their prey to the dogs, and they, mollified by the gift, suffered them to tear the flocks. Must not he who maintains that the Gods can be propitiated argue thus?

Cle. Precisely so.

Ath. And to which of the above-mentioned classes of guardians would any man compare the Gods without absurdity? Will he say that they are like pilots, who are themselves turned away from their duty by 'libations of wine and the savour of fat', and at last overturn both ship and sailors?

Cle. Assuredly not.

Ath. And surely they are not like charioteers who are bribed to give up the victory to other chariots?

Cle. That would be a fearful image of the Gods.

Ath. Nor are they like generals, or physicians, or husbandmen, or shepherds; and no one would compare them to dogs who have been silenced by wolves.

Cle. A thing not to be spoken of.

907 *Ath.* And are not all the Gods the chiefest of all guardians, and do they not guard our highest interests?

Cle. Yes; the chiefest.

Ath. And shall we say that those who guard our noblest interests and are the best of guardians, are inferior in virtue to dogs, and to men even of moderate excellence, who would never betray justice for the sake of gifts which unjust men impiously offer them?

Cle. Certainly not; nor is such a notion to be endured, and he who holds this opinion may be fairly singled out and characterized as of all impious men the wickedest and most impious.

Ath. Then are the three assertions — that the Gods exist, and that they take care of men, and that they can never be persuaded to do injustice — now sufficiently demonstrated? May we say that they are?

Cle. You have our entire assent to your words.

Ath. I have spoken with vehemence because I am zealous against evil men; and I will tell you, dear Cleinias, why I am so. I would not have the wicked think that, having the superiority in argument, they may do as they please and act according to their various imaginations about the Gods; and this zeal has led me to speak too vehemently; but if we have at all succeeded in persuading the men to hate themselves and love their opposites, the prelude of our laws about impiety will not have been spoken in vain.

Cle. So let us hope; and even if we have failed, the style of our argument will not discredit the lawgiver.

Ath. After the prelude shall follow a discourse, which will be the interpreter of the law; this shall proclaim to all impious persons that they must depart from their ways and go over to the pious. And to those who disobey, let the law about impiety be as follows: — If a man is guilty of any impiety in word or deed, anyone who happens to be present shall give information to the authorities, in aid of the law; and let the authorities who first receive the information bring him before the appointed court according to the law; and if an official, after receiving information, refuses to act, he shall be tried for impiety at the instance of anyone who is willing to vindicate the laws; and if anyone be cast, the court shall estimate the punishment of each act 908 of impiety, and let all such criminals be imprisoned. There shall be three prisons in the state: the first of them is to be the common prison in the neighbourhood of the agora for the safekeeping of the generality of offenders; another is to be in the neighbourhood of the nocturnal Council, and is to be called the 'House of Reformation'; another, to be situated in some wild and desolate region in the centre of the country, shall be called by some name expressive of retribution. Now, men fall into impiety from three causes, which have been already mentioned, and from each of these causes arise two sorts of impiety, in all six, which are worth distinguishing, and should not all have the same punishment. For he who does not believe in the Gods, and yet has a righteous nature, hates the wicked and dislikes and refuses to do injustice, and avoids unrighteous men, and loves the righteous. But they who besides believing that the world is devoid of Gods are stricken with intemperance of pleasure and pain, and have at the same time good memories and quick wits, are worse; although both of them are unbelievers, much less injury is done by the one than by the other. The one may talk loosely about the Gods and about sacrifices and oaths, and perhaps by laughing at other men he may make them like himself, if he be not punished. But the other who holds the same opinions and is called a clever man, is full of stratagem and deceit — men of this class deal in prophecy and jugglery of all kinds, and out of their ranks sometimes come tyrants and demagogues and generals and hierophants of private mysteries and the sophists, as they are termed, with their ingenious devices. There are many kinds of unbelievers, but two only for whom legislation is required; one of the hypocritical sort, whose crime is deserving of death many times over, while the other needs only bonds and admonition. In like manner also the notion that the Gods take no thought of men produces two other sorts of crimes, and the notion that they may be propitiated produces two more. Assuming these divisions, let those who have been made what they are only from want of understanding, and not from malice or an evil nature, be

909 placed by the judge in the House of Reformation, and ordered to suffer imprisonment during a period of not less than five years. And in the meantime let them have no intercourse with the other citizens, except with members of the nocturnal Council, and with them let them converse with a view to the improvement of their soul's health. And when the time of their imprisonment has expired, if any of them be of sound mind let him be restored to sane company, but if not, and if he be condemned a second time, let him be punished with death. As to that class of monstrous natures who not only believe that there are no Gods, or that they are negligent, or to be propitiated, but in contempt of mankind conjure the souls of the living and say that they can conjure the dead and promise to charm the Gods with sacrifices and prayers, and will utterly overthrow individuals and whole houses and states for the sake of money — let him who is guilty of any of these things be condemned by the court to be bound according to law in the prison which is in the centre of the land, and let no freeman ever approach him, but let him receive the rations of food appointed by the guardians of the law from the hands of the public slaves; and when he is dead let him be cast beyond the borders unburied, and if any freeman assist in burying him, let him be liable to prosecution for impiety by anyone who is willing to bring a suit against him. But if he leaves behind him children who are fit to be citizens, let the guardians of orphans take care of them, just as they would of any other orphans, from the day on which their father is convicted.

In all these cases there should be one law, which will make men in general less liable to transgress in word or deed, and less foolish, because they will not be allowed to practise religious rites contrary to law. And let this be the simple form of the law: — No man shall have sacred rites in a private house. When he would sacrifice, let him go to the temples and hand over his offerings to the priests and priestesses, who see to the sanctity of such things, and let him pray himself, asking anyone whom he pleases to join with him in prayer. The reason of this as follows: — Gods and temples are not easily instituted, and to establish them rightly is the work of a mighty intellect. And women especially, and men too, when they are sick or in danger, or in any sort of difficulty, or again on their receiving any

910 good fortune, have a way of consecrating the occasion, vowing sacrifices, and promising shrines to Gods, demigods, and sons of Gods;

and when they are awakened by terrible apparitions and dreams or remember visions, they find in altars and temples the remedies of them, and will fill every house and village with them, placing them in open spaces, or wherever they may have had such visions; and such examples should lead us to follow the law now proposed. The law has also regard to the impious, and would not have them fancy that by the secret performance of these actions — by raising temples and by building altars in private houses — they can propitiate the God secretly with sacrifices and prayers, while they are really multiplying their crimes infinitely, bringing guilt from heaven upon themselves, and also upon those who permit them, and who are better men than they are; and the consequence is that the whole state reaps the fruit of their impiety, which, in a certain sense, is deserved. Assuredly God will not blame the legislator, who will enact the following law: — No one shall possess shrines of the Gods in private houses, and he who is found to possess them, and perform any sacred rites not publicly authorized, — supposing the offender to be some man or woman who is not guilty of any other great and impious crime, — shall be informed against by him who is acquainted with the fact, which shall be announced by him to the guardians of the law; and let them issue orders that he or she shall carry away their private rites to the public temples, and if they do not persuade them, let them inflict a penalty on them until they comply. And if a person be proven guilty of impiety, not merely from childish levity, but such as grown-up men may be guilty of, let him be punished with death, whether he have sacrificed to any Gods in public, or in private rites which he has instituted; for his sacrifice is impure. Whether the deed has been done in earnest, or only from childish levity, let the guardians of the law determine, before they bring the matter into court and prosecute the offender for impiety.

The Myth of Er

From the Republic, Book X

ᴥᵹ The Myth of Er, like the *Phaedo* myth, tells of the fate of the soul after death. It has been reserved for the final position in this book because it was chosen by Plato himself as a sort of musical resolution of tension, bringing a sense of finality and peace, at the end of his greatest work. In it not all, it may seem to us, is perfection. In depicting the experiences that await the virtuous, the myth tells nothing of the promised blessedness except to speak vaguely of its delights and beauties and to contrast it with the bodily sufferings and terrors of the vicious. What is ultimately gained by the most deserving souls, the choice of a life of virtue in the next incarnation, is not presented as a thing of wonder. Even the tenth book of the *Laws,* with its promise that the better soul will be rewarded by being borne into the company of its spiritual kin, seems to reach a higher moral level.

But the picture of the afterworld itself, of the universe opened to the view, girdled with a beam of light, pierced through with the mighty spindle of Necessity around which revolve the concentric rings of the heavenly bodies, each with its chanting siren, and of the three Fates busy with their appointed tasks, the barren plain and the river of forgetfulness — all this forms a pageantry of splendor and seeming verisimilitude at which we cannot scoff.

The myth comes at the very end of the *Republic.* Socrates is speaking:

614   Well, I said, I will tell you a tale; not one of the tales which Odysseus tells to the hero Alcinous, yet this too is a tale of a hero, Er the son of Armenius, a Pamphylian by birth. He was slain in battle, and ten days afterwards, when the bodies of the dead were taken up already in a state of corruption, his body was found unaffected by decay, and carried away home to be buried. And on the twelfth day, as he was lying on the funeral pile, he returned to life and told them what he had seen in the other world. He said that when his soul left the body it went on a journey with a great company, and that they came to a mysterious place at which there were two openings in the earth; they were near together, and over against them were two other openings in the heaven above. In the intermediate space there were judges seated, who commanded the just, after they had given judgement on them and had bound their sentences in front of

them, to ascend by the way up through the heaven on the right hand; and in like manner the unjust were bidden by them to descend by the lower way on the left hand; these also bore tokens of all their deeds, but fastened on their backs. He drew near, and they told him that he was to be the messenger who would carry the report of the other world to men, and they bade him hear and see all that was to be heard and seen in that place. Then he beheld and saw on one side the souls departing at either opening of heaven and earth when sentence had been given on them; and at the two other openings other souls, some ascending out of the earth dusty and worn with travel, some descending out of heaven clean and bright. And arriving ever and anon they seemed to have come from a long journey, and they went forth with gladness into the meadow, where they encamped as at a festival; and those who knew one another embraced and conversed, the souls which came from earth curiously inquiring about the things above, and the souls which came from heaven about the things beneath. And they told one another of what had happened by the way, those from below weeping and sorrowing at the remem- 615 brance of the things which they had endured and seen in their journey beneath the earth (now the journey lasted a thousand years), while those from above were describing heavenly delights and visions of inconceivable beauty. The full story, Glaucon, would take too long to tell; but the sum was this: — He said that for every wrong which they had done and every person whom they had injured they had suffered tenfold; or once in a hundred years — such being reckoned to be the length of man's life, and the penalty being thus paid ten times in a thousand years. If, for example, there were any who had been the cause of many deaths by the betrayal of cities or armies, or had cast many into slavery, or been accessory to any other ill treat- ment, for all their offences, and on behalf of each man wronged, they were afflicted with tenfold pain, and the rewards of beneficence and justice and holiness were in the same proportion. I need hardly repeat what he said concerning young children dying almost as soon as they were born. Of piety and impiety to gods and parents, and of murder, there were retributions other and greater far which he described. He mentioned that he was present when one of the spirits asked another, 'Where is Ardiaeus the Great?' (Now this Ardiaeus lived a thousand years before the time of Er: he had been the tyrant of some city of Pamphylia and had murdered his aged father and his elder brother, and was said to have committed many other abominable crimes.) The answer of the other spirit was: 'He comes not hither and will never come. And this', said he, 'was one of the dreadful sights which we ourselves witnessed. We were at the mouth of the cavern, and, having completed all our experiences, were about to reascend, when of a sudden, we saw Ardiaeus and several others, most of whom were tyrants; but there were also some private individuals who had been great criminals: they were just, as they fancied, about to return into the upper world, but the mouth, instead of admitting them, gave a roar, whenever any of these whose wickedness was incurable or who had not been sufficiently punished tried to ascend; and then wild men of fiery aspect, who were standing by **616** and heard the sound, seized and carried them[1] off; but Ardiaeus and others they bound head and foot and hand, and threw them down, and flayed them with scourges, and dragged them along the road outside the entrance, carding them on thorns like wool, and declaring to the passers-by what were their crimes, and that they were being taken away to be cast into Tartarus.' And of all the many terrors of every kind which they had endured, he said that there was none like the terror which each of them felt at that moment, lest they should hear the voice; and when there was silence, one by one they ascended with exceeding joy. These, said Er, were the penalties and retributions, and there were blessings as great.

Now when each band which was in the meadow had tarried seven days, on the eighth they were obliged to proceed on their journey, and, on the fourth day after, he said that they came to a place where they could see from above a line of light, straight as a column, extending right through the whole heaven and through the earth, in colour resembling the rainbow, only brighter and purer; another day's journey brought them to the place, and there, in the midst of the light, they saw the ends of the chains of heaven let down from above; for this light is the belt of heaven, and holds together the circumference of the universe, like the under-girders of a trireme. From these ends is extended the spindle of Necessity, on which all the revolutions turn. The shaft and hook of this spindle are made of adamant, and the whorl is made partly of steel and also partly of other materials. The nature of the whorl is as follows; it is, in outward shape, like the whorl used on earth; and his description of it implied that there is one large hollow whorl which is quite scooped out, and into this is fitted another lesser one, and another, and another, and four others, making eight in all, like vessels which fit into one another; the whorls show their circular edges on the upper side, and on their lower side all together form one continuous whorl. This is pierced by the shaft which is driven home through the centre of the eighth. The first and outermost whorl has the rim broadest, and the seven inner whorls are narrower, in the following proportions — the sixth is next to the first in size, the fourth next to the sixth; then

---

1 [i.e. those who were not incurable, but had further punishment to endure.]

comes the eighth; the seventh is fifth, the fifth is sixth, the third is seventh, last and eighth comes the second. The largest [or fixed stars] is spangled, and the seventh [or sun] is brightest; the eighth [or moon] coloured by the reflected light of the seventh; the second and fifth [Saturn and Mercury] are in colour like one another, and yellower than the preceding; the third [Venus] has the whitest light; the fourth [Mars] is reddish; the sixth [Jupiter] is in whiteness second. Now the whole spindle has the same motion; but, as the whole revolves in one direction, the seven inner circles move slowly in the other, and of these the swiftest is the eighth; next in swiftness are the seventh, sixth, and fifth, which move together; third in swiftness appeared to move, because of this contrary motion, the fourth; the third appeared fourth and the second fifth. The spindle turns on the knees of Necessity; and on the upper surface of each circle stands a siren, who goes round with them, chanting a single tone or note. The eight together form one harmony; and round about, at equal intervals, there is another band, three in number, each sitting upon her throne; these are the Fates, daughters of Necessity, who are clothed in white robes and have chaplets upon their heads, Lachesis and Clotho and Atropos, who accompany with their voices the harmony of the sirens — Lachesis singing of the past, Clotho of the present, Atropos of the future; Clotho from time to time assisting with a touch of her right hand the revolution of the outer circle of the whorl or spindle, and Atropos with her left hand touching and guiding the inner ones, and Lachesis laying hold of either in turn, first with one hand and then with the other.

When Er and the spirits arrived, their duty was to go at once to Lachesis; but first of all there came a prophet who arranged them in order; then he took from the knees of Lachesis lots and samples of lives, and having mounted a high pulpit, spoke as follows: 'Hear the word of Lachesis, the daughter of Necessity. Mortal souls, behold a new cycle of life and mortality. Your genius will not be allotted to you, but you will choose your genius; and let him who draws the first lot have the first choice, and the life which he chooses shall be his destiny. Virtue is free, and as a man honours or dishonours her he will have more or less of her; the responsibility is with the chooser — God is not responsible.' When the Interpreter had thus spoken he scattered lots indifferently among them all, and each of them took up the lot which fell near him, all but Er himself (he was not allowed), and each as he took his lot perceived the number which he had obtained. Then the Interpreter placed on the ground before them the patterns of lives; and there were many more lives than the souls present, and they were of all sorts. There were lives of every animal and of man in every condition. And there were tyrannies

617

618

among them, some lasting out the tyrant's life, others which broke off in the middle and came to an end in poverty and exile and beggary; and there were lives of famous men, some who were famous for their form and beauty as well as for their strength and success in games, or, again, for their birth and the qualities of their ancestors; and some who were the reverse of famous for the opposite qualities. And of women likewise. The disposition of the soul was not, however, included in them, because the soul, when choosing a new life, must of necessity become different. But there was every other quality, and they all mingled with one another, and also with elements of wealth and poverty, and disease and health; and there were also states intermediate in these respects.

And here, my dear Glaucon, is the supreme peril of our human state; and therefore each one of us must take the utmost care to forsake every other kind of knowledge and seek and study one thing only, if peradventure he may be able to discover someone who will make him able to discern between a good and an evil life, and so to choose always and everywhere the better life as he has opportunity. He should consider the bearing of all these things which have been mentioned severally and collectively upon the excellence of a life; he should know what the effect of beauty is, for good or evil, when combined with poverty or wealth in this or that kind of soul, and what are the good and evil consequences of noble and humble birth, of private and public station, of strength and weakness, of cleverness and dullness, and of all the natural and acquired gifts of the soul, and the operation of them when blended with one another; he will then look at the nature of the soul, and from the consideration of all these qualities he will be able to determine which is the better and which is the worse; and so he will choose, giving the name of evil to the life which will tend to make his soul more unjust, and good to the life which will make his soul more just; all else he will disregard. For we 619 have seen and know that this is the best choice both in life and after death. A man must take with him into the world below an adamantine faith in truth and right, that there too he may be undazzled by the desire of wealth or the other allurements of evil, lest he be drawn into tyrannies and similar activities, and do irremediable wrongs to others and suffer yet worse himself; but may know how to choose a life moderate in these respects and avoid the extremes on either side, as far as possible, not only in this life but in all that which is to come. For this way brings men to their greatest happiness.

And according to the report of the messenger from the other world this was what the prophet said at the time: 'Even for the last comer, if he chooses wisely and will live diligently, there is appointed a happy and not undesirable existence. Let not him who chooses first be careless, and let not the last despair.' And when he had spoken, he who had the first choice came forward and in a moment chose the greatest tyranny; his mind having been darkend by folly and sensuality, he had not made any thorough inspection before he chose, and did not perceive that he was fated, among other evils, to devour his own children. But when he had time to examine the lot, and saw what was in it he began to beat his breast and lament over his choice, forgetting the proclamation of the prophet; for, instead of throwing the blame of his misfortune on himself, he accused chance and the gods, and everything rather than himself. Now he was one of those who came from heaven, and in a former life had dwelt in a well-ordered State, virtuous from habit only, and without philosophy. And for the most part it was true of others who were caught in this way, that the greater number of them came from heaven and therefore they had never been schooled by trial, whereas the pilgrims who came from earth having themselves suffered and seen others suffer were not in a hurry to choose. And owing to this inexperience of theirs, and also to the accident of the lot, the majority of the souls exchanged a good destiny for an evil or an evil for a good. For if a man had always on his arrival in this world dedicated himself from the first to sound philosophy, and had been moderately fortunate in the number of the lot, he might, as the messenger reported, be happy here, and also his journey to another life and return to this, instead of being rough and underground, would be smooth and heavenly. Most curious, he said, was the spectacle — sad and laughable and strange; for the choice of the souls was in most cases based on their experience of a previous life. 620 There he saw the soul which had once been Orpheus choosing the life of a swan out of enmity to the race of women, hating to be born of a woman because they had been his murderers; he beheld also the soul of Thamyras choosing the life of a nightingale; birds, on the other hand, like the swan and other musicians, wanting to be men. The soul which obtained the twentieth lot chose the life of a lion, and this was the soul of Ajax the son of Telamon, who would not be a man, remembering the injustice which was done him in the judgement about the arms. The next was Agamemnon, who took the life of an eagle, because, like Ajax, he hated human nature by reason of his sufferings. About the middle came the lot of Atalanta; she, seeing the great fame of an athlete, was unable to resist the temptation: and after her there followed the soul of Epeus the son of Panopeus passing into the nature of a woman skilled in some craft; and far away among the last who chose, the soul of the jester Thersites was putting on the form of a monkey. There came also the soul of Odysseus having yet to make a choice, and his lot happened to be the last of them all. Now the recollection of former toils had disenchanted him of ambition, and he went about for a considerable time in search of the life of a private man who had no cares; he had some difficulty in finding this, which was lying about and had been neglected by everybody else; and when he saw it, he said that he would have done the same had his lot been first instead of last, and gladly chose it. And not only did men pass into animals, but I must also mention that there were animals tame and wild who changed into one another and into corresponding human natures — the righteous into the gentle and the unrighteous into the savage, in all sorts of combinations.

All the souls had now chosen their lives, and they went in the order of their choice to Lachesis, who sent with them the genius whom they had severally chosen, to be the guardian of their lives and the fulfiller of the choice: this genius led the souls first to Clotho, and drew them within the revolution of the spindle impelled by her hand, thus ratifying the destiny of each; and then, when they were fastened to this, carried them to Atropos, who spun the threads and made them irreversible, whence without turning round they passed beneath the throne of Necessity; and when they had all passed, they marched on to the plain of Forgetfulness, in intolerable scorching heat, for the plain was a barren waste destitute of trees and verdure; and then towards evening they encamped by the river of Unmindfulness, whose water no vessel can hold; of this they were all obliged to drink a certain quantity, and those who were not saved by wisdom drank more than was necessary; and each one as he drank forgot all things. Now after they had gone to rest, about the middle of the night there was a thunderstorm and earthquake, and then in an instant they were driven upwards in all manner of ways to their birth, like stars shooting. He himself was hindered from drinking the water. But in what manner or by what means he returned to the body he could not say; only in the morning, awaking suddenly, he found himself lying on the pyre.

And thus, Glaucon, the tale has been saved and has not perished, and will save us if we are obedient to the word spoken; and we shall pass safely over the river of Forgetfulness and our soul will not be defiled. Wherefore my counsel is that we hold fast ever to the heavenly way and follow after justice and virtue always, considering that the soul is immortal and able to endure every sort of good and every sort of evil. Thus shall we live dear to one another and to the gods, both while remaining here and when, like conquerors in the games who go round to gather gifts, we receive our reward. And it shall be well with us both in this life and in the pilgrimage of a thousand years which we have been describing.

Appendix A

ON TRANSLATING PLATO

The sophisticated reader in this semantically self-conscious age may wish to put a searching question to the editor of this book:

"I have no Greek to my name. Consequently, I am dependent upon the English words and sentences that you have put before me in Plato's name. Now, granting the impossibility of an absolutely 'noiseless' translation, I am still somewhat at sea. In any given passage, how can I be sure that I am reading what Plato, a philosopher of fourth-century Athens, rather than what Benjamin Jowett, a theologian of mid-nineteenth-century Oxford, thought about the matter in hand?

"One other closely related point: You have more than once referred with enthusiasm to Plato's literary quality, his style. I find a parallel problem here. How are we English readers to tell when we are looking at Plato's authentic Attic gems and when at Jowett's Oxford imitations?"

In answer to this question an extensive essay might be projected on the model of Matthew Arnold's famous *On Translating Homer*, isolating those characteristics of Plato's literary style in the absence of which an English version of a Platonic dialogue becomes a perversion of its original. Arnold attributes to Homer the following four qualities: (1) Homer is "eminently rapid." (2) He is "eminently plain and direct . . . both in his syntax and in his words." (3) He is "plain and direct in . . . his matter and ideas." (4) And finally, "he is eminently noble." Arnold cites an abundance of Homeric passages to confirm his view, and shows by examples how Homer's translators — from Chapman the exuberant, and Pope the polite, to Newman the grotesque — having persistently violated one or more of the four canons, have thereby variously failed to give us a sufficiently Homeric Homer.

Can we do for Plato's translators something remotely comparable to what Arnold has done for Homer's, using Arnold's formula but reminding ourselves of the important differences between an epic poet and a philosopher? Eventually something of the sort might be devised, given time and space enough. But on this occasion within our limits we must avoid promising anything beyond a charcoal sketch of the imposing edifice that someone may someday erect on the site.

Following Arnold's pattern, let us begin by collecting and formu-

507

lating Platonic qualities corresponding in a broad way to the four Homeric ones of Arnold's choice.

In addition to the basic requirements of clarity and logical coherence, we may list among the essential qualities of Plato's style rhythmic cadence (sometimes employed for aesthetic effect, and again as an engine of satire), pungency of phrase, command of arresting and congruous metaphor, narrative skill, dramatic power, the art of graceful transition and modulation akin to that of a musical composer, and withal an impression of intellectual plenty implying an apparently inexhaustible reserve.

There are also some important negative requirements. We would not allow our translator to "improve" upon his original, either by softening certain passages that might conceivably offend contemporary taste, or by brightening colorless passages — for such indeed occur — with adventitious English paint. Nor should we permit our translator to procure a cheap admiration from his readers through tricks of over-modernizing that destroy aesthetic distance and do violence to the past. Such are the major specifications for the translation of which we are in quest.

Setting aside some admirable versions of a few only among the wide sweep of the more than twenty commonly accepted dialogues, one comes inevitably upon a virtually complete English Plato, which reveals itself, for reasons presently to be offered, as the closest existing approximation to our ideal. This is the fourth and latest (1951) revision, by two distinguished scholars, of Benjamin Jowett's monumental work — itself, as has often been said, an English classic.

Checking this Jowett version against the just-listed qualities of the ideal, one may say, on the positive side, that Plato here retains, to a surprising degree, his literary values. Jowett has, it appears, taught Plato to speak an English which is alive and expressive of shades of thought and feeling, and through his often deliberate freedom in rendering the Greek, has been enabled to do so with exceptional grace and charm. Partisans of "the American language" may now and then brindle at an Anglicism, while modernists with negative tolerance for Victorian embroidery will suffer some distress. But for a moderate reader, willing to listen carefully, these disadvantages are heavily outweighed. For time has mellowed and not outmoded Jowett's English, and it can speak to us with a perennial accent most suitable as a vehicle of Plato's perennial thought. It is a language neither so remote as to lose immediacy nor so close to us as to seem pedestrian; and at times, following Plato's own example, it shakes off all other commitments and speaks as the philosophic muse compels.

But, it will be asked, how will Jowett rate in terms of those other, nonliterary, and — since Plato was essentially a philosopher — overwhelmingly philosophical virtues: logical clarity, terminological consistency, and genuine grasp of the deeper issues of Plato's argument, not to mention the humbler but necessary virtue of "correctness," that is, fidelity to the meaning of the original text?

Answering the last point first, one may note that the correctness of Jowett's version is, with all respect to Jowett, a collective achievement. From its first publication in 1871 until Jowett's death in 1893, labors of improvement were never at a stand. The criticisms and specific corrections offered by countless scholars, at home and abroad, were taken account of in the second and third editions. And in the posthumous fourth edition of 1953, sheltered by the names of two highly accredited Oxford Plato scholars, D. J. Allan and H. E. Dale, an attempt has been made to remove all surviving demonstrable inaccuracies. Wherever doubts about the proper translation exist, these editors have indicated the fact, often suggesting alternative versions, in footnotes which we do not reproduce in the present volume but which are accessible in the original edition to interested readers.

The remaining "philosophical virtues" cannot be here appraised save in summary purview. Platonic interpretation is still in active operation; there is yet no such fundamental agreement as to justify a graduated scale of philosophical precision. Jowett's vision of Plato has been condemned in some quarters as too idealistic, too Hegelian, or too Christian. But this interpretation is limited chiefly to Jowett's introductions to the dialogues, and appears in the translation only to a well-trained eye; an example is the frequent use of the capitalized word "God" where a small letter or the phrase "the divine" might be preferable as less likely to suggest inappropriate Christian associations. Let us then be grateful for the many virtues of our host Benjamin Jowett, whose good wine seems to grow better with the years.

Appendix B

NOTE ON TRANSLITERATION

In this volume Greek words will often be first given in the Greek alphabet and then transliterated into the English alphabet, for the benefit of the reader who lacks Greek. The transliteration will not follow the Latinizing pattern usual in the case of proper names, in which, for example, the Greek diphthong αι (*ai*) becomes *ae* (as in *Hephaestus*), the letter κ (*k*) becomes *c* (as in *Cratylus*), and the ending -ος (*-os*) becomes -*us* (as in both these names). Instead, it will employ the most nearly equivalent letter.

It is suggested that the reader may enjoy memorizing the Greek letters, especially the lower-case letters, and their equivalents, and that by doing so he will find a number of Platonic passages clearer and more interesting.

The letters and equivalents are as shown in the table on the opposite page.

Besides the letters, it is necessary to know the "breathings." Every initial vowel or diphthong has either the rough breathing (') indicating an *h* sound, as in ὅρος (*horos*), or the smooth breathing (') indicating the absence of the *h* sound. The rough breathing will be transliterated as *h*; the smooth breathing will not be transliterated.

The diphthongs are as follows:

αι	(*ai*)	as in C*ai*ro	ηυ	(*ēu*)	as in *eh'-oo*
αυ	(*au*)	like *ou* in *out*	ωυ	(*ōu*)	as in *oh'-oo*
ει	(*ei*)	as in v*ei*n	υι	(*ui*)	as in French h*ui*t
ευ	(*eu*)	like *e* in m*e*t plus			
		oo in m*oo*n			
οι	(*oi*)	as in *oi*l			
ου	(*ou*)	as in t*ou*r			

Most Greek words also have an accent, which may be grave (`), acute (´), or circumflex (^). In ancient Greek these accents indicated different pitches. As pronounced today, they all indicate stress.

Greek Alphabet			English Equivalent	Sound as in these words[1]
A	α	alpha	a	*a*go, or *f*ather
B	β	beta	b	*b*et
Γ	γ	gamma	g or n[2]	*g*o, or si*n*g
Δ	δ	delta	d	*d*o
E	ε	epsilon	e	*e*gg
Z	ζ	zeta	z	ga*z*e
H	η	eta	ē	French f*ê*te
Θ	θ	theta	th	*th*ink
I	ι	iota	i	pol*i*ce
K	κ	kappa	k	*k*id
Λ	λ	lambda	l	*l*et
M	μ	mu	m	*m*et
N	ν	nu	n	*n*et
Ξ	ξ	xi	x	a*x*e
O	ο	omicron	o	*o*bey
Π	π	pi	p	*p*et
P	ρ	rho	r or rh[3]	*r*un
Σ	σ, s[4]	sigma	s	*s*et
T	τ	tau	t	*t*ap
Υ	υ	upsilon	y or u[5]	French t*u*
Φ	φ	phi	ph	*ph*ysics
X	χ	chi	ch	German i*ch*
Ψ	ψ	psi	ps	u*ps*et
Ω	ω	omega	ō	n*o*te

[1] This table of equivalents is adapted from H. W. Smyth, *Greek Grammar for Colleges.*

[2] Gamma standing before kappa, gamma, chi, or xi is pronounced like *n* in *sing* and will be transliterated as *n*.

[3] Every initial rho has the rough breathing (see below) and will be transliterated as *rh*.

[4] Sigma has two forms in the small letters. It is written as *s* only at the ends of words, elsewhere as σ.

[5] Upsilon will be transliterated as *y* when it stands alone but as *u* when it forms part of a diphthong such as *eu*.

Bibliography

Adkins, A. W. H. *Merit and Responsibility: A Study in Greek Values.* Oxford: Clarendon Press, 1960.

Bridges, Robert. *The Testament of Beauty.* New York: Oxford University Press, 1930.

Burnet, John. *Plato's* Phaedo. Oxford: Clarendon Press, 1911.

———. *Plato's* Euthyphro, Apology of Socrates, *and* Crito. Oxford: Clarendon Press, 1924.

Cornford, F. M. *Plato's Cosmology.* New York: Harcourt, Brace, 1937.

———. *Plato's Theory of Knowledge.* New York: Humanities Press, 1951.

Dodds, E. R. *Plato:* Gorgias. Oxford: Clarendon Press, 1959.

Hocking, W. E. *Preface to Philosophy.* New York: Macmillan, 1946.

Jowett, B. *The Dialogues of Plato,* 4th edition, revised by D. J. Allan and H. E. Dale. Oxford: Clarendon Press, 1953.

Jaeger, Werner. *Paideia.* New York: Oxford University Press, Vol. I, 1939; Vol. II, 1943; Vol. III, 1944.

Levinson, Ronald. *In Defense of Plato.* Cambridge, Mass.: Harvard University Press, 1953.

———. "Plato's *Phaedrus* and the New Criticism," *Archiv für Geschichte der Philosophie,* 46 (1964), 293–309.

Morrow, Glenn R. *Plato's Cretan City.* Princeton: Princeton University Press, 1960.

———, ed. Timaeus *by Plato.* New York: Liberal Arts Press, 1949.

Notopoulos, J. A. *The Platonism of Shelley.* Durham, N.C.: Duke University Press, 1949.

Post, L. A. *Thirteen Epistles of Plato.* Oxford: Clarendon Press, 1925.

Richards, I. A. *Republic of Plato.* New York: Norton, 1942.

Ross, Sir David. *Plato's Theory of Ideas.* Oxford: Clarendon Press, 1951.

Shorey, Paul. *What Plato Said.* Chicago: University of Chicago Press, 1933.

Smyth, H. W. *Greek Grammar for Colleges.* New York: American Book Co., 1920.

Whitehead, A. N. *Adventures of Ideas.* New York: Macmillan, 1933.

Woodbridge, F. J. E. *The Son of Apollo.* Boston: Houghton Mifflin, 1929.